NEW DIRECTIONS IN DEVELOPMENT ECONOMICS

The contributions to *New Directions in Development Economics* examine two broad subjects: Part I focuses on economic growth (or its absence) in developing countries, and Part II joins the ongoing debate over the role of the state in promoting development.

Bringing together development experts from four continents, this volume presents the widest possible range of perspectives on the challenges of growth. In addition, it examines the environmental costs of growth; throughout, the contributors emphasize the need to invest in human capital and the environment in order to achieve real growth as opposed to growth measured purely in terms of economic indicators.

Despite the growing dominance of free market policies in the post-communist world, the state still plays a pivotal role in economic development. The chapters in Part II cover both the theoretical background to current state-versus-market discussions and practical issues such as foreign investment incentives and the role of non-governmental organizations in securing democratic participation in development.

New Directions in Development Economics provides an essential reference work for those interested in current debates, as it reflects topical trends of thought and identifies prevailing problems and solutions. Rather than merely highlighting the many dilemmas facing developing countries, the contributors outline possible policy responses that decision makers in both North and South would be well advised to consider.

Mats Lundahl is Professor of Development Economics at the Stockholm School of Economics. **Benno J. Ndulu** is Executive Director of the African Economic Research Consortium and Professor of Economics at the University of Dar-es-Salaam. Both have published widely on development issues, trade policy and long-term growth.

ROUTLEDGE STUDIES IN DEVELOPMENT ECONOMICS

1. **Economic Development in the Middle East**
   Rodney Wilson

2. **Monetary and Financial Policies in Developing Countries**
   Growth and stabilisation
   Akhtar Hossain and Anis Chowdhury

3. **New Directions in Development Economics**
   Growth, environmental concerns and government in the 1990s
   Edited by Mats Lundahl and Benno J. Ndulu

4. **Financial Liberalization and Investment**
   Kanhaya L. Gupta and Robert Lensink

5. **Liberalization in the Developing World**
   Institutional and economic changes in Latin America, Africa and Asia
   Edited by Alex E. Fernández Jilberto and André Mommen

6. **Financial Development and Economic Growth**
   Theory and experiences from developing countries
   Edited by Niels Hermes and Robert Lensink

NEW DIRECTIONS IN DEVELOPMENT ECONOMICS

Growth, environmental concerns and government in the 1990s

Edited by Mats Lundahl and Benno J. Ndulu

London and New York

First published 1996
by Routledge
11 New Fetter Lane, London EC4P 4EE

Simultaneously published in the USA and Canada
by Routledge
29 West 35th Street, New York, NY 10001

Routledge is an International Thomson Publishing company I(T)P

© 1996 Swedish Agency for Research Cooperation with Developing
Countries (SAREC)

Typeset in Garamond by Pure Tech India Limited, Pondicherry

Printed and bound in Great Britain by
Mackays of Chatham PLC, Chatham, Kent

British Library Cataloguing in Publication Data
A catalogue record for this book is available from the British
Library.

Library of Congress Cataloging in Publication Data
A catalogue record for this book has been requested.

ISBN 0–415–12121–3 (hbk)
ISBN 0–415–12122–1 (pbk)

CONTENTS

List of figures   vii
List of tables   ix
Notes on the contributors   xi
Preface   xv
Opening remarks by Alf T. Samuelsson   xvii
Welcome address by Anders Wijkman   xxi

1 INTRODUCTION   1
Mats Lundahl and Benno J. Ndulu

Part I Growth, innovation and the environment

2 MACROPOLICIES FOR THE TRANSITION FROM
STABILIZATION TO GROWTH   29
José María Fanelli and Roberto Frenkel

3 CONSTRAINTS ON AFRICAN GROWTH   55
Arne Bigsten

4 LONG-TERM DEVELOPMENT AND SUSTAINABLE
GROWTH IN SUB-SAHARAN AFRICA   67
Ibrahim A. Elbadawi and Benno J. Ndulu

5 HOW PAINFUL IS THE TRANSITION? REFLECTIONS
ON PATTERNS OF ECONOMIC GROWTH, LONG WAVES
AND THE ICT REVOLUTION   104
Claes Brundenius

6 TECHNOLOGICAL IMPLICATIONS OF STRUCTURAL
ADJUSTMENT: SOME LESSONS FROM INDIA   129
Malur R. Bhagavan

7 DEVELOPMENTAL REGIONALISM   159
Björn Hettne

CONTENTS

8 ENVIRONMENTAL RESOURCES AND ECONOMIC
DEVELOPMENT 176
Partha Dasgupta and Karl-Göran Mäler

9 THE CAPTURE OF GLOBAL ENVIRONMENTAL VALUE 203
David Pearce

10 ENVIRONMENTAL TAX REFORM: THEORY,
INDUSTRIALIZED COUNTRY EXPERIENCE AND
RELEVANCE IN LDCs 224
Thomas Sterner

Part II The role of the state

11 THE GOOD, THE BAD AND THE WOBBLY: STATE
FORMS AND THIRD WORLD ECONOMIC
PERFORMANCE 251
Christer Gunnarsson and Mats Lundahl

12 THE ROLE OF THE AFRICAN STATE IN BUILDING
AGENCIES OF RESTRAINT 282
Paul Collier

13 PARTICIPATION, MARKETS AND DEMOCRACY 299
Deepak Lal

14 STYLIZING ACCUMULATION IN AFRICAN COUNTRIES
AND THE ROLE OF THE STATE IN POLICY MAKING 323
Thandika Mkandawire

15 ECONOMIC RESTRUCTURING, COPING STRATEGIES
AND SOCIAL CHANGE: IMPLICATIONS FOR
INSTITUTIONAL DEVELOPMENT IN AFRICA 352
Yusuf Bangura

16 FROM GATT TO WTO – A POTENTIAL FOR OR
A THREAT TO LDC DEVELOPMENT? 394
Göte Hansson

17 GOVERNMENT, TRADE AND INTERNATIONAL
CAPITAL MOBILITY 425
Ronald Findlay

Index 432

FIGURES

4.1 Rates of growth of GDP per capita: Sub-Saharan Africa
and others   69
4.2 Decadal rates of growth of GDP per capita: Sub-Saharan
African countries   69
4.3 Decadal rates of growth of GDP per capita: other
developing countries   70
4.4 Components of TOTSHOCK: SSA   82
5.1 Historical overview of the growth paths   106
5.2 Real GDP per capita: United States   107
5.3 Real GDP per capita: United Kingdom   107
5.4 Real GDP per capita: Sweden   108
5.5 Real GDP per capita: Germany   108
5.6 Real GDP per capita: Japan   109
5.7 Real GDP per capita: Russia/USSR   109
5.8 Real GDP per capita: Argentina   110
5.9 Real GDP per capita: Brazil   110
5.10 Real GDP per capita: Mexico   111
5.11 Real GDP per capita: Korea   111
5.12 Real GDP per capita: China   112
5.13 Real GDP per capita: India   112
5.14 Patterns of growth: Argentina and Sweden   116
5.15 Patterns of growth: United States, Russia/USSR and Japan,   117
9.1 Conservation failure   213
10.1 Determination of Pigouvian taxes   230
10.2 An analysis of green taxes   231
10.3 Inelastic supply of labour but infinite elasticity for energy   232
10.4 Tax proceeds and demand elasticity   237
10.5 Price and consumption of gasoline in various countries   238
10.6 The percentage structure of taxation in individual countries   242
12.1 Social learning and deterrence   290
12.2 Innovation and system correction of corrupt practices   292
15.1 Linkages in institutional development   383

16.1 Origin of world merchandise exports   405
16.2 Merchandise exports from low- and middle-income countries   406
16.3 Developed economies' pre-Uruguay Round rates and
offered reductions   412
16.4 Merchandise exports of developing regions by product group   417

TABLES

4.1 Definition of variables 71
4.2 Determinants of economic growth 72
4.3 Components of external shock 82
4.A Countries in the sample 94
4.B Instrumental variable regression results of the openness model 95
4.C Instrumental variable regression results of the real exchange
   rate 96
5.1 Real GDP per capita in this century 112–3
5.2 Per capita real GDP growth 114
5.3 Growth rates in Eastern Europe and in the republics of
   the former USSR 117
5.4 Catching up over time 119
5.5 Indicators of ICT diffusion 122
6.1 Structure of imports of manufactured goods 132
6.2 Percentage distribution of workforce by broad skill categories 133
6.3 Scientific and technical workers 135
6.4 Educational levels in 1975 and 1985 136
6.5 Enrolment in higher education in natural science, mathematics,
   engineering and computer science 136
9.1 Land conversions 207
9.2 World population projections 207
9.3(a) OECD agricultural subsidies 209
9.3(b) Agricultural input subsidies in developing countries 209
9.4 Preference valuations for endangered species and prized
   habitats 211
9.5 Changes in carbon with land use conversion 212
9.6 A schema for global environmental markets 215
9.7 Private sector carbon offset deals 218
10.1 Green tax reform in a fictitious two-product economy 234
10.2 Actual tax collected, nominal and average marginal tax rates 240
10.3 The structure of taxation in various groups of countries 241
10.4 Percentage of environmental taxes out of total excise taxes 244

12.1 Agencies of restraint and their possible effects   296
13.1 Growth and type of polity   311

NOTES ON THE CONTRIBUTORS

Yusuf Bangura is Research Coordinator at the United Nations Research Institute for Social Development, where he coordinates a programme on 'Crisis, Adjustment and Social Change'. His research interests are in the field of adjustment, livelihood strategies and institutional problems. He is the author of *Britain and Commonwealth Africa: The politics of international economic relations, 1951–78*, co-editor of *Authoritarianism, Adjustment and Democracy: The politics of economic reform in Africa*, and author of several articles relating to the political economy of the African crisis.

Malur R. Bhagavan heads the section on science, technology and industrialization in the Swedish Agency for Research Cooperation with Developing Countries (SAREC) and is Associate Professor in Industrial Economics and Management at the Royal Institute of Technology in Stockholm. His recent work in the area of industrial and technological policy includes *Technological Advance in the Third World, Technological Change and Restructuring in Asian Industries*, and *New Technologies in Developing Countries: The Challenge in Research and Training.*

Arne Bigsten is Professor of Development Economics at Göteborg University. He has published widely on issues of African economic development. His publications include *Regional Inequality and Development: A Case study of Kenya, Income Distribution and Development: Theory Evidence and Policy* and *Education and Income Determination in Kenya.*

Claes Brundenius is Associate Professor at the Research Policy Institute, University of Lund, Sweden. He has written extensively on development issues in the Third World and in the former centrally planned economies, notably Cuba. He is the co-author (with Andrew Zimbalist) of *The Cuban Economy: Measurement and Analysis of Socialist Performance* and the co-editor (with Bo Göransson) of *New Technologies and Global Restructuring; The Third World at a Crossroads.*

Paul Collier is Professor of Economics at Oxford University and Director of the Centre for the Study of African Economies. His books include

Controlled Open Economies and *Peasants and Governments* (both co-authored with D. L. Bevan and J. W. Gunning).

Partha Dasgupta is Frank Ramsey Professor of Economics at the University of Cambridge; Fellow of St John's College, Cambridge; and Chairman of the Board of the Beijer International Institute of Ecological Economics of the Royal Swedish Academy of Sciences in Stockholm. Over the years his research has ranged over population, environmental, resource and development economics, welfare economic theory, game theory, the theory of the economics of malnutrition and destitution. His most recent book is *An Inquiry into Well-Being and Destitution*. He is a Fellow of the Econometric Society, Fellow of the British Academy and Foreign Member of the Royal Swedish Academy of Sciences.

Ibrahim A. Elbadawi is the Research Coordinator of the African Economic Research Consortium in Nairobi, on leave from the Research Department of the World Bank. He has several publications on issues of macroeconomic adjustment, growth and exchange rate policy in Sub-Saharan Africa. His recent publications include 'Estimating Long-Run Equilibrium Real Exchange Rates' in J. Williamson (ed.) *Estimating Equilibrium Exchange Rates*, and 'Indirect Speculative Attacks and the Black Market for Foreign Exchange: The Example of Sudan', *Revista de Análisis Económico*.

José María Fanelli is Director of the Economics Department at the University of Buenos Aires and Senior Researcher at CEDES (the Center for the Study of State and Society) and CONICET (the National Research Council) in Buenos Aires. He specializes in macroeconomics and monetary economics and has published books and articles on stabilization, structural reform and the financial system in Latin America. Recent publications in English are: chapters in *Stabilization Lessons for Eastern Europe from Latin America; The Perspective of Monetary and External Sector Policy, Economic Lessons for Eastern Europe from Latin America, Foreign Capital in Latin America*.

Ronald Findlay is Ragnar Nurkse Professor of Economics at Columbia University, New York. Most recently he has published *Trade Development and Political Economy: Selected Essays of Ronald Findlay*, and *Factor Proportions. Trade and Growth*, based on the Ohlin Lectures for 1991. He is also the co-editor, with Stanislaw Wellisz, of *The Political Economy of Poverty, Equity and Growth: Five Small Open Economies*.

Roberto Frenkel is Professor of Economics at the University of Buenos Aires and Director of the Centro de Estudios de Estado y Sociedad (CEDES). He specializes in Latin American macroeconomics and has numerous publications on related issues in Spanish and English. Recent publications in English are *Strengthening the Financial Sector in the*

Adjustment Process and chapters in: *The Market and the State in Economic Development in the 1990s, The Rocky Road to Reform,* and UNCTAD *International Monetary and Financial Issues for the 1990s,* Volume I and Volume II.

Christer Gunnarsson is Professor of Economic History and Director of The Centre for East and Southeast Asian Studies at Lund University. He has published on different aspects of development but with focus on institutional factors. His recent publications include *"Village" in the Transformation of Rural Southeast Asia* (with Mason C. Hoadley) and *Growth, Stagnation and Chaos. An institutional analysis of the causes of underdevelopment* (in Swedish, with Mauricio Rojas).

Göte Hansson is Associate Professor at the Department of Economics, School of Economics and Management, Lund University, and the Deputy Dean of the Faculty of Social Science at the same university. He is External Research Fellow at the Centre for Research on Economic Development and International Trade (CREDIT) at Nottingham University. Göte Hansson has written widely on trade, trade policy and development issues. His publications include *Social Clauses and International Trade* (1983), *Harmonization and International Trade, The Ethiopian Economy 1974–1994– Ethiopia Tikdem and After,* and he has edited *Trade, Growth and Development – The Role of Politics and Institutions.*

Björn Hettne, Professor, Department of Peace and Development Research at the University of Göteborg (PADRIGU), has written on colonial history in India, European integration, ethnic conflicts, international relations and development theory. His previous publications are *Development Theory in Transition* (co-author), and *Europe. Dimensions of Peace* (ed.). His most recent publication is *Development Theory and the Three Worlds.*

Deepak Lal is the James Coleman Professor of International Development Studies at the University of California Los Angeles, Professor Emeritus of Political Economy, University College London, and Co-Director of the Trade Policy Unit of the Centre for Policy Studies, London. He has advised a number of governments in developing countries and international organizations. From 1984 to 1997 he was Research Administrator for the World Bank. His books include *The Poverty of 'Development Economics', The Hindu Equilibrium,* and most recently *The Repressed Economy* and *Against Dirigisme.*

Mats Lundahl is Professor of Development Economics at the Stockholm School of Economics. He has published widely on issues of development. His recent publications include *Incentives and Agriculture in East Africa, The Dependent Economy: Lesotho and the Southern African Customs*

Union, Politics or Markets? Essays on Haitian Underdevelopment and *Apartheid in Theory and Practice: An Economic Analysis.*

Karl-Göran Mäler is Professor of Economics at the Stockholm School of Economics and the Director of the Beijer International Institute of Ecological Economics. He is a member of the Royal Swedish Academy of Sciences. He has published a number of books and articles in environmental economics. More recently, he has been working on national income accounts and environmental resources, the valuation of environmental resources using household production functions, transboundary environmental problems and problems on development and environment.

Thandika Mkandawire is the Executive Secretary of CODESRIA (Council for the Development of Social Research in Africa). He has taught economics at the Universities of Stockholm and Zimbabwe. He has published extensively on problems of policy making in Africa. His recent publications (co-authored) are *Between Liberalisation and Repression: The Politics of Adjustment* and *From Stagnation and Adjustment to Human Development.*

Benno J. Ndulu is currently the Executive Director of the African Economic Research Consortium and Professor of Economics on leave of absence from the University of Dar-es-Salaam. His recent writings have focused on economic reforms in Sub-Saharan Africa, trade policy and industrialization, and investment and long-term growth.

David Pearce is Professor of Environmental Economics at University College London and Director of the Centre for Social and Economic Research on the Global Environment (CSERGE). He is the author of over forty books and more than 200 articles in academic journals. His most recent books are: *Blueprint 3: Measuring Sustainable Development*; *The Economic Value of Biodiversity*; *The Causes of Tropical Deforestation*; *World Without End*; and *Economic Values and the Natural World.*

Thomas Sterner is Professor of Environmental Economics at the University of Gothenburg. His most recent books on environmental issues in developing countries include *International Energy Economics* and *Economic Policies for Sustainable Development.*

PREFACE

The essays contained in the present volume, with two exceptions, were presented at the International Colloquium on *New Directions in Development Economics – Growth, Equity and Sustainable Development*, at Hässelby Castle, outside Stockholm, 9–11 March 1994, organized by the Swedish Agency for Research Cooperation with Developing Countries (SAREC). SAREC has for many years been supporting research in the field of development economics in the Third World, e.g. through its Latin America Program (LAP) and its Program for African Social Sciences (PASS), and more recently also via contributions to the African Economic Research Consortium (AERC) in Nairobi. The objective of the colloquium was to contribute to the process of producing lines of theoretical understanding which will be of policy relevance and at the same time sensitive to the imperatives of the developing world, through a discussion unfettered by existing paradigms.

As editors, we are grateful to a number of people, above all to the secretariat of SAREC, in particular Anders Wijkman, Director General, Bo Göransson, secretary of the colloquium, and Marianne Lindström, who handled all the logistics before, during and after the three hectic days at Hässelby. We also want to thank a number of referees, who unfortunately have to remain anonymous, for generously providing us with peer reviews of all the papers presented during the process of selection for publication, as well as our respective secretarial staffs in Stockholm and Nairobi, for struggling with the innumerable practical details of getting the manuscript ready for publication.

Mats Lundahl and Benno J. Ndulu
Stockholm and Nairobi, 1995

OPENING REMARKS

Alf T. Samuelsson
Under-Secretary of State,
Ministry for Foreign Affairs

The theme for this seminar is naturally highly relevant in the context of Swedish development cooperation. Understanding the complex interrelationship between policy reform, appropriate technology, institutional framework, and economic outcome and sustainable development is essential for us in formulating our strategies for development cooperation. These are complicated matters and there are no easy answers or solutions to the problems at hand. We are working in a context of 'learning by doing', where some of the lessons learned are harder than others.

Development assistance has from time to time been heavily criticized and has often had to take the blame for disappointments in economic outcome in some developing countries. Although some of this criticism is valid and should be expressed, in general, the critics tend to overemphasize the role of assistance. Assistance is only one factor influencing the developments within countries. Development cooperation is a means of supporting ongoing processes, but it can never substitute, or even compensate, for inadequate domestic policies. Our cooperation efforts must be seen in a long-term perspective and be based on mutual trust. And our programmes and strategies must be designed to facilitate domestic resource mobilization and to strengthen domestic capacities and institutions. It is therefore important that we improve our understanding of the economic, environmental, technical, institutional and political forces that are needed for attaining sustainable development.

The overall aim of Swedish development cooperation is to improve the standard of living of poor people. This overall aim can be broken down into five subobjectives:

– resource growth
– economic and social equity
– economic and political independence
– democratic development
– far-sighted conservation of natural resources and care of the environment.

These subobjectives must be seen as an integrated whole. They supplement and reinforce each other with the common aim of achieving a higher standard of living and more equitable conditions for poor people. The aim of our cooperation is also to make itself superfluous in the long run, by helping developing countries to solve their own problems and to make it possible for them to participate in the international system on more equal terms. In this context, I would like to stress the importance of the global free trade system. The outcome of the Uruguay Round in GATT is a welcome step forward in integrating the developing countries in a world-wide free trade system, even though it is difficult to analyse the full effects of the agreement at this stage.

The orientation of Swedish development cooperation is increasingly being geared towards various forms of assistance to improve governance in developing countries. Criteria have been established to steer our endeavours in this direction. These criteria are based on the efforts made by the developing countries themselves and will influence our choice of partners and the magnitude of our assistance. The criteria include an assessment of:

- democratic development
- respect for human rights
- economic policy and reforms towards a market economy
- the effectiveness of aid resource utilization
- the utilization and distribution of overall budgetary resources in the recipient country, particularly focusing on the relative share of social expenditure compared with military expenditure.

These criteria help us in our choice of development partners, but they are also prerequisites for attaining sustainable development.

The Swedish budget that was presented in January 1994 points to a number of areas which will be given priority in our coming work. Let me briefly mention these.

First, the promotion of democracy and human rights will remain one of our main priorities. The importance of democracy and respect for human rights in achieving sustainable development is being increasingly recognized in the international community. In most of the countries with which Sweden cooperates, political reforms are under way. Although necessary, these reforms are far from easily undertaken, and it is therefore important that we support the reform processes through our assistance. Priority areas will be support to the legal system and legal institutions, support of various functions within parliaments, support in holding and monitoring elections and support of constitutional reform. Efforts will also be made to strengthen the media to foster professionalism and pluralism.

Second, most of Sweden's cooperating partners are undergoing not only political reforms, but also far-reaching economic reforms. Macroeconomic stabilization and structural reforms are necessary to pave the way for a restoration of growth. Balance of payment support enables us to support the transition to a market economy in recipient countries by increasing their capacity to finance necessary imports, debt servicing and government operations through counterpart payments by importers.

In parallel to the provision of extensive financial support to countries pursuing reforms, we are also working to strengthen domestic capacity in the field of economic analysis and management through support to key institutions such as central banks and Ministries of Finance.

An important element of the support to adjusting countries is additional debt relief. Sweden has for a long time been pressing on an international level for further debt relief for the heavily indebted, reforming low-income countries. The debt service payments for some of these countries are simply not viable, as a majority of their meagre export earnings are being used to repay debt. The debt burdens are in some cases actually posing a major threat to the outcome and continuation of economic reforms. The Swedish government arranged, together with the Swiss government, an international seminar in May 1994 with the aim of achieving a greater international understanding for the need of more far-reaching and sustainable solutions to the debt problem of these countries.

Third, emergency relief will continue to play an important role against the background of a growing number of increasingly complicated disaster situations in different parts of the world. The rising complexities are posing new and difficult challenges for the orientation and design of emergency relief. A new vision and a flexible approach to the linkages between humanitarian, political and peace-keeping activities are strongly needed. Furthermore, we need to clarify and strengthen the linkages between humanitarian efforts, reconstruction efforts and long-term assistance.

Similarly, we need to focus on long-term strategies to avoid or mitigate disaster and emergency situations. There is a great need for improving international coordination in the field of emergency relief.

Fourth, we will strive to improve our work in a number of areas which are of crucial importance in achieving sustainable development. We would like to define sustainable development according to the Brundtland Commission, i.e. 'development satisfying the needs of today, without risking the possibilities of satisfying the needs of coming generations'. The concept of sustainable development is people focused and centres on national and international changes of society from a social, economic, ecological and political point of view. To be able to encompass all these components we need to increase our efforts in the following areas:

- environment and development
- population and development
- agriculture and development
- women and development, and
- children and development.

Fifth, we will be paying more attention to the means of increasing the effectiveness of development cooperation. This is a formidable and necessary task.

Our ability to analyse the environment in which we are working, the prevailing conditions, the priorities set by the recipient country and the realism of our goals will determine the effectiveness of our efforts.

The decisions made concerning the design and magnitude of our cooperation have to be based on the results attained. This might seem obvious, but in the history of development cooperation this has not always been the case. Focusing on results means that we have to define very clearly the goals for all our activities, so that the outcome can be continuously measured against the goals. It also means that we need to improve our analytical toolbox, used to measure results, not only in terms of short-term efficiency but also in terms of long-term effectiveness and development impact. We are at present devoting much time and effort in developing our planning process and methodologies in this area.

An important part of this work is to clarify better our strategies and priorities for cooperation with our main partners. This work is progressing through the successive adoption of Country Strategies for each of our main cooperating partners, encompassing all different types of assistance channelled through the various Swedish aid agencies.

Several studies have been commissioned to look into ways of improving the effectiveness of the execution and administration of Swedish development cooperation. In some cases these studies have resulted in operational proposals that are now being adopted; in others much work remains before changes can be implemented.

WELCOME ADDRESS

Anders Wijkman
Director General, SAREC

Before giving some comments on the theme of this conference, allow me to give a brief presentation of SAREC. When SAREC started in 1975, support capacity building of research was our central task. Strengthening indigenous research was seen as a prerequisite for self-reliance and national development. It was seen as a key factor in the building of knowledge and capacity for development and essential if poor countries were to break out of isolation and have the possibility to participate in international scientific cooperation. Our support was channelled through four major types of programmes:

- bilateral research cooperation
- international research programmes
- regional and special initiatives
- special support for development research at Swedish universities.

Over the years our activities have expanded, in particular those aimed at bilateral capacity-building efforts. We currently have fifteen bilateral programmes, the majority of them in Africa. Our budget is 450 million Swedish kronor, an estimated 60 million US dollars. Since we are active within all major disciplines, this means that we are spread rather thinly.

One obvious observation to be made after almost two decades of work is the extremely small size of the resources allocated for human resources development in most countries of the South, resulting in low capacity. In such a situation it is difficult for a government to start any real development process. Foreign experts are often available but to depend on them means that self-reliance is not possible. Furthermore, the conditions of life and development in southern countries differ very much from the situation in northern countries. The climate is different, soils are different, ecosystems are different, social and cultural habits are different. Hence experts from abroad may have little to contribute; in fact they may often constitute a problem.

When funds for research are unevenly distributed – presently more than 95 per cent of all research in the world takes place in the rich countries – it also follows that research priorities are dominated by northern interests. This is the reason why within SAREC we ask for increased funding both for research and capacity building in poor countries and for a greater interest by northern scientific institutions in the many challenging developmental problems in the South!

One subject area of great concern to us is development economics. We have been able to channel support to a number of capacity-building efforts in this field in Africa as well as Latin America. We see it as a priority to contribute to the development of a better understanding in the countries concerned with the driving forces behind development. Hence our active support for institutions like the African Economic Research Consortium, CODESRIA in Africa, CEDES in Argentina, and CIEPLAN in Chile, to name a few.

The main objective of this conference is to listen to your assessment of where we are today in terms of understanding the dynamics of development. What do we know about development? Why has development succeeded relatively well in some parts of the world and not in others? Where are the 'knowledge gaps'? What role could an institution like SAREC play in the future? To what types of research activities – including capacity building – should we give priority?

Looking back, many different schools of thought regarding development theory and development economics have emerged over the years. During earlier decades polarization was strong between thinkers on the left and on the right. Today the situation is different. Market-friendly approaches have come to dominate the debate more and more. After the collapse of the Soviet system, this tendency is even more pronounced.

When listening to the general discussion one sometimes feels as though history really has come to an end, i.e. that the market economy as we know it is the ultimate development model. Such a conclusion, however, would be premature. Over the last few years a number of problems of paramount importance to everybody concerned with development issues have come to the fore, and no easy answers can be found. I am referring to the ecological crisis as well as to the problem of growing populations. In addition, there is the widening gap between those who have and those who have not.

For a period of time, the issue of equity seemed to be forgotten, and all focus was on growth *per se*. For a number of reasons this situation cannot continue. The gap between the rich and the poor is accelerating and the consequences for social stability, for the environment and also for population growth could be very detrimental.

When reflecting on new strategies to solve these problems, we should of course not lose sight of the significant progress that has been made by the developing world. Average incomes have more than doubled in thirty years, much faster than in the UK during the industrial revolution. Infant mortality has been cut in half. Total fertility rates are down by 40 per cent. In fact many developing countries have been able to bring fertility rates down much faster than was the case in Europe towards the end of the last century.

But for some regions of the South the record is not impressive. In more than thirty-five countries – comprising more than 500 million people – average incomes remain very low or have been declining since the 1960s. In those regions, poverty is a terrible problem. The question is: why have some countries succeeded whereas others have failed?

Larry Summers, the former chief economist of the World Bank, provides some answers in a recent article (Summers and Thomas, 1993). *First*, according to Summers, what is required for any sound development are conditions of peace. *Second*, nations form their own destiny. Poor domestic policies are usually to blame for development failures – much more so than an unfavourable external environment. *Third*, what is required is a proper blend of state and market in the economy. As Keynes once said, 'the important thing for a government is not to do the things which individuals are doing already...but to do those things which at present are not done at all' (Summers and Thomas, 1993, p. 244). Investments in human capital – through education and health services – as well as infrastructure are examples of meaningful activities.

I guess most people would agree with Summers and Thomas' reasoning. When analysing further what constitutes a 'good policy environment' Summers and Thomas point to the value of experience regarding the importance of sound macroeconomic policies as well as a competitive climate for enterprise.

However, there is a great deal of uncertainty as well when it comes to explaining what has worked and what has not worked. Summers and Thomas ask for more research into the whole question of what role state interventionist policies played in the case of the Southeast Asian success stories. Another important research area is the relationship between political and economic reform. Many of the most successful nations have had governments that were authoritarian. What conclusions can be drawn?

Development is not only a question of growth. Far too often, however, development is presented as being successful provided growth rates are high. Human Development Reports have made endeavours in recent years to go beyond the GDP statistics. In developing the Human Development Index, an attempt is made to assess quality of life in a broader sense. These efforts ought to be strengthened.

To measure progress solely as a function of the growth rate of the economy is questionable for a number of reasons. The GDP tells us nothing about the distribution of incomes, nor does it indicate how the welfare system is functioning. Another weakness is that the effects on the environment are neglected. This was a correct approach as long as human activities were relatively small compared with nature. But this is no longer the case. The World Resources Institute and others have shown for individual countries, in particular in the South, that if observance had been given to the negative environmental consequences of economic growth the net national product would be negative instead of positive.

For many years the majority of economists paid little attention to the negative impact on the environment of production and consumption systems. If the problem was recognized, the response was normally one of 'putting the prices right'. But very rarely did prominent economists take the lead on these extremely important issues. Hence it is with great pleasure that we welcome to this conference a few personalities who have made valuable contributions to the efforts to integrate economics and environment!

Let there be no misunderstanding. Economists are absolutely right in stressing the need to 'get the prices right'. One of the main weaknesses of today's system is that it is more or less free to pollute. By internalizing the social costs of production and consumption conservation efforts and efficiency are being encouraged and environmentally friendly systems of production, consumption and transportation will have a real chance to compete. However, let us not forget that some aspects of environmental degradation are difficult to assess in monetary terms. I am referring particularly to damages in the services provided by ecosystems (like local climate control, recycling of nutrients, absorption of waste products, etc.). Here more research is needed to develop the right kind of policy instruments.

More and more people agree that for the South to continue to follow the prevailing growth concept of the North does not provide a solution to its problems. The resulting waste would be colossal and most probably lead to major ecological collapses. Those that would suffer the most would be the poor.

What is urgently needed are new strategies for development, in the North as well as in the South, where the focus is as much on the quality aspects of growth as on quantity. Only by doing more with less could sustainability be accomplished. In a recent paper, the German scientist Ernst von Weizsäcker asked for a quantum leap in the efficiency by which humans use energy and materials. Only through such a 'revolution' will it be possible to provide decent living standards for the billions of poor in the South without destroying the life-support systems (von Weiszäcker, 1994).

The British author Paul Harrison has another approach, i.e. poverty as a cause of environmental degradation. He argues in favour of a better understanding of the real causes behind deforestation and land degradation. According to Harrison, the main problem is poverty and growing populations. As long as there is land available and the poor are not offered better opportunities for survival than what they have, the degradation will continue (Harrison, 1993).

Thus, a key issue for the future will be how to reach the poorest segments of the population. Can adjustment to the 'market-friendly' approach work in the poorest countries – and will such approaches really reach the poor segments of the population, those living on subsistence farming and outside the formal economy?

Other important issues are of course those related to technology and technology transfers. Almost all 'late-industrializers' in both the North and the South have industrialized on the basis of technology transfer, including the countries of Southeast Asia. Such a process can be looked upon as 'technological learning rather than technological innovation'. Key questions are: Why did this process succeed so well in some countries and fail so dismally in others? What role did state intervention and state-imposed technology policy play in the successful cases?

Another dimension of technology is job creation. What can we expect of the future? To what extent will automation penetrate the South? Will the phenomenon of jobless growth occur?

Looking back, technology transfer to the South has largely been a failure in many countries from the point of view of generating large-scale and rapid growth in employment. The so-called appropriate technology movement has tried to meet this challenge by evolving technologies and organizations that can be easily mastered by local populations, that make use of local materials, etc. This movement has had its successes in several parts of the South, but it has not been something that developing country elites have been eager to promote. How can the appropriate technology movement be better supported in the future? What obstacles does it face? What niches can it occupy? These are some of the issues that require better understanding.

Over the last decades education has been acknowledged as a fundamental factor for development. The issues that need to be further discussed are: What should be the balance between technical and non-technical education, between higher education and research, between state intervention and private initiatives?

As well as preparing myself for this conference I have also been participating in preparations for a major seminar in Parliament on population-related problems. It is one of many meetings preceding the Cairo Conference. What has struck me in the preparations so far is that almost everybody is focusing on fertility rates and what could be done to bring them down as quickly as possible. This is of course important. But just as important is to start to think really about how to prepare the planet for another 3 to 4 billion people in the next fifty years. No matter how successful we are in bringing down fertility rates there is no way we can avoid another 3 to 4 billion people. That is how strong the momentum is. This has nothing to do with population policies but is sheer mathematics.

Quite obviously the world is not well prepared for such an increase in the number of people. Imagine all the health care, all the housing, all the schooling – not to mention all the jobs – that would be required to take good care of all those people! Already today we experience enormous difficulties in providing those services and opportunities for a much smaller population. This should put our discussions into the right perspective.

BIBLIOGRAPHY

Harrison, P. (1993) *The Third Revolution*, Penguin, Harmondsworth.

Summers, L. H. and Thomas, V. (1993) 'Recent Lessons of Development', *The World Bank Observer*, vol. 8, no. 2.

von Weizsäcker, E. (1994) 'How to Measure Progress Towards Sustainability', Paper presented at Norwegian Government Symposium on Sustainable Development, Oslo, 19–20 January 1994.

1

INTRODUCTION

Mats Lundahl and Benno J. Ndulu

Economic development usually encompasses issues of growth and distribution. Development takes place when the gross national product (or income) per capita grows at a sustained pace over a long period without simultaneously worsening the distribution of income and increasing the number of absolute poor. Given that economic growth implies using resources, some of which are not renewable, to these requirements should also be added a condition with respect to sustainability. That is, growth should take place in a way that takes the true costs of resource depletion and environmental degradation into account. Growth should not be hampered, but resources must be left to future generations as well.

The essays contained in this volume all attempt to reflect the above definition of economic development. At the same time, they focus on some of the most important issues facing development economics as the present century draws to a close. The first of these issues is economic growth and its costs. Growth – the overriding development concern during the 1950s – has been brought back to the forefront in the 1990s. The so-called New Growth Theory has endogenized technological change, focusing not only on capital formation (as was the case in the 1950s) but also on such determinants as the development of human capital, research and international trade. In order to bring out the complexity of the growth process the economy has been disaggregated into more than one sector. On the empirical side, interest is shifting from short-run stabilization of economies that were in acute crisis in the 1980s to more long-run issues, including structural reforms and institutional requirements, creating a growth-inducing economic environment.

The concern with growth is reflected in the first six essays. The three following ones all discuss the costs of growth in terms of the environment. Environmental issues as such have been dealt with for a long time in economics, notably in the theory of exhaustible resources and in the discussion of externalities in welfare economics and public-choice-oriented literature. The problems of deforestation and soil erosion and more generally the protection of biodiversity remain among the most serious issues facing developing countries today. However, until relatively recently few systematic attempts had been made to bring environmental considerations into the development context.

1

The second half of the book concentrates on problems related to the role of the state. Hand in hand with the emphasis on growth in the 1950s went a belief that the state would be able to promote growth by means of an active, highly interventionist, development policy that substituted an orderly planning procedure for the capricious swings of the market. As is well known, the pudding of central planning has not stood the test of eating. The trend during the past twenty years has been one away from *dirigisme* towards a more market- and incentive-oriented view of how development can be brought about. Still, *laissez-faire* has not carried the day. The notable success of the East Asian economies during recent years and the many incomplete answers to questions about the exact degree and nature of government intervention in these economies has revived the state versus market debate, as reflected in the last seven essays of this volume.

GROWTH, INNOVATION AND THE ENVIRONMENT

Economic growth has occupied a central place in the development literature throughout the past four decades. Growth has led to the prosperity and welfare gains of nation states. Indeed the differentiation of the well-being of economies over time rests mainly on the level of achievements in growth performance. Development strategies have thus invariably focused on the means to achieve high rates of growth as a basis for reducing poverty and improving living standards.

These strategies have experienced major changes over time. The changes have been influenced by developments in the theory of growth and by experience from the actual implementation of growth strategies. The early theories emphasized capital formation as the engine of growth and savings mobilization as the main means for achieving high investment. Productivity growth was considered to be driven largely by exogenous technological progress. Incomes of the world economies were expected to converge unconditionally over time as the poorer nations caught up, given the anticipated higher productivity of capital in these countries. Macroeconomic policy stances were expected to have no influence on the long-term rates of growth as these were driven by exogenously determined rates of technological progress and population growth. Since the 1980s, however, the New Growth Theory has shown that technical change is endogenous to the growth process and that human capital and policy stances do matter for long-term growth. Technological progress benefits from human capital formation, scale economies and access to foreign technologies. This contention is supported by growing disparities in incomes between the developed and the least developed world and the empirical evidence that convergence of incomes is conditional on the improvement of other growth fundamentals.

2

The 1980s also saw a major swing towards concerns with macroeconomic stability in the developing world as a condition for long-term growth. In addition, this shift emphasized market-oriented incentive structures to promote efficiency in resource use and productivity growth. Little attention was paid to other fundamentals. The continued sluggish growth performance in the least developed countries, however, points to the need for addressing the problems related to such issues as well. Moreover, since these countries depend to a large extent on environmental resources for sustaining growth, the increasing loss in biodiversity has raised serious concerns about the protection of environmental resources for future generations.

The six essays that focus on long-term growth highlight the importance of the recent emphasis on macroeconomic stability as a condition for achieving sustained growth. At the same time, these chapters draw attention to several other conditions for growth. They emphasize the need to coordinate stabilization and development policies in order to ensure that short-run corrective measures are consistent with the broader aims of promoting employment, investment and innovation. The essays also point to the importance of appropriate institutional environments that will facilitate resource accumulation and efficient allocation. The main concerns here relate to uncertainty and lack of credible policies which discourage investment and distort resource use.

Also addressed is the need to create a productive structure in developing economies that is capable of responding flexibly to external reversible shocks so as to ensure a continued stable development environment. The essays consider regional integration as a strategy to reach threshold scales of activities, attract investment into marginal regions and coordinate security and resource management in order to reduce risks and uncertainties as well as conserve scarce resources. The role of innovation is considered in the context of long-run cyclical patterns of technological change and with a view to meeting the necessary conditions for keeping up with a rapidly innovating world.

The focus of the three essays on the environment concerns the overexploitation of environmental resources, as well as approaches to resolve the tension in the appropriate utilization of these resources to ensure the well-being of generations over time. All three use the viewpoint of intergenerational equity as their point of departure and emphasize the need to respect resource constraints when pursuing economic development. The essays also consider specific policy instruments to address the distortions arising from the failure of markets and governments so as to ameliorate the rising loss in biodiversity. These initiatives and their potential impacts are reviewed in relation to local market failures, government intervention failures and global appropriation failures.

3

Chapter 2

'Macropolicies for the Transition from Stabilization to Growth', by José María Fanelli and Roberto Frenkel, focuses on coordination of macroeconomic and development policies. Using the Latin American experience of the 1980s and 1990s, the chapter shows how a lack of coordination between macroeconomic and structural policies in situations of undeveloped markets and pervasive market and government failures can lead to persistent macroeconomic instability and uncertainty. This, in turn, discourages investment and innovation, which hinders both growth and productivity gains. The chapter singles out four key factors as the fundamental causes of coordination failures. These are the extremely thin and rationed capital markets, the public sector's tendency to generate unsustainable deficits because of rudimentary systems of taxes and expenditure, a productive structure incapable of responding flexibly to external shocks, and a lack of access to timely financing of resource gaps caused by reversible shocks.

In contrast to the situation in the developed economies where the task of macroeconomic policies is largely that of fine tuning to smooth out cyclical fluctuations in investment and employment rates, macroeconomic policy in developing countries has primarily aimed at correcting short-run current account disequilibria and fiscal imbalances. The preoccupation with restoring equilibrium has led to a dichotomization between stabilization and development policies. The authors emphasize the need to coordinate policies so as to achieve macrostability on a sustained basis while at the same time promoting employment, investment and innovation. They highlight the need for taking into account the longer-run consequences of stabilization policies on economic structure and the effects of structural reforms on short-run stability.

Fanelli and Frenkel review the coordination failures of the 1980s in Latin America during which uncertainty and instability prompted domestic savers to prefer liquid international assets – capital flight. Owing to the limited availability of international credit to governments and domestic private investors, effective investment was lower than its potential. During the 1990s, macroeconomic stabilization policies have reversed the capital flight and expanded short-term inflows. This has generated significant real appreciation of currencies and an allocation of resources that is inconsistent with long-term sustainability of the external equilibrium. In both cases, these undesirable effects are attributed to the fundamental coordination failures.

Fanelli and Frenkel point to four main challenges in the 1990s which are related to the links between macroeconomic policies and development. First, there is the need to raise the rate of investment and savings through a combination of the classical tradition of 'thriftiness', the Keynesian tradition of appealing to the investor's 'animal spirits', the neoclassical tradition

4

of 'allocative efficiency' and the Schumpeterian tradition of 'incentives for innovation'. The second challenge is that of addressing the problem of disarticulation of the financial system in the light of the thinness of financial markets and the lack of robustness of the domestic demand for financial assets. Third is the need for strengthening the fiscal structures in order to close unsustainable fiscal gaps. In this regard, particular attention needs to be paid to the harmonization of the multiple objectives of fiscal policy, particularly between fostering macroeconomic stability and nurturing productive investment. A primary task singled out here is that of improving the revenue productivity of the tax system while minimizing the distortionary allocative effects. Fanelli and Frenkel encourage the reduced use of tax handles in order to avoid 'fiscal rebellion' by instilling a sense of fairness. Expenditure restructuring towards public investment and anti-poverty programmes is encouraged. The fourth and final challenge is to avoid interruption of the growth process through the creation of a productive structure that can flexibly respond to external shocks and through improved access to contingent finance. All together, the Fanelli and Frenkel chapter characterizes the ideal macroeconomic framework for growth as that which ensures a lower degree of uncertainty regarding inflation, an appropriate and stable rate of exchange and an improved fiscal balance in support of higher savings and investment, as well as the sound instrumentation of strategic interventions to compensate for market failures.

Chapter 3

In 'Constraints on African Growth', Arne Bigsten raises research questions with respect to the persistently very poor growth performance of African economies in contrast to other developing regions, which have shown a remarkable ability to catch up with the developed world. The chapter first reviews the results of various studies that explain growth performance. The review singles out three factors – the rate of resource accumulation, technological innovation and efficiency in resource allocation – as being fundamental for sustained growth. It is further argued on the basis of these studies that technological progress benefits from human capital accumulation, the existence of scale economies and access to foreign technologies. The advantage of late-starters is partly related to the opportunity to adopt up-to-date foreign technologies at significantly lower costs than the inventors. Against this background, the African economies are seen to be sliding back in relative terms as a result of low rates of resource accumulation, the absence of scale economies, negative productivity growth and an increasing gap between the technologies applied in Africa and those on the international frontier.

Bigsten then delineates the important areas for further investigation, focusing on the appropriate economic and institutional environment for facilitating the accumulation of resources, their efficient allocation and the introduction of better technologies. In acknowledging the considerable effort and progress in macroeconomic policy reforms, three key areas are singled out for further research. The first task is to determine the extent to which instability and unsustainability of policies discourage investment. The role of a large debt overhang is also highlighted in relation to the pressures for policy change and increased vulnerability to shocks. Uncertainty and lack of credibility are thus pinpointed as important constraints to investment that need further study.

The second issue is the extent to which selective market interventions can be adopted from the East Asian experience to promote export growth. Transparency in the selection of target agents for support and the development of appropriate supportive institutions are emphasized. Also important, in order to reduce transaction costs, is a clear delineation of exchange rules and enforcement of contracts. Finally, Bigsten stresses the importance of research on the political processes that promote policy interventions based on rules rather than discretion. What mechanisms can be adopted to insulate a competent bureaucracy from undue political pressure and interference?

Chapter 4

'Long-Term Development and Sustainable Growth in Sub-Saharan Africa', by Ibrahim Elbadawi and Benno Ndulu, focuses on the constraints and prospects for long-term growth in Sub-Saharan Africa. The analysis is motivated by widely supported empirical evidence that a significant proportion of Africa's poor growth performance is unexplained even after taking into account basic growth fundamentals and policy stances.

The chapter identifies three broad categories of constraints to long-term growth in Sub-Saharan Africa. The first set is what is referred to as the growth fundamentals. The economies are characterized by vastly under-developed infrastructure, weak institutions, rudimentary technology and relatively low human capital development, as well as unstable macroeconomic and political environments that discourage saving and investment. Elbadawi and Ndulu review empirical studies on the relationship between long-term growth and these fundamentals and in addition use their own empirical analysis to confirm the significance of all these factors in explaining the poor growth of Africa and the failure to 'catch up' with the rest of the world.

The second constraint is the structural disarticulation of African economies, which makes them more susceptible to external shocks and limits their capacity to respond to those shocks. The chapter assesses the income effects of external shocks resulting from changes in the external terms of trade, interest rates and net transfers of external resources for a median

African country. In contrast to the conventional wisdom, the results show a significantly higher loss of income from external shocks in Sub-Saharan Africa than in other developing regions. At best, net transfers of foreign resources only partially offset the negative effects of the sustained decline in the external terms of trade. The chapter also looks at the indirect effects of these shocks in the light of the weak response capacity and relatively poor access to timely liquidity to help ride out temporary shocks. These indirect effects include irreversible resource allocation decisions by producers attempting to cope with persistent unpredictable shocks and the stimulation of bad policy response to shocks. Finally, Elbadawi and Ndulu point to the close link between external and fiscal pressures in the African economies and the high debt overhang as crucial factors constraining a prudent response to external shocks.

The third set of constraints relates to the small size of African markets and their poor strategic location *vis-à-vis* the main economic growth poles of the world. The chapter points to the failure to generate the threshold scales necessary for creating strategic complementarities and attracting adequate levels of investment for badly needed modernization and technological progress. It also raises the issue of regional spillover effects from investment in human and physical capital and from civil instability. Finally, it urges policy coordination at the regional level to buttress reforms as well as other forms of regional integration to achieve threshold scales of activities and attract investment.

The Southeast Asian experience is referred to in the context of rethinking industrial strategies as African countries move away from the previous disastrous experience with import substitution and selectively build on past investment. The urge for selectivity and transparency in intervention, the need to exploit comparative advantage in unskilled labour and the necessity of building on human competence and technological capabilities are emphasized as important lessons from this successful experience.

Chapter 5

'How Painful is the Transition? Reflections on Patterns of Economic Growth, Long Waves and the ICT Revolution', by Claes Brundenius, focuses on the role of innovation in the growth process in the context of long-run cyclical patterns of technological change. Such cyclical patterns are characterized by transitions from one 'techno-economic paradigm' (TEP) with a dominant form of technology to another. These transitions involve significant costs.

Brundenius' central thesis is that countries that move rapidly to higher development stages need to adopt new technology relatively early in a Kondratiev cycle or position themselves with foresight on what the new underlying technology of the future will turn on. The empirical evidence presented in the chapter suggests that as technology changes, developing countries that have positioned themselves to benefit from the 'underlying technology' of the next long wave can catch up with the rich countries, while those that lock themselves in dinosaur technologies fall behind. According to Brundenius, the catching-up process crucially depends on the ability to adapt to the rapidly changing conditions of entry into the world market during the transition from one techno-economic paradigm to another. This adaptation requires changes in the institutional, social and response capacity of firms to exploit emerging opportunities.

The author illustrates his contention with a comparison of long-term growth performance among 'pioneers', 'late-comers' and 'late late-comers'. Those now developed countries that were successful in making the painful transition between phases got ahead, while those that did not stagnated in relative terms or even fell back. Through the first four waves, 'late-comers' such as the United States, Germany and Sweden were able to catch up with pioneers (e.g. Britain) and surpass them by engaging in revolutionary technological breakthroughs. These countries are now well positioned to exploit the opportunities of the next techno-economic paradigm (fifth cycle), which will be driven by the information and communication revolution.

Countries in Latin America such as Argentina and Brazil, which posted reasonably fast growth during the first cycle, as well as the former Soviet Union, which posted rapid growth during the fourth cycle, have stumbled, owing to their inability to make the painful transition to new dominant technologies. Other countries, such as India, have stayed behind for the same reason. The only 'late-comers' singled out by Brundenius as having been able to position themselves well for the transition to the fifth cycle recently are those of Southeast Asia.

The evidence presented in Brundenius' chapter poses two key questions for development as the world moves from the fourth Kondratiev cycle, driven by mechanization, to the fifth, which will be spearheaded by information technology. The first issue is that this transition provides an opportunity for developing countries to 'leapfrog' in terms of growth, as shown by the Southeast Asian experience. This opportunity arises from the fact that microelectronics and informatics, which enhance human mental effort, are based on a cheap and undepletable resource – silicon – and the skills for using such technology can be more easily acquired.

The second issue relates to the conditions for successful exploitation of this opportunity. These go beyond the current focus on trade liberalization/ competitive environment as the quickest route to learning. The chapter underscores the need to adopt policies that support the learning process and the response capability of firms. The need for requisite intellectual capacity to be able to benefit from these opportunities can thus not be overemphasized. Furthermore, late-comers may be trapped in the inertia from the previous industrial structure in trying to mimic closely the experience of the leading countries. From this perspective Brundenius concludes that the catching-up prospects for the majority of late-comers are very bleak.

Chapter 6

In 'Technological Implications of Structural Adjustment: Some Lessons from India', Malur Bhagavan reviews the evolution of technological policy in India over the last three and a half decades and poses the transitional challenges a developing country faces in coping with the changes towards a high-tech world. This evolution has taken place in two main phases: the era of the closed economy during which the government played a dominant role in promoting technological progress (1950–1984) and a more recent phase of a liberalized and open economy with a larger number of important actors, including the domestic private sector and foreign firms (1985 to date). Bhagavan argues that the move towards the second phase began in the mid-1960s with a gradual decline of state ownership and control of the commanding heights of the economy. The process has intensified since the mid-1980s and accelerated with the adoption of the structural adjustment programme in 1991.

During the first phase, through its technology policy, India succeeded in building capacity for technological absorption, increasing the ability to use and replicate a great variety of imported standard modern technologies and a few highly modern capital goods. Bhagavan cites the drastic reduction of imports of consumer goods and capital goods as evidence. At a more detailed firm level, further evidence is provided from a set of studies that confirm success in the indigenization of foreign components, product adaptation and diversification. These achievements were a result of efforts in research and development organized in government research laboratories, Indian institutes of technology and in-house research and development in industrial firms. The overall protective structure and technical as well as scientific training, mainly through public programmes, buttressed this effort.

However, Bhagavan voices several concerns with respect to the experience with the technological progress achieved and the technology policy pursued during this phase. First, there is the failure to acquire the capacity to design and innovate new standard technology. Second, there is the failure to indigenize high technology as is evident from the continued growth of technology imports. In both these cases the effort in public institutions and the in-house research and development was inadequate. The firm-level evidence cited shows that the principal concerns of the firms were improvement of product quality, production efficiency and labour productivity. Innovation was seen to be too costly for the firms' limited means, and public laboratories and institutes lacked both resources and a culture of responsiveness to the requirements of the firms. Third, the structure of skills development was biased towards graduate scientists and engineers and against technicians. Making a comparison with the structure in South Korea, Bhagavan sees this inverted skill formation pyramid as an obstacle to technological progress.

With the opening up and liberalization of the Indian economy during the second phase, the participation of foreign firms and high-technology imports have rapidly increased. The number of technology agreements with foreign firms has doubled, spurred by the dismantling of restrictions previously in place. Import restrictions for capital goods have been considerably reduced, licensing for new and expansion of old firms has been abolished, provisions for monopolies and trade confinement have been scrapped and public firms have been exposed to competition and critical review for efficient performance.

Bhagavan raises several doubts with respect to the new policy regime. First, he sees it as intensifying the process of technological polarization and dualism set in motion in the 1980s. On the one hand, medium- and large-scale firms will increase their utilization of imported highly modern technology while abandoning domestic modern technology. On the other, the small-scale sector will continue to use locally produced technology. Thus the gap in know-how between the two will widen. Second, Bhagavan doubts the capability of local producers to absorb high technology effectively in spite of their increased efforts. He sees the challenges when it comes to retraining shop floor engineers and technicians to absorb high-tech skills as formidable. Third, Bhagavan regards the influx of high technology and abandonment of standard technology as an impetus to further postponement of technological effort in design and innovation since far more resources and capabilities are required for this purpose. Fourth, he envisages a likely encroachment into the small-scale sector with the removal of licensing restrictions. The new policy environment opens up this sector for a possible takeover by medium- and large-scale firms. Fifth, as industry shifts to high technology, skilled labour will become increasingly redundant without alternative opportunities for absorption.

In the last section of the chapter Bhagavan considers various options for addressing the challenges. These include strategies for retraining and job relocation, growth in the small-scale sector and its modernization through technology estates, rejigging in-house research and development for absorption of new technology and restructuring education, workforce and national research systems.

Chapter 7

'Developmental Regionalism', by Björn Hettne, focuses on the rise and revitalization of regionalism as a development strategy. Hettne argues that this 'new' regionalism is qualitatively different from earlier attempts at creating regional blocs as free trade areas to address the problem of small market sizes. It facilitates trade flows within the membership of regional organizations, but three key features distinguish it from the old arrangements. First, the new regionalism incorporates the coordination of security systems among the participants as a means for preventing political disintegration and conserving resources committed to resolving civil strife for alternative use in support of development – the peace dividend. Second, these new entities are increasingly being used as a means for solving ecological problems which span national boundaries. Third, the new regionalism offers a way of avoiding marginalization as the globalization of the world economy proceeds rapidly and disparities in development increase across the regions of the world.

Hettne is optimistic about the success of the new regional arrangements in achieving the above objectives. Unlike their old counterparts, they emphasize the concept of 'region' rather than simple participation in global hegemonic arrangements. The end of the cold war has played an important part in this transformation. Moreover, he argues, rather than being imposed from above through governmental acquiescence to hegemonic interests, the new entities are being formed from below with a wide participation of non-governmental interests such as firms, labour unions and other kinds of social movements. The new regional organizations are adapting to the opening up of the global economy. In contrast to the old 'closed regionalism', the new 'open regionalism' seeks to remain consistent with GATT regulations while addressing region-specific concerns. The links across regional interests are bound by these rules and regulations, relieving the tension between regional interests and the process of globalization. They ensure social protection against the potentially disruptive forces of market expansion while permitting the exploitation of opportunities from the globalization process. Hettne likens this arrangement to a decentralized GATT system.

In order to illuminate the applicability of these new features to regional initiatives in the developing world, Hettne highlights the dominant features of the strategy in each initiative. The argument of 'viable economy' is particularly pertinent to Africa and the Caribbean, the main concern being to avoid marginalization. In the case of Africa, he points to the formation of the African Economic Community as a remedy in the long run. In the meantime, however, Hettne emphasizes the importance of a gradual achievement of this ambition through the strengthening of subregional initiatives such as the Southern Africa Development Community (SADC) and the Economic Organization of West African States (ECOWAS) as building blocks. The objectives of these and other initiatives, like the Inter-governmental Authority on Drought and Development (IGADD), go beyond the promotion of trade to encompass political, security and environmental concerns. Hettne identifies the harmonization of economic policies through the adoption of similar economic reforms and political pluralism as conducive to successful integration.

In the case of the Caribbean Basin, Hettne observes the current movement away from the earlier emphasis on structural transformation for national autarky and specialization according to the comparative advantages of each country. Changes in the external world, including the formation of the North American Free Trade Area (NAFTA) and the end of the cold war, have raised the concerns of marginalization and economic viability in spite of the many obstacles to integration in the region. As the region becomes politically more homogeneous, prospects for regionalism become stronger. Hettne concludes that these economic and geopolitical factors will push the Caribbean countries towards joining NAFTA.

The argument of effective global articulation is best exemplified by the countries in Southeast Asia. As the globalization process intensifies and regional blocs emerge, particularly in the developed world, these countries increasingly seek to articulate interests within the region *vis-à-vis* the globalization process. Hettne characterizes this initiative as 'open regionalism' built around a Sino-Japanese core against the 'Fortresses' of Europe and the Americas. GATT rules and regulations are the key instrument for this articulation.

Hettne also exemplifies the peace dividend by pointing to regional initiatives in the Middle East. In spite of the very significant regional homogeneity in language, culture and religion, security in the region remains elusive and conflicts abound. Regional hegemonism has been and still remains strong. Hettne concludes that a regional development process based on the triangle of Israel–Jordan–Palestine is essential for the consolidation of the peace process and development of the whole region.

Finally, there is South Asia. Hettne notes that the strategy of delinking that was dominant in the region is losing ground. Hostilities within the region still abound and some form of regional cooperation has been initiated against regional hegemonism. Developmental regionalism remains embryonic. However, Hettne sees some scope for cooperation in respect to common resource management. He cites the common management of the shared river system as an important imperative for regionalism in the future.

Chapter 8

In 'Environmental Resources and Economic Development', Partha Dasgupta and Karl-Göran Mäler review the relationship between economic development and the appropriate use of environmental resources. The principal objective is to highlight the resolution of intergenerational tensions in the management of environmental resources for economic development. These resources include both renewable and non-renewable stocks. The chapter essentially sets this resolution as a problem of both intertemporal welfare economics and the theory of optimal development. Dasgupta and Mäler point out that the central concern need not be so much the decline in the stock of environmental resources *per se*, but the optimal pattern of use of such resources to realize the well-being of the society over time. Sustainable development in this regard pertains to the strict observation of an intergenerational resource constraint to guarantee the reasonable welfare of future generations.

These concerns arise from several factors. Most poor countries depend heavily on natural resources for their livelihood and yet they are the least able to repair damage to environmental resources. Soil degradation through overcultivation and salinization through irrigation in the absence of adequate drainage are examples of the fragility of the development base in these countries. Lack of credit, insurance and capital markets is also cited as a cause of animal overstocking in these countries – with similar consequences. Until recently, little concern was given to the issue of the deteriorating environmental resource base in the formulation of policies. The same neglect is cited for the discipline of development economics. The authors argue that the recent upsurge of environmental concerns has lopsidedly focused on putting a stop on the decline of the stock of environmental resources without paying adequate attention to the other side of the coin, the well-being of society. This underlies the adoption in this chapter of a more balanced approach to the resolution of this apparent tension.

Dasgupta and Mäler begin by considering a first-best solution to resource use for intergenerational well-being. The underlying assumption is that intergenerational equity is valued as an ethical goal. The adopted optimization procedure results in a well-specified condition for maintaining intergenerational well-being. It requires that the discount rate applied to the consumption stream over time be less than the social rate of return on investment (or capital productivity). If this condition holds, consumption over time will not decline. This, they argue, is contrary to the popular notion of a zero consumption discount rate. It underlines the fact that the rate of discount for well-being differs from the consumption rate of discount.

The authors note, however, that in the real world computing the first-best allocation of the resources may be unattainable and, hence, they consider a second-best scenario involving appropriate social cost–benefit analysis. The problem of global warming is used as an illustrative case. In this analysis Dasgupta and Mäler underscore the need to correct for the problem of market failures resulting, for example, from missing forward markets for property rights and from the existence of transactions costs. They cite the puzzling results of recent simulation studies on the economics of global warming based on simple social cost-benefit analysis. These studies conclude that the social costs of efforts to counter the phenomenon in the near future would exceed the benefits, which will accrue only in the very distant future. Dasgupta and Mäler argue that these results ignore the need to avoid future risks, including the possibility of societal extinction. The use of social rates of discounts that take into account the specific risks and uncertainties related to environmental matters is critical.

To be able to evaluate properly changes in aggregate well-being over time, as required by the approaches suggested above, one needs appropriate measures of the components of well-being. Dasgupta and Mäler point to the weaknesses of the current approaches to measuring real net national income as an indicator of well-being. These ignore social and environmentally related components. An appropriate measure of the real net national product, they argue, needs, on the one hand, to incorporate deduction of the value of environmental damages and depreciation of the natural capital stock and, on the other, to add the recurrent expenditures against environmental damages and the net additions to the environmental defensive capital. The authors further emphasize the use of appropriate shadow prices for goods and services in estimating real net national product. These ought to be derived from the intertemporal optimization of the economy. The prices so obtained can in turn be used at a more operational level to evaluate projects and policies. Dasgupta and Mäler conclude that if these prices are used in this way they would indicate that projects that degrade the environment have lower social profits than they currently tend to show.

The Dasgupta–Mäler chapter provides a useful framework for a balanced approach to evaluating the links between the management of environmental resources and economic development. It sets the tone for the next two chapters, which focus on specific issues of environmental concern and draw on relevant experiences to highlight them.

Chapter 9

'The Capture of Global Environmental Value', by David Pearce, takes up the critical concerns of overexploitation of environmental resources as a result of three economic failures: local market failures, government intervention failures and global appropriation failures. These lead to a less than optimal allocation of global environmental resources. The chapter focuses more specifically on balancing the benefits from land conversion and land conservation as a way of minimizing the loss in biodiversity.

Although Pearce contends that it is unrealistic to expect to save much of the world's biodiversity owing to the rapid increase in sheer population pressure, the loss in biodiversity could be significantly reduced through leveraging the flow of funds under international agreements and exploiting mutually beneficial trade that generates benefits from the conservation of biodiversity. The chapter expresses concern about the current singular emphasis on the flow-of-funds approach to conservation, noting that its requirement, which is estimated at 0.8 per cent of the GNP of the OECD countries, far exceeds total official development assistance, which stands at only 0.36 per cent of GNP. Pearce therefore strongly advocates using complementary measures at local and international levels to foster a balance between land conversion and land conservation as well as refraining from subsidizing the rate of return to land conversion. At the global level provision of the 'missing' global markets for the valuable functions of habitat and species is emphasized.

Using specific examples, Pearce highlights particular schemes falling under private and official ventures. Some of these are regulation induced and others are a result of spontaneous market transactions. He advocates the broader adoption of appropriate domestic policies in both the developing and the developed world since the economic approach to minimizing the loss of global resources has more promise than the flow-of-funds approach. More specifically, it urges the adoption of measures to internalize and capture the significant environmental values in market prices and direct agreements between economic agents. Filling the gap of missing markets locally and globally is an important part of this initiative.

Chapter 10

In 'Environmental Tax Reform: Theory, Industrialized Country Experience and Relevance in LDCs', Thomas Sterner considers different approaches for resolving the potential conflict between growth and depletion of finite environmental resources at the national level. He reviews the options available to policy makers for improving efficiency in the allocation of environmental resources without compromising growth objectives, particularly those related to public expenditure. The main instrument considered by Sterner for achieving the double dividend of environmental protection and increased government revenue is what is referred to as 'green taxes'. While noting the limitations of relying on taxes alone for managing common property resources, the author describes the important role they can play in correcting market failures and enhancing social efficiency in the use of depletable resources.

The chapter reviews the type of tax reforms that could be promoted to attain simultaneously the objectives of revenue generation and environmental protection. The keen environmental protection interest which a country like Sweden has pursued is based on its high reliance on natural-resource-based industries, and intensive utilization of taxes for financing large public expenditure programmes. Sterner compiles a range of environmentally relevant product taxes and assesses their budgetary and environmental protection effects. Key among these are energy-related taxes, including taxes on oil, coal, natural gas, liquid petroleum gas and electricity. Other taxes are those directly levied on vehicle owners and users as well as on tobacco.

Turning to the developing economies, Sterner highlights the limited tax options for revenue generation that these countries have, their meagre resources for environmental protection programmes and the high dependence their populations have on natural resources for their livelihood. This situation, the chapter argues, makes the use of green taxes for multiple objectives particularly attractive. The strategy advocated includes avoiding environmentally destructive subsidies and a consideration of a wider range of green taxes, including those on water, refuse, energy, fertilizer, lumber stumpage and other natural resource rents.

THE ROLE OF THE STATE

One of the most exciting, and consequently most hotly debated, current development issues is what role the state plays and should play in the economy. During the 'Golden Age' of development economics, in the 1950s and 1960s, this role was taken for granted by most economists. Interventionism, founded partly on the Keynesian heritage, and partly on welfare economics, was the rule. Market failures were thought to be ubiquitous in less developed economies and the proper role for the state was to step in and correct these, through an active economic policy in general and through planning in particular.

A host of planning models was developed. Most of these models had in common a very pessimistic view of the possibilities of employing the market mechanism. Growth-oriented constructions, with a strong structural emphasis on a perceived lack of flexibility, saw the day. Comprehensive, highly aggregated macroeconomic models and input–output analysis, based on shadow prices instead of market prices, were all put to use to improve upon the performance of the market mechanism in the Third World.

With time, however, the enthusiasm for planning subsided and the tide turned in favour of the market. Little by little it was discovered that planning in practice and planning in theory amounted to two different exercises that in the worst case had little to do with each other. The ideal planning sequence – formulating the goals, identifying the restrictions, choosing the means, quantifying the plan and implementing it – was always interfered with by politicians, bureaucrats, lobbies, local people, etc. The outcome virtually always fell short of the planners' expectations. In addition, information began to accumulate about mistaken interventionist policies, e.g. in the area of international trade. It was also discovered that the 'planning' view that held the state to represent the citizens at large was not necessarily a realistic one. It was equally possible to have a government that strongly concentrated on pushing for certain groups only – in the worst case only the one(s) contained in the government itself. With the advent of the public choice literature in the 1960s and 1970s, 'government failure' became the new catchword. The total breakdown of the communist system at the beginning of the 1990s put the final nail in the coffin of comprehensive planning.

The market has made a strong comeback during the past twenty years. Still, this does not mean that all government action is 'out'. On the contrary, the most eloquent development success story during the post World War II period is that of Japan and Southeast Asia – and what 'caused' this success is far from completely clear. The available explanations cover a very wide spectrum of views, ranging from 'market fundamentalism' to a conviction that the 'Asian miracle' would not have been possible without extensive government intervention in a number of fields.

Naturally, this tends to raise some important questions. Are there ways for the state to intervene in the development process without simultaneously destroying the market mechanism? Do 'non-traditional' fields for successful government interference exist that have not been sufficiently explored, or should the role of the state be a minimal one? What is 'good governance' all about? Our second set of essays deals with these types of questions.

Chapter 11

'The Good, the Bad and the Wobbly: State Forms and Third World Economic Performance', by Christer Gunnarsson and Mats Lundahl, deals with varieties of government in developing countries. The point of departure is the inefficient state that fails to foster economic development. Gunnarsson and Lundahl distinguish two different reasons for this: on the one hand the lack of willingness; on the other the existence of information and administration costs. Without doubt, the most difficult of these situations is the former, where the government does not have any commitment to development, in particular when it is authoritarian and self-seeking, since this easily makes the state predatory.

Douglass North has pointed out that throughout history the prevailing set of property rights has as a rule tended to produce stagnation rather than growth (labelled 'North's law' by Gunnarsson and Lundahl). The predatory state constitutes a prime example of this, and Gunnarsson and Lundahl therefore set out to explain how this type of state is created, with power concentration first locally and, as the problem of organizing larger groups and units is solved, subsequently on the regional and national level.

The ruler of a predatory state faces a problem with respect to the size of the clique that should be allowed to share the spoils. Gunnarsson and Lundahl discuss how finding the optimal size entails a trade-off between income aspects and security considerations. A smaller clique may lead to a higher income for the ruler but also to a higher probability of being toppled – the 'Latin American' case. But the opposite situation, where the clique size tends to become too large from the survival point of view – the 'African' case – is also possible.

The plunder of the citizens by the government builds on the mechanism of rent seeking, i.e. on the redistribution of an already existing cake. Rent

17

seeking is a game that may be played by individual citizens. It presupposes the existence of a bureaucracy that has the power to decide who will get what. Needless to say, this constitutes a fertile breeding ground for corruption, and Gunnarsson and Lundahl point to some mechanisms that tend to make for a thoroughly corrupt civil service – even out of a small beginning.

In the predatory state, however, the most important rent seeking takes place at the top. It is carried out by the ruler, who, besides being able to seek already existing rents, is in the unique position of having the power to *create* new ones. This, in turn, imposes a cost on the rest of the society. Rent seeking redistributes existing income and assets without in principle creating any new goods and services, and in the process it uses up real resources – the more, the smaller is the already existing claim of the predators and, paradoxically, the less, the larger their past success in plundering. There is, however, a limit to predation. The ruler always has to face the competition of would-be rulers and is also up against a transactions cost constraint on the plunder.

Finally, even predatory rulers have an interest in maintaining the plunder base. They only foster inefficiency when it is in their direct interest to do so. It is only when predation clashes with efficiency that they choose the former. Thus, the question necessarily arises of when the predatory state turns 'productive'. Under certain circumstances it is in the interest of the ruler to enhance private production, and from there the road lies open towards the 'good' or developmental state. What, then, makes for transition from the predatory to the developmental variety of state?

Gunnarsson and Lundahl repudiate arguments based on the 'benevolence' of rulers. This type of argument can hardly explain why rent seeking ceased to be a viable strategy, e.g. in Korea and Taiwan. Instead they point to the importance of external pressure. Rulers are always operating under a competitive constraint. They may be toppled by contenders for power. Sometimes, however, not only the ruler but the entire political unit as well is in danger. This was typically the case in Europe as the modern state emerged there during the sixteenth and seventeenth centuries. The European states competed with and fought each other and a strong army needed a strong economy. The same was true during the wave of industrialization in the late nineteenth century. The modernization of Japan after the Meiji Restoration and today's development states in East Asia are other cases in point.

Chapter 12

Paul Collier's essay, 'The Role of the African State in Building Agencies of Restraint', picks up one of the strands of the Gunnarsson–Lundahl chapter: the widespread corruption in many Third World countries, with concentration on Africa. Collier begins by modelling how equilibrium levels of incidence of a particular corrupt practice (the extent to which the practice

18

has spread) and the proportion of practices that are corrupt are established. The former equilibrium is determined by the social learning or contagion of corrupt behaviour on the one hand and deterrence on the other. The proportion of practices that are corrupt, in turn, is determined by the change in this proportion and the rate of system correction, i.e. the rate at which society is able to close off opportunities for corruption.

Collier argues that after independence both deterrence and system correction broke down in Africa when the restraint ultimately exercised by the colonial authorities disappeared – with the result that African societies became high-corruption societies. The second problem he investigates is how these societies can be put on the road to honesty and governments can be restrained with respect to macroeconomic policy and fiscal composition. Collier emphasizes system correction, by reducing the power and the range of activities of the state, since this would reduce the opportunities for corrupt practices. (Only thereafter can the state be re-expanded.) The effects of a number of mechanisms – donor conditionality, central bank independence, indexation of domestic debt, budget rules, democratization and multinational reciprocal threats – are analysed.

Donor conditionality is likely to be effective only in the short run because donors are seldom in a position where they can make credible long-term threats and promises *ex ante*. The usefulness of donor conditionality is also undermined by the introduction of democracy in Africa, which makes it difficult for a sitting government to make long-term commitments. Possibly, however, there is some scope for *ex post* conditionality in the sense that countries with a bad performance record will receive less aid in the future.

Central bank independence, whereby the central bank sets the inflation target itself or independently pursues a target set by the government, is difficult in Africa, where government is highly centralized and fiscal policy easily gets out of line with a monetary policy designed to combat inflation. Indexation of domestic debt in order to avoid spurts of unanticipated inflation produced by government may be effective in the longer run while the introduction of cash budgets (no more is spent than what comes in) may provide short-term restraint on government spending.

Democracy is the most important long-run mechanism for checking predation and corruption, but its short-run effects are more doubtful. In particular, overspending may easily take place each time elections are approaching. Also, decentralization of spending makes it more difficult to check on corruption at the local level where it is often more rampant than at the centre. Finally, reciprocal multinational threats, exercised through schemes of regional integration (e.g. trade and currency agreements) have an advantage over conditionality in that they involve more national participation and less externally imposed restraint.

The analysis of Collier leads to a logical sequence of restraint, beginning with a reduction of the domain of the state that makes possible the shedding of functions likely to harbour corrupt practices. Conditionality and cash budgets have a role to play here. Their role remains a short-term one, however. In the long run more sustainable mechanisms are called for: reciprocal threats and democracy and, once the scope for corrupt practices has been reduced, deterrence in the form of punishment.

Chapter 13

Deepak Lal's 'Participation, Markets and Democracy' relates to one of the themes touched upon both by Gunnarsson and Lundahl and by Collier: the existence of a non-developmental state. A popular argument in much of the discussion of development assistance has been that in such cases the appropriate strategy is to spend through non-governmental organizations (NGOs), i.e. in a way that does not require state participation on the receiving side. Lal casts very serious doubts on this view and maintains that the ultimate test of the NGO pudding is in the eating. What decides whether operating through NGOs is good or bad is the cost-effectiveness of each particular project – nothing else.

The starting point for Lal's analysis is the assumption that popular participation, e.g. via NGO projects, fosters democracy and that democracy, in turn, leads to good governance and economic development through the market. Lal questions this chain of reasoning and argues that the available evidence does not permit such conclusions to be drawn. Beginning with democracy, he points out that the essential advantage of democracy is that it promotes liberty, which is positive in itself. What is needed for economic development, on the other hand, is a functioning market economy to which the state may contribute by good governance. However, good governance is not necessarily fostered by democracy, nor is it a monopoly of democracy. This, according to Lal, is clearly borne out both by the writings of such classic scholars as Adam Smith and David Hume and by the experience of the developing countries during the post World War II period.

Lal traces the predilection in many quarters for NGOs to the American tradition of political sociology, which holds that civil voluntary associations, of the American variety, provide a check on the tyranny of the ruler or central executive. This remains true. What is questionable, however, is whether the existence of a pluralist democracy, with many such interest groups, leads to efficient markets, as some sociologists and economists have argued. As Mancur Olson has shown, it is difficult to achieve a balance among these groups. Their actions tend not to cancel each other, but smaller groups may have an influence on government actions that bears no relationship to their small size, while the opposite is true for large groups. The overall result of this is to decrease, not increase, efficiency in the economy.

Lal also cites evidence from a large comparative World Bank study, directed by himself and Hla Myint, which indicates that democratic or oligarchic states tend to perform less well in terms of economic growth than states where factional pressures play a subordinate role. In addition, pressure groups are often dominated by those with a relatively high income and not by broader population segments. It may also be the case that broad, popular participation in the political process produces an outcome that nevertheless tends to favour the middle class (the typical median voters) or that broad popular participation is exploited by populist demagogues.

Lal finishes his discussion by making recommendations with respect to World Bank policy *vis-à-vis* NGOs. Since it cannot be proved that working via NGOs necessarily promotes either democracy (and liberty) or economic efficiency and development, the only reasonable policy is to work on a pure case basis. What must be established is the cost-effectiveness in each and every instance. There are no shortcuts or general principles that would make this procedure superfluous.

Chapter 14

'Stylizing Accumulation in African Countries and the Role of the State in Policy Making', by Thandika Mkandawire, tackles the problem of how the stylization of an economy determines the policy conclusions and the research agenda. Mkandawire begins with a characterization of the neoclassical paradigm. This involves, for example, constant returns to scale and substitutability in production, competitive markets with clear, technological change in response to changes in factor prices, absence of financial repression, full employment and flexible wages. In this setting, the role of the state in the development process is simply one of approximating these conditions as closely as possible so that the market mechanism can do the rest.

However, making reference to the failure of the structural adjustment programmes in much of Sub-Saharan Africa, Mkandawire argues that the neoclassical stylization of the economy may be completely out of touch with the African reality and may hence have led to a completely erroneous set of policy recommendations. He then goes on to an alternative stylization – one that builds more on observed facts.

In the alternative stylization, markets are no longer perfect, but market failures are ubiquitous. Economies of scale influence the directions of technological change. The small size of the market in most African countries makes for monopolies unless trade is allowed to act as a countervailing power. Labour markets are characterized by institutional arrangements that differ from those of the neoclassical model. Dualism is present and the wage-setting process in the formal sector is often a highly political one. Monopoly firms may pay higher wages to reduce labour turnover or to appear as 'good citizens'. Financial markets are repressed and market failures due to, for example, imperfect information are frequent. There is no close relationship between savings and interest rates.

Mkandawire goes on to discuss the state explicitly. The two different stylizations of the economy in his view lead to completely different roles for the state. Depending on which of the two stylizations has had the upper hand, the prevailing view among economists has changed. While *dirigisme* was advocated almost universally in the 1950s and 1960s, the following two decades saw a shift towards a more passive role. Government failure was emphasized, and the possibility of an 'evil' state was recognized. Mkandawire argues that the pendulum has swung too far. A more pragmatic view of the state is needed – one that takes into account the East Asian experience and the possibility of a positive symbiosis between state and private enterprise.

The last part of Mkandawire's essay spells out a research agenda, based on the non-neoclassical stylization of the economy. The first component in this agenda is the possibility of learning from the East Asian story. The second component focuses on the politics of policy making and its relation to increased democratization. Third, there are the institutions and functioning of labour markets. Finally, issues of technology and technology policy warrant more research, not least in the light of the New Growth Theory.

Chapter 15

'Economic Restructuring, Coping Strategies and Social Change: Implications for Institutional Development in Africa', by Yusuf Bangura, analyses the relationship of institutions to structural adjustment programmes from the point of view of social change. Here, as in the case of Mkandawire, the point of departure is the neoclassical paradigm and its lack of institutional content. Bangura sketches some of the major criticisms of this paradigm and points out that institutions and economic actions need to be seen as embedded in social relations.

The main section of the essay examines the impact of economic crisis and structural adjustment on the coping strategies of different socioeconomic groups in Africa, i.e. the changes in the composition of income-generating activities: migration, self-employment in the informal or rural sector, wage labour, subsistence activities, etc. This diversified pattern has existed for some time but was intensified and generalized in the 1980s in a dramatic way. Bangura examines how the various coping strategies have operated in the economy and how different groups have fared.

The coping strategies are also associated with changes in social relations. Polarization takes place as people earning their living in diversified ways acquire multiple social identities. Modernization efforts have been truncated and the process has also led to stalemates in the configuration of political power. Old divisions have been sharpened and new ones have been introduced. The main winners are those with access to foreign exchange through their activities. The difference between haves and have-nots has grown in the countryside and divisions between rural and urban areas have been sharpened and made more complex.

The fact that people have several jobs confers multiple social identities on them. This operates on all levels. Academics have been fused with bureaucrats and professionals, rural poor and marginal urban groups tend to resemble each other and the difference between smallholders and workers in the informal urban sector is weakened. This, in turn, makes it difficult to direct policy action towards specific sectors or groups within sectors because the response pattern will differ from the situation where there is a clear separation.

The increased role of the informal sector has made modernization more difficult. Traditional groups and leaders tend to achieve more importance in relation to the modern centralized state, which has lost legitimacy by its failure to display patent development. Religious and ethnic movements of various kinds come to the forefront.

During the process of structural adjustment, according to Bangura, the multilateral organizations have systematically attempted to strengthen politically those groups that are favourably inclined to reform. That, however, has met with resistance from many African governments and also from important interest groups. This tends to produce a political stalemate that makes it difficult to devise clear strategies for (or against) reform, especially since the coping strategies that rest on diversification make it difficult to identify clear-cut winners and losers.

The last section of Bangura's essay deals with the problems of institutional reform. As long as there is a contradiction between the institutions through which economic policy and reform have to work and the wider society, the institutions will remain inefficient and hamper development. Bangura examines how a process of institutional reform must focus on three fundamental dimensions and the relations among them: institutional goals, which may have to be reshaped to conform to social relations, the very crisis of institutionalization, as spelled out above, and the changes in the social relations themselves. These three dimensions cannot be separated. For the process to be effective, moreover, Bangura argues that two critical conditions must be met. African states must retrieve sovereignty in policy making from the multilateral financial institutions and single-run reform must be discarded in favor of an open-minded multi-faceted perspective.

Chapter 16

'From GATT to WTO – A Potential for or a Threat to LDC Development?', by Göte Hansson, concentrates on the international arena and analyses the recent multilateral trade agreement emanating from the Uruguay Round. Hansson concludes that this new agreement is likely to constitute a clear improvement of the institutional framework for international trade. The degree of transparency and predictability of rules will increase and this, in turn, is likely to benefit poor countries with weak international bargaining power.

Hansson notes the increasing consensus, not least in the Third World, with respect to the benefits for the world economy of the new trade agreement, although the latter cannot be expected to be completely positive for all developing countries. The least developed economies, which are often net food importers, may run into problems as a result of the gradual elimination of government support for the agricultural sectors in the OECD countries. On the other hand, dismantling the Multifiber Arrangement may serve as a stimulus to Third World exports.

Whether the developed countries will in the future take policy action to assist their less fortunate brethren remains a somewhat moot point. They made a commitment to this end in the Uruguay Round, but domestic structural problems may create restrictions behind screens of 'environmental problems' or 'cheap labour'. With respect to the highly sensitive area of child labour, Hansson persuasively argues in favour of social and educational measures instead of mere trade restrictions, which are likely to result mainly in the deterioration of the already difficult situation of large low-income families.

Although the overall conclusion emanating from Hansson's analysis is that the Third World is likely to gain from the recent institutional change in the area of international trade, the OECD countries stand out as the great winners in this exercise. If the less developed countries are to be able to make full use of the opportunities offered, they will almost certainly need assistance, not least when it comes to increasing their bargaining and administrative ability.

The agreement with respect to technical obstacles to trade constitutes another problem area for Third World countries. The new agreement could easily contribute to keeping exports of, for example, processed foodstuffs, textiles and consumer durables to the industrialized world. Foreign assistance to enhance the capacity to apply technical standards in export production is clearly needed.

Still, Hansson argues that the problems created by the Uruguay Round should not be exaggerated. The obvious counterfactual is what would have happened if the new agreement had not been concluded. Poor and weak economies would hardly have benefited in a situation likely to have been characterized by increased uncertainty resulting from increased bilateralism in trade and less transparent rules.

Hansson concludes by noting that domestic systemic change within the less developed countries themselves is a necessary but hardly sufficient condition for the situation of these countries to improve. Such change must be complemented with reforms of the international trade and payments systems as well. The Uruguay Round Agreement constitutes but one step in the latter process and without an institutional framework, many Third World countries may find themselves more or less permanently caught in their current difficult trade situation.

Chapter 17

Governments can, however, also act domestically when it comes to influencing international competitiveness. The last chapter, 'Government, Trade and International Capital Mobility', by Ronald Findlay, focuses on the consequences of capital movements in a model where government action can affect the productivity of the private sector. Findlay begins by making the observation that while the role of state action in 'traditional' fields of trade policy (tariffs, quotas, subsidies) has been substantially reduced during the past couple of decades, with the liberalization of the international exchange of goods, governments may still have an impact on productivity and comparative advantage. This takes place through the provision of physical and social infrastructure, notably education, which serves to raise the productivity of the labour force and the capital stock.

Given this starting point, Findlay goes on to sketch a suitable approach to the analysis of this problem, which is of relevance not least for developing countries. In his approach, the state does two things. It provides a public intermediate input that is employed in the production of final goods. It also produces public services directly consumed by the citizens. The private sector, in turn, produces one high-technology (manufactured) good and one low-technology (agricultural) commodity. The two goods are tradables, while the public service is consumed only domestically.

The model has a number of interesting implications. Findlay works with the case where technology and factor endowments are identical across countries, but the relative tastes of the citizens for private goods and public services differ. Economies with relatively stronger preferences for the former tend to spend relatively more on public inputs and export the commodity that is more sensitive to such inputs, i.e. high-technology goods, and import low-technology goods from economies preferring relatively more public services.

What is more, the very trading process tends to increase the difference in comparative advantage, since it contributes to allocating more labour to public input production in the country with stronger preferences for private goods while it draws labour out of this sector in the other type of economy. This tendency may be counteracted by conscious government action, but only by a government that does not reflect the interests of the citizens in its policies, and then of course at the expense of the consumers.

The above takes place when capital and labour are immobile between countries. Opening the model for capital movements produces a capital flow from the high-tech sector (the only one using capital) of the low-tech exporters to the high-tech sector of the high-tech exporters, since the rate of return on capital tends to be higher in the latter. This increases the size of the high-tech sector in the recipient country and decreases it in the capital-exporting country. This effect is further reinforced by the fact that as capital enters the high-tech exporting country, the rate of return to the public input will increase there, while it decreases in the other country. More of this intermediate good will therefore be provided in the former economy and less in the latter. More capital moves across borders until the rate of return is equalized, with real wages being higher in the high-tech exporting country than in the low-tech exporting economy.

CONCLUSIONS

To conclude, the present volume does not purport either to cover the entire area of development economics as we approach the end of the twentieth century or to spell out any definitive conclusions or recipes for development. The idea has been to point to a number of important issues of growth and the costs of growth, on the one hand, and of the role of the state in the development process, on the other. These are among the most important problems facing the development economics profession today.

Even so, the range covered has turned out to be wide. The first group of growth essays covered the coordination of macroeconomic policy and development policy proper, particularly in Latin America, and the poor growth performance of African economies, with special emphasis on constraints and future prospects. They also noted the role of regionalism and that of innovation both in the context of long-run cyclical patterns of technological change and in connection with structural adjustment. The second group concentrated on the environmental cost of growth.

Turning to the essays dealing with the role of the state, the first two covered negative government action and how to get away from that: the predatory type of state and its conversion into the developmental variety as well as problems of corruption and its abolition. Thereafter the focus was shifted to the pros and cons of channelling foreign aid through non-governmental organizations when the recipient government is a non-developmental one, the influence of the stylization of an economy on policy action, the relation between structural adjustment in Africa and the coping strategies and the social relations of the individuals affected by them. Finally, government action related to trade was brought into the picture, through international institutions and domestically, via the provision of different types of public goods. Certainly, all these topics will rank among the leading development issues well into the next century.

Part I

GROWTH, INNOVATION AND THE ENVIRONMENT

2

MACROPOLICIES FOR THE TRANSITION FROM STABILIZATION TO GROWTH

José María Fanelli and Roberto Frenkel

INTRODUCTION[1]

Economics has been called the dismal science. To a certain degree, macroeconomics, as a subdiscipline, can be blamed for this. The central message of macroeconomics is not a popular one among either citizens or economists from other subfields. And this is so for at least two reasons. On the one hand, macroeconomics plays the role of the Freudian superego: its most important task is to tell us what should not be done. On the other hand, the results of following macroeconomists' advice can be particularly disappointing: macroeconomic equilibrium itself, once achieved, does not guarantee economic development.

In the Latin American context, however, this lack of popularity of macroeconomic policies has been greatly enhanced by the characteristics of many of the stabilization packages that were implemented after the debt crisis. They not only reduced growth by inducing significant falls in investment but also deteriorated income distribution.

Macropolicies, i.e. exchange, fiscal, monetary, financial and income policies, mainly focus on the management of short-run disequilibria. But every combination of macropolicies has its own impact on the growth performance of the economy. For example, the more favourable external financial conditions that Latin America is facing in the 1990s have made room for stabilization policies based on the instrumentation of the exchange rate as a nominal anchor of the price system. While these policies have been successful in curbing inflation, they have also caused a real appreciation that has had significant impact on the allocation of investment (i.e. favouring nontradable sectors).

After the debt crisis, however, the issue of the relationship between policies oriented to achieving macroeconomic stability and those aimed at augmenting investment, innovation and employment has been rarely raised in the Latin American context. The macroeconomic instability that followed the crisis was deep and long lasting and, in such a context, it was taken for granted that nothing could be done regarding growth without stabilizing the economy first. This led to an increasing divorce between short-run stabilization and development policies, creating a situation where the latter were completely subordinated to the former.

The contention that stability is a necessary condition for restoring growth is basically correct. But, given this constraint, there was no systematic analysis of the kinds of stabilization policies which could minimize the negative consequences on investment, employment and the process of learning and innovation.

It should be mentioned, however, that this divorce between short-run and long-run policies was not new in the Latin American region. What was new in the 1980s was the intensity and consistency with which this divorce influenced the policy-making process. Indeed, it was during the 1950s that stabilization policies began to be conceived of as being independent of development policies. In those years, the conception of independent stabilization policies was associated with the appearance of external bottlenecks, budget disequilibria and the acceleration of inflation. Likewise, in that period, the first stabilization plans under the surveillance of the IMF were implemented.

This origin of stabilization policies in Latin America made the approach to macropolicies differ from the conception of stabilization adopted in developed countries (and in macroeconomics textbooks). In developed countries the objectives of fiscal, monetary and exchange rate policies were always assumed to be those of achieving full employment and stabilizing investment rates in order to smooth cyclical movements. Only in the post-war period was inflation included as an important target for macropolicy while current account disequilibria were never in the forefront. In Latin America, on the contrary, employment and investment (and sometimes even inflation) have not been the primary goals of stabilization packages. The priority has usually been (and still is) to reduce short-run current account disequilibria. And since the public sector is normally blamed when absorption is too high, an additional objective has always been to achieve fiscal budget equilibrium. When there was a trade-off between employment and inflation on the one hand and fiscal and external equilibria on the other – for example, because of the inflationary and recessive consequences of devaluations and increments in public prices – the target to close the fiscal and external gaps was usually privileged.

The main purpose of this chapter is to analyse macropolicies from the perspective of growth and development. Although our analysis will focus on these real objectives, we will not lose sight of the fact that the primary objective of stabilization policies is to achieve macroequilibrium. The way to overcome the incorrect dichotomy between stabilization and development policies cannot be by ignoring the constraints posed by the need to ensure the coordination of diverse economic activities at the macroeconomic level. Indeed, the problem is to select from the set of policies capable of ensuring macrostability, those that best improve employment and foster innovation and investment.

Such a set of feasible macropolicies depends heavily on the specific characteristics of the macroeconomic situation of the country at hand. Regarding this, it should be kept in mind that the evolution of the Latin American countries in the 1980s showed a series of different disequilibria and that some of them gave rise to explosive paths. In the 1980s, in countries like Argentina, Peru and Bolivia (or presently in Brazil), the amplitude of the existing disequilibria and the perverse characteristics of the dynamic paths (that tended to lead the economy towards hyperinflation) made it extremely difficult even to conceive of a consistent and viable stabilization package, not to mention viable industrial or social policies.

In such a context, the degrees of freedom of economic policy making are basically constrained by the number of disequilibria, their magnitude, and the features of the dynamic paths. The first aim of economic policy turns into that of urgently reducing the disequilibria deactivating possible explosive paths. Under other circumstances the margins for choosing policies are wider. However, in all cases, there is a set of macroeconomic constraints that must be taken into account in order to ensure that the decisions that are being taken at the microeconomic level will be consistent when aggregated.

The present study is organized as follows. In the first section we try to define the characteristics of the macroeconomic problem and its relationship with other policies oriented towards fostering growth and productivity. In the second, we briefly review the most salient features of the recent macroeconomic evolution of the Latin American region as compared with the doomed 1980s. The objective is to show briefly the main macroeconomic problems that the region is now facing and the constraints that they posed to development policies. The third section is devoted to analysing specific macropolicies (namely, fiscal, monetary and financial, and exchange rate policies) and their relationships with the creation of employment and incentives for investment and innovation.

MACROECONOMIC BALANCES AND GROWTH-ORIENTED POLICIES

If the functioning of markets were perfect, economic policy would be redundant. The only task that the government would have to perform would be that of organizing the institutional setting of economic activity (i.e. to ensure the enforcement of contracts, property rights, and so on). Leaving aside extreme positions, however, there is a consensus that, in the real world, markets do not perform all the tasks with the same degree of efficiency. This is so mainly because there are market failures, short-run rigidities and transaction costs, income distribution problems and

31

coordination failures at an aggregate level. Specific economic policies are designed to tackle each of these specific problems. For example, industrial policies cope with market failures such as the existence of externalities; social policies aim at a targeted distribution of welfare; and so on.

The specific task of *macroeconomic policies* is that of managing coordination failures. The main advantage of a market economy is to allow for the decentralization of economic activity and economic decision making. But one of its most important weaknesses is related to this virtue: it may occur that when aggregated, the decisions taken at a microeconomic level are inconsistent at the macroeconomic level.[2] When this occurs, it will not be possible for all economic agents to carry out their planned transactions at the existing prices and, at the macroeconomic level, disequilibria in some key markets will be observed. There are *ex post* market disequilibria because there are *ex ante* coordination failures. And there are macroeconomic policies because it is believed that government intervention can more efficiently correct the disequilibria than can the mechanisms built into the market system.[3]

In principle, one could think that coordination failures are more likely to occur in developing countries – not only because the developing economies suffer from the same market distortions which impede macroequilibrium from being achieved in developed countries (e.g. price rigidities or wrong market signals stemming from capital markets) but also because markets in general are less developed and the development process itself tends to generate structural imbalances and pervasive market disequilibria. In the context of the typical developing country, capital markets are usually extremely thin and rationed; the public sector tends to generate unsustainable deficits because of the rudimentary character of the system of taxes and expenditures; and the productive structure usually shows a lack of flexibility that makes macroeconomic equilibrium much more vulnerable to external shocks. In the recent 'mainstream' literature on stabilization the issue of the effects of stabilization policies on the growth process is downplayed. It is considered that the most important coordination failures are due to government-induced distortions and, consequently, the most important task of stabilization policies is that of removing such distortions. Likewise, there is a sharp distinction between stabilization and growth-oriented structural reform policies.

Behind these arguments, there is a strong presumption among mainstream economists: regardless of the kind of disequilibrium that the economy is experiencing, a market equilibrium always exists and there is a stable path that the economy can follow to reach it if government distortions are removed. Although this may be true in developed economies, in the highly distorted Latin American context this a priori assumption can be misleading. The economies of the region experienced persistent disequilibria – especially after the debt crisis – and sometimes it was not at all clear whether or not an equilibrium existed and, likewise, whether the economy was on a stable path.

Indeed, in the economic policy recommendations stemming from multilateral organizations such as the IMF or the World Bank, there is a certain contradiction in the treatment of this question. The contradiction stems from the fact that, on the one hand, it is assumed that an equilibrium exists and that it can be reached with the appropriate stabilization measures but, on the other, it is said that deep structural changes (i.e. fiscal reform, the opening of the economy, market liberalization) are needed for stability to be sustainable. If under the existing conditions stability cannot last unless key parameters defining the economic structure are changed, then there is no attainable equilibrium under the present circumstances. In fact, stabilization-cum-structural reform is recommended precisely for this reason.

If this is true, it is very difficult to uphold the argument that stabilization and growth policies are independent.[4] If, for stabilization to be sustainable, it is necessary to *reform the economic structure*, it is crucial to take into account the longer-run consequences of stabilization on the economic structure and the effects of structural reform on short-run stability.

When stabilization and structural problems are considered together, many complicated questions arise, basically because in the policy-making process it is necessary to take into account the interactions between income distribution, market failures and coordination failures, in addition to the specific problems that arise in the transition period from stabilization-cum-structural reform to stable growth.[5]

The questions that are posed to macroeconomic policy making can be shown by means of an example. A well-known rule of policy says that for maintaining macrostability, 'countries should try to keep their spending consistent with their permanent income'. This means that in order to maintain full employment and avoid coordination failures – taking into account the necessary intertemporal consistency between income and absorption – countries should borrow in bad times and rescue debt or accumulate financial assets when the good times come. However, this cannot be implemented when some *market failures are present in the economic structure*. To be more specific, if the market failure consists in the inexistence of a long-run capital market (because the domestic credit market is too thin and access to international markets is rationed as it was in the 1980s), this policy advice is useless.

In the absence of a long-term capital market, the proper constraint for a country facing, say, a short-run balance of payments disequilibrium is not that implicit in the intertemporal consistency between future incomes and expenditures but rather the point-in-time liquidity constraint posed by the maximum available amount of external financing. In such a context, macropolicies must be directed at adjusting the financing needs of the economy to the short-run availability of funds. Typically, at least in the Latin American experience, this means that the real exchange rate will be adjusted to the point at which the demand for external credit originating in the current account disequilibrium equals the given supply.

If the balance of payments problem were due to a *temporary* fall in the terms of trade or to a *temporary* increase in capital flight originating in political turmoil, the previously-mentioned exchange rate policy would lead to an *over*shooting of the long-run equilibrium level of the exchange rate. When terms of trade return to their 'equilibrium' level or flight capital is repatriated, if the narrowness of the domestic capital market does not allow for the sterilization of part of the increased capital inflows, there will be an *under*shooting of the long-run level of the exchange rate in the short run.

The consequences on macroeconomic stability of these kinds of dynamics are obvious. However, the consequences on development are no less important. These dynamics will result in ample changes in income distribution (because of the effects on employment and real wages), wide fluctuations in relative prices (especially regarding the real value of tradable *vis-à-vis* non-tradable goods) and huge variations in the real value of government deficits.

In this special case, then, stabilization must take into account not only the need to match income and absorption but also the need to develop a stronger capital market. This means that it is necessary to seek stabilization policies that, at least, do not worsen the existing fragility of the financial system, not only because it is necessary to ensure that investment be financed but also to make macropolicies more efficient.

The lack of attention to the problems presented by structural imbalances is related, to a certain extent, to the recent evolution of development economics. Up to the 1970s, development economics had always emphasized market imperfections and the potential for Pareto-improving government intervention. According to this view, governments could seek out dynamic externalities and exploit divergences between private and social rates of return to investment (Fishlow, 1990).

In the last two decades, however, there has been an increasing criticism of interventionist policies and their theoretical underpinnings. The opportunities opened to 'rent seeking' (Krueger, 1974) and the inward-oriented character of some of the development strategies adopted have received the bulk of such criticism. But, in spite of the correctness of some of the critics to the import-substitution strategy adopted in Latin America, the supporters of the market-friendly approach have not been able to show decisively that government intervention is always and under any circumstance distorting. From the empirical point of view, 'No one has yet shown that the failure of government intervention *necessarily* outweighs market failure' (Fishlow, 1990) and, specifically, it has been especially difficult to show that government intervention has been either damaging or redundant in explaining the successful evolution of countries like Japan, Korea and Taiwan.[6]

On the other hand, adopting the a priori view that market imperfections and dynamic effects cannot be exploited in order to foster development can be theoretically sterile even from the point of view of the neoclassical paradigm. Krugman (1992), for example, after considering that the market-friendly counter-revolution went too far, calls for a counter-counter-revolution in development theory in order to retain for economic analysis the role that the pioneers of development economics had assigned to economies of scale and externalities. He believes that it is probably time once again to focus on market as well as government failures.

In brief, two important points follow from our previous discussion. First, macropolicies are relevant when there exists a coordination failure and coordination failures are likely to be pervasive in developing countries. Second, stabilization and structural reform policies are not independent. It is necessary to take into account the interactions between macroeconomic failures, market failures, income distribution and dynamic effects, not only because some stabilization policies can be damaging to development but also because overcoming some structural deficiencies (like the inexistence of a strong capital market or the weakness of the fiscal structure) is crucial for ensuring a sustainable stabilization.

LIFE AFTER THE DEBT CRISIS: MACROINSTABILITY AND CHANGING EXTERNAL CONSTRAINTS

Disequilibrium and gaps

In order to avoid the a priori assumption about the existence and stability of market equilibrium and stress the structural origin of many of the imbalances present in Latin American countries, we will analyse the recent experience utilizing the concept of gaps.

A gap represents a disequilibrium situation at the macroeconomic level, but one that is not necessarily self-correcting. Disequilibria can be lasting and can also show amplifying tendencies. The dynamics of an economy in disequilibrium depend on the specific structural characteristics of the economy and on the measures authorities can implement to change the trend (in this sense, the description of macropolicies is as important as the characterization of the gaps).

In principle, any macroeconomic disequilibrium qualifies as a potential gap. However, in the recent Latin American experience, two gaps are identified as *basic*: the *external* gap and the *fiscal* gap. Negative shocks originating in either the external or fiscal sectors, or both, account for most of the destabilizing tendencies.

Regarding the dynamics, two main mechanisms transmit and eventually amplify the policies and shocks originating in the basic gaps. One refers to the behaviour of labour and goods markets and consequently to the behaviour of inflation and unemployment and the other to the characteristics of money and financial markets.

The characterization of gaps and transmission mechanisms in the 1980s and early 1990s is, then, the first element that we need in order to set the background of our analysis of economic policies in Latin America. In accounting for the evolution of the macroeconomic disequilibria experienced by Latin America, particular emphasis will be placed on the effects of the changing situation in the international capital market.

The 1980s

During the 1980s Latin America experienced the worst economic crisis of the post-war period. This crisis was triggered by the worsening of the foreign variables faced by the region. However, the magnitude of the negative external shock was widened, at the domestic level, by the extreme weakness of the macroeconomic setting.

In the period that preceded the shock, the public sector was typically running huge deficits, the financial sector showed a marked fragility and there was a tendency for the economy to generate unsustainable current account deficits. These macroeconomic imbalances, in turn, were to a large extent a consequence of the exhaustion of the development model based on both import substitution and the state as the engine of growth that most countries of the region had been following, at least after World War II. In fact, the impact of the debt crisis was so huge because it took place in such a context.

At a more specific level, the anatomy of the crisis and its effects on growth can be succinctly described in terms of the fiscal and external gaps and in terms of the transmission mechanisms that tended to amplify the disequilibria represented by these gaps.

Obviously, the first impact of the negative external shock was to open the external gap. The worsening of the terms of trade, together with the increase in the interest rates in the early 1980s, induced a huge imbalance in the current account. Most countries, with the only important exception of Chile, were unable to finance the increased disequilibria because of the lack of access to voluntary sources of credit and the scarcity of funds stemming from multilateral organizations. Consequently, the possibility of smoothing the adjustment by increasing indebtedness in the short run was precluded and the main objective of macropolicy became that of generating a trade surplus of a magnitude similar to the deficit in the financial services account.

The consequences of trying to generate a trade surplus at any cost were perverse from the point of view of stability and growth, particularly because the exchange rate policy was oriented to increasing the real exchange rate via nominal devaluation. This led to a significant acceleration of inflation and many countries (Peru, Bolivia, Brazil, Argentina) were put on the brink of or directly experienced hyperinflation.

The fact that in most Latin American countries the bulk of the foreign debt is held by the public sector determined that the external shock had a direct impact on the fiscal accounts. The increase in the international interest rate exogenously augmented public expenditures in a context in which the government was already facing severe problems financing the existing public deficit. This meant that there was a simultaneous widening of the fiscal gap together with the opening of the external gap. This had two important consequences at a macroeconomic level. In the first place, given the narrowness of the domestic financial system and the difficulties to accede to external financing, most governments resorted to inflationary finance. This rendered monetary policy passive and greatly helped to validate the inflationary pressures stemming from nominal devaluation. In the second place, the attempts to reduce the deficit fell basically on public investment. The reduction of this kind of expenditure entails the lowest degree of political conflict in the short run. This behaviour of public expenditures is one of the most important causes of the observed reduction in the investment rate. In addition to its direct effects on global investment, the fall in public investment induced a reduction in private investment because of the existence of a 'crowding-in' effect that relates the two.

On the other hand, the increase in the real exchange rate and the public imbalance, together with the acceleration of inflation and the existing indexation mechanisms, acted as transmission belts of the crisis into the weak existing financial sector. Many countries (e.g. Argentina, Chile, Brazil, Mexico, Uruguay) experienced a financial breakdown that made the financing of investment projects extremely difficult.

In this scenario of extreme macroeconomic uncertainty, there was an important reduction in the private savings and investment rates and, together with investment, the process of learning and innovation and the international competitiveness of the economy greatly suffered. Likewise, the process of growth was additionally hampered by the fact that this environment favoured capital flight as a defensive tool against inflation and financial instability.

By the end of the 1980s it was clear that important structural changes would be necessary if the growth process were to regain momentum in the region. In the context of extreme instability, however, it was very difficult to articulate the stabilization efforts with policies oriented towards growth and structural change. Furthermore, the context of the debt crisis was not propitious for rethinking the development strategy since economic policy was almost completely determined by the need to achieve a minimum level of stability. Growth and development lost ground on the economic policy agenda.

The 1990s

The economic situation of the region, however, has greatly changed in the current decade. Most Latin American countries have shown a positive growth rate and a fall in the inflation rate. The main exceptions were Brazil, where macroeconomic instability and political turmoil led to high inflation and a drop in the GDP, and Peru, where the stabilization policy proved to be ineffective at overcoming the ongoing recession despite a decline in the inflation rate.

What is it that changed in Latin America in the 1988–1989 period, when the average growth rate fluctuated around zero and many countries were suffering from inflation rates approaching hyperinflation, and the 1991–1992 period, characterized by positive growth and falling inflation? In answering this question, the role of the structural reform programmes is usually emphasized. However, the most remarkable difference between the aforementioned periods concerns the evolution of the external sector. First, there was a significant fall in the international interest rate. Second, there was a sudden and marked reversion in the direction of capital movements.

The downturn in the interest rate had a very important and positive income effect in terms of the national income of the region and also induced a softening in the external gap via a reduction in the financial services account deficit. While in the 1988–1989 period the net payments of interest and profits abroad amounted to 36 billion dollars, in 1991–1992 these payments totalled 30.2 billion dollars. This positive effect, nonetheless, was compensated for to a certain extent by the decrease in the terms of trade. So, despite the fact that the situation would have been worse if the interest rate had not been declining, it seems that the income effect of the diminishing interest rates was not strong enough to explain the improvement in the Latin American situation as a whole.

It must be taken into account, however, that the fall in the international interest rate has had a substitution effect too. And it surely has had a bearing on the observed reversion in the direction of capital flows. It was via substitution effect that the reduction in the foreign interest rate made the investment in financial assets issued within the region more profitable. This greatly helped to stop capital flight. Likewise, with a lower interest rate, the net return of investments in productive assets rose. This second factor may be very important in explaining not only the spurt in foreign direct investment flowing into various countries of the region, but also the success of privatization in countries like Argentina, where there was an active participation of multinational firms in the process. The figures regarding the reversion of capital flows are impressive; they grew by more than six times in a very short period. As a consequence of the fall in interest payments abroad and the increase in capital inflows, for the first time in nine years (since the debt crisis of the early 1980s), the net transfer abroad effected by the region became negative in 1991 and again so in 1992. While Latin America sent 56.7 billion dollars abroad in the doomed years of 1988–1989, in 1991–1992 it received 35.8 billion dollars.

The softening of the extreme credit rationing that the region was facing during the 1980s allowed many countries to finance a higher current account deficit and, consequently, there was a strong reduction in the trade surplus that the region had been generating during the 1980s in order to finance the net transfer abroad. Indeed, in 1992, for the first time since 1983, Latin America generated a trade deficit.

With the relaxation of the external gap many of the aforementioned mechanisms which contributed to the amplification of the disequilibria during the 1980s were deactivated. First of all, the availability of external credit permitted an expansion of domestic absorption. Indeed, the reversion in capital inflows was so abrupt and significant that there tended to be an excess supply of foreign exchange in many countries, even though the trade and current account deficits were increasing fast. Consequently, the region as a whole accumulated international reserves during the period and most of the countries faced a revaluation of their domestic currencies.

Beyond their consequences on the balance of payments, the expansion of the activity level and the lagging exchange rate proved to have beneficial consequences on macroeconomic stability. Fiscal revenues in many countries showed an upward trend because of the recovery of the activity level. Besides, the overvaluation helped to improve the fiscal balance because an appreciated exchange rate in real terms implies a lower real value for the interest payments on the outstanding public debt. If the positive income effect of the fall in the international interest rate is added to this, it is not surprising that there was an extraordinary improvement in the fiscal equilibrium throughout Latin America in the last two years. Many countries in the region are now running a fiscal *surplus*.

The lagging exchange rate also played an important role in the observed process of disinflation. In most of the countries this is one of the key factors explaining the fall in the inflation rate even in a context of expansion of domestic absorption.

The recovery process, however, is showing two important weaknesses. In the first place, in most cases – and particularly in Argentina and Mexico – the positive evolution of the GDP was more the result of an increasing rate of utilization of existing capacity than a consequence of the widening of it. In the second place, the increase in the activity level was accompanied by a widening in the trade deficit and this could be a source of macroinstability if the international situation worsens.

J. M. FANELLI AND R. FRENKEL

MACROPOLICIES AND DEVELOPMENT IN THE NINETIES

As compared with the 1980s, nowadays the region is in a much better situation to face the challenge of designing economic policies suitable to both stabilization and growth. However, it should be taken into account that history matters and, consequently, many of the sequels of the crisis still remain.

There is a set of key constraints that deserve to be mentioned. First, the rate of investment and domestic savings, which were severely affected by the crisis, are still too low and the recovery has not yet been strong enough to restore the pre-crisis levels. Second, financial systems and capital markets are still weak and small. The degree of monetization is remarkably low while the term maturity of financial instruments is very short. Third, the closing of the fiscal gap does not seem to be sustainable in many countries, either because it is based on the 'repression' of public investment in economic and social infrastructure (Mexico) and/or because it depends heavily on the proceeds coming from privatization (Argentina). Besides, there are countries that did not even attain budget equilibrium in the short run (Brazil). Fourth, the interruption of the growth process, in itself, has had long-lasting and permanent negative consequences on the development process, especially regarding employment generation and increases in productivity.

Indeed, the principal problem confronting the countries of the region is that of designing a new development strategy capable of restoring employment creation, investment and innovation. And policies normally classified under the heading of stabilization (fiscal, monetary and exchange rate policies) will surely play a crucial role in such a strategy. In what follows, we will try to show the main features that these macropolicies should have in the current Latin American situation.

The alternatives open to the selection of the instruments of a specific stabilization package depend heavily on the kinds of macroeconomic disequilibria that the economy at hand is experiencing and the best policies regarding employment and investment should be chosen taking into account these important facts. For example, there exist situations in which it is very difficult for the public sector to have access to capital markets, either foreign or domestic. Under such circumstances, the objective of stabilization will require measures oriented towards the elimination of the existing fiscal deficit and, consequently, the best policies regarding employment and investment should be selected in such a way that fiscal equilibrium is guaranteed.

It is a fact that the Latin American economies differ greatly from the macroeconomic point of view. There exists a spectrum with Brazil at one end and Chile at the other. It is also a fact that the evolution of each national economy showed significant and frequent changes in the last twenty years and that the situation will not be very different in this regard in the near future. If these differences are ignored, incorrect generalizations may be made.[7]

In order to classify the kinds of problems that economic policies face in Latin America, in another paper (Fanelli *et al.*, 1992a) we distinguished three problems that should be resolved in order to restore the growth process. In the first place, to sustain growth, it is necessary to generate sufficient savings – the feature of the process emphasized by the classical or Smithian tradition of thought: the 'wealth of nations' is explained by the thriftiness of their populations. In the second place, it is necessary to ensure that the non-consumed flow of income be invested because one cannot count on savings being automatically channelled into capital formation. This problem is highlighted by the Keynesian tradition, which focuses on two determinants of growth. One is the state of investors' animal spirits, primarily affected by their expectations regarding the future evolution of the economy. The other takes the form of marginal productivity decisions in the allocation of a given flow of savings between real and financial assets. These choices among different possible components of asset-holders' port-folios influence heavily the degree of capital deepening and hence the long-term rate of growth. A third factor influencing the growth rate is the efficiency with which given real resources are allocated. This can be called the neoclassical approach to growth because neoclassical models concentrate on allocative efficiency.

When confronting problems related to development as an evolutionary process – different from mere growth, and where innovation is crucial – however, it is necessary to add a fourth problem highlighted by the Schumpeterian tradition: the need for establishing an economic setting able to generate the incentives and the means for exploring new, potentially better ways of doing things (Nelson, 1991). In this regard, ensuring competition and appropriate public policies related to the education system is crucial.

Fiscal policy[8]

There are many reasons why *fiscal policy will play a key role* in solving the four previously mentioned problems and hence in restoring growth and development. First, in the process of fiscal adjustment public investment has been taken to extremely low levels. Second, in most countries of the region, public savings represent a good part of overall savings. Third, the rate of savings, the allocation of real and financial resources and the incentives for innovation faced by the private sector are affected by both tax and expenditure policies.

Fiscal policy, however, cannot be designed with the only objective of recovering investment and savings and helping the process of innovation. It also has to ensure macrostability. At present, many countries are generating a primary fiscal surplus that is viewed as a necessary condition for maintaining the recently achieved macrostability. The question is, then, that there are trade-offs and complementarities between policies oriented to fulfilling these objectives. Indeed, in the policy recommendations that appear below, we have taken into account the experience of countries like Chile, which succeeded in recovering savings, investment and stability while adjusting the public sector, as compared with others like Mexico or Argentina, where the adjustment of fiscal accounts was not accompanied by the restoration of pre-crisis rates of savings and investment.

It is because of its role in fostering growth and ensuring stability that fiscal policy cannot ignore the interrelationships between stabilization and development. The constraints stemming from such interrelationships, however, do not exhaust the difficulties of designing fiscal policy. An additional and extremely important complication is that the state itself needs to be reformed, and the reform entails not only restructuring but also reconstructing the economic institutions of the public sector. In some countries, the distortionary effects of the crisis and its permanence have been so strong that the public sector has lost a good part of its administrative and management capacities. To make the state more efficient would, obviously, greatly help in attaining growth and stability. However, the state not only has to be economically efficient, it must also be institutionally strong, whatever its size.

This is not an abstract contention. Empirical evidence shows that countries like Colombia and Chile, where the state did not renounce its role as a major investor and where the state institutions suffered a much lower degree of erosion during the adjustment process, had the most successful experiences.

The need for ensuring macroeconomic stability places severe constraints on government behaviour. Although the state has to apply aggressive policies to restore growth, it cannot generate significant deficits as it did in the past. In fact, in many Latin American countries, such as Argentina, Brazil and Peru, the government cannot run fiscal deficits higher than the sum of the available flow of external financing to the public sector plus the proceeds coming from privatization. This is so because today's real flow demand for new issues of domestic assets in the form of either 'bonds' or 'money' is still very low. To preserve financial stability, the rate at which the authorities increase the supply of nominal domestic assets cannot be greater than the sum of the rate of growth plus the rate of inflation. And by assumption, in a stable macroeconomic context the latter must be reduced.

Usually, the policies regarding the reduction of expenditures are much more emphasized than those regarding the revenues side of the government balance sheet as a means of reducing fiscal deficit. It is assumed that an increase in the ratio of tax revenue to GDP would have serious deterrent effects. However, when the overall macroeconomic setting is taken into account, it is possible that the positive effects of an increase in public savings might largely compensate any worsening in the incentive structure, thus contributing heavily to softening the Smithian restriction. Likewise, a disincentive effect on private savings does not mean that the available funds for domestically financing investment would decline because part of the resources saved by the private sector is allocated either to foreign assets or to extremely short-run domestic deposits that cannot sustain long-term credit for investment.

From our point of view, in the present Latin American situation, the first task of fiscal policy should be that of increasing the tax revenue/GDP ratio. A necessary condition for this to be possible is to rationalize and simplify the existing tax structure. In most Latin American countries the tax system shows severe disadjustments for two reasons. One is that the tax systems have been abusively used to attain objectives related to the allocation of resources and to obtain loosely defined distributional aims. The other is that the present structure has resulted from many *ad hoc* modifications over the adjustment period that were closely related to short-run stabilization objectives with little or no concern about the long-run effects on both the efficiency of the tax structure and the amount of taxes collected. In this way, a greater degree of buoyancy of the tax system in the short run was obtained at the cost of a fall in the income elasticity of taxes. In addition, the recurrent resort to tax handles to fill temporal gaps in the fiscal accounts (that usually induced negative effects on income and wealth distribution) severely affected the community's sense of fairness and in some countries gave rise to a sort of 'fiscal rebellion' that contributed to widening the size of the underground economy.

The principal elements of the needed tax reform should be, first, the strengthening of the ability of the government to collect. This calls for a higher amount of resources allocated to improving the financial management, the monitoring and the controlling systems of the central tax bureau. In addition, the administrative and controlling capacity of the tax bureau could be greatly improved by both eliminating those taxes that are unproductive and minimizing the use of multiple rates. This should lead to a decrease in tax evasion and a widening of the tax base. Second, the elimination or reduction to a minimum of temporary or *ad hoc* taxes to make both the amount of taxes that the private sector expects to pay and the amount of government revenues less uncertain. Third, the share of total tax collection made up by direct taxes on income and wealth should be significantly raised. In many Latin American countries, the first objective should be to return to the share observed during the pre-crisis period. Such a policy would improve not only the equity of the tax system but also its income elasticity. In fact, to ensure a high income elasticity of the tax structure is very important because, otherwise, a self-sustained growth process would lead to a renewed fiscal imbalance. Fourth, the use of the tax system to grant incentives to the private sector should not necessarily be avoided but carefully planned and implemented. The tax policies implemented under the import-substitution strategy of development, providing general incentives for real investment and specific incentives intended to foster investment in selected industries or regions, showed mixed results. More often than not, these resulted in tax evasion because of loopholes in the tax legislation. Analogous results showed other policies intended to stimulate savings in the domestic financial system, such as tax exemptions on interest earned by financial assets and on investment in equities. In many cases these policies induced perverse portfolio decisions and fuelled capital flight. However, it must be mentioned that the worst results were observed during periods of high inflation and instability because these conditions both weakened the ability of the state to manage the policies and led to the distortion of the incentives. Even so, a complete reformulation of tax incentives is clearly needed and it could be based on lessons provided by some successful experiences. Tax incentives for savings, investment and allocation in selected activities have been intensively implemented in most of the East Asian cases of rapid industrialization (Tanzi and Shorne, 1992). Three characteristics seem to differentiate East Asian policies from those implemented in Latin America (Amsden, 1991, 1993). The first is targeting: in the East Asian cases incentives have been explicitly related to the achievement of concrete, monitorable performance standards (i.e. exports, investment in R&D, worker training). The second is effective monitoring: the governments have been able to monitor and enforce the committed targets preventing rent-seeking behaviour. This characteristic depends not only on the policy design but on the quality and power of the administration in broader terms (Tanzi and Shorne, 1992). The third characteristic is a stable macroeconomic environment: low inflation and stable relative prices stressed the importance of tax structure in the allocation of resources and precluded the distortions observed in Latin America. The stability of the macroeconomic framework in the East Asian countries seems to have been crucial not only regarding the effectiveness of tax incentives but also regarding the efficacy of other policies, particularly with respect to the financial policies favouring investment in selected industries. This characteristic is one of the most salient features of the East Asian experience *vis-à-vis* Latin America.

On the expenditure side, after more than a decade of adjustment, there is not that much room for further dramatic reductions of government outlays. In fact, in some items such as public investment or those related to the improvement of public sector staff skills, there should be significant rises. Thus the policy reform should aim at significantly improving the allocation of existing expenditures. There are many institutional obstacles, however, that will appear while performing this task. The most important is the existence of a variety of interest groups (e.g. industrial and commercial associations, trade unions, political lobbies). This is one of the most important reasons calling for a strengthening of the state autonomy built on the basis of a democratically generated consensus.

The restructuring of expenditures should be directed at increasing the amount of resources allocated to public investment and anti-poverty programmes. In addition, the structure and design of subsidy policies should be greatly modified in order to reinforce the basis for the process of innovation.

The recovering of the public investment rate should start by strongly supporting well-designed strategies to increase maintenance and operation expenses. The second step to be taken should aim at financing public infrastructure projects, particularly projects for improving the infrastructure closely related to the expansion of exports and the competitiveness of the economy (e.g. roads, harbours, storage capacity), to transport, and to social policies (health, education and poverty reduction). That is, the main purpose of public investment policies should be to stop the process of deterioration that the public sector infrastructure has undergone during the last ten years. Besides, public investment should be increased not only to stop the deterioration of public infrastructure but also to 'prime the pump', thereby reducing the probability that the economy falls into a bottom-of-the-well equilibrium in the post-stabilization period.

One of the much criticized aspects of the growth-promoting policies of the post-war period is that it was very difficult to calculate the costs of such policies because the necessary subsidies were carefully hidden in the budget. We think that such criticism is fairly accurate. The restructuring of the public sector expenditures should induce a radical modification of the form in which subsidies are allocated and recorded in the budget. As we mentioned, the restructuring should be oriented by the successful experience of the East Asian cases. On the one hand, the granting of subsidies should be tightly attached to clearly defined performance criteria and, on the other, the rules for implementing them should neither leave much room for discretionary case-by-case decision making nor absorb as many fiscal resources as in the past. Obviously, the reorganization of the mechanisms for allocating public spending is closely related to the reorganization of the state. Better design and implementation calls for a much more efficient budgeting staff. Many of the mistakes in the past were made precisely because it was administratively easier to grant massive subsidies through public enterprises or the banking system.

The alternative to bad subsidy policies is not a no-subsidy policy but a more efficient one: the problems posed by market failures and income distribution do not disappear just because implementing efficient fiscal policies is a difficult task. In fact, one of the main challenges stems from the fact that while selective promotion policies are needed for development, the policy tools used in the past for growth promotion are now obsolete, either because the economic situation has changed or because they proved to have perverse consequences on both microincentives (work, investment and efficient portfolio selection) and macroequilibrium. So, the reformulation of promotion policies following the lines suggested above should be a high-priority task because they are a necessary condition for the recovery of growth.

Monetary and financial policy

In order to preserve stability most Latin American countries are now trying to follow tight monetary policies, especially regarding the financing of the public deficit by means of issuing money. Likewise, most of them are now trying to liberalize the financial system and in some cases, like in Argentina, Peru and Bolivia, this has led to the development of a parallel financial system based on dollar-denominated assets and liabilities. In spite of these measures, however, the financial system has been unable to generate a market for long-term borrowing and lending which is badly needed to foster investment and to increase the savings rate.

This recent Latin American experience with the management of monetary and financial policies seems to suggest that the consequences of such policies on growth and stability are ambiguous. Tight monetary policies have recently led – via an increment in the domestic interest rate – to an exacerbation of capital inflows and this provoked a further appreciation of the real exchange rate that hindered competitiveness while the increase in the interest rate acted against the objective of increasing investment. Likewise, a good part of the credit generated in the dollar-denominated segment has gone to finance consumption and non-tradable activities. If there were an upward correction of the real exchange rate, there could be an increment in the level of financial fragility of the economy.

We have remarked many times that one of the most important market failures, pervasive throughout the region, is caused by the absence of a long-term capital market. This fact has several consequences on both stabilization and growth. It makes stabilization policies difficult because it implies that capital markets cannot be used in order to smooth cyclical variations in the activity level by means of a coordination of the short-run evolution of income and expenditures, taking 'permanent income' as a standard. When the financial system is fragile and 'bonds' markets are weak, it is very difficult to implement open market operations and sterilization measures which are the primary tools of monetary management.

If the monetary authorities do not have the instruments needed to offset the impulses originating in the balance of payments and the fiscal budget, to maintain short-run monetary stability the stabilization policy should avoid huge fluctuations in the current account deficit and in the public sector borrowing needs. The impossibility of pursuing an independent monetary policy because the needed instruments are not available puts strong constraints on the set of fiscal and exchange rate policies which are compatible with monetary and financial stability. The best way to ensure monetary stability is to have a sustainable exchange rate and a sustainable evolution of fiscal imbalances.

The stability in the evolution of monetary aggregates, however, not only depends on the current account and the budget. One important source of turbulence is the volatility of external capital movements. As previously mentioned, the problems generated by such volatility have been particularly important in the recent Latin American experience, characterized by a marked reversion in the sign of capital movements.

The core of the problem raised by capital movements lies in the fact that the size of the domestic capital markets is too small as compared with the size of capital outflows and inflows. For example, in Argentina, while the total stock of domestically generated financial assets slightly exceeded 25 billion dollars, in only one year, in 1992, the country received capital inflows of about 12 billion dollars. If the authorities had tried to sterilize such an amount of capital inflows, there would have been an increase in the stock of government bonds inconsistent with financial stability. Given that the monetary authorities did not resort to sterilization and adopted a passive monetary policy, the outcome was a strong and unsustainable over-valuation of the real exchange rate.

What the Argentine experience makes clear is that, in a context where the domestic capital market is weak and there is a complete opening of the economy to capital movements, the monetary authorities may have to choose between financial instability and overvaluation of the domestic currency. There are no easy ways to escape from this fate. Nonetheless, the experience of countries like Chile, which combined direct intervention in order to smooth capital inflows (such as fixing minimum terms for foreign lending) and an exchange rate policy oriented to increasing short-term uncertainty (while guaranteeing the real level in the long run), seems to be better than the alternative chosen by Argentina of passively adapting the evolution of monetary aggregates and the exchange rate to capital inflows.

Looking at the past Latin American experience, it seems clear that private markets have never generated a flow of financial intermediation high enough to support a significant rate of investment in productive activities. The available alternatives to correct this market failure are very controversial and it is possible that the best policy will be that of avoiding the imple-mentation of extreme 'solutions' via either generalized government inter-vention or financial liberalization.

In the post-war period, the lack of long-term segments led to the creation of development banks. Likewise, public guarantees and other forms of financing long-term investment projects made up the set of policy tools to promote growth during the successful industrialization period until the mid-1970s. Even at the cost of efficiency losses and distributional biases, the system performed fairly well for forty years. Nonetheless, it proved not to be robust to the conjunction of macroeconomic instability – especially to inflation – misleading budgetary policies and rent seeking.

On the other hand, the experience with radical financial liberalization policies has not been better. There are some recent examples of financial crises – such as those that occurred in the so-called Southern Cone liberalization experiences – which were self-generated by the volatility of deregulated and private financial systems.

In spite of the negative consequences of financial liberalization, in the current Latin American context, it is not possible to return to 'repressed' systems. In the first place, the financial systems have already been deregulated and, in the second place, the existing degree of integration between domestic and international capital markets renders aggressive interventionist policies impossible.

But, as experience has shown, deregulated capital markets have not been a viable 'first-best' solution to the lack of a long-run capital market. Consequently, in order to correct this market failure, government intervention is necessary. One way of doing this is to recover the capacity to channel public, private and external savings to finance private investment by means of development banks or specific investment funds. Carefully administered public development banks could be efficiently used for evolving screening devices for the selection of private investment projects. This was an important feature of the growth strategy in Latin America in the past and in other developing experiences as well. Although many specialists have a negative view of this role of the state because they see it exclusively as a subsidy that worsens resource allocation, we believe that this kind of policy action is badly needed for overcoming a serious market failure.

Exchange rate policy

The level of the **real** exchange rate and its stability is crucial in determining the evolution of the real side of the economy. In the first place, it plays a fundamental role in determining the degree of external competitiveness of the economy and, consequently, in influencing the allocation of resources between the tradable and non-tradable sectors. This, in turn, affects not only the position of the current account in the long run but also the evolution of productivity since external competitiveness has a bearing on changes in technology and the organization of firms. In the second place, because of the importance of trade taxes and public foreign indebtedness, the real exchange rate contributes to determining the real size of public expenditures and revenues and hence the real burden of government deficits. In the third place, especially in developing countries, there is a close relationship between income distribution and the real exchange rate, mainly because of the effects of the latter on real wages. Likewise, in a setting where the existence of 'specific factors' makes the reallocation of resources costly in the short run, changes in the level of the real exchange rate may induce severe losses in terms of employment.

In addition to their role on the real side, the spot and expected **nominal** exchange rates contribute heavily to determining the level and the rate of change of domestic nominal prices on the one hand and the domestic nominal interest rates on the other.

Because of these relationships with the evolution of both *nominal* and *real* variables, the exchange rate policy is a key tool influencing not only short-run stability but also growth. It is not surprising, then, that very frequently the authorities confront difficult trade-offs when setting real *vis-à-vis* nominal targets for the exchange rate.

Another complication with the exchange rate from the point of view of economic policy making is that it is directly influenced by variables that are not under the control of the authorities. An additional complication is that these variables may be highly volatile. Among such variables, fluctuations in international interest rates, changes in the access to external financial markets and the evolution of terms of trade play a central role in Latin America.

Given the many objectives and exogenous variables that have a bearing on the exchange rate policy, there are no clear-cut and general rules that could be followed. Nonetheless, on the basis of the experience of Latin American countries, some remarks could be made about the best policies for augmenting employment and investment while maintaining an acceptable degree of macroeconomic stability.

The best guide for evaluating the level of the real exchange rate is to take into account that the real exchange rate should be *sustainable* in the long run. From the point of view of macropolicy, even though the sustainability criterion might appear to be rather diffuse, it is more operative than the one provided by the concept of 'equilibrium' exchange rate. The equilibrium exchange rate is a theoretical concept that assumes perfect knowledge of the future state of the economy. Besides, even if such an equilibrium level could be calculated, for the economic policy to sustain the real exchange rate at its equilibrium value, perfect capital markets would be necessary. The sustainability criterion attempts to take into account the imperfections of the financial structure and the existence of disequilibria.

One of the main implications of this criterion for economic policy making is that whenever important changes in the aforementioned fundamental determinants of the real exchange rate occur, it is necessary to adapt the level of the real exchange rate to the new situation. It is particularly important to avoid exchange rate policies that imply huge current account disequilibria or perverse effects on the degree of competitiveness of the economy.

Although, in practice, the degree of sustainability of a specific exchange rate can only be assessed on the basis of historical comparisons and uncertain evaluations of the future evolution of the variables which affect the real exchange rate, sustainability as a guide for policy making would have been strong enough to discriminate against some of the most negative policy experiments implemented in Latin America. This criterion, for example, would have ruled out the Southern Cone liberalizations of the late 1970s: the simultaneous opening of the economy and overvaluation of the exchange rate are not compatible with a sustainable current account equilibrium because they tend to generate trade account deficits that can only be sustained by increasing capital inflows. On the other hand, countries that followed more strict real exchange policies seem to have resisted negative shocks better. Even though the debt crisis affected all the countries of the region, the economies that were more severely affected were those that had heavily appreciated the domestic currency in the previous years while countries like Colombia, which had a more stable exchange rate policy, were less affected. Indeed, the present evolution of some Latin American countries would be greatly enhanced if the sustainability criterion were to be applied. This is particularly so in the cases of Mexico and Argentina which are now generating increasing and unsustainable deficits in the current account.

Besides ensuring sustainability, the exchange rate policy should be aimed at minimizing the uncertainty of expectations about the future real exchange rate. The expected exchange rate influences not only the allocation of resources between tradable and non-tradable goods but also investment decisions in general because of its effects on both the activity level and the financial position of agents with different combinations of foreign assets and liabilities in their balance sheets.

However, to set the correct real exchange rate from the point of view of sustainability in a way that minimizes the uncertainty of expectations about the future real exchange rate is not an easy task, especially because the Latin American economies are highly inflationary according to international standards. If domestic inflation is systematically higher than that of the principal trade partners of a country, it will be necessary to adapt the nominal exchange rate permanently in order to maintain the real exchange rate at the targeted level. In other words, an indexing rule will be necessary and, hence, the credibility of the real exchange rate will become a function of the credibility of the real parity rule based on the indexation of the nominal rate.

More or less explicit real parity rules have been followed in Chile and Bolivia. These countries have managed to sustain the post-crisis stabilization longer. Indeed, in these countries it can be considered that the maintenance of the real exchange rate by using the real parity rule constitutes an indicator of the robustness of the degree of stabilization achieved: unlike the cases of Argentina and Mexico, stability does not depend on the nominal exchange rate as an anchor of nominal prices.

In brief, a real parity rule that ensures the sustainability and the credibility of the future exchange rate appears to be the tool best suited to the objectives of maintaining stability and fostering growth. There is one important caveat, nonetheless. When an economy faces a strong destabilizing shock of the kind the Latin American economies experienced in the early 1980s, it could be beneficial to abandon the indexing rule. If the economy is on the brink of hyperinflation with an inertial mechanism built into the price dynamics, recent stabilization experiences strongly suggest that it is worthwhile to use *temporarily* a fixed nominal exchange rate as a nominal anchor for the price system. A discussion of this caveat, however, is beyond the scope of this chapter. With the exception of strong shocks, the real parity rule seems to be the best choice for stability and growth.

CONCLUDING REMARKS

In these concluding remarks we want to stress the main points developed in the previous sections. The chapter has been organized as an attempt to answer the question: what are the best macropolicies from the point of view of growth and development? Our first answer is that the way to overcome the incorrect dichotomy between stabilization and development policies cannot be by ignoring the constraints posed by the need to ensure the coordination of economic activities at the macroeconomic level. So, the problem is to select from the set of policies capable of ensuring macrostability, those that best improve employment and foster innovation, savings and investment. The second point of the answer is that such a set of feasible macropolicies depends on the specific characteristics of the macroeconomic situation of the country at hand.

The fiscal, monetary, financial and exchange policies discussed in the third part of the chapter are focused on the macroeconomic situation of Latin American countries in the 1990s. This situation can be broadly described by two characteristics. First, the economies show the long-lasting effects of the crisis of the 1980s on their macroeconomic performance and on their development potential. Second, since the early 1990s there have been new and more favourable international financial conditions. Both characteristics are considered to specify the kind of problems that have to be resolved in order to restore the growth process and to investigate the ways in which macropolicies can contribute to the task. The first problem relates to the generation of sufficient savings needed to sustain growth. The second problem is to ensure that the non-consumed flow of income be channelled into capital formation raising the rate of investment. The third problem relates to the efficiency with which given real resources are allocated. The fourth problem is the need to establish an economic setting favouring innovation, i.e. an environment able to generate the incentives and the means to explore new, potentially better ways of doing things.

The set of macropolicies presented and discussed in the chapter should contribute in complementary ways to the resolution of the mentioned four problems of development. The ideal macroeconomic framework generated by the successful implementation of those policies should be characterized by, first, stability, i.e. a relatively low and more or less predictable rate of inflation and a smooth cycle, and, second, right and stable rates of exchange and relative prices.[9] None of these attributes is attainable as an isolated effect of any specific policy (such as fiscal or exchange policies) but has to result from the combined effects of the whole set of macropolicies. A third attribute should be a more comfortable fiscal situation needed to make room for policies fostering higher rates of savings and investment. Both savings and investment would be directly favoured by the positive effects of a stable macroeconomic framework and should also be stimulated by fiscal and financial incentives. Fiscal policy, particularly the reconstruction and strengthening of the tax system, is essential to this purpose, not only to make room for macroeconomic sound tax and credit incentives to the private sector, but also to recover the public sector's own capacity to save and invest. Lastly, a fourth attribute should be a more efficient allocation of investment. A lower degree of uncertainty regarding inflation and the sustainability of relative prices, especially the rate of exchange, should have in itself positive effects on the efficiency of investment. But, as in the case of general incentives for savings and investment, a stronger fiscal position is also essential for the sound instrumentation of fiscal and financial incentives to foster innovation and to compensate for market distortion in specific industries.

NOTES

1 Comments on a previous draft by Colin Bradford are gratefully acknowledged. The authors are also thankful for the comments made in the workshop 'Integrating Competitiveness, Sustainability and Social Development', OECD Development Centre, Paris, 17–19 June 1993; particularly those by Gerald Adams, Joseph Ramos and Ricardo Ffrench-Davis. The authors also thank the OECD Development Centre, IDRC (Canada), Mellon Foundation (USA) and SAREC (Sweden) for their support.

2 One of the most significant coordination failures in the 1980s resulted from the behaviour of domestic savers and international banks. As a consequence of uncertainty and instability, the domestic savers' preference for liquid assets in international currency rose, i.e. deposits held in international banks. At the same time and in response to the same incentives, the international banks reduced the availability of credit to governments and potential domestic private investors. As a result of the combination of capital flight and credit rationing, effective investment was lower than the potential investment that could have been financed by domestic savings. Another example of coordination failure is given by the effects

of capital inflows in the 1990s. In some countries capital inflows establish a significant trend to real appreciation, signalling, then, an allocation of resources inconsistent with the long-term sustainability of external equilibrium.

3 Since the 'rational expectations revolution', there have been some discussions in the literature on macroeconomic policies for developed countries on the true existence of coordination failures. Some authors affirmed that macropolicies are, to say the least, redundant. This discussion, nonetheless, was not important for developing countries. There is a consensus among economists that stabilization policies are necessary and relevant in the developing world, at least during the transitional path to a fully developed market economy.

4 On the relationship between stabilization and structural reform from the market-friendly viewpoint, see World Bank (1991).

5 In the literature there has recently been a discussion of the transition period under the heading of 'sequencing', but the arguments have been rather inconclusive. In another paper we focus on this problem; see Fanelli and Frenkel (1993). The relevant literature is cited there.

6 Stiglitz (1993) has recently made a similar point regarding financial markets. Based on analytical arguments and on the experiences of Japan, Taiwan and Korea, this author emphasizes that the relevant policy questions relate to the appropriate design of regulations. Stiglitz argues that government regulation, no less than markets, is beset by problems, but the conclusion, on that account, that there should be less government regulation, is incorrect. The problem arises from the incorrect design of government regulations.

7 Monetary policy can be used to show this point. The degrees of freedom of monetary policy are a function of the amplitude and robustness of the domestic demand for financial assets. This is usually not even mentioned because in the standard textbook exercise the existence of such a demand is taken for granted. However, in some economies of the region, the crises have induced strong changes in the agents' financial behaviour, basically because the crises fuelled capital flight and there was a strong demonetization as a counterpart. But the intensity was not the same in each country and consequently there are different degrees of disarticulation of the financial systems. It is not sensible to expect that the same policy tool (e.g. sterilization) will have similar effects in economies that greatly differ in this respect.

8 The proposals regarding fiscal policies are based on Fanelli et al. (1992b).

9 These attributes are the most salient features in the comparison between Latin American and East Asian countries. The conditions show analogous relevance in comparing Latin American growth performances across more and less stable periods (i.e. before and after the mid-1970s) and also in comparing growth performances between individual Latin American countries after the debt crisis.

REFERENCES

Amsden, Alice H. (1991) 'The Public Sector in Industrialization: Examples from North- and South-East Asia' (mimeo), UNCTAD.
——(1993) 'Asia's Industrial Revolution', *Dissent*, Summer.
Fanelli, J. and Frenkel, R. (1993) 'On Gradualism, Shock Treatment and Sequencing', *International Monetary and Financial Issues for the 1990s*, Volume II, UNCTAD, New York.
Fanelli, J., Frenkel, R. and Taylor, L. (1992a) 'The World Development Report 1991: A Critical Assessment', *International Monetary and Financial Issues for the 1990s*, Volume I, UNCTAD, New York.

Fanelli, J., Frenkel, R. and Rozenwurcel, G. (1992b) 'Growth and Structural Reform in Latin America. Where we Stand', in A. A. Zini Jr (ed.) *The Market and the State in Economic Development in the 1990s*, North-Holland, New York.

Fishlow, Albert (1990) 'The Latin American State', *Journal of Economic Perspectives*, vol. 4, no. 3.

Krueger, Anne O. (1974) 'The Political Economy of the Rent-Seeking Society', *American Economic Review*, June.

Krugman, Paul (1992) 'Toward a Counter-Counterrevolution in Development Theory', *Proceedings of the World Bank Annual Conference on Development Economics*, The World Bank, Washington, DC.

Nelson, Richard (1991) 'Why do Firms Differ, and How does it Matter?', *Strategic Management Journal*, vol. 12.

Stiglitz, Joseph E. (1993) 'The Role of the State in Financial Markets', *Annual Bank Conference on Development Economics*, 3–4 May, The World Bank, Washington, DC.

Tanzi, Vito and Shorne, Parthasarathi (1992) 'The Role of Taxation in the Development of East Asian Economies', in T. Ito, and A. Krueger (eds) *The Political Economy of Taxation*, The University of Chicago Press, Chicago.

World Bank (1991) *The Challenge of Development: World Development Report 1991*, Oxford University Press, New York.

3

CONSTRAINTS ON AFRICAN GROWTH

Arne Bigsten

INTRODUCTION

The purpose of this chapter is to deepen understanding of the challenges of development economics and to identify new research priorities. To my mind, the most important and challenging task at present is to understand why African economies are performing so poorly. This chapter discusses what we know so far, and in what direction I think we should proceed.

THE STARTING POINT

Although development economics as a subdiscipline is relatively new, the ambition of economists to understand economic development is old. The classical economists, from Adam Smith onwards, had more or less well-worked-out theories about long-term economic change. Some took an optimistic view, while others, notably Ricardo, concluded that there would be economic stagnation in the long run. His argument was that the fixed availability of natural resources would eventually force returns on investment to zero, and thus make investment cease. The same pessimistic view about the sustainability of development has been taken by some in more recent discussions. In more optimistic scenarios, however, it has been argued that technological progress will make it possible to increase production in spite of natural resource limitations.

What have we learnt since the time of Smith and Ricardo? Obviously, the world has undergone dramatic economic changes during this period. The industrial revolution which started in England has engulfed a larger and larger share of the world economy. Today all parts of the world have been affected. The frontier between developed and underdeveloped countries has continuously shifted. Even though some countries have had setbacks, the shift has mainly been one way. The number of countries which can be characterized as economically developed has increased dramatically, with some very successful Asian countries as the most recent entrants into the group. Thus we have a certain basis for long-term optimism, even for Third

World countries, which at present have very low incomes, and in many cases have actually seen their low incomes fall.

So far, the limitation of resources has not precluded economic growth, and I doubt it will do so in the future either. When resources that are finite become too expensive, it will surely be possible to shift to technologies that use other finite resources, or renewable resources, instead, while still maintaining an advanced economy. More worrisome are the possible effects of economic activities on the environment, and this pressure is going to increase with the size of the global population. Also, space itself is limited, and crowding is itself welfare reducing (at least for a Scandinavian). Still, the starting point for my discussion here is the belief that environmental effects can be handled in such a way that environmental constraints are not going to prevent countries which are now outside the club of developed countries from joining it.

THE POST-WAR GROWTH EXPERIENCE

The period since World War II has been characterized by a very rapid growth in world output. At the end of the war the United States was economically dominant, with the highest per capita income, but since then Europe, Japan and others have caught up. This seems to indicate that there is a growth advantage in being relatively poor. Tests of the catching-up or convergence hypothesis are numerous. The approach normally used is cross-section regressions of growth rates on initial levels of per capita income (see, for example, Barro, 1991; Baumol, 1986; Mankiw *et al.*, 1992). A negative coefficient on the initial income level is taken to indicate convergence.

Easterly (1994) looks at country experiences in the post-war period of 1950–1985 and finds that, contrary to the hypothesis, many poor countries have seen their incomes stagnate. Out of eighty-seven LDCs in the sample, only forty-one had significantly positive growth rates of per capita income, while all OECD countries had significantly positive growth rates. This seems to indicate that there is at least no general, unconditional process of convergence. However, estimates by Barro (1991) indicate that there is at least convergence conditional on initial incomes and policies. Baumol *et al.* (1989) make the interesting observation that the growth rate first rises and then falls as countries move from low to high per capita incomes. This observation is consistent with the earlier evidence presented by Gerschenkron (1962), who found that backwardness may foster growth and development, but that the development process may not get started if the country is too backward.

Easterly (1993) presents a very interesting model that generates a growth pattern consistent with those empirical observations. His model makes a distinction between the alternative regimes of stagnation or positive growth. In the model, the conditional catch-up effect is counterbalanced by the low

56

savings and slow growth effects that characterize the very poor countries. Once per capita incomes start to increase beyond the needs of subsistence consumption, there is increased room for savings, and thus for investment. The drag of poverty on growth will then gradually be reduced, and the positive catch-up effect will dominate more and more. The evidence reported by Easterly in his paper suggests that it is policies, rather than initial incomes, that determine whether an economy stagnates or not. A high black market premium is found to be particularly likely to cause stagnation. The results also confirm his hypothesis that the rate of growth is low at very low per capita incomes, but then accelerates as income levels increase.

Another cross-section analysis is presented in the World Bank (1993) study of the East Asian miracle. It shows that a sizeable share of the growth advantage can be attributed to the rapid accumulation of physical and human capital, but the study also notes that initial income had a significant relationship with the growth of per capita income. There was evidence, however, that this process of conditional convergence varies among regions. In controlling for education, investment and initial income, the Asian NICs have had a significantly higher rate of growth than all other economies, while Latin America and Sub-Saharan Africa have had significantly lower underlying growth rates, about 1 per cent (World Bank, 1993, p. 52). It is argued that Sub-Saharan Africa has a conditional convergence advantage, but the advantage of low initial income derived in the regression is the average advantage of the whole sample. The negative coefficient for the Africa dummy variable may be an indication that the forces of convergence are not effective there. One may also note that two-thirds of the growth difference between the Asian high-performers and Sub-Saharan Africa are left unexplained by the regression. This suggests that African countries have been less successful in allocating their resources to high-productivity activities, and in introducing new technologies. Easterly and Levine (1994) make a similar cross-country regression of conditional convergence, and they also find that the coefficient for the Africa dummy is significantly negative. The dummy explains 1.4 percentage points of a growth difference between Africa and the non-African economies of 1.8 per cent. One may interpret these results to mean that, so far, Africa has not been able to benefit from being a late-comer to the same extent as has the average LDC.

The evidence provided by this type of regression has been criticized on methodological grounds by Quah (1993). He provides an alternative, dynamic model that suggests that there is no overall tendency towards convergence, although there are pockets showing convergence. Instead, he suggests that the economies of the world are tending towards either very rich or very poor, with the middle-income class vanishing. Many of the countries slipping behind are African.

Most analysts trying to explain intercountry differences in growth rates have looked for country characteristics that can explain the gaps. Easterly *et al.* (1993) advise caution in the interpretation of the results obtained. They note that, while country characteristics are generally very stable over time, growth rates are highly unstable, and that shocks, primarily terms of trade shocks, explain a large part of the growth variance. However, vulnerability to external shocks may also be regarded as a country characteristic. Many African countries obviously show this characteristic.

Thus, whatever the approach, the evidence shows that Africa is slipping behind, not catching up. The question then is, why is Africa not catching up as the convergence hypothesis predicts?

ACCUMULATION AND TECHNOLOGICAL PROGRESS

The rate of growth of an economy is determined by the accumulation of physical and human capital, the efficiency of resource allocation, and the ability to acquire and apply modern technology. This proposition is consistent with all growth theories, although they differ in many other respects.

The traditional neoclassical model of economic growth (Solow, 1957) has been challenged in recent years by the endogenous growth approach. According to the traditional view, the return to capital would be high in the capital-poor countries and capital should move there. This would help the poor to catch up. According to the endogenous view, on the other hand, the increments to physical and human capital tend to make an increased contribution as economies become richer. A small head-start may lead, via scale economies or external economies, to cumulative divergence (see, for example, Krugman, 1981; Romer, 1987; Barro and Sala-i-Martin, 1992; Mankiw *et al.*, 1992). What we have argued above is that at present there seems to be a process of catching up among middle-income countries, while the poorest countries, notably those in Africa, are slipping behind or stagnating. Neither theory is thus obviously confirmed, but the predictions of the endogenous approach seem to be more consistent with the African experience. The endogenous model proposed by Easterly (1994) predicts slow growth at very low income levels, and then gradually increasing growth as per capita incomes increase. Easterly also finds that it is primarily policy and model parameters that determine whether a country can break out of stagnation. In particular, countries which penalize capital accumulation via overvalued exchange rates are more likely to stagnate. The model also predicts that there is a threshold level for certain parameters that must be surpassed for sustained growth to be established. The model thus provides a consistent explanation of why poor countries have difficulties in exploiting the advantage of backwardness.

Both the neoclassical and the endogenous approaches predict that countries with higher investments will have higher growth rates of per capita income. According to the neoclassical model, this is only temporary, while according to the standard endogenous growth model, it may persist. Factor productivity growth was taken by Solow to be exogenous, while in some endogenous growth models it is related to the interaction between knowledge and investment (see the survey by Hammond and Rodriguez-Clare, 1993). Endogenous growth theory focuses on innovations and technological spillovers. The hypothesis is that innovations take place when investors find it profitable, and it is furthermore assumed that the cost of innovations falls as knowledge accumulates. The accumulation of human capital is therefore a crucial determinant of technological progress. It is also suggested that scale economies are important. A large capital stock and a large population may therefore lower the costs of innovation, and thus increase the rate of innovation. Small stocks of physical and human capital are a hindrance to technological progress, so that even if resources were optimally allocated in a small African economy, it might still slip behind because of its small size.

We know that growth varies a lot among countries, but we do not yet have a very clear picture of the processes determining total factor productivity change (Page, 1990; Pack, 1994). One can make a distinction between improvement of international best practice, or 'technological change', and movement towards this, or 'technical efficiency change' (World Bank, 1993, p. 49). Poor countries can in principle grow rapidly through the adoption of up-to-date foreign technologies, which often comes with new equipment. De Long and Summers (1993) show that investment in equipment is particularly closely related to growth. The authors of the 'miracle study' find that most productivity change in low- and middle-income countries is due to changes in technical efficiency. But the average annual rate of technical efficiency change for Sub-Saharan Africa has been an appalling − 3.5 per cent. It is thus slipping further and further away from the international technology frontier.

The picture for Africa is thus very bleak. It is falling behind technologically and the rate of resource accumulation is low. The two aspects are not unrelated, of course. Physical accumulation brings in embodied technologies, while human capital investment facilitates the absorption and development of new technologies. A partial explanation may be that the price of imported capital goods has been high in Sub-Saharan Africa, relative to international standards (see Helleiner, 1993).

The factor-price equalization theorem shows that trade will equalize factor prices once the technology is the same in different countries, provided that the differences in factor proportions are not too large. (Differences in per capita income will still remain, as long as some countries are endowed with more capital per capita than others.) The evidence suggests that the gap is widening between technologies as applied in Africa and those at the international frontier. Anyway, this means that the strong forces of income equalization through international trade implied by the factor-price equalization theorem do not seem to be very effective in African economies.

One reason may be trade policy distortions. Ben-David (1993) shows that at least among more developed countries, there is a strong link between trade liberalization and income convergence.

The policy question then is how the environment in Africa could be changed to facilitate the accumulation of factors and their efficient allocation, and the introduction of better technologies. The experiences of many countries show that economic policies at the microlevel should aim to develop and sustain efficient markets, while macropolicy must be geared to guarantee macroeconomic stability. It has become increasingly obvious that an efficient economy requires a supporting environment of efficient institutions. We turn now to the issues of policy and institutions.

ECONOMIC POLICY

We know that there have been large distortions in the incentive structures in many African economies, and that consequently resources have been poorly allocated. Fischer (1993) shows in a cross-country analysis that growth is negatively related to inflation, budget deficits and distorted foreign exchange markets. Easterly and Levine (1994) obtain similar results and particularly emphasize that growth is slower the higher the black market premium on foreign exchange. Easterly (1993) shows, for a cross-section of fifty-seven countries, that price distortions, in the form of high variance of relative input prices in investment goods across sectors, have a significantly negative effect on economic growth. With recent reductions in distortions in African economies, allocation of the meagre resources has probably improved, but the growth impact has been disappointing. Obviously, much more is required in terms of economic policy to support factor accumulation, technical progress and an efficient allocation of resources. Structural adjustment programmes have been grappling with this, and there has been some progress (see World Bank, 1994).

A necessary, but not sufficient, condition for growth is investment. A major aim of recent adjustment programmes has been to increase private sector investment, and studies of the adjustment experience of a range of countries suggest that recovery of private investment is the distinguishing feature of a successful programme. The sluggishness of investment in African countries cannot be explained by conventional factors such as import constraints and interest rates, but 'the problems lie in the overall environment for investment decision making and intangible perceptions of risk heightened by "unclear" and conflicting signals over economic policy' (Chibber et al., 1992, p. 10). In a review of private investment in LDCs, Chibber et al. (1992) note that, where policies are volatile or unsustainable, and where a large debt burden exists, private investment suffers. A high level of debt increases the vulnerability of a country to shocks. Thus, high debt signals to investors that there is a risk of policy change. Faini and de Melo

(1992) also show in a cross-country study that the recovery of private investment is delayed in countries with a high debt burden. They find too that macroeconomic instability in the form of fluctuating real exchange rates slows down private investment.

Uncertainty and lack of credibility are thus important constraints on investment. These factors make investors shy away from irreversible long-term investments and stimulate short-term speculative behaviour. When there is uncertainty, firms choose to place their money in liquid or financial assets. In a debt-ridden African economy, investment may remain sluggish even if capacity utilization increases. Investment expansion thus requires long-term macroeconomic stability, and for this to be credible, debt burdens in countries such as Zambia, for instance, have to be reduced dramatically. A sound overall macroeconomic environment is thus a basic condition for investment, which is a requirement for growth. But once such an environment has been established, what more can a government do?

A hotly debated issue with regard to the Asian NICs is whether selective, non-neutral market interventions played an essential role in their success. The answer given by the 'miracle study' is a qualified 'no', although several critics argue that it misreads the evidence (see, for example, Amsden, 1994). One area where experiences of the Asian NICs suggest that there might be scope for non-neutral policy is export support. It is essential, though, that interventions be based on economic performance criteria, and that the bureaucracies that handle them are not corrupt. African experiences are often not happy ones. An example of an attempt to intervene in Kenya was the pre-shipment export-financing facility, through which an exporter could get credit on the basis of an export order. However, this system was so much abused that it had to be discontinued in the second half of 1993.

The general experience of African countries seems to be that interventions should not be selective, since this opens the door to various forms of corruption and inefficiency. The reasons for these different results in Africa and Asia must be sought in the structure of institutions. We turn now to this issue.

INSTITUTIONS AND TRANSACTION COSTS

So far we have argued that growth is determined by physical and human capital accumulation, technological progress and the efficiency of resource allocation, and that the outcome is influenced by the economic policy pursued. However, an efficient economic system requires low transaction costs. The character of institutions is a very important determinant of these transaction costs. Thus, the smooth running of the economic system also requires an efficient set of institutions. Resources are required to define the content of exchange transactions and to guarantee compliance with contracts. In developed countries, agents can rather confidently make explicit or implicit contracts with strangers, and this makes specialization possible.

In African economies, one needs to be more careful owing to higher uncertainty. This hinders transactions and reduces the scope for specialization. North (1990, p. 73) argues that the inability of societies to develop simple and cheap methods to guarantee compliance with contracts is the most important source of stagnation in history, and of underdevelopment in the Third World today. Uncertain ownership conditions instead incline people to avoid long-term contracts and to use little fixed capital.

A central question then is why growth-supporting institutions develop. North (1981) argues that, historically, stagnation is the rule rather than growth, which he explains with a theory of the behaviour of the state and the transaction costs of taxation. A government which is primarily concerned with its own survival does not necessarily set up ownership rules that are good for economic growth. It is notable in the successful East Asian countries that economic interventions have largely been related to economic performance criteria. With interest politics at centre stage there is bound to be static inefficiency due to distortions, investors are going to be cautious, and resources are going to be wasted in rent-seeking activities. It would therefore seem reasonable to look for explanations of poor African results in the lack of adequate institution building in the political arena.

THE POLITICAL ARENA

Many observers of African economies have noted the pervasive influence of politics on economics. A characteristic feature is that many of the policy interventions have been discretionary in Africa, while they have been more rule based and institutionalized in the Asian NICs. This selectivity of interventions has paved the way for the high level of corruption and rent seeking in Africa (Bigsten, 1993). Many of the interventions were well intended, but the power elite has also used the system to allocate rents as a means of securing their power positions (see Bigsten and Moene, 1994, and Shleifer and Vishny, 1993). The ethnic diversity of most African countries stimulates this kind of behaviour (see Easterly and Levine, 1994). In extreme cases it may lead to political instability and civil strife. Many of the worst wars in recent decades have been fought in Africa.

Murphy et al. (1991) have analysed how the most talented people in the society choose between becoming entrepreneurs or becoming rent seekers, whose activities reduce growth. They argue that individuals consider the size of the market for both activities, the size of the firm they can manage, and the type of contracts that can be enforced.

> In general, the smaller the market for goods (say, because of poor infrastructure), or the smaller the size of the firm that can be effectively managed (say because the capital market is underdeveloped), or the less the entrepreneur can appropriate from the surplus they generate

(say, because of unclear property rights and/or lack of patent protection), the more likely are the most talented individuals to become rent-seekers who lower the growth rate.

This analysis has relevance for African countries. In Kenya, for example, one finds relatively few African entrepreneurs in active roles in large-scale businesses (Departments of Economics, 1994). They dominate the bottom end of the size distribution of firms, but are virtually absent at the higher echelons, outside the parastatals. To some extent this is due to the history of colonialism, which made it difficult for Africans to accumulate capital. However, Kenya has been independent for thirty years and many competent individuals have emerged, but few have become wealthy through the direct business route. On the other hand, there are many wealthy individuals who have made it economically via the political route. Why does an ambitious person choose the political route to money? If we take the perspective of Murphy *et al.*, we first note that markets are mostly relatively limited, although this can sometimes be compensated for by various forms of government protection. This means that it is easier to capture a large market with political connections. Loans are easier to get if one is well connected. There has been a long list of scandals in Kenya within the so-called 'political banks', which have been used by well-placed politicians to milk the central bank for money. There are also some cases where African entrepreneurs have made it economically – without political backing – only to become blocked by the political elite afterwards. Successful indigenous businesspeople are also considered to be more of a threat than are successful Asian businesspeople, since the latter have no political clout in any case. Thus, paradoxically enough, it is sometimes the independent African businesspeople who are most vulnerable. The insecurity of property rights means that it may be wise to start by establishing a political base.

It is thus very plausible to argue that it is the relative attractiveness of different options, plus an assessment of risks, that determine the choices made by potential African entrepreneurs. There is no lack of entrepreneurial skills as such, but the question is, where are they to be put to use?

Studies of the relationship between democracy and growth have been inconclusive, although growth seems somewhat more likely in countries where the population experience civil and economic liberties (see the review in Alesina and Perotti, 1994). There is a clearly negative effect of political instability on growth. Thus, a vicious circle may emerge where low growth yields political instability. Again it seems essential for countries in low-level equilibria to break out of the stagnation and move to a regime of sustained growth.

A notion that appears many times in the analysis of the Asian miracle is 'shared growth'; that is, the mass of the population must also see the benefits if they are going to participate actively. And not only must the general citizen be included, but also the ruling elite must allow competing elites to progress, and must also allow new competitors to come in. The desire for total control has stifled many initiatives, at least in Kenya.

For shared growth to come about, there is a need for a bureaucracy of high quality which is sufficiently insulated from pressure groups. Such an institutional set-up is not easily created. It is not enough to instill the relevant skills in civil servants. If they are then put into institutions where outside interference determines outcomes, they become frustrated and cynical. To avoid this, the norms and behaviour in the society at large have to change. An open debate may contribute to this, and here African economies have taken strides in the right direction in the last few years. There is thus some hope for improvements.

CONCLUSION

Africa is not catching up with the developed countries. In trying to explain the poor performance of African economies, we have looked at the determinants of basic economic variables, including economic policies, and have discussed the role of institutions and politics as determinants of changes in these variables. It is easy to point out major policy mistakes that have contributed to the poor relative performance of African economies, but even allowing for this, there is a residual to be explained. Explanations for this residual should be sought in the area of institutions (including the political system), although this is admittedly difficult when it comes to quantification of impacts. Future research on economic growth in Africa therefore needs to focus more on this area, and on its interlinkage with traditional economic variables.[1]

NOTES

1 Our discourse has focused on economic growth, but the set of factors discussed also determines the distribution of income. The end result of the economic process is a certain income structure, and institutions also play an important mediating role here. Income distribution analysis could therefore benefit from more explicit attention to the institutional dimension. There are great problems in defining institutional impacts, of course, and this makes it very difficult to measure them. We may also have problems in getting access to the relevant data.

REFERENCES

Alesina, A. and Perotti, R. (1994) 'The Political Economy of Growth: A Critical Survey of the Recent Literature', *World Bank Economic Review*, vol. 8, no. 3, pp. 351–372.

Amsden, A. H. (1994) 'Why Isn't the Whole World Experimenting with the East

Asian Model to Develop?: Review of the East Asian Miracle', *World Development*, vol. 22, no. 4, pp. 627–634.

Barro, R. J. (1991) 'Economic Growth in a Cross-Section of Countries', *Quarterly Journal of Economics*, vol. 106, no. 2, pp. 407–443.

Barro, R. J. and Sala-i-Martin, X. (1992) 'Convergence', *Journal of Political Economy*, vol. 100, no. 2, pp. 223–251.

Baumol, W. J. (1986) 'Productivity Growth, Convergence and Welfare', *American Economic Review*, vol. 76, no. 5, pp. 1072–1085.

Baumol, W., Batey Blackman, S. A. and Wolff, E. N. (1989) *Productivity and American Leadership: The Long View*, MIT Press, Cambridge, MA.

Ben-David, D. (1993) 'Equalizing Exchange: Trade Liberalization and Income Convergence', *Quarterly Journal of Economics*, vol. 108, no. 3, pp. 653–679.

Bigsten, A. (1993) 'Regulation versus Price Reforms in Crisis Management: The Case of Kenya', in M. Blomstrom and M. Lundahl (eds) *Economic Crisis in Africa. Perspectives on Policy Responses*, Routledge, London.

Bigsten, A. and Moene, K. O. (1994) *Growth and Rent Dissipation – The Case of Kenya*, Memorandum no. 207, Department of Economics, University of Gothenburg.

Chibber, A. Dailami, M. and Shafik, N. (eds) (1992) *Reviving Private Investment in Developing Countries. Empirical Studies and Policy Lessons*, North-Holland, Amsterdam.

De Long, J. B. and Summers, L. H. (1993) 'How Strongly Do Developing Economies Benefit From Equipment Investment?', *Journal of Monetary Economics*, vol. 32, no. 3, pp. 395–415.

Departments of Economics, Universities of Gothenburg and Nairobi (1994) *Limitations and Rewards in Kenya's Manufacturing Sector: A Study of Enterprise Development*, World Bank, Washington, DC.

Easterly, W. (1993) 'How Much Do Distortions Affect Growth?', *Journal of Monetary Economics*, vol. 32, no. 2, pp. 187–212.

——(1994) 'Economic Stagnation, Fixed Factors, and Policy Thresholds', *Journal of Monetary Economics*, vol. 33, no. 3, pp. 525–557.

Easterly, W. and Levine, R. (1994) 'Africa's Growth Tragedy', Paper presented at AERC Conference, May, Nairobi.

Easterly, W., Kremer, M., Pritchett, L. and Summers, L. H. (1993) 'Good Policy or Good Luck? Country Growth Performance and Temporary Shocks', *Journal of Monetary Economics*, vol. 32, no. 3, pp. 459–483.

Faini, R. and de Melo, J. (1992) 'Adjustment Investment and the Real Exchange Rate in Developing Countries', in A. Chibber *et al.* (eds) *Reviving Private Investment in Developing Countries. Empirical Studies and Policy Lessons*, North-Holland, Amsterdam.

Fischer, S. (1993) 'The Role of Macroeconomic Factors in Growth', *Journal of Monetary Economics*, vol. 32, no. 3, pp. 485–512.

Gerschenkron, A. (1962) *Economic Backwardness in Historical Perspective*, Harvard University Press, Cambridge, MA.

Hammond, P. J. and Rodriguez-Clare, A. (1993) 'On Endogenizing Long-Term Growth', *Scandinavian Journal of Economics*, vol. 95, no. 4, pp. 391–425.

Helleiner, G. (1993) 'Trade, Trade Policy and Economic Development in Very Low Income Countries', in A. Maizels, M. Nissanke and A. Hewitt (eds) *Economic Crisis in Developing Countries*, Pinter, London.

Krugman, P. (1981) 'Trade, Accumulation and Uneven Development', *Journal of Development Economics*, vol. 8, no. 2, pp. 149–161.

Mankiw, N., Roemer, D. and Weil, D. N. (1992) 'A Contribution to The Empirics of Economic Growth', *Quarterly Journal of Economics*, vol. 107, no. 2, pp. 407–437.

Murphy, K. M., Shleifer, A. and Vishny, R. W. (1991) 'The Allocation of Talent: Implications for Growth', *Quarterly Journal of Economics*, vol. 106, no. 2, pp. 503–530.

North, D. C. (1981) *Structure and Change in Economic History*, Norton, New York.

——(1990) *Institutions, Institutional Change and Economic Performance*, Cambridge University Press, Cambridge.

Pack, H. (1994) 'Endogenous Growth Theory: Intellectual Appeal and Empirical Shortcomings', *Journal of Economic Perspectives*, vol. 8, no. 1, pp. 55–72.

Page Jr, J. M. (1990) 'The Pursuit of Industrial Growth: Policy Initiatives and Economic Consequences', in M. F. G. Scott and D. Lal (eds) *Public Policy and Economic Development: Essays in Honour of Ian Little*, Clarendon Press, Oxford.

Quah, D. (1993) 'Galton's Fallacy and Tests of the Convergence Hypothesis', *Scandinavian Journal of Economics*, vol. 95, no. 4, pp. 427–443.

Romer, P. M. (1987) 'Crazy Explanations for the Productivity Slowdown', in S. Fischer (ed.) *NBER Macroeconomics Annual*, MIT Press, Cambridge, MA.

Shleifer, A. and Vishny, R. W. (1993) 'Corruption', *Quarterly Journal of Economics*, vol. 108, no. 3, pp. 599–617.

Solow, R. M. (1957) 'Technical Change and the Aggregate Production Function', *Review of Economics and Statistics*, vol. 39, no. 3, pp. 312–320.

World Bank (1993) *The East Asian Miracle: Economic Growth and Public Policy*, Oxford University Press, Oxford.

——(1994) *Adjustment in Africa: Reforms, Results and the Road Ahead*, Oxford University Press, Oxford.

4

LONG-TERM DEVELOPMENT AND SUSTAINABLE GROWTH IN SUB-SAHARAN AFRICA

Ibrahim A. Elbadawi and Benno J. Ndulu

INTRODUCTION

This chapter provides evidence of three sets of stylized facts about economic growth and development in Sub-Saharan Africa (SSA) and then attempts to draw some implications for the latter. First, the economies of SSA are characterized by low per capita incomes, low savings and investment, economic distortion, vastly underdeveloped infrastructure, weak institutions, rudimentary technology and relatively uneducated populations which adversely affect growth performance and prospects. Second, the structural disarticulation of the African economies makes them much more susceptible to external shocks, where economic growth and economic performance in general are relatively exogenous. Third, save for a few countries, SSA is mostly composed of countries with small markets and not strategically located *vis-à-vis* the main economic growth poles of the world.

The next section reviews the evidence linking the first set of characteristics to the prolonged economic stagnation of SSA and its rather weak economic convergence towards the growth rates achieved by middle- and high-income countries. This chapter argues that breaking away from this trap requires a significant improvement in both physical and human capacity for production, a stable development environment buttressed by appropriate policy stances, and an institutional capacity capable of initiating, promoting and sustaining change. Governments not only need to invest in physical and human capital, reform and deepen institutions, and expand the technological base, but they should also attempt to build consensus behind reform, so that resources can be freed to finance these new initiatives while trying to maintain sustainable macroeconomic environments. Thus a modified but significant and proactive role for African governments is required. While the empirical regularities of the next section provide important insight into the growth process of SSA over the past decades, these growth fundamentals, however, could only explain part of the variations in SSA's growth. Evidence from endogenous growth-based cross-country regressions involving a large number of countries (both developed and developing) could not eliminate an estimated large and significant negative effect of the African dummy, implying that the behavioural part of these models systematically overpredicts the rates of growth in SSA (Barro and Lee, 1993; Easterly and Levine, 1993). In their attempt to explain this puzzle of the African dummy, Barro and Lee (1993) suggested that the failure to explain the extent of the poor performance in the slow-growing African countries could be rectified by developing a better measure of the terms of trade shocks that allows a direct effect on growth as well as an indirect effect through stimulating bad policies. Furthermore, the relatively small scale of the typical African economy and the absence of sufficiently large and geographically close economies to provide spillover benefits to smaller economies, may be another factor to consider.

The third and fourth sections of this chapter will assess the extent to which growth in SSA might have been disproportionately retarded by these two factors.[1] Finally, the last section contains our conclusions.

BASIC GROWTH FUNDAMENTALS IN SSA

The past two decades have witnessed the severely declining fortunes of many economies of SSA. In a sample of sixty-one mostly low-income developing countries including thirty-two SSA countries,[2] the average annual rate of growth in real per capita GDP for the SSA countries declined from 1.19 per cent in the 1970s to about − 0.99 per cent in the 1980s, with an average of − 0.35 per cent for the two decades. This rather gloomy performance is in sharp contrast to the record of other developing countries included in the sample, where average annual rates of growth of 3.47, 1.82 and 2.33 per cent were achieved for each of the above periods, respectively (Figure 4.1).

In terms of growth sustainability, the story is equally alarming. Out of thirty-two SSA countries considered in this study, only six managed to achieve consecutive average positive rates of growth over the two decades. All other SSA countries have lost at least one decade, and a significant number of these countries have had two consecutive, negative average, decadal growth rates (Figure 4.2). In contrast, none of the twenty-nine non-SSA countries in the sample registered negative growth over the two consecutive decades (Figure 4.3). The median for the number of years (of the two decades of the 1970–1990 period) with per capita growth less than 1 per cent was 11 for SSA compared with only 8 for the group of non-SSA developing countries.

The above record confirms that economic growth in SSA has been disappointing. However, controversy abounds as to the causes behind this economic stagnation. Obviously this debate relates but is not confined to the relative degree of influence of the adverse exogenous shocks and initial

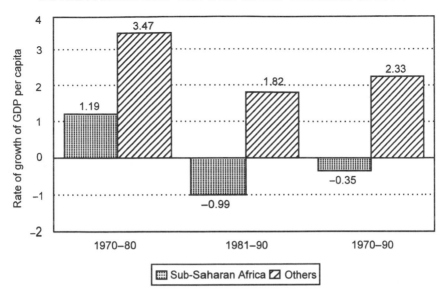

Figure 4.1 Rates of growth of GDP per capita: Sub-Saharan Africa and others

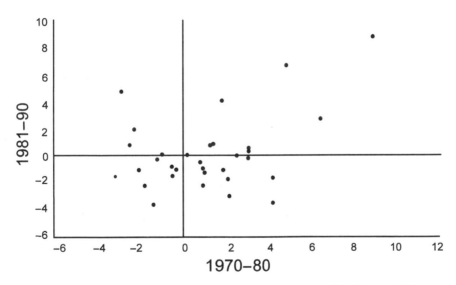

Figure 4.2 Decadal rates of growth of GDP per capita: Sub-Saharan African countries

conditions *vis-à-vis* domestic policy mistakes and ill-conceived development strategies. The recent 'endogenous growth' literature offers a useful analytical framework for assessing the relative importance of the above two sets of growth fundamentals.[3]

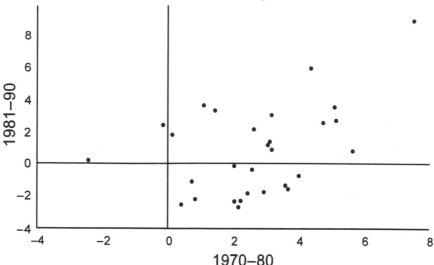

Figure 4.3 Decadal rates of growth of GDP per capita: other developing countries

The basic framework suggested by this literature (e.g. Barro and Lee, 1993) relates real per capita growth rate to 'two kinds of variables: first, initial levels of *state* variables such as the stock of physical capital and the stock of human capital in the form of education and health; and second, *control* or environmental variables'. The latter group in turn can be divided into policy-induced variables such as real exchange rate misalignment (or exchange rate premium), real exchange rate variability, inflation, government consumption, financial depth, trade openness and domestic investment; and exogenous factors, such as external and weather shocks, and wars, civil strife or political instability. Empirical evidence on the relative impacts of the above fundamentals on growth will be reviewed in subsequent subsections. The median growth coefficients of the fundamentals for a set of comparable cross-country studies will then be combined with the median values of these fundamentals for a sample of SSA and other developing countries, to derive a matrix of sources of growth (*à la* Barro and Lee, 1993) that can be used to assess contributions to the overall growth of various fundamentals in a comparative sense for the 1970–1990 period (Table 4.2).

The 'conditional' convergence effect

A number of theories in the growth literature suggest that imbalances between physical and human capital could have important growth implications. It is argued that a high ratio of human capital to physical capital (or initial income)[4] is likely to induce rapid growth in physical capital and output. This is because, other things being equal, a low initial level of

Table 4.1 Definition of variables

Variable	Definition
RPCGDP, RPOP, INFL	RPCGCP, RPOP and INFL for each country have been calculated by regressing the change of the natural logarithms of real per capita GDP, population and a GDP deflator respectively on a time trend and an intercept.
WEATHER	WEATHER variability is proxied by the variability of food yield and is given by the residual of regression of the natural logarithm of cereal yield on a time trend and a constant.
PRIMSCH, SECSCH	PRIMSCH (SECSCH) are constructed as ratio of total students enrolled in primary (secondary) education to estimated number of individuals in the age brackets 6–11 (12–27) years for the year 1970.
MORT	MORT is defined as mortality rate for ages 0 through 4. Average of 1965 and 1985.
RERVAR	RERVAR is defined as (standard deviation/mean) or real exchange rate for each country.
RERMIS	RERMIS is defined as $[(RER_e/RER_a - 1)]$ where RER_a is the actual real exchange rate; RER_e is the equilibrium real exchange rate calculated as follows. Five-year moving averages of the projected real exchange rate using the real exchange rate model in Appendix C were calculated. Let this variable be called RER_p^{ma}. For each country, RER_p^{ma} was rescaled so that it is equal to RER_a for the year in which the absolute value of (exports − imports)/GDP was the maximum. Thus RERMIS is zero for any country for the year in which the absolute value of (exports − imports)/GDP was maximum.
CIVLIB	CIVLIB is an index of civil liberties where 0.01 = highest, 0.07 = lowest.
LLY	LLY is defined as the ratio of liquid liabilities of the financial system (M2) to GDP.
TOTSHK	TOTSHK for year t is calculated as: $[(PX_t/PX_{base} - 1)^* (X/GDP)_{t-1}] - [(PM_t/PM_{base} - 1)^*(M/GDP)_{t-1}]$ where PX and PM are export and import price indices respectively deflated by the US GNP deflator; PX_{base} and PM_{base} are the average PX and PM respectively for the preceding three years; X and M are respectively the exports and imports of goods and non-factor services.
ROISHK	ROISHK for year t is calculated as $-(r_t - r_{base})^* (Debt/GDP)_{beg}$ where r is the real rate of interest calculated by dividing interest payments by total debt and then deflating by the US GNP deflator; r_{base} is the average of r for the preceding three years; $(Debt/GDP)_{beg}$ is the average annual debt to GDP ratio for the period 1970–1975.
NFSHK	NFSHK for year t is calculated as $[(NF_t/NF_{base}) - 1]^* (NF/GDP)_{t-1}$ where NF is the official + private net flows (exclusive of interest payments). NF_{base} is the average of NF for the preceding three years.

Source: African Economic Financial Data, World Debt Tables and the World Bank Database (ANDREX)

Table 4.2 Determinants of economic growth: SSA and others (median annual average values, 1970–1990)

				Sources of Growth	
Growth variables	*(1)* SSA	*(2)* Others	*(3)* Median of estimated effects[b]	*(4)* SSA	*(5)* Others[f]
Basic fundamentals:					
Per capita GDP in 1970	337	795	− 0.008	0.0012	− 0.0018
PRIMSCH	0.40	0.87	0.008	− 0.0019	0.0019
SECSCH	0.07	0.27	0.007	− 0.0007	0.0007
MORTA	0.16	0.10	− 0.078[c]	− 0.0023	0.0023
RPOP	2.94	2.29	−	−	−
Net conversion effect	−	−	−	− 0.0038	0.0031
Rate of investment to GDP[g]	0.19	0.23	0.075	− 0.0023	0.0002
Policy variables:					
Trade openness index (adjusted)	0.989	1.040	+ NS[d]	−	−
RERMIS (mean value)	0.128	0.069	− 0.400	− 0.0118	0.0118
RERVAR	0.120	0.240	−	−	−
INFL	4.992	5.250	− NS[d]	−	−
Ratio of govt consumption to GDP	0.142	0.109	− 0.074	− 0.0010	0.0015
LLY	0.201	0.297	0.036	− 0.0017	0.0017
Exogenous factors:					
Total Shock	− 0.0205	− 0.0146	−	−	−
TOTSHK	− 0.0311	− 0.0160	0.800	− 0.0097	0.0024
ROISHK	− 0.0014	− 0.0045	−	−	−
EFSHK	0.0120	0.0059	−	−	−
Variability of food yield	0.0050	0.0020	−	−	−
CIVLIB[e]	0.0545	0.0400	− 0.173	− 0.0013	0.0013
Growth performance					
Projected RPCGDP[a]	−	−	−	− 0.0314	0.0219
Actual RPCGDP	− 0.0030	0.0154	−	−	−
Deviation of actual RPCGDP from sample median			−	−	−
				− 0.0125	0.0059

Notes:
[a] Sum of above items.
[b] Column 3 refers to the median range of estimated coefficients obtained from ten recent studies that estimate a Barro-type regression for a large number of countries. The studies are Barro and Lee (1993), Easterly and Levine (1993), Easterly (1992), Edwards (1992), Chua (1993a, b) Easterly *et al.* (1992), Khan and Kumar (1993), Levine and Renelt (1992) and King and Levine (1993).
[c] This estimate is the negative of life expectancy.
[d] +NS (− NS) refers to positive (negative) but insignificant effect. Edwards was the exception, where he estimated a significant effect at 0.0225 for OI, but unlike the others he used the rate of total factor productivity as his dependent variable rather than the real per capita GDP growth rate.
[e] The coefficient on civil liberties and coups is in fact due to a similar indicator for 'revolution and coups' – see Barro and Lee (1993).

[f] Columns 4 and 5 are derived by obtaining the difference between columns 1 and 2 respectively and the corresponding median for the whole sample. The differences are then multiplied by column 3.
[g] Memorandum:

Sectoral shares of public investment	1960–1969		1970–1979		1980–1988	
	SSA	OTH	SSA	OTH	SSA	OTH
Agriculture	0.0983	0.0562	0.0885	0.0479	0.0444	0.0357
Education and health	0.1929	0.1451	0.2449	0.1093	0.1124	0.1320
Industry	0.1763	0.1424	0.1490	0.0977	0.0821	0.1059
Infrastructure (transport and communication, water and power)	0.2460	0.3351	0.2111	0.2273	0.1676	0.2736
Total public sector investment/GDP	0.0583	0.0540	0.0893	0.0806	0.0993	0.0844

income relative to education and health indicators (human capital) implies a higher marginal productivity of capital. This should lead to both higher domestic and foreign investment that will raise the capital/labour ratio and generate output growth and higher wages. Other theoretical models predict that a higher level of human capital enhances the ability to absorb new technologies, and hence triggers a higher rate of growth for a given level of physical capital. Unlike the empirically unsubstantiated old notion of convergence which predicts initial income to be negatively correlated with growth,[5] this notion is conditional and only predicts such correlation provided that initial income is low relative to the stock of human capital – the so-called conditional convergence or catch-up effect (see Barro and Sala-i-Martin, 1993, Ch. 4, for a detailed discussion).

Table 4.2 shows that for the 1970–1990 period, the median annual average per capita GDP growth rate for SSA was − 0.3 per cent compared with 1.54 per cent for other developing countries. SSA grew so slowly over the last two decades, despite the fact that it started from very low initial levels of income relative to other developing countries. The median annual average real per capita GDP for SSA was 337 in 1970 compared with 795 for other developing countries. This, however, appears to be balanced by the relatively very low stock of human capital in Africa. For example, the median averages for primary and secondary school enrolment for SSA were 0.40 and 0.07 compared with 0.87 and 0.27 for other developing countries, respectively. The median mortality rate was 0.16 for SSA compared with 0.10 for other developing countries. Furthermore, populations in SSA grew faster at median average annual rates of 2.94 per cent compared with 2.29 per cent for the others.

Using the median estimated coefficients for various growth variables derived from ten studies based on Barro-type cross-country regressions, we computed a decomposition of 'the hopefully exogenous' sources of growth for the sixty-one SSA and other developing countries over the 1970–1990 period (Table 4.2). The results of Table 4.2 show that the annual

average 'net convergence' effect over the two decades of 1970–1990 is about
– 0.38 per cent for SSA. In contrast, the other developing countries, in spite
of their much higher initial levels of incomes compared with the SSA
countries, were able to achieve a positive net convergence effect of 0.31
per cent. Barro and Lee (hereafter BL) also study the determinants of
decadal per capita growth rates for a sample of 100 developing and developed countries, in the context of a formal cross-country regression, and find
that for the fourteen SSA countries that belong to the lowest quintile of
growth rates for the 1965–1985 period,[6] the 'net convergence' effect for the
1965–1975 decade is close to zero, and is only marginally positive (at 0.006)
for the following decade. This provides a stark contrast to the eight fast-
growing East Asian economies which, in spite of their much higher initial
levels of income compared with these African countries, were able to
achieve positive net convergence effects in both decades (with rates of
0.016 and 0.008, respectively).

Easterly (1993) observes that since many low-income countries are
among those stagnating, it is evident that there is no tendency towards
unconditional convergence of incomes, as was shown by BL's analysis and
numerous other authors. Easterly links this phenomenon to the classic
argument of Gerschenkron (1962) 'that backwardness usually fosters rapid
growth but that one may be "too backward" and grow slowly'. In a formal
model that distinguishes between stagnation and positive growth, Easterly
balances the usual 'conditional catch-up' effect by the slow saving and slow
growth effect that characterizes subsistence economies. The interaction of
these two factors in Easterly's model produces a hump-shaped transitional
dynamic of a rising and then falling growth as income rises. Poor economies
bordering on subsistence are dominated by the consumption of necessities
that cannot be postponed to allow for higher national savings (Table 4.2).
This is consistent with the view that one mechanism that explains low
growth for low-income countries is the low saving rates typically observed
in low-income countries (e.g. Rebelo, 1992; Kuznets, 1966). Another implication of Easterly's model is that output is likely to stagnate the lower
the ratio of public to private capital, and that the effect of public investment
on growth is higher, the lower the elasticity of substitution between public
and private capital.[7]

The policy implications from the above selective review are rather obvious but are also very far reaching. Clearly a virtuous cycle exists between
savings and growth and at very low-income levels, public saving is unavoidable and triggers this cycle.[8] Furthermore, public investment in areas that
are weakly substitutable to private investment, such as human capital and
infrastructure, is key to both shaking off stagnation and accelerating economic growth. The public sector should free up resources to finance growth
by saving more, and should strive to level the field for higher growth by
undertaking higher investment in the sectors that are complementary to

private sector activity. Unfortunately the evidence of Table 4.2 suggests that neither has happened in the case of SSA.

Other exogenous and policy-induced growth variables

In the neoclassical growth framework, such as BL's, the control variables, both policy-induced and exogenous, are predicted to influence the position of steady-state growth. Using the evidence of Table 4.2, we will discuss below the theoretical and empirical relevance of both sets of factors to the growth process of the countries in the sample, where the experiences of SSA and other non-SSA developing countries will be compared and contrasted.

Exogenous shocks and sociopolitical instability

Exogenous factors are deemed to have a direct effect on growth depending on the magnitude and direction of the shock. An increase in political uncertainty has an equivalent effect of a decline in the security of property rights, and hence has the same effect on growth as economic distortions. Also, negative exogenous shocks, such as adverse terms of trade or weather shocks, will lower the rate of growth for given levels of state variables, through the direct income effect, but they could also have more subtle substitution effects (see the next section). The evidence of Table 4.2 suggests that SSA has been more negatively impacted by external shocks and political instability. These findings appear consistent with the slower growth of SSA relative to other developing countries.

The overall magnitude of the external shock was negative and higher in SSA at a median annual average of − 2.05 compared with − 1.46 per cent of GDP for other developing countries. In terms of individual components, however, the relative impact of external shocks is a mixed bag. The terms of trade shock was − 3.11 compared with − 1.6 per cent for the others, and the real interest rate shock was much smaller but weaker with − 0.14 and − 0.45 GDP percentage points for SSA and non-SSA, respectively. On the other hand the external finance shocks were positive for both sets of countries, with SSA receiving 1.2 percentage points of GDP compared with only 0.59 for non-SSA developing countries. However, only for the case of TOT shocks was a significant effect on growth estimated in formal empirical models of growth (Easterly, 1992); using the estimated coefficient of 0.8, the median annual average contribution of the TOT to per capita rates of growth (in deviation from the sample median) was − 0.97 per cent for SSA compared with 0.24 per cent for other countries in the sample.

An adverse weather shock could have a devastating effect on growth, especially in SSA given the dominance of agriculture in its countries. Measured indirectly in terms of variability of cereal yield, the weather effect has been more severe in SSA with a variability of 0.5 GDP percentage points relative to 0.2 for other developing countries.

Finally, lack of social order and political instability could also be harmful to growth. During conflicts, much of the limited human, financial and physical resources are devoted to non-civilian, non-developmental ends. Furthermore, political instability and social conflicts usually breed uncertainty, and lack of transparency, which discourage investment.[9] An index of civil liberties contained in Table 4.2 (0.01=highest, 0.07=lowest) shows that SSA has a lower level at 0.0545 compared with 0.04 for the others. The corresponding contribution of political instability to annual rate of growth (relative to the sample median) was − 0.13 per cent (0.13 per cent) for SSA (others). The countries of Africa that have been plagued by ethnic violence and civil wars (e.g. Angola, Chad, Ethiopia, Mozambique, Somalia, Sudan, Uganda and Zaire) were among the worst performers.

Policy variables

Financial depth is a policy variable that is expected to have a positive effect on growth. In the traditional literature (e.g. McKinnon, 1973; Shaw, 1973) financial depth and financial liberalization affect economic growth through higher saving rates and higher investment allocation. The modern interpretation of the role of financial depth in economic growth emphasizes the processing of information on entrepreneurs as a central activity of liberalized capital markets (King and Levine, 1993). There is fairly consistent evidence linking financial depth (but not necessarily financial liberalization) to growth (King and Levine, 1993). Financial depth (LLY) given in terms of the ratio of broad money (M2) to GDP (Table 4.2) has a median of 30 per cent in non-SSA developing countries compared with 20 per cent for SSA, with a contribution to the annual rate of growth (in deviation from the sample median) estimated, respectively, at − 0.17 per cent and 0.17 per cent for SSA and others.

The investment ratio is one of the traditional growth variables reflecting the contribution of capital accumulation to output growth at the steady state.[10] Investment as a ratio to GDP is lower in SSA at 19.4 per cent compared with 22.6 per cent for other developing countries. These ratios translate into estimated contributions to annual growth (in deviation from the sample median) at 0.02 per cent for other countries, compared with − 0.23 per cent for SSA.

The new theories on endogenous growth also suggest that productivity growth will be faster in sectors where protection has been reduced and not on those subject to trade barriers or other forms of regulation. For example, Edwards (1992) developed a formal model which assumes that a country's ability to absorb world technology depends on the openness of the economy and on the country's gap relative to the world in terms of total factor productivity. The empirical implementation of this model using data from a large set of countries provides additional support for the view that, after controlling for other growth variables, countries with more open and less distorted trade regimes have experienced faster growth in total factor productivity than nations with a more distorted external sector. However, almost all other studies have failed to find consistent evidence on the relevance of trade openness to long-term growth (e.g. see BL; Easterly and Levine, 1993; Khan and Kumar, 1993; to mention a few). The results of Table 4.2 suggest that SSA appears to be less open in terms of the ratio of actual trade to GDP relative to the notional trade ratio that adjusts for the scale of the economy, population size and capital flows (see Appendix B). On the other hand, relative to the same measure, other developing countries in the sample are found to be more open. However, the lack of consistent empirical regularities linking growth to trade regimes prompted some authors to argue that macroeconomic consistency, including real exchange rate compatibility, for a given trade regime is much more important to economic performance than the nature of the trade regime, and that the experience of East Asia reveals systematic evidence on the former rather than the latter (e.g. Helleiner, 1993, 1994).

On the other hand, economic distortions imply a lower steady-state position and hence a lower rate of growth for values of the state variables. Economic distortions could be reflected indirectly by the ratio of government consumption to GDP or directly by the rate of real exchange rate overvaluation (or the black market premium), domestic inflation, or the real exchange rate variability. Economic distortions have been shown in the empirical growth literature to have had systematic and deleterious effects on growth, and the evidence of Table 4.2 shows that they are much more acute in SSA than in other developing countries.

Starting with the real exchange rate misalignment (RERMIS), the index of Table 4.2 (see Appendix Table 4.C) gives an overvaluation index of 12.8 percent for SSA, almost double that of other developing countries at 6.9 percent. The real exchange rate misalignment encompasses a wide range of macroeconomic, trade, exchange rate and fiscal policies. As an indicator of domestic policy distortion, real exchange rate overvaluation has adverse effects on long-run growth. Substantial overvaluation discourages the production of tradables, especially exports. To the extent that improved export performance generates economy-wide forward and backward linkages, overall growth could be slowed down. Second, the overvaluation represents a signal of policy incredibility, which discourages investment and precipitates the inefficient allocation of resources. Hence, it is not surprising that economic distortion higher than the sample median in SSA, as reflected by the RERMIS index, resulted in a -1.18 per cent contribution to growth compared with 1.18 per cent for other developing countries.

Government consumption is usually concentrated on non-traded goods and to the extent that it is kept higher than sustainable levels, it will lead to increasing taxes and monetization and hence real exchange rate overvaluation. In a model of constant returns to scale with respect to government inputs and private capital combined but diminishing returns with respect to private capital alone, Barro (1989, 1990) showed that a high level of taxation distorts saving decisions and lower growth. Also the endogenous growth model developed by Easterly (1993) permits distortions between returns on two types of capital to affect growth adversely. This effect of a high and unsustainable level of domestic public consumption should be picked up by the RERMIS index. Over and above this, a high but sustainable level of public consumption may still further decelerate growth. To the extent that unproductive forms of such expenditure crowd out valuable public goods (education, health, infrastructure, etc.) that are complementary to private investment and growth, public consumption could have an independent (of RERMIS) deleterious effect on growth. The average public consumption rate is higher by 4 percentage points of GDP in SSA at 14.4 per cent compared with 10.4 per cent for other developing countries, with the corresponding contribution to growth in deviation from the sample median estimated at − 0.10 per cent for SSA compared with 0.17 per cent for other countries (Table 4.2).

Macroeconomic stability signals to the private sector the sustainability and credibility of macroeconomic policy, while instability compromises the informational content of relative prices as a signal for resource allocation. The rate of domestic inflation (INFL) and the real exchange rate coefficient of variation (RERVAR) averaged, respectively, 4.6 and 31.4 per cent for SSA (Table 4.2). While inflation is slightly higher in other developing countries at 5.25 per cent, the RERVAR is lower at 26.3 per cent.

The significant African dummy – is Africa really different?

The above analysis provides the following broad conclusions. First, SSA has grown more slowly than other developing countries over the last two decades. Second, despite its relatively low initial income levels, SSA could not 'catch up' with other developing countries because of its lower standards of human capital and lower savings. Third, the policy indicators also seem to be consistent with the disappointing growth record of SSA relative to other developing countries. SSA has undertaken less saving, has been more prone to higher real exchange rate overvaluation and variability, has higher public consumption and rather rudimentary financial systems. Fourth, the economies of SSA were more impacted than others by negative, exogenous external and weather shocks and political instability; however, unlike the above, these factors so far have not been systematically established as determinants of growth in formal behavioural models.

As we suggested in the introduction, while the above fairly systematic empirical regularities provide important insight into the growth process of

SSA over the past decades, these growth fundamentals could only explain part of the variations in SSA's growth. The presence of the significant negative African dummy in these endogenous growth-based cross-country regressions implies that the behavioural part of these models systematically overpredicts the rates of growth in SSA (BL; Easterly and Levine, 1993).[11] Despite their careful analysis, however, these authors also concluded that 'after controlling for policies, human capital endowments, terms of trade shocks, and "catchup" factors, Africa grew more slowly for reasons that a cross-country model does not explain. Africa is different.' The following two sections of this chapter will attempt to contribute to this discussion, by analysing two sets of growth variables that could further add to the systematic explanation of growth variables in SSA, and therefore provide an opportunity for assessing the extent to which growth in SSA might have been disproportionately retarded by these two factors.[12]

EXTERNAL SHOCKS AND GROWTH IN SUB-SAHARAN AFRICA

The relative importance of external shocks to Africa's growth performance has been a subject of long and continuing debate. One set of views is held by those who consider the shocks not a significant explanatory factor either because negative shocks tend to be offset by positive shocks or because Africa's exposure to these shocks is no different from that faced by other developing countries. These views place more emphasis on the policy response to shocks as being key to understanding their influence on growth.

A different view emphasizes the high vulnerability of African growth to both the magnitude and variability of external shocks. The economies are considered to be structurally fragile, with a low capability to respond to shocks in a manner that maintains a stable development environment. The fragility is partly due to their high dependence on imports; unstable export revenues; rigidities in supply response limiting their adjustment options and their potential effectiveness; and limited access to timely stabilization and adjustment finance in response to shocks. This view, therefore, considers restructuring African economies to enhance their capabilities to respond flexibly to shocks, reduce the degree of exposure to shocks by diversifying the export base, and sustained and timely resource support towards these ends as being more important than emphasizing a policy response to shocks in a fragile economy.

Below, we first highlight the structural features that enhance the vulnerability of Africa's growth to external shocks; identify the key links between external shocks and growth; measure and identify major types of external shocks experienced by SSA countries; and review empirical evidence for the impacts of and responses to external shocks drawing from African experience and that of other economies with similar structures.

The transmission of external shocks to growth in SSA

A useful starting point for analysing the sensitivity of African growth to external shocks is to identify the key channels of influence of these shocks on growth. In so doing we attempt to take into account the peculiar features of the African economies that exacerbate such sensitivity and distinguish the nature of the effects of the shocks broadly into direct and indirect ones. There are three important characteristic features of African economies of particular importance to the understanding of the high vulnerability of African growth to external shocks. The dependence on imports for production and investment on uncertain revenue from exports, on the one hand, and on autonomous external resources to finance them on the other, underlies the sensitivity of growth to external shocks. Indeed, savings cannot be converted into investment without foreign exchange to import capital goods; and productive capacity cannot be effectively utilized without imports of intermediate goods. In this way both capacity and output expansion are dependent on the availability of foreign exchange. A large proportion of Africa's exports is of primary commodities subject to high volatility in world market prices and supply rigidities. In 1986, for example, 40 per cent of SSA merchandise exports were agricultural compared with 29 per cent for all low-income countries (World Bank, 1988). A large proportion of the external resource inflows into Africa is autonomous, being predominantly official development assistance. Exports in turn are largely supply constrained and also significantly dependent on imports for expansion (Khan and Knight, 1988). This intensifies the significance of the foreign exchange constraint on growth. It is the significant exogeneity of the determinants of the foreign exchange constraints that determines the exogeneity of growth performance and its sensitivity to exogenous shocks.[13]

Another important and relevant structural feature here is the close link between the external and fiscal gaps in these economies. The high debt/GDP ratios reflect a solvency problem arising from the stock-flow disequilibrium between foreign obligation and current incomes. Since nearly all external debt obligations are held by governments, the external crisis has also assumed a fiscal form requiring simultaneous cuts in fiscal expenditures to reduce exposure. To the extent that such cuts have fallen on public investment they reduce capacity growth both directly and indirectly through foregone crowding in of private investment (Fanelli et al., 1992). Where governments have relied on mobilizing revenues through increased transfers from the private sector to service external debt, this has occurred at the expense of crowding out domestic private investment. The important point to note here, as Fanelli et al. (1992) do more generally for developing countries, is that given the prevalence of the severe debt overhang problems African economies face, they have to contend simultaneously with external and fiscal constraints to growth. Unpredictable external shocks make such undertakings more difficult to manage.

In addition to the direct income effects and their impact on savings and investment, negative external shocks in the short to medium term affect investment productivity as economies adjust in a contractionary fashion through capacity utilization changes in response to intensifying foreign exchange bottlenecks. For example, in the cases where economies have to effect a double transfer to service external debt, this has also been at the expense of the much needed infrastructural maintenance critical for investment productivity.

Types and magnitudes of external shocks faced by SSA economies

Three types of external shocks will be the subject of our attention in this section. The first is the terms of trade shocks resulting from changes in the world market prices for African exports and imports. The measurement of the terms of trade shocks will appropriately use export shares and import shares of GDP as weights on the respective prices; the relative importance of the sources of shocks from both the export and import sides will be determined. In the following section, the effects on growth of these TOT shocks will be disentangled into direct effects through a stimulus to government policies and private sector response with respect to expenditure (including investment) and macroeconomic stability. Also a possible asymmetry in the effects depending on whether the shocks predominantly originate from the export or import price side will be investigated. The second type of external shock is that of foreign real interest rate changes and their impact on the debt-servicing burden. The real rate of interest is measured in its 'effective' terms by dividing interest payments by total debt adjusted by the US GNP deflator. The magnitude of the shock is thus measured as a ratio of changes in real interest payments to GDP.

The third type of shock is the net capital flows (private and official) which augment or reduce resource availability (financing in general and in foreign exchange terms in particular) for growth. It is measured as the rate of change of net transfers (gross flows less amortization) weighted by the share of net transfers in GDP.

The three components of external shocks are subsequently combined, having all been measured as proportions of GDP, as the sum of the components. This combination emphasizes the income effects of the external shocks.

Table 4.3 and Figure 4.4 present the median magnitudes of the above external shocks experienced by a sample of thirty-two SSA economies, the median component structure of terms of trade shocks, and comparison (in median terms) with other developing countries for the period 1970–1990.[14]

Table 4.3 Components of external shock: SSA and others

	1970–1975	1976–1979	1980–1985	1986–1990
TOTSHOCK				
SSA	− 0.0392	− 0.0317	− 0.0284	− 0.0253
OTH	− 0.0217	− 0.0161	− 0.0141	− 0.0121
ROISHOCK				
SSA	0.0249	− 0.0088	− 0.0360	0.0141
OTH	0.0206	− 0.0149	− 0.0357	0.0119
NFSHOCK				
SSA	0.0079	0.0184	− 0.0041	0.0054
OTH	0.0084	0.0105	0.0032	− 0.0022
EXTERNAL SHOCK				
SSA	− 0.0064	− 0.0221	− 0.0685	− 0.0058
OTH	0.0073	− 0.0205	− 0.0466	− 0.0024

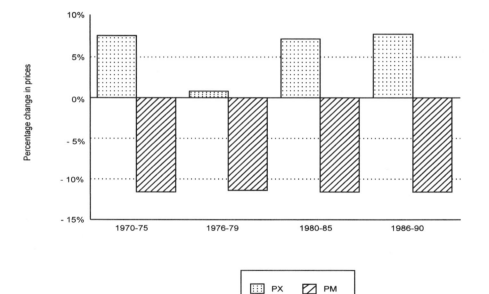

Figure 4.4 Components of TOTSHOCK: SSA

From Table 4.3 and Figure 4.4 we see that:

(a) The terms of trade (TOT) shocks clearly dominate the external shocks faced by SSA countries for the 1970–1990 period as a whole, accounting for an income loss of 3.1 per cent of GDP, which is twice the 1.6 per cent loss for other developing countries in the sample within this period, 1970–1975, 1976–1979 being the most severe periods of TOT shocks. Import price hikes were relatively more

82

significant drivers of negative TOT shocks during these periods owing to a combination of their larger changes and higher shares of imports in GDP.[15]

(b) The foreign interest rate real shock for 1970–1990 was slightly negative at − 0.14 per cent of GDP. The incidence of these negative shocks occurred during 1976–1979 and more significantly 1980–1985 when external real interest rates rose sharply, increasing debt-servicing payments significantly during the period. Comparatively, however, other developing countries suffered relatively more during the same period, to the tune of 0.15 per cent of GDP.

(c) Net transfers (private and official) for the same period constituted a positive shock estimated at 1.2 per cent of GDP. It is notable, however, that while this was largely counter-cyclical during 1970–1975, being mostly stabilization support against the first oil crisis, the absolute decline during 1980–1985 was pro-cyclical reinforcing the negative TOT and interest shocks. Resumption of aid associated with stabilization and adjustment programmes after 1985 explains its significant positive contribution in this period.

(d) Combining all the components of external shocks, SSA suffered a net income loss of 2.05 per cent compared with 1.46 per cent for other developing countries included in the sample.[16]

The effects of external shocks on growth

Empirical studies on the relationship between external shocks and growth in Africa fall under four categories. The first set of studies focuses more generally on the impact of external shocks on real growth. Using cross-sectional analysis these studies evaluate the effects of terms of trade changes and net resource inflows on growth. The focus is on the direct income effects of both, and the interpretation of results typically consolidates the likely offsetting effects of both types of shocks. Barro and Lee (1993), Easterly (1992) and Elbadawi (1992) are good examples of these studies. The main conclusions from these studies, with some variations, are that external shocks do matter but by broadly combining the TOT effects and net inflows, they show that Africa is not significantly different from other developing countries in terms of the intensity of shocks to which it is subjected. These studies also compare the relative importance of policy and external conditions and conclude that policy response matters more than the shocks *per se*. An important exception to this tradition, however, is Pritchett (1992) who undertook various tests, based on the new growth literature, on the role of country characteristics on growth. The tests showed that there is much less correlation between countries' growth rates over decades than there is between country characteristics, and Pritchett therefore concludes that 'shocks, especially those to terms of trade, play a much larger role in explaining variables in growth than previously acknowledged'. Also Wheeler (1984) in an earlier comprehensive cross-sectional study for SSA concluded that environmental variables including TOT and instability had a greater impact on growth than did 'policy' variables. He points out that movements in the TOT and international conditions of demand have had a very powerful impact on the general growth experience of African states through their impacts on foreign exchange earnings.

In contrast to the cross-sectional studies reviewed above, Basu and McLeod (1992) find strong links between terms of trade and growth dynamics on a country-specific basis for twelve LDCs (Latin America and the Philippines) using a stochastic growth model and standard time series tests. Their model highlights the structural features of these economies including the dependence of production on imported inputs that can only be purchased with uncertain export revenues; export supply rigidities for primary products; complementarity of domestic capital and imports; and limited access to flexible international finance to ride out uncertain resource gaps. These are conditions similar to those obtaining in SSA.[17]

Using variance ratios and unit root tests their analysis suggests that terms of trade movements are transient (cyclical and trend stationary) while output series show a much larger random walk component. This stochastic property of LDCs' output growth suggests that occasional shocks could lead to persistent changes in output levels and average growth rates.

The authors' estimates based on a VAR model confirm that transient shocks have a persistent effect on output levels in nine out of eleven countries, with the long-run terms of trade output elasticities ranging from 0.1 to 0.2. The effect is higher for countries with larger trade shares. Terms of trade variability explains 20–50 per cent of the long-term variation in output levels in ten out of twelve countries in the sample. In nearly every one of the countries in the sample, output is negatively associated with the variance of export prices.

The second category focuses on policy responses to external shocks and their impacts on growth. The issues emphasized naturally relate to the relative importance of stabilization and adjustment efforts in response to shocks. Management of commodity price booms and slumps as well as the Dutch-disease impacts of aid are included here. The basic hypothesis being tested is that African economies have typically responded to booms by increasing 'wasteful' expenditure, particularly government consumption, instead of investing or building up reserves; and during slumps they typically pursue a fiscal populist stance by persistence in expenditure at the expense of macroeconomic stability. In both situations, long-term growth suffers. The key agent of mismanagement is taken to be the government which typically taxes windfall and wastes it instead of leaving it in the hands of private agents who are better users. Hill (1963), Ingham (1973) and Bevan et al. (1989, 1990) use case studies to show this hypothesis and in addition

Bevan *et al.* point to the Dutch-disease effects on the efficiency of private activity. At the macroeconomic level, the suggestion here is to pursue a spending strategy consistent with permanent income and avoid boom and bust episodes (Barro and Lee, 1993; Wheeler, 1984; Balassa, 1988; World Bank, 1988).[18]

A recent study by Deaton (1993) subjects the above hypothesis to a very vigorous test using commodity price fluctuations. He observes that the actual behaviour of commodity prices is very strongly autocorrelated at high frequencies and the prices revert to their means only very slowly, suggesting that in the limit, income is a random walk and misfortunes last for long, uncertain periods of time. Under such conditions pursuing stabilization using a simple permanent income rule is futile. In contrast to the case studies cited above, using Pan-African empirical evidence, Deaton (1993) finds the African macroeconomic response to commodity price booms on average to be sensible, with booms generating a great deal of growth and stimulating productive investment.[19] This conclusion holds true even when countries are categorized into 'high taxers' and 'low taxers' based on passing through world market prices to producers. The evidence on the response to slumps, however, points to an asymmetry as shown by investment expenditure inertia in the downturn. This corroborates earlier evidence by Wheeler (1984) who found a strong and significant 'capital habit' during slumps in a cross-sectional study of SSA economies as shown by inflexibility in adjusting the imports of capital goods often at the expense of intermediate imports and hence current production.

The third category of studies emphasized the instability of exports and imports and their impacts on growth. The principal concern for export instability, especially in poorer countries that enjoyed limited access to international credit, was always its effect upon import volume instability (Helleiner, 1986). Import volumes are relatively more constrained by the availability of import capacity than traditional demand factors (Moran, 1989). Discontinuities in the flows of intermediate imports and capital goods, both of which are highly sensitive to fluctuations in import volumes, were clearly damaging to the process of economic growth. Intermediate imports and imports of incentive goods are typically candidates of first cuts under foreign exchange crunch; capital imports, being largely tied to external project finance, persist in times of slump. This makes medium-term growth and savings more vulnerable to instability through variations in capacity utilization.

Using a sample of twenty-four SSA countries for the period 1960–1979, Helleiner (1986) found that import instability significantly affected growth adversely. To the extent that such deceleration in growth led to lower savings and hence investment, longer-term output expansion was also affected. The resultant erosion of the government revenue base meant that public investment in infrastructure and human capacity as well as infrastructural maintenance were prime candidates for expenditure cuts, further weakening the basis for long-term growth. A strong positive correlation between export instability and import instability was obtained for a sample of thirty-one countries considered earlier in SSA during 1970–1990. Both were measured in terms of coefficients of variations. On the other hand, a very weak correlation was obtained between the coefficient of variation of net transfers and import stability suggesting that the timing of resource flows was not counter-cyclical.

The fourth category of studies considers more explicitly the relationship between external shocks and private investment and hence growth. Again, in this regard, empirical evidence from LDCs more generally, and Latin America in particular, will be drawn upon.

Among the factors that explain the investment slump of the 1980s in LDCs, Bleaney and Greenaway (1993) considered cost and availability of capital as well as terms of trade. The relatively high real interest rate during the 1980s increased debt service requirements in LDCs thereby reducing the share of output available for investment. For eleven countries also covered by Greene and Villanueva (1991), Bleaney and Greenaway, using pooled regression, find both real interest rate and terms of trade to be statistically significant in explaining private investment determinants in LDCs. They too, like Greene and Villanueva, find that public investment crowds in private investment (10 per cent public investment crowds in 1.6 per cent private investment).

Cardoso (1993) focuses on the relationship between terms of trade changes and private investment in Latin America. Two mechanisms are identified for the link between the two phenomena. The first is 'the Manaus Opera House effect', which combines the effect of a change in the TOT on real income and hence on investment via the accelerator principle and the specific impact on investment in the export sector through changes in the profitability of activities in this sector. Bad news for the export sector in turn becomes bad news for other sectors if profits are correlated across sectors.

The second mechanism is what she calls the 'IMF effect'. Essentially, a deterioration in the TOT will worsen the current account balance and induce contractionary measures to restore balance either because the deterioration is perceived to be permanent or, if perceived transitory, because it cannot be financed. The required tight money policy to restore balance may raise the cost of capital and reduce investment, may require credit rationing and reduce investment, or may reduce profit flows and ability to self-finance investment. These contractionary measures are validated on the external constraint side either by administered import compression or by a devaluation, both affecting real activity.

Empirical evidence presented confirms a strong positive effect of a terms of trade improvement on private investment. It also confirms the strong complementarity between private and public investment in Latin American countries.

Issues

Drawing on the discussions and the review of empirical evidence above several issues present themselves. First, unless the structural weaknesses of the African economies are redressed, Africa's long-term growth will remain vulnerable to external shocks. Such restructuring needs to strengthen the capacity to respond to shocks in a manner that is conducive to a stable development environment. Diversification of the export base to help stabilize earnings, and transformation of the economies to enhance links between domestic production and domestic resource use and demand, are possibly the most critical measures towards this end.

Second, African economies need a significant reduction in debt overhang to release resources for investment and growth. In view of the dominance of public debt in servicing requirements, such a reduction will, in particular, help boost public investment and, through it, also private investment and the absorptive capacity of these economies for growth. Human capacity is particularly a beneficiary of public investment in education and health.

Third, given the unpredictability and transient nature of terms of trade shocks, access to first-line liquidity to help ride out temporary and unanticipated shocks is critical for maintaining a stable development environment. Such access is virtually not available from commercial sources to African economies and official sources hardly provide these on a timely basis. Transitory deteriorations that are not financed induce the severe contractionary measures that not only affect growth in the short run but also induce neglect of maintenance of capital stock and a reduction in investment with negative consequences on growth in the medium and long term.

Fourth, more long-term deteriorations in terms of trade or international demand for African exports need adjustments. Such adjustments, however, given the supply rigidities, are also long term in nature and require adjustment finance to reduce the social costs of these adjustments. While the traditional advice is to 'finance temporary and adjust to permanent disturbances', adjustment and financing have been shown not to be mutually exclusive. In fact they are complements for reviving economic growth (Gavin, 1992; Elbadawi, 1992).

Fifth, while pursuing stabilization in response to shocks using a simple permanent income rule may prove fruitless given that misfortunes from price fluctuations last for long, uncertain periods of time, bad policy responses to shocks will exacerbate the negative impact of such shocks on growth conditions. The evidence presented shows an asymmetry in responses in periods of upturns and downturns. Spending inertia in the downturn coupled with macroeconomic instability prolong the required adjustments to shocks and worsen growth conditions.

TRADE STRATEGY, REGIONAL INTEGRATION AND GROWTH IN SSA

In the context of the debate on structural adjustment and the broader development strategies for developing countries, the issue of trade liberalization has been the most controversial component of what Williamson (1990) codified as the 'Washington Consensus' on policy reform: a balanced budget, a competitive real exchange rate, liberalization of trade and foreign investment, privatization, and domestic market deregulation. The new trade and growth theory suggests two broad implications (articulated in Krugman, 1992). First, the free-market orthodoxy should not be carried too far because there is an intellectually solid case for some government promotion of industry, and second, there is a need to shift the research on trade and industrial policy away from its focus on government failure or the horrors of import substitution and the distortions imposed by government policy, and towards a concern with market failure. Krugman also argues in the same paper – designed to rehabilitate what he referred to as 'high development theory' – that basically the main 'core of ideas regarding external economies, strategic complementarity, and economic development remain intellectually valid and may continue to have practical applications'.

The relevance of this 'counter-counter-revolution'[20] for the design of a long-term development strategy for Africa will be explored in the remainder of this section in the context of two issues: the viability of industrial policy as a means to create a manufacturing base in SSA, and the possible role for African regional integration in fostering scale economies and spurring growth in SSA.

Industrial policy in SSA: some lessons from East Asia

Krugman, who introduced in the context of the new trade theory the theme of 'import protection as export promotion', has, however, argued in later articles (e.g. Krugman, 1989) that this policy option is likely to be of limited value in developing countries. This is because the success of this policy requires not only economies of scale (internal to the firm), but a sufficiently large domestic market as well. A dissenting view, however, argues that subsidies can be used to attract foreign firms to locate in a small country, not just to supply the domestic market, but to produce for the world market (Jones, 1989). Helleiner (1989) also argues that Krugman seems to have overstated the unimportance of import-substitution policies in developing countries: at the theoretical level, there is 'a high potential for product differentiation (the conventional argument for small country specialization) and the potentially large relative role of domestic sales for individual risk-averse firms; and empirically, because Korea has evidently successfully been doing it'.

Following the same line of argument, Jayawardena (1992), citing the experience of East Asia as a successful application of the 'high development theory', argues for a more explicit interpretation of recent theoretical and empirical findings than does Krugman. Instead of merely cautioning against 'carrying a free-market orthodoxy too far', he suggests that the World Bank and other multilateral agencies might incorporate in structural adjustment lending specific ways of developing sound long-term industrial policies (including both functional and selective interventions) and ensuring that trade liberalization does not impede these interventions.[21]

The new trade theory, albeit with a lot of caveats, seems to lend support to some role for industrial policy. Even though the new trade and growth theories provide a much stronger role for free trade, trade liberalization now is seen not only to increase national income through static efficiency gains, but also to increase the growth rate permanently. However, at the same time the new models also suggest that countries could do even better by intelligently managing their trade.[22] This last implication, in addition to the fact that 'completely liberal' trade strategy, Hong Kong style, has been the exception rather than the rule in the successful experiences of East Asia,[23] has opened the door for recommending, in the context of an otherwise liberal trade regime, some measure of 'selective interventions' to support key industries with a high potential for a limited time, and for picking specialized and high-performance exporters for selective support.[24]

However, as pointed out by Husain (1994),[25] the phenomenal growth of the East Asian countries and the apparent success of state intervention has not been a coincidence. First of all, every country of this group has got the basics right, i.e. they have maintained low inflation, competitive real exchange rates and prudent fiscal policies on a sustained basis over more than twenty years.[26] Second, in addition the East Asian countries have done more. Over the past twenty years they have achieved the highest rate of human capital formation in the world, an average domestic saving rate of about 24 per cent of GDP, rapid agricultural growth, even when agricultural shares in GDP were declining, and a larger decline in the rate of population growth relative to other developing countries. Third, these countries did intervene, heavily and systematically. For example, they kept low deposit rates in the context of a targeted credit program and they gave protection to domestic import-substitution manufacturing. However, these countries have also invested heavily in applied research, allowed and encouraged foreign investment,[27] and developed a fairly transparent and credible regulatory framework. Even more importantly, the East Asian interventions have been transparent with the rules governing eligibility, performance criteria and the referee (usually drawn from both the private sector and government bureaucracy) being sufficiently articulated and in the public domain.

The experience of East Asian countries also shows that their initial industrialization mainly exploited their comparative advantage in unskilled labour. However, as industrial experience grew, real wages rose, and the educational attainments and skills composition of the labour force increased, new industries with comparative advantages emerged (Krueger, 1994). Skill formation and an increase in technological capabilities were thus part of the experience of successful industrialization and not merely a precondition for industrialization. This points to an important feedback from the process of industrialization to building these capabilities and ultimately enabling shifts in comparative advantages.

The above main elements of the East Asian development strategies suggest the following guidelines for Africa. First, regardless of the trade orientation or the chosen development strategy, respecting fundamental macroeconomic balances and static efficiency rules on a sustained basis is an essential prerequisite.[28] Hence, despite some major strides on this front by some key African countries, Africa still needs adjustment (World Bank, 1993). Furthermore, in this context, structural adjustment, especially its macroeconomic component, should not be construed as a development strategy, but merely as a necessary prelude to restoring economic growth. Second, the state cannot create an enabling environment for the private sector without an effective, highly motivated and qualified bureaucracy that is also shielded from direct political capture. Therefore, for Africa, not only are more resources needed to support a more rapid pace of human capital accumulation, but also more consideration of the issue of appropriate governance structure is required. Third, if properly conceived and implemented, industrial policy (and economic intervention in general) can be a successful device for building a new comparative advantage in manufacturing and dealing with potential market failure in the area of policy coordination.[29] In addition, the appropriate timing of the shift from import substitution to export promotion not only minimizes the cost to the economy of the former (Helleiner, 1990), but it also helps maintain the 'threat of competition' on domestic manufacturing and hence enhances technological innovation,[30] even when the import-substitution regime is still in force. Also the transparency of intervention could eliminate rent seeking, which has been one of the most wasteful consequences of most import-substitution experiences in the past.

To recapitulate, the long cycles of terms of trade declines in most of SSA exports (see the previous section), and the success of East Asia in generating a viable manufacturing base through deliberate policy measures, are factors that cannot be taken lightly in rethinking a long-term development strategy for SSA. Clearly it can be argued that Africa needs some careful industrial policy that allows the development of sufficiently large manufacturing sectors, with the potential for strong forward and backward linkages, and hence enough strategic complementarity to lead to concentrated manufacturing. As we show above, however, in terms of the prerequisites for managing successful industrial policy, SSA is very far behind.

Regional integration and growth in SSA

The basic arguments for economic integration as an engine of growth are now sufficiently articulated in the new growth literature and the more recent models of economic geography (e.g. Krugman, 1991). Deeper economic integration in a given region could permit expansion of the regional economy to generate the threshold scales necessary to trigger the much needed strategic complementarity, and to attract adequate levels of investment necessary for the development of modern manufacturing cores and the transfer of technology within the region. Given the relatively small scale (both in terms of output level and population size) of the typical African economy, this insight from economic geography provides a new justification for economic integration in Africa.[31] Having proposed regional economic integration in SSA as an instrument for growth, it is important to examine its implications for national economic policy and trade policy in particular. Several considerations present themselves in this regard.

First, perhaps the most significant contribution of regional integration to growth is in the area of policy coordination/harmonization. Even the sceptics of the value of African *trade* integration argue that several policies beyond trade policy will influence integration and may benefit from being coordinated. To take some obvious ones, transport policy may benefit from being coordinated either through shared airline services or a common rail and road system. Energy policy may benefit from being coordinated if water is used for hydroelectric power. Fiscal policy may benefit from being coordinated since harmonized tax rates reduce smuggling. Additionally, as Bliss (1993) argues, if African governments continue to compete for foreign investment by offering tax holidays, they will get worse terms than if they adopt a common incentive structure. That is, collectively, Africa might be largely in the niche market for certain types of direct foreign investment (Collier and Gunning, 1993).

Second, both the new growth and trade theoretical models as well as related empirical evidence lend support to the above analysis. For example, Baldwin (1993) outlined a simple model that classifies African trade relations in terms of a 'hub and spoke' arrangement, where Europe and North America are the 'hub' and the African nations are the spokes. The basic argument is that despite SSA's advantage in terms of lower labour costs, the rather high cost of trade within Africa due to lack of adequate transportation, banking and insurance services, etc., makes it less profitable for manufacturing firms to locate in SSA. He argues that

> the hub and spoke free trade arrangements have a tendency to marginalize the 'spoke' economies, since production facilities located in the 'spoke' have artificially lower market access than factories in the hub. Consequently, hub and spoke FTAs render an artificial deterrent to investment in the outer economies. Filling in the gaps with spoke-spoke FTAs removes this policy-induced investment deterrent.

Also empirical evidence from the endogenous growth literature suggests important implications on the country-specific growth of regional spillover effects of investment, both on physical and human capital; in addition, the level of regional instability was shown to have had a significant impact on individual country growth performances. In fact, when these regional spill-overs are taken into consideration, the 'African dummy' ceases to be significant in the usual endogenous growth cross-country regressions (Chua, 1993a, b; Ades and Chua, 1993).[32]

Third, in terms of trade policy, regional integration in SSA cannot be a blueprint for the closing of Africa vis-à-vis the rest of the world. The rather dismal failure of the existing regional schemes in enhancing intra-African trade is a testimony to the fact that the economies of SSA are not sufficiently dissimilar to allow generating enough trade within SSA (e.g. de Melo and Panagariya, 1993; Foroutan, 1993). In fact, as argued by Foroutan, even if these regional integration schemes were to adopt a regionally discriminatory trade strategy (e.g. a common external tariff), non-discriminatory trade liberalization is an unavoidable necessary prelude. As articulated in Collier and Gunning (1993), the past failure of regionalism in SSA can at least in part be attributed to the highly protectionist national trade policies in SSA:

> until these barriers are reduced, the transfers generated by regional reciprocity are too powerful to be politically sustainable.... Further, where the compensation schemes are implemented, they introduce substantial distortions. Regional reciprocal discrimination starting from a position of high levels of protection creates very powerful redistributions between countries, while the overall net gains from liberalization are small or even negative because such a small proportion of trade is intra-African.[33]

Therefore, the above analysis suggests that before successful integration schemes can be achieved in SSA, significant trade liberalization may be required at the national level. At one extreme it can be argued that all Africa needs is a non-discriminatory trade liberalization, because the latter could enhance regional integration without actively promoting it. In this case regional integration will merely be confined to policy coordination in the context of a non-discriminatory trade regime. Another arrangement proposed by Collier (1991) and Collier and Gunning (1993) calls for regional custom unions tied to a northern market (the EEC). They argue that this would dominate unilateral trade liberalization in five ways: (i) it would achieve as much as Africa can achieve from global liberalization; (ii) it would establish credibility of trade reform; (iii) it would serve a defensive purpose, ensuring that Africa would not be left out of trade blocs with GATT rules insufficiently enforced; (iv) it might be politically easier to achieve than unilateral reform; and finally (v) it might facilitate the adoption of useful institutions by the regional union.

Finally, considering all sides of the issue, it appears that the following broad regional integration/trade strategy for SSA should merit serious consideration: a strong case exists for policy coordination in the context of regional integration in SSA; a fairly liberal and non-discriminatory trade regime at the national level is a prerequisite for the success and sustainability of regional integration; some discriminatory liberalization arrangement linking Africa's RI to a major trading partner (the EEC) could be a viable trade strategy;[34] and, finally, whatever the trade arrangements may be, some scope has to be left for industrial policy, at least at the regional level (e.g. through a common external tariff, among others).

CONCLUSION

The analysis of the second section confirms that the common wisdom that 'macroeconomic populism' should be avoided is still as valid for Africa as everywhere else. Indeed, credible macroeconomic stabilization and microeconomic and structural reforms remain critical prerequisites for positioning SSA on the road towards a sustainable growth path. However, beyond getting the 'price right' and creating an enabling environment for the private sector, sustainable growth and long-term development in SSA will be determined by the emerging role of the African governments, Africa's external economic relations and progress towards economic integration in Africa.

The analysis of the third section suggests that at best, increased foreign aid can only offset the negative income effects of the sustained decline in Africa's terms of trade. This leaves the more important price effects of the latter, which could precipitate irreversible, devastating allocative decisions by producers. Diversification of the export base to help stabilize earnings, partly through export-based industrialization, is possibly the most critical measure for reducing vulnerability to external shocks in the long term. This needs to be complemented in the short term by improved access to first-line liquidity to help ride out temporary and unanticipated shocks in order to maintain a stable growth environment. Furthermore, the external economic environment in terms of foreign aid and preferential trade arrangements is likely to be less favourable in the future (Grilli, 1993). The short- to medium-run implications of this are that Africa should seek to enhance its competitiveness in existing areas of comparative advantage, by deepening domestic reforms and emphasizing reciprocity with other economic regions, and maybe by enforcing this opening by some binding agreements with these regions (Collier, 1991; Kanbur, 1993).

To deal with the declining terms of trade of its main exports in the longer run in the context of a broader development strategy, Africa may have to consider building new areas of comparative advantage, preferably with the consent of its main economic partners. For this initiative to succeed and not

93

to repeat the failed experiences of the import-substitution strategies, the scale of the economy matters (Krugman, 1991). The analysis of the preceding section also suggests that suboptimal scale may have been a factor behind the slow growth in SSA. Regional economic integration allows the economies of SSA to generate the threshold scale needed to attract the adequate levels of investment necessary for the development of modern manufacturing cores and the transfer of technology within Africa. This insight from economic geography provides a new justification for economic integration in Africa.

APPENDIX A

Table 4.A Countries in the sample

Sub-Saharan Africa		Others	
BDI	Burundi	ARG	Argentina
BEN	Benin	BOL	Bolivia
CAF	Central African Rep.	BRA	Brazil
CIV	Cote d'Ivoire	BUR	Burma
CMR	Cameroon	CHL	Chile
COG	Congo	COL	Colombia
GAB	Gabon	CRI	Costa Rica
GHA	Ghana	DZA	Algeria
GMB	Gambia	EGY	Egypt
GNB	Guinea-Bissau	GTM	Guatemala
HVO	Burkina Faso	GUY	Guyana
KEN	Kenya	HND	Honduras
LSO	Lesotho	HTI	Haiti
MDG	Madagascar	IND	Indonesia
MLI	Mali	IND	India
MRT	Mauritania	JAM	Jamaica
MUS	Mauritius	KOR	Korea, Rep.
MWI	Malawi	LKA	Sri Lanka
NER	Niger	MAR	Morocco
NGA	Nigeria	MEX	Mexico
RWA	Rwanda	MS	Malaysia
SDN	Sudan	PAK	Pakistan
SEN	Senegal	PAN	Panama
SLE	Sierra Leone	PER	Peru
TCD	Chad	PHL	Philippines
TGO	Togo	SLV	El Salvador
ZAR	Zaire	THA	Thailand
ZMB	Zambia	TUR	Turkey
BWA	Botswana	BGD	Bangladesh
SON	Somalia		
TZA	Tanzania		
CPV	Cape Verde		

APPENDIX B

Table 4.B Instrumental variable regression results of the openness model (1970–1990)

Dependent variable = log(UOI)

Regressor	Coefficient (t-statistic)
Constant	5.502*
	(3.797)
log(PCY)	0.392*
	(5.462)
(log(PCY))^2	− 0.0255*
	(− 4.456)
log(POP)	− 0.669*
	(− 3.763)
(log(POP))^2	0.0168
	(3.086)
KFGDP	− 0.454*
	(− 2.710)
R^2	0.1405
No. of obs.	1194
F-statistic	38.839*
Mean sq. error	0.0141

* = significant at 1% level
UOI = Unadjusted trade openness index (exports + imports)/GDP
PCY = per capita GDP
POP = population
KFGDP = capital flow to GDP ratio
The instruments are first lags of the independent variables.
The adjusted openness index (OI) is obtained as the anti-log of the residual from the above regression.

APPENDIX C

The real exchange rate misalignment index is defined as RERMIS = (RER/ERER − I)*100, where RER and ERER are, respectively, the real exchange rate and its corresponding equilibrium rate. The ERER is that rate which ensures equilibrium in the non-traded goods market, and is derived as a function of the fundamentals that determine the supply and demand for these goods (see e.g. Edwards (1989), Elbadawi (1994) and Rodriguez (1989) for a derivation). The theoretical model and the empirical evidence generated in this literature predict that a terms of trade improvement, higher external capital flows or government consumption (expenditure in non-tradables) should lead to RER appreciation (higher RER). On the other hand, a more open trade regime or higher investment (expenditure in tradables) should cause the RER to depreciate (lower RER).

A panel RER regression was estimated for 1970–1990 for sixty-one African and non-African developing countries. The results reported in Table 4.C below strongly corroborate the RER model. In addition the results also show a very significant and positive effect for the African dummy. Other things being equal, RER in SSA appreciated by about 7 per cent relative to the average. The ERER index is computed as follows. Five-year moving averages of the projected real exchange rate using the estimated model of Table 4.2 were calculated. To underscore the importance of external balance, the ERER index is scaled so that it is equal (on average) to the actual RER in the years for which the resource balance was the highest. Finally the scaled ERER index is then used in the above formula to generate the real exchange rate misalignment index. The average RERMIS index for SSA was 12.8 per cent, almost double that of other developing countries at 6.9 per cent (Table 4.1).

Table 4.C Instrumental variable regression results of the real exchange rate model (1970–1990)

Dependent variable log(RER)

Regressor	Coefficient (t-statistic)
Constant	0.356*
	(6.34)
Afdum	0.068*
	(2.89)
Trend	−0.029*
	(−8.01)
logTOT	0.234*
	(3.06)
KFGDP+	0.695**
	(2.42)
logINGDP+	−0.302*
	(−4.20)
logOI	−0.074
	(−3.82)
logINGDP+	0.455
	(−4.87)
R^2	−0.107
No. of obs.	739
Mean sq. error	0.096

* = significant at 1%, ** = significant at 5% level
+ = these variables have been assumed endogenous
Afdum = dummy for SSA countries
Trend = time trend, 1970 = 1
TOT = terms of trade, measured as the ratio of index of dollar value of exports to index of dollar value of imports
KFGDP = capital flows to GDP ratio
INDGDP = gross domestic investment to gross domestic product ratio

OI = actual to projected openness ratio (anti-log of the residual from Table 4.B regression)
GCGDP = government consumption to gross domestic product ratio
The instruments are Afdum, Trend, Constant, first seven lags on KFGDP, INGDP and GCGDP, current values and first seven lags on TOT and OPEN.

NOTES

1 In a forthcoming paper we intend to use indicators of these two potential growth fundamentals, among others, in a variant of an endogenous growth cross-country model to explain the process of growth in SSA, with the ultimate objective of explaining this African dummy.
2 The list of countries in the sample is contained in Appendix A, and Table 4.1 contains the definition of variables involved in the analysis of growth perform-ance in this section.
3 See Barro (1989, 1990, 1991), Easterly (1993), Easterly and Levine (1993), East-erly and Wetzel (1989) and Romer (1989, 1990), among others.
4 Owing to data limitations, in the empirical tradition of the growth literature capital stock is usually replaced by initial income, where it is assumed that for given values of schooling and health, a higher level of initial real per capita GDP reflects a greater stock of physical capital per person (or a larger quantity of natural resources).
5 See, for example, the discussion in Khan and Kumar (1993) and references cited therein.
6 Out of twenty-three countries that constitute the lowest quintile of growth rates in BL, sixteen are from Sub-Saharan Africa. On the other hand, out of the twenty-three fastest growers, only five were Sub-Saharan African countries.
7 Easterly's findings confirm earlier results by Khan and Reinhart (1990), in that longer-term public investment, such as infrastructure, tends to have desirable crowding-in effects on private investment, while public investments competitive with private investment do not.
8 This conclusion should not be taken to suggest that these issues were not given due consideration in the clasical development economics (e.g. Hirschman, 1982; Stern, 1989; Lewis, 1954). However, the analytical articulation of these ideas, especially in relation to the role of human capital, and the explicit linkages of growth to standard macroeconomic and trade models constitute a major con-tribution by the current 'endogenous growth' literature.
9 Clearly the role of the state and good governance cannot be overstated. For example, Reynolds (1983) argues that 'the single most important explanatory variable (for differential growth performance among LDCs) is political organ-ization and the administrative competence of government'.
10 However, for exceptionally low levels of investment efficiency, an increase in the investment ratio can be counter-productive. For example, in a separate regression for the fourteen SSA slow growers in their sample, BL estimate a negative coefficient for I/GDP ratio, which implies a negative investment productivity. One explanation for the low productivity of investment in SSA is the high price of capital goods there relative to international standards (Helleiner, 1993a).
11 However, Easterly and Levine (1993) found that the relationship between growth and common policy indicators is not different from those in the rest of the world.
12 The World Bank (1994) identified further factors that are not adequately cap-tured in formal growth models, but may be important for explaining the process of African growth. These factors include the bias against agriculture, the weak

capacity to manage the fluctuations in the terms of trade, and the difficulties of the political and social transition following independence.

13 This line of reasoning clearly associates overall growth with export growth. However, as suggested by Krueger (1981), the theoretical reasons for this association remain rather unclear, since efficient import substitution can also relieve the problem of the foreign exchange constraint (see also Helleiner, 1990, 1993b, for a review of the empirical evidence on this issue). In the case of SSA, since there are no significant import-substituting sectors to speak of, the export sector remains the sole source of foreign exchange.

14 Our estimates of the relative magnitudes of external shocks in SSA and other developing countries differ from some of the earlier studies (e.g. Easterly *et al.*, 1992; World Bank, 1994) because we use the median rather than the mean of the sample to represent a typical situation to avoid strong outliers which usually dominate the averages in the context of cross-country comparisons. This is particularly important for terms of trade shocks where there are a few large countries which are oil exporters and benefit from large increases in oil prices while the bulk of the small ones (incomewise) are adversely affected by such large price increases.

15 The year of 1991 even showed further terms of trade losses in SSA (The *Economist*, 11 January 1992). See also Helleiner (1994) for a detailed account of individual country experiences.

16 Accounting only for official development assistance (ODA), Helleiner (1994) calculated that out of fifteen SSA countries that lost from terms of trade deterioration over the 1980 decade, only six received increased ODA that more than compensated their losses.

17 Gavin (1992) also develops an intertemporal export–import two-sector model in which production, unlike consumption, takes time to adjust to TOT shocks. He shows that a negative TOT shock leads to real exchange rate overshooting and a substantial slowdown in income in the short to medium runs, before a gradual increase in output towards the equilibrium level. He used this finding to argue that, in order to avoid costly and excessive adjustment in the short run, a case for appropriate external financing could be made even in the case of permanent shocks. See also Gavin (1993) for applications to Nigeria and Esfahani (1991) for an analysis of semi-industrialized economies.

18 However, a more recent important qualification to this principle, 'finance transitory disturbances and adjust to permanent disturbances', is formalized by Gavin (1992). (See footnote 5.)

19 Sub-Saharan African growth was generally as good as that of any other developing region in the 1960s, early 1970s and again in the 1976–1978 period, all periods of a buoyant global economy. See also Cuddington and Urzua (1989) and Cuddington and Wei (1992) for a further analysis of the time series characteristics of terms of trade for developing countries.

20 The term is ascribed to Krugman (1992), who argues for a 'counter-counter-revolution to restore some of the distinctive focus that characterized development economics before 1960'.

21 Japan's view of industrial policy is also consistent with the belief in targeted protection of immature industries (Overseas Economic Cooperation Fund, 1991).

22 As shown by Krugman (1989), as long as exporting requires an indivisible investment in infrastructure, for example, this argument applies even to primary commodity-producing developing countries.

23 For example, see Helleiner (1990) and the summary on the lessons from East Asian experiences quoted from Sachs (1987).

24 See World Bank (1991) for the debate within the World Bank on these issues, and Taylor (1991).

25 See World Bank (1993) for a more detailed analysis of the East Asian experiences, and a critical analysis of this analysis in Amsden (1994). Another useful volume in the literature is Lindauer and Roemer (1993).

26 Decadal averages for some key policy indicators calculated by Easterly and Levine (1994) reveal that Africa considerably lags behind East Asia and the Pacific. For example, SSA averaged a fiscal deficit ratio of about 5% compared with 2.5% for East Asia and about 40% premium compared with only 5% for East Asia, while financial depth in SSA is less than 50% of that of East Asia.

27 However, South Korea opened up to foreign investment only in the later stages of its industrialization effort when it needed high technology. In its earlier stages, like Japan, it was extremely restrictive.

28 A remarkable degree of convergence exists on this particular issue among authors of otherwise divergent intellectual persuasions (e.g. Helleiner, 1993a).

29 Krugman (1992) articulated the need for giving more attention in the policy debate and the research agenda to the consequences of market failures on growth and development, to balance the current lop-sided attention accorded to the problems of policy mistakes and government intervention.

30 Baldwin (1993) emphasized the importance of the following arguments in the African context: 'in an attempt to promote domestic industry, government strove to protect existing firms from competition. The idea was that the protection would raise the returns to introducing productivity-enhancing technology and thereby promote technical progress and growth. The weak link in this chain of reasoning is the last one. Unless existing firms are *threatened* [emphasis is ours] by new technologies, they have very little incentive to continually invest in productivity-boosting knowledge.' However, an interesting theoretical scepticism of the link between productivity and liberalization is provided by Rodrik (1992).

31 In the case of SSA, there could also be substantial gains from regional integration in the sphere of agriculture as well. This has been one of the main results of recent research by IFPRI in southern Africa, in particular the analysis of Cleaver (1993) on an agricultural development strategy for SSA.

32 Also Barro and Lee (1993) provide an interesting finding on three African countries (Botswana, Lesotho and Mozambique), which are neighbours or enclaves of South Africa. The first two are amongst the fast growers in the BL sample, while the last is amongst the slow growers. BL argue that controlling for other effects, 'the adjacency of this developed country could provide spill over benefits, such as ready access to capital and skilled managers, which would spur economic growth'. Obviously, in the case of Mozambique, the regional spillover effect has not been enough. However, the remarkable thing is that in all three countries, even in the case of Mozambique, growth residuals are positive and highly significant.

33 This sharply contrasts with the situation of European economic integration, where the level of intra-regional trade is quite substantial, while initially trade protection within the region is much smaller than the one within SSA.

34 However, these Collier–Gunning arguments need to be contrasted with the long-standing concerns over the formation of regional trade blocs, of which Prebisch warned so long ago. They can be devices for reducing the overall strength of the poorer countries and the carving of the world into 'spheres of influence' again.

REFERENCES

Ades, A. and Chua, H. (1993) 'Regional Instability and Economic Growth: Thy Neighbor's Curse', *Center Discussion Paper* No. 704, Economic Growth Center, Yale University.

Amsden, A. (1994) 'The World Bank's The Easian Miracle: Economic Growth and Public Policy', ed. special section, *World Development*, vol. 22, no. 4, April.

Balassa, B. (1988) 'Temporary Windfalls and Compensation Arrangements', Policy Planning and Research WPS28, The World Bank, Washington, DC.

Baldwin, R. (1993) 'Review of Theoretical Developments on Regional Integration', A paper presented at an AERC Conference on Trade Liberalization & Regional Integration in SSA, Nairobi, December, 1993.

Barro, R. (1989) 'A Cross-Country Study of Growth, Saving and Government', *NBER Working Paper* No. 2855, NBER, Cambridge, MA.

——(1990) 'Government Spending in a Simple Model of Endogenous Growth', *Journal of Political Economy*, vol. 98, pp. S103–S125.

——(1991) 'Economic Growth in a Cross Section of Countries', *Quarterly Journal of Economics*, vol. 106, pp. 407–444.

Barro, R. and Lee, J. (1993) 'Losers and Winners in Economic Growth', A paper presented at the Annual Conference on Development Economics, The World Bank, 3–4 May, 1993.

Barro, R. and Sala-i-Martin, X. (1992) 'Convergence', *Journal of Political Economy*, vol. 100, pp. 223–251, April.

——(1993). 'Economic Growth', Unpublished manuscript, Harvard University.

Basu, P. and McLeod, D. (1992) 'Terms of Trade Fluctuations and Economic Growth in Developing Economies', *Journal of Development Economics*, vol. 37, pp. 89–110.

Bevan, D., Collier, P. and Gunning, J. (1989) *Peasants and Governments: An Economic Analysis*, Clarendon Press, Oxford.

——(1990) *Controlled Open Economies: A Neoclassical Approach to Structuralism*, Clarendon Press, Oxford.

Bleaney, M. and Greenaway, D. (1993) 'Adjustment to External Imbalance and Investment Slumps in Developing Countries', *European Economic Review*, vol. 37, pp. 577–585.

Bliss, C. (1993) 'Comment', in J. de Melo and A. Panagariya (eds) *New Dimensions in Regional Integration*, Cambridge University Press for the Centre for Economic Policy Research.

Cardoso, E. (1993) 'Macroeconomic Environment and Capital Formation in Latin America', Ch. 7 in L. Serven and A. Solimano (eds) *Striving for Growth After Adjustment: The Role of Capital Formation*, World Bank Regional and Sectoral Studies, Washington, DC.

Chua, H. (1993a) 'Regional Spillovers and Economic Growth', *Center Discussion Paper* No. 700, Economic Growth Center, Yale University.

——(1993b) 'Regional Public Capital and Economic Growth', Unpublished mimeo, Economic Growth Center, Yale University.

Cleaver, K. (1993) 'A Strategy to Develop Agriculture in Sub-Saharan Africa and a Focus for the World Bank', *Technical Paper* 203, The World Bank.

Collier, P. (1991) 'Africa's External Economic Relations 1960–90', *African Affairs*, vol. 90, pp. 339–356.

Collier, P. and Gunning, J. (1993) 'Linkages Between Trade Policy and Regional Integration', A paper presented at an AERC conference on Trade Liberalization & Regional Integration in SSA, Nairobi, December.

Cuddington, J. and Urzua, C. (1989) 'Trends and Cycles in the Net Barter Terms of Trade: A New Approach', *The Economic Journal*, vol. 99, pp. 426–442.

Cuddington, J. and Wei, J. H. (1992) 'An Empirical Analysis of Real Commodity Price Trends: Aggregation, Model Selection and Implications', *Estudios Economicos*, vol. 7, no. 2.

Deaton, A. (1993) 'Commodity Prices, Stabilization and Growth in Africa', mimeo, Princeton University, Institute for Policy Reform.

de Melo, J. and Panagariya, A. (eds) (1993) *New Dimensions in Regional Integration*, Cambridge University Press for the Centre for Economic Policy Research.

Easterly, W. (1992) 'Projection of Growth Rates', Outreach 5, World Bank, Policy Research Department, Washington, DC.

—— (1994) 'Economic Stagnation, Fixed Factors, and Policy Thresholds', *Journal of Monetary Economics*, vol. 32, no. 3.

Easterly, W. and Levine, R. (1993) 'Is Africa Different? Evidence from Growth Regressions', Mimeo, World Bank, Washington, DC.

—— (1994) 'Africa Growth Tragedy', An invited paper presented at the Biannual Conference of the African Economic Research Consortium, Nairobi, May 29.

Easterly, W. and Wetzel, D. L. (1989) 'Policy Determinants of Growth: Survey of Theory and Evidence', *PPR Working Paper* No. 343, World Bank, Washington, DC.

Easterly, W., Kremer, M. Pritchett, L. and Summers, L. (1992) 'Good Policy or Good Luck? Country Growth Performance and Temporary Shocks', Mimeo, World Bank, Washington, DC.

Edwards, S. (1992) 'Trade Orientations, Distortions and Growth in Developing Countries', *Journal of Development Economics*, vol. 39, no. 1.

Elbadawi, I. (1992) 'World Bank Adjustment Lending and Economic Performance in SSA in the 1980s: A Comparison of Early Adjusters, Late Adjusters, and Nonadjusters', Policy Research WPS #7007, The World Bank.

—— (1994) 'Estimating Long-Run Equilibrium Real Exchange Rates', in J. Williams (ed.) *Estimating Equilibrium Exchange Rates*, Longman, London.

Esfahani, H. (1991) 'Exports, Imports and Economic Growth in Semi-Industrialized Countries', *Journal of Development Economics*, vol. 35, no. 1, pp. 93–116.

Fanelli, J., Frenkel, R. and Taylor, L. (1992) 'The World Development Report 1991: A Critical Assessment', in *UNCTAD, International Monetary and Financial Issues for the 1990s*, Volume 1, United Nations, New York.

Foroutan, F. (1993) 'Regional Integration in Sub-Saharan Africa: Past Experience and Future Prospects', in J. de Melo and A. Panagariya (eds) *New Dimensions in Regional Integration*, Cambridge University Press for the Centre for Economic Policy Research.

Gavin, M. (1992) 'Income Effects of Adjustment to a Terms of Trade Disturbance and the Demand for Adjustment Finance', *Journal of Development Economics*, vol. 37, pp. 127–153.

—— (1993) 'Adjusting to a Terms of Trade Shock: Nigeria, 1972–88', in R. Dornbusch (ed.) *Concepts and Case Studies in Economic Performance*, Oxford University Press.

Gerschenkron, A. (1962) *Economic Backwardness in Historical Perspective*, Harvard University Press, Cambridge, MA.

Greene, J. and Villanueva, D. (1991) 'Private Investment in Development Countries', *IMF Staff Papers*, vol. 38, pp. 33–38.

Grilli, E. R. (1993) *The European Community and Developing Countries*, Cambridge University Press, Cambridge.

Helleiner, G. (1986) 'Outward Orientation, Import Instability and African Economic Growth: An Empirical Investigation', in S. Lall and F. Stewart (eds) *Theory and Reality in Development*, Macmillan, London.

—— (1989) 'Comments to Krugman (1989)', in G. Calvo et al. (eds), *Debts, Stabilization and Development*, Blackwell, Oxford.

—— (1990) 'Trade Strategy in Medium-Term Adjustment', *World Development*, vol. 18, no. 6, pp. 879–897.

—— (1993a) 'Trade, Aid and Relative Price Changes in Sub-Saharan Africa in the 1980s', *Journal of International Development*, vol. 5, no. 2.

——(1993b) 'Trade, Trade Policy and Economic Development in very Low-Income Countries', in M. Nissanke and A. Hewitt (eds) *Overcoming Economic Crisis in Developing Countries*, Pinter, London.

——(1994) 'External Resource Flows, Debt Relief and Economic Development in Sub-Saharan Africa', in G. Cornia and G. Helleiner (eds) *From Adjustment to Development in Sub-Saharan Africa: Conflict, Controversy, Convergence, Consensus?*, Macmillan, London.

Hill, P. (1963) *The Migrant Cocoa Farmers of Southern Ghana: A Study in Rural Capitalism*, Cambridge University Press, Cambridge.

Hirschman, A. (1982) 'The Rise and Decline of Development Economics', in M. Gersowitz *et al.* (eds) *The Theory and Experience of Economic Development: Essay in Honour of Sir W. Arthur Lewis*, pp. 372–390, Urwin and Urwin, Boston.

Husain, I. (1994) 'The Future of Structural Adjustment in Africa: Some lessons from South East Asia', A lecture presented at the World Bank Regional Office, Nairobi, Kenya, January.

Ingham, B. (1973) 'Ghana Cocoa Farmers – Income Expenditure Relationships', *Journal of Development Studies*, vol. 9, no. 3, pp. 365–372.

Jayawardena, L. (1992) 'Comments to Krugman (1992)', *World Bank Economic Review*.

Jones, R. (1989) 'Comments to Krugman (1989)', in G. Calvo *et al.* (eds), *Debts, Stabilization and Development*, Blackwell, Oxford.

Kanbur, R. (1993) 'EC-Africa Relations: A Review of Enzo R. Grilli', *The European Community and Developing Countries*, Cambridge University Press.

Khan, M. and Knight, M. (1988) 'Import Compression and Export Performance in Developing Countries', *The Review of Economics and Statistics*, vol. 70, no. 2, pp. 315–321.

Khan, M. and Kumar, M. (1993) 'Public and Private Investment and the Convergence of Per Capita Incomes in Developing Countries', *IMF Working Paper/WP* 193/51, June 1993.

Khan, M. and Reinhart, C. (1990) 'Private Investment and Economic Growth in Developing Countries', *World Development*, vol. 18, pp. 19–27.

King, R. and Levine, R. (1993) 'Finance, Entrepreneurship, and Growth', A paper presented at World Bank Conference on How do National Policies Affect Long-run Growth?, February, 1993.

Krueger, A. O. (1981) 'Export-led industrial growth reconsidered', in Wontack Hons and Lawrence B. Krause (eds) *Trade and Growth in the Advanced Developing Countries in the Pacific Basin*, pp. 3–27, Korea Development Institute, Seoul.

——(1994) 'Developing Countries and Deep Integration of the World Economy', Mimeo, Stanford University, Stanford, CA.

Krugman, P. (1989) 'New Trade Theory and Less Developed Countries', in G. Calvo, *et al.* (eds) *Debt, Stabilization and Development*, Blackwell, Oxford.

——(1991) *Geography and Trade*, MIT Press, Cambridge, MA.

——(1992) 'Toward a Counter-Counterrevolution in Development Theory', *World Bank Economic Review*, Proceedings of the World Bank Annual Conference on Development Economics.

Kuznets, S. (1966) *Modern Economic Growth*, Yale University Press, New Haven, CT.

Levine, R. and Renelt, D. (1992) 'A Sensitivity Analysis of Cross-country Growth Regressions', *American Economic Review*, vol. 82, pp. 942–963.

Lewis, W. A. L. (1954) 'Economic Development with Unlimited Supplies of Labour', in *Selected Economic Writings of W. Arthur Lewis*, pp. 311–363.

Lindauer, D. and Roemer, M. (1993) *Development in Asia and Africa: Legacies and Opportunities*, Harvard Institute for International Development, September.

McKinnon, R. (1973) *Money and Capital in Economic Development*, Brookings Institution, Washington, DC.

Moran, C. (1989) 'Imports under a Foreign Constraint', *The World Bank Economic Review*, vol. 3, no. 2.

Overseas Economic Cooperation Fund (1991) 'Issues Related to the World Bank's Approach to Structural Adjustment – Proposal from a Major Partner', Occasional Paper 1, Tokyo.

Rebelo, S. (1992) 'Growth in Open Economies', *Carnegie-Rochester Series on Public Policy*, vol. 36, pp. 5–46.

Reynolds, L. G. (1983), 'The Spread of Economic Growth to the Third World', *Journal of Economic Literature*, vol. 21, pp. 941–980 (Summer).

Rodriguez, C. (1989) 'Macroeconomic Policies for Structural Adjustment', Policy Research Working Paper no. 247, World Bank, Washington, DC.

Rodrik, D. (1992) 'Closing the Productivity Gap: Does Trade Liberalization Really Help?', in G. Helleiner (ed.) *Trade Policy, Industrialization and Development: New Perspectives*, Clarendon Press, Oxford.

Romer, P. (1989) 'What Determines the Rate of Growth of Technological Change?', *PPR Working Paper* No. 279, World Bank, Washington, DC.

—— (1990) 'Endogenous Technological Change', *Journal of Political Economy*, vol. 98, pp. S71–S102.

Sachs, J. D. (1987) 'Trade and Exchange Rate Policies in Growth-oriented Adjustment Programs', in Vittorio Corbo, *et al.* (eds) *Growth-Oriented Adjustment Programs*, pp. 291–325, IMF/World Bank, Washington, DC.

Shaw, E. (1973) *Financial Deepening in Economic Development*, Oxford University Press, New York.

Stern, N. (1989) 'Development Economics: A Survey', *Economic Journal: The Journal of the Royal Economic Society*, vol. 99, pp. 597–685 (Summer).

Taylor, L. (1991), *Income Distribution, Inflation, and Growth: Lectures on Structuralist Macroeconomic Theory*, MIT Press, Cambridge, MA.

Wheeler, D. (1984) 'Sources of Stagnation in Sub-Saharan Africa', *World Development*, vol. 12, no. 1, pp. 1–23.

Williamson, J. (ed.) (1990) *Latin American Adjustment: How much has happened?*, Institute for International Economics, Washington, DC.

World Bank (1988) *World Development Report*, Oxford University Press, New York.

—— (1991) 'Industrialization in Newly Industrializing Countries: Case Studies of Korea, India and Indonesia', Volume 1, World Bank, Operations Evaluation Department.

—— (1993) *The East Asian Miracle: Economic Growth and Public Policy*, Oxford University Press, New York.

—— (1994) *Adjustment in Africa: Reforms, Results and the Road Ahead*, Oxford University Press, New York.

5

HOW PAINFUL IS THE TRANSITION?

Reflections on patterns of economic growth, long waves and the ICT revolution

Claes Brundenius

In the light of late-comer success stories in primarily East and Southeast Asia, there is a growing debate on the implication of these success stories for development theories (see e.g. Abramovitz, 1986; Amsden, 1989, 1993; Wade, 1990; World Bank, 1993). Relevant in this context is also the revived debate on whether there exist long cycles, or waves, in global economic development and to what extent the existence of such long waves affects conditions for 'catching up' by late-comers. This also leads the discussion on to what extent national economies have to go through 'painful transition stages' to successively new 'techno-economic systems or paradigms' (see e.g. Freeman, 1986, 1987, 1989, 1993; Freeman and Perez, 1988; Perez and Soete, 1988).

This also leads to the discussion on possible 'windows of opportunities', and other possibilities for 'leapfrogging' by developing countries in connection with the presumed blessings of the new ICT (Information and Communication Technology) revolution (Perez and Soete, 1988). New technologies have often before in history been seen as revolutionary remedies that will save humans from the spectre of misery and starvation (the 'green revolution' is a case in point), but in spite of these 'revolutionary breakthroughs' the income gap has steadily widened between the rich and the poor countries.

Simultaneously with these debates there has been a renewed interest in growth accounting, as witnessed by the 'new' growth theories, which give long overdue recognition of R&D innovation and human capital as important sources of growth. The 'new' growth theories thus, in contrast to the neoclassical tradition, treat technological change endogenously, allowing for education and knowledge to produce positive externalities and increasing returns (see e.g. Romer, 1986; Lucas, 1988).

The debate on late-comer industrialization and 'catching up' is actually an old debate on 'why growth rates differ' that Denison started in the 1960s (see e.g. Denison, 1962, 1967) and theories of technology gaps (with, for example, productivity levels as proxies) as a major explanation (see e.g. Abramovitz, 1986; Fagerberg, 1987). These discussions are also reflected in the recent studies of the Technology Economy Programme of the OECD (see e.g. OECD, 1991a, b, 1992).

In writing this chapter I have been inspired by a recent article by Takashi Hikino and Alice Amsden on the experience of, and conditions for, late industrializers in an historical perspective (Hikino and Amsden, 1993). They argue that *patterns* of growth in the long run tend to converge. That this is so is clearly evidenced by the Western countries after World War II. Hikino and Amsden examine late-comers like the United States (in relation to England), the Nordic countries (in particular Sweden) in relation to the United States, but scrutinize in more detail the characteristics of 'late' late-comers such as Japan, South Korea, and Taiwan, and also to some extent Brazil and Mexico.

Hikino and Amsden are intrigued by the fact that these late late-comers have **not**

> enjoyed the asset of pioneering technology [and that] this character-
> istic marks a critical departure from the past experiences of the leading
> enterprises of Britain, and then the United States and Germany [and
> other Western countries; my observation], which conquered world
> markets by successfully generating *new* manufacturing technology
> [my emphasis].

By contrast the late late-comers after World War II have industrialized as 'learners', borrowing and improving already existing technology. A basic idea then is that countries can be grouped by different historical growth paths (see Figure 5.1), with the UK showing a linear secular trend, while others are 'staying behind', 'stumbling back', 'sneaking up', or 'soaring ahead'.

Group I thus includes the innovators of the second industrial revolution (in particular the United States). Group II comprises countries that started from behind but caught up with the 'world frontier' at the time (the Nordic countries, in particular Sweden). Groups III and VI include countries that 'had the opportunity', but for some reason or other 'stumbled back' (like Argentina, Uruguay and the Philippines). Group IV refers to countries that for different reasons 'stayed behind' (like India and Pakistan) and Group V, finally, refers to learners, or twentieth-century followers that are not only 'sneaking up' but apparently also 'soaring ahead'. It is not clear to me where/if Russia/USSR fits into this general picture of 'paths of development'.

Levels of development are measured in presumably comparable 'international dollars', based on purchasing power parity (PPP), used by Maddison in his study on the world economy in the twentieth century (Maddison, 1989). Comparing relative per capita income levels (in relation to 'world'

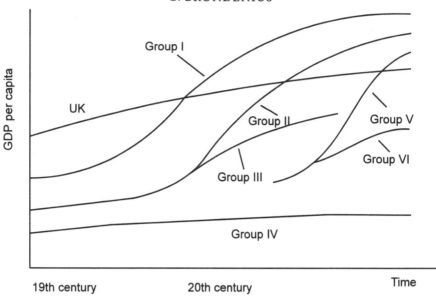

Figure 5.1 Historical overview of the growth paths
Notes:
Group I: 'Convergence Club': innovators
Group II: 'Convergence Club': nine-teenth-century followers
Group III: Nineteenth-century cases of 'stumbling back'
Group IV: Underdeveloped or 'staying behind'
Group V: Learners or twentieth-century followers that are 'sneaking' up
Group VI: Twentieth-century cases of 'stumbling back'
Source: Hikino and Amsden (1993)

GDP per capita) for selected years in this century, and for a selected group of countries, Hikino and Amsden find that some countries, indeed, appear to be following the paths described above. However, I believe that it is not sufficient to select some random years in order to prove this hypothesis. In order to do that it is essential to have long time series that would make it possible to identify sharp declines or upswings over time. And that is why I have ventured to construct such long time series of real per capita income (1900–1993) for a selected number of countries, which all fall, I believe, into the groups used by Hikino and Amsden (cf. Figure 5.1).

PATTERNS OF LONG-TERM GROWTH

I have selected fourteen countries that should represent *grosso modo* the groups used by Hikino and Amsden in their study: the United Kingdom, the United States, Sweden, Germany, Japan, Russia/USSR, Argentina, Brazil, Chile, Mexico, China, India, Taiwan and the Republic of Korea. No African country has been included at this stage for lack of sufficiently long time series (see the Appendix note for a discussion of methods and reliability of data).

Some of the results of this exercise are shown graphically (log scale) in Figures 5.2–5.13, and numerically in Table 5.1 for selected years. The benchmark year is 1980 with PPP levels of per capita GDP based on estimates taken from the studies mentioned above. The diagrams and the

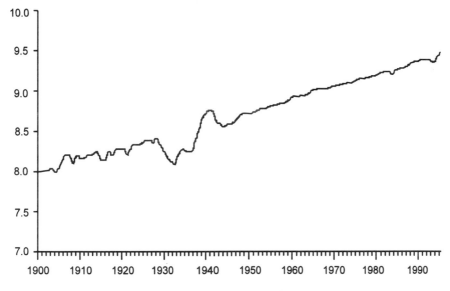

Figure 5.2 Real GDP per capita: United States, 1900–1993

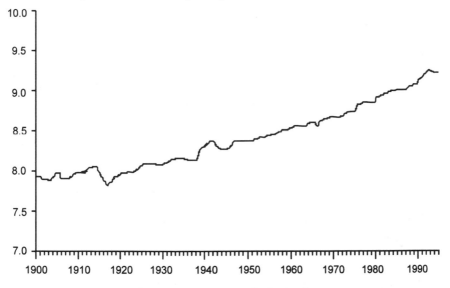

Figure 5.3 Real GDP per capita: United Kingdom, 1900–1993

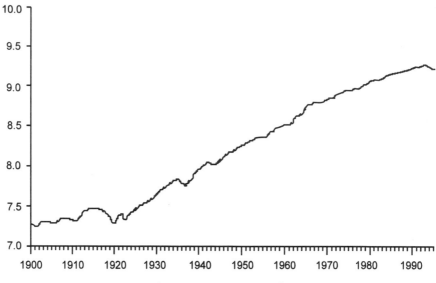

Figure 5.4 Real GDP per capita: Sweden, 1900–1993

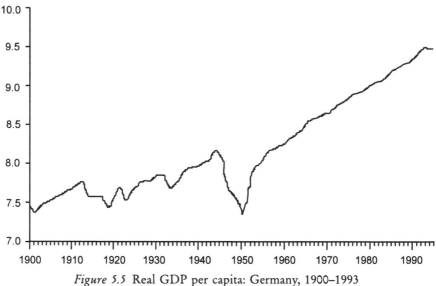

Figure 5.5 Real GDP per capita: Germany, 1900–1993

figures in Table 5.1 should thus be comparable and allow for cross-country comparisons of growth paths over time. It is clear that growth patterns differ significantly over time, although external shocks such as major wars or civil wars (like in Russia) seem to be major explanations of differences.

Table 5.1 suggests that the income gap between industrialized and developing countries, measured in PPP, increased steadily during the first three-

Figure 5.6 Real GDP per capita: Japan, 1900–1993

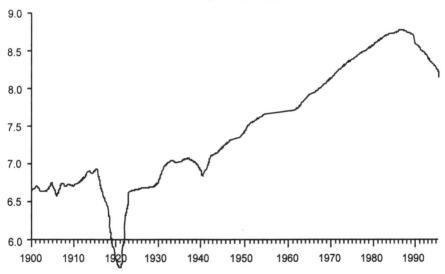

Figure 5.7 Real GDP per capita: Russia/USSR, 1900–1993

quarters of this century but has since then stagnated, or even declined. Take India as a case in point. The gap between, for instance, the United States and India was in 1900 7.7 times, in 1929 12.2 times, in 1950 18.7 times and by 1973 it had increased to 21.4 times. By 1987, however, this gap had decreased to 20.5 times and by 1993 to 17.8 times, still a tremendously big gap but at least it seems to be decreasing. On the other hand, there are no

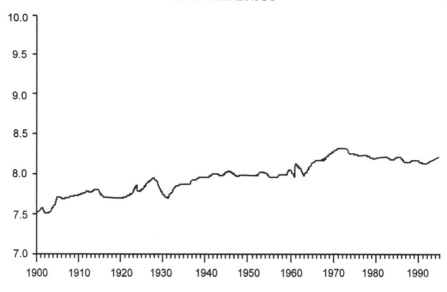

Figure 5.8 Real GDP per capita: Argentina, 1900–1993

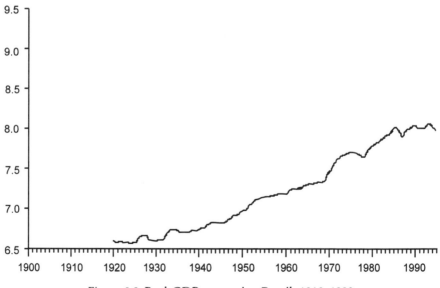

Figure 5.9 Real GDP per capita: Brazil, 1918–1993

doubt still many countries and regions in the world that are less dynamic than India, and the full picture has to wait until we get more country results.

What is quite clear, however, is that there are several cases of catching up in this century. Japan has done it, and Korea and Taiwan are on their way to

110

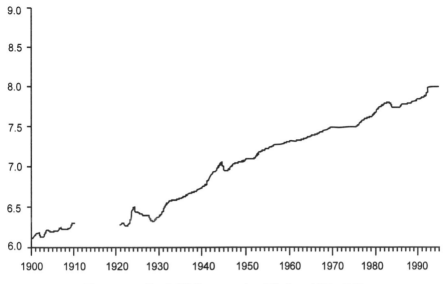

Figure 5.10 Real GDP per capita: Mexico, 1900–1993

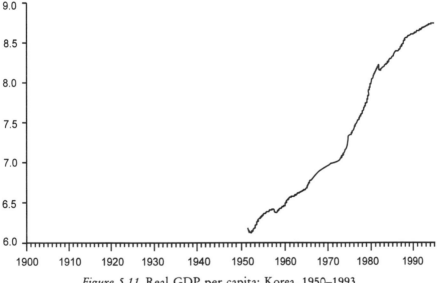

Figure 5.11 Real GDP per capita: Korea, 1950–1993

catching up with the 'world frontier'. Russia/USSR is an example of an attempt that ended in failure and the world is now watching China with bewilderment and (perhaps) mixed feelings. Will this giant, with a fifth of the population of the planet, be able to sustain two-digit growth and catch up with the world leaders within a generation or less, and with what consequences?

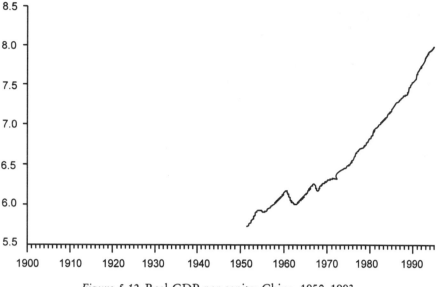

Figure 5.12 Real GDP per capita: China, 1950–1993

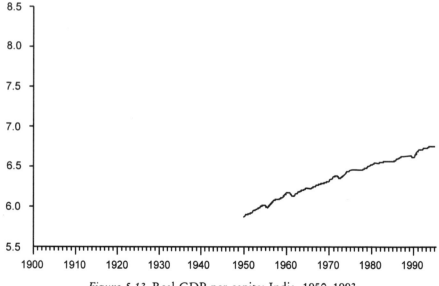

Figure 5.13 Real GDP per capita: India, 1950–1993

PATTERNS OF GROWTH AND LONG WAVES

What conclusions can be drawn from economic growth records and catching up in the past? Table 5.2 shows growth rates for the sample countries. It should be stressed that the figures before 1950, especially for the Asian

Table 5.1 Real GDP per capita in this century, selected countries and years (1980 PPP dollars)

	1900	1929	1950	1973	1993
USA	2910	4908	6696	10,978	14,182
UK	2800	3200	4171	7413	9213
Sweden	1482	2244	3898	8288	9844
Germany	1694	2339	2725	8252	12,476
Japan	670	1151	1104	6553	11,042
USSR/Russia	796	1043	2263	5062	3601
Argentina	1918	2687	2442	3933	3470
Brazil	436*	654*	1068	2505	2842
Chile	956*	1928*	2350	3309	4570
Mexico	466	741	1241	2363	2817
Korea	549*	749*	563	1790	5895
Taiwan	434*	631*	526	2087	6597
China	401*	444*	338	774	2636
India	378*	403*	359	513	795
Weighted Average	799	1182	1519	2874	3906

* Estimates by Maddison (1989; Table 1.3)
Source: Brundenius (1993)

countries (except Japan), are less reliable than those after 1950. There do seem to be some definite patterns, however, that confirm the Hikino and Amsden hypothesis.

Per capita income of the 'world' (here represented by the weighted average of the sample) increased at a rate of 1.7 per cent in this century (which, incidentally, is also the US rate). Some of the countries in the sample are above this rate: Sweden, Germany, and above all Japan, among the OECD countries, Brazil and Mexico in Latin America, and in Asia both Korea and China, while Argentina and India are trailing ('stumbling back' or 'staying behind'). There are large fluctuations in these patterns. Growth rates were as a rule higher in the second half of the century, especially during the 'golden age of growth' between 1950 and 1973 when 'world' per capita expanded at an unprecedented, sustained rate of growth of 2.8 per cent. Generally speaking, Latin America expanded more rapidly in the first half of the century, while the contrary is the case in Asia. Latin America is suffering from severe 'transitional pains' at the end of this century with the possible exception of the 'new miracle'(?) in Chile (after 1987).

Could the diverging growth paths described for the twelve countries in Figures 5.2–5.13 be linked to, and to any degree be explained by, the long-wave theory? Before discussing various possible hypotheses, let me start with a few words about the revival of theories of long cycles and techno-logical change. After a long unprecedented period of growth in the world economy (in practically all parts of the world) there was disturbing turbulence in the world economy in the 1970s, following the breakdown of Bretton Woods and the subsequent oil crises (in 1973 and 1979). In the 1980s there was here and there some recovery of growth rates, in most cases until around 1989 when the world economy again seemed to be heading for a major depression like that in the 1930s.

Table 5.2 Per capita real GDP growth, 1900–1993 (annual average compound growth rates)

	1900/1929	1929/1950	1950/1973	1973/1987	1987/1993
USA	1.8	1.5	2.2	1.5	0.8
UK	0.5	1.3	2.5	1.5	0.1
Sweden	1.4	2.7	3.3	1.6	− 0.8
Germany	1.1	0.7	4.9	2.0	2.4
Japan	1.9	− 0.2	8.1	2.8	2.3
USSR/Russia	0.9	3.8	3.6	1.2	− 8.0
Argentina	1.2	− 0.5	2.1	− 0.9	0.1
Brazil	2.2	1.3	3.8	2.2	− 3.0
Chile	2.4	0.9	1.5	0.2	5.1
Mexico	1.6	2.5	2.8	0.9	0.8
Korea	1.1	− 1.3	5.0	6.2	6.1
Taiwan	1.3	− 0.9	6.2	6.0	5.6
China	0.4	− 1.3	3.7	6.0	7.1
India	0.2	− 0.5	1.6	1.8	3.1
Weighted Average	1.4	1.2	2.8	1.8	1.0

Source: As Table 5.1

The revival of interest in long cycles in economic development is hence not astonishing. The long-cycle theories are generally referred to as 'Kondratiev cycles', or 'Kondratiev long waves', although the Russian economist Kondratiev (who died prematurely in Stalin's gulag in the 1930s) was not the originator of the idea. There were many others (like Pareto, Parvus, and van Geldern) who even before World War I, like Kondratiev, studied secular movements of long time series of price data, identifying such long waves. The revival of interest in the long-wave theory is, however, primarily linked to Schumpeter and the 'neo-Schumpeterians' (e.g. Mensch, Freeman, Soete, Perez and van Duijn).

Schumpeter stressed the cyclical pattern of technological change and the role of innovations in the growth process. He identified four phases of the growth cycle: prosperity, recession, depression and recovery. Schumpeter linked his innovation cycles to Kondratiev's price cycles. The dynamic element of capitalism was, in his view, paradoxically as it may seem, its inherent tendency towards self-destruction since 'the capitalist process not only destroys its own institutional framework but it also creates the conditions for another' (Schumpeter, 1942, p. 162). For Schumpeter, technological change is uneven by nature because 'innovations appear, if at all, discontinuously in groups or swarms' (Schumpeter, 1939, p. 223).

By juxtaposing Schumpeter's innovation cycles on Kondratiev's price cycles one gets two diametrically opposed cycles, indicating a dialectical relationship between the two, where the intersecting points could be interpreted as identifying serious critical stages in the growth path. These crossing points could thus represent the 'painful transition from one techno-economic paradigm to another', paraphrasing Chris Freeman (1989). Humans would hence now be experiencing the downswing of the fourth Kondratiev cycle with a consequent upswing of a corresponding Schumpeter innovation cycle with a swarming of innovations in generic, notably ICT (Information and Communication Technology) related technologies. This change from a saturated model, based on a specific techno-economic set up or paradigm, to another model or system invariably implies profound structural adjustments, institutional changes and other 'transitional pains' as necessary corollaries.

The long-wave theory is appealing as a conceptual model of secular change. It makes sense to talk of successive techno-economic systems, or paradigms (TEP), that are running out of steam and hence have to be replaced. In Chris Freeman's view

> changes of TEP are based on combinations of **radical** product, process and organizational innovations. They occur relatively seldom (perhaps twice in a century) but when they do occur they necessitate changes in the institutional and social framework, as well as in most enterprises if their potential is to be fully exploited.
>
> (Freeman, 1987, p. 67).

It is these changes in the institutional framework that have been the concern of many scholars when discussing the dilemmas of developing countries (see e.g. Perez, 1989). It is logical that when the 'world economy' (to a large extent defined by and shaped to the image of the 'world leaders') goes through a transition to new TEP, the *conditions of entry* on the world market are rapidly changing.

The failure of Argentina to catch up with the United States at the beginning of the century, in spite of its initially relatively high level, is a case in point. Figure 5.14 gives an illustration of the growth paths of Argentina and Sweden between 1900 and 1993. As can be seen, the income level of Argentina was higher until the depression in the 1930s that marked the end of the third Kondratiev cycle, 'the age of steel, electrification and imperialism' (Freeman, 1989). One interpretation of the different growth patterns of Argentina and Sweden could be that Sweden, in contrast to Argentina, did meet the transition requirements imposed by the new TEP (the Fourth Kondratiev cycle), for instance through the restructuring of industry and exports, through new institutions and structural adjustment to

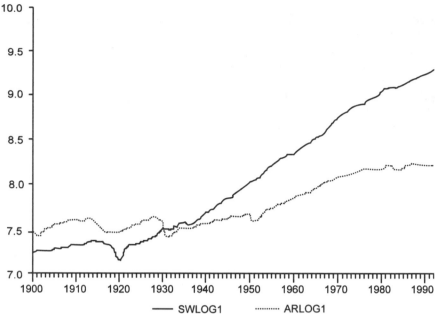

Figure 5.14 Patterns of growth: Argentina and Sweden, 1900–1993
Note: Real GDP per capita (log scale)

cope with a new international economic environment as result of a dominating new techno-economic paradigm. Another example of an attempt to catch up that eventually ended in failure, and that could be linked to the long-wave theory, is the Soviet Union which will be briefly discussed below.

LONG WAVES AND THE DEMISE OF THE SOVIET MODEL OF GROWTH

Not so long ago the Western world was stunned and worried by the advances of Soviet technology. In 1957 the Soviets launched the Sputnik – the first artificial satellite – challenging the United States to conquer space. Few could have guessed that three decades later the whole Soviet system would collapse. What are the reasons for the demise of a system that, for good or worse, to some extent represented a growth model for many developing countries? What went wrong? Can long-wave theory give some hints?

Even if recent studies suggest that growth rates in the former Soviet Union, and in Eastern Europe, probably were inflated, the growth record still seems to have been impressive, by all accounts, at least until the late 1960s (see Table 5.3). But growth was primarily based on the fourth Kondratiev (or even third Kondratiev) technologies that were becoming increasingly obsolete in the West at the time. In the 1970s it became evident that the growth model was not only becoming rapidly saturated, but also based on the ruthless exploitation of natural resources with no, or little, concern for the environment. Figure 5.15 gives a good illustration of the failure of the Soviet Union to keep pace with the United States and how it was eventually overtaken by Japan in the 1960s.

Table 5.3 A painful transition: growth rates in Eastern Europe and in the republics of the former USSR*

	1960/1970	1970/1980	1980/1989	1990	1991	1992	1993**
USSR	5.9	4.1	2.5	–	–	–	–
Russia	–	–	–	– 4.0	– 14.3	– 22.0	– 15.0
Ukraine	–	–	–	– 3.6	– 11.2	– 16.0	– 12.0
Czechoslovakia	3.6	4.2	1.8	–	–	–	–
Czech Republic	–	–	–	0.8	– 14.9	– 7.1	– 0.5
Slovakia	–	–	–	– 3.8	– 15.3	– 6.0	– 6.5
Hungary	5.1	4.5	1.2	– 3.3	– 11.9	– 5.0	– 2.0
Poland	5.1	5.4	0.8	– 11.6	– 7.6	1.0	4.0

* Until 1989 annual average compound growth rates of net material product (constant prices); after 1989 annual rate of growth of real GDP or GNP
** Preliminary
Sources: Brundenius (1993), updated with figures given in UNECE (1993)

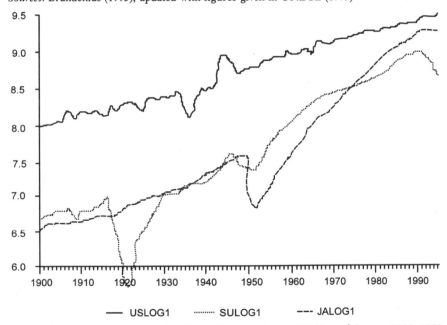

— USLOG1   ⋯⋯ SULOG1   --- JALOG1

Figure 5.15 Patterns of growth: United States, Russia/USSR and Japan, 1900–1993
Note: Real GDP per capita (log scale)

In the Soviet model of growth there was an obsession with fulfillment of *quantitative* goals through capital extension rather than increasing capital intensity (increasing the K/L ratio). Thus there were few incentives for technical innovation in the system, and in the long run the system became untenable. Growth rates were impressive during the first five-year plans and in the immediate reconstruction after the war. But technology and organization of work were based on mass-scale and Fordist assembly line principles with technology to a large extent imported, or imitated, from the West (Bailes, 1978; Sutton, 1968, 1971), and the model was then exported to Eastern Europe and many developing countries.

Lenin had been a great admirer of American technological advance and firmly believed that the combination of Western technology and communist principles of planning and social relations would provide an invincible formula for Soviet eternal superiority. Large-scale production with enormous concentration of power in huge state monopolies and trusts, modelled after US monopoly capitalism of the 1920s, was the ideal for the organization of the state-owned production units in the USSR (Sutton, 1968).

The main problem with this strategy was that it was based on a static view of technological change (as well as of capitalist development). The Soviet model of accumulation was in the fourth Kondratiev upswing based on energy- and resource-intensive technologies. It is true that this was also the case in the West but in the Soviet centrally planned economy, with prices arbitrarily set by the government, it was more problematic since there were no checks on imbalances in the system – such as waste and depletion of resources, pollution and other environmental costs. So when the bill came to the West in 1973 – in the form of quadrupled energy prices – for decades of ruthless exploitation of energy and raw material resources, it gave clear signals for the system to change and to initiate 'the painful transition to a new techno-economic paradigm'.

In contrast, no such signals were perceived in the Soviet system. For decades it had assumed that crises, such as recessions and depressions, had been phenomena typical of capitalism. But when *perestroika* and *glasnost* came with Gorbachev in 1986 it was simply too late to modify a system that had long been obsolete.

Russia and Eastern Europe have now embarked upon a road that will supposedly lead to the restoration of some kind of market economy but the transition appears to be not only painful but also long. Growth rates have been negative since 1989 and it is hard to see any light in the tunnel, with the possible exception of Poland and the Czech Republic (see Table 5.3).

LONG WAVES AND CATCHING UP

What conclusions can be drawn from the discussion so far? First of all it does seem reasonable to think in terms of long waves or cycles in the world economy although it is not so easy to demonstrate. The long cycle (40–50 years) should not be confused with the medium-length Juglar cycle (8–9 years), or the shorter Kitchin cycle (3–4 years), that result, according to conventional theory, from fluctuations in investments and commodity inventories, respectively. Such cycles are much easier to identify. It is clear, however, that long-term growth rates have differed in this century with upswings in the first and third quarters of the century, and with downswings in the second and last quarters of the century. However, the downswing at the end of this century looks less significant than the one in the second quarter of the century that led to the Great Depression. Although the current world recession is serious it does not seem likely that it will end up like the major depression of the 1930s.

This, however, does not exclude the possibility that there are, indeed, long cycles that could be the result of new, pervasive, generic technologies that have such a wide range of applications that they affect the conditions of production and distribution in all or almost all sectors of the economy, thus changing the 'techno-economic paradigm'. In the final analysis this also means that the entry conditions on the world market, a *sine qua non* for catching up, are permanently changing. Thus countries with inward growth strategies, with little or no exposure to competition on global export markets, seem to be losers in the long run. Since entry conditions on the export markets are permanently changing, conditions for catching up are also constantly changing. Thus, the conditions for catching up at the end of the twentieth century are entirely different than they were fifty or a hundred years ago. Not only is the distance to the 'world frontier' bigger but catching up is also like trying to catch up with a moving target. Still, some countries have managed to catch up in this century while many have failed.

Table 5.4 Catching up over time (years to reach a subsequent level), selected countries

	$500 to 1,000	$1,000 to 3,000	$3,000 to 6,000	$6,000 to 10,000
UK	?	93	52	24
USA	?	50	42	27
Germany	?	68	26	20
Sweden	50	72	22	21
Japan	39	44	9	16
USSR/Russia	?	44	31	?
Argentina	?	114	?	?
Brazil	49	35	?	?
Mexico	41	53	?	?
Korea	14	18	9	?
China	24	14	?	?
India	25	?	?	?

Source: Same as Table 5.1

Table 5.4 gives an idea of how many years it has taken, approximately, for different late-comers to move between thresholds, or different levels of development (measured in 1980 PPP dollars per capita). A first critical step seems to be between 500 and 1000 PPP$, the pre-take-off stage in the Rostowian sense. The 'take-off' (from 1000 to 3000 PPP$) required much more time in the past than in the case of late-comers in the second half of the century, notably Japan, Korea and China. It is then tempting to suggest that 'stumbling back' (like Argentina) and 'staying behind' (like India) has to do with the failure to cope with the institutional requirements to be met by the change to successively new techno-economic systems or paradigms (TEP).

CATCHING UP AND THE INFORMATION AND COMMUNICATION REVOLUTION

If the TEP theory holds, it is then also logical to suggest that there can never be one single production function, or growth model, that could be universally applied. The variables and parameters change over time, from country to country, and from period to period. At some point during catching up, working hours and the investment rate, for instance, are no doubt more important than skills and human capital formation, while at some later stage the opposite may be true. Thus, today, coping with the institutional requirements of the ICT revolution may have top priority in catching up.

According to the TEP theory, each Kondratiev cycle is dependent on a key factor that has to be cheap and in, if not unlimited, at least abundant supply, and it should have a potential for pervasiveness. Such characteristics today hold for microelectronics, which prepared the ground for the ICT revolution, leading the way towards the fifth upswing (in the 1990s?). In the fourth Kondratiev upturn it was cheap and abundant energy (oil) that constituted this key factor. Before that, for the third Kondratiev cycle, the role of key factor was played by low-cost steel and electric power, for the second Kondratiev cycle, it was low-cost coal and steam-powered transportation that constituted the key factor, and it has been suggested that low-cost machine-tending and cotton-growing labour played the role of key factor in the first industrial revolution, or first Kondratiev cycle (Perez, 1985).

The phase of each new long wave depends on the extent to which there is harmony, or disharmony, 'match or mismatch between the socio-economic institutional framework and the requirements of the wave of technical change that is shaping the economic sphere' (Perez, 1989).

All shifts in TEP are thus connected with revolutionary technological breakthroughs. Microelectronics is not surprisingly considered to be by far the most revolutionary of the new generic technologies in the last decades because of its potential impact on productivity growth, and its pervasiveness throughout the economy. By the end of the 'golden age of growth' (roughly 1950–1973), industrial technology had started to shift away from mass-scale and assembly line production (intensive in energy as well as material), to a much more flexible and information-intensive pattern of production, associated with computerized control and communications systems.

What is then so specific about the fifth Kondratiev cycle? First of all, it is based on microelectronics and informatics that bring about the *automation revolution*, and automation is quite distinct from mechanization (a characteristic of the fourth wave) since it is concerned with replacing and/or aiding human mental effort, not human physical effort. Second, and which is perhaps even better news, the cheap and abundant key factor in the microelectronics-led upswing in the fifth Kondratiev cycle – silicon – is not only cheap but virtually inexhaustible, in contrast with oil as a key factor in the fourth Kondratiev cycle.

But what prospects are there then for developing countries to catch up with the world frontier riding on this new wave? Carlota Perez suggests that a shift in TEP always opens new 'windows of opportunities' for latecomers: 'This is partly because the new technologies allow "leapfrogging" for some of the countries that do not carry the inertia of the previous industrial structure' (Perez, 1985, p. 457). The problem, however, is that most developing countries have fallen into the trap of closely following the experience of leading countries, thus repeating the same mistakes, and ending up with more inertia rather than less. There are possible exceptions like Japan, Korea and Taiwan but that is another story.

Information and communication technology is today being diffused world-wide with enormous speed, but primarily in the already 'developed' world. The OECD has estimated that the world-wide ICT market, broadly defined (IT hardware, telecommunications equipment and software), is doubling every fifth year, from an estimated 350 million dollars in 1985, to 663 million in 1990 and 1.3 billion dollars by 1995. Table 5.5 gives an overview of the ICT density in various countries in the mid-1970s and by the end of the 1980s. The table gives quite a revealing picture of the noble art of catching up and the not so noble art of lagging behind. Both Latin America and, above all, Russia and Eastern Europe have lagged behind (especially in computer diffusion), and countries like China and India are also way behind the leaders, while Korea and Taiwan are rapidly catching up.

But why then such differences in performance? Staffan Jacobsson has in a recent study compared government policy and the performance of the new technology industries in India and Korea (Jacobsson, 1993), and concludes that what is at stake for governments is **not** whether to intervene and protect infant industries, nor whether to liberalize trade and open up markets (elimination of protection). In both India and Korea state intervention has been strong but with quite different results. What **is** at stake is the *selectivity* and, above all, *timing* of state intervention.

121

A trade liberalization is therefore only one, but a difficult, phase in a long process of fostering firms, the success of which depends greatly on how previous policy regimes have succeeded in creating a powerful response capacity among firms. The assumption that a complete and rapid elimination of protection equals the quickest route to learning is therefore fallacious. A liberalization needs to be preceded by policies designed to support the learning process and the response capacity for quite some time.

(Jacobsson, 1993, p. 268)

Table 5.5 Indicators of ICT diffusion world-wide, mid-1970s and end of the 1980s (index US = 100)

	Telephone lines 1976		Telephone lines 1989		Computer power 1988	
	Density*	Index	Density*	Index	Density**	Index
USA	37.4	100.0	50.9	100.0	132.2	100.0
UK	25.1	67.1	44.4	87.2	60.9	46.1
Germany	23.1	61.8	48.2	94.7	37.6	28.5
Sweden	52.9	141.4	68.8	135.2	42.8	32.4
Japan	30.3	81.0	42.1	82.7	48.8	37.0
USSR	5.2	13.9	11.9	23.4	0.60	0.5
Argentina	6.5	17.4	11.0	21.6	n.a.	n.a.
Brazil	2.3	6.1	6.3	12.3	2.54	1.9
Mexico	3.1	8.3	6.1	12.0	1.91	1.4
Korea	3.5	9.4	31.5	61.9	7.09	5.4
Taiwan	6.0	16.0	31.0	60.9	8.42	6.4
China	0.34	0.9	0.60	1.2	0.17	0.1
India	0.24	0.7	0.55	1.1	0.15	0.1

* Main lines/100 inhabitants
** MIPS (Millions of Instructions Per Second)/1000 inhabitants
Sources: ITU Statistics (14th and 19th editions); Statistical Yearbook of the Rep. of China, 1991; Juliusen and Juliusen, 1991)

Bo Göransson has, in another recent study, focused on the telecommunications equipment industry, compared catching-up strategies in Brazil, India and Korea, and arrived at similar conclusions. He sees two distinctly different types of strategies pursued by the three countries.

Korea has carried out a selective and dynamic approach, building on pragmatism, while Brazil and India have followed a less flexible policy, demanding adherence to the overriding goal of far-reaching substitution of imports by local manufacture. In other words, Brazil and India have not compromised on policy but on product, while Korea has compromised on policy but not on product.

(Göransson, 1994, p. 184)

TOWARDS SOFTNOMICS IN THE NEXT CENTURY?

If the long-wave theory helps to give some insight into the question of why some countries are leaders, some are stumbling back, others seem to be catching up sooner or later, while some seem to be inexorably lagging behind, then a natural follow-up question is what is next? If Japan, and perhaps in the near future also countries like Korea and Taiwan (and perhaps China), will not only catch up with the world frontier but even become the *new* techno-economic leaders, then it seems logical that these late late-comers will also have to conquer the world markets with *new*, not borrowed technology, in the next century (compare the hypothesis of Hikino and Amsden discussed earlier).

An answer might lie in an Asian response to the ICT revolution. Already in the late 1960s Japan, for instance, started preparing itself for the coming information society, with a gradual shift from hardware to software development, and from applied to basic research. 'Softnomization' became a catch-word to describe the age that Japan and other advanced countries are entering, and a Softnomics Center was set up in Tokyo in 1984 under the auspices of the Ministry of Finance (Nelson, 1993).

'Softnomization' is defined as the 'tendency of software such as information and services to outweigh in market value hardware such as goods and energy' (Softnomics Center 1985, quoted in Nelson, 1993). The strategy of softnomization seems to rest on three pillars: the conviction that high-technology societies will gradually become more information intense, that they will require successively more intellectual than physical input, and that there will be a continuing rapid globalization of the world economy. Following this strategy Japan's past, current and future development is divided into four phases: the hardware-oriented age (from roughly 1960); the softnomization quickening period (from 1970 to 1974), the software-oriented age (from roughly 1985); and the heyday of softnomics (or *Sofutonomikkusu* in Japanese), around 2000.

But if 'softnomics' might represent the future for many parts of the world what is there in it for the developing countries? Although Carlota Perez believes that there is an opening 'window of opportunity' for the developing countries in the software market (Perez, 1985), I am afraid the picture is not that bright. It is true that the software industry is accelerating at an impressive speed but the opportunities for developing countries are bleak, I believe, except for the already successful late-comers and perhaps for some Latin American countries like Brazil and Chile.

The Japanese government has forecast that the software market in the world will grow from an estimated 220 billion dollars in 1990 to 960 billion dollars by the year 2000, or at a breakneck rate of 16 per cent per year

123

(quoted in IITA, 1993). It is not very likely, however, that outsiders will manage to take large pieces of this cake.

In 1990 it was estimated that the Triad (USA, EC and Japan) accounted for 92.4 per cent of the total world market (with 46.4 per cent, 27.2 per cent and 18.7 per cent, respectively). Only 7.6 per cent was outside the Triad in 1990, and even 'tigers' like Korea and Taiwan had only 0.36 per cent and 0.32 per cent, respectively, of the world market (IITA, 1993). So if soft-nomics were to mark the beginning of the new century, the prospects for most developing countries of catching up by leapfrogging through software look quite dim, at least as producers and exporters.

APPENDIX: A NOTE ON METHODS AND RELIABILITY OF DATA

I will here briefly discuss and describe the methods and problems involved in an exercise, attempting not only to make cross-country comparisons of growth rates but also to compare *levels* of development over time. First of all, we have the problem with growth indices. In order to depict real growth, nominal growth has to be deflated by some national price index. This is also done in most countries but the reliability is, of course, questionable in countries with two-digit monthly inflation. Growth series of GNP (or GDP) have sometimes been criticized for not deducting the costs for maintenance of the current capital stock, i.e. depreciation, and it has been questioned why the *net* national product (NNP) is not used instead. Helleiner's answer is that this is simply far too difficult (Helleiner, 1990, p. 14). This is no doubt true but I do not think this omission (depreciation) is so serious at any rate. At least judging from long time series of US data, the difference in growth between the two (GNP and NNP) is minimal (see US Bureau of the Census, 1960, Tables F 1–5, F 6–9).

A more serious critique of conventional national accounting is that it is based on so-called *throughput growth* only (Goodland, 1991), i.e. a growth accounting that does not castigate wasteful and environmentally destructive management of resources (Brundenius, 1993). This, of course, has to do with the sustainability argument, also brought up by Helleiner in his critique of traditional measuring of economic performance (Helleiner, 1990, pp. 12–15). However, in the absence of a new accounting system that would allow for the calculation of a 'green' GDP (or NDP for that matter) we have to settle for conventional growth accounting for the time being. Even when a new (or at least parallel) accounting method is universally agreed upon (it is a politically and ideologically hot issue, of course), it would still require time (if at all possible) to reconstruct time series based on the new concept. Then we have the problem with the benchmark references. In order to be comparable over time, country levels have to be measured in the same units and cross-country compared at least at one point in time. Traditionally this has been done by taking a reference year (more or less at random) and then converting GNP (or GDP) into dollars using current exchange rates (CER). This is, of course, acceptable when exchange rates do not fluctuate very much, and when they are neither overvalued nor undervalued (in relation to the dollar) to any large extent. This was the case with the OECD area until the abandoning of the Bretton Woods system in 1971 but since then the problem of using CER when comparing per capita income levels has become increasingly acute. In addition, the problem of comparing income levels in developed countries with those of developing countries has always existed (due to the violent swings in exchange rates in many developing countries).

Using the CER method tends to create a bias against less developed countries (i.e. it tends to exaggerate income gaps between those at the upper end and those at the lower end), since the CER income levels do not always reflect actual purchasing power of the national currencies. The research community (and international agencies) have long been aware of this dilemma and there have been many attempts in this century to make international comparisons of income levels based on purchasing power parity. The most famous early attempt is perhaps Colin Clark's pioneering study on conditions of economic progress (Clark, 1957). Already in the early 1950s the OEEC (the predecessor of the OECD) initiated work, under the guidance of Gilbert and Kravis, on comparing national products of some Western European countries with those of the United States (Gilbert and Kravis, 1954).

In the 1970s Kravis and associates continued and expanded the work under the UN-sponsored International Comparison Programme (Kravis *et al.*, 1978, 1982) and have since produced a series of reports, successively including more countries and additional benchmark years. After Kravis' retirement the work has been continued by his associates Alan Heston and Robert Summers. This work is nowadays coordinated with similar work at the OECD and at the UN Commission of the European Communities (Eurostat IV, 1987).

Angus Maddison has drawn heavily upon the results of these studies in his work on the world economy, earlier referred to (Maddison, 1989). I have in this exercise basically used the same method as Maddison: that is, applying growth indices to a benchmark year GDP expressed in 1980 PPP dollars. However, I have changed some of the benchmark real GDP figures in the light of new estimates published in the continuous updates of the so-called Penn World Table (see Summers and Heston, 1992). The benchmark real GDP per capita figures for 1980 are as a rule taken from the Penn World Tables except in the cases of OECD members, for which I have rather relied on the now available 1980 PPP level in the OECD series on PPP dollar levels in current prices 1970–1991 (OECD, 1993a, Table VII:2).

125

I have also constructed longer time series (back in time) for Argentina, Brazil, Mexico and Russia/USSR, drawing on studies by ECLAC (in the case of Argentina and Brazil), by the Banco de México (in the case of Mexico) and Nutter and Bergson and Kuznets (in the case of Russia/USSR). All data have been updated until the end of 1993, based on results (for 1993 preliminary) reported by OECD (1993a), ECLAC (1993), ESCAP (1993) and UNECE (1993).

REFERENCES

Abramovitz, M. (1986) 'Catching Up, Forging Ahead and Falling Behind', *Journal of Economic History*, vol. XLVI, no. 2.
——(1991) 'The Postwar Productivity Spurt and Slowdown. Factors of Potential and Realisation', in *Technology and Productivity: The Challenge for Economic Policy*, OECD, Paris.
Amsden, A. (1989) *Asia's Next Giant. South Korea and Late Industrialization*, Oxford University Press, New York.
——(1993) 'Why Isn't the Whole World Using the Asian Model to Develop?', Review of the World Bank's East Asian Miracle Report, draft.
Bailes, K. E. (1978) *Technology and Society under Lenin and Stalin*, Princeton University Press, Princeton, NJ.
Banco de México (1969) *Producto Bruto Interno y Series Basicas, 1895–1967*, Bank of Mexico, Mexico City, January.
Bergson, A. and Kuznets, S. (1963) *Economic Trends in the Soviet Union*, Harvard University Press, Cambridge, MA.
Brundenius, C. (1993) 'Global Restructuring, New Technologies and the Demise of the Second World: Challenges for the Third World', in C. Brundenius and B. Göransson (eds) *New Technologies and Global Restructuring: The Third World at a Crossroads*, London and Los Angeles.
Clark, C. (1957) *Conditions of Economic Progress*, Macmillan, London.
Denison, E. D. (1962) *The Sources of Economic Growth and the Alternatives Before Us*, Committee for Economic Development, New York.
——(1967) *Why Growth Rates Differ*, The Brookings Institution, Washington, DC.
ECLAC (1991) *Sustainable Development: Changing Production Patterns, Social Equity and the Environment*, Santiago de Chile.
——(1992) *Social Equity and Changing Production Patterns: An Integrated Approach*, Santiago de Chile.
——(1993) *Preliminary Overview of the Economy of Latin America and the Caribbean 1993*, Santiago de Chile.
ESCAP, (1993) *Economic and Social Survey of Asia and the Pacific 1992 (Parts I and II)*, United Nations, New York.
Eurostat IV (1987) *World Comparison of Purchasing Power Parities*, Phase IV of the International Comparison Project, Part Two: Detailed Results for 60 Countries, UN Commission of the European Communities, New York.
Fagerberg, J. (1987) 'A Technology Gap Approach to Why Growth Rates Differ', *Research Policy*, vol. 16, nos 2–4.
——(1988) 'Why Growth Rates Differ', in G. Dosi et al. (eds) *Technical Change and Economic Theory*, Pinter, London and New York.
Freeman, C. (ed.) (1986) *Design, Innovation and Long Cycles in Economic Development*, Pinter, London.

—— (1987) *Technology Policy and Economic Performance: Lessons from Japan*, Pinter, London and New York.

—— (1989) 'New Technology and Catching Up', in C. Cooper and R. Kaplinsky (eds) 'Technology and Development in the Third Industrial Revolution', *European Journal of Development Research*, vol. 1, no. 1.

—— (1993) 'Technical Change and Future Trends in the World Economy', *Futures*, no. 6.

Freeman, C. and Perez, C. (1988) 'Structural Crises of Adjustment: Business Cycles and Investment Behaviour', in G. Dosi *et al.* (eds) *Technical Change and Economic Theory*, Pinter, London and New York.

Gilbert, M. and Kravis, I. B. (1954) *An International Comparison of National Products and the Purchasing Power of Currencies*, OEEC, Paris.

Goodland, R. (1991) 'The Case that the World has Reached Limits: More Precisely that Current Throughput Growth in the Global Economy cannot be Sustained', in R. Goodland *et al.* (eds) *Environmentally Sustainable Economic Development: Building on Brundtland*, UNESCO, Paris.

Göransson, B. (1994) *Catching Up in Technology. Case Studies from the Telecommunications Equipment Industry*, Taylor Graham, London and Los Angeles.

Helleiner, G. K. (1990) *The New Global Economy and the Developing Countries: Essays in International Economics and Development*, Edward Elgar, Aldershot.

Hikino, T. and Amsden, A. (1993) 'Staying Behind, Stumbling Back, Sneaking Up, Soaring Ahead: Late Industrialization in Historical Perspective', in W. J. Baumol *et al.* (eds) *International Convergence of Productivity with Some Evidence from History*, Oxford University Press.

IITA (1993) *A Proposal for the Promotion of Software Industry in Korea*, Institute for Technology Assessment, Electronics and Telecommunications Research Institute, Daejon, draft, December.

Jacobsson, S. (1991) 'The Extent, Nature and Timing of Industrial Policy for Infant Industries', in C. Brundenius and B. Göransson (eds) *New Technologies and Global Restructuring. The Third World at a Crossroads*, Taylor Graham, London and Los Angeles.

Juliusen, K. P. and Juliusen K. (1991) *The Computer Industry Almanac 1990*, Brady, New York.

Kravis, I. B., Heston, A. and Summers, R. (1978) *International Comparisons of Real Product and Purchasing Power*, Johns Hopkins University Press, Baltimore and London.

—— (1982) *World Product and Income. International Comparisons of Real Gross Product*, Johns Hopkins University Press, Baltimore and London.

Lucas, R. E. (1988) 'On the Mechanics of Economic Development', *Journal of Monetary Economics*, vol. 22.

Maddison, A. (1989) *The World Economy in the Twentieth Century*, OECD, Paris.

Mensch, G. (1979) *Stalemate in Technology: Innovations Overcome the Depression*, Ballinger, New York.

Nelson, P. (1993) *Japan's Information Society Concept: Influence in China and Singapore*, Department of Economic History, University of Lund, draft.

Nutter, G. W. (1962) *Growth of Industrial Production in the Soviet Union*, Princeton University Press, Princeton, NJ.

OECD (1991a) *Technology in a Changing World*, The Technology/Economy Programme, OECD, Paris.

—— (1991b) *Technology and Productivity, The Challenge for Economic Policy*, The Technology/Economy Programme, OECD, Paris.

—— (1992) *Technology and the Economy, The Key Relationships*, The Technology/Economy Programme, OECD, Paris.

127

——(1993a) *National Accounts. Main Aggregates 1960–91*, OECD, Paris.

——(1993b) *OECD Economic Outlook*, No. 54, December.

Perez, C. (1985) 'Microelectronics, Long Waves and World Structural Change: New Perspectives for Developing Countries', *World Development*, vol. 13, no. 3.

——(1989) *Institutional Implications of the Present Wave of Technical Change for the Developing Countries*, The World Bank, Washington, DC.

Perez, C. and Soete, L. (1988) 'Catching Up in Technology: Entry Barriers and Windows of Opportunity', in G. Dosi *et al.*, (eds) *Technical Change and Economic Theory*, Pinter, London.

Romer, P. M. (1986) 'Increasing Returns and Long-Run Growth', *Journal of Political Economy*, vol. 94, October.

Schumpeter, J. A. (1939) *Business Cycles: A Theoretical, Historical and Statistical Analysis of the Capitalist Process*, McGraw-Hill, New York.

——(1942) *Capitalism, Socialism and Democracy*, Harper and Brother, New York.

Summers, R. and Heston, V. P. (1988) 'A New Set of International Comparisons of Real Product and Price Levels Estimates for 130 Countries, 1950–85', *Review of Income and Wealth*, vol. 34, no. 1.

——(1992) 'The Penn World Table (Mark 5): An Expanded Set of International Comparisons, 1950–88', *The Quarterly Journal of Economics*, vol. CVI, May, no. 2.

Sutton, A. C. (1968) *Western Technology and Soviet Economic Development: 1917 to 1930*, Stanford University Press, Stanford, CA.

——(1971) *Western Technology and Soviet Economic Development: 1930 to 1945*, Stanford University Press, Stanford, CA.

UNECE (1993) *Economic Survey of Europe, 1992–93*, UN Economic Commission for Europe, Geneva and New York.

US Bureau of the Census (1960) *Historical Statistics of the United States from Colonial Times to 1957*, Washington, DC.

van Duijn, J. J. (1983) *The Long Wave in Economic Life*, Allen and Unwin, Boston and Sydney.

Wade, R. (1990) *Governing the Market. Economic Theory and the Role of Government in East Asian Industrialization*, Princeton University Press, Princeton, NJ.

World Bank (1993) *The East Asian Miracle. Economic Growth and Public Policy*, Oxford University Press, New York.

6

TECHNOLOGICAL IMPLICATIONS OF STRUCTURAL ADJUSTMENT

Some lessons from India

Malur R. Bhagavan

THE TECHNOLOGICAL SCENE ON THE EVE OF STRUCTURAL ADJUSTMENT

With the benefit of hindsight we can see *four major periods* in the evolution of the industrial and technological policies of the Indian state, each period defined by departures from some of the positions taken in the previous period. The *first* period, 1950–1965, was marked by the state acquiring and keeping the lead in the producer goods sector, i.e. capital goods and some key intermediate goods, leaving almost the entire consumer goods and the non-strategic parts of the intermediate goods sectors to private Indian and foreign capital. During the *second* period, 1966–1984, the emphasis on state ownership and control of the strategic parts of Indian industry gradually declined, and the strategy of self-reliantly catching up with the West technologically was abandoned in practice (though not in rhetoric). The *third* period, which spans the years 1985–1991, signalled the retreat of the state from the 'commanding heights of the economy'. It initiated the entry of the private sector into areas formerly reserved exclusively for the public sector. It also witnessed a strengthening of the strategy of 'import liberalization for modernization of industry' which was set in motion already during the latter half of the second period. The onset of the so-called 'stabilization and structural adjustment programme' in July 1991 heralds the start of the *fourth* period. (For a detailed presentation of the Indian government's industrial policies over the last forty years, the reader is referred to Sandesara, 1992.)

The conventional division of India's so-called 'mixed economy' into 'public' and 'private' sectors can be misleading. They are two sides of the same coin. It should be borne in mind that from independence (1947) onwards the strategic aim of those who wielded real (as opposed to nominal) power was to make India into a strong nation state on the foundations of a strong capitalist economy. There was a convergence of views between the state and domestic private capital as to their respective roles in this endeavour: the state would provide highly subsidized transport, communications and social infrastructure, as well as basic materials and energy (e.g. steel, chemicals, coal and electricity) required by industry (both private and public), impose barriers against imports and create highly protected domestic markets for the output of domestic industry; the private sector would accumulate capital and grow by supplying the domestic market for consumer goods.

State intervention on behalf of domestic industry has been and will continue to be the key issue in the process of successfully industrializing any country, let alone India, as the literature on the economic development of Europe, North America and East Asia repeatedly demonstrates. (See the critique of the World Bank's 1993 report on 'The East Asian Miracle' in the special section of *World Development*, April 1994.)

The question then is not whether the state should intervene, but how and how much. As background to the analysis in this chapter of how structural adjustment is likely to affect industry and technology in India, we will in this section briefly review the technological outcome of state intervention practised over the last four decades.

During the first policy period (1950–1965), with its three first five-year plans single-mindedly concentrating on building domestic manufacturing capacity in capital goods, India had strong technical collaboration with both the West and the erstwhile communist bloc. But with the onset of the second policy period in the mid-1960s, technology transfer from the communist bloc began to decline in favour of increasing collaboration with Western transnational corporations. By the mid-1980s, when the third policy period with its strong bias towards liberalization had been ushered in, the former Soviet Union and Eastern Europe were out of the picture altogether. Already by then, technology agreements with the OECD region ran to several thousand. Since then, the demand for and the approval of technology agreements have greatly accelerated, as is evident if we note that during 1985–1990 the total number of *new* agreements approved was 5203, which was 80 per cent more than the 2916 approved over the preceding five-year period 1980–1984 (India-DSIR, 1992). These figures bear eloquent witness to the fruition of the quiet and implicit policy embarked upon in the early 1970s of abandoning the quest for self-reliant indigenous technological development. Official industrial statistics in India are now graced by a new concept of classification, the 'foreign collaborated firm', as in Wipro-Sun, HPL-HP, PSI-Bull, etc. (Vyasulu, 1993).

Let us now turn to the question of what actually has been achieved on the basis of this massive import of technology.

Analytical framework

The concept of *modern technology* we adopt is a broad one. Its 'embodied' or 'hardware' form consists of tools, machinery, equipment and vehicles, which together make up the category of *capital goods*. Its 'disembodied' or 'software' form encompasses the *knowledge and skills* required for the use, maintenance, repair, production, adaptation and innovation of capital goods, which are often also labelled in the literature as 'the know-how and the know-why of processes and products'. In our usage, knowledge and skills refer not only to scientific, engineering and technical abilities, but also to the skills associated with organization, management and information. Hereafter we use the terms 'knowledge' and 'skills' interchangeably.

We find it analytically useful to classify modern technology into two broad types, standard-modern and highly-modern, on the basis of five indicators: automation, science-relatedness, research intensity, dominant innovative skills and leading sectors (Freeman, 1982). These two broad types, which we hereafter denote by 'standard-tech' and 'high-tech', are characterized respectively by 'medium' and 'high' values in their degrees of automation, science-relatedness and research intensity. For a detailed exposition of this approach to technology analysis the reader is referred to Bhagavan (1990).

The range of professional skills required for the regular use, maintenance, repair and production of the capital goods belonging to these two types of technologies depends of course on the specific industrial and infrastructural branches that one is looking at. In general, they comprise a large number, but not all, of the skill categories listed under the International Standard Classification of Occupations (see its Appendix 2), *excluding* those that come under sales, services and agriculture.

A country's capacity to *innovate* in standard and high tech presupposes the existence of a good base in the skills mentioned above. However, that is not enough. In addition, one has to acquire capacity in certain areas which are specifically *innovation oriented*. Research scientists and research engineers represent the class of people with leading innovative skills. For much of the century-long duration of the standard modern era in the West (1860–1960), the research scientist and the research engineer worked individualistically without being tied to 'systems approaches'. The transition from standard to high tech, both in 'old' products (say textile machinery) and in entirely new ones (say digital telecommunications), depends crucially on systems approaches to solving problems. The innovations associated with the high-tech area, and with the transition from standard to high tech in already-known products, appear impossible without professionalized R&D entities in which research scientists and engineers, as well as system and symbol analysts, work as teams.

Roughly speaking, the transition from the standard-modern to the highly-modern era began in Western Europe and North America in the 1960s. Some examples of the leading sectors that exemplify standard-tech capital goods and skills are steel, railways, electricals, automobiles, plastics, synthetic textiles and synthetic dyes. However, all these 'old' products have made the transition and are now available in their high-tech avatars. Examples of entirely new leading sectors that have arisen with high tech are microelectronics, computers, digital and satellite-based telecommunications, robotics, informatics, biotechnology (based on genetic engineering) and new materials.

Acquiring capacity for using and replicating imported standard-modern technology

In the following we will summarize the factors and measures that helped India acquire, within the space of thirty years (1950–1980), the capacity to use and replicate a great variety of imported standard-modern capital goods, as well as a few highly-modern ones.

However, what has signally failed is the apparent effort to acquire the capacity to design and innovate new standard tech, let alone the very much more complex high tech. On paper, of course, the Indian state formulated a host of measures to generate this capacity. But no serious efforts were made to enforce these measures systematically and to create the environment that would oblige both the public and private sectors, as well as government-funded R&D establishments, to undertake technology design and technology innovation.

Table 6.1 shows that imports of consumer goods had been drastically reduced already by the early 1970s in comparison with the other two sectors. By then India was meeting most of the domestic demand for consumer goods by domestic production, importing mainly a small range of consumer durables for its high-income stratum that it was not yet making itself.

Table 6.1 Structure of imports of manufactured goods: percentage distribution of value of imports by broad sectors

Year	Capital goods	Intermediate goods	Consumer goods
1970	16.7	73.6	6.8
1981	13.4	77.5	9.1

Sources: United Nations Yearbook of International Trade Statistics, various issues

Machinery dominated the import composition of capital goods, accounting for nearly 90 per cent by 1981. The average annual growth rates of imports of machinery and transport equipment were also very high right to the end of the 1970s, reaching nearly 17 per cent by 1980.

Since, by the early 1980s, India had achieved a large capacity in the domestic manufacture of capital goods, the question arises as to why imports of capital goods did not decline much from the 1970s' level. The answer lies in the fact that although India had achieved near self-sufficiency in replicating standard tech by the late 1970s, it was very far from doing so in high tech, which was what the capital goods imports in the 1980s and beyond concentrated on. Nearly 30 per cent of the capital goods imports in the early 1980s consisted of high tech like electrical power machinery and switch gear, telecommunication equipment, computers, aircraft and ships (Bhagavan, 1990). In comparing the monetary values of imports, one should remember that the cost of even one high-tech capital good, say a long-range civilian jet aircraft, may be several orders of magnitude higher than that of a large number of consumer durables, say dishwashers.

India began exporting standard-tech capital goods from the late 1970s onwards, accounting by 1984 for 10 per cent of the total value of exports (Lall, 1990).

Skill structure of the workforce

One of the key indicators of a country's technological level is the skill composition of its workforce. The historical pattern is that employment in modern industry and infrastructure overtakes that in agriculture, as a country becomes more industrialized. And since substantial parts of industrial and infrastructural work require machine-related skills, a relative increase in industrial and infrastructural employment can be taken to be a rough and ready indicator of an increase in the skill level of the workforce.

Table 6.2 Percentage distribution of workforce by broad skill categories

Country	Year	ISCO major groups (percentages)						
		1	*2*	*3*	*4*	*5*	*6*	*7/8/9*
India	1971	2.7	0.9	2.8	4.0	3.3	72.5	12.9
	1981	2.7	0.9	2.8	3.9	2.6	66.1	13.0
South Korea	1970	3.1	0.9	5.8	9.9	6.5	49.6	21.2
	1989	6.7	1.4	12.1	14.3	10.5	18.8	33.6

Notes:
The above percentages do not always add up to 100, because we have excluded from the table the categories 'workers not classifiable by occupation' and 'unemployed'.
For India, 1981 is the latest year for which published data were available in United Nations sources at the time of writing.
By 'workforce' we mean those categorized as 'economically active population' by the UN Statistical Office.
1 = Professional, technical and related workers
2 = Administrative and managerial workers
3 = Clerical and related workers
4 = Sales workers
5 = Service workers
6 = Agriculture, animal husbandry and related workers
7/8/9 = Production and related workers, transport equipment and labourers
Sources: ILO, Yearbook of Labour Statistics, 1990 and 1991

Looking at Table 6.2, we note that South Korea conforms to this pattern, but not India. Between 1970 and 1989, there was a massive shift downwards in agriculture's share of employment in South Korea by 30 percentage points (category 6), accompanied by a shift upwards in the share of industry and infrastructure by 12 percentage points (categories 7, 8 and 9). In India, there has been no shift at all in industry's and infrastructure's share of employment over the period 1971–1981. It is immobile at 13 per cent, while that in agriculture has decreased by more than 6 percentage points. That decrease is in effect a corresponding rise in unemployment, as the other sectors have also stayed motionless, as is clear from Table 6.2. Although the Indian data refer to 1981, the well-documented fact that there has been virtually no growth in employment in the organized registered sector of industry during the 1980s (Ghose, 1993) lets us infer that industry's and infrastructure's *share* of total employment in the early 1990s is very likely to be less than it was in the early 1980s. Thus, at a very aggregated level, we can venture the opinion that there has been no *structural* shift within the Indian workforce in the direction of increasing total machine-related skill content.

Professional, technical and managerial personnel are of strategic importance in industrial and technological advance. Here too India seems not to have undergone the kind of structural change that rapid technological progress requires. The figures for categories 1 and 2 in Table 6.2 demonstrate that over the ten-year period 1971–1981 these two categories stood structurally still at 3.6 per cent of the total workforce. There is no factor in the Indian economy that indicates that this figure may have moved up in the decade of the 1980s. Rather the opposite. The measure of Indian non-performance becomes clear when compared with South Korea's strong shift towards higher skills as revealed by the 4 percentage point increase in categories 1 and 2 over the period 1970–1989.

Scientific and technological workers

Under the strategy of relatively rapid industrialization that India adopted after independence, there arose a sharply increasing demand for large numbers of literate workers skilled in basic industrial skills. The tradition of recruiting unskilled (and most often illiterate) labourers, and training them on the job to acquire the skills that any particular enterprise required, proved wholly inadequate. It was argued that the expanding secondary education system would meet this challenge.

On an average, about 15 per cent of the employees in industry and infrastructure belong to the skilled category. In theory, the supply of recruits into this group should therefore be easily ensurable by Indian secondary schools even at their current very low proportional intakes. One may be tempted to conclude that the supply of recruits for skilled work does not pose a problem in India. However, industrial employers would, in the first instance, be looking for *vocationally* trained candidates rather than fresh secondary school leavers. Therefore a better measure of the actual recruiting base would be the output of vocational schools that train pupils over several years in one or more industrial skills.

In the early 1980s, India was producing around 400,000 vocational school leavers per year, which was roughly 7 per cent of employment in manufacturing. This should be compared with South Korea's 840,000, corresponding to 40 per cent of manufacturing jobs (Lall, 1990). As mentioned earlier, the 1980s in India were the years of 'jobless growth'. So in terms of absorptive capacity, even the very modest output by Indian vocational schools (in comparison with South Korea's absolute figures, let alone on a per capita basis) was already too high for Indian industry.

Technicians take a midway position between skilled workers and graduate scientists and engineers. Their role is crucial in industrial development. Ideally, their work should consist of diagnosing and putting right major faults in a range of sophisticated equipment, and liaising between the planning, designing and engineering sections, leaving the actual implementation of the designs to skilled workers. However, in the absence of any significant design work in Indian industry at present, the technical-liaising dimension has remained dormant. Instead, technicians' present primary duties are as foremen and supervisors, exercising technical and social control over factory floor labour. In other words, the talents and training of technicians are being underutilized.

Table 6.3 Scientific and technical workers (employed)

Country	Year	Scientists and engineers		Technicians	
		No. (000)	per million popn	No. (000)	per million popn
India	1990	2471	2995	639	774
South Korea	1981	94	2478	1931	50,828

Source: UNESCO, Statistical Yearbook, 1991

One among several illustrations of the telling contrasts in skill levels and skill use between sluggish and dynamic industrial sectors is provided by the figures for technicians in India and South Korea. From Table 6.3 one can see that whereas there were more than 50,000 technicians per million of the population in South Korea as early as 1981, there were less than 800 technicians per million of the population in India as late as 1990.

But when it comes to graduate scientists and engineers, the Indian figures are roughly on a par with South Korea's, at around 3000 per million of the total population (Table 6.3). The two countries are also on a par in proportional enrolment in higher education and specifically in science and engineering (Tables 6.4 and 6.5).

The inverted educational pyramid

The Indian performance in enrolment in secondary education is very poor, not least when compared with the leaders among the late industrializers like South Korea. It can be seen from Table 6.4 that by the mid-1980s, while South Korea was approaching near universal secondary education, India had not even managed to get halfway to that goal.

Table 6.4 Educational levels in 1975 and 1985: numbers enrolled as percentage of age group

Country	Secondary education		Higher education	
	1975	1985	1975	1985
India	28	38	8.6	6.4
South Korea	56	90	10.3	34.2

Source: UNESCO, Statistical Yearbook, 1991

In the debate about the role of human resources in development, it is now increasingly acknowledged that without universal primary and secondary education it is not possible to generate the process of self-sustaining development. With universal secondary education, every child approaching adulthood will have internalized the primary knowledge base and the basic techniques of learning, with which he or she can acquire a whole range of new knowledge and skills. It is not a coincidence that the OECD countries and the dynamic East Asian economies (of which South Korea is used here as a reference example to compare and contrast with India) first concentrated on attaining universal secondary education, before making higher education more widely accessible. In terms of financial resources, India has done the opposite: it has poured more public money into higher education *on a proportional basis* than into primary and secondary education. It shares this feature of the 'inverted educational pyramid' with many other developing countries (Upendranath, 1993a). But now with the structural adjustment programme (SAP) there are firm indications that this lop-sided behaviour will be put right and primary and secondary education will begin to get more of the education budget.

Table 6.5 Enrolment in higher education in natural science, mathematics, engineering and computer science

Country	Year	Number (000)	As % of total enrolment in higher ed.
India	1985	1234	27.6
South Korea	1989	384	24.3

Source: UNESCO, Statistical Yearbook, 1991

The imperatives that lie behind this skewed policy of promoting higher education, while grossly neglecting primary and secondary education, are those of the politically powerful middle class (Upendranath, 1993a). It wants higher education for its offspring partly for reasons of social status and partly because it is the minimum qualification required for any white collar job. But the contradiction of supplying degrees in excess of the needs of a sluggish economy has been transparent for a long time in the form of graduate unemployment. It is reported that about 1.2 million science and engineering graduates and technicians were registered as unemployed in 1990.

The difference between quantity and quality is nowhere more apparent than in the realms of the work done by scientists, engineers and technicians. For instance, although India is reputed to have the world's third largest combined *stock* of these three professions, its industrial productivity has still recently been negative and the quality of its industrial products open to serious misgiving. These negative outcomes have their origins in the following conditions under which higher education has been, and continues to be, conducted: first, and perhaps most devastating, is that non-academic, non-merit factors are decisive in gaining entry into professional courses; second, the predominantly book-bound orientation of the training, with rote learning and exam passing almost totally displacing problem-solving approaches; third, out of the countless number of universities and colleges, only a tiny fraction have the resources to provide basic laboratories and workshops to back up theoretical work – for the others with no experimental facilities, science simply becomes theology; and fourth, with higher education having exploded in numbers beyond imagining, there simply are not enough places in industry and other professional sectors to place undergraduates for short periods of practical training. And on top of all this, there is the annual brain-drain of promising young talent to technologically greener pastures elsewhere. To quote from the *Far Eastern Economic Review* (1992):

> Out of the 190 recognised universities, the world-class science and engineering institutions number only about a dozen. These schools turn out 2,000–3,000 graduates a year. About a third opt for management careers or the civil service. Another third emigrate to the US, Canada and Singapore.

INDIAN R&D: NOT TECHNOLOGY INNOVATION, BUT TECHNOLOGY ABSORPTION

The explicit involvement of the government of India in funding targeted scientific and industrial research predates independence in 1947. In 1942, following the British model, the then colonial government in New Delhi established a Council of Scientific and Industrial Research (CSIR) to oversee and be in charge of a few national laboratories, created at that time to investigate whether imported industrial raw materials could be replaced by local ones to overcome the problems created by the ongoing World War II. Recognizing the central importance of technology to economic development, the government of independent India rapidly expanded the number of national research laboratories and institutes under the CSIR umbrella to over forty by the late 1960s. They were spread over major cities in the country and covered a wide field in the natural and engineering sciences. Their mandate was to do both 'pure' and 'applied' research, and in particular to address the technological problems of industry and contribute to technological innovation. Since then, the exercise has been repeated in other fields like agriculture, forestry, marine resources, medicine, electronics and biotechnology, with each new area being placed under a separate ministerial department that funds and controls the corresponding national laboratories and institutes.

Government research laboratories

Total R&D funding in India grew very rapidly during the 1980s, increasing by nearly a factor of six over the period 1981–1991, from slightly over Rs 7 billion in 1981 to Rs 42 billion in 1991 (US$ 2.3 billion at the then exchange rate). Of the 1991 funding 80 per cent was spent in government labs and public sector enterprises, with the private sector accounting for the remaining 20 per cent (India-DST, 1992). Over half of the government funding, Rs 18 billion, went to three organizations: The Defence Research and Development Organization (with its huge number of R&D units), the Department of Atomic Energy and the Department of Space Research.

In order to ensure that top-class engineers would be available for leading industrial development work, the Indian government, with generous financial and technical assistance from the West, created five Indian Institutes of Technology (IIT). Like the national labs, they too were geographically spread out, with two in the north and one each in the east, south and west. Besides providing undergraduate and postgraduate education in the engineering sciences, they were charged with the responsibility of being in the forefront of technological research.

The third approach towards promoting technological research was very much more diffuse. It was to try and coax both public and private sector industries into establishing in-house R&D units with import tax rebates and generous amortization rates for R&D equipment.

The scientific establishment in India routinely bemoans the fact that India spends less than its role models in East Asia on R&D as a proportion of its total GDP. For instance, in 1990, Japan, South Korea, Taiwan and India spent, respectively, US$ 85.6 billion (2.98 per cent of GDP), 3.2 billion (1.83

per cent), 2 billion (1.41 per cent) and 2.5 billion (0.88 per cent) on R&D. What they conveniently forget to mention is that the overwhelming part of the East Asian funding comes from the domestic private sector, which really makes sure that it gets value for its money (Sigurdson, 1990). A corollary of this is the stunning performance of the East Asians in making technical changes, in generating technological innovations and putting new products and processes on the market. Considering the truly colossal sums spent on civilian R&D by the government over the last four decades, India has little to show in terms of civilian innovation that is its own. From toothbrushes to tractors, from shoe polish to ships, from bicycles to buses, any improvements that the Indian customer may have enjoyed are still the result of continuing imports of technology. The Indian customer is also unaware of any incremental technical improvement in commodities of regular use that government-funded R&D may have hit upon. Not that private sector R&D has done any better.

Whatever else they may have accomplished, it is now clear that the government research labs and institutes have been less than marginal in promoting technical change and innovation in Indian industry and infrastructure. The labs charge industry with deliberately ignoring their contributions in preference to imported technology. Industry claims that the labs have concentrated on work which is of no relevance to industry. The accusations fly back and forth. What the verdict of the present Indian government is can be inferred from the fact that it imparted a sharp shock to the government research labs and institutes in 1992 by not approving the expected automatic annual increase in their budget allocation, hinting that the future would be pretty dire. The Ministry of Finance has told them to generate 30 per cent of their budget from commissioned work from the private sector. At the time of writing, several of them have set up marketing units and task forces to try and sell their know-how to private industry.

A recent empirical study into industrial R&D in India (Alam 1993) finds that

> a large number of firms were unhappy with their experiences with these [government] laboratories and institutes. Most felt that the facilities available with these institutes were adequate, but that their approach to research for industry was not very positive. The most common feeling was that the national laboratories and research institutes were not used to commercial culture and did not appreciate the importance of completing jobs on time. This has led to frustration and losses for the firms. Firms also felt that the facilities available with these laboratories are grossly underutilized and could be used by industry for testing prototypes etc.

The IITs seem to have fared somewhat better than the CSIR labs in responding to industry's needs. To quote from the same report (Alam,

1993): 'Our case studies reveal that...industry sponsored research projects [at the IITs] aimed at solving specific problems.' Be that as it may, of the original two-part intention that the IITs should not only produce the very best engineering graduates but also retain the intellectually brightest of them to do technological R&D within the country, only the first appears to have been seriously tried. Apparently about a thousand IIT graduates leave India each year for North America.

In-house R&D in industrial firms

That brings us to a consideration of in-house R&D in industry. A look at the macrostatistics gathered and annually published by the Indian government tells us that the number of industrial firms with some kind of in-house R&D has been steadily increasing over the last two decades and is now nearing the figure of 1,200. It also tells us that the total amount spent by them on R&D as a proportion of their total sales is about 0.66 per cent, averaged over the six-year period 1985–1990 (India-DST, 1992).

Considerable amounts of case study material and analyses, at both the micro and macrolevels, are now available on why Indian industrial firms, both public and private, invest in R&D and what fruit that investment has borne. We will summarize below the main findings of a number of these studies (Alam, 1993; Desai, 1988, 1990; Gumaste, 1988; Kathuria, 1989; Katrak, 1989; Kumar, 1987; Lall, 1987; Tyabji, 1993), which also investigate the effect of government policy on promoting R&D at the firm level.

Empirical studies of several hundred firms were conducted by some of the above-mentioned authors. They covered the fields of ceramics, electronics, electricals, machinery, automobiles, metallurgy, metal working, chemical engineering, minerals and mining, paper, textiles, leather and food processing. The firms identified the following activities as the principal objectives of their R&D work: product adaptation, product diversification, indigenization of components, indigenization of raw materials and testing. Of these, the first three were mentioned the most often.

Some firms also claimed that they did some 'product development'. On a closer look, what this claim boiled down to is minor modifications of imported articles, or their imitation or an expansion of the product line by introducing new imports.

One of the measures that the government insisted on being implemented, within foreign technology agreements, was the rapid replacement of imported part components by locally manufactured ones. This process of 'indigenization' of component manufacture, as it has come to be called, also required the rapid absorption of increasing volumes of foreign technology. The R&D units became the principal vehicles for indigenization.

On analysing their data, the authors find that the primary objective of firms in setting up R&D units was to develop in-house skills to understand how the imported capital goods function (know-how), why they do what they do (know-why), what their strengths and weaknesses are, and what the critical points are that one has to be aware of. This process is called *technology absorption*.

It is very important to note that technological innovation, which among other things involves acquisition of design capacity, does not feature among the R&D goals of the firms studied. Product adaptation, which usually involves some incremental technical change, is the first step towards product innovation.

With most of the attention being focused on absorbing the know-how, the learning of know-why receded into the background. Without know-why it is not possible successfully to attempt change and adaptation in imported technology to suit local conditions. Nor was such change the first priority of most firm owners. Improvements in product quality, production efficiency and labour productivity were much more of central concern; these could be tackled on the basis of the know-how that came with the imported technology.

Firms in electronics and electricals spend more on R&D as a percentage of sales than other firms, with metal industries spending least, while machinery and chemicals take intermediate positions. Roughly the same pattern holds for royalty and other payments for disembodied technology (i.e. technological knowledge) as a proportion of sales. A plausible hypothesis that would explain both these patterns is that the *rate of technical change* in electronics and electricals is much higher than in other areas, leading to frequent imports of new technology, which in turn necessitates a continuous strengthening of the firm's technology absorption capability.

A sharp increase has been noted in the total volume of payments made for foreign technical knowledge (disembodied technology). But, at the same time, the authors of the case studies find, somewhat to their surprise, that the more generous terms allowed for payments for technological knowledge since 1985 and 1991 have not led to any significant increases in the import of technological knowledge by individual firms as individual firms. The increase in the total volume of payments would then mean that substantial numbers of new firms have entered the market as knowledge buyers.

A prime reason why the costs of individual agreements have not risen to the degree expected is that firms are buying only very specific bits of hardware and software, and not a whole composite machinery. This ability to 'unpackage' technology and buy only that which cannot be locally generated is a promising sign of the growing industrial maturity of the country.

It seems as though the limiting factor on R&D investment was not the terms set by the government but quite simply the level of the financial resources available to firms. In fact, most case studies underline the fact that on average an Indian firm spends far too little on knowledge imports and in-house R&D to be able really to attempt technological innovation. The firms are fully aware of this limitation. Their purpose in establishing in-house R&D is first and foremost to absorb technology. One of India's leading industrialists is quoted as saying that

> none of this [i.e. in-house R&D] is research. It's mostly reverse engineering. Basic research would mean a lot of time reinventing the wheel, and the funds required are such that most Indian companies can't compete – Honda's R&D expenditure is more than my annual turnover.
>
> (*Far Eastern Economic Review*, 1992).

Firms point out that a technology agreement makes it easier to source the capital goods and production inputs, through the foreign partner's know-ledge of and contacts in the supplying market. Indian firms usually do not have the resources to build up such information and market capabilities. In other words, technology agreements are often even less significant than they are made out to be: they are less the vehicles for upgrading techno-logical knowledge than a practical and relatively inexpensive way of sour-cing capital goods and inputs. An extreme is reached when, as in some leather and textile firms, the foreign collaboration agreement is nothing more than a means of obtaining market intelligence.

Impact of policy on firm-level R&D

Analyses of macropolicy factors that promoted or inhibited R&D activities at the firm level revealed the following trends. The smallness of the size of most Indian firms in comparison with those in the OECD region is an inhibiting factor when it comes to significant investments in R&D. In contrast to that, firms' export capacity and market competitiveness had no significant impact in either direction. The more liberal rules introduced in 1985 and 1991 for foreign equity holdings in Indian firms, as well as for imports of technology, seem to have started eroding the earlier rationale for investing in R&D. However, it was also noted that firms which increased their imports of technology and production inputs also invested more in R&D to generate the appropriate kinds and levels of technology absorption capacity.

THE IMPOSITION OF THE STABILIZATION AND STRUCTURAL ADJUSTMENT PROGRAMME (SSAP)

The making of the 1991 crisis as the prelude to SSAP

The liberalization of imports and foreign exchange transactions, sanctioned by the 1985 policies, ate rapidly into India's foreign exchange reserves. The sudden increase in the import bill of oil caused by the Gulf War, though brief, was another severe drain. In the aftermath of the Gulf War, forex remittances from Indian workers from the Gulf states dried up. With the confidence in the Indian economy declining, Indians resident abroad began withdrawing their forex deposits from Indian banks. By the summer of 1991 the forex reserves were down to a level insufficient even to cover essential imports for a few weeks!

The total external debt had meanwhile climbed to 70 billion dollars, corresponding to nearly a quarter of the total GDP, giving India the dubious distinction of being the third largest debtor nation in the Third World after Brazil and Mexico. With the forex reserves at rock bottom, India found itself for the first time in the position of having to default on its debt servicing which had now climbed to 22 per cent of export income, a move that would have choked off all future avenues for foreign loan and credit facilities.

Five years after the optimistic projections made by the Indian government in 1985 while launching its liberalization policies, its fiscal crisis had not got any better, but worse. A measure of that crisis is the fact that the accumulated domestic borrowing of the Indian government (financed largely out of the savings of middle-class households held in banks, bonds and sundry financial institutions and instruments) had reached a staggering 55 per cent of the GDP by 1991. In the same year, consumer price inflation had risen to 14 per cent from 8 per cent in 1985.

The balance of payments crisis and the fiscal crisis of the state are deeply structural and cannot be resolved by short-term measures. But a quick short-term 'fix' had to be found to stave off impending disaster and it came in the shape of yet another massive loan from the International Monetary Fund. But that loan was conditional on the Indian government's commitment to implementing the IMF's standard prescription of stabilization and structural adjustment.

This is not the place to recount the details of the measures proposed within the SSAP for various sectors of the Indian economy and society. For a meticulous, if somewhat positivist, summary that captures the essentials, the reader is referred to Das (1993).

The thrust of the stabilization policies is to devalue the currency to make exports cheaper and imports dearer, to check inflation through a squeeze on money supply, credits, wages and incomes, and to stimulate investment and demand through tax reductions.

The principal long-term aims of the structural adjustment programme (SAP) are to reshape the economy along 'free-market' lines which would drastically curtail the role of the state in the ownership and control of economic assets and activities, give the private sector (both domestic and foreign) the dominant role in all sectors of the economy, promote unimpeded imports of foreign goods, services, investment and technology, provide special incentives to promote exports, end all subsidies and sharply reduce state financing of social services like education, health and transport.

A vigorous debate is taking place among Indian academics, policy makers and government officials on the pros and cons of the SAP. A great deal has been written and published. To obtain a quick overview of the positions taken, the reader is referred to ILO-ARTEP (1992), Raghuram (1992), Gupta (1993) and Nayyar (1993).

To sum up, then, 'liberalization' and the SAP were not bolts from the blue. Between the 'closing' of the economy in the early 1950s and its near total 'opening' in the early 1990s, one can discern a gradual political–economic process, the turn towards the 'opening' already being taken by the mid-1970s. The fiscal crisis of the state and the balance of payments crisis, which came to a head in 1991, are but the latest episodes in a long drawn-out struggle between the main contenders for economic and political power (Bardhan, 1984; Patnaik, 1986; Curien, 1986; Bhagavan, 1987).

The new industrial and technological policies under the SAP

The new industrial policy introduced by the Indian government as part of the SAP extends and completes the 'liberalization' measures of 1985. We summarize its main features and the associated technological measures below.

The licensing system has been abolished for all branches of mining and manufacturing industry except those involving strategic and security concerns, social and environmental concerns, hazardous chemicals and elite consumer durables. These exceptions comprise the following: defence, aerospace, explosives and fossil fuels; alcohol, tobacco and asbestos; sugar, animal fats and oils; leather, furs and skins; chemically treated wood products, paper and newsprint; pharmaceuticals; motor cars, entertainment electronics and household white goods (refrigerators, washing machines, air conditioners, etc.).

The small-scale sector would, however, be automatically exempt from licensing for any of the above eighteen branches which fall within the list of commodities already exclusively reserved for it through earlier policies.

The upper limit on investment in plant and machinery has been raised from Rs 3.5 million to 6 million for small-scale units in general, and to 7 million for so-called ancillary units of bigger firms and for export-oriented small-scale firms. Other firms can now hold up to a quarter of the total investment in any small-scale unit.

No licensing is required for the expansion of existing production capacities, or for adding new product lines within the existing commodity area of the firm (so-called broad-banding).

Permission to import capital goods would be automatic for projects which ensure foreign exchange through foreign investment, provided their CIF value was less than 25 per cent of the total value of the plant and equipment, subject to a ceiling of Rs 20 million.

A virtual 'open door' policy for foreign investment, with an upper limit of 51 per cent of the equity in any given firm, comes into effect in thirty-four so-called 'high-priority industries', which covers a great many major branches in capital, intermediate and consumer goods sectors, as well as in tourism (see the Appendix). To qualify for such automatic clearance, the foreign exchange cost of the imported capital goods must be covered by the foreign equity.

Technology agreements with foreign suppliers would be automatically approved for the above-mentioned thirty-four high-priority industries, subject to upper limits of Rs 10 million for lumpsum payments and 8 per cent of sales for royalty payments. These payments, for which foreign exchange would be automatically approved, would last for a maximum of ten years from the date of agreement, or seven years after the commencement of production. Non-priority industries would also enjoy this privilege of automatic approval provided they did not claim the same 'free' access to foreign exchange technology payments that the priority industries have a right to.

No permission would be required for hiring foreign technical personnel.

The eight industries hitherto reserved exclusively for the public sector would now be open to the private sector. They are in defence; atomic energy and associated fuels and materials; fossil fuels; the mining of ferrous and non-ferrous ores, as well as some strategic and precious metals; and railway transport.

Public sector firms would be subjected to critical review, which would not exclude the possibilities of closure, liquidation, rehabilitation or privatization. The criteria that would guide any action in these directions would be related to inefficiency in performance, low levels in technology, smallness of scale, low social priority, and not least the existence of well-developed private sector capacities supplying the same commodities. The government has announced its intention to sell 20 per cent of its holdings in the public sector, while simultaneously directing public sector firms to generate more internal resources.

Public sector firms would from now on be held to agreed levels of performance through binding memoranda of understanding. Their boards would be made more professional and autonomous, and given greater power.

The central provisions of the Monopolies and Restrictive Trade Practices (MRTP) Act have been scrapped. Mergers and takeovers are now freely permitted. Prior government approval for expanding present undertakings or for starting new ones is no longer necessary.

Both imports and exports have been greatly liberalized. Only very few commodities are banned outright from import and export, while between sixty and seventy are placed on the restricted list for exports and imports respectively. *Capital goods are being particularly favoured* both with easier import rules for a great majority of items and enhanced incentives for their exports.

The above policies have been launched with the conviction that they will lead to rapid rates of industrial growth and exports, through, first, high inflows of foreign investment and technology, second, higher investment by the domestic private sector, third, increased efficiency in both the public and the private sectors, and fourth, increased competitiveness in domestic and foreign markets both in terms of price and quality.

INDUSTRIAL RESTRUCTURING IN THE WAKE OF STRUCTURAL ADJUSTMENT

As we have indicated in earlier sections of this chapter, the process of liberalizing and opening up the Indian economy was a gradual one which picked up speed in the second half of the 1980s. Under the influence of this process, Indian industry and infrastructure began to undergo a shift and a restructuring in the 1980s relative to the character they had acquired by the late 1970s. The structural adujustment policies introduced in 1991 are likely to intensify and accelerate the trends set in motion in the 1980s. Of the various elements that make up the new industrial policy package of the Indian government that were described in the last section, the following can be expected to have the greatest impact:

- Abolition of the licensing system, in conjunction with the abolition of the restrictions on the growth in investment size, production capacity and product lines of individual enterprises.
- Automatic approval of majority equity holdings by foreign capital, and of foreign technology collaboration agreements, in the thirty-four high-priority areas listed in the Appendix.
- Unrestricted imports of capital goods, technical knowledge and managerial expertise, in a large number of industrial and infrastructural branches, on the condition that these are paid for in convertible hard foreign exchange brought in through foreign investment by the enterprise in question.
- Allowing up to one-quarter of the investment capital of a small firm to be owned by other firms.
- Enforcing penalties on the public sector for non-performance.

We will now examine the differential impacts that the new policies are likely to have on the restructuring process that had been set in motion before 1991.

Oligopoly: *plus ça change...*

From the mid-1980s onwards, the consumer goods sector, for both non-durables and durables, has shown much more dynamism than the intermediate and capital goods sectors. At present it also leads the other two in terms of the share of total industrial output and profits. This performance is traceable to the macroeconomic policy shift of the Indian state in the mid-1980s to stimulate consumer demand by the urban and rural middle-income groups. With restrictions on investment size, production capacity and product lines gone, the fight between the big industrial cum trading houses will greatly intensify to grab as much of the consumer goods cake as possible.

The scene is set for the further spreading of the cancer of oligopoly that has affected the Indian body industrial and economic so long, with its ills of market rigging, price fixing, indifference to quality and predilection for kickbacks.

Scale encroachment

The impressive growth of the small-scale sector over the last four decades has taken place under the protection offered by two policies. First, the reservation of certain commodities for the small-scale sector from which the large firms were excluded. Second, severe restrictions on how much of a small firm's capital can be owned by other firms. While 'commodity reservation' is still in place in the new industrial policy, the capital ownership restriction has been substantially weakened. One can foresee how, through the '25 per cent rule' mentioned above, large companies will increase the scope and magnitude of their control, de facto if not de jure, of the more dynamic and profitable small firms, something that has been conducted so far on a modest scale by undercover proxy ownership. This in turn will indirectly further erode the protection offered by commodity reservation. The small firms that come under the grip of large ones will perforce follow the economic rationale of the latter in replacing labour-intensive technology by a labour-displacing one, and local resources by non-local ones.

These moves will further entrench and accelerate the decades-old process of concentration of the more profitable goods in the hands of a limited number of large firms, with the small-scale sector left to produce for the poor majority. The brunt of this scale encroachment will be borne mainly by the following, historically most dynamic branches of the small-scale sector, which today account for between 40 and 90 per cent of the branch-wise value added (see Table 4.2 in Sandesara, 1992): food processing, beverages, tobacco, textiles, wood and leather products, and simpler metal products and parts, including household utensils.

Production for the domestic market vs the foreign market: what's sauce for the goose is sauce for the gander

Among the thirty-four so-called 'high-priority' areas that the Indian government has opened up for majority equity ownership by foreign capital, there is not a single consumer goods branch! This is not a coincidence. It is entirely consistent with the post-independence industrialization strategy of the Indian state to safeguard the consumer goods sector for domestic private capital.

On the other hand, the success of the new industrial and economic policy package is entirely predicated on being able to attract hard currency investment and high tech from the OECD and East Asian regions, to improve the competitiveness of Indian industrial goods, in particular of consumer durables, on the world market. It is hoped that foreign investors will be prepared to accept a non-controlling role in Indian firms in return for attractive profits in export markets.

However, it is no secret that the OECD and East Asian investors are primarily interested in getting into the growing middle- and upper-income markets *within* India. They are less motivated about helping Indian firms improve their export competitiveness.

The interplay of these diverse interests is likely to lead to a major restructuring of the *large-scale* sector in Indian industry along the following lines. It applies to both the private and public sectors, in all the three use-based sectors. (Those illustrative examples mentioned below which belong to the intermediate and capital goods sectors are taken from the Indian government's priority list reproduced in the Appendix):

1 Firms which are mainly geared to the domestic market, with *no* foreign investment but using imported earlier standard-tech designs.

   Examples: Textiles, beverages, radios, television sets, refrigerators, watches, pharmaceuticals; chemicals, fertilizers, paper and pulp, rubber, cement, building materials; machine tools, industrial and agricultural machinery, passenger and commercial vehicles, railway equipment.
2 Firms with foreign investment and imported high tech, producing largely for the domestic market, but also attempting to export a part of their output.

   Examples: Colour television, videos, compact discs, washing machines, household gadgets, passenger vehicles, pharmaceuticals; chemicals, prefabricated building materials; electrical, electronic and telecommunication equipment.
3 Primarily export-oriented companies, with foreign investment and imported high tech.

   Examples: A range of the latest microprocessor-based consumer durables and household gadgets; chemicals; computers, computerized equipment in electricals and electronics.

The retrenching of the public sector

Until the mid-1980s, the public sector had been assured a privileged and pampered place in the industrial and technological advance of India. That era is coming to a close. The new policy directive is to hold public sector firms firmly accountable for their future non-performance, entailing the real possibility of cutbacks and closures. In addition, there is the stated policy intention of privatizing 20 per cent of the government holdings in public sector firms. In the none too distant future this may mean that the public sector will have to vacate its place in a range of industries and technologies. Into which of these gaps the private sector, both domestic and foreign, will step depends on their perceived profitability. Clearly, many will not be profitable. This heralds a radical reordering of the industrial scene in India, the contours of which are not yet discernible. The old self-imposed imperative of wanting to make nearly everything from mirrors to missiles has lost its relevance.

TECHNOLOGICAL IMPLICATIONS OF STRUCTURAL ADJUSTMENT AND SOME POLICY CONCLUSIONS

In the first section of this chapter we reviewed the main features of the technological scene in India on the eve of structural adjustment. We noticed there that the characteristics attained during the 'closed economy and strong state intervention era' had begun to alter under the pressure of liberalizing and opening up the economy in the 1980s. Chief among the features in the late 1980s were lack of dynamism in technology absorption, absence of technological innovation and design capacity, spread of technological dualism, lack of significant structural change in the skill composition of the workforce, poor educational base, etc. We will argue below that the new policy regime introduced by the SAP is likely to entrench these negative features rather than help to overcome them.

The increasing dualism and polarization in the area of technology and skills is one of the outcomes of the conflict between rival interests: domestic capital vs foreign capital, the Indian state vs the Bretton Woods institutions, production for the domestic market vs the export market, the public sector vs the private sector, the 'sick' public sector vs the 'healthy' public sector, the large scale vs the small scale, etc.

One among several major consequences of these processes will be that medium- and large-scale firms will speed up their retooling with imported high tech, abandoning domestically produced standard tech as fast as they can afford to. In contrast, the small-scale sector will continue to depend on locally produced technology, becoming by stages its principal customer.

Acquisition of new skills: strategy for retraining

As indicated earlier in our analytical framework, high tech is characterized by high values in the degree of automation, science-relatedness and research intensity. The high values of these three features are now built into most industrial and infrastructural branches of the OECD countries, and present OECD research is geared to making them ever higher. Any *contemporary* technology from the OECD that India acquires with foreign equity will be of this kind, irrespective of whether the product or the process is 'classical' or not, e.g. metallurgy, industrial machinery, vehicles, cement, wood, glass, rubber, paper, printing, food processing, beverages, seeds, etc. (see the Indian government's list of 'the privileged thirty four' in the Appendix).

One immediate consequence will be that Indian firms will have to retrain their engineers and technicians to use, maintain and repair the new technology. Various branches of high tech share a common base in certain *new generic* fields of knowledge in science and engineering. There is therefore good ground for thinking that a substantial part of the retraining should be common to most firms, while the more narrowly specialized activity-specific skills could be imparted inside the firm. Since top quality and hands-on practicality are of the essence in such retraining, there are but a few institutions in India which can be entrusted with this task.

A number of questions have to be addressed urgently: who should mount common retraining courses, how should the costs be shared, where should the courses be located, is there any credible national expertise available to impart the training or is one obliged to rely heavily on expatriate expertise, etc.? The private and the public sector should jointly create an independent-minded task force, with no vested interests, to consider the questions and draft a strategy for retraining on a national basis.

The technological capabilities of workers below the level of technicians and the question of productivity

Usually, the introduction of high tech renders most semi-skilled, and some skilled, work redundant. (The limited number of skilled workers who will be retained by firms in the transition to high tech will have to undergo retraining of the kind offered to technicians.) Since, under the present, relatively just Indian labour laws, workers cannot in effect be retrenched, the private and the public sector will have to find other areas of work for them. This will be a huge challenge and a growing one. There are as yet no signs that any constructive, humane and productive strategy has been crafted to deal with this challenge.

It would be a tremendous waste of the existing technological capacity of India if the technical capabilities of 'potentially redundant' workers are not used productively. Theoretically, there are three ways in which their capacities can be so used.

First, if one has confidence in the official prognosis that the SAP will usher in an era of very high growth rates, the new industrial enterprises, both large and small, may be expected to absorb some of the retrenched workforce. But one cannot be sanguine about it. The 1980s' relatively high annual rates of industrial growth of 8 per cent occurred with almost no growth in jobs in the registered organized industrial sector. Growth in output was achieved through higher labour and technological productivities. The high-tech transition will in all likelihood attempt to continue this trend of high output growth with low job growth; that is in fact what it will have to do, if all that is asked of it in terms of high productivity, efficiency, quality and market competitiveness has to be delivered. So this route is likely to remain closed for the redundant workforce.

From the recent computations of Ghose (1993) one can infer that labour productivity in manufacturing during the second half of the 1980s maintained the increased positive levels it had attained in the first half. This trend seems less due to increasing skill content of the workforce than to increasing capital intensity of the means of production, retrenchment of labour and the phenomenon of jobless growth.

Further, as we have argued elsewhere (Bhagavan, 1992), productivity is not merely a function of shop floor efficiency, but also of crucial externalities like transport and energy infrastructure. It is not a coincidence that the boost in investment in railways, electric power generation and fossil fuel production preceded the 1980s' increases in both industrial output and productivity.

The *second route* is through small-scale industry. It is traditionally more labour intensive than large industry. It would be ideally suited to the levels of skill that the workers have. But to absorb labour at the rate required, it will have to grow at a much greater pace than it is now doing. But the wind is apparently blowing in the opposite direction. Potential small-scale investors are fighting shy of getting in, saying that the competition is fierce and market demand is stagnant.

The *third route* is a return to Keynes, with massive public investment in modern energy, transport and communication infrastructure, public civil engineering projects and social services. This will create massive numbers of new jobs, while at the same time conserving, upgrading and increasing the technological capabilities of the workforce.

In the present age of SAP-hegemony the third route may sound like science fiction, given the fierce hostility of the begetters of the SAP, the IMF and the World Bank, to anything that smells remotely Keynesian. But they may be forced to temper their market-fundamentalism under the pressure of the new employment-creating forces gathering pace in Western Europe. At the European Union (EU) summit meeting held in Corfu, Greece, in June 1994, the heads of the EU governments endorsed the neo-Keynesian proposals contained in the White Paper of Mr Jacques Delors, President of the European Commission, to create massive numbers of new jobs based on new skills. This is to be accomplished mainly through the Trans-European Networks (TENS) Programme comprising eleven transport and communication projects. To quote from the *Guardian* (June 1994), 'the summit agreed to step up governments' role in stimulating "the unprecedented technological revolution" which can lead to developments in teleworking, distance learning, road and air traffic management, health care networks and electronic tendering'. The Delors proposals are the product of the new economic thinking that has emerged in Western Europe over the last few years to grapple with the task of recovering from the disaster of the Reagan–Thatcher era of 'new liberalism' (Lane, 1993; Keegan, 1993; Lipietz, 1993).

Technology estates for small industry

Since technological dualism will continue to deepen in India, the question arises as to how to cater for the technological upgrading of the small-scale sector, which as we have seen above will be even more crucial in the SAP-era than it was before the SAP. The market, as one knows too well by now, will not do it unassisted. In fact, the small-scale sector in India owes its existence and growth to state protection. Because of its tremendous heterogeneity and extremely wide geographical dispersal, national technology suppliers cannot individually effectively inform and service this sector.

This prompts the suggestion that the state actively promotes the idea of small industrialists' associations themselves establishing technology estates in all medium-sized towns to provide technological information to the local small investors in the local language. The information should be backed up by regular demonstrations of nationally produced hardware and software. As these estates find their feet, they will also take on the role of channels of communication between the users and the domestic producers of technology, which it is to be hoped will bring about user-driven improvements, incremental or otherwise.

Technology absorption: how to rejig in-house R&D?

About 1200 industrial firms in India have in-house R&D units. The most highly skilled work they do is technology absorption. Technology design and innovation are at present beyond their capabilities and resources. In the transition to imported high tech, these R&D units are already confronting, and will continue to confront, the challenge of reskilling themselves to absorb the new technology. The kind of reskilling called for often involves a shift in their technological paradigm. It will demand of them that they not only theoretically understand the new concepts and the new way of reasoning, but also translate that understanding into shop floor practice.

The present in-house R&D units, which have evolved slowly to deal with the pre-high-tech situation, cannot be 'rejigged' overnight to take on the new challenge. There is little doubt that their capacity to absorb technology will go through a longish period of serious decline. Older professionals who are the intellectual leaders in their R&D units are likely to find that they cannot make the transition. A vicious circle of stress conditions leading to poor performance will set in.

Although the decline cannot be arrested in the short term, certain measures need to be put in place fairly soon to create the R&D capacity in the medium term that firms will need, if high tech is not to remain for ever a 'black box with buttons attached' for Indian industry. To this end, the private and public sectors should together commission experts (preferably from high-tech exporting countries) to analyze the entire complex of problems and suggest strategies for overcoming them.

Mere increases in hardware and software resources, in salaries and perks, and in intra-firm status, will not by themselves be sufficient to generate the motivation and the ambition to solve problems, which only intellectual passion can. Therefore one of the keys will be finding fresh, new recruits with the right cast of mind from the alumni of India's few high-quality science and engineering faculties to join the R&D teams. That will not be an easy task given the preference of the brightest professionals to emigrate to North America or Singapore.

Education, labour and the national research system

The likely impact of structural adjustment on the public funding of education in developing countries in general is best summarized in the following words from a World Bank study (Noss, 1992):

> Adjustment measures (undertaken with or without World Bank assistance) affect education through changes at the macro and micro levels of the economy. Adjustment at the macro level often implies a combination of budget containment measures for the public education system, limited access to post primary public education and higher user fees for education services at the secondary and tertiary levels. At the micro level, changes in household incomes and prices (user fees, reduced student subsidies) directly influence the demand for education by altering the opportunity cost of attending school. Household incomes also affect health and nutrition status, and thus indirectly influence attendance and learning. Finally, adjustment affects education through changes in markets and infrastructure (resulting from currency devaluation, fiscal and monetary restraint, and price liberalisation) that affect supply of education services and the opportunity cost of attending school.

In plain English what the above-mentioned measures could mean for secondary and higher education in India is, first, cuts in public funding, accompanied by the charging of fees, second, a decrease in the number of pupils and students from poorer households, third, a further deterioration of the public education system, and fourth, the strengthening of private education to the benefit of the higher-income households.

To go down the route charted by the SAP in the area of education is to jump from the frying pan into the fire. India's development ideology notwithstanding, the Indian government has over the last forty years neglected primary and secondary education in comparison with higher (tertiary) education. Since the education system has been and continues to be almost entirely in the hands of the Indian state, it cannot disclaim responsibility for the inequities and the utter lack of quality that have developed at all levels in the system (Shatrugna, 1993; Upendranath, 1993b).

The industrial and technological progress of India needs precisely the opposite of what the SAP recommends in education. A rapid advance on a broad front is only possible if the educational and technical levels of all the young in India are raised as a matter of the greatest urgency. And that is impossible in the Indian context without increased massive support from the state, but a support that is administered in a radically different way than at present. The need of the hour is not SAP-inspired dismantling of the public education system, but a revolutionary transformation of it to raise the quantity and quality of really skilled young people. What the present system is imparting is not education, but bits of ritual paper certifying that this or that exam has been passed with this or that grade.

India's neighbours in East Asia are worth notice. Their spectacular success in both economic and social development would not have been possible without their single-minded simultaneous pursuit of universalization of and high quality in primary and secondary education. In quality tests in science and mathematics administered in the early 1990s to high school pupils across a representative sample of the OECD and the developing countries, with India included, South Korea topped the list, with Japan coming next, Western Europe and North America on their heels, and India so far behind as to be invisible in the race.

That said, there is most definitely a need for draconian measures to convert the present higher education system from its present degraded state of being one vast conveyor belt graduate factory into a system that actually imparts knowledge. A restructuring of public funding based on the criteria of social equity, quality and merit, while simultaneously encouraging higher-income groups to take advantage of privatized institutions, would be the strategy to follow.

The present system of government national laboratories and institutes has outlived its original rationale. It is demonstrably not contributing to significant innovation in science and technology. Its impact on industry has been minimal. The move by the present Indian government progressively to reduce its commitment to this moribund system is a wise one. However, that does not mean that the state can afford not to fund scientific and technological R&D. Quite the contrary. Again, as with the educational system as a whole, the state needs to pump vastly more resources into R&D but along the lines of an entirely new strategy. What the new national R&D system should look like and how it should be put together are issues that should be publicly debated in India. The ideas that have recently emerged in the advanced industrialized countries on 'national innovation systems' would be of seminal value in such a debate and in arriving at future policy decisions (Nelson, 1993).

ACKNOWLEDGEMENTS

This is a shortened and revised version of a study that was commissioned by the South Asia Multidisciplinary Advisory Team (SAAT) of the International Labour Organization (ILO), based in New Delhi, whose support is gratefully acknowledged. It is a pleasure to thank Dr Rizwanul Islam and Dr Ajit Kumar Ghose of ILO-SAAT for their critical reading of the manuscript and valuable suggestions. Thanks are also due to two anonymous referees for their helpful comments.

APPENDIX: HIGH-PRIORITY INDUSTRIES WHICH QUALIFY FOR 51 PER CENT FOREIGN EQUITY HOLDING AND FOR AUTOMATIC APPROVAL OF FOREIGN TECHNOLOGY AGREEMENTS

1 Metallurgy
2 Boilers and steam generators
3 Prime movers (other than electrical generators)
4 Electrical equipment
5 Transportation equipment
6 Industrial machinery
7 Machine tools
8 Agricultural machinery
9 Earth moving machinery
10 Industrial instruments
11 Scientific and electro-medical instruments, and laboratory equipment
12 Nitrogenous and phosphatic fertilizers
13 Chemicals (other than fertilizers)
14 Drugs and pharmaceuticals
15 Paper and pulp, including paper products and industrial laminates
16 Automobile tyres and tubes
17 Plate glass
18 Ceramics
19 Cement products

20 High-technology reproduction and multiplication equipment
21 Carbon and carbon products
22 Pre-tensioned high-pressure RCC pipes
23 Rubber machinery
24 Printing machinery
25 Welding electrodes other than those for welding mild steel
26 Industrial synthetic diamonds
27 Photosynthesis improvers
28 Extraction and upgrading of minor oils
29 Pre-fabricated building material
30 Soya products
31 High-yielding hybrid seeds and synthetic seeds
32 All food processing, excluding flour, milk food and malted food, and excluding items reserved for the small-scale sector
33 Packaging for food processing industries, excluding items reserved for the small-scale sector
34 Hotel and tourism-related industry

REFERENCES

Alam, G. (1993) 'Research and Development by Indian Industry: A Study of the Determinants of its Size and Scope', Mimeo, Centre for Technology Studies, New Delhi.

Bardhan, P. (1984) *The Political Economy of Development in India*, Basil Blackwell, Oxford.

Bhagavan, M. R. (1987) 'A Critique of India's Economic Policies and Strategies', *Monthly Review* (New York), vol. 39, no. 3, July-August.

—— (1990) *Technological Advance in the Third World*, Zed Books, London.

—— (1992) 'Technological Change and Restructuring in Asian Industries: Implications for Human Resources Development', in M. Muqtada and A. Hildeman (eds) *Labour Markets and Human Resource Planning in Asia: Perspectives and Evidence*, UNDP and ARTEP/ILO, Geneva and New Delhi.

Curien, C. T. (1986) 'Caught in Contradictions of Mixed Economy', *Economic and Political Weekly* (Bombay), 12 April.

Das, T. K. (1993) 'Structural Reforms and Stabilisation Policies in India: Rationale and Medium-Term Outlook', in S. P. Gupta (ed.) *Liberalisation: Its Impact on the Indian Economy*, Macmillan, Delhi.

Desai, A. V. (1988) *Technology Absorption in Indian Industry*, Wiley Eastern, New Delhi.

—— (1990) 'Recent Technology Imports into India: Results of a Survey', *Development and Change*, vol. XXI, pp. 723–749.

Far Eastern Economic Review (1992) 'Time to catch up: India tries to bring science closer to business' (Dateline: Hamish McDonald in Bangalore), 10 December, pp. 45–46.

Freeman, C. (1982) *The Economics of Industrial Innovation*, Second Edition, Pinter, London.

Ghose, A. K. (1993) 'Employment in Organised Manufacturing in India', Mimeo, ARTEP/ILO, New Delhi.

Guardian Weekly (1994) 'Last words go to people and jobs' (Dateline: John Carvel in Corfu), 3 July, p. 5.

Gumaste, V. (1988) 'Anatomy of In-House R&D: A Case Study of Indian Automobile Industry', *Economic and Political Weekly* (Bombay), vol. XXIII, Review of Management, pp. M67–72.

Gupta, S. P. (ed.) (1993) *Liberalisation: Its Impact on the Indian Economy*, Macmillan, Delhi.

ILO-ARTEP (1992) Social Dimensions of Structural Adjustment in India, New Delhi.

India-DSIR (1992) Dept of Scientific and Industrial Research, Government of India, Annual Register of Foreign Collaborations, 1992 and preceding issues.

India-DST (1992) Dept of Science and Technology, Government of India, Research and Development Statistics, 1990–91 and preceding years.

Kathuria, S. (1989) 'Market Structure and Innovation', *Economic and Political Weekly* (Bombay), 26 August.

Katrak, H. (1989) 'Imported Technologies and R&D in a Newly Industrializing Country: The Experience of Indian Enterprises', *Journal of Development Economics*, vol. 31, July.

——(1990) 'Import of Technology and the Technological Effort of Indian Enterprises', *World Development*, vol. 18, no. 3.

Keegan, W. (1993) *The Spectre of Capitalism: The future of the world economy after the fall of communism*, Radius, London.

Kumar, N. (1987) 'Technology Imports and Local Research and Development in Indian Manufacturing', *The Developing Economies*, September.

Lall, S. (1987) *Learning to Industrialize: The Acquisition of Technological Capability by India*, Macmillan, Basingstoke.

——(1990) *Building Industrial Competitiveness in Developing Countries*, OECD Development Centre, Paris.

Lane, R. E. (1993) *The Market Experience*, Cambridge.

Lipietz, A. (1993) *Towards a New Economic Order: Post-Fordism, Ecology and Democracy*, Polity Press, London.

Nayyar, D. (1993) 'Indian Economy at the Cross Roads: Illusions and Realities', *Economic and Political Weekly* (Bombay), 10 April.

Nelson, R. R. (1993) *National Innovation Systems: A Comparative Analysis*, Oxford University Press, New York.

Noss, A. (1992) 'Education and Adjustment', World Bank Staff Paper, Washington, DC.

Patnaik, P. (1986) 'New Turn in Economic Policy: Contexts and Prospects', *Economic and Political Weekly* (Bombay), 7 June.

Raghuram, S. (ed.) (1992) *Development Policy: Issues and Challenges for the 90s*, HIVOS, Bangalore.

Sandesara, J. C. (1992) *Industrial Policy and Planning 1947–91*, Sage Publications, New Delhi.

Shatrugna, M. (1993) 'Education, Equity and Privatization', Mimeo, Seminar paper presented at the Institute of Public Enterprise, Hyderabad.

Sigurdson, J. (1990) 'The Internationalization of R&D: An interpretation of forces and responses', in J. Sigurdson (ed.) *Measuring the Dynamics of Technological Change*, Pinter, London.

Tyabji, N. (1993) 'Technological Collaborations and Partial Absorption: The failure of Indian industry in the 1980s', Mimeo, Madras Institute of Development Studies, Madras.

Upendranath, C. (1993a) 'Political Economy of Education in India', Mimeo, Institute for Social and Economic Change, Bangalore.

—— (1993b), 'SAP and Education: Issues related to equity', Mimeo, Institute for Social and Economic Change, Bangalore.

Vyasulu, V. (1993) 'The New Economic Policy and Technological Change: Towards New Initiatives', Mimeo, Institute of Public Enterprise, Hyderabad.

World Bank (1993) *The East Asian Miracle: Economic Growth and Public Policy*, Washington, DC.

World Development (1994) Special Section edited by Alice H. Amsden, vol. 22, no. 4, April.

7

DEVELOPMENTAL REGIONALISM

Björn Hettne

WORLD ORDER, REGIONALISM AND DEVELOPMENT

The 'new world order' is a fashionable concept today, just as 'the new international economic order' was in the 1970s (Cox, 1979; Krasner, 1985). Both are essentially ideological concepts, expressing particular interests. The latter was an articulation of the Third World preference for a more interventionist and redistributive world economy, the former has come to mean a market-oriented mode of allocation backed by US hegemonic power. Thus, albeit ideologically very different, both concepts suggest a world order determining the rules of the game of the international economic system.

The recent financial disturbances in Europe underline the importance of a certain degree of security and continuity for sustained economic development. An economic system presupposes a social order, i.e. a coherent system of rules, accepted by the actors making up the system. The market system of exchange does not in itself constitute an order. It is confined by a particular order and expressing its underlying value system, or normative content. Therefore, concrete market systems differ among themselves to the extent that their underlying social orders differ. In a transition between different orders, the market can only reflect the confusion and turbulence of this transition, but it will not by itself create order. Rather the self-seeking behaviour called 'maximization', if consistently adhered to, would lead to 'the end of organized society as we know it' (Kenneth Arrow, quoted in Hodgson, 1993, p. 4). The urge for order is thus becoming a major issue in world politics, and a crucial research field in international political economy, where it is emphasized that sustained economic transactions necessitate an institutional framework, sometimes specified as a 'hegemonic' position of one of the major political powers (Keohane, 1980, 1984; Cox, 1983; Gilpin, 1987). The 'hegemonic stability' thesis says that the post-war open world economy was institutionalized through the Bretton Woods system, which in turn was upheld by the hegemonic power of the USA.

Hegemony in this sense can be seen as a substitute for a world government guaranteeing the smooth functioning of a transnational economy. Hegemonic decline spells economic turbulence and political anarchy. Being less pessimistic, one could think of other post-hegemonic scenarios, for instance a regionalization of the world economy and the world order, by which is meant the political and legal framework within which economic transactions take place. It was generally assumed that a breakdown in the GATT negotiations would have led to trade war and economic chaos. It might, however, also have been a step towards a regionalized world order, i.e. a qualitatively different social order, less liberal, more neomercantilist (Hettne, 1993a, b; Hettne and Inotai, 1994).

This chapter argues that some kind of regionalization will come anyhow, and that this will have an impact on the pattern of and the conditions for development in the 1990s. I am here concerned only with this particular scenario. Whether the world is becoming regionalized or not, it is at least obvious that new regional formations are emerging and that old regional organizations are reactivated. There is also a renewed academic interest in regionalism, indicating that something has happened. The current interest in regionalism, often summarized as 'the new regionalism' comes from several disciplines and has led to some unavoidable conceptual confusion. The 'new' regionalism certainly includes trade arrangements (de Melo and Panagariya, 1993; Anderson and Blackhurst, 1993; Salvatore, 1993) but it goes much beyond that. Regional integration implies, for instance, a security dimension, which is quite essential to the dynamics of the integration process. It does not make sense to distinguish the 'economics' of integration, on the one hand, from the 'politics' of disintegration, on the other. Integration and disintegration form part of the same dialectical process and should be dealt with within a single theoretical framework. To develop such a framework, a 'political economy of integration and disintegration', is a challenge for the social sciences. Regional integration also involves ecological issues. Few serious ecological problems can be solved within the framework of the nation state. Some ecological problems are bilateral, some are global, quite a few are regional. A third dimension of the new regionalism is the development strategy implied in regional integration activities such as the conscious fostering of complementarities, industrial projects, joint investments in transport, infrastructure, etc. This, what I call developmental regionalism, is the focus of this essay.

I would thus like to make a very clear distinction between the new regionalism and the kind of regional integration in various parts of the world we have seen so far. These experiences have been largely negative; the regions were not natural economic regions but formed by security interests; they were usually confined to trade agreements of limited relevance for countries with similar types of economies; uneven development and centre-periphery polarization were reproduced within the region.

The new regionalism differs from the old regionalism, both concepts used as ideal types, in the following respects:

1 Whereas the old regionalism was formed in a bipolar cold war context, the new is taking shape in a multi-polar world order, in which the former superpowers, in spite of their military superiority and of course in varying degrees, are being degraded to regional powers, competing with other emerging regional powers.

2 Whereas the old regionalism was created 'from above' (i.e. by the superpowers), the new is a more spontaneous process from within the region and also 'from below' (in the sense that the constituent states themselves are main actors). There are also other actors such as firms, labour unions and different kinds of social movements which are playing an increasingly important role.

3 Whereas the old regionalism, as far as economic integration is concerned, was inward oriented and protectionist, the new is often described as 'open', and thus compatible with an interdependent world economy. However, the idea of a certain degree of preferential treatment with the region is indicated or implied. How this somewhat contradictory balance between universal GATT regulations and specific regional concerns will be kept is left open. In my definition of new regionalism, I rather stress this ambiguity between 'opened' and 'closed' regionalism.

4 Whereas the old regionalism was specific with regard to objectives, some organizations were security oriented and others were economically oriented, the new is a more comprehensive, multi-dimensional process. This includes trade and economic integration, but also the environment, social policy, security and democracy: the whole issue of accountability and legitimacy.

5 Whereas the old regionalism only concerned relations between formally sovereign states, the new forms part of a global structural transformation in which non-state actors are active and manifest themselves at several levels of the global system. It can therefore not be understood only from the point of view of the single region. It can be defined as a world order concept, since any particular regionalization process has systemic repercussions within and between single regions throughout the world, thus shaping the way in which the world is organized.

This definition implies that the new regionalism is different from the three much discussed trading blocs, or, rather, the three trading blocs differ in terms of what I call 'regionness' (Hettne and Inotai, 1994). The basic idea here is 'subjectification', from region as geographical entity to region as acting subject, or what the late Dudley Seers referred to as 'extended nationalism' (Seers, 1983).

The European Community is now changing from being simply a free trade area into becoming some kind of political union with a relatively high degree of 'regionness'. Highly diverging political strategies are competing to shape the future Europe, most importantly the 'social capitalism' of continental Europe versus the Anglo-Saxon neoliberal form. Europe represents the most advanced regional arrangement the world has seen, and thus serves as a paradigm for the new regionalism even if it naturally differs a lot from one part of the world to another. Europe is often referred to as an example to follow by other regional organizations, such as ASEAN, SAARC and OAU, to judge from recent summit meetings of these organizations. In more negative terms, the integration process in Europe is rather seen as a threat to the global trade system, the so-called 'Fortress Europe', and therefore a pretext for organizing competing regional trade systems, such as NAFTA or EAEC (the East Asian organization proposed by the Malaysian prime minister).

NAFTA, the recently concluded trade agreement between the USA, Canada and Mexico, is a free trade area, nothing less and nothing more. The issue of a social dimension is not raised, neither is the security dimension. There is little to suggest that a genuine regional identity is emerging among the traditionally not very closely related subregions. On the other hand these subregions are themselves heterogeneous, in a way that is reminiscent of the region at large. This facilitates further regionalization at least to the extent that nationalist particularism is a stumbling block. In view of the strong integration of the Caribbean and Central American subregions in the North American market, their participation in NAFTA is a matter of time. Going further south we can note a stronger hesitation towards 'North Americanization' resulting in the MERCOSUR project.

The Asia-Pacific is so far neither a free trade area nor a region. Most countries in this 'region' (if it can be so called) are dependent and committed to a wide-open world economy, what often is called global interdependence, and regionalism is merely a precautionary strategy. If an eventual fragmentation of the world economy occurs, it is better to be prepared. Asia-Pacific is becoming the new centre of global capitalism. It can also be seen as an emerging, albeit still non-existing, trade bloc under the leadership of Japan, depending on the relative degrees of cooperation and conflict among competing capitalisms: North America, Europe and Asia-Pacific. It contains several potential regional formations, the shapes of which are still uncertain due to unresolved security dilemmas.

The eventual conclusion of the GATT negotiations guarantees that the trading blocs continue to keep their borders relatively open, but this does not eliminate continued regionalism in one form or the other. Rather, the agreement was concluded among the three trading blocs, and other countries, for instance India, had no impact whatsoever on the treaty. In India large anti-GATT demonstrations took place. The conclusion drawn among the 'outsiders' was rather that continued efforts at regionalization 'at home' were imperative.

Regionalism and globalism are related to each other in a rather intricate way. A trading bloc is compatible with GATT rules, and the emerging three blocs can be seen as a kind of decentralized GATT system. A 'Fortress', whether European or North American, is, of course, not compatible with GATT regulations. The new regionalism is emerging in the grey area between the free trade area model, on the one hand, and the Fortress model, on the other. It may go either way, and some regional projects are introverted, others more extroverted (open regionalism).

Regional cooperation as such is not a new idea, but it is now possible to see the emergence of a 'new regionalism' throughout the world. Basic insights and innovations in social science remain relevant, even if they have to be adapted to new situations. Therefore it is sometimes inspiring to return to the social science classics. I have been particularly inspired by the work of the Hungarian economic historian Karl Polanyi, from whom I have borrowed two ideas which are relevant in this context: the concept of the 'double movement', and 'regionalism' as opposed to 'universal capitalism'.

According to Polanyi (1957), modern society must be understood as a result of both market expansion ('the first movement') and the self-protection of society against the disruptive and destabilizing effects of the market ('the second movement'). As market exchange can only be amoral, or morally neutral, it is for the political regime to deal with the consequences of the way in which an unregulated market operates. Thus, society tends to change in accordance with the double movement. After a phase of disembedment, the economy tends to be re-embedded in society. Paradoxically, even the process of disembedment presupposes a strong and consciously active state (Hodgson, 1993). The market cannot liberate itself.

The second idea borrowed from Polanyi is the idea of regionalism itself, first developed in an article from the year 1945. This was just after the conclusion of a great war, when the eventual shape of the new world order was an open question, a situation rather similar to the one we are just living through after the cold war. The USA was then preparing itself for the role as the guardian of the still-to-be-born Bretton Woods system. Polanyi warned against the inherent instability of a liberal world order based on the market and hegemonic powers, and recommended a regional world order with some element of planning as a more stable system.

What is, then, the connection between the two ideas: regionalism and the double movement? Previously, the self-protection of society was carried out mainly by the state, on the level of the nation state. This is no longer possible (for small and weak states it never was), and it is my contention that the current phenomenon of the more introverted and protective variety of regionalism should be seen as a manifestation of the second movement, the self-protection of society, on the level of the region, as a social reaction against the global market expansion which took place in the 1980s and is the predominant trend today.

In the current transformation of the world economy, regionalism can thus be seen as a modifying force with regard to the mainstream interdependence scenario. In the very long run this contradiction may be transcended, and a regionalized world order/world economy may be seen as a step towards an institutionalized integrated world order. In the medium-run perspective, however, national development strategies may have to adapt to the dynamics of a more regionalized world. In any case the regional factor will play a more important role in shaping future patterns of development and conditions for development assistance.

THE STRATEGY OF DEVELOPMENTAL REGIONALISM

Development is only one dimension of the new regionalism, which has many causes and serves many purposes, but it is the one we focus upon here. Regionalism as development policy has been tried in all parts of the world, and it seems to be a more or less general consensus that it has been a failure.

It is therefore essential to grasp the difference between the 'old' and the 'new' regionalism from a developmental perspective. Why has regional cooperation failed to generate development, and how can the regional strategy be made more relevant? First, the old regionalism was often imposed from outside for geopolitical reasons, and in such cases there were few incentives for economic cooperation, particularly if the 'natural' economic region was divided in accordance with the cold war pattern. Second, the attempts at regional cooperation/integration that actually took place were often inherited from colonial schemes and did not go far beyond the signing of free trade treaties between what essentially had been colonial empires. Trade was never a sufficient field of cooperation owing to the lack of complementarities between neighbouring countries. The outcome was rarely encouraging, as the global pattern of uneven development was reproduced within the region with political tensions as a result. However, a distinction should be made between exchange-based free trade areas (such as the Latin American Free Trade Area) and common markets also involving conscious efforts to specialize production (such as the Central American Common Market and the Andean Pact). The former approach is based on considerations of static comparative advantage, the latter more dynamic (Mytelka, 1992). Neither was very successful, though.

In contrast, the 'new' regionalism is more political, and its approach to free trade cautious, far from autarkic but more selective in its external relations. It is careful to see to the interests of the region as a whole, for instance in the case of natural resources. It is well known that ecological and political borders rarely coincide and it is, furthermore, increasingly realized that few serious ecological problems can be solved within the framework of the nation state. Some problems are bilateral, some are global, quite a few are regional. The regional are often related to water: coastal waters, rivers and ground water. Examples are the South China Sea, Barents Sea, the South Asian river systems, the Mekong River system, the Nile, Euphrates–Tigris, and the uneven exploitation of ground water resources in the areas around Jordan. As is evident these issues cannot be studied in separation from the question of regional security.

Another imperative for regional cooperation is the increasingly tense and destabilized security situation in regions where individual countries are becoming black holes. Third, the current transformation of the world economy and the emergence of economic blocs make it necessary for the many excluded countries to stick together in order not to be completely dwarfed. In addition to these imperatives related to the current transformation of world economy and world order, we must of course add the classical arguments, such as territorial size, economies of scale and externalities.

The levels of regionness between regions in the process of being formed will continue to be uneven, but only the future will decide which levels will be reached by which regional formations, and where the balance between regionalization and globalization will be struck.

Developmental regionalism may provide solutions to many development problems for the South:

- Self-reliance was never viable on the national level (at least for most countries) but may be a feasible development strategy on the regional (collective self-reliance). This is the *viable economy argument*. It could be further extended to the 'societal viability' argument (or social sustainability argument). The emphasis on soundness of the artificially isolated economic system, separated from society, has created a new social dualism. The purpose of the new regionalism is to prevent such cases of national disintegration by including social security concerns, whereas neoliberal 'market regionalism' reinforces processes of transnational integration and national disintegration.
- The viable economy argument is particularly relevant in the case of microstates, who either have to cooperate or become client states of the 'core countries' or tourist resorts for the richer states. This is the *argument of sufficient size*. This argument which has been elaborated in the Caribbean context has lost some of its force but cannot be neglected.
- Collective bargaining on the level of the region could improve the economic position of marginalized Third World countries in the world system, or protect the structural position of successful export countries. This is the *argument of effective articulation* in the world economy.
- Regional conflict resolution will eliminate distorted investment patterns as the security fund could be tapped for more productive use. This is the *peace dividend argument*.

– The issues of development, security and peace, and ecological sustainability form one integrated complex, at the same time as they constitute as many imperatives for deepening regional cooperation, if not regional integration. This is the *sustainability argument*.

THE ARGUMENTS ILLUMINATED

The arguments for developmental regionalism apply in varying degrees to all world regions, but in order to illuminate them further we shall relate specific arguments to the regions where they seem most significant.

The viable economy argument: Africa

In Sub-Saharan Africa (SSA) there has been little regional integration, simply because there is little to integrate in the first place. Therefore, there is an urgent need for a broader and more dynamic concept of development, beyond 'stabilization'. Again this is only possible within a framework of regional cooperation. The 'dynamic approach' to regional integration (Robson, 1968) must be re-emphasized and the model of 'development integration' (Østergaard, 1993) further developed. Above all, this must become a political imperative among African leaders as the only way to halt the continued marginalization of the continent. This also implies a more realistic view on political intervention in the economic process than has been the case during the last decade. If the great discovery of the 1980s was that political intervention is not necessarily good, the discovery of the 1990s may be that it is not necessarily bad either. 'Developmental regionalism' has thus been the main issue in Africa. The nation state system is more or less dead, and the concept of a national development process is dying with it. The cruel choice seems to be: regionalization or recolonization.

At the 1991 OAU summit in Abuja it was repeatedly stressed that the ongoing integration of Europe called for a collective response from the member states, in the form of an *African Economic Community* (AEC). The theme of the summit was the threatening marginalization of Africa, to which regionalism was then seen as the remedy. Many previous initiatives have of course been taken in this direction, for instance the *Lagos Plan of Action* (1980), but undoubtedly the issue now has assumed a special urgency. The implementation of the AEC will take decades, and the first five-year period will, realistically, be devoted to the strengthening of existing regional economic communities as building blocs in the creation of a continentwide unity. Promising efforts are being made.

One important subregional initiative in the context of the new regionalism, at least in terms of declared objectives, is SADCC (*Southern Africa Development Cooperation Conference*), covering ten countries. The main function of SADCC (now SADC, i.e. Southern Africa Development Community) was originally to reduce the dependence on South Africa, a regional power with evident designs of regional control through the destabilization of 'hostile' regimes. Thus, it is a fairly clear example of 'the new regionalism', since SADCC was not simply based on the common market concept but had wider political objectives. So far, however, the instruments have been lacking and no substantial supranational powers conferred (Tostensen, 1992). Attempts are now being made to upgrade the level of regional integration by establishing a formal treaty. The most recent SADC documents indicate an awareness of the need for political intervention to prevent regional economic disparities from destabilizing the security situation. The areas to be covered by SADC are (1) food security, land and agriculture; (2) infrastructure and services; (3) industry, trade, investment and finance; (4) human resources development, science and technology; (5) natural resources and environment; (6) social welfare, information and culture; (7) politics, diplomacy, international relations, peace and security.

After apartheid has been declared a 'closed book', the agenda for regional cooperation in southern Africa will change fundamentally – and the incentives will perhaps become positive rather than negative.

Much depends on the character of a post-apartheid regime, not only for southern Africa but for the whole of Sub-Saharan Africa. Three possible scenarios can be mentioned (Martin, 1991): (1) 'regional restabilization' under South African dominance, (2) regional breakup, peripheralization and bilateralization of internal and external relations, and (3) a neoregional alternative implying regional restructuring based on a symmetric and self-reliant pattern of development. The last one is a very optimistic scenario.

However, the prospects for regional cooperation are beginning to look brighter, partly as a result of the weakening of the previously so almighty nation states as the dominant political institutions. In the Horn of Africa, for instance, the record of conflict is longer than the record of cooperation, but in recent years joint efforts have been made to combat an enemy that in the long run may prove more formidable than even war, namely the deteriorating environment. What is more, the two threats are most likely linked (Molvaer, 1990, 1991). Thus, there is an urgent need for regional cooperation. The countries in the region (Somalia, Djibouti, Ethiopia, Eritrea and Sudan) have (in January 1986) established the *Intergovernmental Authority on Drought and Development* (IGADD). Normally, there must be an embryonic regional framework to build upon. However, even in the Horn, a pattern of regional cooperation is slowly beginning to emerge. For the first time in decades the countries in the region do not have any open conflicts among themselves (*Horn of Africa Bulletin*, vol. 5, no. 4, July–Aug., 1993).

In West Africa, where the major regional initiative ECOWAS has been more or less paralysed for a long time, there are signs of economic and political homogenization and a somewhat more active regionalism.

National repressive regimes are crumbling, the 'socialist' experiments are over, and even old 'liberal' autocracies such as Côte d'Ivoire are slowly democratizing. The delinking of the state apparatus from elite interests may lead to a strengthening of the regional as well as the local level – the regional because of the development imperative, the local because this is where the democratic forces are.

Of importance here is the ongoing democratization, the so-called 'second liberation', in Africa, including South Africa, which, to the extent that there is a democratic political culture underneath the authoritarian model, will increase the political homogeneity of the region, although the political winds are unpredictable (Riley, 1992).

Similarly, economic policies are 'harmonized' owing to the dramatically increased dependence on the IMF and the World Bank, as well as the donor countries. The new political conditionalities can be criticized from many points of view, but they undoubtedly harmonize the political cultures in the various nation states. The problem is whether the externally imposed economic policies are consistent with internal political pluralism in unstable states.

The argument of sufficient size: the Caribbean Basin

In a world of growing interdependence and increasing specialization the problem of size in economic development is no longer that much discussed. This is not to say that it traditionally has been of great concern. Whereas orthodox liberal theory abstracted from the existence of national boundaries and presupposed a free flow of the factors of production, socialist theory was typically linked to the peculiar (and now discredited) experience of the Soviet Union. The recommendations implied in these two orthodoxies were: either to specialize and reap the benefits from comparative advantages and economies of scale, or to develop towards national autarky through the establishment of heavy industries, making the maximum use of the national market and domestic resources.

The discussion on size and self-reliance became a theoretical field of special concern for Caribbean economists. One important contribution was that of W. G. Demas who saw structural transformation as the essential ingredient of self-sustained economic growth (Demas, 1965). As such a transformation is hard to achieve in a small economy, integration of the region in a common market system was advocated. Such a policy (the creation of CARIFTA – the Caribbean Free Trade Association) has not been very successful, however, for reasons largely connected with the problem of dependence (Axline, 1979). Consequently, the attention of the Caribbean economists turned towards dependence. It is against this intellectual background that one should see the work of Clive Thomas (Thomas, 1974), who rejected regional integration under capitalism as a viable strategy and instead tried to develop a strategy for planned transition to social-ism with special reference to small dependent national economies. Here he could draw upon the long Caribbean debate. Today regionalism is again given more urgency in the region, albeit not in a socialist framework.

The Caribbean and the smaller Central American states have strong incentives for regional cooperation, and the change of regime in Nicaragua has increased the regional political homogeneity and consequently the scope for regional initiatives. So has the settlement of the border conflict between Honduras and El Salvador. The crucial issue is whether the countries can develop a common approach to the emerging USA–Canada–Mexico bloc, or whether they will join this bloc as individual client states, and thus become 'North Americanized'.

The USA traditionally follows a policy of bilateralism which does not facilitate regional cooperation. On the other hand the European connection through the Lomé framework is pushing these countries towards a wider community. The European Single Market has provided incentives both for a Caribbean deepening towards a more integrated market (1993) and for an enlargement. In the Caribbean, the thirteen-member regional organization CARICOM now contains less than 6 million people. There are only 32 million people in the greater Caribbean. The next step would therefore be to form a Caribbean Basin region including Central America. There is widespread concern that the Caribbean risks being marginalized in a world of large trading blocs (*Caribbean Information*, vol. 14, no. 1). Conse-quently, the islands are more or less ready for a degree of regional integra-tion beyond the old colonially based cultural areas.

The disappearance of the Soviet factor will further eliminate artificial cold war frontiers and increase the political homogeneity of the region. At the same time, changes in the external world are creating new difficulties. The privileged treatment of some countries in a position to play the geopolitical card will disappear. All the countries of the region will now have to cooperate regionally.

The Caribbean countries face in an extreme form problems that are common to all exporters which, in an era of changing structure of trade, are dependent on trade preferences (Stevens, 1991). In the emerging world economy the Caribbean prospects are bleak. In fact this region may be one of the main losers from '1992'. In no region are the arguments for region-alism stronger, in no region are the obstacles to regionalism greater. Be-tween the many islands there are cleavages due to colonial history and language, within the islands there are what has been called 'dual societies', characterized by their lack of common civic culture. Thus not only the region but the societies within the region and within each country are fragmented and divided. For this reason it is realistic to expect that econ-omic, as well as geopolitical, factors will push the Caribbean, just like Central America, towards NAFTA, either as a group or as single countries.

This view has already been widely expressed in the region (*Caribbean Information*, vol. 15, no. 6). A similar dilemma can be identified also in continental Latin America, where countries such as Chile have a choice to be 'North Americanized' or to join the Latin alternative, MERCOSUR (Dreifuss, 1993).

The argument of effective global articulation: Southeast Asia

Southeast Asia has been divided into two economic and political blocs, one extroverted and the other introverted: ASEAN (Indonesia, Thailand, Singapore, Malaysia, the Philippines and – since 1984 – Brunei) and the 'Indochinese' area or Mekong River Basin (Vietnam, Kampuchea and Laos). The latter subregion has been under communist rule with Vietnam exercising subregional hegemony. This role is now played down at the same time as market-oriented economic policies (*doimoi*) are tried. Thus, the introverted region is opening up.

Vietnam, and behind it the Soviet Union, was earlier seen as a grave threat by the ASEAN countries. This security complex is the reason why ASEAN has worked rather well as a regional organization. The source of common cause and identity was thus partly an external threat, and there were few incentives for economic cooperation. Only recently (January 1993) a free trade agreement was agreed to be realized within a fifteen-year period. Many doubt that this free trade zone will be realized. ASEAN countries are direct competitors in many areas and it will take a long time for them to develop into complementary economies. From the very beginning ASEAN was a political, rather than an economic, organization (Yamakage, 1990), and now the political preconditions are rapidly changing.

The countries in ASEAN could be described as capitalist in economic terms and conservative in political terms, although, for instance, Singapore and Indonesia differ significantly in their economic policies. The economic integration that has taken place so far is rather modest, and the figure for intra-region trade is still only about 20 per cent.

The national economies are outward oriented, and the political systems are formally democratic but in practice more or less authoritarian. Developmental authoritarianism in fact constitutes the homogenizing political factor. The ASEAN countries are in various phases of an NIC-type development path. Problems on the international market usually reinforce domestic authoritarianism due to the strong two-way causal relationship between economic growth and political stability. Economic growth and redistribution is a precondition for ethnic peace, political stability a precondition for the economic confidence expressed by international capital towards the region.

This 'open regionalism' is thus a way to articulate interests within the region *vis-à-vis* the globalization process. There are, however, also expressions of a more exclusive regionalism. In 1990 the Malaysian prime minister Mahathir (in frustration over drawn-out GATT negotiations) urged Japan to act as the leader of an East Asian Economic Grouping (EAEG), which would create an East Asian and Southeast Asian superbloc with a Sino-Japanese core. EAEG (it has since been modestly renamed East Asia Economic Caucus – EAEC) would be a sort of response to the threat of European and North American 'fortresses'. The EAEC proposal is slowly gaining support among other ASEAN countries, whereas the East Asian countries, particularly Japan and South Korea, have taken a more sceptical attitude. So has the USA and the World Bank.

A more comprehensive alternative to 'closed regionalism' is the fifteen-member-strong forum for *Asia Pacific Economic Cooperation* (APEC) which was set up in 1989 and will be further developed in case GATT fails. Thus, it has regional and interregional trade expansion as its main goal (*Asiaweek*, 28 August 1992). APEC can be compared with 'the Atlantic project' in Europe. It is a transregional network providing a bridge for the USA in the area, and therefore supported by US-oriented regimes and opposed by spokespeople for a genuinely Asian regionalism.

The peace dividend argument: the Middle East

The Middle East 'region', which can be seen as a region mainly in the geographical sense, is in many ways the most complex of the Third World regions. Regionalism is therefore bound to emerge and resurge in different manifestations and constellations, and has to transcend many contradictions. The region is extremely diverse in ethnic terms, at the same time as it is largely dominated by one religion and (with a few important exceptions) one linguistic culture. Great ambitions towards regional unity coexist with constant conflicts between states and ethnic groups.

Of importance is the frustrated, but yet surviving, idea of an Arab Nation, nurtured not least by Arabic Christian minorities – particularly in the initial period of Arab nationalism – and today politically articulated in Syrian and Iraqi Ba'athism. This idea, badly injured by the Gulf War, corresponds to a potential 'regional civil society' among the Arabs, today at best a sleeping potentiality. With the rise of political Islamic movements in the 1980s and 1990s, it looks as though Islam today has gained the upper hand over pan-Arabism, and therefore a broader 'community' for identity purposes is provided at the same time as the internal cleavages remain.

Peace is thus a necessity for development. Since conflict is the main characteristic of the region, the best way of approaching the regional issue is through the regional complex concept, suggested by Barry Buzan (1991). It is the region of 'realist thinking' *par préférence*. The artificial boundaries, the competing elites, and the lack of democratic tradition make the power play between heavily armed states as close to Machiavelli's world as one can come. Superpower involvement during the cold war followed the same cynical logic.

The problem of regional hegemonism has a long historical tradition and there are several competing powers with a potential for regional leadership or hegemony, but also with decisive handicaps in performing that particular role. Iraq was the strongest candidate before the war that crippled it. Syria and Egypt, the remaining Arab contenders, have become too much involved with the West to be credible in the poor Arab world. Turkey is an outsider, being a member of NATO and nurturing ambitions to become a European state, but now instead finding a new role in Central Asia. Iran is feared throughout the region as non-Arabic, Shiite (i.e. non-Sunnite) and expansionist.

Finally, we have the pervasive Arab–Israeli conflict, which to a large extent has marked the political culture of the region.

It is very difficult to foresee what a new security system in the Middle East may look like. Ironically, Sadam Hussein is still needed for balance of power purposes, since no alternative military government is coming forward to guarantee the status quo. What now binds the countries together is their fear of Iraq becoming the regional hegemonic power. The problems to be solved are, however, many: first of all to contain the power and influence of Iran, to find a solution to the Palestine question, and to reduce the gap between the rich Gulf states and the poor Arab masses. Then there is a host of minority and human rights problems of which the most urgent is the Kurd question affecting a number of neighbouring countries.

The major problem, thus, lies in the field of security. Peace will open a new world, and therefore the recent breakthrough in the Israel–Palestine peace process is extremely important. A regional development process based on the Israel–Jordan–Palestine triangle is essential for the consolidation of the peace process, and again for further development in the whole region, even if the pattern of conflict is more complex than this brief treatment can clarify.

The sustainability argument: South Asia

In 1985 South Asian regional cooperation after five years of preparations at last got its own organization: South Asian Association for Regional Cooperation (SAARC). The initiative originated from Bangladesh with a proposal made by President Ziaur Rahman in 1980. Significantly, academic scholars from the region have been very active developing the concept. India was rather lukewarm, while the smaller countries in regional cooperation saw a possibility to coordinate their resistance to Indian control (Muni, 1985, 1992). Regional cooperation has in fact been initiated as a counterforce to regional hegemonism.

South Asia is thus one of the last regions to wake up to the challenge of the new regionalism. It has been called 'a region without regionalism' (Palmer,

1991, p. 75). It has been a region of distrust and conflict, penetrated by external powers, which, as a matter of fact, have been invited by the states of the region as part of their internal hostilities. Until the mid-1980s there was no regional cooperation whatsoever. To the extent that one can say that South Asia had reached a certain level of regionness, its network of relations was mainly conflictive. The region has experienced no less than three wars between the two major powers. The dominant power has a record of bilateral conflict with most of the other states in the region. Thus there are quite a number of obstacles to overcome. Currently, the region is being marginalized in the world economy. The concept of 'Asia' has more and more come to mean East and Southeast Asia (Chambers, 1993).

So far, SAARC's main constraints are the Indo-Pakistan and the Indo-Sri Lanka tensions. The world is going through dramatic structural changes, and there are two different types of options for the South Asian countries – regional or national. In principle there is little difference between the two levels, since the regional diversity is reflected within the individual states as well. There is no rationale for an Indian or Pakistani nation which does not apply to the South Asian region as a whole. The reason to search for regional solutions is that bilateral suspicion makes any other solution fragile.

The overall trend in the region is towards occasionally crisis-ridden muddling-through democracies, where the threats from intrastate heterogeneity are more problematic than interstate conflicts. However, to an increasing degree, internal and external issues become interwoven.

Regional cooperation in the economic field, or developmental regionalism, is at best embryonic. The economic rationale is not overwhelming, but has to be created (Adiseshiah, 1987). The slow process of economic convergence has at least started. In the field of resource management, which is of concern here, there is, owing to the shared river systems, strong interdependencies which so far have been a source of conflict rather than cooperation. They may also be turned into regionalist imperatives.

CONCLUSION

In the current transformation of the world economy, regionalism can thus be seen as an alternative to the interdependence scenario. In the very long run this contradiction may be transcended, and a regionalized world order/world economy may be seen as a step towards an institutionalized integrated world order. In the medium-run perspective, national development strategies may have to adapt to a more regionalized world. In any case the regional factor will play a more important role in shaping future patterns of development and conditions for development assistance.

Developmental regionalism is a package that, although with variations as to its content, is relevant in all emerging regions, even in the marginalized areas. Even if 'delinking' is no longer on the agenda, its general orientation

173

may be more or less offensive/defensive, or extroverted/introverted. It contains the traditional arguments for regional cooperation such as territorial size and economies of scale, but, more significantly, adds some which are expressing new concerns and uncertainties in the current transformation of the world order and world economy.

REFERENCES

Adiseshia, M. (1987) 'The Economic Rationale of SAARC', *South Asia Journal*, vol. 1, no. 1.

Anderson, Kym and Blackhurst, Richard (eds) (1993) *Regional Integration and the Global Trading System*, Harvester Wheatsheaf, Hemel Hempstead.

Axline, A. (1979) *Caribbean Integration. The Politics of Integration*, Pinter, London.

Buzan, B. (1991) *People, States and Fear: An Agenda for International Security Studies in the Post-Cold War Era*, Harvester Wheatsheaf, Hemel Hempstead.

Chambers, Valerie (1993) 'ASEAN-EC Relations: the Intersection of two Regional Groupings or the Rise of Economic Rivals', *Journal of Asian Business*, vol. 9, no. 2, pp. 55–276.

Cox, R. W. (1979) 'Ideologies and the New International Economic Order: Reflections on some recent literature', *International Organization*, vol. 33, no. 2, pp. 257–267.

—— (1983) 'Gramsci, Hegemony and International Relations. An Essay in Method', *Millenium*, vol. 12, no. 2, pp. 162–175.

Demas, W. G. (1965) *The Economics of Development in Small Countries with Special Reference to the Caribbean*, McGill University Press, Montreal.

de Melo, Jaime and Panagariya, Arvind (eds) (1993) *New Dimensions in Regional Inegration*, Cambridge University Press, Cambridge.

Dreifuss, A. (1993) 'Mercosul: A Point of View', Paper presented at the GEMDEV-EADI Seminar on Intégration – désintégration régionale à l'echelle des continents, 13–14 May 1993.

Gilpin, R. (1981, 1987) *The Political Economy of International Relations*, Princeton University Press, Princeton, NJ.

Hettne, B. (1993a) 'The Concept of Neomercantilism', in Lars Magnusson (ed.) *Mercantilist Economies*, Kluwer, Boston.

—— (1993b) 'Neo-Mercantilism: The Pursuit of Regionness', *Cooperation and Conflict*, vol. 28, no. 3, pp. 211–232.

Hettne, B. and Inotai, A. (1994) *The New Regionalism*, WIDER, Helsinki.

Hodgson, G. M. (1993) *Economics and Evolution*, Polity Press, Cambridge.

Keohane, R. O. (1980) 'The Theory of Hegemonic Stability and Changes in International Economic Regimes, 1966–77', in O. R. Holsti *et al.* (eds) *Change in the International System*, Westview Press, Boulder, CO.

—— (1984) *After Hegemony: Cooperation and Discord in the World Political Economy*, Princeton University Press, Princeton, NJ.

Krasner, S. D. (1985) *Structural Conflict: The Third World Against Global Liberalism*, University of California Press, Berkeley, Los Angeles, London.

Martin, William G. (1991) 'The Future of Southern Africa: What Prospects After Majority Rule?', *Review of African Political Economy*, no. 50, pp. 115–134.

Molvaer, R. K. (1990) 'Environmental Cooperation in the Horn of Africa. A UNEP Perspective', *Bulletin of Peace Proposals*, vol. 21, no. 2, pp. 135–142.

—— (1991) 'Environmentally Induced Conflicts? A Discussion Based on Studies from the Horn of Africa', *Bulletin of Peace Proposals*, vol. 22, no. 2, pp. 175–188.

Muni, S. D. (1985) 'SARC: Building Regions from Below', *Asian Survey*, vol. XXV, no. 4 (April).

——(1992) 'Changing Global Order and Cooperative Regionalism: The Case of Southern Asia', in Helena Lindolm (ed.) *Approaches to the Study of International Political Economy*, Padrigu, Göteborg.

Mytelka, Lynn K. (1992) *South-South Cooperation in a Global Perspective*, OECD Development Centre, Paris.

Østergaard, Tom (1993) 'Classical Models of Regional Integration – What Relevance for Southern Africa?', in Bertil Odén (ed.) *Southern Africa after Apartheid. Regional Integration and External Resources*, The Scandinavian Institute of African Studies, Uppsala.

Palmer, N. D. (1991) *The New Regionalism in Asia and the Pacific*, Lexington Books, Lexington, MA.

Polanyi, K. (1945) 'Universal Capitalism or Regional Planning', *The London Quarterly of World Affairs*, January.

——(1957) *The Great Transformation*, Beacon Press, Boston.

Riley, Stephen P. (1992) 'Political Adjustment or Domestic Pressure: Democratic politics and political choice in Africa', *Third World Quarterly*, vol. 13, no. 3.

Robson, Peter (1968) *Economic Integration in Africa*, George Allen and Unwin, London.

Salvatore, Dominick (ed.) (1993) *Protectionism and World Welfare*, Cambridge University Press, Cambridge.

Seers, D. (1983) *The Political Economy of Nationalism*, Oxford University Press, Oxford.

Stevens, Christopher (1991) 'The Caribbean and Europe 1992: Endgame?', *Development Policy Review*, vol. 3, no. 3.

Thomas, C. Y. (1974) *Dependence and Transformation: The Economics of the Transition to Socialism*, Monthly Review Press, New York.

Tostensen, Arne (1992) *What Role for SADCC in the Post-Apartheid Era?* Scandinavian Institute of African Studies, Uppsala.

Yamakage, S. (1990) 'Asean from a Regional Perspective', *Indonesian Quarterly*, vol. XV, no. 5, p. 430.

8

ENVIRONMENTAL RESOURCES AND ECONOMIC DEVELOPMENT[1]

Partha Dasgupta and Karl-Göran Mäler

THE RESOURCE BASIS OF RURAL PRODUCTION

People in poor countries are for the most part agrarian and pastoral folk. In 1988, rural people accounted for about 65 per cent of the population of what the World Bank classifies as low-income countries. The proportion of the total labour force in agriculture was a bit in excess of this. The share of agriculture in the gross domestic product of these countries was 30 per cent. These figures should be contrasted with those from industrial market economies, which are 6 per cent and 2 per cent, respectively.[2]

Poor countries are for the most part *biomass-based subsistence economies*, in that their rural folk eke out a living from products obtained directly from plants and animals. For example, in their informative study of life in a microwatershed of the Alaknanda River in the central Himalayas in India, the (Indian) Centre for Science and Environment (CSE, 1990) reports that, of the total number of hours worked by the villagers sampled, 30 per cent was devoted to cultivation, 20 per cent to fodder collection, and about 25 per cent was spread evenly between fuel collection, animal care and grazing. Some 20 per cent of time was spent on household chores, of which cooking took up the greatest portion, and the remaining 5 per cent was involved in other activities, such as marketing. In their work on Central and West Africa, Falconer and Arnold (1989) and Falconer (1990) have shown how vital forest products are to the lives of rural folk. Come what may, poor countries can be expected to remain largely rural economies for a long while yet.

The dependence of poor countries on their natural resources, such as soil and its cover, water, forests, animals and fisheries, should be self-evident: ignore the environmental resource base, and we are bound to obtain a misleading picture of productive activity in rural communities there. Nevertheless, if there has been a single thread running through forty years of investigation into the poverty of poor countries, it has been the neglect of this resource base. Until very recently, environmental resources made

176

but perfunctory appearances in government planning models, and they were cheerfully ignored in most of what goes by the name of development economics.[3]

The situation is now different. As regards timing, the shift in attitude can probably be identified with the publication of the Brundtland Report (World Commission, 1987), and today no account of economic development would be regarded as adequate if the environmental resource base were absent from it. This chapter, therefore, is about the environment and emerging development issues. Our intention is not to attempt a survey of articles and books on the subject. We will instead weave an account of a central aspect of the lives of the rural poor in poor countries on the basis of a wide-ranging analytical and empirical literature that has developed quite independently of the subject of development economics and the Brundtland Report.

WHAT ARE ENVIRONMENTAL RESOURCES?

Environmental problems are almost always associated with resources that are regenerative (we could call them *renewable natural resources*), but that are in danger of exhaustion from excessive use.[4] The earth's atmosphere is a paradigm of such resources. In the normal course of events, the atmosphere's composition regenerates itself. But the speed of regeneration depends upon, among other things, the current state of the atmosphere and the rate at which pollutants are deposited. It also depends upon the nature of the pollutants. (Smoke discharge is different from the release of chemicals or radioactive material.) Before all else, we need a way of measuring such resources. In the foregoing example, we have to think of an atmospheric quality index. The net rate of regeneration of the stock is the rate at which this quality index changes over time. Regeneration rates of atmospheric quality are complex, often ill-understood matters. This is because there is a great deal of synergism associated with the interaction of different types of pollutants in the atmospheric sink, so that, for example, the underlying relationships are almost certainly non-linear, and, for certain compositions, perhaps greatly so. What are called 'non-linear dose–response relationships' in the ecological literature are instances of this.[5] But these are merely qualifications, and the analytical point we are making, that pollution problems involve the degradation of renewable natural resources, is both true and useful (see Ehrlich et al., 1977).

Animal, bird, plant and fish populations are other examples of renewable natural resources, and there are now a number of studies addressing the reproductive behaviour of different species under a variety of 'environmental' conditions, including the presence of parasitic and symbiotic neighbours.[6] Land is also such a commodity, for the quality of arable and grazing land can be maintained only by careful use. Population pressures can result in an extended period of overuse. By overuse we mean not only an unsustainable shortening of fallow periods, but also deforestation, and the cultivation and grazing of marginal lands. This causes the quality of land to deteriorate, until it eventually becomes a wasteland.

The symbiotic relationship between soil quality and vegetation cover is central to the innumerable problems facing Sub-Saharan Africa, most especially the Sahel.[7] The management of the drylands in general has to be sensitive to such relationships. It is, for example, useful to distinguish between, on the one hand, a reduction in soil nutrients and humus, and, on the other, the loss of soil due to wind and water runoff. The depletion of soil nutrients can be countered by fertilizers (which, however, can have adverse effects elsewhere in the ecological system), but in the drylands, a loss in topsoil cannot be made good. (In river valleys the alluvial topsoil is augmented annually by silt brought by the rivers from mountain slopes. This is the obverse of water runoff caused by a lack of vegetation cover.) Under natural conditions of vegetation cover, it can take anything between 100 and 500 years for the formation of 1 cm of topsoil. Admittedly, what we are calling 'erosion' is a redistribution of soil. But even when the relocation is from one agricultural field to another, there are adjustment costs. Moreover, the relocation is often into the oceans and non-agricultural land. This amounts to erosion.[8]

Soil degradation can occur if the wrong crops are cultivated. Contrary to general belief, in subtropical conditions most export crops tend to be less damaging to soils than are cereals and root crops. (Groundnuts and cotton are exceptions.) Many export crops, such as coffee, cocoa, oil palm and tea, grow on trees and bushes that enjoy a continuous root structure and provide continuous canopy cover. With grasses planted underneath, the rate of soil erosion that is associated with such crops is known to be substantially less than the rate of erosion associated with basic food crops (see Repetto, 1988, Table 2). But problems are compounded upon problems in poor countries. In many cultures the men control cash income while the women control food. Studies in Nigeria, Kenya, India and Nepal suggest that, to the extent that women's incomes decline as the proportion of cash cropping increases, the family's nutritional status (most especially the nutritional status of children) deteriorates (Gross and Underwood, 1971; von Braun and Kennedy, 1986; Kennedy and Oniang'o, 1990). The indirect effects of public policy assume a bewildering variety in poor countries, where ecological and technological factors intermingle with norms of behaviour that respond only very slowly to changing circumstances.[9]

The link between irrigation and the process by which land becomes increasingly saline has also been much noted in the ecological literature (see Ehrlich et al., 1977). In the absence of adequate drainage, continued irrigation slowly but remorselessly destroys agricultural land owing to the salts left behind by evaporating water. The surface area of agricultural land removed from cultivation world-wide through salinization is thought by some to equal the amount added by irrigation (see United Nations, 1990). Desalinization of agricultural land is even today an enormously expensive operation.

The environment is affected by the fact that the rural poor are particularly constrained in their access to credit, insurance and capital markets. Because of such constraints, domestic animals assume a singularly important role as an asset (see e.g. Binswanger and Rosenzweig, 1986; Rosenzweig and Wolpin, 1985; Hoff and Stiglitz, 1990; Dasgupta, 1993). But they are prone to dying when rainfall is scarce. In Sub-Saharan Africa farmers and nomads therefore carry extra cattle as an insurance against droughts. Herds are larger than they would be were capital and insurance markets open to the rural poor. This imposes an additional strain on grazing lands, most especially during periods of drought. That this link between capital and credit markets (or rather, their absence) and the degradation of the environmental resource base is quantitatively significant (World Bank, 1992) should come as no surprise. The environment is itself a gigantic capital asset. The portfolio of assets that a household manages depends on what is available to it. In fact, one can go beyond these rather obvious links and argue that even the fertility rate is related to the extent of the local environmental resource base, such as fuelwood and water sources. Later we will not only see why we should expect this to be so, but also study its implications for public policy.

Underground basins of water have the characteristic of a renewable natural resource if they are recharged over the annual cycle. The required analysis is a bit more problematic though, in that we are interested in both its quality and its quantity. Under normal circumstances, an aquifer undergoes a self-cleansing process as pollutants are deposited into it. (Here, the symbiotic role of microbes, as in the case of soil, is important.) But the effectiveness of the process depends on the nature of pollutants and the rate at which they are discharged. Moreover, the recharge rate depends not only on annual precipitation and the extent of underground flows, but also on the rate of evaporation. This in turn is a function of the extent of soil cover. In the drylands, reduced soil cover beyond a point lowers both soil moisture and the rate of recharge of underground basins, which in turn reduces the soil cover still more, which in turn implies a reduced rate of recharge, and so on.[10] With a lowered underground water table, the cost of water extraction rises.

In fact, aquifers display another characteristic. On occasion the issue is not one of depositing pollutants into them. If, as a consequence of excessive extraction, the ground water level is allowed to drop to too low a level, there can be saltwater intrusion in coastal aquifers, and this can result in the destruction of the basin.

Environmental resources, such as forests, the atmosphere and the seas, have multiple competing uses. This accentuates management problems. Thus forests are a source of timber, bark, sap and, more particularly, pharmaceuticals. Tropical forests also provide a habitat for a rich genetic pool. In addition, forests influence the local and regional climate, preserve soil cover on site, and, in the case of watersheds, protect soil downstream from floods. Increased runoff of rainwater arising from deforestation helps strip soil away, depriving agriculture of nutrients and clogging water reservoirs and irrigation systems. The social value of a forest typically exceeds the value of its direct products, and on occasion exceeds it greatly (see Ehrlich *et al.*, 1977; Dasgupta, 1982a; Hamilton and King, 1983; Anderson, 1987).

It is as well to remember that the kinds of resources we are thinking of here are on occasion of direct use in consumption (as with fisheries), on occasion in production (as with plankton, which serves as food for fish species), and sometimes in both (as with drinking and irrigation water). Their stock is measured in different ways, depending on the resource: in mass units (e.g. biomass units for forests, cowdung and crop residues), in quality indices (e.g. water and air quality indices), in volume units (e.g. acre feet for aquifers), and so on. When we express concern about environmental matters, we in effect point to a decline in their stock. But a decline in their stock, on its own, is not a reason for concern. This is seen most clearly in the context of exhaustible resources, such as fossil fuels. Not to reduce their stocks is not to use them at all, and this is unlikely to be the right thing to do. In the sections to follow we will appeal to modern welfare economic theory to study the basis upon which their optimal patterns of use should be discussed. But even a casual reading of the foregoing examples suggests that a number of issues in environmental economics are 'capital theoretic'.

SOCIAL OBJECTIVES, 1: SUSTAINABLE DEVELOPMENT

World Commission (1987) popularized the phrase 'sustainable development' in connection with the use of environmental resources, and it continues to be the focal point of much of the writings on the environment. Unfortunately, the emerging literature has in great measure been developed independently of both intertemporal welfare economics and the theory of optimal development, two subjects that have provided for over twenty-five years a language in which we may usefully ask questions regarding intergenerational justice. In the event, most writings on sustainable development start from scratch and some proceed to get things hopelessly wrong. It would be difficult to find another field of research endeavour in the social sciences that has displayed such intellectual regress.

Much attention has been given to defining 'sustainable development'. Consider, for example, the following:

'we can summarize the necessary conditions for sustainable development as constancy of the natural capital stock; more strictly, the requirement for non-negative changes in the stock of natural resources, such as soil and soil quality, ground and surface water and their quality, land biomass, water biomass, and the waste-assimilation capacity of the receiving environments.

(Pearce *et al.*, 1988, p. 6)

Or consider instead the passage cited by Solow (1991) from a UNESCO document: 'every generation should leave water, air and soil resources as pure and unpolluted as when it came on earth'.

Both passages involve a category mistake, the mistake being to identify the determinants of well-being (e.g. the means of production of well-being) with the constituents of well-being (e.g. health, welfare and freedoms). But leaving that aside for the moment, the point is not that sustainable development, as it is defined by these authors, is an undesirable goal; rather, it is an impossible goal. In any event, the focus of concern should be present and future well-being, and methods of determining how well-being is affected by policy. History, introspection and experience with analytical models since the early 1960s tell us that reasonable development paths would involve patterns of resource substitution over time.

To be sure, a number of authors writing on sustainable development have recognized that the starting point ought to be the realization of well-being over time. But the thought that, barring exhaustible resources, a just distribution of well-being implies that all capital stocks ought to be preserved, retains an emotional pull. For example, elaborating on the notion of sustainable development, von Amsberg (1993, pp. 15–16) writes:

'Under [the] guidelines for intergenerational resource distribution, the endowment of every generation would include the sustainable yield of the earth's natural capital plus the benefits from resource depletion of natural capital if adequate compensation is made to future generations ... owning land would only include the right to harvest the sustainable yield of the land while leaving the capital value intact... the guidelines for intergenerational resource distribution could be implemented through a sustainability constraint.... The purpose of the sustainability constraint is to ensure some minimum level of welfare of future generations and a guarantee that a basic stock of natural capital is passed on to the next generation.

Two constraints? No doubt *some* index of natural capital would have to be preserved if a minimum level of welfare for the future is to be guaranteed.

Why then introduce it as an additional constraint? Preservation of the index ought to be derivable from the optimization exercise.

A second weakness of the formulation is this: it offers no ethical argument for imposing either of the side constraints. A more general (and intellectually firmer) approach would be to allow future generations' well-being to be reflected in a function that is defined over the well-being of all generations. In other words, the idea is to appeal to an aggregate social well-being function. Such a tactic would enable us also to experiment with different degrees of substitutibility between different generations' levels of well-being. The demands on the present generation could well be stiffer in this framework than that it be required merely to ensure that some minimum level of well-being is guaranteed for future generations.[11] This point of view was adopted by the late Tjalling Koopmans in his formulation of the problem of intergenerational justice.

SOCIAL OBJECTIVES, 2: OPTIMAL DEVELOPMENT, DISCOUNT RATES AND SUSTAINABILITY

In a remarkable set of contributions, Koopmans (1960, 1965, 1967, 1972a, b) conducted a series of thought-experiments on intertemporal choice so as to see the implications of alternative sets of ethical assumptions in plausible worlds.[12] Underlying Koopmans' programme of research was the premise that no ethical judgement in such abstract exercises as those involving resource use should be taken as being decisive. We should instead play off one set of ethical assumptions against another within plausible scenarios, see what their implications are for the distribution of well-being, and then appeal to our varied intuitive senses before arguing policy. For example, he showed (Koopmans, 1965, 1967) that we can have no direct intuition about the validity of discounting future well-being unless we know something concrete about feasible development paths. As the set of feasible paths in a world with an indefinite future is enormously complicated, the reasonable thing would be to work with alternative discount rates on well-being and see what they imply.[13] Although seemingly innocuous, this suggestion represents a radical break with a philosophical tradition, stretching from Ramsey (1928) to Parfit (1984), that has argued against discounting future well-being without first having studied its distributional consequences across generations in plausible worlds. That this tradition is otiose was demonstrated by Mirrlees (1967) and Chakravarty (1969), who showed that in plausible economic models, not to discount future well-being could imply that the present generation be asked to save and invest around 50 per cent of gross national product. This is a stiff requirement when GNP is low.

For simplicity of exposition, let us assume that population size is constant over time (t), and that generation t's well-being is an increasing function of its level of consumption (C_t), which we denote by $W(C_t)$. We assume time to be continuous. Let Γ_C be the set of feasible consumption paths – from the present to the indefinite future – and let Γ_W be the corresponding set of well-being paths. We take it that there is no uncertainty, and that Γ_W is bounded. Imagine that there is an underlying ethical preference ordering defined over Γ_W. Alternative policies are therefore to be evaluated in terms of this ordering. Koopmans (1960) showed that under a plausible set of assumptions, this ordering can be represented by a numerical functional (which we may call *aggregate well-being*) possessing the 'utilitarian' form:

$$\int_0^\infty W(C_t)\exp(-\delta t)\mathrm{d}t, \quad \text{where } \delta > 0.^{14} \tag{8.1}$$

Now (8.1) may look like classical utilitarianism, but it is not. There is nothing in the Koopmans axioms to force a utilitarian interpretation upon W. Moreover, (8.1) involves discounting future well-being at a constant rate $(\delta > 0)$. In short, positive discounting of well-being is seen to be an implication of a set of ethical axioms that, at face value at least, would appear to have nothing to do with discounting.

When conducting analytical experiments with alternative assumptions embedded in (8.1), it makes sense to go beyond the Koopmans axioms and allow for consideration of the case where $\delta = 0$. It also makes sense to go beyond the axioms and to consider unbounded well-being functions. This way we are able to test models to see what all this implies for public policy and the choice of discount rates in social cost–benefit analysis. On the other hand, purposeless generality should be avoided. So we will assume that $W(C)$ is strictly concave, to give shape to the idea that intergenerational equity is valued as an ethical goal.[15]

It is as well to begin by noting that discount rates in use in social cost–benefit analysis are 'consumption discount rates'. In first-best situations, they equal 'income discount rates'. (They are also sometimes, misleadingly, called 'social discount rates', and are different from market interest rates in second-best situations; see below.) If consumption is expected to grow, then the discount rate used in cost–benefit analysis would be positive even if δ were taken to be zero. This follows from the strict concavity of $W(C)$. To see this, recall that, in discrete time the consumption rate of discount at time t is the marginal social rate of substitution between consumption at times t and $t+1$ minus 1. This means that it is the percentage rate of decline in discounted marginal well-being over the interval $[t, t+1]$. Let ρ_t denote this. Reverting to continuous time and the 'utilitarian' form in (8.1), it is an easy matter to confirm that

$$\rho_t = \rho(C_t) = \delta + \alpha(C_t)(\mathrm{d}C_t/\mathrm{d}t)/C_t \tag{8.2}$$

where $\alpha(C_t) > 0$ is the elasticity of marginal well-being at t (see e.g. Arrow and Kurz, 1970). Moreover, along a full optimum, the consumption rate of discount equals the productivity of capital (i.e. the social rate of return on investment). This is the famous Ramsey rule.

Isoelasticity offers a simple, flexible form of $W(.)$. So let us assume that

$$W(C) = -C^{-\alpha}, \quad \text{where } \alpha \text{ is a positive constant.} \tag{8.3}$$

In this case the optimality criterion reflected in (8.1) depends only upon two parameters: α and δ. Obviously, the larger is δ, the lower is the weight awarded to future generations' well-being relative to that of the present generation. The moral of Mirrlees' (1967) computations was that introducing this sort of bias would be a way of countering the advantages to be enjoyed by future generations, should the productivity of capital and technological progress prove to be powerful engines of growth in well-being.

Nevertheless, consider the case $\delta = 0$. As an example, let us assume that $\alpha = 2.5$ (a not implausible figure if $W(C)$ were to be based on revealed preferences). If the rate of growth of optimum consumption at t is, say, 2 per cent, then $\rho_t = 5$ per cent. It will be noticed that the larger α is, the more egalitarian is the optimal consumption path. As $\alpha \to \infty$, the well-being functional represented in (8.1) resembles more and more the Rawlsian maxi–min principle as applied to the intergenerational distribution of consumption (and thus well-being). This in turn means that, even in productive economies, optimal growth in consumption is slow if α is large. In the limit, as $\alpha \to \infty$, optimal growth is zero. From equation (8.2), we can now see why the consumption rate of discount is bounded (and how it manages to equal the productivity of capital) even in these extreme parametric terrains. (On this, see Dasgupta and Heal, 1979, Chapters 9–10.)

Social discount rates are percentage rates of change of intertemporal relative shadow prices. It follows that, unless the optimizing economy is in a steady state, social discount rates typically depend upon the numeraire that has been adopted.[16] As equation (8.2) makes clear, the well-being discount rate differs from consumption rates of discount. This is not an obvious point, and it continues to be misunderstood in a good deal of the environmental literature that is critical of social cost–benefit analysis (see e.g. Daly and Cobb, 1991). Modern philosophers writing on the matter make the same mistake and conflate well-being and consumption rates of discount. They argue that δ should be zero and then criticize the practice of discounting future flows of consumption in social cost–benefit analysis (see e.g. Parfit, 1984; Cowen and Parfit, 1992).

Although simple, the Koopmans formulation spans a rich variety of ethical considerations. Among other things, it tells us that consumption rates of discount do not reflect primary value judgements: they are derived notions. They are essential when we try to implement optimal policies by means of cost–benefit analysis of projects.

184

Notice that in equation (8.3), $W(C)$ is unbounded below. If $\delta = 0$, this ensures that very low consumption rates are penalized by the optimality criterion reflected in (8.1). On the other hand, if δ were positive, low consumption rates by generations sufficiently far in the future would not be penalized by (8.1). This means that unless the economy is sufficiently productive, optimal consumption will tend to zero in the very long run. As an illustration of how critical δ can be, Dasgupta and Heal (1974) and Solow (1974a) showed in a model economy with exhaustible resources that optimal consumption declines to zero in the very long run if $\delta > 0$, but that it increases to infinity if $\delta = 0$. It is in such examples that notions of sustainable development can offer some cutting power. If by sustainable development we wish to mean that the chosen consumption path should as a minimum never fall short of some stipulated, positive level, then it follows that the value of δ would need to be adjusted downward in a suitable manner to ensure that the optimal consumption path meets with the requirement. This was the substance of Solow's remark (see Solow, 1974b) that, in the economics of exhaustible resources, the choice of δ can be a matter of considerable moment.

On the other hand, by sustainable development we could mean something else: we could mean that well-being (and, therefore, consumption) must never be allowed to decline. This is a stiffer requirement than the one we have just considered. If δ is less than the productivity of capital, the valuation criterion reflected in (8.1) ensures that the optimal consumption path will satisfy the requirement. This follows immediately from equation (8.2) and the Ramsey rule. We may therefore conclude that the Koopmans programme is all encompassing, and that concepts of 'sustainability' are useful in pruning out of consideration those consumption paths that are ethically indefensible on prima facie grounds.

SECOND-BEST OPTIMA, GLOBAL WARMING AND RISK

Analysing full optima (i.e. first-best allocations) helps fix ideas. In reality, a vast array of forward markets are missing (due to an absence of property rights, transaction costs, or whatever). It is a reason why, typically, market rates of interest ought not to be used in discounting future incomes in the social evaluation of projects and policies.

The phenomenon of global warming offers a good instance of what this can imply. The atmosphere is a global commons *par excellence*, and greenhouse emissions are a byproduct of production and consumption activities. In short, there is 'market failure'. Social cost–benefit analysis needs to be undertaken with these failures in mind. Consider then that a number of simulation studies on the economics of global warming (e.g. Nordhaus, 1990) have indicated that the social costs of doing much to counter the

185

phenomenon in the near future would far exceed the benefits, because the benefits (e.g. avoiding the submergence of fixed capital in low-lying areas, and declines in agricultural outputs) would appear only in the distant future (namely, a hundred years and more). In these studies future costs and benefits, when expressed in terms of income, are discounted at a positive rate over all future periods, even when doing nothing to combat global warming is among the options that are being considered.

These results, quite rightly, appear as something of a puzzle to many. They imagine that global warming will result eventually in declines and dislocations of incomes, production and people; and yet they are informed that 'economic logic' has been shown to cast a damper on the idea that anything really drastic needs to be done in the immediate future to counter it. Perhaps then, or so it is on occasion thought, when deliberating environmental matters, we ought to use social rates of discount that are different from those in use in the evaluation of other types of economic activity.

We have seen earlier why this would be a wrong thought. On the other hand, using a constant discount rate for the purposes of simulation in the economics of global warming is not sound either. If global warming is expected to lead to declines in (weighted) global consumption over some extended period in the distant future, then the logic underlying formula (8.2) would say that over this same extended period consumption rates of interest could well be *negative*. If this were so (and it would certainly be so if $\delta = 0$), then from our current viewpoint future losses due to global warming could well be amplified; they would not be reduced to negligible figures by the relentless application of a constant and positive discount rate. It is then entirely possible that far more aggressive policies than are implied by current simulation models to combat global warming are warranted.

Introducing risk into the theory of optimal development raises additional questions, and avoiding future risks that would arise from global warming provides another reason why more aggressive current action may be called for. The theory of rational choice under uncertainty (i.e. the von Neumann–Morgenstern–Savage theory) instructs us to expand the space of commodities and services by including in their description the event at which they are made available. It tells us that the appropriate generalization of (8.1) is the expected value of the sums of flows of (possibly discounted) well-being.

Optimal development when future technology is uncertain has been much studied within this framework (see e.g. Phelps, 1962; Mirrlees, 1965, 1974; Levhari and Srinivasan, 1969; Hahn, 1970; Dasgupta and Heal, 1974; Dasgupta et al., 1977). Risk of extinction of the human race provides an additional reason for discounting future well-being. If the possibility of extinction is judged to be approximately a Poisson process, then the modification is especially simple: it involves increasing the well-being discount rate by the probability rate of extinction (see e.g. Mirrlees, 1967; Dasgupta, 1982a).

Uncertainty about future possibilities and the fact that economic decisions can have irreversible impacts, together provide us with a reason to value flexibility (Arrow and Fisher, 1974; Henry, 1974). The underlying idea is that the present generation should choose its policies in a way that helps preserve future generations' options. Environmentalists have frequently interpreted the idea of sustainable development in this light.

One way of formulating the idea of keeping future options open is to study the structure of Γ_C (which, recall, is the set of feasible consumption paths, from the present to infinity) in terms of the resource and capital base a generation inherits from the past, and to consider only those actions on the part of the generation that, as a minimum, preserve Γ_C. Thus, writing by K and S the stocks of manufactured capital (including knowledge and skills) and environmental resources, respectively, let $\Gamma_C^t(K, S)$ denote the set of feasible consumption paths defined over $[t, \infty)$. To preserve future generations' options would be to insist that $\Gamma_C^t \subseteq \Gamma_C^{t+1}$ for $t \geq 0$. This idea was suggested by Dasgupta and Heal (1979, Chapter 9) and subsequently explored by Solow (1991).

There are two problems with it. First, but for the simplest of economies (e.g. the one-good economy in Solow, 1956), $\Gamma_C^t(K, S)$ is so complicated a set that nothing directly can be gleaned about the nature of policies that preserve options. Second, and more importantly, it is an unsatisfactory approach to the notion of intergenerational justice, because it pays no heed to the *worth* of options. But worth cannot be measured except in terms of well-being. So we are back full circle to notions of aggregate well-being. To be sure, uncertainties about current stocks (e.g. numbers of species), and about future needs, wants, technology, climate and so forth, need to be introduced; say, in terms of the expected value of aggregate well-being. But this is only to remind us of a central truth: the worth of keeping future generations' options open should be seen as a derived value. In other words, the worth should be assessed in terms of an overarching notion of aggregate well-being. The theory of option values is based on this insight.

PROJECT EVALUATION AND THE MEASUREMENT OF NET NATIONAL PRODUCT

There are two ways of assessing changes in aggregate well-being. One would be to measure the value of changes in the constituents of well-being (utility and freedoms), and the other would be to measure the value of the alterations in the commodity determinants of well-being (goods and services that are inputs in the production of well-being). The former procedure measures the value of alterations in various 'outputs' (e.g. indices of health, education, and other social indicators), and the latter evaluates the aggregate value of changes in the 'inputs' of the production of well-being (i.e. real national income). A key theorem in modern resource allocation theory is that, provided certain technical restrictions are met, for any conception of aggregate well-being, and for any set of technological, transaction, information and ecological constraints, there exists a set of shadow (or accounting) prices of goods and services that can be used in the estimation of real national product. The index in question has the following property: small investment projects that improve the index are at once those that increase aggregate well-being.[17] We may state the matter more generally: provided the set of accounting prices is unaffected, an improvement in the index due to an alteration in economic activities reflects an increase in aggregate well-being. This is the sense in which real national income measures aggregate well-being. Moreover, the sense persists no matter what is the basis upon which aggregate well-being is founded. In particular, the use of national income in measuring changes in aggregate well-being is *not* restricted to utilitarian ethics.

The theorem should be well known, but it often goes unrecognized in development economics, and today the use of real national income as an indicator of economic development is held in disrepute. For example, Anand and Ravallion (1993) criticize the use of national income in assessing relative well-being in poor countries, on the grounds that income is a measure of opulence, and not of well-being (nor, as they say, of 'capability'; see Sen, 1992). They assert that using the former for the purposes of measuring the latter constitutes a philosophical error, and imply that development planners would have been better placed to make recommendations in poor countries if they had only read their Aristotle. The authors divide national income into personal income and public services, and show that there are a number of countries with a better-than-average personal income per head that display worse-than-average social indicators, such as health and basic education.

But it has long been a tenet of resource allocation theory that public health and basic education ought not to be a matter of private consumption alone. One reason for this view is that they both display strong externalities, and are at once merit goods (Musgrave, 1959). Another reason is that the credit and savings markets work especially badly for the poor in poor countries. In short, the theory has always informed us that a community's personal consumption would not tell us much about its health and education statistics. As this is standard fare in public economics, one can but conclude that if the majority of poor countries have a bad record in the provision of public services, it is not due to philosophical error on the part of their leaderships, nor a lack of knowledge of resource allocation theory: it is something else. In any event, reliance on national income as an indicator of aggregate well-being does not reflect any particular brand of ethics. Its justification rests on a technical result in economics, and is independent of the ethical stance that is adopted.

To be sure, if real national income is to reflect aggregate well-being, accounting prices should be used. Recall that the accounting price of a resource is the increase in the maximum value of aggregate well-being if a unit more of the resource were made available costlessly. (It is a Lagrange multiplier.) Accounting prices are, therefore, the differences between market prices and optimum taxes and subsidies. This provides us with the sense in which it is important for poor countries to 'get their prices right'. Moreover, by real national product for an intertemporal economy, we mean real *net* national product (NNP). The accounting value of the depreciation of fixed capital (and by this we mean both manufactured and natural capital) needs to be deducted if the index of national product is to play the role we are assigning to it here (see Dasgupta and Heal, 1979; Dasgupta and Mäler, 1991; Mäler, 1991). Thus, NNP, when correctly measured, reads as follows:

$$NNP = Consumption + net\ investment\ in\ physical\ capital + the\ value\ of$$
$$the\ net\ change\ in\ human\ capital + the\ value\ of\ the\ net\ change$$
$$in\ the\ stock\ of\ natural\ capital - the\ value\ of\ current$$
$$environmental\ damages \qquad (8.4)$$

We are regarding consumption as the numeraire in our measure of NNP. So the 'values' referred to in equation (8.4) are consumption values, and they are evaluated with the help of shadow prices. In the Appendix we will present an account of how net national product ought ideally to be computed in an intertemporal economy. We will study an optimizing economy there. The optimization exercise enables one to estimate accounting prices. These prices can then in principle be used for the purposes of project and policy evaluation even in an economy that is currently far from the optimum (see e.g. Little and Mirrlees, 1974; Squire and Van der Taak, 1975).

An alternative way is to think of public policy as a sequence of reforms. Accounting prices in this framework would be estimated from the *prevailing* structure of production and consumption (and not from the optimum). If the economy has a convex structure, then a sequence of such reforms would in principle take the economy ultimately to the optimum (see e.g. Dasgupta *et al.*, 1972; Ahmad and Stern, 1990). Expression (8.4) reflects the correct notion of NNP in both frameworks.[18]

It is useful to note here that the convention of regarding expenditures on public health and education as part of final demand implicitly equates the cost of their provision with the contribution they make to aggregate well-being. This in all probability results in an underestimate in poor countries.[19] We should note as well that current defensive expenditure against damages to the flow of environmental amenities ought to be included in the estimation of final demand. Similarly, investment in the stock of environmental defensive capital should be included in NNP.

By 'investment', we mean the value of net changes in capital assets, and not changes in the value of these assets. This means that anticipated capital gains (or losses) should not be included in NNP. As an example, the value of the *net* decrease in the stock of oil and natural gas (net of new discoveries, that is) ought to be deducted from GNP when NNP is estimated. The answer to the question as to how we should estimate NNP should not be a matter of opinion today: it is a matter of fact.

Current estimates of NNP are biased because depreciation of environmental resources is not deducted from GNP. Stated another way, NNP estimates are biased because a biased set of prices is in use. Prices imputed to environmental resources on site are usually zero. This amounts to regarding the depreciation of environmental capital as zero. But these resources are scarce goods, so we know that their shadow prices are positive. Profits attributed to projects that degrade the environment are therefore higher than the social profits they generate. This means in turn that wrong sets of projects get chosen – in both the private and public sectors.

The extent of the bias will obviously vary from project to project, and from country to country. But it can be substantial. In their work on the depreciation of natural resources in Costa Rica, Solorzano *et al.* (1991) have estimated that in 1989 the depreciation of three resources – forests, soil and fisheries – amounted to about 10 per cent of gross domestic product and over a third of gross capital accumulation. Resource-intensive projects look better than they actually are. Installed technologies are usually unfriendly towards the environment.

APPENDIX: NET NATIONAL PRODUCT IN A DYNAMIC ECONOMY

The economics of optimal control

We will show in this appendix how shadow prices can be used in judging the relative desirability of alternative economic activities. Of particular interest to us is social cost–benefit analysis of investment projects. The measurement of real national income is intimately connected to this. The index we seek is net national product (NNP) as a measure of aggregate well-being.[20] We will show that the question of how we should measure it for the purposes of social cost–benefit analysis is not a matter of opinion, it has an unambiguous answer. We need a formal model to establish this. In this appendix we present what we hope is a canonical model of an optimizing economy for doing so.[21]

Our aim here is to display the connection between accounting prices, rules for project evaluation, and national product accounting in a context that is simple, but that has sufficient structure to allow us to obtain a number of prescriptions alluded to in the body of the chapter. In order to keep to what, for our purposes in this chapter, are essential matters, we will ignore the kinds of 'second-best' constraints (e.g. market disequilibria) that have been the centre of attention in the literature on project evaluation in poor countries; as, for example, in Dasgupta *et al.* (1972) and Little and Mirrlees (1974). The principles we will develop here carry over to disequilibrium situations. For expositional ease, we will restrict ourselves to a closed economy.

We will take it that the aggregate well-being function*al* is the (possibly discounted) integral of the flow of instantaneous social well-being (as in (8.1)). Let us begin by recalling the main features of intertemporal optimization exercises.[22] The theory of intertemporal planning tells us to choose current controls (e.g. current consumptions and the mix of current investments) in such a way as to maximize the current-value Hamiltonian of the underlying optimization problem. As is well known, the current-value Hamiltonian is the sum of the flow of current well-being and the shadow value of all net investments currently being undertaken. (The optimization exercise generates the entire set of intertemporal shadow prices.[23]) It will be seen in the next section that the current-value Hamiltonian measures the 'well-being return' on the value of all capital assets. In short, it is a measure of the return on wealth. This provides us with the necessary connection between the current-value Hamiltonian and real net national product. NNP is merely a linearized version of the current-value Hamiltonian, the linearization amounting to representing the current flow of well-being by the shadow value of all the determinants of current well-being. In the simplest of cases, where current well-being depends solely on current consumption, NNP reduces to the sum of the accounting value of an economy's consumptions and the accounting value of the changes in its stocks of real capital assets.

The Hamiltonian calculus in fact implies something more. It implies that the present discounted sum of today's current-value Hamiltonian is equal to the maximum present discounted value of the flow of social well-being (equation (A13) below). This was not seen immediately as an implication of the mathematical theory of programming, although it should have been transparent from the work of Arrow and Kurz (1970) and Solow (1974a). Each of these matters will be illustrated in our formal model.

NNP in a deterministic environment

We consider an economy that has a multi-purpose, manufactured, perfectly durable capital good, whose stock is denoted by K_1. If L_1 is the labour effort combined with this, the flow of output is taken to be $Y = F(K_1, L_1)$, where $F(.)$ is an aggregate production function.[24] The economy enjoys in addition two sorts of environmental resource stocks: clean air, K_2, and forests, K_3.

Clean air is valued directly, whereas forests have two derived values: they help keep the atmosphere (or air) 'clean', and they provide fuelwood, which too is valued directly (for warmth or for cooking). Finally, we take it that there is a flow of environmental amenities, Z, which directly affects aggregate well-being.

Forests enjoy a natural regeneration rate, but labour effort can increase it. Thus we denote by $H(L_2)$ the rate of regeneration of forests, where L_2 is labour input for this task, and where $H(.)$ is, for low values of L_2 at least, an increasing function. Let X denote the rate of consumption of fuelwood. Collecting this involves labour effort. Let this be L_3. Presumably, the larger the forest stock the less is the effort required (in calorie requirements, say). We remarked on this earlier. We thus assume that $X = N(K_3, L_3)$, where $N(.)$ is an increasing concave function of its two arguments.

Output Y is a basic consumption good, and this consumption is also valued directly. However, we take it that the production of Y involves pollution as a byproduct. This reduces the quality of the atmosphere both as a stock and as a flow of amenities. We assume, however, that it is possible to take defensive measures against both these ill-effects. First, society can invest in technologies (e.g. stack-gas scrubbers) for reducing the emission of pollutants, and we denote the stock of this defensive capital by K_4. If P denotes the emission of pollutants, we have $P = A(K_4, Y)$, where A is a convex function, decreasing in K_4 and increasing in Y. Second, society can mitigate damages to the flow of amenities by expending a portion of final output, at a rate R. We assume that the resulting flow of amenities has the functional form $Z = J(R,P)$, where J is increasing in R and decreasing in P.

There are thus four things that can be done with output Y: it can be consumed (we denote the rate of consumption by C); it can be reinvested to increase the stock of K_1; it can be invested in the accumulation of K_4; and it can be used, at rate R, to counter the damages to the flow of environmental amenities. Let Q denote the expenditure on the accumulation of K_4.

Now, the environment as a stock tries to regenerate itself at a rate which is an increasing function of the stock of forests, $G(K_3)$. The net rate of regeneration is the difference between this and the emission of pollutants from production of Y. We can therefore express the dynamics of the economy in terms of the following equations:

$$dK_1/dt = F(K_1, L_1) - C - Q - R \tag{A1}$$

$$dK_2/dt = G(K_3) - A(K_4, F[K_1, L_1]) \tag{A2}$$

$$dK_3/dt = H(L_2) - X \tag{A3}$$

$$dK_4/dt = Q \tag{A4}$$

$$X = N(K_3, L_3) \tag{A5}$$

$$Z = J[R, A(K_4, F[K_1, L_1])]. \tag{A6}$$

The current flow of aggregate well-being, W, is taken to be an increasing function of aggregate consumption, C; the output of fuelwood, X; the flow of environmental amenities, Z; and the quality of the atmospheric stock, K_2. However, it is a decreasing function of total labour effort, $L = L_1 + L_2 + L_3$. (As noted in the text, labour effort could be measured in calories.) We thus have $W(C, X, Z, K_2, L_1 + L_2 + L_3)$.

Stocks of the four types of assets are given at the initial date; the instantaneous control variables are C, Q, R, X, Z, L_1, L_2 and L_3. The objective is to maximize the (discounted) sum of the flow of aggregate well-being over the indefinite future; that is

$$\int_0^\infty W(C, X, Z, K_2, L_1 + L_2 + L_3)\exp(-\delta t)dt,$$

where $\delta > 0$.

We take well-being to be the numeraire. Letting p, q, r and s denote the (spot) shadow prices of the four capital goods, K_1, K_2, K_3 and K_4 respectively, and letting v be the imputed marginal value of the flow of environmental amenities, we can use equations (A1)–(A6) to express the current-value Hamiltonian, V, of the optimization problem as

$$\begin{aligned} V =&\, W(C, N(K_3, L_3), Z, K_2, L_1 + L_2 + L_3) + p[F(K_1, L_1) - C - Q - R] \\ &+ q[G(K_3) - A(K_4, F[K_1, L_1]) - A(K_4, F[K_1, L_1])] + r[H(L_2) \qquad \text{(A7)} \\ &- N(K_3, L_3)] + sQ + v(J[R, A(K_4, F[K_1, L_1])] - Z). \end{aligned}$$

Recall that the theory of optimum control instructs us to choose the control variables at each date so as to maximize (A7).[25] Writing by W_C the partial derivative of W with respect to C, and so forth, it is then immediate that along an optimal programme the control variables and the shadow prices must satisfy the conditions

$$\begin{aligned} &\text{(i) } W_C = p; \quad \text{(ii) } W_X N_2 + W_L = rN_2; \quad \text{(iii) } W_Z = v; \\ &\text{(iv) } W_L = [qA_2 - vJ_2 - p]F_2; \quad \text{(v) } W_L = -rdH(L_2)/dL_2; \qquad \text{(A8)} \\ &\text{(vi) } p = vJ_1; \quad \text{(vii) } p = s.[26] \end{aligned}$$

Moreover, the accounting prices p, q, r, and s satisfy the auxiliary conditions

$$\begin{aligned} &\text{(1) } dp/dt = -\partial V/\partial K_1 + \delta p; \quad \text{(2) } dq/dt = -\partial V/\partial K_2 + \delta q; \\ &\text{(3) } dr/dt = -\partial V/\partial K_3 + \delta r; \quad \text{(4) } ds/dt = -\partial V/\partial K_4 + \delta s. \end{aligned} \qquad \text{(A9)}$$

Interpreting these conditions is today a routine matter. Conditions (A8) tell us what kinds of information we need for estimating accounting prices;

(A9) are the intertemporal arbitrage conditions that must be satisfied by accounting prices. We may now derive the correct expression for net national product (NNP) from equation (A7): it is the linear support of the Hamiltonian, the normal to the support being given by the vector of accounting prices.

It will pay us now to introduce time into the notation. Let us denote by O_t^* the vector of all the non-price arguments in the Hamiltonian function along the optimal programme at date t. Thus

$$O_t^* = (C_t^*, Z_t^*, Q_t^*, R_t^*, K_{1t}^*, K_{2t}^*, K_{3t}^*, K_{4t}^*, L_{1t}^*, L_{2t}^*, L_{3t}^*).$$

Write $I_{it} \equiv dK_{it}/dt$, for $i = 1, 2, 3, 4$. Consider now a small perturbation at t round O_t^*. Denote the perturbed programme as an unstarred vector, and dO_t as the perturbation itself. It follows from taking the Taylor expansion around O^* that the current-value Hamiltonian along the perturbed programme is

$$V(O_t) = V(O_t^*) + W_C dC_t + W_X dX_t + W_Z dZ_t + W_L(dL_{1t} + dL_{2t} + dL_{3t})$$
$$+ p dI_{1t} + q dI_{2t} + r dI_{3t} + s dI_{4t},$$

where

$$Z^* = J[R^*, A(K_4^*, F[K_1^*, L_1^*])]. \tag{A10}$$

Equation (A10) tells us how to measure net national product. Let $\{O_t\}$ denote an arbitrary intertemporal programme. NNP at date t, which we write as NNP_t, in the optimizing economy, measured in well-being numeraire, is the term representing the linear support term in expression (A10). So,

$$NNP_t = W_C C_t + W_X X_t + W_Z J[R_t, A(K_{4t}, F[K_{1t}, L_{1t}])] + W_L(L_{1t} + L_{2t} + L_{3t})$$
$$+ p dK_1/dt + q dK_2/dt + r dK_3/dt + s dK_4/dt. \text{[27]} \tag{A11}$$

Notice that all resources and outputs are valued at the prices that sustain the optimal programme $\{O_t^*\}$.[28] In order to stress the points we want to make here, we have chosen to work with a most aggregate model. Ideally, (income) distributional issues will find reflection in the well-being functional. These considerations can easily be translated into the estimates of shadow prices (see Dasgupta et al., 1972).

Why should expression (A11) be regarded as the correct measure of net national product? The clue lies in expression (A10). Suppose we are involved in the choice of projects. A marginal project is a perturbation on the current programme. Suppressing the index for time once again, the project is the ten-vector (dC, dX, dR, dL_1, dL_2, dL_3, dI_1, dI_2, dI_3, dI_4), where $I_i = dK_i/dt$, ($i = 1, 2, 3, 4$); and dC, and so on, are small changes in C, and so forth. If the project records an increase in NNP_t (the increase will be marginal of course), it will record an increase in the current-value Hamiltonian, evaluated at the prices supporting the optimal programme. Recall that optimal control theory asks us to maximize the current-value Hamiltonian. Moreover, we are assuming that the planning problem is concave. So, choosing projects that increase NNP (i.e. they are socially profitable) increases the current-value Hamiltonian as well and, therefore, they should be regarded as desirable. Along an optimal programme the social profitability of the last project is nil. Therefore, its contribution to NNP is nil. This follows from the fact that the controls are chosen so as to maximize expression (A7). This is the justification. All this is well known, and our purpose here is to obtain some additional insights. Expression (A11) tells us:

(a) If wages were equal to the marginal ill-being of work effort, wages would not be part of NNP. In short, the shadow wage bill ought to be deducted from gross output when we estimate NNP. (If labour is supplied inelastically, it is a matter of indifference whether the wage bill in this optimizing economy is deducted from NNP.) On the other hand, were we to recognize a part of the wage bill as a return on the accumulation of human capital, that part would be included in NNP.

(b) Current defensive expenditure, R, against damages to the flow of environmental amenities should be included in the estimation of final demand (see the third term in expression (A9)).

(c) Investments in the stock of environmental defensive capital should be included in NNP (see the final term of expression (A11)).

(d) Expenditures that enhance the environment find expression in the value imputed to changes in the environmental resource stock. We may conclude that this change should not be included in estimates of NNP (notice the absence of sQ in expression (A11)).

(e) The value of changes in the environmental resource base (K_2 and K_3) should be included in NNP. However, anticipated capital gains (or losses) are not part of NNP.

The Hamiltonian and sustainable well-being

Differentiate expression (A7) and use conditions (A9) to confirm that along the optimal programme

$$dV_t^*/dt = \delta(p\,dK_1/dt + q\,dK_2/dt + r\,dK_3/dt + s\,dK_4/dt)$$
$$= \delta(V_t^* - W_t^*),$$

(A12)

where W_t^* is the flow of optimal aggregate well-being.

This is a differential equation in V_t^* which integrates to

$$V_t^* = \delta_t \int_t^\infty W_\tau^* \exp[-\delta(\tau - t)]d\tau,$$

and thus

$$V_t^* \int_t^\infty \exp[-\delta(\tau - t)]d\tau = \int_t^\infty W_t^* \exp[-\delta(\tau - t)]d\tau. \qquad (A13)$$

Equation (A13) says that the present discounted value of a constant flow of today's current-value Hamiltonian measures the maximum present value of the flow of social well-being.

Define $K \equiv pK_1 + qK_2 + rK_3 + sK_4$ as the aggregate capital stock in the economy. The first part of equation (A12) can then be written as

$$V_t^* = \delta K_t.$$

In short, the current-value Hamiltonian measures the 'well-being return' on the economy's aggregate capital stock, inclusive of the environmental re-source base.

Future uncertainty

We will now extend the analysis for the case where there is future uncertainty. As an example, we could imagine the discovery and installation of cleaner production technologies which make existing abatement technologies less valuable. For simplicity of exposition, we will assume that such discoveries are uninfluenced by policy, e.g. research and development policy.[29]

It is most informative to consider discrete events. We may imagine that at some random future date, T, an event occurs which is expected to affect the value of the then existing stocks of capital. We consider the problem from the vantage point of the present, which we denote by $t = 0$, where t, as always, denotes time. Let us assume that there is a (subjective) probability density function, π^t, over the date of its occurrence. (We are thus supposing for expositional ease that the event will occur at some future date.) From this we may define the cumulative function Φ^t.

We take it that the social good is reflected by the expected value of the sum of the discounted flow of future aggregate well-being. If the event in question were to occur at date T, the economy in question would enter a new production and ecological regime. We shall continue to rely on the notation developed in the previous section. As is proper, we use dynamic programming, and proceed to work backwards. Thus, let K_i^T (with $i = 1, 2, 3, 4$) denote the stocks of the four assets at date T. Following an optimal economic policy subsequent to the occurrence of the event would yield an expected flow of aggregate well-being. This flow we discount back to T. This capitalized value of the flow of well-being will clearly be a function of K_i^T. Let us denote this by $B(K_1^T, K_2^T, K_3^T, K_4^T)$. It is now possible to show that until the event occurs (i.e. for $t < T$), the optimal policy is to pretend that the event will never occur, and to assume that the flow of aggregate well-being is given, not by $W(.)$, but by $(1 - \Phi^t)W(.) + \pi^t B(.)$ (see Dasgupta and Heal, 1974). Suppressing the subscript for time, we may then conclude from the analysis of the previous section that NNP at any date prior to the occurrence of the event is given by the expression

$$\text{NNP} = (1 - \Phi)[W_C C + W_X X + W_Z J[R, A(K_4, F[K_1, L_1])] \qquad (A15)$$
$$+ W_L(L_1 + L_2 + L_3) + p dK_1/dt + q dK_2/dt + r dK_3/dt + s dK_4/dt].$$

Notice that if the event is not expected to occur ever, then $\pi^t = 0$ for all t, and consequently, $(1 - \Phi^t) = 1$ for all t. In this case expression (A15) reduces to expression (A11). Notice that the accounting prices that appear in expression (A15) are Arrow–Debreu contingent commodity prices. Notice too that whilst we have used the same notation for the accounting prices in expressions (A11) and (A15), their values are quite different. This is because future possibilities in the two economies are different.

NOTES

1 This chapter is a shortened version of Partha Dasgupta and Karl-Göran Mäler's article 'Poverty, Institutions and the Environmental Resource Base', in the *Handbook of Development Economics*, vol. 3, eds T. N. Srinivasan and J. Behrman, North Holland, Amsterdam. The authors want to express their appreciation of comments from Scott Barrett, Jere Behrman, John Dixon, Lawrence Lau, Mohan Munasinghe, Theo Panayotou, Kirit Parikh and T. N. Srinivasan.

2 International figures, such as these, are known to contain large margins of error. Nevertheless, they offer orders of magnitude. For this reason, we will allude to them. However, we will not make use of them for any other purpose.

3 There were exceptions of course (e.g. CSE, 1982, 1985; Dasgupta, 1982a). Moreover, agricultural and fisheries economists have routinely studied environmental matters. In the text, we are referring to a neglect of environmental matters in what could be called 'official' development economics.

4 Minerals and fossil fuels are not renewable (they are pristine examples of exhaustible resources), but they raise a different set of issues. For an account of what resource allocation theory looks like when we include exhaustible resources in the production process, see Dasgupta and Heal (1979), Hartwick and Olewiler (1986) and Tietenberg (1988). For a non-technical account of the theory and the historical role that has been played by the substitution of new energy resources for old, see Dasgupta (1989).

5 The economic issues arising from such non-linearities are analysed in Dasgupta (1982a).

6 Ehrlich and Roughgarden (1987) is an excellent treatise on these matters.

7 Anderson (1987) contains an authoritative case study of this.
8 One notable, and controversial, estimate of world-wide productivity declines in livestock and agriculture in the drylands due to soil losses was offered in UNEP (1984). The figure was an annual loss of $26 billion. For a discussion of the UNEP estimate, see Gigengack et al. (1990). The estimate by Mabbut (1984), that approximately 40% of the productive drylands of the world are currently under threat from desertification, probably gives an idea of the magnitude of the problem. For accounts of the economics and ecology of drylands, see Falloux and Mukendi (1988) and Dixon et al. (1989, 1990). We will discuss the notion of environmental stress in the final section.
9 See Dasgupta (1993) for further discussion of these linkages.
10 See, for example, Falkenmark (1986, 1989), Olsen (1987), Nelson (1988), Reij et al. (1988) and Falkenmark and Chapman (1989).
11 This issue was the focus of Dasgupta and Heal (1974) and Solow (1974a). See Dasgupta and Heal (1979, Chapters 9–10) for an elaboration.
12 For an account of this programme, see Dasgupta and Heal (1979, Chapters 9–10).
13 Dasgupta and Heal (1974) and Solow (1974a) provide exercises of this sort in economies with exhaustible resources.
14 Koopmans' theorems were proved under the assumption that time is discrete. In Koopmans (1972a, b) the ethical axioms are imposed directly on Γ_C, and $W(.)$ is obtained as a numerical representation.
15 For simplicity of exposition, we will begin by focusing on a full optimum. Social cost–benefit analysis in second-best circumstances was the subject of discussion in Dasgupta et al. (1972) and Little and Mirrlees (1974).
16 Therefore, unless the numeraire has been specified, the term 'social discount rate' is devoid of meaning.
17 See Dasgupta (1993, Chapters *7 and *10). The technical restrictions amount to the requirement that the Kuhn–Tucker theorem is usable, i.e. that both the set of feasible allocations and the ethical ordering reflected by the aggregate well-being function are convex. The assumption of convexity is dubious for pollution problems. Nevertheless, in a wide range of circumstances, it is possible to separate out the 'non-convex' sector, estimate real national income (or product) for the 'convex' sector, and present an estimate of the desired index as a combination of the real product of the convex sector and estimates of stocks and their changes in the non-convex sectors. This is a simple inference from Weitzman (1970) and Portes (1971).
18 For a simplified exposition of the connection between these two modes of analysis (reforms and optimization), see Dasgupta (1982a, Chapter 5).
19 If education is regarded as a merit good, and not merely as instrumental in raising productivity, then its accounting price would be that much higher.
20 There are other purposes to which the idea of national product has been put; for example, as a measure of economic activity. They require different treatments. We are not concerned with them here.
21 This appendix is taken from Dasgupta and Mäler (1991) and Mäler (1991).
22 The best economics treatment of all this is still Arrow and Kurz (1970).
23 The current-value Hamiltonian in general also contains terms reflecting the social cost of breaking any additional (second-best) constraint that happens to characterize the optimization problem. As mentioned in the text, we ignore such additional constraints for the sake of expositional ease.
24 In what follows we assume that all functions satisfy conditions which ensure that the planning problem defined below is a concave programme. We are not going to spell out each and every such assumption, because they will be familiar to the reader. For example, we assume that $F(.)$ is concave.

25 Notice that we have used equation (A5) to eliminate X, and so we are left with six direct control variables.

26 F_2 stands for the partial derivative of F with respect to its second argument, L_1; and as mentioned earlier, $L = L_1 + L_2 + L_3$. We have used this same notation for the derivatives of $N(.)$, $J(.)$ and $A(.)$.

27 We may divide the whole expression by W_C to express NNP in aggregate consumption numeraire. It should also be recalled that by assumption W_L is *negative*.

28 But recall the alternative framework in which accounting prices are estimated from the prevailing structure of production and consumption. See Dasgupta *et al.* (1972).

29 Research and development policy can be easily incorporated into our analysis (see Dasgupta *et al.* 1977). The following account builds on Dasgupta and Heal (1974), Dasgupta and Stiglitz (1981) and Dasgupta (1982b). These earlier contributions, however, did not address the measurement of NNP, our present concern.

REFERENCES

Ahmad, E. and Stern, N. (1990) *The Theory and Practice of Tax Reform for Developing Countries*, Cambridge University Press, Cambridge.

Anand, S. and Ravallion, M. (1993) 'Human Development in Poor Countries: On the Role of Private Incomes and Public Services', *Journal of Economic Perspectives*, 7.

Anderson, D. (1987) *The Economics of Afforestation*, Johns Hopkins University Press, Baltimore, MD.

Arrow, K. J. and Fisher, A. (1974) 'Preservation, Uncertainty and Irreversibility', *Quarterly Journal of Economics*, 88.

Arrow, K. J. and Kurz, M. (1970) *Public Investment, the Rate of Return and Optimal Fiscal Policy*, Johns Hopkins University Press, Baltimore, MD.

Binswanger, H. and Rosenzweig, M. (1986) 'Credit Markets, Wealth and Endowments in Rural South India', Report No. 59, Agriculture and Rural Development Department, World Bank.

Chakravarty, S. (1969) *Capital and Development Planning*, MIT Press, Cambridge, MA.

Cowen, T. and Parfit, D. (1992): 'Against the Social Discount Rate', in P. Laslett and J. S. Fishkin (eds) *Justice Between Age Groups and Generations*, Yale University Press, New Haven, CT.

CSE (1982, 1985) *The State of India's Environment: A Citizens' Report*, Centre for Science and Environment, New Delhi.

Daly, H. E. and Cobb, J. B. (1990) *Human–Nature Interactions in a Central Himalayan Village*, Centre for Science and Environment, New Delhi.

—— (1991) *For the Common Good: Redirecting the Economy towards Community, the Environment, and a Sustainable Future*, Greenprint, London.

Dasgupta, P. (1982a) *The Control of Resources*, Basil Blackwell, Oxford.

—— (1982b) 'Resource Depletion, Research and Development, and the Social Rate of Discount', in R. C. Lind (ed.) *Discounting for Time and Risk in Energy Policy*, Johns Hopkins University Press, Baltimore, MD.

—— (1989) 'Exhaustible Resources', in L. Friday and R. Laskey (eds) *The Fragile Environment*, Cambridge University Press, Cambridge.

—— (1993) *An Inquiry into Well-Being and Destitution*, Clarendon Press, Oxford.

Dasgupta, P. and Heal, G. M. (1974): 'The Optimal Depletion of Exhaustible Resources', *Review of Economic Studies* (Symposium on the Economics of Exhaustible Resources), 41.

—— (1979) *Economic Theory and Exhaustible Resources*, Cambridge University Press, Cambridge.

Dasgupta, P. and Mäler, K.-G. (1991) 'The Environment and Emerging Development Issues', *Proceedings of the Annual World Bank Conference on Development Economics* (Supplement to the *World Bank Economic Review* and the *World Bank Research Observer*).

Dasgupta, P. and Stiglitz, J. E. (1981) 'Resource Depletion under Technological Uncertainty', *Econometrica*, 49.

Dasgupta, P., Marglin, S. and Sen, A. (1972): *Guidelines for Project Evaluation*, United Nations, New York.

Dasgupta, P., Heal, G. M. and Majumdar, M. (1977) 'Resource Depletion and Research and Development', in M. Intriligator (ed.) *Frontiers of Quantitative Economics*, Volume III, North-Holland, Amsterdam.

Dixon, J. A., James, D. E. and Sherman, P. B. (1989) *The Economics of Dryland Management*, Earthscan Publications, London.

—— (eds) (1990) *Dryland Management: Economic Case Studies*, Earthscan Publications, London.

Ehrlich, P. and Roughgarden, J. (1987) *The Science of Ecology*, Macmillan, New York.

Ehrlich, P., Ehrlich, A. and Holdren, J. (1977): *Ecoscience: Population, Resources and the Environment*, San Francisco: W. H. Freeman.

Falconer, J. (1990) *The Major Significance of 'Minor' Forest Products*, FAO, Rome.

Falconer, J. and Arnold, J. E. M. (1989) *Household Food Security and Forestry: An Analysis of Socio-Economic Issues*, FAO, Rome.

Falkenmark, M. (1986) 'Fresh Water: Time for a Modified Approach', *Ambio*, 15.

—— (1989) 'The Massive Water Scarcity Now Facing Africa: Why Isn't It Being Addressed?', *Ambio*, 18.

Falkenmark, M. and Chapman, T. (eds) (1989) *Comparative Hydrology: An Ecological Approach to Land and Water Resources*, UNESCO, Paris.

Falloux, F. and Mukendi A. (eds) 'Desertification Control and Renewable Resource Management in the Sahelian and Sudanian Zones of West Africa', World Bank Technical Paper no. 70.

Gigengack, A. R. *et al.* (1990) 'Global Modelling of Dryland Degradation', in J. A. Dixon, D. E. James and P. B. Sherman (eds) *Dryland Management: Economic Case Studies*, Earthscan Publications, London.

Gross, D. R. and Underwood, B. A. (1971) 'Technological Change and Caloric Cost: Sisal Agriculture in North-Eastern Brazil', *American Anthropologist*, 73.

Hahn, F. H. (1970) 'Savings and Uncertainty', *Review of Economic Studies*, 37.

Hamilton, L. S. and King, P. N. (1983) *Tropical Forested Watersheds: Hydrologic and Soils Response to Major Uses or Conversions*, Westview Press, Boulder, CO.

Hartwick, J. and Olewiler, N. (1986) *The Economics of Natural Resource Use*, Harper & Row, New York.

Henry, C. (1974) 'Investment Decisions under Uncertainty: The Irreversibility Effect', *American Economic Review*, 64.

Hoff, K. and Stiglitz, J. E. (1990) 'Introduction: Imperfect Information and Rural Credit Markets: Puzzles and Policy Perspectives', *World Bank Economic Review*, 4.

Kennedy, E. and Oniang'o, R. (1990) 'Health and Nutrition Effects of Sugarcane Production in South-Western Kenya', *Food and Nutrition Bulletin*, 12.

Koopmans, T. C. (1960) 'Stationary Ordinal Utility and Impatience', *Econometrica*, 28.

——(1965) 'On the Concept of Optimal Economic Growth', *Pontificiae Academiae Scientiarum Scripta Varia*, 28. Reprinted in *The Econometric Approach to Development Planning* (1966) North-Holland, Amsterdam.

——(1967) 'Objectives, Constraints and Outcomes in Optimal Growth Models', *Econometrica*, 35.

——(1972a) 'Representation of Preference Orderings with Independent Components of Consumption', in C. B. McGuire and R. Radner (eds) *Decision and Organization*, North-Holland, Amsterdam.

——(1972b) 'Representation of Preference Orderings over Time', in C. B. McGuire and R. Radner (eds) *Decision and Organization*, North-Holland, Amsterdam.

Levhari, D. and Srinivasan, T. N. (1969) 'Optimal Savings Under Uncertainty', *Review of Economic Studies*, 36.

Little, I. M. D. and Mirrlees, J. A. (1974) *Project Appraisal and Planning for Developing Countries*, Heinemann, London.

Mabbut, J. (1984) 'A New Global Assessment of the Status and Trends of Desertification', *Environmental Conservation*, 11.

Mäler, K.-G. (1991) 'National Accounting and Environmental Resources', *Journal of Environmental Economics and Resources*, 1.

Mirrlees, J. A. (1965) 'Optimum Accumulation Under Uncertainty', Mimeo, Faculty of Economics, University of Cambridge.

——(1967) 'Optimal Growth when Technology is Changing', *Review of Economic Studies*, 34.

——(1974) 'Optimum Accumulation under Uncertainty: the Case of Stationary Returns on Investment', in J. Dreze (ed.) *Allocation under Uncertainty: Equilibrium and Optimality*, Macmillan, London.

Musgrave, R. (1959) *Theory of Public Finance*, McGraw-Hill, New York.

Nelson, R. (1988) 'Dryland Management: The "Desertification" Problem', World Bank Environmental Department Paper No. 8.

Nordhaus, W. D. (1990) 'To Slow or Not to Slow: The Economics of the Greenhouse Effect', Mimeo, Department of Economics, Yale University.

Olsen, W. K. (1987) 'Manmade "Drought" in Rayalaseema', *Economic and Political Weekly*, 22.

Parfit, D. (1984) *Reasons and Persons*, Oxford University Press, Oxford.

Pearce, D., Barbier, E. and Markandya, A. (1988) 'Sustainable Development and Cost-Benefit Analysis', Paper presented at the Canadian Assessment Workshop on Integrating Economic and Environment Assessment.

Phelps, E. S. (1962) 'The Accumulation of Risky Capital: A Sequential Analysis', *Econometrica*, 30.

Portes, R. (1971) 'Decentralized Planning Procedures and Centrally Planned Economics', *American Economics Review* (Papers & Proceedings), 61.

Ramsey, F. (1928) 'A Mathematical Theory of Saving', *Economic Journal*, 38.

Reij, C., Mulder, P. and Begemann, L. (1988) 'Water Harvesting for Plant Production', World Bank Technical Paper No. 91.

Repetto, R. (1988) 'Economic Policy Reform for Natural Resource Conservation', World Bank Environment Department Working Paper No. 4.

Rosenzweig, M. and Wolpin, K. I. (1985) 'Specific Experience, Household Structure and Intergenerational Transfers: Farm Family Land and Labour Arrangements in Developing Countries', *Quarterly Journal of Economics*, 100.

Sen, A. (1992) *Inequality Reexamined*, Clarendon Press, Oxford.

Solorzano, R. *et al.* (1991) *Accounts Overdue: Natural Resource Depreciation in Costa Rica*, World Resources Institute, Washington, DC.

Solow, R. M. (1956) 'A Contribution to the Theory of Economic Growth', *Quarterly Journal of Economics*, 70.

—— (1974a) 'Intergenerational Equity and Exhaustible Resources', *Review of Economic Studies* (Symposium on the Economics of Exhaustible Resources), 41.

—— (1974b) 'The Economics of Resources, or the Resources of Economics', *American Economic Review* (Papers & Proceedings), 64.

—— (1991) 'Sustainability – An Economist's Perspective', Department of Economics, Massachusetts Institute of Technology.

Squire, L. and Van der Taak, H. (1975) *Economic Analysis of Projects*, Johns Hopkins University Press, Baltimore, MD.

Tietenberg, T. (1988) *Environmental and Natural Resource Economics*, Second Edition, Scott, Forsman, Glenview, IL.

UNEP (1984) *General Assessment of Progress in the Implementation of the Plan of Action to Combat Desertification 1978-1984*, Report of the Executive Director, United Nations Environment Programme, Nairobi.

United Nations (1990) *Overall Socioeconomic Perspectives of the World Economy to the Year 2000*, UN Department of International Economic and Social Affairs, New York.

von Amsberg, J. (1993) 'Project Evaluation and the Depletion of Natural Capital: An Application of the Sustainability Principle', World Bank Environment Department Working Paper No. 56.

von Braun, J. and Kennedy, E.(1986) 'Commercialization of Subsistence Agriculture: Income and Nutritional Effects in Developing Countries', Working Paper on Commercialization of Agriculture and Nutrition No. 1, International Food Research Institute, Washington, DC.

Weitzman, M. L. (1970) 'Optimal Growth with Scale-Economies in the Creation of Overhead Capital', *Review of Economic Studies*, 37.

World Bank (1992) *World Development Report*, Oxford University Press, New York.

World Commission (1987) *Our Common Future*, Oxford University Press, New York.

9

THE CAPTURE OF GLOBAL ENVIRONMENTAL VALUE

David Pearce

INTRODUCTION AND THEME

As the twentieth century closes there is a recognition that many environmental problems have the properties of a global public good, or, perhaps better expressed, a global public 'bad'. If goods create human well-being, bads detract from it. Public goods are shared by all because their consumption by one person (or one country) entails their consumption by another person (or another country). For a good to be truly public it must also be effectively impossible to exclude these 'joint consumers' through pricing or other means (see Stevens, 1993). A global public bad, then, is a loss of global well-being brought about by the actions of individuals and nations and which it is impossible, or very difficult, for any one individual or country to avoid. The solutions to such problems tend to involve a deliberate change in property rights, usually through the creation of an international agreement to protect the global environment. Effectively, such agreements convert what were global *open access* resources into global *common property* resources. With open access there are no owners. With common property there are communal owners and their success in controlling the problem will depend on the design of incentives to maintain the agreement (Bromley, 1991).[1]

Two such agreements relating to global resources were negotiated at the Earth Summit in Rio de Janeiro in June 1992: the Framework Convention on Climate Change, and the Convention on Biological Diversity (for the texts of these Conventions, see Johnson, 1993). Before that, the Montreal Protocol on the protection of the earth's ozone layer had already been negotiated in 1987 (Munasinghe and King, 1991).[2] These agreements can be interpreted as signs that the world has come to its senses with respect to global pollution.

But there is one major underlying problem and, not surprisingly, it lies with the issue of making the relevant resource transfers from North to South.

First, it has to be questioned whether global agreements carry with them the financial power to make other than cosmetic differences to the state of the global environment. The targets agreed under the Conventions are modest enough, and their very modesty, when contrasted with the scale of the problems they seek to address, is testimony to the concern of the negotiators that 'saving the world' should not be too expensive a business.[3] In its 'Pilot Phase' for example, the Global Environment Facility will have disbursed funds of around $1 billion in a three-year period, i.e. $300–400 million p.a. In its operational phase, which commenced in 1994, it will have some $2 billion over a similar period. By comparison with the scale of the problems, the sums are trivial. In comparison with official aid flows they are perhaps 1.5 per cent of the total.

Second, if transfers are made to secure a global good, are these transfers to be seen as part of conventional development aid, or are they intrinsically something different? Conventional aid is aimed at development *within* nations. A reasonable, first-order, test of the potential success of such aid is that the economic benefits to the developing nation should exceed any costs it bears from the development action. This is orthodox benefit–cost analysis as embodied in numerous guidelines, manuals and texts. But intervening to secure the *global good* may not be consistent with conventional aid criteria: for example, benefits to the developing nation may be less than the costs, but the *global benefits* may exceed the net costs. From the global standpoint, the intervention is worthwhile. From the developing country standpoint, it is not unless its 'share' of global benefits exceeds the net 'domestic' costs. Self-evidently, the transfer must overcompensate the developing nation for the excess domestic costs. But developing nations may see greater gains by diverting resources to lobby developed nations and international agencies to make the global transfers more 'development oriented'. Indeed, that is exactly what has happened in the debate over prospective international transfers under the Rio Conventions, and under the non-binding and extremely wide-ranging document *Agenda 21* agreed at Rio.

Third, persuading developing countries to undertake actions for the global benefit may be difficult given the often starkly contrasting priorities of the developing and developed world. For most developing countries the priorities are food, shelter, energy, health and education – the 'basic needs' – and the prospect of economic growth. The conservation of biological diversity will often appear a low priority against such a backdrop, while even global warming control strikes few chords outside of the island and deltaic states.

These problems suggest the following interim conclusions:

(a) that 'official' transfers to secure global benefit are going to be small in any event, and that, if global problems matter, other sources of transfer have to be tapped;

(b) that transfers for global benefit must exploit, wherever possible, 'gains from trade', but with the trades having spin-offs in the form of development opportunities, i.e. all parties must be better off.

This chapter explores this theme and tries to identify the potential for 'low-cost' and 'win–win' solutions to global issues. While false optimism should not be generated, we conclude that there is a vast scope for mutually beneficial North–South 'trades' and that, by and large, the institutions to achieve them are already in place. In so far as new resource transfers are needed, the same focus – on mutually beneficial trades against the backdrop of the international agreements in place – will show how existing modest official flows can be leveraged to produce financial flows of some significance. We use the control of greenhouse gases and biodiversity conservation as our examples.

ENVIRONMENTALLY SENSITIVE RESOURCE TRANSFERS

While much has been done to make the flow of funds going from rich to poor countries more sensitive to environmental impacts, and more targeted at resource conservation and the enhancement of environmental quality, the actual flow that can be identified as truly 'green' remains unknown. The OECD countries spend approximately 1–1.5 per cent of their GNPs on their *own* environmental protection – a combination of public and private expenditures (OECD, 1991). If they spent that same fraction on conserving the global environment and the environments of the poor countries that cannot afford better environments, total 'green' resource flows might be some $100–150 billion per annum.[4] This is very similar to the actual total official development finance (ODF) of all kinds of $70 billion in 1991, plus around $55 billion of private flows (foreign direct investment, bank lending, etc.), or some $130 billion in total (OECD, 1992). Put another way, if the OECD countries spent as much on global and developing country environmental protection as they spend on their own environments, they would double the total resource flows to the developing countries.

The World Bank (1992) estimates that *additional* costs of some $70 billion p.a. will be needed by the year 2000 to meet selected *local* environmental programmes in the developing world – water and sanitation, air emissions control, effluent and solid waste management, soil conservation and family planning. To conserve and expand by 50 per cent the protected areas of the developing world would, they estimate, cost another $2.5 billion p.a. Addressing global and local LDC problems, then, is unlikely to cost more than, say, $100 billion per year. If that was all to be paid for by the OECD countries, it would add a cost of about 0.8 per cent of GNP to public and private resource transfers in the year 2000.[5] While much of the cost could be met from sustained economic growth in the developing world, a significant sum would remain as transfers from rich to poor countries. It has then to be borne in mind that the total *official* development assistance from OECD countries has remained at a fairly constant 0.35 per cent of OECD GNP since 1970 (OECD, 1992). In other words, if much of the cost of improving the global and local LDC environments has to come from *official* aid, the prospects look grim. If foreign aid has not changed as a proportion of the rich world's income in response to poverty, it hardly seems likely that it will respond differently to environmental concerns. Whether this view is just or not, it suggests the urgent need for a different approach – one based on the idea of mutual benefit and which does not require the maximization of the official, government content of North–South resource flows but which, instead, exhausts the opportunities for mutually beneficial trades.

THE FUNDAMENTAL CAUSES OF GLOBAL ENVIRONMENTAL CHANGE

This section sets out an elementary framework for assessing the potential for mutually beneficial trades in global environmental benefits. We choose biological diversity as the context. The fundamental forces giving rise to biodiversity loss arise from two factors:

(a) competition between humans and non-humans for the remaining ecological niches on land and in coastal regions; and
(b) 'failures' in the workings of the international and national economic systems.

Of course, other causes are at work as well. In a comprehensive view we would need to add misdirected past policies by bilateral and multilateral aid agencies, corruption, the indifference of much big business to environmental concerns, the results of international indebtedness and perhaps poverty itself. But, contrary perhaps to widespread opinion, these factors are not well understood and a popular mythology has emerged about them, usually more in keeping with preconceived political agendas than with any respect for proper research and judgement.

Niche competition

Most of the competition for space between humans and nature shows up in the conversion of land to agriculture, aquaculture, infrastructure, urban development, industry and unsustainable forestry. Table 9.1 shows land use conversions by world region between 1977 and 1987.

The loss of the world's forests, rich sources of biodiversity, is apparent, especially in Asia and South America. Unless the reasons for these conversions are understood, the outlook for the conservation of biodiversity is bleak.

Population pressure is clearly a force of some considerable importance. Whereas humans compete only marginally for niche space in the world's oceans, they compete directly with other species for land and coastal waters space. The story about world population change is by now well known. Table 9.2 records World Bank projections for the next 160 years. World population is expected to stabilize at around 12 billion people towards the end of the next century, but this is more than twice the number of people on earth today. The fastest growth rate is in Africa, currently growing at 2.9 per cent p.a. and heading for a population of 3 billion people towards the end of the next century, around five times the population of today.

Table 9.1 Land conversions 1977/9–1987/9 (million hectares)

	Cropland	Pasture	Forest	Other
Africa	+8	−4	−25	+22
North and Central America	+3	+11	+7	−20
South America	+14	+20	−41	+11
Asia	+4	−2	−29	+29
Europe	−2	−3	+2	+4

Note: Other land includes roads, uncultivated land, wetlands, built-on land.
Source: Estimated from World Resources Institute (1992, Table 17.1)

Table 9.2 World population projections (billion)

	1990	2100	2150
World population	5.4	12.0	12.2
% in:			
Asia/Oceania	59.4	57.0	56.8
North & South America	13.7	11.0	10.8
Africa	11.9	23.9	24.5
Europe	15.0	8.1	7.9

Source: World Bank

These figures suggest that sheer pressure of human beings on space will displace other living species. Some authors have argued that the *benefits* of this process probably outweigh the costs (e.g. Simon, 1981, 1986), but one suspects that such views arise from a lack of appreciation of the economic values embodied in biodiversity (Pearce and Moran, 1994). The displacement hypothesis should, however, be tested empirically. Brown and Pearce (1994a) bring together the findings of a number of studies on the factors that are statistically linked to one major environmental change – tropical deforestation. There it is suggested that population change is indeed a factor that is linked to forest loss.

The economic theory of species extinction was developed mainly in the water context and very largely in terms of the fishery (see Clark, 1990). There it is comparatively straightforward to see that a combination of *open access property rights* (no one owning the sea) and profitability (the difference between revenues and the cost of fishing effort) does much to explain overfishing and the loss of mammalian species. Once the theory is moved to land, the additional factor is the sheer competition for niche occupancy, and the theory needs to change, as Swanson (1994) has so elegantly demonstrated. Rather than saying open access explains excess harvesting effort, the question is why nation states allow open access conditions to prevail. Put another way, why do governments not invest more in conservation land uses? There are three immediate reasons and they comprise the second major strand in the explanation for biodiversity loss: an *economic theory of biodiversity loss*.

Economic failure as a cause of environmental loss

Local market failure

First, underinvestment arises for the classic economic reason of 'market failure'. What this means is that the interplay of market forces will not secure the economically correct balance of land conversion and land conservation. This is because those who convert the land do not have to compensate those who suffer the *local* consequences of that conversion – extra pollution and sedimentation of waters from deforestation, for example. The corrective solutions to this problem are well known – a tax on land conversion, zoning to restrict detrimental land uses, environmental standards, and so on. From this it follows that we cannot rely on market forces to save the world's biodiversity as long as biodiversity loss is one of the incidental effects of those market forces. Notice, however, that the measures needed to correct this market failure do not result in *zero* biodiversity loss. In the economist's language there is an 'optimal' rate of loss. It is less than what happens now, but it is not zero.

Intervention failure

Second, and a more recent explanation, is 'intervention failure' or 'government failure' – the deliberate intervention by governments in the working of market forces. As we shall see, this can coexist with market failure: both forces are at work at the same time. The examples are, by now, well known (Pearce and Warford, 1993) and include the subsidies to forest conversion for livestock in Brazil up to the end of the 1980s; the subsidies to beef in Botswana, inflated by preferential tariffs in the European Community; hedgerow removal and overintensive farming arising from above-equilibrium guaranteed prices under the European Common Agricultural Policy; the underpricing of irrigation water whether in California or Pakistan, and so on. What government intervention does is to distort the competitive playing field. We are used to hearing businesspeople using this language, but, while they often see environmental regulations as the means of hampering their competitive efficiency, the truth is that the same argument shows powerfully why the conservation of biological diversity is an uphill struggle. Governments effectively subsidize the rate of return to land conversion, tilting the economic balance against conservation.

Table 9.3(a) OECD agricultural subsidies (producer subsidy equivalents %)[6]

	1981–1984	*1985–1988*	*1989–1992*
Australia	11	12	12
Canada	30	47	45
EC	32	47	46
Japan	63	74	68
Sweden	38	55	57
United States	27	35	27
OECD	33	46	43

Source: OECD (1993)

Table 9.3(b) Agricultural input subsidies in developing countries

	Irrigation: subsidy as a % of price	*Pesticides: subsidy as a % of retail cost*
Bangladesh	82*	
Indonesia	86	82
Rep. of Korea	82	
Nepal	93	
Philippines	78	
Thailand	95	
China		19
Colombia		44
Ecuador		41
Egypt		83
Ghana		67
Senegal		89

* Operating costs only
Source: Pearce and Warford (1993)

Table 9.3 assembles some information on the scale of the distortions that governments introduce. Such distortions are widespread. While some OECD countries tax their agricultural sectors, most subsidize agriculture. Moreover, the extent of subsidy has *increased* in many cases. In the developing world, agricultural prices tend to be kept *below* their comparable border price, but *input prices* are subsidized.

Global appropriation failure

The rate of return to biodiversity conservation is distorted by what economists call 'missing markets'. What this means in the biodiversity context is that systems of habitat and species are serving valuable functions which are not marketed. Effectively, then, no one values these functions because there is no obvious mechanism for capturing the values. Local market failure described this phenomenon within the context of the country or local area. But there are *missing global markets* as well. We can consider two such global markets which are highly relevant to biodiversity: what economists call the 'non-use' or 'existence' value possessed by individuals in one country for wildlife and habitat in other countries, and the carbon storage values of tropical forests. *Global appropriation failure* (or GAF for short) arises because these values are not easily captured or appropriated by the countries in possession of biological diversity.

Non-use values

Economists use methods of measuring individual preferences, as revealed through individuals' 'willingness to pay' to conserve biodiversity. The methodologies include *contingent valuation* (CVM), which functions through sophisticated questionnaires which ask people their willingness to pay, and other techniques such as the *travel cost method*, the *hedonic property price* approach and the *production function* approach (Pearce, 1993). The economic values that are captured in this way are likely to be a mix of potential use value and non-use values. Use values relate to the valuation placed on the resource because the respondent makes use of it or might wish to make use of it in the future. Non-use values, or 'passive use values' as they are also called, relate to positive willingness to pay even if the respondent makes no use of the resource and has no intention of making use of it.

'Global valuations' of this kind are still few and far between. Table 9.4 assembles the results of some CVMs in several countries. These report willingness to pay for species and habitat conservation in the respondents' own country. These studies remain controversial, especially in light of the findings of the recent 'blue ribbon' panel on contingent valuation in the USA (Arrow *et al.*, 1993), although that same panel basically gave CVM a good bill of health provided rigorous rules of investigation are pursued. While we cannot say that similar kinds of expressed values will arise for the protection of biodiversity in other countries, even a benchmark figure of, say, $10 p.a. for the rich countries of Europe and North America would produce a fund of $4 billion p.a., around four times the mooted size of the fund that will be available to the Global Environment Facility in its operational phase as the financial mechanism under the two Rio Conventions and its continuing role in capturing global values from the international waters context (see later), and perhaps ten times what the fund will have available for helping with biodiversity conservation under the Rio Convention.

Table 9.4 Preference valuations for endangered species and prized habitats (1990 US$ p.a. per person)

	Species	
Norway:	Brown bear, wolf and wolverine	15.0
USA:	Bald eagle	12.4
	Emerald shiner	4.5
	Grizzly bear	18.5
	Bighorn sheep	8.6
	Whooping crane	1.2
	Blue whale	9.3
	Bottlenose dolphin	7.0
	California sea otter	8.1
	Northern elephant seal	8.1
	Humpback whales[1]	40–48 (without information) 49–64 (with information)
	Habitat	
USA:	Grand Canyon (visibility)	27.0
	Colorado wilderness	9.3–21.2
Australia:	Nadgee Nature Reserve, NSW	28.1
	Kakadu Conservation Zone, NT[2]	40.0 (minor damage) 93.0 (major damage)
UK:	Nature reserves[3]	40.0 ('experts' only)
Norway:	Conservation of rivers	59.0–107.0

Notes:
[1] Respondents divided into two groups, one of which was given video information.
[2] Two scenarios of mining development damage were given to respondents.
[3] Survey of informed 'expert' individuals only.
Source: Pearce (1993)

Carbon storage

All forests store carbon so that, if cleared for agriculture, there will be a release of carbon dioxide which will contribute to the accelerated greenhouse effect and hence global warming. In order to derive a value for the 'carbon credit' that should be ascribed to a tropical forest, we need to know (a) the net carbon released when forests are converted to other uses, and (b) the economic value of 1 tonne of carbon released to the atmosphere.

Carbon will be released at different rates according to the method of clearance and subsequent land use. With burning there will be an immediate release of CO_2 into the atmosphere, and some of the remaining carbon will be locked in ash and charcoal which is resistant to decay. The slash not converted by fire into CO_2 or charcoal and ash decays over time, releasing most of its carbon to the atmosphere within 10–20 years. Studies of tropical forests indicate that significant amounts of cleared vegetation become lumber, slash, charcoal and ash; the proportion differs for closed and open forests: the smaller stature and drier climate of open forests result in the combustion of a higher proportion of the vegetation.

If tropical forested land is converted to pasture or permanent agriculture, then the amount of carbon stored in secondary vegetation is equivalent to the carbon content of the biomass of crops planted, or the grass grown on the pasture. If a secondary forest is allowed to grow, then carbon will accumulate, and maximum biomass density is attained after a relatively short time.

Table 9.5 illustrates the net carbon storage effects of land use conversion from tropical forests (closed primary, closed secondary, or open forests) to shifting cultivation, permanent agriculture, or pasture. The negative figures represent emissions of carbon; for example, conversion from closed primary forest to shifting agriculture results in a net loss of 194 tC/ha. The greatest loss of carbon involves change of land use from primary closed forest to permanent agriculture. These figures represent the once-and-for-all change that will occur in carbon storage as a result of the various land use conversions.

Table 9.5 Changes in carbon with land use conversion (tC/ha)

	Original C	Shifting Agriculture*	Permanent Agriculture	Pasture
Original C		79	63	63
Closed primary	283	− 204	− 220	− 220
Closed secondary	194	− 106	− 152	− 122
Open forest	115	− 36	− 52	− 52

* Shifting agriculture represents carbon in biomass and soils in second year of shifting cultivation cycle
Source: Brown and Pearce (1994b)

The data suggest that, allowing for the carbon fixed by subsequent land uses, carbon released from deforestation of secondary and primary tropical forest is of the order of 100-200 tonnes of carbon per hectare.[7]

The carbon released from burning tropical forests contributes to global warming, and we now have several estimates of the minimum economic damage done by global warming, leaving aside catastrophic events. Recent work by Fankhauser (1993) suggests a 'central' value of $20 of damage for every tonne of carbon released. Applying this figure to the data in Table 9.5, we can conclude that converting an open forest to agriculture or pasture would result in global warming damage of, say, $600–1000 per hectare; conversion of closed secondary forest would cause damage of $2000–3000 per hectare; and conversion of primary forest to agriculture would give rise to damage of about $4000–4400 per hectare. Note that these estimates allow for carbon fixation in the subsequent land use.

How do these estimates relate to the development benefits of land use conversion? We can illustrate this with respect to the Amazon region of Brazil. Schneider (1992) reports upper bound values of $300 per hectare for land in Rondonia. The figures suggest carbon credit values 2–15 times the price of land in Rondonia. These 'carbon credits' also compare favourably with the value of forest land for timber in, say Indonesia, where estimates are of the order of $2000–2500 per hectare. All this suggests the scope for a global bargain. The land is worth $300 per hectare to the forest colonist but several times this to the world at large. If the North can transfer a sum of money greater than $300 but less than the damage cost from global warming, there are mutual gains to be obtained.

Note that if the transfers did take place at, say, $500 per hectare, then the cost per tonne of carbon reduced is of the order of $5 ($500/100 tC/ha). These unit costs compare favourably with those to be achieved by carbon emission reduction policies through fossil fuel conversion. *Avoiding deforestation* becomes a legitimate and potentially important means of reducing global warming rates.

A synthesis

Figure 9.1 brings together the economic analysis of conservation 'failure'. The vertical axis shows money ($). The horizontal axes show the extent of land conversion, the main factor involved in biodiversity loss, and the 'amount' of biodiversity (BD) conserved. Land conversion and BD are therefore inversely related.

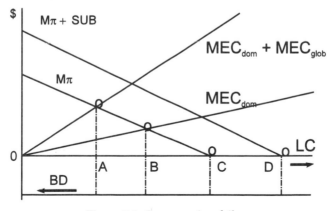

Figure 9.1 Conservation failure

213

The curves shown are *marginal* benefit and cost functions. Thus, $M\pi$ is the marginal profit accruing to the country from land conversion. $M\pi + SUB$ shows the effect of subsidizing land conversion. More land is converted, with the result that there is less biodiversity. MEC_{dom} is the marginal external damage from land conversion which is borne by the country itself, say in the form of loss of watershed protection, reduced medicinal plants, etc. $MEC_{dom} + MEC_{glob}$ shows the externality from land conversion but now including the loss in global benefit.

Inspection of the diagram shows that point A is the overall optimum where the optimal amount of local and global externality occurs. Point B is the domestic optimum allowing for domestic externalities only. Point C is the free-market solution when there are no subsidies, and point D is the solution when there are subsidies. The distance CD is 'intervention failure'; distance BC is domestic market failure; and distance AB is global market failure. The gap between A and D describes the overall level of failure due to the market, intervention and global failure. Clearly, this distance could be very large.

Note that the more land is conserved, the greater the opportunity cost of that conservation. In Kenya, for example, it has been estimated that land conservation for biodiversity purposes (including wildlife tourism) costs Kenya around 2.5 per cent of its GNP (Norton-Griffiths, 1995).

There are clear opportunities for 'no-regret' or 'win–win' situations that can be brought about by the removal of market and government failure, as discussed above. Terminology like 'win–win' may be something of an exaggeration – subsidy measures often have their own social purposes – but it is often true. A great deal of biodiversity can be conserved by 'getting domestic policies right'. This must not be used to argue that resource transfers are not appropriate: there should still be resource transfers from North to South regardless of the existence of no-regret measures. Equally, it cannot be argued that *all* biodiversity conservation requires financial transfers. North and South perspectives often differ on this issue, as is revealed in the text of the Rio Biodiversity Convention. Article 11 clearly attempts to locate some responsibility in the developing world for biodiversity loss through domestic distortions:

> Each contracting party shall, as far as possible and as appropriate, adopt economically and socially sound measures that act as incentives for the conservation and sustainable use of components of biological diversity.

By implication, the removal of distortions constitutes such a 'sound measure'. But Article 20.4 asserts:

> The extent to which developing country Parties will effectively im-
> plement their commitments under this Convention will depend on the

effective implementation by developed country Parties of their commitments under this Convention related to financial resources and transfer of technology and will fully take into account the fact that economic and social development and the eradication of poverty are the first and overriding priorities of the developing country Parties.

In other words, the developing world places responsibility for conservation on the developed world through transfer mechanisms, and implies that there are no domestic distortions.

CREATING GLOBAL ENVIRONMENTAL MARKETS

We can now focus on global appropriation failure. There are several ways in which global appropriation failure can be corrected through creating global environmental markets (GEMs). We distinguish between private and public ('official') ventures, and between those that are regulation-induced and those that are 'spontaneous market' initiatives. Public regulation-induced activity arises because of international agreements, such as the Biodiversity and Climate Change Conventions. Table 9.6 sets out the resulting schema. The examples listed are dealt with more fully below.

Table 9.6 A schema for global environmental markets

	Regulation-induced	*Spontaneous market*
Public/official ventures	Examples: government to government measures under joint implementation provisions of the Rio treaties: Norway, Mexico, Poland, GEF	Example: government involvement in market ventures: Swiss Green Export aid; debt-for-nature swaps
Private sector ventures	Examples: carbon offsets against carbon taxes and externality adders	Examples: purchase of exotic capital – Merck and Costa Rica

Regulation-induced markets

The first way in which markets are emerging is via the existence of regulations or anticipated regulations. In turn, these regulations are international and national but since implementation is always at the national level we can treat them together.

Government–government trades

An example of an international regulation is the Framework Climate Convention negotiated at Rio in 1992. Under the Convention each ratifying

215

country will have an obligation to cut back on CO_2 emissions, but the Convention quite explicitly recognizes that it is often cheaper for one country to cut back on emissions in another country, besides making its own domestic effort to cut back. Similarly, it may be cheaper to create 'sinks' for CO_2 in another country compared with cutting back domestically (Barrett, 1993a, b). This scope for 'carbon offsets' or 'joint implementation' is potentially large, and the first joint implementation agreement has already been agreed between Norway, Poland and Mexico, through the medium of the Global Environment Facility (GEF). Norway agrees to create additional financing (through the revenues from its own carbon tax) for GEF carbon-reducing projects in Mexico (energy-efficient lighting) and Poland (converting from coal burning to natural gas) (Global Environment Facility, 1992). The US Environmental Defense Fund is understood to be in the process (1993) of developing a reforestation project in Russia. The US government announced the *Forest for the Future Initiative* (FFI) in January 1993 under which carbon offset agreements will be negotiated between the USA and several countries, including Mexico, Russia, Guatemala, Indonesia and Papua New Guinea. The aim is for the US Environmental Protection Agency to broker deals involving the private sector.

As yet, the procedures for joint implementation under the Convention are not agreed and it is likely that more deals will develop once the ground rules have been established.

Private sector trades

The European Community Draft Directive on a carbon tax and other European legislation also provide an incentive to trade in this way, as does state regulation on pollution by electric utilities in the USA. While not strictly a private enterprise trade, in the *Netherlands*, the state electricity generating board (SEP) has established a non-profit-making enterprise (FACE – Forests Absorbing Carbon Dioxide Emissions) and is planning to invest in forest rehabilitation to absorb CO_2 in Czechoslovakia, Indonesia, Ecuador, Costa Rica and the Netherlands itself. The FACE Foundation already has a contract with Innoprise in Sabah, Malaysia, for the regeneration of degraded forest lands.

In the US case the offset deals are currently not *directly* linked to legislation, but several have occurred which are clearly a mix of anticipation of regulation and 'global good citizenship' (Newcombe and de Lucia, 1993). These include the *New England Electric System*'s investment in carbon sequestration in Sabah, Malaysia, through the reduction of carbon waste from inefficient logging activities. The forest products enterprise is run by Innoprise. New England Electric estimate that some 300,000 to 600,000 tonnes of carbon (C) will be offset at a cost of below \$2 tC. Rain Forest

Alliance will assist in monitoring the project. New England Electric regard the Innoprise project as the first of a series aimed at assisting with the Corporation's plan to reduce CO_2 emissions by 45 per cent by the year 2000. *PacifiCorp*, an electric utility in Oregon, is considering reforestation projects and urban tree planting programmes in the USA, and an international sequestration project (Dixon *et al.*, 1993). Two pilot projects have been announced: (a) a rural reforestation project in southern Oregon which funds planting subject to a constraint of no harvesting for 45–65 years, at an estimated cost of around $5 tC; and (b) an urban tree programme in Salt Lake City, Utah, at a provisionally estimated cost of $15-30 tC sequestered. *Tenaska* Corporation is considering sequestration projects in the Russian boreal forests. Ultimately, some 20,000 ha of forests may be created in the Saratov and Volgograd regions at a cost of $1-2 tC. Russian partners in the venture include the Russian Forest Service, the Ministry of Ecology and others.

While these investments are aimed at CO_2 reduction, sequestration clearly has the potential for generating joint benefits, i.e. for saving biodiversity as well through the recreation of habitats. Much depends here on the *nature* of the offset. If the aim is CO_2 fixation alone, there will be a temptation to invest in fast-growing species which could be to the detriment of biodiversity. It is important therefore to extend the offset concept so that larger credits are given for investments which produce joint biodiversity–CO_2 reduction benefits.

The US Energy Policy Act of 1992 requires the Energy Information Administration to develop guidelines for the establishment of a database on greenhouse gas offsets, together with an offset 'bank'. The Keystone Center in the USA is also establishing an interchange of information with a number of electric utilities to explore the issues involved in establishing offset deals.

Global good citizenship

Several offset deals appear to have been undertaken quite independently of legislation or anticipation of regulation. *Applied Energy Services* (AES) of Virginia has also undertaken sequestration investments in Guatemala (agroforestry) and Paraguay and is in the process of setting up another project in the Amazon Basin. The Guatemala project is designed to offset emissions from an 1800 MW coal-fired power plant being built in Uncasville, Connecticut. The intermediary for the project is the World Resources Institute and in Guatemala the implementing agency is CARE. The project involves tree planting by some 40,000 farm families. Carbon sequestration is estimated to be 15.5 million tons of carbon. The $14 million cost includes $2 million contribution from AES; $1.2 million from the government of Guatemala; $1.8 million from CARE; with the balance coming in kind from US

AID and the Peace Corps. Note that the motivations for involvement vary. AES's involvement relates to its concern to offset CO_2 emissions, whereas other partners are concerned with the local development and environmental benefits the deal brings. Dixon *et al.* (1993) report the sequestration cost as $9 tC overall, but inspection of the data suggests it may be less than this; $9 tC would be expensive for carbon sequestration alone, but there are other benefits from the scheme, including local economic benefits. In the Paraguay deal, AES is planning to advance money to the (US) Nature Conservancy for investment in some 57,000 ha of endangered tropical forest. AES expects to sequester some 13 million tC at around $1.5 per tC. Local benefits include ecotourism, scientific research, recreation, agroforestry and watershed protection.

Table 9.7 summarizes the private sector carbon offset deals to date (mid-1993).

Table 9.7 Private sector carbon offset deals

Company	Project	Other participants	Million tC sequestered	Total cost $ million	$ tC sequestered
AES	Agroforestry Guatemala	US CARE Govt of Guatemala	15–58 over 40 years	14	(a) 0.5–2* (b) 1–4 (c) 9
AES	Agroforestry Paraguay	US Nature Conservancy, FMB	13 over 30 years	2	(a) 0.2 (b) 0.4 (c) < 1.5
NEES	Forestry Malaysia	Rain Forest Alliance COPEC	0.3–0.6, period not stated	0.45	(a) n.a. (b) n.a. (c) < 2
SEP	Reforestation, Malaysia	Innoprise	? over 25 years	1.3	(a) n.a. (b) n.a. (c) n.a.
Tenaska	Reforestation, Russia	Trexler, Min. of Ecology, Russian Forest Service, etc.	0.5 over 25 years	0.5?	(a) n.a. (b) n.a. (c) 1–2
PacifiCorp	Forestry, Oregon	Trexler	0.06 p.a.	0.1 p.a.	(a) n.a. (b) n.a. (c) 5
PacifiCorp	Urban trees, Utah	Trexler, TreeUtah	?	0.1 p.a.	(a) n.a. (b) n.a. (c) 15–30

Notes:
(a) Assumes 10% discount rate applied to total cost to obtain an annuity which is then applied to carbon fixed per annum, assuming equal distribution of carbon sequestered over the time horizon indicated.
(b) Assumes 4% discount rate applied to costs.
(c) cost per tC as reported in Dixon *et al.* (1993).
* Barrett (1993a) estimates the total cost of sequestration at $0.73 tC
Source: adapted from Dixon *et al.* (1993) and Bann (1993)

'Exotic capital'

Financial transfers may take place without any regulatory 'push'. The consumer demand for green products has already resulted in companies deciding to invest in conservation either for direct profit or because of a mix of profit and conservation motives. The Body Shop is an illustration of the mixed motive, as is Merck's royalty deal with Costa Rica for pharmaceutical plants and Pro-Natura's expanding venture in marketing indigenous tropical forest products. There is, in other words, an incentive to purchase or lease 'exotic capital' in the same way as a company would buy or lease any other form of capital.

The deal between *Merck & Co*, the world's largest pharmaceutical company, and INBio (the National Biodiversity Institute of Costa Rica) is already well documented and studied (Gámez *et al.*, 1993; Sittenfield and Gámez, 1993; Blum, 1993). Under the agreement, INBio collects and processes plant, insect and soil samples in Costa Rica and supplies them to Merck for assessment. In return, Merck pays Costa Rica $1 million plus a share of any royalties should any successful drug be developed from the supplied material. The royalty agreement is reputed to be of the order of 1 per cent to 3 per cent and to be shared between INBio and the Costa Rican government. Patent rights to any successful drug would remain with Merck. Biodiversity is protected in two ways – by conferring commercial value on the biodiversity, and through the earmarking of some of the payments for the Ministry of Natural Resources.

How far is the Merck–INBio deal likely to be repeated? Several caveats are in order to offset some of the enthusiasm over this single deal. First, Costa Rica is in the vanguard of biodiversity conservation, as its strong record in debt-for-nature swaps shows. Second, Costa Rica has a strong scientific base and a considerable degree of political stability. Both of these characteristics need to be present and their combination is not typical of that many developing countries. Third, the economic value of such deals is minimal *unless* the royalties are actually paid and that will mean success in developing drugs from the relevant genetic material. The chances of such developments are small – perhaps one in 1–10,000 of plant species screened (Pearce and Moran, 1994). INBio has undertaken to supply 10,000 samples under the initial agreement. There is therefore a chance of one such drug being developed. But successful drugs could result in many hundreds of millions of dollars in revenues. Finally, there are two views on the extent to which deals of this kind could be given added impetus by the Biodiversity Convention. The Convention stresses the role of intellectual property rights in securing conservation and is sufficiently vaguely worded for there to be wide interpretation of its provisions. But it also appears to threaten stringent conditions concerning those rights and technology transfer and it remains to be seen how the relevant Protocols are worded. If so, parties to the Convention may find private deals being turned into overtly more political affairs with major constraints on what can be negotiated (Blum, 1993).

Other examples of direct deals on 'biodiversity prospecting' include California's Shaman Pharmaceuticals (Brazil and Argentina) and the UK's Biotics Ltd (general purchase and royalty deals), while Mexico and Indonesia are looking closely at the commercialization of biodiversity resources.

The demand for direct investment in conservation is not confined to the private sector. The demand for conservation by NGOs is revealed through debt-for-nature swaps, which are further examples of these exotic capital trades (for an overview see Pearce and Moran (1994) and Deacon and Murphy (1992)).

Buying down private risk

Newcombe and de Lucia (1993) have drawn attention to another, potentially very large private trade which has global environmental benefits. Investment by the private sector in the developing world is invariably constrained by risk factors such as exchange rate risks, repayment risks, political risks and so on. In so far as this investment benefits the global environment, as with, say, the development of natural gas to displace coal, the existence of the risks reduces the flow of investment and hence the global environmental benefits. But these risks might be shared ('bought down') by having an international agency, such as the Global Environment Facility, provide some funds or services which help reduce the risk. Given the scale of private investment flows, the potential here is enormous. Nor is there any reason why it should not benefit biodiversity, either indirectly as a joint benefit of other investments in, for example, raising agricultural productivity and hence in reducing the pressure for land degradation, or directly through afforestation schemes.

CONCLUSIONS

With population set to double in the next eighty years or so, it is unrealistic to expect to save the world's biodiversity. Much of it will be lost. But much of it can be saved. There is a major role to be played by regulations and agreements, but the prospects for real action must lie in (a) leveraging the flow of funds that will occur under international agreements, and (b) exploiting every possibility for mutual economic gain that also generates biodiversity conservation benefits. The idea of exploiting mutual economic gain will strike many as morally unacceptable, but the same viewpoint – while heartfelt – partly explains why we have the problem in the first place. Taking the moral high ground may be satisfying for the moralist, but it has not yet produced the wave of resources needed to contain the problem, nor is it likely to. The answer is to pioneer on all fronts. The economic approach looks especially promising. This chapter has argued that there is substantial potential for mutual gain through 'global trades'. This should not divert attention from the continuing need to correct domestic policies in the developing and developed world alike. All forms of economic failure need to be addressed.

NOTES

1 Garret Hardin's 'tragedy of the commons' confused open access and common property. The 'tragedy' of mutual overuse and destruction relates to open access not common property. See Hardin (1968).

2 Arguably, the Montreal Protocol and the Climate Change Convention deal with truly global public goods – the ozone layer and the earth's carbon cycle – whereas the Biodiversity Convention deals with a mixed public–private good. Biological diversity is a private good in so far as its uses are competitive (e.g. ecotourism vs local and international hunting), and a public good in so far as it generates some kind of 'primary value' upon which other values depend. An example of primary value would be the link between diversity and ecological stability – see Perrings and Pearce (1993). Note that an attempt to get a similar convention on conserving the world's forests was not successful at Rio. In contrast, a convention on 'desertification' – interpreted as dryland degradation – has been negotiated (1993).

3 Indeed, the USA did not originally sign the Biodiversity Convention for this reason, and other countries, notably the United Kingdom, also had qualms about signing. Ratification may be even more problematic.

4 1–1.5 per cent of OECD GNP of $10 trillion.

5 Assuming 3 per cent economic growth, OECD's $10 trillion GNP would rise to around $12 trillion in 2000; $100 billion as a percentage of $12 trillion is then 0.8 per cent.

6 A PSE equals

$$Q(P - PW) + DP - LV + OS$$

and a percentage PSE equals

$$PSE/[Q(P - PW_{nc}) + DP - LV]$$

where Q = volume of production; P = domestic producer price; PW_{nc} = border price in national currency; DP = direct payments; LV = levies on production; OS = other support.

7 A refinement to these estimates would estimate the present value of the carbon releases by discounting future carbon releases. That is, all the carbon is not released in the initial burning. There may be subsequent burnings, and there may be some slower release of carbon over time.

REFERENCES

Arrow, K., Solow, R., Portney, P., Leamer, E., Radner, R. and Schuman, H. (1993) *Report of the NOAA Panel on Contingent Valuation*, National Oceanic and Atmospheric Administration, US Department of Commerce, Washington, DC.

Bann, C. (1993) *The Private Sector and Global Warming Mitigation*, Centre for Social and Economic Research on the Global Environment, University College London, Mimeo.

Barrett, S. (1993a) *Joint Implementation for Achieving National Abatement Commitments in the Framework Convention on Climate Change*, Report to the Environment Directorate, Organization for Economic Cooperation and Development (OECD), Paris; London Business School and Centre for Social and Economic Research on the Global Environment, University College London, Mimeo.

——(1993b) *A Strategic Analysis of 'Joint Implementation' Mechanisms in the Framework Convention on Climate Change*, Report to the United Nations Conference on Trade and Development (UNCTAD), Geneva; London Business School and Centre for Social and Economic Research on the Global Environment, University College London, Mimeo.

Blum, E. (1993) 'Making Biodiversity Conservation Profitable: A Case Study of the Merck.INBio Agreement', *Environment*, vol. 35, no. 4, May.

Bromley, D. W. (1991) *Environment and Economy: Property Rights and Public Policy*, Blackwell, Oxford.

Brown, K and Pearce, D. W. (1994a) *The Causes of Deforestation*, University College London Press, London.

——(1994b) 'The Economic Value of Carbon Storage in Tropical Forests', in S. Weiss (ed.) *The Economics of Project Appraisal and the Environment*, Edward Elgar, London, pp. 102–123.

Clark, C. (1990) *Mathematical Bioeconomics*, Second Edition, Wiley, New York.

Deacon, R. and Murphy, P. (1992) 'The Structure of an Environmental Transaction: The Debt-for-Nature Swap', Department of Economics, University of California at Santa Barbara, Mimeo.

Dixon, R., Andrasko, K., Sussman, F., Trexler, M. and Vinson, T. (1993), 'Forest Sector Carbon Offset Projects: Near-Term Opportunities to Mitigate Greenhouse Gas Emissions', *Water, Air and Soil Pollution*, Special Issue.

Fankhauser, S. (1993) 'Global Warming Damage Costs: Some Monetary Estimates', Centre for Social and Economic Research on the Global Environment, University College London, Mimeo.

Gámez, R., Piva, A., Sittenfield, A., Leon, E., Jimenez, J. and Mirabelli, G. (1993) 'Costa Rica's Conservation Program and National Biodiversity Institute (INBio)', in W. Reid *et al.* (eds) *Biodiversity Prospecting: Using Genetic Resources for Sustainable Development*, World Resources Institute, Washington, DC.

Global Environment Facility (1992) *Memorandum of Understanding on Norwegian Funding of Pilot Demonstration Projects for Joint Implementation Arrangements under the Climate Convention*, GEF, World Bank, Washington, DC, Mimeo.

Hardin, G. (1968) 'The Tragedy of the Commons', *Science*, vol. 162, 13 December.

Johnson, S. (1993) *The Earth Summit*, Graham and Trotman, London.

Munasinghe, M. and King, K. (1991) *Issues and Options in Implementing the Montreal Protocol in Developing Countries*, World Bank Environment Working Paper No. 49, World Bank, Washington, DC.

Newcombe, K. and de Lucia, R. (1993) 'Mobilizing Private Capital Against Global Warming: A Business Concept and Policy Issues', Global Environment Facility, Washington, DC, Mimeo.

Norton-Griffiths, M. (1995) 'The Opportunity Costs of Biodiversity Conservation' *Ecological Economics*, vol. 12, pp. 125–139.

OECD (Organisation for Economic Cooperation and Development) (1991) *OECD Environmental Data: Compendium 1991*, OECD, Paris.

——(1992) *Development Cooperation: 1992 Report*, OECD, Paris.

——(1993) *Agricultural Policies, Markets and Trade: Monitoring and Outlook 1993*, OECD, Paris.

Pearce, D. W. (1993) *Economic Values and the Natural World*, Earthscan, London.

Pearce, D. W. and Moran, D. (1994) *The Economic Value of Biological Diversity*, Earthscan, London.

Pearce, D. W. and Warford, J. (1993) *World Without End: Economics, Environment and Sustainable Development*, Oxford University Press, New York and Oxford.

Perrings, P. and Pearce, D. W. (1994) 'Biodiversity Conservation and Economic Development', *Environmental and Resource Economics*.

Schneider, R. (1992) *Brazil: An Analysis of Environmental Problems in Amazonia*, World Bank, Washington, DC.

Simon, J. (1981) *The Ultimate Resource*, Martin Robertson, Oxford.

——(1986) *Theory of Population and Economic Growth*, Blackwell, Oxford.

Sittenfield, A. and Gámez, R. (1993) 'Biodiversity Prospecting in INBio', in W. Reid et al. (eds) *Biodiversity Prospecting: Using Genetic Resources for Sustainable Development*, World Resources Institute, Washington, DC.

Stevens, J. (1993) *The Economics of Collective Choice*, Westview Press, Boulder, CO.

Swanson, T. (1994) *The International Regulation of Extinction*, Macmillan, London.

World Bank (1992) *World Development Report 1992*, Oxford University Press, Oxford.

World Resources Institute (1992) *World Resources 1992–1993*, Oxford University Press, Oxford.

10

ENVIRONMENTAL TAX REFORM

Theory, industrialized country experience
and relevance in LDCs

Thomas Sterner

INTRODUCTION

Sustainable development of the economy requires at least two things: first that economic activities such as industry, fisheries, forestry and agriculture are carried on in a way that is compatible with the natural preconditions of the local ecology, and second that the development of the economy itself is coherent requiring, among many other things, a certain degree of long-run balance in current accounts and government accounts. The first of these is ecological management and the second economic management. We shall discuss in this chapter some issues that are related to both types of management. Our principal focus will be on taxation which we think is a potent instrument of environmental policy and also has the advantage of bringing in much needed public revenue.

Demands for reform together with the difficulty of raising revenue have consistently led to public deficits. In many developing countries aid has come to be a major source of finance for the government creating a fiscal dependency which is not desirable – neither because of the dependency created on other countries, nor because it gives the ruling elite a feeling of independence or autonomy. If they are not dependent on finance from their electorate this in practice reduces their accountability and even legitimacy.

As part of the general reform process sweeping across the world, often under such names as structural adjustment, there are a couple of general guiding principles such as the importance of 'getting the prices right', limiting the intervention of government to appropriate areas. The issue of what actually constitutes 'right' prices is, however, quite complex since there is often a delicate trade-off between considerations of allocative efficiency and distributional aspects.

Most of the reforms recommended in Third World countries have implications for their budget. Cutting tariffs may reduce one popular source of income, likewise the reduction in the role of parastatals, and thereby the potential of non-tax income for the state. Many countries find that aid is being cut too and governments in the Third World are faced with a very difficult situation. This can be visualized as if they were faced with two lists: one of reforms, income transfers and projects that need to be financed, subsidized or supported; and one of possible sources of income. We will not dwell on the first list but merely say that it is a long list of urgent issues ranging from law and order through education to infrastructure, catastrophe relief, health and so forth. The second list is, however, sadly short. Apart from the world community (in the form of aid), there is little else to tax. Taxing private income is in many countries a difficult alternative: the poor are too poor and the rich too powerful. Taxing trade is distortive to the economy. Taxing foreign capital, profits, property, etc., implies a risk of scaring away international capital and thus of slowing down growth and lowering employment. Commodity taxation has some, limited, potential because the main staple items of the economy such as food and housing are consumed by the very poor and indeed there are in many cases demands for subsidies rather than taxes on these items. Taxing luxuries is ideal both from an allocative and a distributional viewpoint, but it actually provides very little revenue!

Given this situation, visualized as a long list of items worthy and needy of subsidies and a short list of 'taxables' – and given the long-run need to balance the budget – it is natural to focus on the idea of taxing goods or services that create environmental or resource problems. Such taxes may have a 'double dividend' in that they both help reduce an environmental problem (such as water scarcity, urban air pollution, overuse of pesticides, etc.) and help finance the budget.

GROWTH, SUSTAINABILITY AND ENVIRONMENTAL POLICIES

Economic and population growth have brought us up against a whole series of natural resource constraints and many of the problems we face can be thought of as natural resource management problems. The economist immediately thinks of rising scarcity rents as in the models inspired by Hotelling (1931). According to these models a natural resource will not just get depleted since the owner will have an interest in saving some as scarcity increases. This leads to rising prices and the prices in their turn act as a rationing mechanism encouraging technological improvements that lead to economizing with the scarce resource and if possible to substitution by other resources.

The trouble with many environmentally important resources is that they have no owner or at least lack effective ownership control and thus this mechanism does not work. This is clearly the case for the atmosphere. We inherited an atmosphere with a certain concentration of gases including carbon dioxide to which we are adapted. We are now using the atmosphere as a waste disposal site for our combustion byproducts such as carbon dioxide. In a sense we are thereby mining a 'resource' which we could call 'the absence of too high a level of carbon in the atmosphere'. However, this resource (as opposed to ordinary fossil resources of oil and coal) has no owner and thus fetches no price in the market place.

This is the motivation for economic policy in this area: to correct for this 'market failure' by substituting other mechanisms such as taxes or other rules that will ration demand to the necessary levels. We should, however, notice that environmental management requires a whole set of policy instruments of which taxation is only one. There are numerous cases, such as the management of small common property resources, in which national taxation is not only ineffective but even counterproductive since such resources can only be managed at the local level. This applies to many local fisheries, hunting grounds, pastures, forests, irrigation systems as well as other systems of water supply and so forth; see for instance Ostrom (1990) for a careful analysis of the type of policies and institutions that may successfully be applied for common property resource management.

At the other end of the scale, global problems are again not easily amenable to national policy instruments. They may, however, be very interesting from a Third World perspective since 'management of the global commons' may very well imply large transfers of resources from the industrialized countries.

Both these topics – of local as well as global commons – are extremely important and at least the latter may have some relevance also for national taxation. We will, however, in this chapter concentrate on the type of environmental or natural resource problems that can most easily be delineated within a national perspective and thus be dealt with by, for instance, national taxes. For a recent survey of environmental policies in developed and developing countries see Sterner (1994).

THE CHOICE OF ENVIRONMENTAL POLICY INSTRUMENTS

In the simplest textbook models, quantitative regulations (requiring production or emissions to diminish) and price mechanisms (adding a tax to reflect external costs) have much the same effect. However, there are many factors which may modify this result in practice. One of the most essential reasons why economists prefer the market mechanism is that it has a vastly superior static efficiency when cost functions differ strongly between units.

However, if we do not know the cost functions we run the risk of choosing the wrong tax level. The cost of this can be quite high and depends very much on the elasticities (slopes) of the supply and demand curves.

With very steep slopes for environmental costs (when we have serious and maybe irreversible changes such as death due to toxic chemicals) the cost of choosing a wrong tax level may be too high and other instruments may be preferable.

Sometimes the tax level can be corrected by trial and error. But if clean-up requires large and long-run investments or if the environmental costs of being wrong are high (higher than the costs of excessive clean-up) then the basic message is that we will not want to rely on taxes (alone). In this case regulation would be preferable but there is still a chance of using the market mechanism by creating a market for the regulated units of emission themselves!

Such rights are generally called tradable emission permits (TEPs). There are numerous other policy instruments such as subsidies, deposit–refund systems, legal systems of liability and insurance, etc., that can all play important roles depending on the exact circumstances. In choosing a policy instrument we need to consider not only the environmental problem at hand but also the economic and social context and ask ourselves questions such as: is this a market with competition? Is it an area of rapid technological progress? What are the informational requirements? How will the costs of control and enforcement depend on the choice of policy instrument? There is not sufficient space to go into these issues here but clearly there are many different kinds of consideration that may be relevant for the choice of policy instrument. These include cost efficiency (in a static as well as a dynamic framework), administrative, transaction and information costs, the creation of barriers to entry – particularly in non-competitive markets – and finally various aspects concerned with the perceived distribution of costs and thus the 'fairness' and acceptability of the instrument chosen. The spatial distribution of emissions, and in general of economic activities, is another very important factor since the collection of taxes as well as the incidence of pollution may well have important effects on the regional distribution of income. Cost efficiency would here be taken to mean that the same effect cannot be achieved at a lower cost through some other mechanism, while the concept of 'optimality' when applied to policy instruments would include the other considerations mentioned above.

Pigouvian taxes

Taxes are thus not the only instrument available and they are not always suitable. They are, however, in many instances superior to regulations and we will therefore continue to concentrate on taxes. Early economists, such as Pigou, already recognized that taxes could be used to correct for (negative) externalities such as are associated with environmental problems of pollution or of crowding on common property. In the context of Third World countries we will mainly be concerned with product taxes levied on environmental grounds, but in some cases pure taxation of emissions and effluents could also be warranted.

In Figure 10.1 the free-market equilibrium is found where the supply curve MC_p, which only takes ordinary, private, costs into account, crosses the demand curve. At this point, however, environmental costs $(E_1 + E_2)$ are incurred but not taken into consideration. The true social optimum is instead found where total social marginal costs MC_S $(= MC_p + MC_e)$ crosses the demand curve giving a volume of q_2 instead of q_1. Note that the new point does imply a loss of consumers' surplus $(= A)$ and producers' surplus $(= B)$ but that these are more than outweighed by the decrease in environmental costs E_1.

Notice that there are still environmental costs $(= E_2)$ and that these exactly correspond to the taxes paid $(= T)$.[1] This analysis does not take into account the use of these proceeds, nor whether this additional tax revenue may be positive for the economy. It is a partial analysis which rather treats the environment as any other service such as water for which the company would pay. By this analogy some observers argue that the proceeds should be used to maintain the supply of the environmental service in question. This would obviously give additional environmental benefits but these must be weighed against other uses of the public funds acquired. Note that these issues fall outside what is traditionally meant by Pigouvian taxation and that the tax itself causes an improvement in the environmental situation irrespective of how the tax proceeds are used. Notice, however, that there is an asymmetry implicit in the fact that the environmental benefits E_1 are of a public good nature while the allocative costs $A + B$ are of a traditional private nature. We will return to this point later.

We should also remind the reader that these environmental improvements could generally be reached by other policy instruments which may or may not give the state revenue (or imply costs for the state). Examples of such instruments are command-and-control regulations, subsidies, tradable permits (auctioned or grandfathered, etc.). The choice between these instruments depends on a large number of criteria such as their efficiency, flexibility and costs as described above.

THE THEORY OF OPTIMAL TAXATION: A BRIEF OVERVIEW

Leaving environmental issues completely aside for a moment, we turn, very briefly, to the issue of taxation. (This is not the place for an extensive presentation of the theory of optimal taxation: we will simply enumerate some main results.) In the simplified world of textbook economics the first goal of optimal taxation is to create a tax system that will induce a minimum of distortions to economic behaviour (compared with a situation without taxes – and thus without public spending). This is the rationale behind the so-called 'lumpsum' taxes. They are taxes that in no way depend on any other economic variables and thus can in no way affect economic behaviour. It is, however, not possible to construct (even less enforce) such taxes, although the so-called 'poll tax' (which is a tax per person irrespective of income etc.) comes rather close. It is clearly regressive and generally thought of as unfair.

This has led taxation theorists to reconsider commodity taxation. The so-called Ramsey rule states that tax rates should be so chosen that the 'excess burden' is minimized. The excess burden is the burden caused by a reallocation of resources in the economy caused by the tax system. It is often measured through the loss in consumer and producer surplus caused by tax-induced changes in consumer prices. Such losses are clearly smaller for goods that are subject to inelastic demand since changes in quantities traded will be small. The actual calculation of optimal taxes is quite complicated and we are forced to make various simplifying assumptions. Two results are often quoted. If we assume that all cross-price elasticities are zero then product taxes should be the inverse of demand elasticities. On the other hand, if we assume separability in the utility function between labour/leisure and consumption then a broad-based uniform tax on all products (or on income) is preferable.

To differentiate taxes is, however, not easy. If we seek to tax inelastic products where tax proceeds will be high and excess burden low we need considerable amounts of information. In practice these elasticities will not be easy to ascertain – and they may well be variable, so that the administrative costs of a complex differentiated commodity tax system could well be considerable. Naturally progressive income taxes have similar problems – or costs – associated with the costs of gathering information and control since the incentive for tax evasion rises with marginal tax rates.

Distributive considerations

Another problem with the Ramsey rule is that the goods with inelastic demand curves tend to be necessities and particularly high taxation on these goods (and lower taxation on goods with more elastic demand) will thereby in practice imply a higher (regressive) taxation of low-income earners. If we have, as is the case in many societies, an ambition to tax higher incomes more heavily than lower ones (a progressive tax system) then there would seem to be no way round a direct income tax. We should note that differentiated income taxes, like differentiated commodity taxes, require considerable amounts of information, control and administrative effort. Progressive incomes that are designed to satisfy distributional notions generally imply high marginal tax rates. This, in turn, implies considerable costs for the collection of information and administration and also problems with the incentive structure since various opportunities for rent-seeking behaviour are created.

In practice most countries have varying mixtures of income tax and commodity taxes and the level of differentiation is in general quite limited.

GREEN TAX REFORM: THE 'DOUBLE DIVIDEND' ARGUMENT

Considering the difficulties and costs of raising tax revenue it has been suggested that there is a 'double dividend' to environmental taxation. Not only would green taxes help to solve an environmental problem but at the same time they would raise revenue in a way that implies little or no excess burden to the economy. If t in Figure 10.1 is the optimal Pigouvian tax this implies that it is the tax level at which the difference between the consumers' and producers' surplus on the one hand and environmental costs on the other is minimized. The tax receipts are treated as a purely incidental transfer. If instead these are assigned a value (due to the avoided excess burden that would be incurred through some other form of tax collection) then the optimum tax level would shift to a higher value than t (and the resulting optimum would imply quantities that were smaller than q_2).

It has also been shown by Sandmo (1975) that if society puts a value on tax revenue then the optimal tax on a polluting good may be decomposed into two components, one which is akin to the Pigouvian externality tax and then a further component determined by the state's need for tax revenue which is basically the taxation to which all goods in the economy (polluting or not) are subject. In everyday terminology this amounts to adding on (for instance) value-added taxes to environmental or natural resource taxes.

Some enthusiasts for green tax reform want to go one step further and claim that green tax reform can solve all kinds of problems by improving

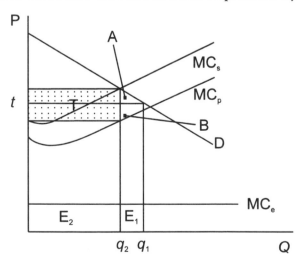

Figure 10.1 Determination of Pigouvian taxes

230

the tax system to reduce tax evasion, improving incentives for work and thus reducing unemployment and budget deficits in addition to addressing environmental problems. As shown in a recent series of articles by Bovenberg and others (Bovenberg and van der Ploeg, 1992, 1993) this will generally be promising too much.

The idea behind the double dividend argument can be illustrated as in Figure 10.2. By 'tilting' the factor price ratio between work and 'environmental services' or between 'clean' and 'dirty' goods one would use more of the former and less of the latter but stay at the same utility level (or in fact a higher one when taking the reduced externalities into account). For simplicity we will here assume that the 'clean' good is produced using principally labour while the 'dirty' good is produced using principally some environmentally noxious form of energy (typically together with capital equipment) so that we can associate shifts in consumption with shifts in production and technology. Making 'labour' cheaper and coal or oil more expensive the price ratio would go from D_2C_1 to D_1C_2, moving the economy from α characterized by the consumption of 'dirty' products using environmentally noxious production factors along the utility curve U_1 to a position δ in which there is more consumption of 'clean' goods and where labour is used more extensively thereby increasing employment and reducing environmental degradation.

There are however several problems with this argument. These are related to the character of technology and to the markets for labour and environmentally degrading factors of production, say energy for short. They are also related to the public good nature of the environment and to the productivity of the environmentally degrading factors.

There is clearly a risk (illustrated in Figure 10.3) that labour supply will be relatively inelastic, so that reduced taxes on labour get absorbed into

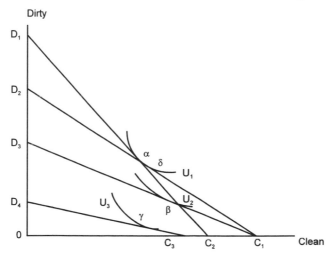

Figure 10.2 An analysis of green taxes

231

higher wage claims and thus the initial effect on the labour market is weak. If, furthermore, energy is internationally traded at a fixed price then the domestic price will rise owing to the tax and the demand for energy will be reduced, and the outcome of the shift in tax will be a combination of less energy with the same amount of labour giving a smaller level of production and utility. Note that this actually implies a *lower* real wage which may further reduce (rather than increase) labour supply in the long run.

Putting this the other way round, one might say that the double dividend argument builds on the fallacy that taxing 'the environment' is costless. There may indeed be some rather important cases when there is some truth to this – at least in the spirit of Ricardo – since the environmental factors may have owners whose land rents can be taxed without any other allocative effects on the economy. This *might* have some relevance for the oil 'sheikhs' (although the international political consequences of trying to tax them might just as well turn out to be *very* costly). In general, however, the 'environment' as such has no money and the incidence of the tax always falls on people in some way. This may for instance be through reduced productivity or even loss of employment in 'dirty' industries or through loss of consumer surplus in consumption. Either way the 'real' income goes down and this might (with a positively sloping supply curve for labour) lead to a reduced supply of labour and thus to further decreases in production.

One might argue that these costs are outweighed by environmental benefits due to reduced externalities, bringing us back to the Pigouvian argument (in Figure 10.1) which is in principle correct but we should, in

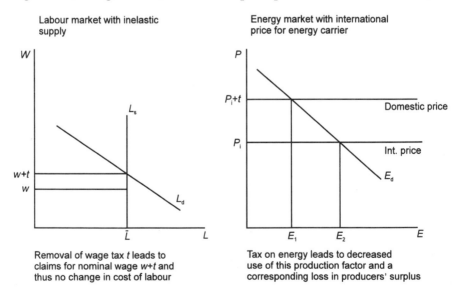

Labour market with inelastic supply

Energy market with international price for energy carrier

Removal of wage tax *t* leads to claims for nominal wage *w+t* and thus no change in cost of labour

Tax on energy leads to decreased use of this production factor and a corresponding loss in producers' surplus

Figure 10.3 Inelastic supply of labour but infinite elasticity for energy

this context, observe a further point which complicates the issues: these environmental benefits (such as cleaner air) often take the form of public goods while the cost of adjustment (shifting consumption to cleaner goods or shifting production techniques away from the use of environmentally hazardous factors) usually implies private costs. There is thus again an instance of the problem of optimal supply of public goods and the optimum may actually in this sense be below the Pigouvian level since the weight attached to the (private) costs of clean-up will be higher than the weight attached to the (public) benefits thereof.

To get a better picture of the effects of a 'green' tax reform we refer back to Figure 10.2. Note that we also assume that we have a state sector which needs to collect a certain tax T to finance a certain amount of public consumption G. This can be done either through income taxes (these may alternatively be thought of as uniform consumption taxes on both goods) or through taxes on just one of the goods – naturally the 'dirty' one.

The budget line D_1C_2 shows the initial situation in which households pay a uniform tax t. Thus $(1 - t)Y = P_cC_2 = P_dD_1$, where Y is income, P_c the price of the clean good and P_d the price of the dirty good. If the income tax is removed the consumer budget is increased to Y pushing the budget line to C_1, but the price of the dirty good increases more than proportionally which explains the total shift in the budget line to D_3C_1. This will imply that the consumer's optimum will move from α on U_1 to β on the lower utility level U_2.[2] Note that this assumes that the demand for the dirty good is at least partially price elastic. If this is not the case then it would be possible for the consumer to stay at α and the proceeds of the tax $t_D D_\alpha$ would be enough to finance G. Note that even a small decline in consumption of D as a result of the rise in P_D would lead to a further need for raising the tax t_D.

We now see that the shift is not on the same utility frontier from α to δ, but to β, on a lower one. The consumers have thus experienced the equivalent of a loss in real income. The reason for this is the erosion of the tax base when it is narrower, which illustrates the importance of the fundamental tenet in optimal taxation that the tax base should be as broad as possible. *If labour supply is upward sloping this would furthermore lead to a reduction in labour supply ultimately bringing us towards a point such as γ on the even lower utility curve U_3. (If labour supply slopes the other way then the labour market reaction would in fact help improve matters instead.)*

A simple numerical illustration

The above arguments, related to Figure 10.2, can be illustrated by way of a simple numerical example. Assume n identical agents in the economy work 100 hours each at a wage of \$10 giving them individual gross incomes of \$1000 each. (The totals for the economy are thus simply given by multiplying by n and we will focus on the representative agent.) This money can be spent either on the environmentally friendly product 'computer games' which sell at a price of $10 each, or on the environmentally noxious product 'gasoline' which has an international price of $5 per litre. Government also requires finance to fund culture for a total of $250n$ per year. Initially the tax rate is 25% on income ($250 per person) so that the consumers are left with $750 each which they spend buying 50 litres of gasoline (for $250) and 50 computer games (costing $500);[3] see Table 10.1, first row.

The income tax is then removed and replaced by a tax of $10 per litre of gasoline (bringing its total price to $15). This reduces consumption in the second row of the table to 25 litres per person[4] at a total cost of $375, of which $250 is tax used to fund culture. Left for the consumption of computer games is now $625.

Table 10.1 Green tax reform in a fictitious two-product economy

Price computer games	Price + tax of gasoline	Consump. gasoline	Consump. computer games	Net income	Income tax	Gasoline tax	Tax/ public spending
10	5	50*5 = 250	50*10 = 500	750	250		250
10	5 + 10 = 15	25*15 = 375	62.5*10 = 625	1000		250	250

Notice that the consumption of 25 litres of gasoline and 62.5 computer games would at the original prices have cost $125 + 625 = 750. This consumption package would thus have been possible – but was not chosen. It corresponds to a point such as β in Figure 10.2.[5] Thus the choice of a narrow-based tax is, as expected, not optimal. And as already mentioned this loss of consumer surplus can be seen as a real loss in salary and could in principle provoke reductions in labour supply which would further worsen the situation.

TAX REFORMS IN REAL WORLD ECONOMIES

The above arguments have naturally built on a number of simplifying assumptions. One of them was that a uniform tax rate on labour income (or on consumption of all goods) is optimal and the other that the supply of labour depends on the net wage. However, we have not seriously discussed the causes of unemployment.

In reality there are a number of other factors influencing the choice of tax rate. Among these we have traditionally had various considerations concerning income distribution and equity. Real tax systems have evolved through a long historical process in which the search for efficiency and equity have been two factors but not always the most powerful since others, such as rent seeking from a number of special interests in society, have carried considerable weight in practice.

Real economies are obviously characterized by tax systems which are far from optimal in the textbook sense. Real economies are also beset by a number of problems such as unemployment which are in various complex ways related to numerous factors including the tax system. We may therefore find a country where the marginal tax rate is extremely high, reducing heavily incentives for work. If these marginal tax rates can be reduced as part of a package in which environmental taxes are levied partly to take their place then this type of green tax reform may indeed have a type of double dividend.

The economist may still wish to keep these issues separate. Welfare is of course improved by a better environment. It may in many cases be optimal to use Pigouvian taxes as a policy instrument and the fact that these give extra revenue is an advantage since it lowers somewhat the need for other taxation. Aside from this, the economy in general is best served by an optimal tax structure which may for instance imply more uniform taxes applied to a broader base and less use of extremely high marginal taxes which have strongly adverse incentive effects. Thus each of these two reforms would be worth while in its own right and unless there are particular reasons for combining them they should be kept separate. Since the political agenda at any one moment is limited there may, however, on occasion be political–economic reasons for the type of packaging of reforms suggested above. In fact if the present tax structure implies severe distortions then the situation might be improved when such a tax structure is replaced by environmental taxes, even if the latter are somewhat 'too high'. In this case there would, in principle, be an even better alternative: namely, a reform which just focused on abolishing the distorting taxes and applying an appropriate combination of Pigouvian taxes[6] and other broad-based income or consumption taxes.

IMPLEMENTATION IN ONE COUNTRY: PROBLEMS OF COMPETITIVENESS

Turning back once again to taxation in general we are left with three or four broad categories of tax: proportional and progressive income taxes, and commodity taxes. To avoid double taxation, to simplify tax administration and to encourage rather than hamper exports, it is common for most commodity taxation to take the form of value-added taxes. This implies that tax is only paid on the 'value added' in each stage of production and that exporting companies can deduct all the VAT (however, imports are subject to VAT in the country where the products are sold, thus ensuring neutrality in competition). The other form of commodity taxes is referred to as excise taxes and they are usually not deductible.

For taxes on factors of production, it may be argued that it is particularly important not to disturb the allocation of productive resources as it would have been in the absence of (fiscally motivated) taxation, because by so doing we would automatically lower productivity. Only factors of production that are offered in inelastic supply should be taxed.[7] One example of such factors of production is the rent from scarce resources in a fixed supply such as land (this is Ricardo's famous case for taxing the landowners: it would have no effect on resource allocation since they do not actually participate in the productive process but just live off a scarcity value, and cannot reduce their supply of land). It is also sometimes argued that labour supply is inelastic and that labour taxes do not ultimately affect the long-run price of labour as a factor of production – they simply reduce (affect) the net pay received by the workers. If this is correct then labour (and land) would be the only two factors of production which should be taxed. Other factors (such as intermediate goods) should only be subject to VAT and Pigouvian taxes where appropriate. There may, however, be quite a temptation, considering the (sometimes global) public goods character of the environment and the private (national) character of costs due to loss in competitiveness, to leave out Pigouvian taxes or replace them by VAT in order to boost competitiveness and attractiveness for investors. This leads to a free-rider problem that can only be solved by international negotiation. The reader should also note that the critical objection to taxing intermediate goods rests on the assumption that the economy can operate a broad-based tax such as VAT. Many LDCs cannot do this and taxing some key intermediates such as energy and transport may actually be a second-best proxy for a more general tax; see Heggie and Fon (1991) for further details.

THE CHOICE OF ENVIRONMENTAL TAX BASE

Some observers doubt the efficacy of environmental taxes saying that either they will have no effect on the environment or – if they do – they will not provide a useful base for tax revenues. The first of these concerns is illustrated by Figure 10.4(b) where the demand curve for the environmentally hazardous product (or service) is very inelastic. In this case we do get tax revenues but the taxes will indeed not solve the environmental problem, just diminish it marginally. However, the fact that the demand curve is so inelastic is in this case a way of saying that this is a problem that is very hard to solve and no other policy instrument would necessarily do it better than a tax.

Figure 10.4(a) illustrates the second case – the environmental problem is solved and then there are no tax proceeds. This may in fact very well occur in some cases and may be an indication that the tax instrument is questionable in these cases. Tax legislation is generally quite a complex and time-consuming procedure and one would want to look for simpler instruments to deal with what is essentially an easily solvable problem. In case there are other reasons for using market instruments (such as large potential gains in cost due to differences in environmental control costs) then tradable permits, administrative charges and various other mechanisms might still be more appropriate than a true tax.

We believe, however, that there is a very important class of problems where Figure 10.4(c) is most appropriate. First the demand curve is elastic so the tax helps to reduce consumption (and thereby emissions) considerably; then there is a less elastic portion of the curve corresponding to consumption that is very hard to substitute for and thus we will receive considerable tax proceeds as well. This would seem to be very relevant for the areas of energy and transport. Other areas depend on the national context but may include water and sanitation, waste disposal (including hazardous wastes, chemicals, etc.), and various issues related to natural resources such as stumpage fees, soil erosion, land taxes, mineral rents and so forth.

THE EFFECTS OF ENVIRONMENTAL TAXATION

When it comes to analysing the long-run effects of environmental taxation the main difficulty is that few countries really have any long-run experience

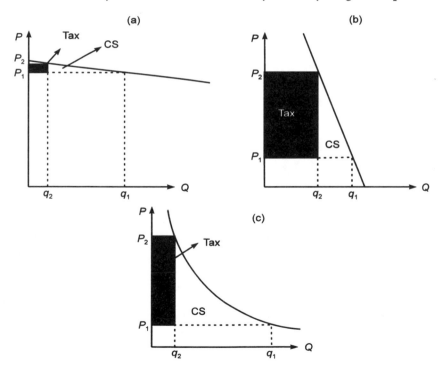

Figure 10.4 Tax proceeds and demand elasticity

237

to analyse. However, the area of gasoline demand gives us a good opportunity. Although gasoline taxation has not always been enforced for environmental reasons we can still use the differences in tax levels and their effects on consumption patterns as evidence of how environmental policies in this area would affect behaviour.

The evidence shows clearly that gasoline demand is quite price elastic: price elasticities are generally in the order of − 0.6 to − 1.0 depending on the type of data and model used. This can be illustrated as in Figure 10.5 which shows that countries with cheap gasoline tend to use more of it than countries with expensive gasoline. For a more rigorous treatment the reader is referred to Sterner (1990, 1991), Sterner and Dahl (1991) or Sterner and Franzén (1994).

It is sometimes believed that economic flexibility and thus also price elasticities would be lower in developing countries. When it comes to gasoline demand this does not seem to be the case; see for instance Dahl (1982, 1992), Belhaj and Sterner (1994), Rogat and Sterner (1994). If there are differences in the elasticities they are fairly marginal. At least it is clear that gasoline demand is still very responsive to differences in price levels.

As shown in Sterner (1992) practically the whole increase in fossil fuel consumption in Africa, and indeed to some extent in the whole Third World, is accounted for by a handful of countries in which the domestic price of energy − and gasoline in particular − is very low. In general these are actually the oil-producing and oil-exporting countries such as Mexico, Venezuela, Nigeria, Egypt and Libya.

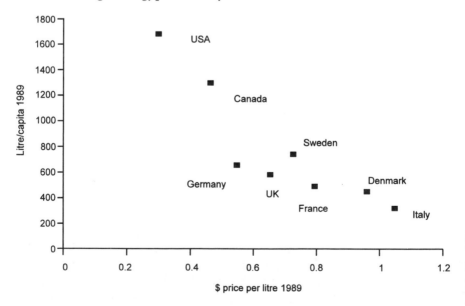

Figure 10.5 Price and consumption of gasoline in various countries, 1989

The enormous economic waste caused, in these countries, by subsidies (rather than taxes) on petroleum products and other energy carriers has also been analysed forcefully in Kosmo (1987) and Larsen and Shah (1992) who show that the world could earn a net increase in welfare amounting to between US$22 and 33 billion (depending on various assumptions about elasticities) just by abolishing subsidies on fossil fuel consumption. Similar (although generally smaller) subsidies occur in a number of other areas such as electricity and water supply as well as fertilizers, pesticides and a number of other inputs that may be damaging for the environment. The removal of these subsidies has been analysed and recommended in numerous World Bank reports and should be seen as a first, necessary, step towards the imposition of Pigouvian taxes.

TAXATION IN DEVELOPING COUNTRIES

There is by now quite a literature analysing the specific theoretical and empirical aspects of optimal taxation when applied to developing countries. The reader is referred to Newbery and Stern (1987) as a good general reference which, like much of this literature, has been written at the in-itiative of the World Bank. Recent World Bank papers analysing the structure of taxation in developing countries include de Melo et al. (1992), Bogetíc and Hassan (1993), Easterly and Rebelo (1992) and Rajaram (1992). There are also a considerable number which focus on the use of fiscal instruments in conjunction with environmental issues: for instance, Eskeland (1993) on taxes to curb air pollution in Mexico, Bahl (1992) and Heggie and Fon (1991) on the use of road pricing in LDCs, Estache and Zheng (1992) on managing pollution in Brazil through the use of taxes and Ahmed (1991) with a similar analysis for Indonesia. Finally Anderson (1990) provides something of a general overview of the field.

Naturally the starting point for this literature is the same optimal taxation theory as referred to in our brief introduction above. There are, however, a number of specific factors in the developing country context that are particularly important since they modify the trade-offs between various types of taxes. Among the most obvious differences compared with countries with higher income levels is the lack of administrative capacity for complex systems and the general difficulties associated with income tax.

As shown by Easterly and Rebelo (1992) many LDCs do on paper have an impressive range of progressiveness in their income tax schedule making it look, also on paper, like a very effective mechanism. In fact, however, as the reader can see in Table 10.2, very little revenue is really collected. The first column shows that, in most LDCs, income tax generally realizes revenues amounting to less than 5% of GDP. In the case of Madagascar, de Melo et al. (1992) show that in spite of quite high statutory tax levels, little tax is actually collected and revenues could just as well be collected with low (roughly 5%) broad-based taxes which would have a much lower excess burden. In part these discrepancies are due to various loopholes and in part to lax enforcement and control. However, they are simply related to the structure of many LDC economies. With a large subsistence or informal sector and pervasive poverty in broad layers of the population there are few people who are even eligible for income taxation. In the case of Kenya for instance there were in 1981 (the latest year in the 1991 CBS statistical abstract) only 65,000 individuals paying income tax! As a share of over 15 million inhabitants, this is less than one-half of 1 per cent! Under such conditions it is indeed quite impressive that income taxes actually make up as much as 30 per cent of central government income in Kenya. To increase this share further is hardly realistic.

Table 10.2 Actual tax collected, nominal and average marginal tax rates

	Marginal taxes (statutory)	Marginal taxes (weighted average)	Actual tax revenue
Argentina	6–54	0	0.02
Peru	2–65	0.3	0.1
Guatemala	5–48	0.9	0.4
Egypt	2–73	1	0.6
Ghana	5–60	1.3	0.9
Pakistan	15–60	2.6	1
Philippines	1–35	2.3	1
Indonesia	15–35	4	1.1
India	33–62	5.4	1.3
Sri Lanka	9–62	2.8	1.4
Chile	8–54	3.3	1.6
Colombia	7–49	2	1.8
Mexico	3–55	3.9	2.2
Côte d'Ivoire	2–72	4	2.3
Thailand	7–65	4.5	2.3
Korea	7–70	4.9	2.6
Tunisia	5–89	4	2.6
Tanzania	20–95	6.9	2.8
Malaysia	6–55	5.2	3.1
Morocco	0.3–80	10.2	3.2
Brazil	5–60	5.8	3.4
Senegal	5–65	5.8	3.4
Zambia	5–80	9.8	4.1
Jamaica	30–58	13	7.6
Turkey	36–65	12.2	7.6
Singapore	4–40	18.1	10.3
Zimbabwe	12–63	16.7	10.9

Source: Adapted from Easterly and Rebelo (1992).

As can be seen from Table 10.3, there is quite a difference in tax structure between developing and developed countries. Naturally there is also a considerable amount of individual variation between countries. This is illustrated in Figure 10.6 which shows the share, in different countries, of VAT and income taxes (including social security and payroll taxes) typically used in OECD countries compared with taxes on capital, trade and other taxes typically used in developing countries. In spite of these individual variations there are a number of general points to notice. First, it is clear that social security contributions, income taxes (on individual income) and other payroll taxes play a much less prominent role in most LDCs and for reasons mentioned above this is probably inevitable in the short to medium term.

Table 10.3 The structure of taxation in various groups of countries (% of total taxes)

Average:	Income	Corporate	Property	Excise	VAT	Trade	Others
World	22.04	12.32	1.80	11.18	13.28	18.25	19.34
OECD	49.61	7.33	2.57	10.51	17.34	2.13	9.73
LDC	14.21	13.74	1.59	11.37	12.12	22.83	22.07
Africa	11.69	16.40	0.91	10.24	11.90	29.39	17.55
Asia	10.93	12.47	1.16	13.65	10.37	26.79	22.71
E. Eur +*	25.43	14.26	1.24	9.99	20.44	10.64	17.79
Middle East	6.73	9.78	1.27	7.12	0.11	16.34	56.99
Latin America	15.18	12.60	2.89	13.20	12.09	20.83	20.13

* Eastern Europe plus the Soviet Union.

Second, we see that taxes on corporate income play quite an important role in a number of Third World countries. While this might be natural in countries such as Botswana or Nigeria which can capitalize on scarce mineral resources, it is an untenable strategy *vis à vis* manufacturing capital since firms may relocate in the face of heavy taxation. The same will partly apply for public enterprise and non-tax revenues in general. These are presumably to be seen as 'vices' that countries with considerable mineral or similar endowments can allow themselves but which would not be successful in less fortunate environments.

Taxes on international trade are (in spite of the World Bank's recent efforts) still very high on average in the Third World and particularly in Africa (almost 30 per cent as compared with 2 per cent in the industrialized OECD countries). Presumably one of the reasons is the relatively low cost of tax collection. In an environment where the informal sector dominates even many ordinary market transactions, where poverty makes income and commodity taxation difficult, the temptation to tax imports (and in some cases exports) must be considerable. There are often a very limited number of ports or other points of entry for imported goods and thus control is relatively easy. The effects on economic allocation and efficiency are, however, considerable and thus this is a tax item that should preferably be reduced.

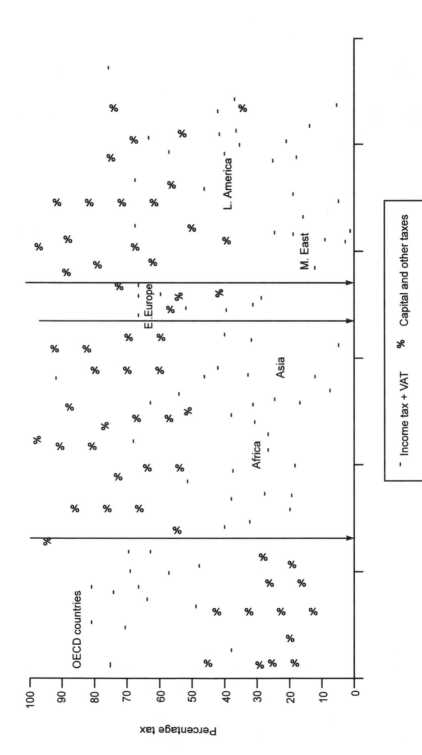

Figure 10.6 The percentage structure of taxation in individual countries

The only main item left now is domestic taxes on goods and services which comprise more or less general VAT and various excise taxes. As we can see in Table 10.3 many LDCs already make considerable use of VAT. As shown by Bogetíc and Hassan (1993) considerable further gains in both fiscal revenue and allocative efficiency of the economy can be made by making VAT more broad based and by using as few rates as possible (preferably single rate only).

GREEN TAX REFORM IN THE LDCS

In spite of the possibility of somewhat increasing VAT (and perhaps even tariff duty) revenues by using low and uniform rates applied to a broad base, it is still clearly a major problem for economic policy makers in the Third World to find sufficient sources of taxation which do not distort the economy and do not lead to evasion or capital flight (or to inevitable electoral defeat!) and which still raise enough revenue to meet the long list of needs faced by the typical developing country.

It is in this context that the use of environmental and natural resource taxation can be particularly useful. The case for such taxation is further strengthened by the fact that most developing countries are very dependent on their natural resources, on agriculture, fishing, forestry and on an intact environment. Poor people are in fact very much more sensitive to certain dimensions of environmental quality (such as clean water) than richer people who can afford to protect themselves (by drinking bottled water) or cure illnesses and discomfort (by moving, going to the doctor, etc.). Given the restraints on public funds most developing country governments find they can save little money to spend on environmental programmes. In this context, again, such instruments as environmental taxes are not an extra burden to the budget but in fact ways of solving environmental problems and protecting natural resources which at the same time help finance the general budget.

Eskeland (1993) shows that higher fuel taxes, primarily intended to improve the air in Mexico City by supporting a programme that will lead to a 70 per cent reduction in emissions from vehicles in 1995, would also collect around $350 million in Mexico City alone – a welcome contribution to the Mexican state budget!

One might ask, finally, why no 'green' taxes have been tried in the developing world. The answer is of course that they have, although not explicitly using that name! As can be seen in Table 10.3, excise taxes account for roughly the same share of tax revenues in all categories of country. Most of these excise taxes are in fact on tobacco, petroleum products and alcohol. Just like in Sweden and in the OECD in general we find that these taxes play quite an important part in a large number of countries. According to Tanzi (1987) these three taxes provide an average of almost 10 per cent of

Table 10.4 Percentage of environmental taxes out of total excise taxes, 1984

Country	Alcohol	Tobacco	Petroleum	Total
Argentina	0	3	62	65
Benin	n.a.	n.a.	50	50
Bolivia	13	10	75	98
Brazil	0	n.a.	45	46
Burkina Faso	n.a.	n.a.	55	55
Burundi	99	n.a.	n.a.	99
Central African Rep.	66	n.a.	34	100
Chad	n.a.	n.a.	72	72
Colombia	2	n.a.	98	100
Costa Rica	14	3	9	26
Côte d'Ivoire	n.a.	16	64	80
Cyprus	8	26	29	63
Dominican Republic	41	13	44	98
Ecuador	21	14	54	89
Ethiopia	27	4	25	56
Grenada	84	16	n.a.	100
Guatemala	47	23	23	93
Honduras	50	18	13	81
India	n.a.	11	17	28
Indonesia	2	90	0	92
Liberia	15	n.a.	n.a.	15
Malaysia	15	6	35	56
Mali	3	5	82	90
Mauritania	6	5	81	92
Mauritius	63	25	n.a.	88
Mexico	9	14	26	49
Morocco	9	50	29	88
Nepal	n.a.	40	n.a.	40
Niger	17	10	72	99
Panama	27	n.a.	58	85
Paraguay	26	13	n.a.	39
Peru	8	19	68	95
Rep. of Korea	39	n.a.	n.a.	39
Rwanda	100	n.a.	n.a.	100
Senegal	12	18	54	84
Sierra Leone	14	45	30	89
Singapore	17	7	41	65
Sudan	7	8	7	22
Tanzania	n.a.	71	n.a.	71
Thailand	23	26	44	93
Togo	n.a.	n.a.	100	100
Trinidad and Tobago	56	n.a.	44	100
Turkey	n.a.	n.a.	3	3
Venezuela	43	30	26	99
Zaire	11	74	n.a.	85
Zambia	47	12	34	93
Average	28	23	44	74

Source: IMF Government Financial Statistics

total tax revenue in the fifty (mainly developing) countries surveyed (1984). Table 10.4 shows that these three taxes do indeed constitute the lion's share of all the excise taxes. In several countries, such as Burundi, Bolivia, Zambia and the Dominican Republic, these three sources alone accounted for 25–35% of total taxes!

The latest issue of the IMF Government Financial Statistics only gives details of these taxes for a rather small number of countries, making a comparison with 1984 difficult. In some of the countries for which there are data (including Zaire, Sri Lanka, Sierra Leone and Ethiopia) we find that the share of excise taxes increased during the 1980s and this particularly applies to the three items mentioned above (principally tobacco) but there are also some countries such as India, Burkina Faso, Korea and Cyprus where no such increase was apparent.

Bahl (1992) shows that total transport taxes (including fuel taxes, vehicle taxes and road user charges) account for more than 10 per cent of total tax revenue in his selection of nineteen LDCs (it is, however, worth noting that his selection does not include any oil countries). In practically all of these countries he found that these total fees accounted for more than total road expenditures (160 per cent of road expenditures on average) thus showing that the transport sector was, in this sense, providing a 'net contribution' to the public sector! The above shows that some of these countries already have, in a certain sense, a 'greener' tax structure than many OECD countries. This should, however, not be taken to mean that these taxes have been motivated by any environmental considerations. It is likely that various other motives have been dominant including the following: large, relatively inelastic tax base; relative ease (low cost) of tax administration and collection; balance of trade arguments (for those countries where the goods are imported). In the case of gasoline there is the further argument that it serves as a charge for the use of publicly financed road services etc. Alcohol and tobacco (and possibly gasoline) may also be seen as luxury items.

Tobacco and alcohol also have certain obvious characteristics (concerning moral or ethical values pertaining to their use) that make them particularly amenable as objects of taxation. The same appears to apply to the traditional drug Khat which has come to be more and more heavily taxed in Djibouti. This particular tax item now brings in twice as much revenue as tobacco tax and almost provides 10 per cent of total tax proceeds in Djibouti!

CONCLUSIONS AND SUGGESTIONS FOR FURTHER RESEARCH

We have shown that green taxes should be a fairly attractive policy option for a range of environmental problems in most developing countries. Although many such countries already use some environmental taxes (although not always using the adjective 'environmental') it should be possible to find other, additional, environmental or natural resource taxes if a systematic inventory of environmental problems and natural resource scarcity was undertaken with a view to selecting policy instruments that are not only useful for the problem at hand but also appealing from a fiscal viewpoint. Obvious candidates are water, refuse, industrial effluents and other polluting emissions, energy, fertilizer, timber stumpage and similar natural resource rents which we already know are very low in most countries (in fact even negative as shown in the study by Larsen and Shah). The first step towards a 'greener' system of taxation must of course be the elimination of subsidies for activities that are environmentally destructive (and often economically disastrous as well).[8]

A number of important issues relating to the potential for green tax reform in developing countries need further research. Among these are the issues of distributive effects, dynamic incentive effects and the costs of control, monitoring and enforcement, staffing and the respective roles of local and central government (or of specialized government agencies) in the setting of tax rates, the collection of taxes and the use of tax revenue. The acceptability of taxes (and hence the degree of tax evasion and the costs of control and revenue collection) may depend quite crucially on how these issues are solved. For environmentally motivated taxes to be accepted there must be a high degree of credibility in their role as environmental policy instruments. Since environmental conditions have a tendency to vary with geographical location, there may in many cases be strong arguments for geographical differentiation and hence maybe for decentralized tax administration. In at least some countries, where central government influence and taxation dwarfs the power of local government, this may be quite a welcome change for other reasons related to the constitutional division of power within these countries.

On the other hand, the long-range transport of pollution and the risk that environmental rules will be used as an element of local competition for investment serve as arguments for centralized decision making in at least some areas of environmental policy making. Estache and Zheng (1992) provide an illustrative analysis of the type of balance required between environmental policy instruments used by the federal and state governments in the case of Brazil.

Finally the relationships between environmental taxes and expenditures need more work as does the political economy of the tax-setting procedures within the various economies.

NOTES

1 Note that this only applies when the marginal cost of environmental damage MC_e is constant. With rising marginal costs, tax proceeds will generally exceed environmental damage. On the other hand the cost of choosing too low a tax level (or of not using a Pigouvian tax at all) will also be higher.

2 Note that β is also on the first budget line C_2D_1 which implies that it would have been attainable under the first set of prices. The fact that α is chosen instead shows that α is preferred to β.

3 Note that we could get the same result without income tax but with a uniform product tax of 33%.

4 These figures correspond to an income elasticity of 1 and a price elasticity of -0.9.

5 Had the price elasticity of gasoline demand been 0 then demand would still have been 50 litres and a gasoline tax of $5 (bringing the price to $10) would have been sufficient to give tax proceeds of $250. This would have cost $50*10 = 500 leaving another $500 for computer games. Thus the consumption would have been exactly the same as in the case with income tax. This corresponds to α in Figure 10.2.

6 Note that the issues of the public good character of the environment should also be taken into account.

7 This applies to taxation motivated by the need for revenue, not Pigouvian taxes. In other words, we have, once again, the inverse elasticity rule. The same principle applies to both the utility and production functions. The economy will settle at the point of tangency between such a function and the relative price line. We therefore want to avoid changing this relative slope through taxation.

8 Ahmed (1991) provides a more detailed description of how subsidies are being removed in Indonesia and suggests the use of various environmental taxes including levies on forest logging, pollution, irrigation water and even urban congestion.

REFERENCES

Ahmed, S. (1991) 'Fiscal Policy for Managing Indonesia's Environment', World Bank Working Papers (WPS 786).

Anderson, D. (1990) 'Environmental Policy and the Public Revenue in Developing Countries', World Bank Environmental Working Paper No. 36.

Bahl, R. (1992) 'The Administration of Road User Taxes in Developing Countries' (WPS 986).

Belhaj, M. and Sterner, T. (1994) 'The Determinants of Gasoline Demand in Africa', Mimeo, Dept of Economics, Gothenburg.

Bogetíc, Z. and Hassan, F. (1993) 'Determinants of Value-Added Tax Revenue: A Cross-Section Analysis' (WPS 1203).

Bovenberg, A. L. and van der Ploeg, F. (1992) 'Environmental Policy, Public Finance and the Labour Market in a Second Best World', *Journal of Public Economics* (forthcoming).

——(1993) 'Does a Tougher Environmental Policy Raise Unemployment? Optimal taxation, public goods and environmental policy with rationing of labour supply', Centre for Economic Policy Research, Discussion Paper No. 869.

Dahl, C. (1982) 'Do Gasoline Demand Elasticities Vary?', *Land Economics*, August, pp. 373–382.

——(1992) 'A Survey of Energy Demand Elasticities for the Developing World', *Journal of Energy and Development*, Autumn, vol. XVIII, no. 1.

Dahl, C. and Sterner, T. (1991) 'A Survey of Econometric Gasoline Demand Elasticities', *International Journal of Energy Systems*, vol. 11, no. 2.

de Melo, J., Roland-Holst, D. and Haddad, M. (1992) 'Tax Evasion and Tax Reform in a Low-Income Economy' (WPS 918).

Easterly, W. and Rebelo, S. (1992) 'Marginal Income Tax Rates and Economic Growth in Developing Countries' (WPS 1050).

Eskeland, G. S. (1993) 'A Presumptive Pigouvian Tax on Gasoline: Analysis of an Air Pollution Control Program for Mexico City' (WPS 1076).

Estache, A. and Zheng, K. (1992) 'Managing Pollution Control in Brazil – The Potential Use of Taxes and Fines by Federal and State Government' (WPS 929).

Heggie, I. G. and Fon, V. (1991) 'Optimal User Charges and Cost Recovery for Roads in Developing Countries' (WPS 780).

Hotelling, H. (1931) 'The Economics of Exhaustible Resources', *Journal of Political Economy*, vol. 39, pp. 137–175.

Kenya Central Bureau of Statistics (1991) *Statistical abstract.*

Kosmo, M. (1987) *Money to burn? The high cost of energy subsidies*, World Resources Institute.

Larsen, B. and Shah, A. (1992) 'World Fossil Fuel Subsidies and Global Carbon Emissions' (WPS 1002).

Miljörapporten (1993) No. 8, Tomorrow Media, Stockholm.

Newbery, D. and Stern, N. (1987) *The Theory of Taxation for Developing Countries*, Oxford University Press.

Ostrom, E. (1990) *Governing the Commons*, Cambridge University Press, Cambridge.

Rajaram, A. (1992) 'Tariff and Tax Reform: Do World Bank Recommendations Integrate Revenue and Protection Objectives?' (WPS 1018).

Rogat, J. and Sterner, T. (1994) 'The Determinants of Gasoline Demand in Latin America', Mimeo, Dept of Economics, Gothenburg.

Sandmo, A. (1975) 'Optimal Taxation in the Presence of Externalities', *Swedish Journal of Economics*, vol. 77, pp. 86–98.

SOU 1989:33 *Reformerad Inkomstbeskattning.*

SOU 1991:59 *Sätt värde på Miljön.*

SOU 1991:90 *Konkurrensneutral Energibeskattning.*

SOU 1992:53 *Skatt på Dieselolja.*

Sterner, T. (1990) *The Pricing of and Demand for Gasoline*, The Swedish Transport Research Board, Stockholm, May.

——(1991) 'Gasoline Demand in the OECD: Choice of model and data set in pooled estimations', *Opec Review*, vol. XV, no. 2.

——(1992) 'Economic and Environmental Policies for Sustainability', in U. Svedin and B. Aniansson (eds) *Society and the Environment: A Swedish Perspective*, Kluwer, Dordrecht.

——(1994) *Economic Policies for Sustainable Development*, Kluwer.

Sterner, T. and Dahl, C. (1991) 'Analyzing Gasoline Demand Elasticities', *Energy Economics*, vol. 13, no. 3, July.

Sterner, T. and Franzén, M. (1994) 'Long-run Demand Elasticities for gasoline', in T. Barker *et al.* (eds) *Global Warming and Energy Elasticities*, Routledge, London.

Tanzi, V. (1987) 'Quantitative Characteristics of Tax Systems of Developing Countries', in D. Newbery and N. Stern (eds) *The Theory of Taxation for Developing Countries*, Oxford University Press.

Part II

THE ROLE OF THE STATE

11

THE GOOD, THE BAD AND THE WOBBLY

State forms and Third World economic performance*

Christer Gunnarsson and Mats Lundahl

SWINGS OF A PENDULUM: ECONOMISTS' VIEWS OF THE STATE

Economic theory has never been particularly successful in modelling the behaviour of the state. This, however, does not mean that economists are not interested in government. Quite the contrary; at least since Adam Smith, the question of the appropriate balance between the invisible hand of the market and the more visible actions of the state has been very much at the centre of the debate on economic policy (Gunnarsson, 1987; Krueger, 1990). This debate has continued up to the present time, with the emphasis by and large on whether state intervention into the market is 'good' or 'bad' (Lal, 1983, Chapter 1; Killick, 1990, Chapters 2–3).

When it comes to modelling the behaviour of the state, however, much less has been accomplished. For a long time, behaviour was postulated rather than analysed explicitly, i.e. the state was taken to be either 'all good' or 'all bad'. That state behaviour has been postulated rather than analysed is a quite natural corollary to the adoption of methodological individualism of neoclassical economics and to its study of utility-maximizing individuals within given institutions. In this setting, where the main concern has been how resources are being allocated as a result of the individual uncoordinated behaviour of producers, consumers and factor owners, it should of course come as no surprise that an explicit theory of state or government behaviour is lacking. (The lack of a theory of the state in Keynesian and Keynesian-inspired macroeconomics, with its emphasis on government intervention, is more surprising.) It is only with the advent of public choice and related approaches that political behaviour as such has been more or less elaborately modelled – with very mixed results.

To some extent the assumptions about the state in neoclassical economics can be defended on the grounds that neoclassical theory is basically concerned with modern, industrialized and democratic societies, among which variations in state forms are likely to be of minor importance. However, from economic history we learn that in the real world there have been a great variety of state formations which remain unaccounted for by neoclassical theory. With this variation in mind it should be obvious that state behaviour cannot be postulated. Instead, what is needed is a theory of the state that can help in explaining this variation in state forms. It would be rather erroneous, however, to say that the discipline of economic history offers such a theory on the basis of empirical generalizations. The fact that it has not yet arrived at constructs which can be used to explain the variety of state forms is a major weakness of economic history (North, 1979, p. 254).

In the case of development economics, we find ourselves in a somewhat 'intermediate' position. Ever since the beginning of its existence as a branch of economic science, development economics has been far more history oriented than economics in general. Many aspects of the process of underdevelopment and development simply cannot be understood unless they are put into a historical perspective. Also, it has had to cover a more diverse spectrum of economies, and then not least with respect to the character of the state, than the Western, industrialized market economies. This, however, does not necessarily mean that development economists have done an outstanding job when it comes to modelling state behaviour. Rather, exactly as for economics in general, the development debate has been laden with normative statements and postulates, according to which the state can either do no wrong or no right (Streeten, 1992, p. 24). Little has been said about why, in the real world, some states, in fact, 'do right' and others 'do wrong'.

This point is made clear once we look at the development literature from the 1950s onwards. The early discussion of the state tended to take for granted that the state should and would step in when the market for some reason failed to allocate resources optimally and correct for market failures. This view was influenced, on the one hand, by the Keynesian interventionism that had developed as a consequence of the experiences of the Great Depression and World War II and, on the other, by the development of welfare economics, including an interest in distributional issues.

The theoretical underpinning was straightforward. The central theorem of welfare economics – that a situation with general equilibrium is simultaneously a Pareto optimum – requires a number of restrictive assumptions with respect to the existence of futures markets, perfect information, absence of monopolies, economies of scale, collective goods and externalities, etc., that are not likely to be fulfilled in practice, and even if a Pareto optimum could be attained it would not necessarily be 'better' from a distributional point of view than a situation which is not optimal. In addition, the Keynesian approach stresses that there is nothing in the market system which guarantees that all markets will clear, notably not the labour market.

These arguments received increased emphasis in the context of less developed countries. The experience that these countries had had of the depression was even less fortunate than that of the industrialized economies. Their concentration on primary production was perceived as conducive to a secular deterioration of their terms of trade and no help was to be expected from the protected markets in the rich countries when it came to industrializing their economies. A number of vicious circles contributed to keeping production and incomes down.

Thus, the market was the source of underdevelopment, not its solution. It was only natural, then, that substituting planning and administrative control for market mechanisms seemed to be the rational way to develop. Development was taken to be the same as industrialization and it was assumed that the state had to take on great responsibilities for initiating the process of industrialization. Theoretical arguments for this forced import-substitution type of industrialization were provided by the structuralist school, according to which the market could not be expected to trigger an industrial take-off (Prebisch, 1950; Nurkse, 1953; Myrdal, 1957). Another support for government intervention was, however, found in Alexander Gerschenkron's (1952) typology of nineteenth-century European industrialization. In Gerschenkron's world, the market was not all bad. On the contrary, the problem was that in backward economies, there were failures and short-comings in the way the market actually operated. Therefore, depending on the relative degree of backwardness, i.e. the relative extent of 'market failure' in industrialization, the state in late industrializing economies would have to take effective measures to promote industrialization even to the point of substituting for the market.

The 1950s and 1960s saw a rapid proliferation of planning models at all levels where the fundamental explicit or implicit assumption was that the state could do a better job than the market when it came to allocating resources optimally. Not only did this imply a growing public sector, but, in addition, many governments proceeded to regulate prices, trade, interest and credit, wages, investments, allocations of foreign currency, etc. The importance of microeconomic incentives via the market was played down and the government took on an important role as a direct producer. The state that was assumed to achieve all this was clearly one that was expected to 'do no wrong'.

During the past two decades, however, the pendulum has swung in the other direction. Criticism against interventionism and, above all, planning had never been lacking. The so-called socialist controversy during the 1920s and 1930s gave vent to concerns about lack of information and lack of incentives in the planned economy, among other things (von Mises, 1935; von Hayek, 1945), and the study of economic regulation and interest groups in the 1960s and 1970s, the development of public choice theory during the same period, monetarism, rational expectations and 'new classical macro-economics' and the 'counter-revolution' in development theory by neoclassically minded economists all contributed to shifting the focus away from market failures to government failures instead.[1] Today the market is 'in', while planning (definitely) and interventionism (to a lesser extent) are 'out'. Empirically, the advocates of the market point to the demise of communism in Eastern Europe as well as to the manifest difficulties of the few still surviving centrally planned economies. In development economics, a symbolic turning point had been reached in 1984 when Arthur Lewis (1984, p. 8) made the observation that a convincing theory of growth for developing countries requires a theory of government, one 'where government would appear as much the problem as the solution'.

The debate, however, does not end there. Matters would be simple if it could be shown once and for all that economic success is associated with a minimum of state intervention. There would be little need to model the behaviour of the state if such a general postulate about non-intervention could be shown to hold good. Then implementation would be the only thing left to achieve. Unfortunately, the evidence remains far from conclusive. Today it seems as if the pendulum has begun to swing back again, towards a critique of the non-interventionist postulate. In part, this stems from observations of the effects of the implementation of ultra-minimalism in the former Soviet Union. In equal part, however, the East Asian miracle economies pose a challenge to the minimalist postulate. Different explanations have been offered, ranging from more or less complete emphasis on the virtues of the free market and the 'small' state to a 'symbiosis' between a very active government, which has managed to overcome the inherent myopia of the market, and private enterprise (Johnson, 1982; Amsden, 1989; Bradford, 1986; Woronoff, 1986; Burenstam Linder, 1986; Harris, 1986; Wade, 1990; Gunnarsson, 1993a; World Bank, 1993). Is it really the case that what made for rapid development in East Asia was that governments have intervened to make it *easier* for the markets to work or even that the state has taken the *lead* in the development process by introducing regulations that violated market principles in the short run but which made exporters highly competitive in high-income elasticity markets in the long run? If the latter is true, i.e. if the correction of 'market failures' has constituted a starting point for industrialization, then we have indeed experienced 'a reaction too far'[2] against interventionism and 'dirigisme' and the neo-orthodox conventional wisdom of the 'free marketeers' must be seriously questioned. Then the postulate that the state can 'do nothing right' will be invalidated.

In any case, we should be able by now to agree that states could be both 'good' and 'bad', and that success and failure cannot easily be measured by the degree of state intervention. But we cannot be content with this as a conclusion. Rather it should serve as a point of departure for further analysis. As Ronald Findlay (1990, p. 195) has noted:

> The common theme...in much recent social science literature,...is the rediscovery by a number of authors, Marxists as well as 'mainstream' scholars, of the 'autonomy of the state', which makes it necessary to treat it as a dynamic independent force instead of as a passive agent of society at large and its various interest groups contending 'horizontally', as in liberal pluralist theory, or as the 'executive committee of the ruling class' as in vulgar Marxism.

If we recognize the importance of the state we would like to know why state forms differ, why in some cases 'the autonomy of the state' is real, while in other cases the state is little more than a 'wobbly' reflection of contending interest groups or classes. We would also like to know why some 'autonomous' states bring about efficiency-enhancing interventions and why some bring their societies to the brink of economic disaster.

The purpose of the present chapter is not only to discuss the effects in terms of economic performance of various state types themselves. It also seeks to answer questions such as why all states are not 'good', and why it is so often rational for political leaders to be 'bad'. In other words, it seeks an answer to what Robert Bates has called 'the obvious question: Why should reasonable men adopt public policies that have harmful consequences for the societies they govern?' (Bates, 1981, p. 3). The chapter is to be regarded as an 'essay in persuasion' in the spirit of John Maynard Keynes (1931) or a piece of 'economic rhetoric' in the spirit of Donald McCloskey (1986). It seeks to advance a hypothesis rather than to come up with conclusive proof. The argument is developed by means of theoretical analysis and by reference to historical evidence. The point of departure is Anne Krueger's discussion of inefficient states and Deepak Lal's and Hla Myint's typology of state forms. Thereafter, we explore a theory of the predatory state, basing ourselves on a framework for analysing the state suggested by Douglass North. In the final sections we analyse the logic of the latter's antithesis, i.e. the developmental state.

VARIETIES OF INEFFICIENT STATES

States and governments can be inefficient for very different reasons. This makes it difficult to 'bring the state back in' (Evans et al., 1985) in a simple, generalized fashion which applies to all kinds of situations. Anne Krueger (1993, p. 53) has observed that the rationale for interventionism to overcome market failures builds on two premises: first, that the government's objective is to achieve economic efficiency, including growth; and second, that there are no information costs, administrative barriers or other obstacles to implementation. Thus, it is assumed that (1) governments have a genuine willingness to develop their economies, and (2) that implementation is costless. Government failures may then arise if either or both of these premises prove to be false, but under circumstances that are essentially different from one another.

The simplest case is the one where the government has good intentions but where information-related or administrative obstacles result in policy mistakes. The government may very well be a 'benevolent social guardian', to use Krueger's terminology, but it may not understand what it is doing or it may face obstacles that prevent efficient outcomes from being realized. Even the most cursory reference to the economic policy discussion of any industrialized nation indicates that at times there are almost as many views as there are economists. Of course, not all these economists can be correctly informed, and depending on who has the ear of the government, more or less efficient policies result.

Transaction or administration costs are important as well. The government could underestimate the complexity of the tasks it entrusts to the bureaucracy. The bureaucracy can be expected to have goals that to a varying extent differ from that of the government. Technical complications that are only imperfectly understood arise, especially in the context of an insufficiently trained staff. Civil servants are given no incentives to produce efficient results, especially when they work in a state monopoly setting. Coordination of units is costly and time consuming. Administrative interventions alter the income distribution in the economy in a way which may give incentives for the private agents to influence the implementation process in ways that were never intended by the planners (Blomqvist and Lundahl, 1992, pp. 237–238, Krueger, 1993, p. 67). All together, transaction costs loom much larger in the real world than in the planners' paradise of perfect computation and perfect implementation.

If lack of information, difficulties in implementation or sheer stupidity had been the only problems facing the government, the problem in a sense would have been a minor one that could have been solved, at least in part, as information was accumulated and ways had been found to train personnel, remove disincentives for efficiency, etc. Unfortunately, however, the story does not end here. First, difficulties of implementation also involve aspects of political power. The social benefits of well-intended policies may be lost to individuals or groups who are in a position to reap disproportionally large private benefits. This is what Jagdish Bhagwati (1982) refers to as 'intervention-triggered' directly unproductive profit-seeking (DUP) activities. But such activities could also be 'intervention-seeking', i.e. influential individuals or groups can pressure the government to implement policies that are not optimal from the point of view of society. This is quite similar to the familiar Marxist critique of the structuralist project, namely that planning is unlikely to yield success because of the prevailing class and power structures in developing countries (Baran, 1957). In either case it cannot be assumed that the state is autonomous enough to carry out a coherent development strategy.

Perhaps even worse, there are indeed cases when governments for various reasons fail to meet the requirements of a benevolent social guardian. In those cases, we have an autonomous state power which is used for pursuing goals other than development. Here, among other things, we find the predatory state in full action. Then the question arises as to what these other goals are, and whether the goal structure differs between states. Another question is how socially damaging the pursuit of these other goals is. In other words, is the predatory state always a brake on incentives, resource allocation and economic growth at large, or are there circumstances when a predatory state can be swiftly transformed into a developmental state? Is there a fundamental rationality underlying state behaviour which, depending on the circumstances, can be expressed in either predatory or developmental action?

This calls for some economic typology of states. We will not attempt any exhaustive survey here. Rather, we will rely on the classification suggested by Deepak Lal and Hla Myint (1996), since this points directly to the core of the present chapter. Lal and Myint distinguish between two basic types of states: autonomous and factional. The factional state is a 'wobbly' state in which some interest group or coalition 'in some contingent manner succeed in capturing the state or in which there is some form of pressure-group equilibrium'. The factional state may be democratic or authoritarian but in either case it is normally a weak state. In the following we will exclude the democratic state on the grounds that it is rare in developing countries. Furthermore, in democratic societies, the free competition for political power imposes checks on predation. So, the factional state that may be of interest for our purposes is the authoritarian one where rent-seeking coalitions can engage in activities which force the government to behave in a predatory manner. Thus, in some contrast to Lal and Myint, we regard this kind of factional state as a potentially predatory state.

The autonomous state depicted by Lal and Myint pictures one which may be either guardian or predatory. The 'clean' form of the predatory state is the one concentrating on the self-seeking extraction of resources for the members of the government and their associates. The predatory state can be either absolutist, i.e. controlled by a single ruler whose objective is net revenue maximization, or bureaucratic–authoritarian, attempting to maximize the number of bureaucrats or public employment. The guardian state, on the other hand, can be either benevolent (or Platonic), i.e. attempt to maximize the welfare of its subjects, or despotic (or Nietzschean), i.e. create its own rules, knowing what is best for the populace.

On the face of it, it seems easy to distinguish the 'good' from the 'bad', i.e. the predatory self-seeking state from the benevolent. However, one should be careful not to confuse outcomes and motives, or *ex ante* and *ex post* assessments. A predatory state is one whose policies can be shown to have benefited a monolithic self-seeking ruler and/or a bureaucratic elite. But self-seeking behaviour cannot be taken *ex ante* to be synonymous with predation. A despotic ruler with fundamental motives other than plunder may in hindsight be regarded as nothing but a self-seeking predator. On the other hand, the policies of a self-seeking ruler may in retrospect be judged as 'developmental'.

What we have in mind when we talk about a 'developmental state' is surely an authoritarian state that to a large extent is insulated from society. It is normally a despotic state which is expected to 'know what is best'. Although such rulers take great measures to promote industrial development they can be just as self-seeking as the ruler of any predatory state. Unless we accept that some self-seeking rulers do try to promote economic development, while others take the road to predation, we will be left with the rather empty conclusion that all development-oriented states are benevolent. The East Asian developmental states are cases in point. Any *ex post* assessment would suggest that these states are benevolent in that 'they appear to have had the economic welfare of their people sufficiently high among their objectives' (Krueger, 1993, p. 61). An *ex ante* judgement some thirty years ago would have seen these regimes as despotic, self-seeking and with a strong concentration on predation.

There are two ways of explaining why potential predators become developmental. One is to assume that it pays for a self-seeking state to encourage economic growth since this increases its revenue. We will develop this possibility later. However, this is hardly a good characterization of the developmental state, since it assumes that the state is a passive follower of the market. Thus, it cannot be assumed to be autonomous enough to function as a leading actor, which after all would be required of a developmental state.

Another way is to see to the goals of the state policy, whether it is for 'power' or 'plenty', to paraphrase Jacob Viner's (1948) discussion of mercantilism. It can be hypothesized that when power alone is the guide of state policies there is little to prevent it from turning predatory.[3] When welfare alone is the goal, it often turns out to be a failure. In the first case it turns predatory because there is no real threat to the power of the ruler. In the second case, the goal is not strong enough to make sure that the policy is actually carried out.

The developmental state is for both power and plenty. In this case, we do not find a state which chooses freely between predation and benevolence. Instead, it is an actual or potential rent seeker which turns developmental in order to stay in power. Thus, development is a basis for power and power makes sure that developmental policies are carried out. Thus, the developmental state resembles the 'Nietzschean' state depicted by Lal and Myint.

There is a problem, however, with such a distinction between power and plenty. For rulers in pre-industrial societies, power and wealth are two sides of the same coin. The purpose of power is to accumulate wealth and the purpose of wealth is to grant the status and grandeur that are the prime symbols of power. (At times, it is hardly possible to draw even a conceptual borderline. As Christopher Clapham (1988, pp. 47–48) has pointed out, in patrimonial societies (à la Max Weber), where authority is ascribed to a *person* (the ruler) and not to an office-holder, there is in principle no difference between the wealth of the state and the personal wealth of the ruler.) Thus, an analysis of why predatory rulers turn developmental cannot be phrased in terms of a switch from power to plenty. Instead, what is important is that the underlying conditions of the state policy are changing so that the concepts of power and plenty are given a new content. Societies change and predatory states become developmental when it is no longer possible to remain in power without fostering economic development and/ or when personal wealth is no longer the foremost symbol of power.

In the following, we will concentrate on the dichotomy between predatory and developmental states. We will attempt to establish the logic of the predatory state and explain why predatory states are more common than developmental states. Surely, all inefficient states cannot be characterized as predatory. However, any *ex post* assessment would indicate that in history a majority of inefficient states have indeed tended to be predatory. This is why we will attempt to explore the logic of the predatory state before we go on to its antithesis: the developmental state.

NORTH'S LAW

The creation of a state is an essential precondition for economic growth. The state, however, is the source of man-made economic decline. This paradox should have made the state central to economic history: Models of the state should be an explicit part of any analysis of secular changes.

(North, 1979, p. 249)

The implications of this familiar statement by Douglass North go a great deal further than just to indicate that the influence of the state could be either positive or negative, depending on the particular circumstances. North also pointed to what is one of the most central functions of governments, that of defining, in the last instance, the property rights that will prevail in the economy and which are central for shaping the incentives to which the agents of the economy will respond. What is more, 'there is no guarantee that the government will find it to be in its interest to protect those property rights which encourage efficiency... as against those in which the property rights protected may thwart growth altogether' (North and Thomas, 1973, p. 7). Empirically, it is mainly the latter situation that has prevailed: 'Property rights that produce sustained economic growth have seldom held sway throughout history' (North, 1979, p. 251).

The latter statement can suitably be referred to as 'North's law'. The elementary point made by North can be explored in the following manner. The fundamental economic task of the state is to establish and give credibility and legitimacy to laws, rules and other institutional arrangements which make human exchange possible, i.e. to guarantee property rights and to protect the validity of contracts. Efficient property rights, i.e. property rights that make for an efficient allocation of resources and rapid economic growth, are the exception, not the rule, throughout the course of economic history. On the other hand, says North (1979, p. 251),

> even the most casual survey of the human experience makes clear that there have been political-economic units that achieved substantial economic growth for long periods of time.... This phenomenon is not confined to the 200 years since the Industrial Revolution.... There is nothing new about sustained economic growth.

North's law and the exceptions to it point to at least two fundamental issues: (1) Why do states tend to produce inefficient property rights? (2) What gives rise to states that constitute exceptions to this general pattern? Surely, all inefficient states cannot be characterized as predatory.

THE PREDATORY STATE

Predatory states are usually established in steps. Following Max Weber, North defines the state as 'an organization with a comparative advantage in violence,[4] extending over a geographic area whose boundaries are determined by its power to tax constituents ... the key to understanding the state involves the potential use of violence to gain control over resources' (North, 1981, p. 21). Here is of course a missing link in neoclassical economics. The theory cannot account for political power, let alone for violence which is the basis for power.

Power is exercised in every society, including primitive societies, and on local levels. But this form of authority is not what we normally mean by a state. It is associated with personal exchange and small group size (Olson, 1991, pp. 133–135). Transactions between people can be made on the basis of personal contacts. People carry out transactions with those they know personally and feel they can trust. Few or any formal rules are needed. Family relationships, but also friendship, religious norms, threats of physical violence, etc., act as mechanisms of social control and as a guarantee that agreements will be carried out. Distinct political and economic spheres hardly exist in such a society. Political authority is locally based and intertwined and involved with economic transactions.

Initially, the area over which control can be wielded tends to be small. What is likely to arise is what William Stokes (1952, p. 447) has termed *machetismo*, which implies that anybody who can 'command the authority represented by the machete', i.e. anybody who can assemble enough local armed followers, has to be reckoned with politically in an area where no state exists. This power will be purely local.

That the area is likely to be small follows from Mancur Olson's (1965, 1982, 1983) logic of collective action. It is easier for small than for large groups to rally around what they perceive as a common cause (a benefit which is perceived as collective for the members of the group). As the size of the group grows, so does the free-rider problem that has to be handled. The group members will to an increasing extent expect the other members of the group to act on their behalf and those with a smaller share of the common benefit will 'exploit' those with larger shares who have stronger incentives to incur the costs involved.

Typically, only a limited number of people can thus be organized and if this number is too small to guarantee power, selective incentives, notably payments of various kinds, will have to be brought into the picture. Gordon Tullock (1974, 1987) has pointed out that 'revolutionary' action by large popular groups seldom takes place but that the majority of government changes involving violence are of the palace coup variety, led by individuals who have a strong *personal* interest in the outcome. The same kind of argument applies in the present case and this, in turn, has two important consequences. In the first place, it creates leaders (*caudillos*, chiefs, etc.) who take larger risks than the ordinary members of the group (and who are those who organize the group) because of the selective incentives they have to do so. Second, it makes income considerations important for the group and the rule that it will establish is then likely to become predatory (Olson, 1991, pp. 136–137).

There is also a second reason for the latter. In a situation where no state exists, so that no property rights have yet been established and where people prefer a higher material standard of living over a lower, there is no good reason why these preferences should not be allowed to govern political action as well. If no group has the upper hand, some kind of Hobbesian 'state of nature' should apply, with no restraint on human behaviour but where 'every man would constantly be open to violent invasion of his life and property'.[5] This is changed by the emergence of a ruler or ruling group, in a way which also necessarily involves violence, or at least the threat of it. In order to arrive at the collective benefit of the group in question, presumably a material one, some kind of property rights will have to be created which guarantee that the benefit materializes, and as stressed by North (1979, p. 250): 'The essence of property rights is the right to exclude.' This can hardly be done unless some kind of sanctions exist and these will have to be backed by a violence potential in order to be credible.

Since power is only local in the above setting, i.e. since no group can be expected to have a pronounced *absolute* advantage in violence over other groups, or at least as long as that advantage has not yet been revealed, in the next step there is likely to be competition for power, presumably in a wider geographical setting as the various local groups find that their interests clash. Coalitions will be formed and with enough time to overcome their organization problem (Olson, 1982, Chapter 3), larger, and hence more powerful, interest groups will be formed.

As markets widen, exchange becomes less personal and the division of labour increases. There is also a demand for violence to be exercised on a large-scale basis. It is here that the state in its essential form begins to take shape. The problem pointed to by Olson, of organizing *large* interest groups, is then overcome. The state is needed to establish universally acceptable rights which make complicated transactions possible. Property rights have to be formally defined and enforced to lower transaction costs. The state is the ultimate guarantor for those institutions which make up the foundation of economic development, i.e. extended exchange, division of labour and widening of the market. Conflicts are likely to arise in matters of property rights and validity of contracts. In changing economies, there is a latent risk of conflict which asks to be reconciled by a 'third party' which can enforce the rule of law.

So, third party enforcement is required for economic development. However, competition for political power, for the monopoly over the means of large-scale violence, constitutes the other side of the coin. In the long run, power can be wielded over fairly large territories. The competitive process ends with one group taking precedence over its competitors. How long this will take varies considerably from case to case and depends on the relative strength of the competing groups. In the worst case a territory is drawn into a 'game' between a number of groups that keep blocking each other all the time, or where loyalties are highly volatile, so that no dominant coalition arises, i.e. a game with an empty core. In this situation, the turnover of rulers and governments is rapid, as was often the case in Latin America during the nineteenth and/or the early twentieth century, in such countries as Bolivia, Peru, Ecuador, Mexico, Costa Rica, El Salvador, Haiti and the Dominican Republic, with the number of coups, countercoups, uprisings and revolutions sometimes running in the hundreds (Bienen and van de Walle, 1991, Appendix, for data). In other cases, again, stable, typically dictatorial, rule is established for long periods of time.[6]

The political units of Europe during the Middle Ages were of similar character. By the year 1500 there were some 500 political entities run by a ruler with some claim to be in the possession of a monopoly of violence in a territory large enough to be called a state (Harris, 1990, p. 29). But in those communities power remained personal. It was attached to the ruler as a person, not to an impersonal agency or institutional arrangement called the state. Only a few resembled the modern state form, the nation state that was to be developed over the following centuries.

These states were predatory in a typical form. The definition of a pre-datory state is that the ruler attempts to maximize revenue, subject to some constraints. Most important among these constraints is that he (or she) must remain in power in order to extract revenue from the citizens. Continued rule, however, can never be guaranteed but always remains a probability, falling somewhere between zero and one. Thus, the ruler is continuously faced with the problem of how much income he or she can extract from his or her citizens without being thrown out of office (Lundahl, 1985). The major problem here is that in such societies loyalty to the ruler cannot be assumed. It has to be reaffirmed each time it is required.

This problem poses a dilemma for the ruler, who must decide how many more individuals should be cut in on the deal, i.e. the ruler must find an optimal size of the ruling clique, knowing that whatever size is chosen determines both income and the probability of his or her remaining in power. A small clique means low income, because then the ruler does not have enough people to enforce collection of (legal and illegal) taxes from the citizens. Gross tax revenue can then be expected to rise with clique size, albeit at a decreasing rate, while collection costs should rise at an increasing rate. This defines an optimal clique size in terms of ruler income.

The size of the clique also determines the probability of remaining in power. A ruler with few backers runs a high risk of being thrown out by outside rivals. As the clique size increases, this probability decreases, since the ruler's violence potential increases simultaneously. However, increasing the clique size also increases the risk of disloyalty among those who already belong to the 'in' group, i.e. it increases the probability that factions will form that oppose the ruler and plan to overthrow him or her. Hence, after a certain point, the clique size becomes *too* large. The risk of being over-thrown increases again, but this time mainly in the form of palace coups.

Unfortunately, for the ruler, the optimum clique size in terms of revenue will normally not coincide with the optimum in terms of safety. The ruler is therefore faced with a dilemma where he or she must decide whether at the margin to prefer safety to income or vice versa. Two situations are possible: (1) increasing the clique size increases income but lowers safety; (2) increas-ing the clique size increases safety but lowers income. Both these situations can arise in practice.

Presumably, the Latin American cases presented above are examples of the latter situation. The economies were not rich enough to allow rule to be based on large cliques. Hence they remained small, and so did the rewards for many groups, both inside and outside the presidential palaces, that were eagerly waiting to get closer to the flesh pots. As a result of this, presidents with strong preferences for income ended up with cliques that were too small to allow them to remain in power other than for short periods.

Examples of the former situation, where the clique size grows too large to ensure political survival, are found in contemporary Africa. Between

1963 and 1975, military coups turned into virtually the only way of deposing rulers (Decalo, 1990). Even though they were small in absolute terms, the African armies were too large for the income they made possible for the rulers to extract. Poor transportation and dispersed population made revenue collection difficult and increased revenue could only be obtained at sharply increasing costs, e.g. in terms of increasing the size of the army. At the same time, African armies tend to offer a picture of very split and polarized loyalties to different, competing, officers (Decalo, 1990, p. 6), which, in a situation where average rewards were low, of course made the coup problem increase rapidly with army size.

THE THREE LEVELS OF RENT SEEKING

In the predatory state, the ruler is the largest rent seeker of all, almost by definition. The ruler is in the position to maximize income, within certain constraints (North, 1981, Chapter 3; Levi, 1988, Chapter 2). The methods that the ruler can choose to employ are almost infinite.[7] There seem to be few limits to human invention and innovativeness in this field. It is, however, possible to classify the methods into two groups. Jagdish Bhagwati (1982), in his seminal article on directly unproductive profit-seeking (rent-seeking) activities, makes a distinction between two different categories of such activities: intervention triggered and intervention seeking, respectively. In the former case, private individuals (companies, lobbies, etc.) engage in lobbying to capture rents, revenues, quotas, etc., that have already been put in place by the government for whatever reason. In the latter, they perceive opportunities for profit that materialize *if* the state intervenes in the resource allocation in a certain way and hence lobby to make the government intervene in the desired way for them.

Rent-seeking activities are activities that take place in all societies, including the most democratic ones. They simply constitute non-market methods of competing for scarce resources. However, in the predatory state they acquire special significance. They also contribute to the creation and maintenance of this type of state. It is not difficult to see why. Rent seeking may take place on different levels. The lowest one is where private actors take advantage of actual or potential government interventions in the way described by Bhagwati. The process, however, does not necessarily end there. Rent seeking presupposes the existence of bureaucrats and politicians or, putting it simply: 'It takes two to tango.' To be able to extract the rents created by political behaviour, the private actors must somehow convince the bureaucrats or politicians that they deserve to be put in a privileged position. This, in turn, opens for a shift of the rents to another level in the economy: the bureaucratic or political one.

If the authority to decide where the rents are going to end up has been more or less routinely delegated from the government to its civil service the road lies open for the interested parties to acquire them through bribes if they can find officials who are willing to receive money, i.e. if they can find corrupt bureaucrats. As Jens Christopher Andvig and Karl Ove Moene (1990) have shown, under certain circumstances, even a small beginning can easily result in a society where most of the civil servants are corrupt.

The expected value for a bureaucrat to follow a corrupt strategy can be expected to vary with the size of the bribes offered, the size of the bureaucrat's salary, the probability of detection, the rate at which future incomes are discounted (the bureaucrat may lose his or her job) and also with the incidence of corruption in society (if caught in the act by a colleague who is also corrupt, the bureaucrat does not lose his or her job but simply part of the bribe he or she has collected). In this situation, e.g. when the costs to the bureaucrat of providing the corrupt services vary between bureaucrats in a fashion that can be described by a normal distribution, multiple and sometimes unstable equilibria may arise which give rise to tipping points where, for example, an increase in the size of the bribe offered makes the economy 'jump' from a state with few corrupt bureaucrats to many (and vice versa).

It may help to visualize the bell-shaped distribution of costs. In the situation where few bureaucrats are corrupt we find ourselves somewhere in the left-hand tail, the tail where costs are low and where few bureaucrats are to be found. There it takes only low bribes to make it worth while to be corrupt. Should the size of bribes increase we will move rightwards and eventually reach the point where the curve starts to bend more sharply upwards, i.e. cost levels where many more bureaucrats are found. Small increases in bribe size will then push many civil servants into the corrupt camp.

What is more, even if the increase in bribe size should be only temporary, it may well be the case that once the size falls to its previous level, the economy ends up in an equilibrium where the number of corrupt bureaucrats is far higher than at the outset (although lower than when the higher bribe level prevailed). The reason is that the higher bribe through increasing the number of corrupt bureaucrats also decreased the probability of detection. Since the reduction of the bribe takes place in the latter situation, fewer bureaucrats are induced to become honest than were corrupted by a bribe increase of the corresponding size. A temporary change in the bribe level can thus give rise to a permanent change in the level of corruption.

In this situation, in principle the rents are passed on from the private agents of the economy to the government bureaucracy who can 'auction' them off to the highest bidder, i.e. auction them *away* from the competing citizens. The monopoly rents are dissipated into the hands of the bureaucrats. With an honest, innocent and naïve government, the process would end here, but this is not necessarily the case. If the state already is of the predatory variety (which is what we have assumed in the foregoing), it will make sure that the bureaucrats act as mere agents for the ruling clique in the process of rent collection, leave some formally illegal benefits for the civil servants, but make certain that the bulk of what is collected ends up on the highest level. (Even if at the outset the state is not predatory, the discovery that rents exist at lower levels may provide a strong incentive to capture them.) The logic of corruption described above may enter government circles as well and a tipping point, turning an honest government into a predatory one, may be reached.

Once corruption has reached the top layer of government, either because the ruling coalition was predatory from the beginning or because it became so as rents filtered upwards in the system, it becomes a serious problem. Now, in addition to the intervention-triggered and intervention-seeking processes analysed by Bhagwati, a third possibility enters the picture, that of intervention-*creating* activities designed to produce rents that can be appropriated by the ruler and his clique (Lundahl and Vedovato, 1989, p. 55). This opens a Pandora's box of opportunities for the predators who, if their security can be guaranteed, now in principle can design any variety of schemes to plunder the citizens, although they may have to hide or obfuscate some of them.[8]

THE PARADOX OF THE PREDATORY STATE

Rent seeking is connected with costs for society. It implies an inefficient allocation of resources that is likely to be inimical to growth as well.[9] This is clearly visible at the level where private citizens work on bureaucrats or politicians to obtain favours, simply because it draws resources out of the production of goods and services that are demanded in the economy, resources which in principle produce nothing but a redistribution of an already existing pie in favour of those who undertake the profit-seeking activities.

The same logic operates higher up in the rent-seeking hierarchy. For the economy as a whole, the costs implied in this distortion of the resource allocation may be considerable. They may amount to a lot more than what those who undertake the activities gain, because they have to be borne mainly by other parties. The rent-seeking activities create a 'cost externality'. The logic is simple (Olson, 1982, pp. 41–44). Let us assume that a ruler can gain 100 million dollars by redistributing income in his or her own favour and that annual income without the redistribution amounts to 1 per cent of the national income. Redistribution cannot take place without costs, however, in the form of a lower GDP, as the allocation of resources is distorted. How large will these costs be? This is of course impossible to say, but it is easy to arrive at an estimate of what the maximum that the ruler is prepared to impose on society will be. In our example, redistribution pays as long as the loss the ruler makes as a result of the decrease of GDP does not exceed 100 million. Assuming that a share equal to the ruler's share of GDP, i.e. 1 per cent, of whatever loss of GDP that results from redistribution accrues to the ruler, he or she will then be prepared to let GDP fall by 100 × 100 = 10,000 million = 10 billion dollars.

Two conclusions can be drawn from this simple exercise. In the first place, in the case of a small predatory clique that takes power there are hardly any limits to the efficiency losses that its members are prepared to inflict on society; 1 per cent of GDP is a very large share for a newcomer to the flesh pots. The second conclusion is slightly more subtle. Given that the *arriviste* clique is able to remain in power for some period, one would expect its share of GDP to increase, and the increase will be larger the more successful the clique is in its predatory operations. In the case of complete success, the entire GDP, i.e. 100 per cent, accrues to the clique.

At this point, there is no more to be redistributed. By the same token, the clique no longer has any incentives to inflict costs on society, since this amounts to hurting none but the clique members themselves. On the contrary, once the perfect stage of rent seeking has been reached, it will do its best to ensure that the allocation of resources becomes as efficient as possible. Instead of a stagnating economy we will see a growing one.

This constitutes the ultimate paradox of the predatory state. *Ceteris paribus*, a new ruler will inflict potentially very large efficiency losses on society, but as the duration of his or her rule increases, provided that the ruler's success in plundering the nation increases, the allocation of resources will become more and more efficient and ultimately, when the entire national economy has been converted into his or her private property, there will be no more incentives for inefficiency. From this it also follows that, from the resource allocation point of view, *ceteris paribus*, a long-lived predatory dictator is to be preferred to the unstable situation where short-lived cliques succeed each other in power.[10] It may also provide an explanation of the finding of Henry Bienen and Nicolas van de Walle that 'the length of time a leader has been in power is the best predictor of how long he will continue to hold power' (Bienen and van de Walle, 1991, p. 13), at least in the case of predatory regimes. With the passage of time successful predatory rulers become less and less prone to interfere with the economy. More and more people are employed directly by them and there are fewer and fewer clashes with the economic interests of other groups.

LIMITATIONS ON PREDATION

An obvious question that arises from our discussion of the predatory state is why *all* states are not predatory. A possible answer is that in fact they *are* but that the circumstances under which they have to operate at times make it impossible for them to extract revenue to the maximum extent. 'Rulers refrain from extraction because of the constraints to which they are subject', argues Margaret Levi (1988, p. 4), echoing North (1979). These constraints are of two kinds: the bargaining power of the ruler, which to a large extent, but not exclusively, is a function of the availability of alternative rulers, and the transaction costs involved in extracting revenue from the citizens.

The availability of alternative rulers is basically a question of the resources of the incumbent ruler in relation to those of competitors: economic resources, political resources and ultimately, of course, violence potential (Levi, 1988, Chapter 2). Rulers who do not dispose of enough economic resources themselves may have to enter into alliances with powerful economic groups. Political resources, in turn, are those connected with the possibility of employing patronage, material rewards, punishments, ideology, etc., to mobilize support for the ruler and prevent support for the competitors. Finally, the use of economic and political resources must be backed by a credible threat of violence. Together, this determines the ruler's bargaining power *vis-à-vis* the citizens.

The transaction costs facing the ruler are of different types. Unless the extraction of resources from the citizens is to rest simply on naked force, explicit or implicit contracts must be concluded with them. These contracts have to be negotiated, which in turn requires information about the resources to be included (their quantity and quality) and also the actual bargaining itself, i.e. the setting of the terms of the contract. Thereafter, the agreement must be enforced, which calls for measuring the revenue sources and monitoring compliance, both of which are connected with agency costs. Finally, non-complying citizens must be identified, tracked down and punished.

The availability of alternative rulers and the existence of transaction costs obviously go a long way towards explaining why rulers do not always act as predators in the sense that they maximize their incomes. This they can do only within the constraints given by these two factors. There is, however, also a third factor to note in the context – one which is related to transaction costs or which can even be incorporated under that heading. It is important to remember that even though Olson's logic of collective action predicts that cliques or rulers intent on redistribution are likely to harm efficiency and growth, this is a 'by-product distortion' (*à la* Max Corden, 1974, p. 13) of their behaviour. It is not necessarily their wish. As pointed out by Lal and Myint (1996, Chapter 6),

> Predators will share an interest in the enlargement of the incomes of their prey (say, through economic growth, promoted by the provision of public goods – of which the most important is law and order) in so far as this raises the potential flow of their own income.

Thráinn Eggertsson (1990, p. 247) agrees:

> Although little can be said a priori about the utility function of those who control the state, it is unreasonable to assume that, other things being equal, they either prefer or are indifferent to economic decline

in their country. This conclusion should be independent of our model of the state, be it one assuming a contract state or a predatory state. For example, a ruler of a predatory state who seeks to maximize her wealth by taxing her subjects, will, other things being equal, attempt to maximize the tax base, the national income.

Predatory rulers do not *necessarily* reduce efficiency. They do so only when it is in their interest to do so, i.e. when this contributes to minimizing the transaction costs of extracting a given income or when it enhances their safety.

In other cases, reducing transaction costs should increase efficiency. There is especially one such instance that is of interest in the present context and that is the promotion of exchange transactions on a voluntary basis through the design of suitable institutions. The underlying logic for this is that of exchange and trade. By becoming involved in exchange transactions with other agents in commodity and factor markets, the agents in the economy can enhance their possible consumption set beyond what they could achieve in isolation. By the same token, the ability of rulers to extract an income for themselves and their clique increases, and it is only when this clashes with the methods actually used in the extraction process that we should expect the latter to carry the day and efficiency to be lowered. Hence, we should expect rulers in principle to have an interest in promoting exchange.

THE PRODUCTIVE PREDATORY STATE

The contradictory views of the ruler create a 'productive' predatory state. A predatory state may have a gain to make by enhancing the efficiency of private producers, but there is also a 'tension between these two aspects of the state, the "productive" and the "predatory"' (Findlay, 1990, p. 201). Ronald Findlay and John Wilson have produced a model which incorporates both these aspects and which builds precisely on the argument advanced above.[11] In their model, national income is produced by private producers using private inputs. The state enters the picture in two capacities. It taxes the citizens to obtain an income, but it also provides a public good: 'public expenditure on administration, law and order, roads, justice and so on acts as an "externality" to private economic activities, enhancing the *private* output from *private* inputs' (Findlay, 1990, p. 201).

The function of the public good is to facilitate private production. Without it a certain national income is possible. The presence of the public good, in turn, increases private production, e.g. by facilitating exchange, but only up to certain point, where the marginal product of labour in the public sector equals that in the private sector. Thereafter, private production falls again, as labour becomes less productive in the production of public goods than in the production of private output.

However, the ruler is not likely to maximize national income. Rather, the ruler will behave either as the Lal–Myint absolutist, i.e. maximize the surplus accruing to the state from tax revenues after having deducted the wage payments to labour in the public sector, or maximize employment in the public sector, i.e. behave like the Lal–Myint bureaucratic authoritarian. In the former case, with a given tax rate that is proportional to the national income, the total tax revenue curve peaks for some public employment, while the total expenditure curve (the after-tax wage payments) rises monotonically. The surplus maximum then is reached when marginal public revenue equals marginal public expenditure, i.e. on the rising part of the tax revenue curve. The size of the public sector becomes smaller than what is optimal from the national income point of view. In the bureaucratic–authoritarian case, on the other hand, government expenditure will increase until it has absorbed all the available revenue. This takes place when the tax and expenditure curves cut each other, i.e. at a larger size of the public sector than in the absolutist case, possibly one which is larger than the one maximizing national income.[12]

Thus, even when a state is predatory, we should expect it – for selfish reasons – to produce some public goods that are wanted by the citizens, because it allows the latter to cut down on their production and transaction costs. The state that acts both as a predator and a provider of goods and services that raise the efficiency of the economy exists. What we should *not* expect is that the *level* of production is optimal. On the other hand, provided that the state has a selfish interest in providing public goods, we cannot of course exclude the possibility that the optimum level of public employment from the point of view of the ruler is very close to the optimum from the national income point of view, i.e. even predatory states could be 'good'. Next we will turn to the circumstances under which this is likely to occur.

THE GOOD STATE

Supposedly, the developmental state is the antithesis of the predatory state. In any case, what we have in mind is a state that takes strong and direct measures to bring about economic development. Thus, it is an autonomous entity with powers to carry out intended policies, and it acts as the 'guardian' of a common 'national' or other interest. How, then, do we explain that such obvious exceptions to North's law actually exist, in fact to the extent that, in some form or another, there is always a developmental state present in most cases of sustained modern economic growth?

A casual explanation would suggest that the developmental state is identical to a benevolent social guardian whose prime concern is the well-being of its fellow citizens. An answer is then to be found in the personal character of the ruler. This is, however, a misleading presumption. In fact, the personal character of the ruler would be of greater importance in predatory monolithic autocratic states. In such cases, benevolence on the part of a merciful ruler might somewhat mitigate the effects of revenue maximization.

Some of the rulers of those states we call developmental have, however, been known to possess only a minimum of compassion for their people. For instance, Chiang Kai-shek was, rightly or wrongly, known as one of the world's worst predators during his reign in (parts of) China. In contrast, as a ruler of Taiwan, he became the incarnation of a 'developmentalist'. At the other extreme we find Kwame Nkrumah of Ghana, who had a clean record with regard to predation and corruption. In hindsight, it is easy to see, however, that the state bureaucracy moulded by Nkrumah for developmental purposes was swiftly turned into a devastating instrument of predation.

Of course, any 'good' ruler needs a minimum of benevolence, but benevolence as such cannot explain a ruler's good behaviour. Thus, we are left with the task of explaining why potential predators may turn developmental. One explanation begins with North's and Levi's assumption that the state is a revenue maximizer that can choose between rent seeking and growth policies as means for achieving maximization. Alice Amsden (1993, p. 14) has suggested that the choice the state makes between predation and developmentalism depends on 'its perceptions of the likelihood of its succeeding in industrializing'. As highlighted by the Findlay–Wilson model, the state will seek to enrich itself through rent seeking rather than through capital accumulation if the perceived probability of success of the former alternative exceeds that of the latter and vice versa.

This is a reasonable argument, but only as far as it goes. Amsden herself (1993, p. 14), in fact, brings up the difficulty underlying this explanation when she goes on to say that 'neither Korea nor Taiwan were regarded as very likely candidates of successful development in the early 1960s, yet their states eventually became developmental'. To be more exact, the prospects for development in the two countries were exceedingly gloomy, not least due to previous predatory state performances. Thus, why would predatory states turn developmental under such circumstances if they had a free choice?

To get further we must rephrase the question and ask why, at a critical moment, rent seeking ceased to be a feasible strategy for the Korean and Taiwanese states, not merely from the point of view of revenue maximization, but for the very survival of the state as well. The explanation begins with the assumption that the state is also a state among other states, i.e. its choice of policies is guided as much by foreign pressures as by domestic challenges. In order to do this we must thus bring in the concept of the 'nation state'.

In principle, the nation state is present at two levels. On the one hand, it serves as the guarantor of the institutional structure that enables exchange to take place within its borders. On the other hand, a state exists in an environment of competing states. Historically, a fundamental break with predation was made when the state began to define the area under its control as a political and economic unit called 'the nation'. The European nation states arose out of a combination of domestic rivalry for power and external pressures. A fundamental task was to define and protect the property rights of its inhabitants against threats from foreign forces.

Thus, the state took on the role of a 'national interest' in a competitive political environment. Both the medieval states in Europe and many contemporary Third World states should be seen as states with few limitations on them but the capacity of their inhabitants to pay taxes. In particular, the external pressure was lacking. Europe consisted of tributary societies and its subjects complied with the dictates of revenue-seeking rulers. The same is true for Imperial China and for major parts of the pre-industrial world. Arbitrary rule and favouritism are legion.

THE ROLE OF EXTERNAL PRESSURE

The existence of a predatory state leads to a society in which institutions are not established to facilitate impersonal exchange since, as suggested by North, the ruler is deterred by a transaction cost constraint and a competitive constraint. However, North's law pictures ruler logic in a society in which ruling the state is a personal affair and in which the ruler is unconstrained by foreign pressures. It pictures the logic of the feudal states of Europe, of the dynasties of Asia and of the privatized predatory state in many present-day developing countries. It is not relevant, however, for societies where not only the ruler but also *the entire political unit* is in danger. In such societies, the state has a choice between expanding the stock of wealth or becoming extinct. It is here that we may find 'the developmental state', i.e. an agent that works for the fostering of the wealth of the national economy in competition with foreign nations and for the exclusion of foreigners from the property rights of the national economy. It is here that we find the developmental states of East Asia (Gunnarsson, 1993b).

Gustav Schmoller (1896, p. 50) once argued that mercantilism 'is nothing but state-making – not state-making in a narrow sense but state-making and national-economy-making at the same time'. Under mercantilism, many monopolies were established to encourage the creation of new enterprises or the appearance of new trades. Via the monopoly trade the political elite could, at a low cost, appropriate a substantial part of the revenue. A symbiotic relationship was developed between the elites of the political and the economic spheres, a *mercantilist partnership* from which both economic and political actors could profit. In this partnership the state guaranteed the property rights of traders and manufacturers at the same time as it restrained the dispersion of property rights by means of taxation and by the granting of privileges.

We have something of a paradox here. As it seems, mercantilism was basically protectionist and, one would assume, anti-trade oriented. But this would be a misunderstanding. The kind of protectionism employed by the states in mercantilist Europe was largely oriented towards the encouragement of trade and industry. It was outward oriented and concerned with policies that would increase the revenue of the state. It did not recognize the principle of international division of labour, but it was in favour of widening the market.

What about rent seeking under such a system? Surely, as Gordon Tullock (1974, 1987) and others (Krueger, 1974, Brennan and Buchanan, 1980; North, 1981; Bhagwati, 1982; Levi, 1988; Magee *et al.*, 1989) have demonstrated, the scope for corruption and rent seeking would be substantial within the system of allocation of special privileges. Seen in this way, the mercantilist state would be no different from the predatory Third World state. Still, there is a fundamental difference between the predatory and the mercantilist state. True, the latter was governed by despotic rulers, but its principal goal was that of increasing output which in the final analysis made a developmental state.

The developmental state can be monolithic, despotic and dictatorial, but not personal. In addition, one should not assume that the degree of exploitation is automatically reduced once the state ceases to be predatory. In fact, it is reasonable to hypothesize that tax rates may even be raised in periods of nation building. The important thing, however, is that acquired rents are not dissipated among a ruler and his or her associates but that accumulated surpluses are put back into productive work.

Why then were the rulers so determined to encourage the growth of trade and industry? Why was it not more rational for the state to implement institutions which maintained the status quo in the same vein as for the predatory state? To understand this, we must take into account the international political aspect of the nation state in the European context. 'War made the state, and the state made war', writes George Tilly (1975, p. 42). The process of nation building involved a capacity to make war. However, wars are costly, and financing was extremely difficult and constrained by the limited surplus capacity of the economy. Improvements in agricultural technology, commercialization and, most important, industrialization were the prime factors by which surplus-creating capacity could be raised. Thus, economic development became an imperative in the process of nation building.

The political competition between European states was also important during the wave of industrialization in the nineteenth century. The mercantilist strategy was renovated and packaged in the form of nineteenth-century nationalism. The development projects all over Europe during the second half of the nineteenth century were all encouraged by nationalist governments. It was realized that, although political power grew out of the barrel of a gun, guns had to be paid for. A strong army needed a strong economy. A developmental state must work both for 'power' and for 'plenty', and in ways that not only benefit the rulers but also enhance wealth and power on a national scale.

The modernization drive in Japan after the Meiji Restoration followed the same growth imperative. It is clear as well that national economic motives have constituted perhaps the most important force behind the economic metamorphosis of South Korea and Taiwan. It has been considered elementary that the state must take on the role of the leading actor in the economy. The governments have encouraged private enterprise and their role has been to 'protect domestic industries from external competition and to promote their competitiveness in the foreign market'.[13]

The developmental state in East Asia is clearly autonomous. It possesses strong powers and great administrative capacity. However, autonomy *per se* cannot explain why the state has become developmental rather than predatory. This choice can only be explained by the presence of a deadly external threat in combination with a domestic challenge. China and North Korea were immediate and obvious enemies, but in fact the entire East and Southeast Asian region was extremely conflict ridden during the 1950s. Thus, this factor, which made observers predict a gloomy future for the region, also posed a decisive challenge for the governments. The Marxian imperative 'accumulate or perish' reflected a new and very painful reality for the states. Development became a necessity. Only those regimes that abandoned predation for accumulation could survive.

Thus, Douglass North's predatory state, constrained as it is by high transaction costs and rivals for the reins of power, exists in a system without foreign pressures which combine with domestic challenges. In constrast, the developmental state exists in a world perceived as one of highly competitive states. The more closed the system, the more likely it is that predatory states are being perpetuated. The more severe the foreign threats, the more likely that the state takes a developmental orientation. The latter term is synonymous with the fostering of *national* economic development, and in East Asia the demand for national development was brought about by the external communist threat imposed on the governments. In this, we find a striking similarity with the mercantilist state of Western Europe which also materialized in a highly competitive environment.[14]

The common factor which explains why Western Europe and East Asia have developed in this way is that the states in both regions were pressured from abroad by competitive and dangerous neighbours. Thus, it was political competition in both regions that made it necessary for the elites to protect a national interest instead of furthering their own special interest which so often has been the case in history and which remains the case in the present-day Third World.

But what about other developing countries? Are they not exposed to foreign threats that would make predatory states redundant? It is true that all developing countries have been faced with a 'developmental challenge', but few have succeeded. However, this challenge has been one 'for plenty', for economic modernization and wealth as goals in themselves. Many are the benevolent social guardians who have had to surrender to predatory rent seekers. Thus, policies for 'plenty' cannot be a force strong enough to withstand the force of 'power'. There has been no need to combine 'power' and 'plenty'. Obviously, when power can be upheld without plenty there is no reason why the state should be expected not to be predatory. Thus, the predatory Third World state is likely to linger on as long as foreign pressures remain limited.

CONCLUSIONS

The theme of this chapter has been a familiar one: that of the proper role of the state in the economy. To a large extent, those in favour of or against state intervention have always had a tendency to take extreme positions. The pendulum has swung from extreme market pessimism to utter state anathema. The state is taken to be either 'all good' or 'all bad'.

In the theoretical debate, which is also highly ideological, state intervention is seen in either maximalist or minimalist terms, i.e. either as a prerequisite for development or as a major source of development failure. The truth is, of course, that in the real world states are both 'good' and 'bad' – both a prerequisite for development and a source of economic decline. In the present chapter, we have tried to go beyond such rather obvious judgements. Instead, we have made an attempt to establish the logic behind 'good' and 'bad' state behaviour and to find out what causes the switch from predatory behaviour to 'developmentalism'. Why do some rulers appear to have reasons to promote development while others resort to predatory behaviour?

We have argued that the difference between 'good' and 'bad' state behaviour is not a question of the size of the state *per se*. Nor can differences in state behaviour be measured in terms of whether the ruler is benevolent or not. There is only a thin dividing line between the predatory state and the developmental state. The rationality of the leaders of a developmental state may be the same as for the ruler of a predatory state.

The concepts of 'power' and 'plenty', borrowed from Jacob Viner, were brought in to shed light on the distinction between predatory and developmental states. It was argued that what makes a developmental state is not only that it is 'for plenty', meaning that its prime goal is to encourage growth and development as opposed to a predatory state that supposedly is only 'for power' (as a means of enrichment). Used in this way, the concepts are utterly *ad hoc* and devoid of content. Instead, we have argued that all states are for both power and plenty. They all work for the accumulation of wealth and for the strengthening of their power base. The crux of the matter is, however, that a predatory state can turn developmental once the external setting changes so that the concepts of power and plenty need to be redefined by the ruler. All predatory states are based on personal rule; power is attached to the ruler as a person and it is this person's private wealth and power that form the basis of state behaviour.

A developmental state, on the other hand, cannot be based on personal rule. It may be despotic (and often is), ruthless and power hungry, but its rule can never be totally vested in the power of a person. A developmental state is a state that takes on the task of accumulating the wealth and power of its entire nation in relation to other nation states. Thus, in a developmental state, power and plenty are concepts which refer to national entities rather than to persons.

The logic of this argument says, of course, that any government that seeks to promote the development of its national economy may deserve to be called a developmental state. In fact, this is a reasonable conclusion. The term cannot be reserved for the success stories alone. Also, developmentalism has its failures and all failures cannot be interpreted in terms of a lack of will on the part of the state.

The developmental state is never just a passive follower of the market. To some extent, it always interferes with the play of market forces and attempts to correct for what is taken to be market failure. Thus, Gerschenkron's postulate about the role of the state for industrialization in backward economies seems to hold water. A problem which needs to be investigated further, however, is why such interventions sometimes turn out to be efficient vehicles of developmentalism, while in other cases they constitute the very symbols of inefficient and even predatory intervention. Why have market regulations with respect to imports, agricultural prices, foreign currency, credits, etc., helped in turning Taiwan into an industrial market economy while identical regulations have hampered the development of market economies in Africa? Why is it that interventions à la Gerschenkron do not work everywhere?

Alice Amsden (1992) has suggested that there is a threshold below which the Gerschenkron thesis does not apply. In the poorest countries, incomes are too low to allow technology gaps to be closed by means of interventions. But it is not only a question of low incomes per se. More important, it seems, is the distribution of income. Uneven distribution tends to undermine the power of the state, since influential groups then have the power to manipulate the state in their own interest. This can be linked to the argument in the present chapter. It can be hypothesized that in societies with an extremely skewed income distribution, 'power' and 'plenty' can be defined in personal terms by the ruler and the elite. As we have seen, in such societies almost any intervention may be turned into an instrument of predation.

In too many Third World countries incomes are not only very low but also unevenly distributed. This is a problem in itself since it tends to obstruct development. A market economy requires 'equality of opportunity'. In order to create that, some form of redistribution of assets is usually needed. In East Asia, income distribution was made relatively equal, mainly as a result of the implementation of comprehensive land reform. In most developing countries, in contrast, the degree of inequality of opportunity has remained extremely high. Industrialization has served to aggravate inequality and social cleavages. As a result, many governments have gradually been losing legitimacy, sometimes to the point where the entire political sphere is being perverted by private interests.

This means of course that institutional arrangements aimed at redistribution may be needed for the growth of the market economy in the Third World. However, such redistribution can only be achieved by the state, and as long as inequality as such constitutes the other side of predatory rule there is little hope for any change in policies. Economic development requires a process of nation building. Therefore, it deserves to be repeated that it is not until accumulation and power are defined on a national basis that one can expect governments to be other than predatory.

NOTES

* Thanks are due to Evald Nalin for helpful comments on a previous version and to Deborah Cheifetz-Pira for correcting our English.
1 Compare the literature referred to in Toye (1987), Findlay (1990), Krueger (1990) and Killick (1990).
2 Compare the title of Killick (1990). See also Colclough and Manor (1993).
3 Compare, however, the distinction made by Wintrobe (1990) between 'tinpot' and 'totalitarian' dictators. The former want to stay in power in order to enjoy the private incomes connected with office, while the goal of the latter is to maximize their power over the population.
4 What he actually means is an *absolute* advantage. A state which is less productive in everything, including violence, than, say, some private organization, but least inferior in the field of violence, of course has a comparative advantage in the latter, but this would not make it possible to control the private organization. The latter would presumably take over the state or at least have a decisive influence on how it is run.
5 Macpherson (1985, p. 40). The original is Hobbes (1985, Chapter 13).
6 Compare Bienen and van de Walle (1991, p. 91) for a list of rulers between 1801 and 1987 who held power for at least twenty-five years. Out of thirty, twenty-two came from developing countries.
7 For an overview of some of the repertoire, see Lundahl (1984) and Lundahl and Vedovato (1989).
8 For examples of such schemes and for the role of obfuscation in a concrete instance – that of Haiti – see Danielson and Lundahl (1994).
9 See Lundahl and Vedovato (1989), for some mechanisms.
10 Compare also Olson (1993), who argues that it is better to have a stationary dictator who organizes plunder in the form of taxes than competitive 'roving bandits' who by their uncoordinated plunder leave far less to the population.
11 Findlay and Wilson (1987). Compare also Olson (1991).

12 Findlay (1990) demonstrates how the tax rate can be endogenized in the models as well.
13 Hung-mao Tien, 'Origins and Development of Taiwan's Democratic Change', Paper presented at the Annual Meeting of the Association of Asian Studies, Washington, DC, 17–19 March 1989. Quoted in Chou (1991).
14 Compare also Findlay (1992), on this point.

REFERENCES

Amsden, Alice H. (1989) *Asia's Next Giant: South Korea and Late Industrialization*, Oxford University Press, New York.
—— (1992) 'A Theory of Government Intervention in Late Industrialization', in Louis Putterman and Dietrich Rueschmeyer (eds) *State and Market in Development. Synergy or Rivalry?*, Lynne Rienner, Boulder, CO and London.
—— (1993) 'The Quality of State Intervention and Industrial Development', Paper presented at EADI Conference, Berlin, 15–18 September.
Andvig, Jens Christopher and Moene, Karl Ove (1990) 'How Corruption May Corrupt', *Journal of Economic Behavior and Organization*, vol. 13.
Baran, Paul A. (1957) *The Political Economy of Growth*, Monthly Review Press, New York and London.
Bates, Robert H. (1981) *Markets and States in Tropical Africa. The Political Basis of Agricultural Policies*, University of California Press, Berkeley, CA.
Bhagwati, Jagdish N. (1982) 'Directly Unproductive, Profit-seeking (DUP) Activities', *Journal of Political Economy*, vol. 90.
Bienen, Henry S. and van de Walle, Nicolas (1991) *Of Time and Power. Leadership Duration in the Modern World*, Stanford University Press, Stanford, CA.
Blomqvist, Hans C. and Lundahl, Mats (1992) *Ekonomisk utveckling. En introduktion till u-ländernas ekonomiska problem*, SNS Förlag, Stockholm.
Bradford, Colin I. (1986) 'East Asian Model: Myths and Lessons', in John P. Lewis and Valeriana Kallab (eds) *Development Strategies Reconsidered*, Overseas Development Council, Washington, DC.
Brennan, Geoffrey and Buchanan, James M. (1980) *The Power to Tax: Analytical Foundations of a Fiscal Constitution*, Cambridge University Press, Cambridge.
Burenstam Linder, Staffan (1986) *The Pacific Century: Economic and Political Consequences of Asian Pacific Dynamism*, Stanford University Press, Stanford, CA.
Chou, Yu-jen (1991) 'The Role of the State in Revising Taiwan's Trade Policy', *Public Administration*, vol. 23.
Clapham, Christopher (1988) *Third World Politics. An Introduction*, Routledge, London.
Colclough, Christopher and Manor, James (eds) (1993) *States or Markets? Neoliberalism and the Development Policy Debate*, Clarendon Press, Oxford.
Corden, W. Max (1974) *Trade Policy and Economic Welfare*, Clarendon Press, Oxford.
Danielson, Anders and Lundahl, Mats (1994) 'Endogenous Policy Formation and the Principle of Optimal Obfuscation: Theory and Some Evidence from Haiti and Jamaica', *Comparative Economic Studies*, vol. 51.
Decalo, Samuel (1990) *Coups and Army Rule in Africa: Motivations and Constraints*, Second Edition, Westview Press, Boulder, CO and London.
Eggertsson, Thráinn (1990) *Economic Behavior and Institutions*, Cambridge University Press, Cambridge.
Evans, Peter B., Rueschmeyer, Dietrich and Skocpol, Theda (eds) (1985) *Bringing the State Back In*, Cambridge University Press, Cambridge.

Findlay, Ronald (1990) 'The New Political Economy: Its Explanatory Power for LDCs', *Economics and Politics*, vol. 2.

——(1992) 'The Roots of Divergence: Western Economic History in Comparative Perspective', *American Economic Review*, vol. 82.

Findlay, Ronald and Wilson, John D. (1987) 'The Political Economy of Leviathan', in Assaf Razin and Efraim Sadka (eds) *Economic Policy in Theory and Practice*, Macmillan, London.

Gerschenkron, Alexander (1952) 'Economic Backwardness in Historical Perspective', in Bert F. Hoselitz (ed.) *The Progress of Underdeveloped Areas*, University of Chicago Press, Chicago.

Gunnarsson, Christer (1987) 'Den nya politiska ekonomin och staten i underutvecklade länder', in *Ekonomisk-historiska vingslag. Festskrift tillägnad G. Fridlizius, L. Jörberg*, Skrifter utgivna av Ekonomisk-historiska föreningen, Lund.

——(1993a) 'Dirigisme or Free-Trade Regime? A Historical and Institutional Interpretation of the Taiwanese Success Story', in Göte Hansson (ed.) *Trade, Growth and Development: The Role of Politics and Institutions*, Routledge, London and New York.

——(1993b) 'Mercantilism Old and New, A Transaction Cost Theory and Developmental States in Europe and East Asia', Paper presented at the Conference on Public Choice Theories and Third World Experiences, London, 17–19 September.

Harris, Nigel (1986) *The End of the Third World. Newly Industrializing Countries and the Decline of an Ideology*, I. B. Tauris, London.

——(1990) *National Liberation*, Penguin, Harmondsworth.

Hobbes, Thomas (1985) *Leviathan*, ed. with an introduction by C. B. Macpherson, Penguin, London.

Johnson, Chalmers (1982) *MITI and the Japanese Miracle: The Growth of Industrial Policy, 1925–1975*, Stanford University Press, Stanford, CA.

Keynes, John Maynard (1931) *Essays in Persuasion*, Macmillan, London.

Killick, Tony (1990) *A Reaction Too Far. Economic Theory and the Role of the State in Developing Countries*, Overseas Development Institute, London.

Krueger, Anne O. (1974) 'The Political Economy of the Rent-Seeking Society', *American Economic Review*, vol. 64.

——(1990) 'Economists' Changing Perceptions of Government', *Weltwirtschaftliches Archiv*, vol. 126.

——(1993) *Political Economy of Policy Reform in Developing Countries*, MIT Press, Cambridge, MA and London.

Lal, Deepak (1983) *The Poverty of 'Development Economics'*, Institute of Economic Affairs, London.

Lal, Deepak and Hla Myint (1996) *The Political Economy of Poverty, Equity and Growth*, Clarendon Press, Oxford.

Levi, Margaret (1988) *Of Rule and Revenue*, University of California Press, Berkeley, CA.

Lewis, W. Arthur (1984) 'The State of Development Theory', *American Economic Review*, vol. 84.

Lundahl, Mats (1984) 'Papa Doc: Innovator in the Predatory State', *Scandia*, vol. 50.

——(1985) 'Government and Inefficiency in the Haitian Economy: The Nineteenth Century Legacy', in Michael B. Connolly and John McDermott (eds) *The Economics of the Caribbean Basin*, Praeger, New York.

Lundahl, Mats and Vedovato, Claudio (1989) 'The State and Economic Development in Haiti and the Dominican Republic', *Scandinavian Economic History Review*, vol. 37.

McCloskey, Donald (1986) *The Rhetoric of Economics*, Wheatsheaf, Brighton.

Macpherson, C. B. (1985) 'Introduction', in Thomas Hobbes, *Leviathan*, ed. C. B. Macpherson, Penguin, London.
Magee, Stephen P., Brock, William, A. and Young, Leslie (1989) *Black Hole Tariffs and Endogenous Policy Theory*, Cambridge University Press, Cambridge.
Myrdal, Gunnar (1957) *Economic Theory and Under-developed Regions*, Duckworth, London.
North, Douglass C. (1979) 'A Framework for Analyzing the State in Economic History', *Explorations in Economic History*, vol. 16.
——(1981) *Structure and Change in Economic History*, W. W. Norton, New York and London.
North, Douglass C. and Thomas, Robert Paul (1973) *The Rise of the Western World. A New Economic History*, Cambridge University Press, London and New York.
Nurkse, Ragnar (1953) *Problems of Capital Formation in Underdeveloped Countries*, Basil Blackwell, Oxford.
Olson, Mancur (1965) *The Logic of Collective Action. Public Goods and the Theory of Groups*, Harvard University Press, Cambridge, MA and London.
——(1982) *The Rise and Decline of Nations. Economic Growth, Stagflation and Social Rigidities*, Yale University Press, New Haven, CT and London.
——(1983) 'The Political Economy of Comparative Growth Rates', in Dennis C. Mueller (ed.) *The Political Economy of Growth*, Yale University Press, New Haven, CT and London.
——(1991) 'Autocracy, Democracy, and Prosperity', in Richard J. Zeckhauser (ed.) *Strategy and Choice*, MIT Press, Cambridge, MA and London.
——(1993) 'Dictatorship, Democracy, and Development', *American Political Science Review*, vol. 87.
Prebisch, Raúl (1950) *The Economic Development of Latin America and Its Principal Problems*, United Nations, New York.
Schmoller, Gustav (1896) *The Mercantile System and its Historical Significance*, Macmillan, New York and London.
Stokes, William S. (1952) 'Violence as a Power Factor in Latin American Politics', *Western Political Quarterly*, vol. 5.
Streeten, Paul (1992) 'Against Minimalism', in Louis Putterman and Dietrich Rueschmeyer (eds) *State and Market in Development*, Lynne Rienner, Boulder, CO and London.
Tilly, George (1975) 'Reflections on the History of European State-Making', in George Tilly (ed.) *The Formation of Nation States in Europe*, Princeton University Press, Princeton, NJ.
Toye, John (1987) *Dilemmas of Development: Reflections on the Counter-Revolution in Development Theory and Policy*, Basil Blackwell, Oxford.
Tullock, Gordon (1974) *The Social Dilemma: The Economics of War and Revolution*, Virginia State University Press, Blacksburg, VA.
——(1987) *Autocracy*, Kluwer, Dordrecht.
Viner, Jacob (1948) 'Power versus Plenty as Objectives of Foreign Policy in the 17th and 18th Centuries', *World Politics*, vol. 1.
von Hayek, Friedrich A. (1945) 'The Price System as a Mechanism for Using Knowledge', *American Economic Review*, vol. 35.
von Mises, Ludwig (1935) 'Economic Calculation in the Socialist Commonwealth', in Friedrich A. von Hayek (ed.) *Collectivist Economic Planning*, Routledge & Kegan Paul, London.
Wade, Robert (1990) *Governing the Market: Economic Theory and the Role of Government in East Asian Industrialization*, Princeton University Press, Princeton, NJ.

Wintrobe, Ronald (1990) 'The Tinpot and the Totalitarian: An Economic Theory of Dictatorship', *American Political Science Review*, vol. 84.

World Bank (1993) *The East Asian Miracle: Economic Growth and Public Policy*, Oxford University Press, New York.

Woronoff, Jon (1986) *Asia's 'Miracle' Economies*, M. E. Sharpe, New York and London.

12

THE ROLE OF THE AFRICAN STATE IN BUILDING AGENCIES OF RESTRAINT[1]

Paul Collier

INTRODUCTION

In this chapter I discuss three African economic problems, all deterrents to private investment, in which a central aspect is the difficulty in restraining some agent within the economy. The first is the probability attached to the reversal of economic reforms. Now that many African governments have liberalized their economies to a considerable degree, surveys of actual and potential investors identify the perceived risk of policy reversal as the most potent deterrent to foreign investment.[2] Investment is low because the stated intentions of governments are not sufficiently credible. The second is the prevalence of corruption among public employees. While this is a phenomenon common to many countries, Schleifer and Vishny (1993) argue that the economic costs of corruption are higher in Africa because the abuse of regulations is competitive. Where the government is cohesively corrupt the price it will charge firms for permissions will be set at the point of revenue maximization. Where, as they claim to be the African case, public officials are corrupt in an uncoordinated way, then the attempt by each of several officials to extract the maximum rent from a permission which each must give yields in aggregate a level of charges much higher than consistent with collusive revenue maximization. Investment is low because government lacks the power either to prevent its employees being corrupt or to enforce coordination in such corruption by centralizing it. Mauro (1993) adds an Economist Intelligence Unit index of perceived corruption as an explanatory variable and finds that it significantly reduces investment. The third is the difficulties of contract enforcement and of verification of information between private agents. In some countries the civil legal system does not function well enough to permit assets to be used as collateral for loans,[3] thus curtailing finance for investment. In some countries the accounts produced by firms are too unreliable for reported profits to be used as a basis for the valuation of the firm. If the firm cannot be valued as a going concern it becomes less marketable, so that investment in it becomes illiquid and therefore less attractive.

AGENCIES OF RESTRAINT AND THEIR
LIMITATIONS IN AFRICA

In each of these three processes of discouragement of investment, the usual solution is the provision of an *agency of restraint*. The problem of incredible policy pronouncements calls for government to provide agencies which bind the government itself in the sphere of macroeconomic or trade policy. Independent central banks and reciprocal threat arrangements such as the European Union are major instances of the creation by governments of self-imposed restraints. The agencies which restrain public employee corruption are those which detect and punish transgressions, namely the police and the criminal courts. Here the government is providing agencies which restrain its own employees. The agencies which enforce contracts and verify accounts are the civil legal system and the audit profession. Here, the former restraint agency is provided by the government while the latter is privately provided, though both enable private agents to restrain themselves. In Africa quite often none of these agencies have worked well and I now turn to why this might be the case and what alternatives are available.

Agencies which restrain the government

All governments need some mechanisms to check their power. I distinguish between mechanisms which aim to restrain macroeconomic policy and those which are concerned with the composition of public expenditure and revenue. Prior to independence, the ultimate agency of restraint in Africa for both of these functions was clearly the colonial authorities. Independence necessarily removed this restraint, and the ensuing economic history of Africa is, in part, interpretable as the consequence of the un-leashing of unrestrained government. During the past decade there have been a variety of attempts to reintroduce agencies of restraint. In this section I consider some of them.

A government can only create a domestic agency of restraint upon its own behaviour if it is clearly subject to the rule of law, and a necessary condition for this is likely to be a well-functioning democracy. Without this then legally conferred powers of control over government behaviour are themselves insecure or even fictions. This may explain why the relationship between greater legal autonomy of the central bank and lower inflation holds true for developed but not for developing countries (Cukierman *et al.*, 1992). In most African countries democracy is still too fragile or too recent to provide a credible context for domestic agencies of policy re-straint. Hence, even where such agencies happen to work, they fail to provide a solution to the current problem of limited government reputation. The time needed for new domestic agencies to acquire reputations for effectiveness is liable to be no shorter than the time needed for an initially untrusted government to become trusted.

An apparent exception to the failure of domestic agencies of restraint is the recent experience of budget rules. One of the early and remarkably successful stabilizations, Indonesia during the 1960s, was ostensibly achieved by a balanced budget rule in the constitution. A different budgetary rule has been a central feature of two recent African stabilizations, Uganda and Zambia. In both, the adoption of a cash budget was highly effective, bringing down the inflation rate from over 100 per cent to zero within three months of implementation. Whereas the Indonesian budget rule was constitutionally based but rather vague on detailed interpretation, a cash budget rule is merely an internal Ministry of Finance decision (to the extent that it is not part of donor conditionality). However, cash budgeting is a very specific procedure rather than a target: the Ministry spends only what it has received in the previous day (Zambia) or month (Uganda). Because the rule is procedurally based, it is easier to maintain it than some less exacting, but arbitrary, target level of deficit.

Many African governments promulgated into their constitutions rules imposing limits on borrowing from the central bank. These limits were not excessive and so approximated to the Indonesian constitution. The limits were, however, raised without significant protest. If central bank borrowing is seen as arcane by the political process, then constitutional rules can be relaxed with ease however well entrenched they appear to be. The cash budget procedure is not sustainable long term because it is unnecessarily severe. Already in Uganda there is pressure to lengthen the reference period from one month to six months. Cash budgeting denies the government the legitimate non-tax revenue provided by non-inflationary seigniorage and so is self-evidently overkill, yet to incorporate a permitted deficit introduces precisely that element of discretion the procedure excludes.

A further strategy for the creation of a domestic agency of restraint is to build 'poison pills' generally associated with financial liberalization. The revenue needs of the expanding African state led not only to the punitive taxation of agriculture but also to the repression of financial markets and, outside of the CFA zone, the imposition of increasingly tight exchange controls. Removal of relative price distortions was a central feature of the reforms of the 1980s. A number of governments have gone further, however, introducing market-determined interest rates on the government's domestic borrowing and liberalizing the capital account. Other things being equal, these policies increase budgetary outlays for interest payments and reduce the relative attractiveness of domestic money in asset portfolios; for these reasons, their adoption may be interpreted by the private sector as a signal of the government's underlying fiscal strength. Similar reasoning applies to a decision to index domestic government debt to the price level or to pay an adjustable interest rate on long-term debt. If successful, such signals help stabilization by reducing expected inflation and interest rates and producing an increase in the demand for domestic money.

These policies are risky, however, in the sense that inflationary shocks, whether random or systematic, are passed on much more strongly to the fiscal deficit. They are therefore treacherous for governments whose ability to cut spending or raise other taxes in the short run is limited. A similar analysis applies to capital account liberalization. Independent of its efficiency implications, an open capital account means a more rapid and transparent transmission of macroeconomic shocks to the balance of payments. Both policies are poison pills, in the sense that they derive part of their efficacy from the increased costs of fiscal irresponsibility: with an open capital account and debt indexation, the exchange rate will collapse and debt service expenditure will escalate. However, because the external environment is highly volatile, these same consequences can occur despite fiscal responsibility.

Finally, democracy itself is not only a necessary condition for specialist domestic agencies of restraint such as central banks to function; it can itself function directly as an agency of restraint. In developed countries this is surely the major mechanism restraining government predation. Notions of fairness among the electorate place limits upon the extent to which taxation and expenditure can be selective and upon the predation of governing parties. Over time, electorates have even learned a little about the political business cycle.

African electorates probably provide less of a restraint upon government because they seldom have the opportunity to evict a government and are usually more ethnically divided. For example, in Nigeria during the Shagari regime electoral politics and a free press failed to restrain fiscal irresponsibility and corruption. A measure of the weak check provided by democratic control is that fiscal probity clearly weakens very substantially in the run-up to African elections (Zambia, Ghana, Kenya). The move to democracy may inhibit governments from gross unfairness in revenue and expenditure allocations, but is likely to make the problem of maintaining macroeconomic stability more acute.

If agencies which restrain the government cannot be constructed domestically by African governments then they may, perhaps, be provided externally. During the 1980s an attempt was made to use aid to construct such an agency. African critiques of donor conditionality as being an infringement of sovereignty and neocolonialist are surely, in this sense, correct, and yet what most such critiques fail to acknowledge is that the restoration of some agency of restraint is desirable and that in present African political circumstances the choices are limited.

The emergence of conditionality in the 1980s was a natural function of the macroeconomic difficulties experienced by both recipient and donor governments, in either case increasing the relative bargaining power of the donor, and the increasing scepticism of the donors about the fundamental priorities of African governments. Conditionality is therefore here to stay, at least in the medium term; the alternative to conditional aid is not a continuation of unconditional aid but rather a substantial reduction in the amount of aid. However, being non-participatory, donor conditionality is a purely external agency of restraint, and as such is highly vulnerable to the gut nationalism present in all societies and which is exploitable by populist governments. Classic instances of this were the exchange rate debates in Nigeria during 1986 and Tanzania in the early 1980s, when issues of sovereignty intruded into and came to dominate debates about economic management.

The scope for donor conditionality varies considerably between countries. The very low-income, resource-scarce economies such as Uganda, Tanzania and Ghana will be major aid recipients for the foreseeable future and so a long-term relationship can potentially be built. By contrast, Zimbabwe and some of the mineral exporters are only substantial aid recipients during periods of aid-funded policy reform. The latter, aid-for-reform packages evidently contain a serious risk of time inconsistency: conditionality may be able to induce reform but can have little influence upon whether it is sustained. The recent collapse of the Nigerian reform programme is an example of the impotence of the donors in the mineral-rich economy. In contrast, the pressure exerted by the gradual exodus of donors in the Tanzanian exchange rate debate culminated in the resignation of President Nyerere in 1985 and the adoption of major and sustained reforms.

However, even for those countries in which aid is prospectively large enough to provide a basis for sustained leverage, it is not clear that donors can or should fulfil this role. Since donors cannot credibly offer reformers sustained higher aid, they must threaten that policy reversals will be punished with aid cut-offs. That is, threats are more effective than promises in achieving sustainable reforms, since governments need a credibly less favourable consequence from abandoning than from persisting with it. For example, two years of aid suspension in Kenya produced more economic reform than ten years of aid-for-reform packages. Overt threats are, however, rather raw intrusions on sovereignty, and conditionality becomes less feasible as Africa democratizes because the government ceases to be in a position where it can always deliver on commitments. This may still leave room for a looser, *ex post* conditionality in which countries which adopt poor policies find that they attract less aid. This is a role for which the bilateral aid programmes are likely to become more selective. They are not expected to fund more than a few countries and so are in a better position to appear to shop around between governments. Clearly, the higher is the elasticity of aid with respect to performance, the more effective is this *ex post* form of conditionality. Recipient governments would learn that to attract aid they would need to deliver what donors want. It is noteworthy that the prime movers in the Kenyan aid saga were not the multilaterals but the bilaterals. However, such a switch from overt conditionality to implicit conditionality through greater responsiveness of aid to past performance is not only made more necessary by democratization, but also made less effective. In the context of the poor and erratic economic performance which has prevailed and is likely to continue in much of Africa, democracy implies that governments must expect short lives. In this case they have less incentive to invest in reputation than the dictatorships and one-party states which they are replacing. The switch to democracy therefore implies that for donor restraint upon policy to be effective aid will need to remain explicitly conditioned to current and prospective performance, rather than implicitly conditioned on past performance. Yet democracy will make the execution of explicit conditionality threats increasingly uncomfortable for donors and so make the threats decreasingly credible.

The range of government actions upon which conditions are attached has gradually expanded from macroeconomic aggregates such as the budget deficit and trade policy to the composition of government expenditure and taxation. This evolution is in part a sign of the success of conditionality in reducing overall government expenditure. Assuming governments and donors to have different preferences, if the government is denied access to the inflation tax then it will choose to curtail expenditures to which donors attach higher priority. To prevent this donors will therefore start to condition upon the composition of expenditure as well as its overall level. However, this conditioning requires far more information than macroeconomic objectives, both for the donor specification to be sensible and for it to be enforced. Analogous to the tax avoidance industry, there might be a process of growing complexity of conditioning on budget heads as the government attempts to maintain its objectives by hiding expenditures more deeply in the budget. This is a game in which the donors have an eventual informational disadvantage and so are unlikely to win.

Donor conditionality is a purely external agency of restraint, and an independent central bank is purely domestic. Now consider a hybrid, namely reciprocal threats between countries. This is the predominant form of agencies of restraint in the developed world. The European Union, and the European Monetary System, for example, are essentially reciprocal threats governing trade and monetary policies. NAFTA is an extension of reciprocal threats to include a developing country. The one institution in Africa which is based on the reciprocal threat model is the Franc Zone. Despite flaws which gradually emerged and are discussed in the next subsection, the Franc Zone delivered a substantial degree of restraint which can be seen by the contrast between the rising and variable inflation rates of Anglophone Africa and the low and stable inflation rates of the Franc Zone.

The advantages of a reciprocal threat over conditionality are, first, that being participatory it is less of an affront to sovereignty, and second, that being rule based it is more credible and consistent than the *ad hoc* conditions negotiated with donors. The Franc Zone, which has become Africa's longest enduring economic institution, is a hybrid between a reciprocal threat agency and donor conditionality because of the participation of France along with the other member states. The French guarantee of convertibility provides a conditional benefit equivalent to the withdrawal of aid threat.

The two currency unions which form the Franc Zone had their equivalents in the currency boards of Anglophone Africa and the Anglophone Caribbean. In the Caribbean the currency boards have survived and the inflation performance is as good as that in the Franc Zone. In Anglophone Africa the boards were dismantled shortly after independence and national central banks established. This was not inevitable, nor is it irreversible. The regional currency boards could be revived and linked to a European currency such as the ECU, creating institutions analogous to the Franc Zone. Currency boards offer the same benefits as an independent central bank while being politically more sustainable.

While the Franc Zone and currency boards are concerned with fiscal and exchange rate policies, it should be possible to build equivalent agencies concerned with trade policy. Here there are two recent models, NAFTA and the associate membership which Morocco has negotiated with the European Union. There is currently a revival of interest in regional trade negotiations in Africa in response to NAFTA. However, the essential feature of NAFTA, namely that it is a North–South agreement, has been missed by African negotiators who remain preoccupied with intra-African trade. A purely African trade agreement lacks much capacity for reciprocal threats because intra-African trade is likely to be intrinsically modest given the economic characteristics of countries (see Foroutan and Pritchett, 1993).

Agencies which restrain public sector corruption

Donor conditionality has increasingly been used against the large-scale corruption practised by senior politicians and in this task it has been partially effective. As discussed above, on the argument of Schleifer and Vishny (1993) this sort of corruption is not in economic terms very damaging because senior politicians have no incentive to push corruption to the level at which it powerfully discourages investment. Here I focus not upon corruption at the top but rather the more pervasive and uncoordinated corruption which Schleifer and Vishny regard as particularly characterizing Africa. However, top-level and lower-level corruption may be connected. It has been argued that in Africa a corrupt leadership weakens the deterrence system (Klitgaard, 1988).

The African public sector is corrupt relative to its own past standards and so something must have changed, at least temporarily. Two recent models provide an explanation for why a temporary increase in the incentive for corruption may produce a permanent increase: hysteresis in corruption. Andvig and Moene (1990) present a model of corruption in which the change is a temporary increase in the proffered bribe. The predisposition to honesty is normally distributed across bureaucrats: low bribes find few takers, but at higher levels the supply of corrupt bureaucrats is elastic. The effectiveness of deterrence is weakened if more bureaucrats are corrupt because the danger of detection by an honest bureaucrat diminishes. Hence, temporarily high bribes increase the supply of corrupt bureaucrats which can be self-perpetuating because of the reduced effectiveness of deterrence. Tirole (1992) models the interaction between collective reputation and individual incentives. Each public employee has a reputation which is based partly on the imperfect observation of his or her own past behaviour and partly upon the prevalence of corruption in society. In an honest society the general presumption towards trust makes honesty a high-yield investment, whereas in a corrupt society the presumption towards suspicion makes honesty a low-yield investment. A temporary reduction in detection effort can flip the society from the low-corruption equilibrium to the high equilibrium which then persists.

I now set out a further model with the same feature of hysteresis. Whereas Tirole focuses upon corrupt *agents* who have reputations, the present model focuses upon corrupt *practices* which are, in effect, skills which have to be acquired. Corruption occurs through innovations in practices which then spread through social learning of various types. As in Andvig and Moene there is a deterrence mechanism which is weakened by the spread of corruption, but a further anti-corruption mechanism is introduced, namely *system correction*: the redesigning of procedures to make some practices infeasible.

The equilibrium level of corruption in a bureaucracy is that at which the rate of increase through the processes of innovation and social learning is precisely offset by deterrence and system correction. I first show why there is likely to be a tipping point between the stable equilibria of honesty and high corruption and then suggest why Africa has made a transition between these equilibria.

I begin by analysing the equilibrium incidence of a corrupt practice if it is not eliminated by system correction. Denoting the proportion of those in a particular activity who are corrupt by C, the change in corruption, dC, is given by

$$dC = L(C) - D(C) \qquad (12.1)$$

where $L(C)$ denotes the rate of social learning and $D(C)$ the effect of deterrence.

Now consider the possible process of social learning, starting from an honest bureaucracy in which all deterrence has been removed. Bureaucrats are identical but start from a position of ignorance about how to operate the corrupt practice. Because of the secrecy of corruption, the practice is only learned through interaction with someone who is already operating it. If the whole population pairs off randomly each instant, the proportion of meetings involving a corrupt person and a non-corrupt person is $C(1 - C)$. If each of these meetings carries a risk r that the non-corrupt person will learn the practice, then

$$L(C) = rC(1 - C)$$
$$L(0) = L(1) = 0; \quad L(1/2) = L_{max}. \tag{12.2}$$

Such social learning gives rise to an unstable equilibrium of honesty and a stable equilibrium of complete corruption.

We now add a process of deterrence, $D(C)$. The effectiveness of deterrence can reasonably be assumed to be a function of the extent to which the practice has already been adopted. A given total expenditure upon a deterrence system is less effective the more widespread is corruption due to dilution: expenditure per infraction reduces proportionately with the number of infractions. Additionally, as suggested by Andvig and Moene, as a practice becomes more common colleagues are less likely to assist the deterrence authorities.

These two effects, social learning and deterrence, are brought together in Figure 12.1 where the horizontal axis is the incidence of corruption, that is the extent to which the practice has already spread over the population, and the vertical axis shows the rate of change in the incidence. $L(C)$ shows the single-peaked social learning effect, $D(C)$ shows the negative monotonic effect of a given amount of deterrence expenditure. The two functions are superimposed in the same space: since social learning increases the incidence of corruption whereas deterrence reduces it, equilibrium levels of corruption occur where the two loci intersect.

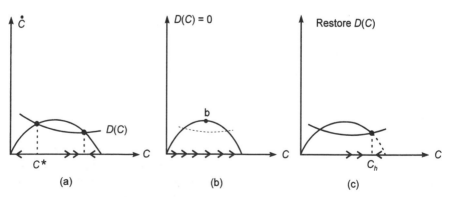

Figure 12.1 Social learning and deterrence

290

A given level of expenditure upon deterrence, $D(C)$, is consistent with both honesty and high corruption, with a tipping point at C^*. Suppose that starting from honesty the deterrence procedure is temporarily removed. If deterrence is reintroduced before corruption rises to C^*, the deterrence effect is sufficiently strong relative to social learning that honesty is re-established. However, if deterrence is reimposed only once corruption has increased beyond C^*, e.g. at point b in Figure 12.1, then far from corruption collapsing back to zero, its growth is not even reversed: growth continues to C.

System correction contains corruption not by punishment but by innovation. Abuses, once discovered, are not just punished; the system is changed to prevent recurrence. All bureaucratic systems need continuous modification because employees gradually learn how to exploit procedures to their advantage.

Figure 12.1 has modelled the equilibrium incidence of a particular corrupt practice. The extent to which a public service is corrupt, however, depends upon both the incidence and the proportion of practices which are corrupt. The latter proportion is determined through an equilibrium between the opposing forces of the pace of innovation in the corruption of practices and the rate at which system correction closes off these opportunities. The domain of innovation is determined by the functions which the public service undertakes and so the set of blueprints of potential corrupt practices is finite. Consider a society in which, starting from an honest public service, the process of system correction is removed. Innovation would occur first in the most lucrative corruption of practices. As these are exhausted, further corruption requires that bureaucrats innovate less remuneratively. This is reinforced by the argument of Schleifer and Vishny that uncoordinated corruption in complementary practices, such as they postulate occurs in Africa, reduces the overall return to corruption. Hence, as more practices become corrupt, the incentive to discover further means by which more practices can be corrupted diminishes. To formulate the concepts of the rate of innovation and the proportion of practices which are corrupt, we must have some aggregation procedure over practices. The concept of the incidence of corruption within a practice used bureaucrats as its unit of measure and the natural extension here is to use labour time: the proportion of practices which are corrupt is the proportion of labour time spent on those practices. Thus defined, the pace of innovation slows as an increasing proportion of practices become corrupted.

The pace at which a system can be corrected depends, in part, upon how much is wrong with it. Whereas deterrence becomes harder the greater the incidence of corruption, system correction becomes easier because there are more procedures in obvious need of being corrected. Thus, for a given expenditure upon system correction (e.g. a given level of staffing of procedure design functions), the greater the proportion of practices which are corrupt, the faster the rate at which opportunities for corruption can be closed off. Whereas system correction closes off existing opportunities for corruption, it restores opportunities for innovation. An analogy would be the relationship between the tax avoidance industry and the revision of fiscal legislation: each round of legislation closes existing loopholes but restores the return to innovation in tax avoidance schemes.

In Figure 12.2 these opposing effects on the proportion of practices which are corrupt are brought together. The horizontal axis shows the proportion of practices which are corrupt (P), and the vertical axis shows the change in the proportion. The $I(P)$ function depicts the rate of innovation of corrupt practices as a function of the proportion that are already corrupt. The $S(P)$ function depicts the rate of system correction for a given level of expenditure. A unique, stable equilibrium proportion of practices are corrupt, given the two functions.

In the above analysis it is practices rather than people which are corrupt. That is, the process of social learning is practice specific. The overall severity of corruption is determined by the proportion of practices which are corrupt and the incidence of corruption in each of these practices. The incidence is practice specific because not all practices have been corrupt for the same duration, and social learning takes time to reach the equilibrium incidence, C^*. Efficient system correction should target the longest-standing corrupt practices because these have the highest incidence of corruption. At least in the early stages, the incidence of corruption accelerates with time, so that the overall extent of corruption in a bureaucracy is highly disproportionately caused by the older corrupt practices.

To summarize, the honest bureaucracy is doubly defended. Deterrence prevents the spread of innovations, but even were the deterrence to fail, the incidence of a corrupt practice would not reach its high-equilibrium level because system correction would close off the opportunity. This double defence can be seen at work in honest bureaucracies: enquiries into public corruption invariably address not just the identity of the guilty, but how the system might be modified to prevent recurrence.

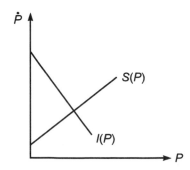

Figure 12.2 Innovation and system correction of corrupt practices

The highly corrupt bureaucracy need not be spending less effort on either of these defence mechanisms than the honest bureaucracy. Rather, at some time in the past its defence mechanisms may have temporarily broken down. After independence both deterrence and system correction at least temporarily broke down in Africa. Deterrence requires scrutiny from the police and the press and judgement by the courts. The suppression of the press and the assault upon judicial independence weakened this deterrence system (Ekpo, 1979), as did the introduction of African elites who regarded patronage as a social obligation. The rapid change in the composition of the top ranks of the bureaucracy reduced, at least temporarily, the capacity for system redesign. In many cases procedures ossified, permitting a gradual avoidance of control procedures, an example being the eventual mass hiring of 'group employees' (casual workers) on a permanent basis by line ministries because the recruitment of such workers was not centrally controlled.[4]

A second instance of the lack of system correction is the gradual erosion of the Franc Zone as an agency restraining government fiscal policy. The rules initially constituted a good attempt at controlling fiscal aggregates but they were not in full conformity with the fixed exchange rate commitment. Governments gradually learned how to circumvent the fiscal control through the parastatals: for example, a parastatal might sell services at a loss to the government and finance it by borrowing from the banks. Governments were also able to run up very large arrears in domestic payments; in effect this created (involuntary) domestic debt without the expenditures appearing on the government books. In this instance the lack of system correction was responsible for the erosion of a previously effective agency of restraint upon government, and a consequent decrease in government policy credibility.

Given that corruption is now a severe problem in Africa, it is quite possible that the effort devoted to the defence mechanisms has been fully restored. African governments may well now be prosecuting as large a proportion of public officials, and changing procedures as rapidly, as is done in public bureaucracies in other parts of the world. Unfortunately, they now face a much more daunting problem.

How can the high-corruption bureaucracy switch back to the honest bureaucracy? Tirole argues on the basis of his model that temporary anti-corruption campaigns will be ineffective and this is indeed an implication of all three models. To the extent that people have reputations for corruption which are partly based on their individual past behaviour and partly on the society to which they belong, a successful transformation could be achieved by the replacement of current employees with an identifiably new cohort with a different behaviour pattern. For example, were the goal of public honesty visibly to capture the imagination of a particular student cohort, then its mass recruitment in place of existing employees might furnish such recruits with sufficient public expectations of honesty for the private incentive to switch in favour of honesty. To the extent that corruption is determined not by expectations of those who use the bureaucracy but by the capacity of employees to defeat defence mechanisms, then the model set out above suggests that deterrence effort becomes less effective both absolutely and relative to system correction effort as the extent of corruption increases. An example of a laborious but effective system correction is the redesign of the collection of airport taxes. In countries with low degrees of corruption such taxes are built into the ticket price charged by airlines. In countries with a high degree of corruption where this would function badly, travellers must now purchase from one public employee a stamp placed on the ticket. This is verified in a public place by a second employee, and a hole punched in it to prevent recycling by a third employee at a further stage. Given time employees will discover collusive strategies to defeat even this system, so part of the civil service needs to be employed on periodically redesigning it.

Agencies for restraining private agents

The third problem which I suggested might be viewed as being due to a malfunctioning of agencies of restraint was the inability of private agents to make credible statements either with respect to contracts in which assets are pledged as collateral, or with respect to valuations of enterprises. For assets to function as collateral requires an uncorrupt and efficient civil legal system; for valuations to be credible requires an uncorrupt and efficient audit system, and in parts of Africa neither of these is currently available.

The deterioration of audit procedures demonstrates that there is nothing peculiar to the public sector about corruption. The audit profession is in some respects more vulnerable to corruption than the public sector because it is hired and selected by the firm which it is to scrutinize. The decline of the trustworthiness of audits can be viewed both as a change in the value of reputation, along the lines of Tirole, and as technical progress in dishonesty, along the lines of the model set out in the last section. Following Tirole, only if the audit firm has a reputation for honesty which it is valuable to protect has the auditor an incentive to behave honestly. Once this reputation is lost then the firm is typecast as dishonest and has an incentive to remain so. If most auditors are dishonest, a new entrant, while not being typecast due to previous corrupt actions, is nevertheless perceived as liable to be dishonest, thereby being unable to provide an audit which will be fully trusted. If the firm cannot purchase an audit which will be trusted, the incentives are entirely in favour of it selecting a dishonest auditor. If any audited figure is suspect and so discounted, starting from an honest set of figures is a considerable disadvantage. Following the model of the previous section, in countries in which audits work reasonably well, the auditors are themselves subject to professional scrutiny. Samples of their work are checked within the profession, and additionally where companies are subsequently exposed by the press or the banks as having fooled auditors the latter can become legally liable for misleading shareholders.

The government has an interest in an honest audit profession both because this reduces the cost of transactions in a way equivalent to infrastructure, and because the government is itself a user of audits through their input into tax collection. The deterioration in self-regulation of the profession is therefore a legitimate matter of government concern. As with the reduction in public employee corruption, a strategy of reform might usefully work both from the Tirole perspective of changing the incentive to acquire reputation and from the perspective of system correction. The former would suggest that a distinct and readily distinguishable category of auditors should be created which is thereby not tarnished with the negative externality of the low reputation of other auditors. Perhaps one method whereby this might be achieved is to create a new category of international accreditation, with audits being required to indicate whether they are conducted by such accredited staff. The system correction perspective would suggest that audits need to be made more exacting. For example, to inhibit over- and under-invoicing, much greater fieldwork might be required to verify true prices as is currently done internationally by firms such as SGS. The two approaches are complementary in that it is easier to introduce such practices on a small scale, so that a category of superauditors could be expected to follow the new practices. Once firms have the option of purchasing audits which are publicly recognized as reliable, then the signal conveyed by the selection of auditors produces an incentive for them to hire the non-corrupt category of auditors, and the shift in demand thereby provides auditors with an incentive to invest in the upgrade to the higher professional category.

Turning from the audit profession to the civil law, the corruption of the judiciary is another example of the breakdown of professional self-regulation and so the same approach is appropriate. A category of judges needs to be ring-fenced from the reputational externalities of their colleagues, and at the same time subjected to new practices which check for competence and honesty. This creation of elite groups within professions is already being attempted with some success in parts of the public sector, notably quasi-autonomous revenue authorities. However, the principle needs to be extended from revenue collection to service delivery. Perhaps the reason why governments have been more prepared to face the political difficulties associated with the creation of professional elites in the areas of revenue collection than service delivery, is that they have a stronger interest in increasing revenue than in improving service delivery. However, socially, arguably improving the efficiency of service delivery achieves welfare gains more surely than does increased revenue collection.

CONCLUSION: SEQUENCING RESTRAINT

In the previous section I have suggested that there are three agency problems: that of the government with its future self, that of the government with its own employees, and that of private agents with each other. The first of these divides into macroeconomic restraints, essentially on the budget deficit, and microeconomic restraints upon the composition of expenditure and taxation. I have reviewed a variety of mechanisms for resolving these agency problems: deterrence, system correction, professional ring-fencing, conditionality, central bank independence, budget rules, poison pills, democracy and reciprocal threats.

Table 12.1 Agencies of restraint and their possible effects

	Corruption	*Macro-policy*	*Fiscal composition*
Deterrence	Long term +	..	..
System correction	Short term +	..	..
Ring-fencing	Short term +	..	..
Conditionality	Short term +	Short term +	Short term +
Cash budget	..	Short term +	..
Central banks	..	..	..
Poison pills	..	+	..
Reciprocal threats	..	Long term +	..
Democracy	Long term +	Short term −	Long term +

.. no effect
+ improvement
− deterioration

Table 12.1 summarizes this discussion and attempts to classify each intervention according to its short- and long-term effectiveness for dealing with the three agency problems. Since both the problem faced by the government in creating trustworthy employees and that faced by private agents in creating trustworthy auditors and judges is essentially one of corruption, they are treated together.

Deterrence, I have suggested, is only of use as a long-term mechanism of maintaining an honest public sector, when that has already been established by system correction and the ring-fencing of new professional elites. Central banks are ineffective as restraints upon African governments. Multinational reciprocal threat institutions are not an immediate option but offer a long-term means of restraining fiscal and trade policies. Finally, democracy, while probably increasing the difficulty of maintaining macroeconomic balance in the short term, offers the only long-term check on the composition of revenue and expenditure.

Tentatively, this suggests a sequence of how restraint agencies might need to evolve. Starting from a high-corruption, fiscal deficit, poor fiscal composition economy, the short-term strategy would be for the state to implement a cash budget within which expenditures upon system correction and professional elite ring-fencing were given priority. Underpinning these changes would be donor conditionality. None of these strategies has other than a short-term effect. They do, however, create an environment in which longer-term mechanisms which are better at locking in than at achieving desirable public sector characteristics can be useful. The creation of multi-national reciprocal threat institutions would replace donor conditionality as the mechanism for maintaining sound macroeconomic policies (and might well do this more effectively). The pressures brought by democracy would be the only mechanism restraining fiscal composition and this might be less effective than donor conditionality. However, democratization is under-mining the efficacy of this detailed form of conditionality which requires a higher level of information than donors are well placed to acquire.

To conclude, I am proposing an evolution from a phase of system correction, elite ring-fencing, conditionality and cash budgets, to a more sustainable, but not directly attainable, stage of democracy, scrutiny and reciprocal threats.

NOTES

1 I wish to thank Dr Stephen O'Connell for his contributions to this essay.
2 For example, a survey of 150 actual and potential foreign investors into five East African countries conducted by Economisti Associati for the World Bank in 1994 found non-commercial risk to be the highest rated of twelve potential deterrents to investment, and within non-commercial risk the fear of policy reversal was the foremost of five categories (World Bank, 1994).
3 For example, in an interview with the author the manager of an investment bank in East Africa described loans as being as risky as equity because of the legal difficulties of foreclosure.
4 I am indebted to Tate Davis for this example.

REFERENCES

Andvig, J. C. and Moene, K. O. (1990) 'How Corruption may Corrupt', *Journal of Economic Behaviour and Organisation*, vol. 13.
Cukierman, A., Webb, S. B. and Negapti, B. (1992) 'Measuring the Independence of Central Banks and its Effect on Policy Outcomes', *World Bank Economic Review*, vol. 6, pp. 353–398.
Ekpo, M. (1979) *Bureaucratic Corruption in Sub-Saharan Africa: Toward a Search of Causes and Consequences*, University Press of America, Washington, DC.
Foroutan, F. and Pritchett, L. (1993) 'Intra Sub-Saharan Trade: Is it Too Little?', *Journal of African Economies*, vol. 2. pp. 74–105.
Mauro, P. (1993) 'Corruption, Country Risk and Growth,' Mimeo, Department of Economics, Harvard University, Cambridge, MA.
Schleifer, A. and Vishny, R. W. (1993) 'Corruption', *Quarterly Journal of Economics*, vol. 4108, pp. 599–617.

Tirole J. (1992) 'Persistence of Corruption', Institute for Policy Reform Working Paper 55, Washington, DC.

World Bank (1994) 'Survey of Investor Attitudes to East Africa', Mimeo, Africa Technical Department, World Bank, Washington, DC.

13

PARTICIPATION, MARKETS AND DEMOCRACY

Deepak Lal*

For forms of government, let fools contest;
whatever's best administered, is best.
(Alexander Pope: Essay on Man)

INTRODUCTION AND SYNOPSIS

A most remarkable movement from the plan to the market – both in development thinking and practice – has characterized the last two decades. This in turn has opened up new questions about the sustainability of a market economy, not least about the necessary bulwarks against the unavoidable political pressures for its subversion. An emerging theme amongst both practitioners and analysts of developing countries is the role of popular participation, and in particular of non-governmental organizations (NGOs) in both the promotion of democracy (seen as essential for better governance) and the maintenance of a market economy. This chapter seeks to set the resulting debate in its historical and intellectual context, and thereby provides a critique of what may turn out to be yet another development fad.[1] It also attempts to provide some guidelines on how an official multilateral agency such as the World Bank should deal with NGOs. This introduction provides a synopsis of the argument.

The debates surveyed in this chapter are of relevance for World Bank operations in two ways. First, in its policy-based lending operations the Bank is being urged to complement its strictly economic conditionality with political conditions which favour the development of popular participation through civil associations and the development of democracy, it being assumed that such participation and democracy will further the aims of good governance and thus promote development. To sort out this debate the first section of the chapter outlines two rival views of the relationship between the state, society and the economy. It particularly commends the view of the classical economists of the Scottish Enlightenment, who made a vital distinction between the forms of government and the characteristics of good government.

As the bank is charged with identifying the latter whilst not taking a view on the former, this distinction is of some operational significance. Particularly as is argued in the first and second parts of this chapter, there is no necessary empirical relationship between the form of government and successful development. A particular form of government – democracy – and its associated freedom of association and free speech may, however, be considered to be valuable in promoting another end – liberty –, which is distinct from the end of attaining opulence (in classical terminology) which from experience is best promoted by the market. Hence, while democracy promotes liberty, it may not promote opulence, which depends upon an efficient market economy, and which in turn does not require a democratic form of government for its maintenance. This implies that the World Bank can (as it has in the past) concentrate on the characteristics of good government (policies) without getting entangled in the dangerous question of the ideal form of government.

The second way in which the debates about participation impinge on World Bank operations is through the claim that both the design and implementation of World Bank projects and policy-based lending will be improved through the active association of NGOs. The second part of this chapter shows how this view is based on the American pluralist tradition of political sociology. It outlines the views of the new political economy which takes a less benign view of the role of pressure groups (NGOs) in promoting opulence, and also of another strand of political sociology which views the populism promoted by mass participation as also a possible enemy of liberty. Hence this part concludes that mass participation through pressure groups in a democracy may harm rather than aid the attainment of the ends of both opulence and liberty.

The last part of the chapter summarizes the discussion and also draws the implications for World Bank operations. In particular it emphasizes that there is no presumption, one way or the other, about the benefits from associating NGOs with particular World Bank operations. The test must be the contingent one of cost-effectiveness. Thus the use of NGOs in project lending – which largely finances public goods – must depend upon the actual merits of each case, namely whether this provides the least-cost mode of provision.

THE STATE, ECONOMY AND SOCIETY – TWO RIVAL VIEWS

Questions concerning ethics, politics and economics are necessarily intertwined in thinking about the interconnections between participation, democracy and markets. To fix ideas it may be useful to begin with a summary of the links that the founders of the subject of political economy – Adam Smith and David Hume – saw between ethics, economics and politics.[2]

Both Smith (in *The Moral Sentiments*) and Hume recognized benevolence as the primary moral virtue. But they also recognized its scarcity. However, fortunately, as Adam Smith was at pains to show in the *Wealth of Nations*, a market economy which promotes a country's 'opulence' does not have to depend upon this moral virtue for its functioning. A market order merely requires a vast number of people to deal and live together, even if they have no personal relationships, as long as they do not violate the 'laws of justice'.

The resulting commercial society does promote some moral virtues – hard work, prudence, thrift and self-reliance (which have been labelled the 'vigorous virtues').[3] But as they benefit the agent rather than others, they are inferior to the primary virtue – altruism. Nevertheless, as these lower-order virtues promote general prosperity, they do unintentionally help others. Hence the market economy and the resulting commercial society is neither immoral nor amoral.

A good government on this classical liberal view is one which promotes 'opulence' through a policy of promoting natural liberty by establishing laws of justice which guarantee free exchange and peaceful competition, the improvement of morality being left to non-governmental institutions. It would be counterproductive for the state to legislate morality.

This classical liberal view of the state seen as a civil association, as noted by Michael Oakeshott (1993), goes back to ancient Greece. On this view the state is seen as the custodian of laws which do not seek to impose any preferred pattern of ends (including abstractions such as the general (social) welfare, or fundamental rights), but which merely facilitate individuals to pursue their own ends.

This view of the state and its relationship to society and the economy has been challenged in Western thought and practice, according to Oakeshott, by a rival conception of the state as an enterprise association – a view which has its roots in the Judaeo-Christian tradition. The state is now seen as the manager of an enterprise seeking to use the law for its own substantive purposes, and in particular for the legislation of morality. Since the truce declared in the eighteenth century in the European wars of religion, the major substantive purposes sought by states seen as enterprise associations are 'nation building' and 'the promotion of some form of egalitarianism'.[4] Historically, both have led to *dirigisme* and the suppression or control of the market. This needs further elaboration.

The mercantilist system which provided the foil for Adam Smith's great work, arose, as Eli Heckscher has shown (in his monumental study *Mercantilism*), from the desire of the Renaissance princes of Europe to consolidate their power by incorporating various feuding and seemingly disorderly groups, which constituted the relatively weak states they inherited from the ruins of the Roman Empire, into a 'nation'. Its purpose was to achieve 'unification and power', making the 'State's purposes decisive in a uniform economic sphere and to make all economic activity subservient to considerations corresponding to the requirements of the State'. The same nationalist motive also underlay the very similar system of mercantilist industrial and trade controls that were established in much of the post-war Third World.

In both cases the unintended consequences of these controls instituted to establish 'order' was to breed 'disorder'. As economic controls became onerous people attempted to escape them through various forms of evasion and avoidance. As in eighteenth-century Europe, in the post-war Third World *dirigisme* bred corruption, rent-seeking, tax evasion and illegal activities in underground economies. The most serious consequence for the state was an erosion of its fiscal base and the accompanying prospect of the unMarxian withering away of the state. In both cases economic liberalization was undertaken to restore the fiscal base, and thence government control over what had become ungovernable economies. In some cases the changeover could only occur through revolution – most notably in France.[5]

But the ensuing period of economic liberalism during the nineteenth century's great Age of Reform was short lived in part due to the rise of another substantive purpose that most European states came to adopt – the egalitarian ideal promulgated by the Enlightenment. Governments in many developing countries also came to espouse this ideal of socialism. The apotheosis of this version of the state viewed as an enterprise association were the communist countries seeking to legislate the socialist ideal of equalizing people. The collapse of their economies under similar but even more severe strains than those that beset less collectivist neomercantilist economies is now history. But the desire to promote egalitarianism through state action still lingers on as part of social-democratic political agendas in many countries.

The locus and nature of the argument of those who want to use the state to promote egalitarianism has, however, shifted in a subtle way. In the past such activists, who sought to transform society through state action, usually argued in favour of some form of revolution whereby the 'anointed' would seize power and irreversibly transform society, if necessary by indoctrination to create a New Man.[6] With the revolutionary route at least tarnished by the hideous outcomes in communist countries – which even fellow travellers now concede – a new constitutional mania[7] has set in. This emphasizes substantive social and economic rights in addition to the well-known rights to liberty – freedom of speech, contract and association being amongst the most important – emphasized by classical liberals. It seeks to use the law to enforce these 'rights' based partly on 'needs', and partly on the 'equality of respect' desired by a heterogeneity of self-selected minorities differentiated by ethnicity, gender and/or sexual orientation. But no less than in the collectivist societies that have failed, this attempt to define and legislate a newly discovered and dense structure of rights (including for some activists those of non-human plants and animals) requires a vast expansion of the government's power over people's lives. Their implementation, moreover, requires – at the least – some doctoring of the market mechanism. Fortunately to date in most Western societies this 'rights-chatter' has just remained that, but it is an important strand in the participation and democracy debate, as we shall see.

While the philosophers of the Scottish Enlightenment were quite emphatic about the characteristics of good government, they were undogmatic about its particular form. They were, however, clearheaded about the nature of Political Man, and saw clearly why the implicit assumption about the character of the agents running a state viewed as an idealistic enterprise association, namely that they were Platonic Guardians, was fallacious. Nor were they starry eyed about the propensities of majoritarian democracies to serve the public weal. Thus Hume, in his essay 'Of the Independence of Parliament', noted:

> Political writers have established it as a maxim that, in contriving any system of government and fixing the several checks and controls of the constitution, every man ought to be supposed a knave and to have no other end, in all his actions, than private interest. By this interest we must govern him and, by means of it, make him, notwithstanding his insatiable avarice and ambition, co-operate to public good. Without this, say they, we shall in vain boast of the advantages of any constitution and shall find in the end that we have no security for our liberties or possessions except the goodwill of our rulers; that is we shall have no security at all.
>
> It is therefore, a just political maxim that every man must be supposed a knave, though at the same time it appears somewhat strange that a maxim should be true in politics which is false in fact. But to satisfy us on this head we may consider that men are generally more honest in their private than their public capacity, and will go greater lengths to serve a party than when their own private interest alone is concerned.
>
> To which we may add that every court or senate is determined by the greater number of voices, so that, if self-interest influences only the majority (as it will always do), the whole senate follows the allurements of this separate interest and acts as if it contained not one member who had any regard to public interest and liberty.

As we shall see, Hume was prescient about the predatory nature of majoritarian democracies.

However, the obvious bankruptcy of totalitarian communism, as well as the *dirigiste* neomercantilism of many developing country governments, has led many in the West to assume that this offers support for their own institutional arrangements which supposedly combine a market economy with majoritarian representative democracy. Issues of good governance, which since Adam Smith have been known to determine the relative wealth of nations, are assumed to be coterminous with the establishment of Western-style democracies in the Third and Second World.

However, despite the moral virtues of democracy in preventing that corruption of absolute power in autocracies decried by Lord Acton, the historical evidence does not support any necessary connection between a particular form of government and the promotion of prosperity. In the post-war period one only has to consider the Far Eastern 'Gang of Four', or the more successful economies in Latin America – Chile, Mexico, and until the 1980s Brazil – to realize, as Lee Kwan Yew has recently been proclaiming from the housetops, that there is no causal relationship between democracy and development.[8] Even in the rocky transition from the plan to the market, as the contrasting experiences of Russia and China show, glasnost may not help perestroika! This does not mean that authoritarianism or military autocracies are necessarily good for development either.

The essential point is that various types of government, as long as they maintain the essentials of a market order, can promote development. But if (as I do) one also attaches a positive value to liberty, then democracy is to be preferred as a form of government, not because of its instrumental value in promoting prosperity, but because it promotes the different but equally valuable end of liberty. As usual De Tocqueville is both prescient and succinct. 'It is true', he writes in *The Ancien Régime*,

> that in the long run liberty always leads those who know how to keep it to comfort, well-being, often to riches: but there are times when it impedes the attainment of such goods; and other times when despotism alone can momentarily guarantee their enjoyment. Men who take up liberty for its material rewards, then, have never kept it for long... what in all times has attracted some men so strongly to liberty has been itself alone, its own particular charm, independent of the benefits it brings; the pleasure of being able to speak, act, and breathe without constraint, under no other rule but that of God and law. Who seeks in liberty something other than itself is born to be a slave.

PARTICIPATION AND DEMOCRACY – SOCIOLOGISTS VS ECONOMISTS

De Tocqueville, however, is even more relevant for our subject as the progenitor of what has become the school of 'pluralist democracy' amongst American political sociologists. This is another important strand in the current debates about participation, markets and democracy. Any textbook on political sociology will inform the reader that there are three theoretical perspectives on the subject: the class model (due to Marx and his followers);

the elite model (due to Pareto, Mosca, Michels and Weber) and the American pluralist model which harks back to De Tocqueville's classic *Democracy in America*. The first has been discredited by the collapse of communism. The second by the failures of *dirigiste* modernizing elites in many parts of the Third World. This leaves the third – almost by default – as the remaining theoretical perspective that American political sociologists are now seeking to apply to the Third World.

In his great book *Democracy in America*, De Tocqueville maintained that:

> all the causes which contribute to the maintenance of a democratic republic in the United States are reducible to three heads: I. The peculiar and accidental situation in which Providence has placed the Americans. II. The laws. III. The manners and customs of the people.
>
> (Volume I, Chapter XVII)

Of these he assigned the greatest weight to customs. He wrote:

> These three great causes serve, no doubt to regulate and direct American democracy; but if they were to be classed in their proper order, I should say that physical circumstances are less efficient than the laws, and the laws infinitely less so than the customs of the people. I am convinced that the most advantageous situation and the best possible laws cannot maintain a constitution in spite of the customs of a country; while the latter may turn to some advantage the most unfavorable positions and the worst laws.

Amongst the customs that De Tocqueville identified as being most important for maintaining democracy in America were the myriad civil voluntary associations he found in the country.

> The political associations that exist in the United States are only a single feature in the midst of the immense assemblage of associations in that country. Americans of all ages, all conditions, and all dispositions constantly form associations. They have not only commercial and manufacturing companies, in which all take part, but associations of a thousand other kinds, religious, moral, serious, futile, general or restricted, enormous or diminutive. The Americans make associations to give entertainments, to found seminaries, to build inns, to construct churches, to diffuse books, to send missionaries to the antipodes; in this manner they found hospitals, prisons, and schools. If it is proposed to inculcate some truth or to foster some feeling by the encouragement of a great example, they form a society. Wherever at the head of some new undertaking you see the government in France, or a man of rank in England, in the United States you will be sure to find an association.
>
> (Volume II, Chapter V)

This myriad of voluntary associations (or NGOs as they would be called today), moreover, provided the bulwark against the tyranny of the central executive in democracies, according to De Tocqueville, once the traditional aristocracy which, with its sense of *noblesse oblige*, usually stood between the rulers and the ruled in the Ancien Regimes in Europe, had been extinguished with the rise of democracy. These voluntary associations were necessary as an intermediating layer between the ruling elites and the masses to prevent the abuse of power by the elites, and to allow the ordinary citizen to participate in the political process. Thus, he wrote:

> In aristocratic nations secondary bodies form natural associations which hold abuses of power in check. In countries where such associations do not exist, if private people did not artificially and temporarily create something like them, I see no other dike to hold back tyranny of whatever sort, and a great nation might with impunity be oppressed by some tiny faction or by a single man.

Despite the critique of the American pluralist model which follows, it is of the greatest importance to note that this essentially political role of voluntary associations in maintaining freedom, which was De Tocqueville's main concern and principal insight, still remains valid. It requires the freedom to associate and of free speech to be maintained. But whether a polity dominated by voluntary associations, or what we would today call pressure groups or interest groups, necessarily serves the cause of the market economy and thence development, is an open question. But in answering it is of vital importance to note that such associations, because they must have substantive purposes to exist, must necessarily be enterprise associations.

However, starting with Bentley (1908) and culminating in the works of Truman (1953) and Latham (1952), an influential strand of American political sociology has argued that free competition amongst pressure groups leads through a process similar to Adam Smith's 'invisible hand' to subserving the general welfare, even though each group is only promoting its own particular interest. Perfect competition amongst interest groups, with the state acting as an umpire, is thus the political analogue of the perfect competition paradigm of the economist. As in the economic model with free entry and exit, the size of the associations would not necessarily pose a problem, because any untoward pressure by one group would call forth pressure by a countervailing group, if necessary being newly created for this purpose. Thus, as Truman, for example, saw it,

> in the first place, ... most pressure groups would be weak and divided in those circumstances in which they asked for too much from society, since their members also had 'overlapping' memberships in other groups with different interests and would thus oppose excessive demands ... in the second place, there were 'potential groups' that would

arise and organize to do battle with the special interests if the special interests got too far out of line.

(Olson, 1965, p. 124)

This school therefore thinks that the pressure group equilibrium would be just and desirable.

This school, moreover, tended to put group interests above the interests of the individuals which composed the group. As Bentley (1908, p. 211) stated: 'There is no group without its interest. An interest, as the term will be used here, is the equivalent of a group.' This thought also underlies the notion of the 'corporatist state' which has found much favour with continental European thinkers since the nineteenth century. But corporatism is no friend of the market. In fact many supporters of the pluralist model look upon the growth of economically motivated pressure groups as providing desirable restraints on the market. Thus Truman (1953, p. 61) wrote:

> There are ... a number of reasons for the prevalence of associations growing out of economic institutions.... There has been a series of disturbances and dislocations consequent upon the utopian attempt, as Polanyi calls it, to set up a completely self-regulating market system. This attempt involved a policy of treating fictitious factors of land, labor and capital as if they were real, ignoring the fact that they stood for human beings or influences closely affecting the welfare of humans. Applications of this policy inevitably meant suffering and dislocation – unemployment, wide fluctuations in prices, waste, and so forth. These disturbances inevitably produced associations – of owners, of workers, of farmers – operating upon government to mitigate and control the ravages of the system through tariffs, subsidies, wage guarantees, social insurance and the like.

This benign view of pressure groups has been questioned by Mancur Olson. Instead of assuming that all interests can be organized with equal facility, he asks the basic question for an economist: what are the costs and benefits for individuals to join various interest groups?

Unlike the rather vague objectives assigned to participation in pressure group activity by political sociologists, Olson rightly looks upon these groups at least in the economic sphere as engaging in attempts to use the political process to obtain special economic benefits for their members. These can in general be described as 'subsidies'. This pressure group politics is of necessity redistributive economics. Olson argued that small, concentrated interest groups are more likely to form and succeed in their aim of influencing the democratic political process to their ends than larger, more diffused groups. For the pay-off from any given 'benefit' acquired through the political process for any individual member of a pressure group diminishes with the size of the group. Also the larger the group the more difficult it becomes for it to coalesce to subserve its aims because of the ubiquitousness of the free-rider problem in organizing collective action. A member who will benefit from the collective 'benefit', even if the member does not participate in its acquisition, will attempt to shirk bearing his or her share of the costs of the collective action if he or she can get away with it. An example of the relevance of Olson's theory is the stylized fact that in developing countries with a preponderance of farmers, agriculture is taxed for the benefit of urban consumers, while in developed countries it is subsidized at the cost of a much larger number of urban consumers.

Those larger pressure groups which do form and are effective, such as trade unions, attract members according to Olson by offering 'selective benefits', not collective benefits. Thus members may have to join trade unions if union membership is a condition for obtaining a particular job. But this is likely to leave the common interests of many large groups unorganized. As Olson (1965) concludes:

> Only when groups are small, or when they are fortunate enough to have an independent source of selective incentives, will they organize or act to achieve their objectives.... But the large unorganized groups [with common interests] not only provide evidence for the basic argument of this study: they also suffer if it is true.
>
> (p. 167)

Thus, far from being the benign social equilibrium of the political sociologists, for the economist, a pressure group equilibrium may not serve the common weal.

Olson later (1982) went on to argue that because of the deadweight costs of the taxes and subsidies associated with a pressure group equilibrium, an economy riddled with pressure groups is likely to bear a heavy burden of such costs, and hence likely to have sluggish growth. He blamed the decline of nations on the growth of interest groups whose aim must necessarily be to use the political process to redistribute income to themselves. This by necessity – given the fixed economic pie at any point of time – is a zero-sum game, a Hobbesian war of all against all. Whether this view is consonant with economic history remains controversial as witness the conflicting claims in the collection of essays in Mueller (1983).

A more serious challenge to Olson's malign view of interest group activity has been provided by Gary Becker, who has sought to provide a rigorous formulation of a model of competition amongst pressure groups for political influence. He partially restores the more benign view of such participation of the political sociologists.

Becker models the influence exerted by pressure groups in terms of costs and benefits – much as Olson – and reaches similar conclusions about the efficacy of smaller over larger groups, because of the problem of controlling free-riding. But his introduction of the deadweight costs of the taxes and subsidies, which comprise the pressure group equilibrium, and which effect the individual's utility, allows him to put a more benign picture on the Cournot–Nash non-cooperative political game he models. In this game the influence of pressure groups (divided into those who pay taxes and those who receive subsidies) is assumed to be a zero sum. As in the political sociology literature there is a countervailing 'potential' taxpayer group to every group that seeks subsidies, and as the overall political budget constraint implies that the amount raised in taxes equals the amount spent in subsidies: 'aggregate influence is zero; increased influence of some groups decreases the influence of others by equal amounts' (Becker, 1983, p. 376). Moreover, because of the deadweight costs of both taxation and subsidization the game is negative sum in these instruments.

These assumptions allow him to derive a number of remarkable 'second-best' efficiency theorems about the pressure group equilibrium. Thus because an increase in the deadweight costs of taxes (subsidies) raises the costs (reduces the benefits), it discourages pressure by the relevant pressure group. Then:

> if the gain to groups that benefit exceeds the loss to groups that suffer, and if access to political influence were the same for all groups, gainers could exert more political pressures than losers, and a policy would tend to be implemented.
>
> (Becker, 1988, p. 101)

This, as he notes, is the famous compensation principle for Pareto optimality in welfare economics, and remarkably it is now resurrected without actual compensation having to be paid! Equally remarkable is the theorem that: 'political policies that raise efficiency are more likely to be adopted than policies that lower efficiency' (Becker, 1983, p. 384).

But as Becker (1988, pp. 91–92) himself notes in passing:

> Aggregate efficiency should be defined not only net of deadweight costs and benefits of taxes and subsidies, but also net of expenditures on the production of political pressure ... since these expenditures are only 'rent-seeking' inputs in the determination of policies. Therefore, efficiency would be raised if all groups could agree to reduce their expenditures on political influence.

But this admission undercuts much of the benign character of the pressure group equilibrium. For with perfect competition amongst pressure groups, we would also expect perfect competition amongst the rent seekers. That, as is well known, will lead to them spending an amount in rent seeking equal to the total rents sought. This, plus whatever expenditures 'taxpayers' have to expend to counter the predatoriness of those seeking subsidies, amounts to the deadweight rectangles of rent-seeking costs which will invariably outweigh any of the conventional Harberger triangle losses which the

Becker framework seeks to minimize. The Becker efficiency conclusions about a pressure group equilibrium would thus seem less than robust, and once the deadweight costs of rent seeking are included it would seem that the more gloomy view taken by Olson about the anti-growth and anti-development effects of an economy dominated by pressure groups is more persuasive.

Further doubt on the benign view that emerges from Becker of a pressure-group-dominated economy – or as I prefer to call it, a factional state – is cast by another of his theorems which follows directly from his assumptions that both taxpayers and subsidy recipients are interested in reducing the deadweight costs of taxes and subsidies. Not surprisingly the commodity tax structure that will then be chosen in his pressure group equilibrium will follow the so-called Ramsey tax rule – that is, tax rates will be related inversely to the elasticity of demand for the good, as this minimizes the Harberger triangle loss for collecting any given revenue. But as Brennan and Buchanan (1980) have shown, the Ramsey tax rule is also the one which will be adopted by what I call an autonomous revenue-maximizing predatory state. This is not merely coincidental. It underlies the basically predatory nature of a distributivist pressure-group-dominated democracy! That the Ramsey rule would also be followed by Platonic Guardians, who by assumption seek to limit revenues to fund essential public goods, offers cold comfort to more cynical political economists who see revenue maximization as the hallmark of predatoriness.

Further doubt is cast on the benign view of a polity and economy dominated by pressure groups by the imperfect empirical evidence which is available about the outcomes in economies dominated by them, as well as by the divergences between theory and actuality about the characteristics of existing pressure groups.

On the first, the Lal–Myint comparative study on the political economy of poverty, equity and growth attempted to classify the twenty-one countries studied into self-explanatory categories defining the central attribute of their polity during the period 1950–1985. The two major categories were of states which were classed as autonomous and factional. In the former the state was seen to stand above the factional pressures exerted by its constituents, and to subserve its own ends. In terms of these ends this category subdivided into the benevolent Platonic Guardian (or one should also add the darker Nietzschean) state attempting to maximize some social welfare function as it saw it, and the more self-serving predatory state seeking to maximize the revenue which the 'monarch' could spend at his or her pleasure. The second category of factional states were those where the states subserved the interests of those who succeeded in capturing the government. The main difference between the two types – oligarchic and majoritarian democratic – distinguished within the category was based on the composition of the polity. Table 13.1 provides the classification of the countries in these broad categories, and a rank ordering by growth rates. It is apparent that, first, any inference about any strong correlation (let alone causation) between forms of government and economic performance is insecure, but that, second, by and large, the performance of the autonomous states tends to be better than that of the factional ones.[9]

Table 13.1 Growth and type of polity (ranked in terms of growth performance)

Region		Growth rate	Autonomous Plat.	Predatory Rev. Max	Bureau Max	Factional Olig.	Dem.
As	Hong Kong	8.9	✓				
As	Singapore	8.3	✓				
As	Malaysia	6.9					✓
As	Thailand	6.7		✓			
LA	Brazil	6.6		✓			
LA	Mexico	5.7			✓		
ME	Malta ⎫	5.6					✓
ME	Turkey ⎭	5.6	✓				
ME	Egypt	5.4			✓		
As	Indonesia	5.3		✓			
LA	Costa Rica	5.0					✓
LA	Colombia	4.7				✓	
As	Sri Lanka	4.7					✓
Af	Malawi	4.3	✓				
LA	Peru	4.1				✓	
Af	Nigeria	3.7					✓
LA	Jamaica	3.3					✓
As	Mauritius	2.9				✓	
Af	Madagascar	2.0				✓	
Af	Ghana	1.3		✓			
LA	Uruguay	1.1					✓

Note: Plat. – Platonic; Rev. Max – Revenue Maximizing; Bureau Max – Bureaucratic Maximizing; Olig. – Oligopoly; Dem. – Democratic.

The second piece of factual evidence which casts some doubt on the perfectly competitive pressure group model is the finding for both developed and developing countries that, apart from the large associations that can utilize selective incentives to gain recruits, most other associations tend to be dominated by relatively more affluent, better educated and middle- or upper middle–class members. As the political scientist Schattschneider put it succinctly: 'The flaw in the pluralist heaven is that the heavenly chorus sings with such an upper class accent. Probably about 90 per cent of the people cannot get into the pressure group system' (1975, pp. 34–35).

As usual an economist has tried to provide an explanation. The political sociologists explained this finding by arguing that 'the higher status

individual has a greater stake in politics, he has greater skills, more resources, great awareness of political matters, he is exposed to more communication about politics, he interacts with others who participate' (Verba
and Nie, 1972, p. 126). By contrast Hirschman (1982) argues that it is
because high-status individuals are also relatively high-income ones, that
they are likely to have satiated their wants for various private goods. They
'may [then] engage in politics because they have become disenchanted with
the pursuit of happiness via the private route' (p. 75). Moreover, unlike the
free-riders who populate the Olsonian collective action universe, Hirschman's high-status political activists participate

> because there is much fulfillment associated with the citizen's exer-
> tions for the public happiness. These exertions are in effect often
> compared with the pleasurable experiences of eating and drinking....
> It is in the very struggle for justice and liberty that the thirst is
> quenched and the craving is gratified. Who then, would want to miss
> all that active pleasure and get a free ride to what is at best the
> comfortable, and usually somewhat disappointing, outcome of these
> processes?
>
> (p. 91)

Though this might explain why many of the principals of NGOs may be
altruistic, it does not tell us whether their actions serve the interests of the
economy or polity. Certainly in some European countries, e.g. Britain, it is
arguable whether the influence of the 'chattering classes' has helped rather
than hindered their economic development (see Weiner, 1981; Letwin,
1992).

Finally, there is the role of mass participation and its effects on electoral
politics. Here studies of participation in voting in those democratic
countries without compulsory voting have shown: first, that voters are
generally badly informed in most democracies, and second, that in many
democracies the percentage voting in elections is not very much more than
half of those eligible to vote.

Economists have again provided a 'rational choice' explanation of this
ignorance and apathy in voting behaviour. Given that the act of voting
involves some positive costs to the individual, whereas the probability of
the individual's vote affecting the electoral outcome is infinitesimally small,
the paradox, as Downs (1957) noted, is not why there is a low voter turnout, but any turnout at all! A similar argument applies to the costs and
benefits of being well informed.

The role of parties, party allegiance and the 'competitive struggle for the
people's vote', which Schumpeter (1950, p. 269) identified as the most
distinctive feature of democracy, then plays a central role in Downs' theory
of democracy. Its most important positive conclusion (of course dependent
on the simplifying assumptions on which it is based) is the so-called median

voter theorem (which was first derived by Hotelling, 1929). This shows that if voters can be ranked along a single dimension (usually defined as the left–right spectrum), have single peaked preferences, and there are only two political parties, then in a majoritarian democracy both parties will have an interest in converging on programmes that appeal to the median voter. This has been used by Stigler (1988a, b) and Meltzer and Richards (1981), amongst others in the economic field, to explain both the growth of government transfers in democracies as well as their inevitable capture by the middle class (the so-called median voter).

One implication of these median voter models of the growth of distributivist welfare states – which in effect become transfer states – is that the political pressure for redistribution and hence the growth of government will decrease with growing prosperity. For with growth, as well as the operation of the transfer state, the median income comes to be closer to the mean, it being noted that, as in the pressure group model, because of the deadweight costs associated with the taxes and subsidies of the transfer state, it will not be in the interest of the median voter to redistribute all the income above the median to him- or herself. Peltzman (1988) has provided a richer model in the median voter tradition which removes some of the shortcomings of the simpler versions. He has also tested it with cross-country regressions which include many developing countries and found it provides a fairly good explanation of the growth of government. The Lal–Myint study found that the Peltzman model also provided a statistically significant explanation for the differences in the levels of government non-defence expenditures in the twenty-one countries studied.

The relatively jaundiced view of the economic effects of majoritarian democracies, emerging from this strand of the new political economy, is complemented by that of a number of political sociologists, e.g. Lipset (1959), who do not see a very high level of political participation to be in the interest of democracy. The example of Hitler's Germany weighs particularly heavily on their minds. The rise of the Nazis through the ballot box was based on their activating many previously inactive groups. This school therefore fears that if non-elite political participation is too widespread, demagogues may exploit the badly informed by playing to the 'irrational' impulses of the masses. A similar view is taken by those who see 'populism' as the bane of Latin American politics and the cause of much of its bad economic performance in recent decades (see Dornbusch and Edwards, 1989).

By contrast other political sociologists adopt a common belief amongst the unreflective that, as Verba and Nie put it: 'Where few take part in decisions there is little democracy; the more participation there is in decisions, the more democracy there is' (1972, p. 1). If this is merely made a definition of democracy then one cannot cavil with it. But then one has to ask, with the political economists and those political sociologists who take a darker view of the consequences of such mass participation, whether the Hobbesian state of nature such a 'democracy' might engender on Olson's view, or the loss of liberty itself on Lipset's view, makes this 'democracy' worth having.

IMPLICATIONS FOR WORLD BANK POLICY

Thus at the end of the above discussion, we are left to swim in very treacherous waters, when we try to work through the effects of those slippery but seemingly obvious concepts 'participation' and 'democracy'. To avoid drowning in them it may be best, as the great Scottish philosophers emphasized, to concentrate not on forms of government but the characteristics of good government – on policies. As the World Bank is charged with advising on the latter and forbidden to deal with the former, it should find this view congenial.

The most important aspect of good government for economic development (and hopefully for liberty), as we have noted, is for the state to view its functions as those of a civil and not an enterprise association. This means that, besides providing the essential public goods at the least cost in terms of revenue, it should not engage in the promotion of any particular morality – be it based on egalitarianism, or fundamental rights.

As redistributive political games are necessarily zero sum, and also involve deadweight costs, a good government will not exacerbate the natural proclivity of human beings to use the political market place to achieve what they cannot obtain through the private market place. The damage that the politicization of economic life can cause for development has been a persistent theme in the writings of Lord Bauer (1970, 1978). His initially lonely position has been amply justified by experience in the last two decades. To the extent the cry for greater participation in the mechanics of development is one for accentuating these redistributive games, it needs to be eschewed.

We have also argued that more recent versions of this game have come to be based on so-called social and economic rights, whose upholding, it is claimed, must form the basis for the 'real' participation of the masses and hence 'genuine' democracy. But democracy as we have argued can only have instrumental value, and if combined with the state viewed as an enterprise association can be inimical to the ultimate ends of promoting both popular 'opulence' and liberty.

This does not mean that 'participation' viewed as affirming the classical liberal freedoms to associate and speak one's mind is not valuable. It is – as it promotes liberty. But this is a different end, though no less valuable than opulence. The latter, experience has shown, is best promoted by markets. But because participation – in the above limited sense – and markets are thus instrumentally desirable, it does not follow, as some seek to claim, that the latter require the former. This is just another reflection of the fact that there is no necessary causal link between democracy and development. We may wish to promote the former because it at least helps to prevent tyranny and hence promotes liberty – a valued end. But it is a fallacy to give in to the natural human failing to believe that all good things go together – so that democracy will promote development. But neither, I hasten to add, is there any necessary link between authoritarianism and development.

Nor does it appear essential for either democracy or development to promote voluntary civil associations, despite the claims of the pluralist American tradition. Particularly in an enterprise state, they can (as discussed above) become the instruments of competitive rent seeking with inimical effects on economic development. By their very nature these pressure groups must themselves be enterprise associations. For the state to promote any of them would amount to its endorsing the aims of that particular enterprise – something which a state viewed as a civil association is charged not do.

But in a such a state, there would also be no need to take any baleful view of these associations, though there is always the danger, as with religious associations which seek to convert the state into an enterprise association, that they may seek to use the political process to subvert the state as a civil association by attempting to take it over. The bulwarks that can feasibly be erected against such outcomes, and others which subvert the state seen as a civil association, are the subject matter of much current research in so-called constitutional economics, but it lies beyond the scope of this chapter.

Nor would there be a presumption, one way or the other, about using these voluntary private (enterprise) associations in the provision of public goods (including programmes which alleviate absolute poverty, which classical liberalism views as a public good).[10] This would depend on the actual merits of the case, as judged by the standard efficiency criterion: is this the least-cost way of providing a particular level of the relevant public good? As most World Bank project lending provides finance for investments in public goods, the association of so-called NGOs in World Bank projects must remain an empirical and contingent matter. There can be no general presumption about its desirability. As we have argued, any attempt to do so through the notions of 'participation' and 'democracy' remains seriously flawed.

But are there specific types of World Bank projects in which involving NGOs might on the basis of existing evidence be useful? And can anything be said about the types of NGOs that the World Bank might find useful in its work?

A World Bank report by Holt (1991) identified three conditions for participation (defined as 'the poor's influence in decisionmaking in poverty reduction programs') as a necessary component of effective and sustainable poverty reduction programmes. These were:

(a) when the poor possess information not known to outsiders that is necessary for program success;

(b) when collective action is required for effective management;

(c) when the government must rely on poor people to expand the public resources that are put into projects.

Amongst the sectors identified as having benefited from participation were: agriculture (including forestry, livestock, irrigation and agricultural extension); rural water supply; urban development (including urban water supply); environment and resettlement; and credit (group lending schemes and microenterprise).

Of the three criteria listed above the importance of (a) and (c) cannot be gainsaid. But these used to be part of standard procedures for the design of World Bank projects. There may be critical technical local knowledge (to be distinguished from preferences), for instance about local ecology or customs, on which the success of a particular investment project will depend. But certainly in the 1970s when I was associated with the World Bank's project evaluation work, particularly in agriculture, obtaining this local knowledge through site visits at the design stage of the project was considered standard practice. Assuming this has not changed, to label this process as 'participation' is to use emotive language, which, given the slippery nature of the concept of 'participation' discussed above, is likely to aid neither clarity of thought nor the relief of poverty.

Similarly, in many social sectors such as health and education it has been part of World Bank practice, in the project design, to include some form of cost recovery from project beneficiaries, as this provides at least some surrogate for the 'willingness to pay' criterion which ensures the efficiency of market provision of private goods. So there is again nothing new about criterion (c).

More worrying is criterion (b), particularly if it is implied that the collective action required for the provision and maintenance of public goods should be through some form of popular participation. As the discussion in the previous sections has highlighted there is no presumption that such participation will necessarily enhance efficiency or even help the poorest. Nor, when the local knowledge which is required for the proper design of public goods projects concerns subjective individual preferences, is there any participatory mechanism which will ensure that these can be objectively ascertained, and more seriously, as social choice theory has emphasized, be aggregated into any meaningful social welfare function.

Thus there seems little that participation can add, beyond what has been standard World Bank good practice in designing projects: namely, obtaining all the relevant local information and designing appropriate incentive mechanisms (which most often mimic those of the market) for the maintenance and use of public goods projects. Whether or not particular NGOs can help in this process must be a contingent matter.

Perhaps more help in providing some general guidelines for World Bank relations with NGOs may be provided by some typology of NGOs? A useful one is provided by Clark (1991). He divides them into six types:

1 Relief and welfare agencies, e.g. Catholic Relief, various missionary societies.
2 Technical innovation organizations, e.g. the Intermediate Technology Group.
3 Public sector contractors, e.g. NGOs funded by Northern governments to work on Southern government and official aid agency projects, like CARE.
4 Popular development agencies. 'Northern NGOs and their Southern intermediary counterparts which concentrate on self-help, social development, and grass roots democracy', e.g. local OXFAM, CEDI and FASE in Brazil.
5 Grassroots development organizations: 'Locally based Southern NGOs whose members are the poor and oppressed themselves, and which attempt to shape a popular development process'.
6 Advocacy groups and networks, 'which have no field projects but which exist primarily for education and lobbying', e.g. environmental pressure groups in the North and South.

One useful purpose served by this typology is that given the discussion in previous sections, whilst the type of associations under 5 and 6 may form a very important part of creating a civil society and maintaining essential liberties, their endorsement by the World Bank would clearly be inappropriate. On the other hand the associations under 2 and 3, are service associations (to coin a label), and their use on particular projects must depend upon the merits of the particular case. For here there is a paucity of evidence on the general effectiveness of such NGOs. As Clark – an OXFAM employee – notes:

> there is surprisingly little objective reporting of NGO projects. Northern NGOs' own writings generally concentrate on the success stories and, being aimed largely at their supporting publics, serve a propaganda purpose. The NGOs tend to commission few objective evaluations, ... and so may not even know much about their successes or failures.
>
> (1991, p. 52)

One of the few evaluations available is by Tendler (1982) of seventy-five USAID NGO projects. This, though not as rigorous as the standard project evaluation methodology (which is hopefully still being followed by the World Bank), does dispel some of the common myths about these 'service'

NGOs. Thus, for instance, she found that NGOs do not benefit the poorest of the poor. The beneficiaries were most often in the middle and upper range of the income distribution, as many NGOs have moved away from their initial strictly relief and welfare projects (with careful targeting of beneficiaries) 'towards conventional development projects'. Also what was described as participation by the poor in the projects was also a myth. Distinguishing between 'participation' and 'decentralization' she found that there was greater decentralization in these projects but the decision making was dominated by NGO staff and the local elite. Lest it be thought this was undesirable she also found that projects which reached the poorest were usually designed by do-gooding outsiders! The study thus confirms many of the theoretical points we have made in earlier sections.

If as we have argued there may still be a case based on contingent factors on associating particular 'service' NGOs with World Bank projects, one essential piece of missing information that is required is on the past track record of the NGO in delivering the requisite services. For this purpose just as the World Bank evaluates its own past projects, it might be desirable to get independent audits done of the past performance of NGOs seeking to be associated with World Bank projects. As according to the OECD over 30 per cent of NGOs' annual funds come from official sources, it would not compromise their independence if official and multilateral institutions were to demand such an audit.

This leaves the associations under 1 and 4. These are largely religious and/or relief associations. Subject of course to the proviso about an audit of past performance, there is some reason to believe that on some type of poverty alleviation projects they may have a comparative advantage. As historically the churches have been the main organizations for alleviating destitution and what can be called conjunctural poverty (due in agrarian economies to the vagaries of nature),[11] they are likely to have organizations for both identifying the poorest as well as monitoring any benefits they receive. This is of importance in overcoming the adverse incentive effects that have bedevilled many poverty alleviation schemes. They may, therefore, provide a more effective channel for disbursing foreign aid aimed at dealing with destitution and conjunctural poverty. But churches are *par excellence* enterprise associations, which have sought in the past and in some cases still seek to take over the state. Thus, in countries where the church is at odds with the state there is a danger that if foreign aid donors channel their aid to help the destitute through such churches, they will be looked upon as partisans in a local political struggle. Once again, therefore, the World Bank could find itself in treacherous waters.

Besides the church, self-help organizations like rotating credit associations (of which Bangladesh's Grammen Bank is a notable example), and the friendly societies which grew up in eighteenth- and nineteenth-century Britain to deal with destitution and conjunctural poverty, have been of importance.[12] As these are part of the civil associations rightly lauded by De Tocqueville, which help in maintaining liberty, and furthermore promote the classical liberal vigorous virtue of self-reliance, they are to be commended. But whether public action and support is required for them to flourish is dubious. As the experience in the West has shown, the establishment of welfare states which sought to substitute public for private benevolence has led to the nationalization of these associations.[13] These intermediate institutions of civil society were forced to surrender their functions and authority to professional elites and the bureaucracies of centralizing states. For their current Third World counterparts too, the public embrace of either foreign aid institutions or their own governments could (for reasons of political economy) be the kiss of death!

Hence our rather gloomy conclusion that apart from a case-by-case appraisal of the desirability of associating the service associations identified above, World Bank involvement with other NGOs is likely to promote neither efficiency nor liberty (nor their associated instruments – markets and democracy).

NOTES

* This essay has greatly benefited from the comments of members of a seminar at the World Bank on an earlier draft.

1 See Lal (1983) and Little (1982) for a discussion of development fads of the 1950s through the 1970s. See Bebbington and Farrington (1993), Drabek (1987) and Stevulak and Thompson (1993) for references to the literature and discussions on the role of NGOs in development. Amongst the World Bank material on the subject in addition to the last reference above, see also Salmen and Eaves (1989) and Ribe et al. (1990). Barry (1970, 1978) remains an excellent critique of the political sociology literature on participation and democracy, and which also takes a fairly cool look at the early political economy literature on the subject. Ostrom et al. (1988) is also a useful collection relevant to the subject of this chapter. Finally, an excellent paper by Gerson (1993) examines popular participation in economic theory and practice. Besides providing a useful summary and critique of the quantitative studies of the effects of participation on project effectiveness (e.g. by Esman and Uphofff (1984) and Finsterbusch and Van Wicklin (1989)) he also surveys the available World Bank evidence. A number of points he makes may be noted as they complement the argument of this chapter. First, as general equilibrium theory has shown, for non-public goods the market provides the most comprehensive and efficient form of popular participation. Moreover, it is the 'willingness to pay' criterion embedded in the market which economists try to evoke and implement when considering the provision of public goods. Second, the belief that participation provides some easy way to elicit the preferences of beneficiaries of public goods is belied by Arrow's famous impossibility theorem about aggregating individual preferences into a social choice function without violating some unexceptional conditions such as non-dictatorship! Third, that some form of cost recovery, through the contribution of time or money by beneficiaries, is an effective form of participation, even in the provision of public goods.

2 An excellent account of this is in Muller (1993).

3 This is Shirley Letwin's term to describe the 'moral' content of Thatcherism.

4 This corresponds to what Oakeshott (1993) calls the productivist and distributionist versions of the modern embodiments of the enterprise association, whose religious version was epitomized by Calvinist Geneva, and in our own times is provided by Khomeni's Iran. Each of these collective forms conjures up some notion of perfection, believed to be 'the common good'. Of these three versions Oakeshott (p. 92) notes: 'first a "religious" version, where "perfection" is understood as "righteousness" or "moral virtue"; secondly a "productivist" version, where "perfection" is understood as a condition of "prosperity" or "abundance" or "wealth"; and thirdly a "distributionist" version, where "perfection" is understood as "security" or "welfare". These three versions of the politics of collectivism succeed one another in the history of modern Europe.... And in our own time the politics of collectivism may be seen to be composed of a mixture in which each of these versions has its place.'

5 This is based on Lal and Myint (1996). On the French Revolution see Aftalion (1990).

6 Sen (1973) characterizes the Chinese Cultural Revolution in these terms and with some implicit approbation!

7 This term and the following argument is due to Ken Minogue (1993).

8 See Gourevitch (1993) for a further elaboration of the tenuous link between forms of government and their promotion of markets.

9 Nor is there any connection between military regimes, and *mutatis mutandis*, authoritarian regimes and development. For a detailed study of the links between the military and development see Alexander Berg and Elliot Berg (1991).

10 See Lal (1993) for a substantiation of this point, as well as a general discussion based on the findings of the Lal–Myint study on poverty and development.

11 In Lal (1993) following Illiffe I distinguish between three types of poverty. The first is the *mass structural poverty* which has been the fate of much of the human race until the era of modern economic growth. This, as the experience of current developed and a growing number of developing countries shows, can be cured by efficient growth. World Bank policy advice and project lending which helps in this process necessarily alleviates this historic hard core of poverty. This still leaves the problems of *destitution* and *conjunctural poverty* which have traditionally composed the problem of poverty that public policy has sought to alleviate. In the agrarian economies of the past, labour was scarce relative to land, and hence destitution was due to a lack of labour power to work land (either their own – because of disabilities – or from family members – because they had none). This is still true of parts of Africa. With population expansion and growing land scarcity destitutes emerged who lacked land, work or adequate wages to support their dependants. Finally, throughout history there has been conjunctural poverty where people have fallen over the brink (albeit temporarily) because of climatic crises or political turmoil. In industrial economies, the trade cycle has added another form of conjunctural poverty associated with cyclical unemployment.

12 See Green (1993).

13 Green (1993) provides a detailed account of the British experience.

REFERENCES

Aftalion, F. (1990) *The French Revolution – An Economic Interpretation*, Cambridge University Press, Cambridge.

Barry, B. (1970, 1978) *Sociologists, Economists and Democracy*, Chicago University Press, Chicago.

Bauer, P. T. (1971, 1976) *Dissent on Development*, Harvard University Press.

Bebbington, A. and Farrington, J. (1993) 'Governments, NGOs and Agricultural Development', *Journal of Development Studies*, January.

Becker, G. (1983) 'A Theory of Competition Among Pressure Groups for Political Influence', *Quarterly Journal of Economics*, August.

—— (1988) 'Public Policies, Pressure Groups, and Deadweight Costs', in G. Stigler (ed.) *Chicago Studies in Political Economy*, Chicago University Press, Chicago.

Bentley, A. F. (1908) *The Process of Government*, Chicago University Press, Chicago.

Berg, A. and Berg, E. (1991) 'The Political Economy of the Military', in G. Psacharopoulos (ed.) *Essays on Poverty, Equity and Growth*, Pergamon, Oxford.

Brennan, G. and Buchanan, J. (1980) *The Power to Tax*, Cambridge University Press, Cambridge.

Clark, J. (1991) *Democratizing Development – The Role of Voluntary Organizations*, Earthscan, London.

Dornbusch, R. and Edwards, S. (1989) 'Macroeconomic Populism in Latin America', Working Paper 2986, National Bureau of Economic Research, Cambridge, MA.

Downs, A. (1957) *An Economic Theory of Democracy*, Harper Bros, New York.

Drabek, A. G. (ed.) (1987) 'Development Alternatives: The Challenge for NGOs', *World Development*, vol. 15 supplement, August.

Esman, M. and Uphoff, N. T. (1984) *Local Organizations – Intermediaries in Rural Development*, Cornell University Press.

Finsterbusch, K. and Van Wicklin III, W. A. (1989) 'Beneficiary Participation in Development Projects – Empirical Tests of Popular Theories', *Economic Development and Cultural Change*, April.

Gerson, P. R. (1993) 'Popular Participation in Economic Theory and Practice', OPRIE, World Bank, Mimeo.

Gourevitch, P. A. (1993) 'Democracy and Economic Policy: Elective Affinities and Circumstantial Conjunctures', *World Development*, August.

Green, D. G. (1993) *Reinventing Civil Society – The Rediscovery of Welfare Without Politics*, IEA, London.

Hirschman, A. O. (1982) *Shifting Involvements*, Princeton University Press.

Holt, S. L. (1991) 'The Role of Institutions in Poverty Reduction', PRE WPS #627, World Bank, March.

Hotelling, H. (1929) 'Stability of Competition', *Economic Journal*.

Lal, D. (1983) *The Poverty of 'Development Economics'*, IEA, London.

—— (1996) 'Poverty and Development', in H. Siebert (ed.) *The Ethical Foundations of a Market Economy*, J. C. B. Mohr, Tubingen

Lal, D. and Myint, H. (1996) *The Political Economy of Poverty, Equity and Growth – A Comparative Study*, Clarendon Press, Oxford.

Latham, E. (1952) *The Group Basis of Politics*, Cornell University Press.

Letwin, S. (1992) *The Anatomy of Thatcherism*, Fontana, London.

Lipset, S. M. (1959) *Political Man*, Heinemann, London.

Little, I. M. D. (1982) *Economic Development*, Basic Books, New York.

Meltzer, A. and Richard, S. (1981) 'A Rational Theory of the Size of Government', *Journal of Political Economy*, vol. 21.

Minogue, K. (1993) *The Constitutional Mania*, Policy Study No. 134, Centre for Policy Studies, London.

Mueller, D. C. (ed.) (1983) *The Political Economy of Growth*, Yale University Press.

Muller, J. Z. (1993) *Adam Smith in His Time and Ours*, Free Press, New York.

Oakeshott, M. (1973) *On Human Conduct*, Clarendon Press, Oxford.

—— (1993) *Morality and Politics in Modern Europe*, Yale University Press.

Olson, M. (1965) *The Logic of Collective Action*, Harvard University Press.

—— (1982) *The Rise and Decline of Nations*, Yale University Press.

Ostrom, V., Feny, D. and Picht, H. (eds) (1988) *Rethinking Institutional Analysis and Development*, International Center for Economic Growth, ICS Press, San Francisco.

Peltzman, S. (1988) 'The Growth of Government,' in G. Stigler (ed.) *Chicago Studies in Political Economy*, Chicago University Press, Chicago.

Ribe, H. *et al.* (1990) 'How Adjustment Programs Can Help the Poor', World Bank Discussion Paper, No. 71.

Salmen, L. F. and Eaves, A. P. (1989) 'World Bank Work With Nongovernmental Organizations', PPR WPS #305, World Bank, December.

Schattschneider, E. E. (1975) *The Semi Sovereign People*, Dryden, IL.

Schumpeter, J. A. (1950) *Capitalism, Socialism and Democracy*, Harper and Row, New York.

Sen, A. K. (1973) *On Economic Inequality*, Oxford University Press.

Stevulak, C. and Thompson, A. (1993) 'Approaches for World Bank Staff on Working with NGOs', Discussion draft, World Bank, June.

Stigler, G. (1988a) 'Directors Law of Public Income Redistribution', in G. Stigler (ed.) *Chicago Studies in Political Economy*, Chicago University Press, Chicago.

—— (ed.) (1988b) *Chicago Studies in Political Economy*, Chicago University Press, Chicago.

Tendler, J. (1982) 'Turning Private Voluntary Organisations Into Development Agencies: Questions for Evaluation', Program Evaluation Discussion Paper No. 12, USAID, April.

Truman, D. B. (1953) *The Government Process*, Knopf, New York.

Verba, S. and Nie, N. H. (1972) *Participation in America*, Harper and Row, New York.

Weiner, M. (1981) *English Culture and the Decline of the Industrial Spirit*, Cambridge University Press, Cambridge.

14

STYLIZING ACCUMULATION IN AFRICAN COUNTRIES AND THE ROLE OF THE STATE IN POLICY MAKING

Thandika Mkandawire

The perception of the role of the state in the process of development has shifted considerably over the years. While in the early years of development economics its pervasive role was considered as both necessary and inevitable, the neoliberal onslaught of the 1980s and 1990s was to dislodge the state from this privileged and self-evident position. Although the pendulum seems to be slightly swinging back again as the success of a number of developing countries revives interest in the 'developmental state' as a potentially positive factor in development, even these 'success stories' raise divergencies in the interpretations of the necessity and efficacy of the state. The role one assigns to the state is, both normatively and positively, embedded in one's stylization of markets because it is this stylization which determines whether or not the state has a positive role to play and what one expects will happen when the state moves in this or that policy direction.

As far back as Adam Smith it has generally been assumed that the study of the economic system presupposes an autonomous, law-governed market mechanism and economists encapsulated in the notion of the 'invisible hand'. And as Milgate and Eatwell (1983) argue most disputes in economics have not, therefore, been on whether there are systematic and persistent forces at work in the economy, but rather over the nature of those forces. More significantly, the role of the state has depended on what were the perceived capacities, limits and tendencies of these forces in achieving certain desired goals. If this is true of the disputes about the nature and functioning of markets in the developed economies, it is, *a fortiori*, true of those of the underdeveloped countries about which there has always been the argument about whether or not such economies are characterized by structures or processes that so attenuate or condition market forces as to warrant special study and theorization (development economics) or whether these economies obeyed the same laws as the advanced ones and could therefore be understood through standard analytical tools and assumptions (the 'monoeconomics' assumption).

It is in light of these observations that this chapter argues that (a) the currently dominant 'stylization' of African economies generates a jaundiced view of the state which has paralysed thinking about policy and research on policy in Africa; (b) one of the reasons for the dismal failure of the current wave of liberalization programmes is the misspecification of these 'spontaneous' processes; and (c) there is a need to break the closure of the research agenda which the axiomatic scheme informing much of the current analysis of African economies imposes.

CAPITAL ACCUMULATION

Whatever else is said about the process of development, capital accumulation is a central player in the drama. Not surprisingly a major task of development economies has been the elaboration of models of accumulation, the most fecund of these being the Lewis 'labour surplus model' (1954) which generated a vast programme of research and theoretical elaboration and for its author the Nobel Prize in economics.. To fix ideas we will resort to a heuristically useful formulation by Joan Robinson in which she suggested that in considering causal accumulation models one had to start not from equilibrium relations but 'from rules and motives governing human behaviour' (Robinson, 1964). This, she argued, is essential because we cannot understand the objectives and effects of state policies until we understand the operation of the 'free' economy that they attempt to modify. One had, therefore, to spell out a number of determinants of the accumulation processes in a given economy. Robinson (1964) identified the following as major determinants of accumulation:

1 Technical conditions
2 Investment policy
3 Thriftiness conditions
4 Competitive conditions
5 The wage bargain
6 Financial conditions
7 The initial stock of capital goods and the state of expectations formed by past experience.

In typical Keynesian fashion, Robinson's stylization was confined to a 'closed economy'. A more realistic model of African economies would have to be necessarily 'open'. We therefore need to add:

8 The external conditions.

It is on the basis of the stylization of these determinants that one formulates one's vision or model of the economy and, explicitly or implicitly, delineates the role of the state.

In this chapter, we will not consider all the 'determinants' mentioned above. Instead, for illustrative purposes, we will only touch on a few partly to indicate the potentially different scenarios, the possible roles of the state and the kind of research questions implicit in the different scenarios. Some of the determinants are considered simultaneously (as they are in real life economic situations where 'everything depends on everything else').

NEOCLASSICAL STYLIZATION

In neoclassical models it is assumed that there are constant returns to scale and smooth production functions with infinite substitutionability. Investments are equal savings. All markets are assumed perfectly competitive and are all cleared. On the assumption of perfect information the initial capital stock is the right one formed by past experiences. So far as the developing countries are concerned, explanations of technological change in the 'North' and its transfer and dissemination in the 'South' are key to understanding both market structure and technology conditions in the latter. Explaining technological innovations in terms of factor prices, this view focuses the technological choice question in the advanced capitalist economies on the rising wage/interest ratio leading to the rising capital/labour ratio (K/L) which is then explained as primarily a technological response to actual or anticipated relative increases in wages. This in turn is viewed as primarily the result of the pace of capital accumulation chronically exceeding that of the growth of the labour supply under full employment conditions. Since the possibilities of maintaining the profit rate by labour adjustments along a given neoclassical production function are limited, a continual search for labour-saving technologies is required, leading to a rising K/L as a result of the biased innovation and the choice of more capital-intensive variants of each new technology (Felix, 1974, 1977).

With such a view of technological change as the point of departure, one can claim that 'late-industrializers' can borrow from a freely accessible 'technological shelf' containing all types of vintages. This view of technological change has implications for labour markets. The predictions of the model are that there will be full employment since high interest rates will force producers to use labour-intensive technologies and the supply and demand interactions in the labour market will determine market-clearing wage rates. Failure to clear the market is attributed to the 'distortions' caused by the *dirigisme* of the state which is part of the rent-seeking or patron–clientalism syndrome which has induced the state to introduce minimum wages, food subsidies and the rights of workers that have reduced 'labour market flexibility' etc. Freeman (1992) has labelled this position 'distortionist' since it is based on a search for 'distortions' and hinges on, among other things, the claims about state interventions: they misallocate labour.

The policy proposals that follow from such analysis include calls for greater 'labour market flexibility', the more undemocratic 'putting a crunch on wages' by repressing labour movements, and the more corporativist calls for labour to assume its 'national responsibilities' and put off its demands to a later stage when the development task has been completed. In practice, the role of the state is reduced to breaking institutions (e.g. labour movements) that 'distort' labour markets. Indeed it is usually with respect to labour markets that calls for a 'strong state' which can discipline labour are made.

With respect to financial markets, the clearest statement of the neoclassical view was by McKinnon (1973) who argued that one source of the tribulations of the developing countries was 'financial repression', referring to interventionist financial policies which impose interest ceilings or rational credit. According to this doctrine, left to themselves, financial markets would lead to a greater volume of financial assets and activity (financial deepening). Higher interest rates would increase the willingness to save and hold savings in financial assets. Reliance on markets would, as in all other spheres, improve overall economic efficiency by subjecting enterprises to greater financial discipline and improving the quality of investment. Not only would the 'unrepressed' financial markets operate in this way, this was how financial markets spontaneously operate.

As far as international financial markets are concerned, it is presumed that they function as perfectly as any market can realistically be expected to. This view is reinforced by the greater 'globalization' of the 1970s and 1980s in international financial markets. Individual countries can readily borrow from these markets if only they get their policies right. The right policies include the liberalization of the domestic markets which have been 'distorted' by the state's financially repressive measures. And as part of the conditionality of the international financial institutions many African countries have proceed to do just that. Essentially, the new view assigns little value to domestic financial policy except as a quixotic attempt to stem the tide of internationalization and as ineluctably leading to loss of access to global financial markets and capital flight.

To be fair, there are sometimes injections of 'realism' in this stylization by conceding certain 'imperfections' and rigidities but these concessions only underscore the importance attached to the underlying model as the benchmark for examining the deviations from the predicted or expected outcomes. Usually, subsequent analysis and policy prescription blithely proceed oblivious of them. The temptation to ignore these rigidities as sources of 'market failure' is enhanced by the glaring evidence of 'government failure' in Africa. Even more pernicious to policy making is that by the time 'rules of thumb' are extracted for policy makers, the complexities and qualifications of certain key assumptions will have been toned down, trivialized or simply forgotten. This is compounded by ideological imperatives that push the analysis towards the desired conclusion regardless of the type of empirical evidence marshalled.

It is this neoclassical stylization of African economies that has informed policy analysis in Africa at least since the 'Berg Report' (World Bank, 1981). It underpinned much of the earlier zealousness about how 'getting prices right' would get things moving in Africa. More significant for arguments in this chapter is the fact that it undergirds the dominant perception of the role of the state in the process of development.

What have been the outcomes? There is considerable evidence of failure of the SAP to induce growth.[1] Mosley and Weeks (1993) summarize the evidence thus:

(a) Based on statistics through 1991, the SSA region as a whole had not recovered from its development disaster, though there was improvement for some countries;
(b) whether a country did better or worse than the average for the region shows little correlation with the category of 'adjusting countries' as variously defined by the World Bank.

Even more serious was the fact that while this approach created vast space for foreign 'donor *dirigisme*', it left African states with virtually nothing useful to do during the most serious economic crises faced by their countries since they achieved political independence.[2] As responses to market reforms failed to yield the expected results or, when they did, yielded them in such derisory magnitudes, there was a realization, albeit grudging, that there may be other constraints to the market besides state interventions. This has led to the realization that one source of the failure of neoliberal policies in Africa, both as economic policy and political practice, was that they were based on a gross misspecification of the underlying economic structure.

ALTERNATIVE STYLIZATION

The alternative stylization dates back to the 'pioneers of development' or what Krugman (1992) has termed 'high development theory'. Some of its features were also to be central to the Latin American 'structuralist' and 'Dependence' schools which, unwarrantedly, extracted 'stagnationist' conclusions from them. These features have been revived or evoked in the 'counter counter-revolution' literature reinterpreting the historical experience of the 'success stories' in essentially non-neoclassical fashion. Some have been formalized in new growth theories[3] and structuralist development models (Krugman, 1992; Taylor, 1991). A common feature of these models is that instead of deriving macroeconomic analysis from the optimization games that idealized firms or households are supposed to play, one starts from the viewpoint that 'macroeconomics matters at its own level in the hierarchy of theories, and that the regularities one builds into macro models require justification much more from historical and institutional analysis (some microeconomic)' (Taylor, 1991, p. 10).

To make the essay self-contained, we will briefly restate these stylized facts which are seen as intrinsic to the process of accumulation in the developing countries and suggest possible positive roles for the state.

Market structure and technical conditions

We will start with technical and market conditions. By market structure we mean the 'constraints on the behaviour of a set of quasi-firms arising from their rivalry in selling a particular product (or type of product in the case of "near substitutes" ' (Robinson, 1964). The 'stylized fact' of market structures in the developing countries is that they tend to be imperfect and prone to 'market failures' as evidenced by the prevalence of monopolistic or oligopolistic markets. African markets are usually characterized by a dualism in their competitive conditions. On the one hand there are the 'formal', more or less oligopolistic firms, while on the other hand, there are the numerous, small-scale, highly competitive firms in the 'informal' sector. This dualism is not exclusively the result of state policies that 'distort' markets, as is suggested in conventional neoclassical diagnosis, but also a result of certain structural features of the domestic and international economies.

The oligopolistic character of the market is a reflection of such factors as the presence of transnational firms which are, by their very nature, oligopolies; economies of scale which will tend to lead to the establishment of units of production which, given the size of the markets of African economies, can sustain only a few enterprises (Felix, 1977); technological dependence which reduces the capacity of developing countries to tailor the size of production units to their own demands (Merhav, 1969); or the 'product cycles' which induce transnational firms to transfer their production technologies to the developing countries in a 'packaged form' (Vernon, 1966; Vaitsos, 1974).

These features of the market received considerable attention in the 1970s before the 'oil crisis' and at a time when direct foreign investment was a key component of capital flows. Since the explanation of such flows relied heavily on factors which gave rise to concentration and large scale, it tended to rely on studies of industrial structures and tended to assume that a necessary condition of direct investment was that the investing firm enjoyed some monopolistic advantage not possessed by potential local competitors (Lall and Streeten, 1977). Lall and Streeten note that while work by some economists had made these assumptions almost commonplace in the literature, the more conventional analysis of foreign investment based on neoclassical trade theory has simply abstracted away from these. And in much of the current literature little attention is paid to these features. The replacement of direct foreign investment by bank lending and the greater financial liberalization in the 1980s lent even greater weight to neoclassical perceptions about how international financial markets operated and led to a downplaying of the structural constraints on the operation of markets (Helleiner, 1988)

Technical conditions

There are at least two interrelated formulations of the nature of technical conditions and how they impact on market structure and accumulation in developing countries. The first of these, and probably the most consequential, is the economies of scale scenario on technical change. The second cluster of explanations relates to transfer of technology and the third relates to market size of the economy as a whole or for a set of goods.

The scale scenario

The 'pioneers of development' tended to assume the prevalence of economies of scale which impinged on the ability to establish profitable industries in developing countries.[4] In more recent years, economists such as David Felix (1974, 1977) and Taylor (1991) have used this assumption to generate models of accumulation that have characteristics that are very different from those of the neoclassical ones.

There is a vast amount of literature on the empirical significance of the scale scenario. In much of the 'orthodox' discussion or modelling of industrialization and state policies in the developing countries, the economies of scale are assumed away almost as a matter of course although there are times when they are rather incongruously dragged in to justify the need for an export-oriented strategy.[5] Significantly, the economies of scale assumptions are now being used as a basic assumption in models of trade among developed countries (Helpman and Krugman, 1985; Krugman, 1990). Hopefully, they will be rigorously integrated into models of accumulation in the developing countries.

The scale scenario immediately suggests one effect of technological dependence, namely that if technical obsolescence in the advanced capitalist countries is in large part due to movement along an economy of scale vector, more of the technology successively discarded by the advanced economies will therefore be market inefficient in the technologically dependent periphery economies than is implied in the neoclassical view. Furthermore, such economies will be characterized by relatively high levels of technical concentration than would be accounted for by their overall levels of economic development (Felix, 1974, 1977). The effects of such technical concentration on the degree of competitiveness in the economy are discussed later.

329

Market size argument

A further argument for the contention that monopoly is congenital to accumulation in African economies is based on the market size of the African economies coupled with the technological dependence described above. In general the size of the market for a country of 5 million people is no larger than the market of a European provincial town with 100,000 inhabitants. The technological dependence determines the scale of production and, in the absence of capital goods, this necessarily leads to imitation of techniques evolved in the advanced capitalist economies with their vastly larger markets (Merhav, 1969). And given the lilliputian size of the African markets, only a few firms will dominate the production of a given commodity. Thus in Zimbabwe the four largest firms in most categories produced more than 50 per cent of the industry's value added while in Zambia and Tanzania one or two firms produced all the output of several categories (Seidman, 1986). In Côte d'Ivoire in 1983 72 per cent of all value added and a similar proportion of exports originated in just forty-eight industries, less than 10 per cent of the estimated total, with the leading enterprises alone responsible for 47 per cent of MVA in 1982 (Riddell, 1990). In Malawi and Kenya the Herfindal indices of industrial concentration were very high (65 per cent and 89 percent respectively) (Adam *et al.*, 1992). These two economies were considered 'market-oriented economies' and, until recently, held up as 'success stories' with few 'market distortions'. The smallness of the market size and its further fragmentation by the structure of income distribution and the commercial activities of the monopoly firms all have the effect of further accentuating the degree of monopoly in the economies. It is often asserted that trade, by making these markets 'contested', removes these constraints on competition due to market size. However, although trade may indeed dilute the monopolistic characteristics of the market induced by the smallness of markets and technological dependence, it cannot entirely remove them for a host of reasons including the fact that a large number of goods are not 'tradable' under realistic assumptions about transaction costs.

In general then the 'stylized facts' spelt out here point to the fact that monopoly is an intrinsic outcome of irreversible sociotechnological developments which constitute an important component of the objective basis of government policy in most African countries. The barriers to meaningful competition are often substantially outside the control of individual governments. By all this we do not deny that at times governments adopt wrong policies based on some theories of development, rent seeking, muddleheadedness, miscalculation, ideological presuppositions, etc. Indeed, the structurally induced oligopolistic characteristic of the economy can be further enhanced or 'frozen' by the agency of, for example, a domestic capitalist class demanding an interventionist state to mediate its relation with foreign capital and to facilitate its access to 'rents' by diluting competitive pressure through acquisition of special privileges such as import licences, exclusive access to inputs or markets, etc. Indeed it is the combination of intrinsic monopolistic tendencies and rent seeking or patron-clientalism that has bedevilled the performance of many an African economy. Most of the analysis of sources of 'market distortions' has been confined to this internal and political source of monopoly (Bates, 1981). What we wish to stress is that policies which create or strengthen monopoly positions do not rest only on interventionist theories, rent seeking, or the purely subjective thrust of state policies. And even more significantly we wish to stress the fact that liberalization in the presence of the structural determinants outlined above may not always be welfare augmenting and that the regulatory role of the state may exist independently of the rent-seeking proclivities of the incumbents.

Wage bargaining and labour markets

A second set of stylized facts relates to the labour market. Labour markets are important not because they are just one-commodity markets, but because it is these markets which often define the politics of a particular pattern of accumulation. It is within these markets that the distributional properties of the accumulation regime are sharply brought out (through labour mobility, social segmentation, wage setting and human capital investments, etc.). It is also in these markets that political responses to particular policies are often most sharply articulated, determining the 'political feasibility' of macroeconomic policies. It is often with respect to labour markets that questions about democratic or authoritarian 'developmental states' are raised. This is because wages are 'a horse of a somewhat different colour' (Ranis, 1973, p. 144).

The first problem relates to the state, labour organizations and the characterization and performance of labour markets. In the current 'no-nonsense' approach to policy making, the greatest impatience with African states in so far as policy making is concerned is often exhibited with respect to their alleged 'softness' in labour markets. The states are seen as too beholden to labour movements to be able to 'discipline' labour or 'put a crunch on wages'. Organized labour is said to have exerted its organizational capacity to extract from the state favourable minimum wages or to force employers to 'buy peace' by paying wages above market clearing ones. To compound matters, an outstanding feature of African labour markets is the relatively high share of public sector employment in total non-agricultural employment (54.4 per cent as compared with 43.9 in developing countries as a whole). From this fact it is often concluded that the state's 'leverage' effects on domestic wage unit costs are considerable, usually in a distortionary direction (Heller and Tait, 1984).

Much of this is stated with little empirical evidence about the relationship of minimum wages to real wages or the downward rigidity of wages in African markets, or the impact of unionization on wages. The verisimilitude of this position with respect to African labour seemed particularly firm in the immediate post-independence period when removal of racial discrimination and the 'indigenization' programmes combined to push up the wages of the indigenous civil servants. However, much of this changed during the 1980s when real wages in the public sector fell dramatically, in a number of cases reversing all the earlier gains (Adesina, 1992; Lindauer et al., 1988). And in the economy as a whole, during the last fifteen years wages have been flexible downwards without any signs of renewed employment growth (Vandermoortele, 1991).

In terms of alternative stylization of labour markets we note, first, that some of the features of the labour market attributed to state policy seem to be a structural feature of capitalism in its infancy. Mosley and Williamson have observed that perhaps the most noticeable forms of inequality during early capitalist development are 'urban wage stretching, widening pay differentials, and wage gaps' (Mosley and Williamson, 1977). And contrary to expectations of a constant wage for unskilled labour suggested by the 'labour surplus' model of Lewis (1954), we find hierarchical wage structures and increasing wage rates in the presence of unemployment and labour surplus. From a research and policy point of view, the important question is: what are the mechanisms that spontaneously generate such structures, what are the social structures that accommodate, generate, exacerbate or mediate them and what are the roles of various actors – states, labour, capital – in shaping these structures?

Second, studies in the developed or developing countries suggest much more complex relationships between degrees of centralization of wage bargaining and changes in wages, wage push being least evident at the extreme ends where bargaining is either highly decentralized or highly centralized (Nelson, 1991). In a study on Kenya, House and Rempel (1976) found that the index of unionization was not able to explain the differences in interfirm unskilled labour wages. Instead they found that the 'ability to pay' and the size of the firm, together with the level of concentration, were statistically more significant. The 'ability to pay' is determined by the technology adopted by firms and by these firms' pricing policies. The capital-intensive technology diminishes the proportion of total labour costs so that increases in wages do not lead to comparable increases in average costs. The 'mark-up' pricing policies of the monopoly firms further enable the firms to make greater wage concessions in such forms as 'bonuses' and social security. Of course, the 'ability to pay' does not explain why monopoly firms do in fact pay higher wages. Here we enter an area that has given room more to speculation than to analysis. Some suggest that monopoly firms, especially the foreign ones, desire to appear as 'good citizens' (Weiss,

1966). Arthur Lewis has suggested a purely 'soulful corporation' argument to explain the high wages paid by the large monopolies when he states: 'the more powerful social conscience among capitalists causes them to wish to share the fruits of progress and limit profit ratios' (Lewis, 1966). One should also add that monopoly firms do not look at wage levels passively. Thus in the labour markets with training costs, employers may offer wages in excess of market clearing to reduce costly labour turnover (Stiglitz, 1974; Bardhan, 1991). Besides being used as instruments for obtaining the best labour and for maintaining labour stability, wages can be used as an instrument to weaken actual or potential competitors or as barriers to entry.

The point of these conjectures is that the 'distortionist view' of labour markets is based on a 'stylization' of labour markets that eschews a whole range of both theoretical and empirical material that calls for more detailed knowledge of African labour markets. The persistence of large wage differentials would seem to suggest the inappropriateness of the competitive hypothesis of wage determination and would give support to other modes such as the 'efficiency wage' models or models that take into account the technological factors, market structures and 'fair wage' considerations.

Investment policy and financial conditions

Investment, be it of firms or the state, determines the rate of accumulation. The questions of what determines decisions to invest in general, and, where foreign investors are concerned, the decisions to invest in a particular country, remain some of the great unknowns in economic theory. In conventional thinking following Say's law, it has often been simply assumed that investment equals savings. Consequently any measures that raise savings automatically raise investment. This is, of course, true *ex post*. However, for policy makers, it is the *ex ante* relationships that are most interesting and these depend on such factors as: (a) the competitiveness or performance of financial markets; (b) the structural pattern of the relationship between the distribution of the 'urge' to borrow and the distribution of 'borrowing power'; and (c) the general level of interest rates and their impact on both savings and investment (Robinson, 1964). Given the extent of 'globalization' these considerations would have to include international and domestic factors.

African financial markets are 'repressed', highly segmented and not competitive. This much is well known. However, we know little about the 'thriftiness' and the determinants of credit to or 'borrowing power' of different actors in the market. As far as the relationship between interest rates and savings is concerned, empirical evidence suggests that the assumptions of 'financial repression' are not always empirically founded. The robustness of this neoclassical theoretical arsenal has received serious challenges on both theoretical and empirical grounds. First, there is the observation that market failures are likely to be more pervasive in financial markets largely due to problems of 'imperfect information' (Stiglitz, 1993). Second, there is the fact that financial structures are embedded in industrial structures, so it should come as no surprise that in an economy such as that assumed by the alternative stylization of African accumulation processes, markets do not operate according to the neoclassical principle.

Third, with respect to interest rates there is a growing realization that their relationship to investment and therefore accumulation is more complex than suggested by the 'financial repression' doctrine – a realization that has led one of the 'fathers' of the doctrine (McKinnon) to suggest that the cure of financial repression may be worse than the disease and to argue that the 'government should probably impose a ceiling on the standard loan (and deposit) rate of interest' to avoid perverse investment patterns induced by high interest rates (McKinnon, 1988). High interest rates can adversely affect incentives and mix of applicants by way of 'Gresham's law of financial markets' in which high 'risk-loving banks drive out more prudent ones' (Stiglitz, 1993). The financial débâcles of banks in Kenya in the early 1990s are suggestive of this process in the context of financial liberalization.[6]

And finally empirical research suggests that in spite of the theoretical strength of the case against financial repression much of the empirical work attempting to show its adverse effects on saving has not been successful – low or negative real rates of return in financial assets have only a marginally significant effect on national and household savings (Giovanni, 1983; Khartala, 1993). Evidence from African countries (Ghana, Kenya, Malawi, Tanzania and Zambia) leads to similar results (Nissanke, 1990; Mwega et al., 1992).[7]

The message here is that the relationship between savings and real interest rate is at best ambiguous and that one needs a much broader understanding of the 'thriftiness conditions' prevailing in different countries. On the investment side, the privatization 'débâcle' in Africa clearly suggests how little was known about the investment policies of the private sector, the relationship between public and private investments, the 'thriftiness' propensities and the financial markets within which they operated (Mkandawire, 1994). One result that was not expected to accompany adjustment was the collapse of private investment as the contraction of the state did not induce the expected 'crowding in' of the private sector. This should have come as no surprise. The historical behaviour of the much touted 'high performers' points to the importance of 'financial repression' and the creation of state-led financial institutions as tools in industrialization (Amsden and Euh, 1993; Koo and Kim, 1992). It was partly on the basis of this understanding that many African governments set up 'development banks' that would supplement or override private capital markets and private decisions recognized to be suboptimal.[8] In the wave of liberalization, rather than improve their performance (given their generally poor performance), these institutions have simply been dismantled.

334

With respect to international finance, the writing on developing countries has tended to assume two polar opposites. One is the 'closed' Keynesian economy assumption implicit in earlier development models which has become less credible owing to the sheer weight of globalization of financial markets and the pressures to 'open' the economies imposed through various conditionalities that accompany stabilization and structural adjustment problems. The currently dominant one is that internationalization of capital has made underlying financial markets describable by the neoclassical model.

In reality, financial markets do not operate as symmetrically as is assumed. Many developing countries are often unable to attract capital, even after instituting major policy reforms that would be expected to enhance the environment for foreign investors. The 'missing markets' and the 'bandwagon effects' among private investors may effectively constrain the access of developing countries to international markets (Collins, 1992). It would seem that African countries have fallen into a 'low-income trap' in international lending in which there is no relationship existing between good policy and lending. Improvements in economic policy in this regime do not increase a country's access to the international capital market (Lensik and van Bergeijk, 1991). It should be noted, in addition, that different regions of the developing world belong to particular financial blocs. Thus while for Latin America the operative markets were in the USA with their relatively low interest rates, those for Africa were the European markets with higher interest rates.

One needs more information about an individual country's standing in international financial markets and in the risk evaluation exercises conducted by international financial institutions. Most African countries have usually simply assumed that the international institutions, under whose tutelage they are making economic reforms, are well informed about such matters and that when they impose financial reforms and promise inflows of private investment following their stamp of approval, they know what they are talking about. To the great surprise of African policy makers, the adoption of far-reaching financial reforms has not opened the doors to new capital from supposedly perfectly functioning international financial markets. Indeed, in a number of cases, the very opposite has occurred. The liberalization has simply laid the unidirectional red carpet for departing capital.

To the extent that there is evidence of credit rationing in the international financial market, evidenced partly by widely different rates of profit, there is a case that policies which affect the domestic return to investment may be more effective than is suggested by the open economy models (Epstein and Gintis, 1992).

THE STATE

In the pioneering theories of development formulated by Rosenstein-Rodan (1943), Nurske (1953), Scitovsky (1954) and Hirschman (1958) it was assumed that the markets in these countries, where they existed at all, were too thin or were characterized by all kinds of rigidities which tended to attenuate the effectiveness of the market system and indeed led to all kinds of 'market failures' which, in turn, necessitated state intervention. Given various real cases or a priori assumptions of 'market failure' in underdeveloped economies, the state was to carry out planning, circumvent or overcome structural constraints and the myopia of the market, and generally shoulder the major burden of social and economic transformation. And above all, it was to mediate the relations among its citizens and between the nation and the outside world. And so side by side with debates on economic development there was an elaborate science of 'political development' or 'modernization' which sought to identify state structures that would be supportive of development. The state was assigned an important role as the key agent of the 'modernization' of 'traditional societies' encumbered with all kinds of cultural, psychological superfluous baggage that putatively constituted 'barriers' to development.

Many factors favoured this inclination towards an interventionist state in the development process (Mkandawire, 1990). First, there was the colonial heritage. The colonial state was interventionist by definition whether this was to protect imperial interests, restrict indigenous populations or provide 'colonial welfare' as in the post World War II period. Second, there were the lessons of the Keynesian macroeconomic management of the economy which had undercut the neoclassical *laissez-faire* ideologies. This had demonstrated the need for state intervention in cases of 'market failure'. Third, there was the experience of rapid industrialization by the Soviet Union as a planned economy. Fourth, there was the historical record which suggested that 'late-industrializers' tended to have a more prominent role for the state than their predecessors (Kemp, 1983). Fifth, there was the 'mood' of the practitioners of development. Most of them were generally sympathetic to the new states and tended to view their practices either uncritically or paternalistically. And sixth, there were the statist and developmentalist ideologies of the nationalist movements which, faced with weak national private capital, saw the state as the only vehicle for ensuring the national control of the economy or initiating the development process.

In the 1970s and 1980s there was a radical shift in perception of the role of the state in development. The economic crisis of the 1970s, the demise of the theoretical armour for state intervention, the ideological hegemony of neoconservatism in key funding institutions and donor countries, the palpable failure of 'development planning' in many countries, the egregious abuse of state power by kleptocratic elites, the crisis of accumulation in the socialist countries, the changing 'mood' towards Third World countries (the Afro-pessimism, the anti-Third-Worldism, etc.), the pessimism or cynicism of the development aid establishment about the integrity of its counterparts in the recipient countries – all these pointed to 'government failure' as more insidious than the 'market failure' which state policies had purportedly been designed to correct. Once again, in pre-Keynesian fashion, the leading assumption about the economy was that normally left to themselves, markets performed smoothly and that state intervention or 'government failure' was the source of 'distortions'. The perfect competition economy was to be the benchmark against which real economies would be judged (Lal, 1983).

On the assumption of pre-existing perfectly competitive markets, the presence of the state posed particular problems relating to how one could account for such an eminently inefficient set of activities as state policies when the market was demonstrably able to sort out such things as resource allocation among classes and over space and time. In this perspective, *ex ante*, the efficiency of the market is ubiquitous and the inefficiency and non-neutrality of the state is *ex post* (Pitelis, 1991). Much of the political analysis of the African state takes this as its point of departure. The self-imposed underlying puzzle then was inevitably the 'good economics–bad politics' disjuncture. What was it in African countries that made policy makers go against what is obviously rational economic policy of relying on markets and instead pursue policies that could not but lead to ruin? Assuming, as the 'Washington consensus' suggests, that economists have correctly diagnosed the African malaise and have written out the proven prescriptions for it, why are African policy makers refusing to take the dose? Or in Bates' words: 'Why should reasonable men adopt public policies that have harmful consequences for the societies they govern?' (1981, p. 3). A considerable amount of literature has been spawned to address these questions.[9] The answers have included the personality of the leaders, the technical incompetence of bloated bureaucracies, the distributionistic proclivities of the ruling elite stemming from patrimonial-clientalistic policies, the rent seeking and corruption, etc.

Even more significant is that this approach has led to a particularly jaundiced view of the state. From being treated as a benevolent institution struggling to correct 'market failures' and generally maximizing social welfare, it became the villain in the development drama, a veritable bull in a china shop, distorting markets, creating monopolies, blunting incentives and generally being a bane on society. It constituted the unrelentingly destructive 'visible foot' under which lay the 'invisible hand' raring to go. It was now the 'rentier state', the 'kleptocratic state', the 'crony state', the 'overextended state', the 'parasitic state', the 'predatory state', the 'lame leviathan', etc. The list of epithets is long.

Studying the state became an essentially debunking exercise. Indeed if one were to identify the one factor that has marred the political analysis of African states (especially among North American scholars), it would surely be this presumption that the neoclassical characterization of African markets was essentially correct and this provides a useful point of departure for judging state policies. This leaves little room for acknowledging that there could be justifiable doubts by African policy makers as to the appropriateness of the policies suggested by international financial institutions, and that there might be legitimate grounds for state intervention. Since the analysis leaves virtually nothing useful for the state to do (except perhaps to run roughshod over local interest groups' claims), it fails to inform about conditions under which the state can play a positive role. It is essentially reduced to a minimalist role so eloquently described by Streeten (1992) since whatever it does easily falls into the category of 'rent seeking' or corruption. Cynicism about states and policy makers has become the affected stance of world-weary advisers. And yet, paradoxically, while all this is being said, a lot is expected of the dethroned state which is called upon to assume roles that are *ex deficione*, beyond its capacity or political will. It is urged to reduce itself, to stabilize the economy, to privatize the economy, to create an 'enabling environment' for the private sector, to engage in 'good governance', to democratize, service the national debt, etc. A state whose managers live off the financial windfalls of state interventionism is rather incongruously expected to implement precisely those policies which would work against their self-interests. It is as if, in a sudden feat of altruism or nationalist zeal, these same state managers were to put aside their otherwise rational pursuits of rents and implement market-friendly and therefore rent-hostile policies. This is an obviously theoretically unsatisfactory solution since it violates the much touted parsimony of the assumptions of the core model about human nature and politics as essentially greed driven.

Clearly, all the many assaults have not been able to dislodge the state from its privileged position in the development agenda, given the overwhelming evidence of the centrality of the state in 'late-developers'. Consequently, there are now discernible changes in the perception of the state and its relationship to the market – away from a 'reaction too far' (to use Killick's (1989) felicitous title) towards a more 'pragmatic' and nuanced view of the state. Part of this shift comes from the growing recognition of the failure of neoliberal solutions to generate recovery and growth in the poor countries. 'Getting prices right', which underpinned policy advice in the 1980s, has proved too simplistic and now is supposed to be accompanied by a whole series of other things including 'getting governance right'. In addition, the historical record suggests that contrary to the rather tendentious presentation of the successful cases as paragons of neoliberal economies, the true image of these cases was that their states had 'governed' the market in ways that were far removed from the orthodox interpretation of their history. The cases of South Korea and Taiwan, once paraded as examples of *laissez-faire*, have turned out to be suggestive of entirely different roles for 'developmental states' (Amsden, 1985; Applebaum and Henderson, 1992; Penrose, 1992; Putterman and Rueschemeyer, 1992; Wade, 1990; World Bank, 1993).

Theoretical developments in economics have also revived interest in some of the issues that were central to development studies. These include problems of human capital, possibilities of the state 'crowding in' private investment, market imperfections and failures, trade and economies of scale, protectionism, etc. Both the widespread acceptance of the role of private investment (local or multinational) on the one hand, and the poor response of the private sector to liberalization reforms on the other hand, have drawn attention to the need theoretically and empirically to elaborate new approaches to problems of the state, the private sector and the markets beyond simple assertions about 'rolling back the state'.

TOWARDS A RESEARCH AGENDA[10]

In this section, we suggest some research issues. The intention is not to provide an exhaustive list of priorities. Rather it is to underscore the need of broadening or refocusing the agenda back to developmental concerns and the potentially positive role the state can play, given the nature of the markets in Africa and the exigencies of accumulation.

It may be otiose to point out that each paradigm bears within it its own research agenda and protocols of evaluation of research. Its major premises determine what are the most important questions to be addressed. The neoclassical research programme has concentrated largely on 'distortions' and the static allocative losses engendered by these 'distortions'.[11] The research is now directed towards macroeconomic variables as the focus has shifted towards fiscal deficits, exchange rates, etc., presumably on the assumption that there is fundamentally nothing wrong with markets.

One of the ironies of this preponderance of the neoclassical view has been the demise of the study of African economies. This statement may seem surprising in light of the vast amount of money being devoted to economic research,[12] the work of the many peripatetic consultants and the many 'Reports' churned out by international agencies. Much of this research evolves around the stabilization and adjustment concerns as posed by the paradigm that currently informs the major funding agencies. A considerable amount of heat is generated by a rather mindless testing of models which have only a remote empirical relationship to the countries or in establishing the 'distortions' caused by state policies or in solving the self-inflicted neoclassical dilemma of reconciling the existence of an interventionist state with rapid growth or in recounting the experiences of African economies in such a way that the proffered solutions are the only ones that make sense.[13]

Learning from others

Paradigms are a prism through which the light of historical experiences is refracted. African policy makers have been reminded of the success of the

East Asian miracle countries. The lessons, filtered through the neoclassical prism, have been that these economies followed the path prescribed by neoclassical economies. There have been several responses to the evidence that the historical record tells a different tale: (a) that the state stimulated the market; (b) that state policies were so 'porous' as not to have interfered with the underlying market forces; (c) that state policies were self-cancelling so as to render overall policy neutral with respect to export or import activities; (d) that the success would have been greater without state intervention. These tortuously constructed explanations merely underline the non-falsifiability of the neoclassical account.[14]

The other argument is that *dirigisme* worked in Asia because of a number of structural and conjuctural factors that may not be replicable in Africa. These factors include the 'softness' of African states, excessive 'rent seeking' (or corruption), the greater diligence of Asians (in contrast to the indolence of Africans?), a less favourable international conjuncture which may not allow states to engage in the kind of policies pursued by the 'miracle' economies. Indeed this is essentially the gist of the 'lessons' that the World Bank has drawn for Africa from the East Asian development strategies (World Bank, 1993). But these assertions only beg the question. First, the claims about the incapacity of African countries to learn from the East Asian experience are in many ways ahistorical and simple prejudice. In any case, it is not clear why Africans should be expected to learn more easily from Washington and London than from Tokyo or Seoul. Second, even if that particular model of *dirigisme* is not replicable in Africa, this does mean that the neoliberal solution is the only alternative, assuming that it is a solution at all. It may mean that *dirigisme* would have to work on entirely different economic variables. After all there are other successful forms of *dirigisme* other than the Asian one and even the Asian form exhibits much greater differentiation than is allowed for in the stylized presentation of the East Asian experience.

It is now evident that state intervention was important in the Southeast Asian 'miracle'. However, for such an intervention to be successful, it is essential to have knowledge of how, in its 'self-regulating' mode, the market functions in a specific country or during a specific conjuncture. Implicit in this is a research agenda that would open up economic policy to 'market structure' frameworks and that would allow the modelling of the circumstances of African economies in order to be able to make prescriptions authoritatively. The advantage of such a research approach would be that it would be able to identify those 'imperfections' that can be harnessed or those that must be corrected. Policy making in South Korea suggests the importance of such an approach. Thus, recognizing the existence of 'chaebols', the state developed macroeconomic policy which gave a status to the industrial and market structure in which these 'chaebols' were basic. Indeed, in the case of Southeast Asia, the World Bank talks of the state organizing or stimulating 'contests', a much more deliberate and goal-oriented form of competition than the textbook one. On what market structures are such contests predicated? What are the risks? And what are the instruments used in such 'contests'? The neoclassical research agenda has simply obviated these questions through a talismanic chant about the efficacy of markets and the wrongheadedness of virtually any state intervention beyond that of Adam Smith's 'watchman' role.

The politics of economic strategies

Research on the politics of policy making has been frozen by the deductive approach by which it is simply asserted that certain political coalitions must exist if one can identify a set of policies which favour that coalition. By this method, politics is studied by an 'as if' approach – governments pursue policies which favour urban coalitions 'as if' such coalitions existed and were pursuing their interests and had leverage on state policies. There is no need to establish empirically the existence of such coalitions. One of the paradoxes of the 'new political economy' is that while it has brought politics back into thinking about economic policy, it has done so by negating much that is central to political science and politics in their classical sense. It has produced 'a political economy without politics' (Toye, 1987; Staniland, 1985). In its pluralistic view of a whole range of interest groups, each struggle to influence state policies, the question of power (beyond purely organizational capacity), of moral agency, of ideology, of affective relationship, etc., has been obscured.

In addition, the extreme instrumentalization of the state as merely serving the interests of rent-seeking groups has tended to ignore or downplay other roles of the state. For one, the state in many cases is engaged in the pursuit of 'national interests' which may transcend the interests of any particular or immediate interest group. Such pursuits may involve the state in ensuring the reproduction of a particular social system or the cohesion of the nation even at the expense of the immediate interests of those who will benefit most from the continuity of the system or nation. This is the case with the adoption by the state of measures that ensure its legitimacy and that of the system as a whole or provision of the infrastructure and enabling environment for accumulation in general. It is only by recognition of these roles that one can explain the existence of 'developmental states' that are engaged in the pursuit of broad accumulation goals.[15] Some of the state's motivation in carrying out these non-rent-seeking activities goes beyond the simple calculus of economics – involving nationalism, solidarity, militarism, religious fundamentalism, chauvinism, etc. These subjective aspects of politics and ideology formation need to be understood if the complexity of state behaviour is to be fully grasped. In addition, states are usually engaged in the management of conflict and wise economic policy is the one that is

341

cognisant of these realities rather than one that demands that society submit to the imperatives of an abstract economic model or prescription.[16]

Some of the most important political experiments taking place in Africa today are the attempts at democratization. A major question for Africa is this: since most of the successful *dirigiste* development strategies have been authoritarian, can Africa learn from these strategies and yet somehow sustain the current fledgling democratic thrust? Can one unpack the strategies and pick out only those elements that are compatible with democratic governance? And if not, are there other strategies that are compatible with or supportive of 'democratic developmental states'? What are the current political trajectories of African countries, what form of governance will they generate and how conducive to rapid growth will it be, and what social regime of accumulation will they spawn?

Labour markets

We noted above the importance of the stylization of labour markets in understanding accumulation regimes and processes. Banuri and Amadeo (1991) note that while it has become commonplace, in the macroeconomic literature on industrialized countries, to regard the differences in the labour market institutions as critical determinants of macroeconomic performance, 'the far greater variety of institutional arrangements in the Third World has almost entirely been neglected as an explanator of the equally divergent macroeconomic performance' (p. 171). The study of the economics of labour markets in Africa is generally quite uninformative and underdeveloped (House, 1992). Things are no better with respect to the politics and sociology of labour markets – on the organizational strength of different actors in the labour market, on the ethnic, gender or age segmentation of these markets, etc. (Adesina, 1992). Africa exhibits a wide range of labour market institutions which have different implications on the stability or even feasibility of certain policy options. Failure to understand these institutions has often led to political instability which in some cases has brought the whole process of development to a grinding halt. The suggestion for 'shock treatment' so as to get to the point of no return before political opposition has been galvanized to torpedo the reform is one instance of such myopic counse often given to African governments since it all too often ignores the prospect of 'big bang' reaction of the labour market forces hurt by these measures to seek to undo the reforms.

There are two issues to be considered in the stylization of markets. The first problem relates to how the labour market should be disaggregated. Since the 1970s, following the ILO/UNDP Mission to Kenya (ILO, 1972), the most common division of the labour market has been that between the 'formal' and 'informal' sector. Although this division has served to highlight an important aspect of segmentation of the labour markets in Africa, it has been marred by our lack of understanding of (a) the dynamic of each submarket and (b) the interaction of the two sectors. The catch-all sub-sector – the 'informal sector' – in many ways is a measure of our ignorance of labour markets in Africa.

The second problem relates to the overall characterization of African labour markets. Banuri and Amadeo (1991) suggest a qualitative taxonomy which places countries into one of four different categories or 'models' of labour market institutions in increasing order of centralization: 'decentralized', 'pluralist', 'polarized' and 'social corporatist'. It may be that African economies may generate different taxonomies. However, this can only be settled by research. After all, African labour markets have often thrown up so many puzzles that they have led to important contributions to labour market theory. Treatment of African labour markets has gravitated between African exceptionalism and the universality of the African experience. In the colonial days, the high labour turnover led to the postulation of 'backward bending supply curves', and in the post-colonial period, the persistence of rural–urban migration even in the face of increasing urban unemployment led to the Harris–Todaro (1970) thesis on expected incomes as the driving force behind decisions to migrate, while the persistence of wage differentials and unemployment led Stiglitz (1974) to the 'labour turnover' thesis about wage setting.[17] Whatever one thinks about these studies, they sought to generate models and policies based on specific reading and stylization of African labour markets.

Technology and industry

Partly because of its unwieldiness, technology has generally been assumed as 'exogenous'. Bell and Pavitt (1992) note that both the import-substitution and outward-looking or export-oriented strategies tended to assume that technological dynamism was a more or less automatic byproduct of the trade regime. Advocates of import substitution assumed that technological dynamism was inherent in the protected sector and would increase as the production structure was deepened to include capital goods. The export-oriented strategy assumed that competitive pressures would be sufficient to induce technological dynamism. Bell and Pavitt argue that both views were mistaken in assuming that trade policy, important as it is, would ensure the most efficient levels of investment and the capacity to generate technological dynamism, and conclude and urge that the policy debate explicitly address the problems of these capabilities. Although their conclusions are correct, I believe there were some important differences in attitudes towards technology policy between these two major strategies. The major countries pursuing import substitution tended to have fairly explicit policies about inducing technological transfer and dynamism. This expressed itself in the rather significant research interest in issues of technology.

With the ascendancy of neoclassical economics within key policy-making institutions, interest in technology has been removed from the primary agenda largely on the assumption of infinite possibilities of substitution ('well-behaved' production functions). And yet the whole point of the debate on technology in the development literature was that the neoclassical world of well-behaved production functions was completely unrealistic and failed to deal with problems of fixed proportions of limited choice, of discontinuities in production structures of increasing returns to scale, of monopolization of technology, etc.[18] Interest in technology in theoretical models has been revived by the 'endogenous growth' (Barros, 1993) and 'industrial policy' (Lall, 1994) literature. This literature points to the need for in-depth studies of industrial structures in Africa to identify 'winners' and 'losers' or growth-promoting industrial and technology policy, to understand industry's differentiated relation with agriculture in the process of accumulation, and to identify human resources investment and technological strategies that African nations or subregions can adopt to secure, through 'protected export promotion', a fair share in the strategic sectors of the world economy without forfeiting the gains from trade (Liang, 1992).

One should add here that important elements of technology may be inherently non-tradable. This may demand selective government intervention rather than the neutral incentive stance counselled by neoclassical economics because the welfare losses from the lack of coordination and integrated decision making with imperfect tradability under increasing returns to scale may be relatively large, in comparison with the empirical estimates of losses of misallocation under policy-induced distortions that the neoclassicals have marshalled (Bardhan, 1991). All this argues for the state explicitly to devise and implement technology and industrial policy. Or to cite Bardhan (1991, p. 62):

> If managing the local acquisition of technological capability, more than factor accumulation or allocation, is at the core of industrialisation, the catalytic role of strategic and selective intervention is imperative in information gathering, in encountering indivisibilities, in effective assimilation of new knowledge, in bargaining terms of technology agreements, in underwriting risks and raising credit, in providing marketing infrastructure, in co-ordinating rationalisation in established industries, in minimising social costs of dislocation in industrial organisation, and in general, in sailing the uncharted waters of potential dynamic comparative advantage, as the recent history of Japan and South Korea amply demonstrates.

CONCLUSION

One of the salutary contributions of the onslaught on the state by the neoliberal school has been its underscoring of the real dangers of 'government failure' and the kind of distortions or rent-seeking activities that the state intervention can engender. These warnings about 'government failure' were a useful antidote to the simplistic social engineering images of the role of the state in the development process that was inherent to much of the pioneering literature on development economics. Unfortunately, driven by ideological imperatives to roll back the state, these reminders of 'government failure' were often couched in a form that disparaged or overlooked any evidence of 'market failure' as really existing economies were judged against perfect competition models towards which the removal of state interventionism would presumably lead.

The alternative stylization of accumulation in Africa seems to us descriptively superior and provides a sturdier base for research and for 'exorcising undesirable remediable trends' within economies (Felix, 1977). Such a stylization does suggest areas in which state interventionism may, at least on theoretical grounds, be justified. There is no presumption here that to every case of 'market failure', there will be an adequate or optimal state response to compensate or correct that failure. Indeed, one can identify cases where the cure may be worse than the ailment.[19] The point here is that there is a potentially positive role of the state and that state intervention cannot be defined, a priori, as good or bad, 'developmental' or 'predatory'. Rather, its role should be tailored to its political capacity to reach a societal consensus and its technical capacity in relationship to the real economy within which it exists rather than in relationship to a misplaced abstraction. This, in turn, means a more open-ended research agenda rather than the furtive search for 'distortions' caused by the state that dominates current research.

NOTES

1 One draft of a World Bank report that circulated in the donor community was bluntly entitled 'Why Structural Adjustment Has Not Succeeded in Africa' (Elbadawi et al., 1992). That title was apparently considered too direct. And the document was published later under a much more anodine and less telling title.

2 One outcome of this has been the paralysis of state institutions and the demoralization of the local bureaucracy now stigmatized as corrupt, bloated and self-seeking and, consequently, side-stepped by international bureacrats that currently steer key ministries.

3 A good survey of these theories and their implications for developing countries is contained in Barros (1993).

4 See most specifically Rosenstein-Rodan (1943), Scitovsky (1954) and Hirschman (1958).

5 Thus Balassa (1971) argues for an export-oriented strategy on the grounds that 'exports or manufactured goods enable firms to lower costs by employing large scale production methods'. But as Toye (1989) observes: 'If one assumes, as Balassa does, significant economies of scale in a major sector of the economy, one is assuming a particular type of market imperfection. Thus market imperfection cannot be willed out of existence without self contradiction.'

6 Since writing this, a Mexican financial crisis has taken place, raising fundamental questions about the functioning of 'emerging markets'.

7 The African Development Bank (1994), in its annual report devoted to financial liberalization, notes: 'There is no empirical support for McKinnon's virtuous circle model working through the portfolio effect of growth on savings. Since total savings and investments are not positively related to interest rates, it is not surprising that the growth rates of the African countries surveyed also appear to be invariant with respect to the real rate of interest' (African Development Bank, 1994, p. 247).

8 Ironically, these are the same arguments that have been used to set up the World Bank itself.

9 See for instance the various papers in Ergas (1987), Callaghy and Ravenhill (1993), Widner (1992), Sahn (1994). See also Herbst (1993), Sandbrook (1993).

10 The inclusion of this section is not only a reflection of the author's professional engagement in organizing research in Africa and the incurable penchant always to seek out 'research issues', but also an expression of the genuine concern of one who sees major policy recommendations being made often on the basis of little knowledge about the histories of the countries, their economic, political and social dynamics, their aspirations, etc.

11 It would seem that by the lights of the neoclassical paradigm what matters is not the magnitude of these costs but their existence. How else can one explain the continuation of the research programme despite evidence that the calculated costs of these distortions are not high?

12 Economic research in Africa is today the best financed of all social science research. Special funds, subscribed to by virtually all the major donors, have been set up to build or enhance the analytical capacity of African economists and policy makers. The research is, however, highly concentrated organizationally and in terms of research direction. The favoured theme is macroeconomics narrowly understood to relate to problems of stabilization and adjustment. There are few studies on factors of growth, problems of equity, market structures or technological changes.

13 A reading of a number of 'country studies' by the World Bank often gives the impression that the authors started with a solution and then went on to reconstruct the economic history of the country being studied so that the solution becomes inevitable. The result is a certain repetitiveness of the accounts and where one knows the country concerned one cannot but be overwhelmed by a nagging feeling that one is being subjected to unrestrained tendentious reading of the economy in question.

14 The non-falsifiability of this type of analysis is most evident in the discussions of structural adjustment in African economies. If an 'adjusting' economy is not doing well by the lights of the international financial institutions then it is not adjusting enough, while if a non-adjusting country is doing well, then either its policies stimulated the market and were, therefore, superfluous, or the performance would have been higher had the economy actually adjusted. And so we have the situation in which countries are listed as 'good' or 'strong adjusters' in one report only to be dropped from the list in the next report for no apparent reason other than that their economic performance was poor in the next.

15 Judging from the literature on 'developmental states', one gets the impression that such states do not exist in Africa. Part of the problem is the tautological connotations given to the notion when used to describe states *post factum* as 'developmental states'. If a state is managing an economy that is growing then it is 'developmental', and if the economy is stagnant or declining then the state is 'non-developmental' even if the roots of the crisis are exogenous or the state self-

consciously pursues policies which are explicitly aimed at enhancing accumulation but somehow fails to yield growth for whatever reasons.

16 For a useful survey of how different societies seek to manage some of these conflicts see Banuri and Amadeo (1991).

17 It is significant that Collier (1993) identifies these insights obtained from the study of African labour markets as a major contribution that the study of African economies has made to economics as a discipline.

18 There is a revival in interest in technology in Africa but this relates more to issues of environment than accumulation processes.

19 The literature on Africa is replete with anecdotal accounts of 'white elephants' that states have created supposedly to correct 'market failures'. The wittiest and most virulent of these accounts are often written by Africans themselves.

REFERENCES

Adam, C., Cavendish, W. and Mistry, P. (1992) *Adjusting Privatisation: Case Studies from Developing Countries*, James Currey, London.

Adesina, Jimi (1992) *Labour Movements and Policy-making in Africa*, CODESRIA: Working Paper 1/1992, Dakar.

African Development Bank (1994) *African Development Report*, African Development Bank, Abidjan.

Amadeo, E. and Banuri, T. (1991) 'Worlds Within the Third World: Labour Market Institutions in Asia and Latin America', in Tarig Banuri (ed.) *Economic Liberalisation: No Panacea*, Clarendon Press, Oxford, pp. 29–55.

Amsden, A. H. (1985) 'The State and Taiwan's Economic Development', in P. Evans *et al.* (eds) *Bringing the State Back In*, Cambridge University Press, Cambridge.

Amsden, A. H. and Euh, Y. (1993) 'South Korea's 1980s Financial Reform: Goodbye Financial Repression (maybe), Hello New Institutional Restraints', *World Development*, vol. 21, no. 3.

Appelbaum, J. and Henderson, J. (eds) (1992) *States and Development in the Asian Pacific Rim*, Sage, London.

Balassa, B. (1971) 'Trade Policies in Developing Countries', *American Economic Review*, vol. 61.

Banuri, T. and Amadeo, E. (1991) 'Worlds Within the Third World: Labour Market Institutions in Asia and Latin America', in Tarig Banuri (ed.) *Economic Liberalisation: No Panacea*, Clarendon Press, Oxford.

Bardhan, P. (1991) 'Alternative Approaches to Development Economics', in H. Chenery and T. N. Srinivasan (eds) *A Handbook in Development Economics*, North-Holland, New York.

Barros, A. (1993) 'Some Implications of New Growth Theory for Economic Development', *Journal of International Development*, vol. 5, no. 5, pp. 531–558.

Bates, R. (1981), *Markets and States in Tropical Africa*, University of California Press, Berkeley and Los Angeles.

Bell, M. and Pavitt, K. (1992) 'Accumulating Technological Capability in Developing Countries', in Proceedings of the World Bank Annual Conference on Development Economics, Supplement to the *World Bank Economic Review* and *The World Bank Researcher Observer*.

Callaghy, T. and Ravenhill, T. (eds) (1993) *Hemmed In: Responses to Africa's Economic Decline*, Columbia University Press, New York.

Collier, Paul (1993) 'Africa and the Study of Economics', in R. Bates *et al.* (eds) *Africa and the Disciplines: The Contributions of Research in Africa to the Social Sciences and Humanities*, University of Chicago Press, Chicago.

Collins, S. (1992) 'Capital Flows to Developing Countries: Implications for the Economies in Transition', in Proceedings of the World Bank Annual Conference on Development Economics, Supplement to the *World Bank Economic Review* and *The World Bank Researcher Observer.*

Elbadawi, I., Ghura, D and Uwujaren, G. (1992) 'Why Structural Adjustment Has Not Succeeded in Africa', Policy Research, *Working Papers*, Transition and Macro-Adjustment, WPS 1000, Country Economics Department, World Bank, Washington, DC, October.

Epstein, G. and Gintis, H. (1992) 'International Capital Markets and the Limits of National Economic Policy', in T. Banuri and Juliet Schor (eds) *Financial Openness and National Autonomy,* Oxford, Clarendon Press.

Ergas, Z. (ed.) (1997) *The African State in Transition,* Macmillan, London.

Felix, D. (1974) 'Technological Dualism in Late Industrialisers: On Theory, History and Policy', *Journal of Economic History,* vol. 34, pp. 204–209.

—— (1977) 'The Technological Factor in Socio-Economic Dualism: Toward an Economy-of-Scale Paradigm for Development Theory', in M. Nash (ed.) *Essays on Economic Development and Cultural Change in Honour of Bert Hoselitz,* Chicago University Press, Chicago.

Freeman, R. (1992) 'Labour Market Institutions and Policies: Help or Hindrance to Economic Development', in Proceedings of the World Bank Annual Conference on Development Economics, Supplement to the *World Bank Economic Review* and *The World Bank Researcher Observer.*

Giovanni, A. (1983) 'The Interest Elasticity of Savings in Developing Countries: The Existing Evidence', *World Development,* vol. 11, no. 7, pp. 601–607.

Harris, J. R. and Todaro, M. P. (1970) 'Migration, Unemployment and Development: A Two-sector Analysis', *American Economic Review,* vol. 69, no. 1.

Helleiner, G. (1988) 'Transnational Corporations and Direct Foreign Investment', in H. Chenery and T. N. Srinivasan (eds) *Handbook of Development Economics,* Volume 2, North-Holland, Amsterdam.

Heller, Peter S. and Tait, Alan (1984) *Government Employment and Pay: Some International Comparisons,* International Monetary Fund Occasional Paper 52, Washington, DC.

Helpman, E. and Krugman, P. (1985) *Market Structure and Foreign Trade: Increasing Returns, Imperfect Competition and The International Economy,* MIT Press, Cambridge, MA.

Herbst, J. (1993) *The Politics of Reform in Ghana, 1982–1991,* University of California Press, Berkeley, CA.

Hirschman, Albert (1958) *Strategy of Economic Development,* Yale University Press, New Haven, CT.

House, W. (1992) 'Priorities for Urban Labour Market Research in Anglophone Africa', *The Journal of Development Areas,* vol. 27. pp. 49–68.

House, W. and Rempel, H. (1976) 'The Determinants of the Changes in the Structure of Wages and Employment in the Manufacturing Sector of the Kenya Economy', *Journal of Development Economics,* vol. 3.

ILO (1972) *Employment, Incomes and Equality: A Strategy for Increasing Productive Employment in Kenya,* ILO, Geneva.

Kemp, Tom (1983) *Industrialisation in the Non-Western World,* Longman, London.

Khartala, Dean (1993) 'Assessing the Impact of Interest Rates in Less Developing Countries', *World Development,* vol. 21, no. 3.

Killick, Tony (1989) *A Reaction Too Far: Economic Theory and the Role of the State in Developing Countries,* Overseas Development Institute, London.

Koo, H. and Kim, E. M. (1992) 'The Developmental State and Capital Accumulation in South Korea', in J. Appelbaum, and J. Henderson (eds) *States and Development in the Asian Pacific Rim*, Sage, London.

Krugman, Paul (1990) *Rethinking International Trade*, MIT Press, Cambridge, MA.

——(1992) 'Toward a Counter-Counterrevolution in Development Theory', in Proceedings of the World Bank Annual Conference on Development Economics. Supplement to the *World Bank Economic Review* and *The World Bank Researcher Observer*.

Lal, Deepak (1983) *The Poverty of "Development Economics"*, Institution of International Affairs, London.

Lall, S. (1994) 'Industrial Policy: The Role of Government in Promoting Industrial and Technological Development', *UNCTAD Review*, pp. 65–89.

Lall, S. and Streeten, P. (1977) *Foreign Investment, Transnationals and Developing Countries*, Macmillan, London.

Lensik, R. and van Bergeijk, P. (1991) 'The Determinants of Developing Countries' Access to the International Capital Markets', *Journal of Development Studies*, vol. 28, no. 1.

Lewis, Arthur (1966) *Development Planning*, Harper and Row.

Lewis, W. A. (1954) 'Economic Development with Unlimited Supplies of Labour', *The Manchester School*, vol. 22, no. 2; reprinted in A. N. Agarwala and S. P. Singh (eds) (1958) *The Economics of Underdevelopment*, Oxford University Press, Oxford.

Liang, N. (1992) 'Beyond Import Substitution and Export Promotion: A New Typology of Trade Strategies', *Journal of Development Studies*, vol. 28, no. 3.

Lindauer, David, Meesok, Oey and Suebsaeng, Parita (1988) 'Government Wage Policy in Africa: Some Findings and Policy Issues', *World Development Research Observer*, vol. 3, no. 1, pp. 1–25.

McKinnon, R. (1973) *Money and Capital in Economic Development*, Brookings Institution, Washington, DC.

——(1988) 'Financial Liberalisation in Retrospect: Interest Rate Policies in the LDC', in G. Ranis and T. Schults (eds) *The State of Development Economics: Progress and Perspectives*, Basil Blackwell, Oxford.

Merhav, M. (1969) *Technological Dependence, Monopoly and Growth*, Pergamon, New York.

Milgate, M. and Eatwell, J. (1983) 'Unemployment and the Market Mechanism', in John Eatwell and Murray Milgate (eds) *Keynes's Economics: The Theory of Value and Distribution*, Oxford University Press.

Mkandawire, Thandika (1990) 'The Crisis in Economic Development Theory', *Africa Development*, vol. XV, no. 3.4.

——(1994) 'The Political Economy of Privatisation in Africa', in A. Cornia and G. Helleiner (eds) *From Adjustment to Development in Africa*, Macmillan, London.

Mosley, Paul and Weeks, John (1993) 'Has Recovery Begun? Africa's Adjustment in the 1980s Revisited', *World Development*, vol. 21, no. 10.

Mosley, S. and Williamson, Jeffrey (1977) 'Class Pay Differentials and Early Capitalist Development', in Mannish Nash (ed.) *Essays on Economic Development and Cultural Change in Honour of Bert Hoselizt*, University of Chicago Press, Chicago.

Mwega, F. M., Ngola, S. M. and Mwangi, N. (1992) 'Real Interest Rates and the Mobilisation of Private Savings in Africa', AERC Research Paper No. 2.

Nelson, Joan (1991) 'Organised Labour, Politics, and Labour Market Flexibility in Developing Countries', *World Bank Research Observer*, vol 6, no. 1, pp. 37–56.

Nissanke, M. (1990) 'Mobilising Domestic Resources for African Development and Diversification: Structural Impediments in the Formal Financial System', Mimeo, Owen Elizabeth House, Oxford.

Nurske, R. (1953) *Problems of Capital Formation in Underdeveloped Countries*, Basil Blackwell, Oxford.

Penrose, Edith (1992) 'Economic Liberalism: Openness and Integration – But What Kind?', *Development Policy Review*, vol 10, no. 3.

Pitelis, C. (1991) *Market and Non-market Hierarchies: Theory of Institutional Failure*, Basil Blackwell, Oxford.

Putterman, L. and Rueschemeyer, D. (eds) (1992) *State and Market in Development: Synergy or Rivalry?*, Rienner, Boulder, CO.

Ranis, G. (1973) 'Unemployment and Factor Price Distortions', in R. Jolly *et al.* (eds) *Third World Employment: Problems and Strategy*, Penguin, London.

Riddell, Roger (1990) 'Cote D'Ivoire', in R. Riddell (ed.) *Manufacturing Africa*, James Currey, London.

Robinson, Joan (1964) 'A Model of Accumulation', in Joseph Stiglitz and Hirofumi Uzawa (eds) *Readings in the Modern Theory of Economic Growth*, MIT Press, Cambridge, MA.

Rosenstein-Rodan, P. (1943) 'Problems of Industrialisation in Eastern and South-Eastern Europe', *Economic Journal*, vol. 53, no. 2–3; reprinted in A. N. Agarwala and S. P. Singh (eds) (1958) *The Economics of Underdevelopment*, Oxford University Press, Oxford.

Sahn, D. (ed.) (1994) *Adjusting to Policy Failure in African Economies*, Cornell University Press, Ithaca, NY.

Sandbrook, R. (1993) *The Politics of Africa's Economic Stagnation*, Cambridge University Press, Cambridge.

Scitovsky (1954) 'Two Concepts of External Economies', *Journal of Political Economy*, vol. 62, no. 2.

Seidman, A. (1986) 'The Need for an Appropriate Industrial Strategy to Support Peasant Agriculture', *Journal of Modern African Studies*, vol. 24, no. 4.

Staniland, M. (1985) *What is Political Economy? A Study of Social Theory and Underdevelopment*, Yale University Press, New Haven, CT.

Stiglitz, J. (1974) 'Alternative Theories of Wage Determination: The Labour Turnover Model', *Quarterly Journal of Economics*, vol. 88, no. 2.

Stiglitz, J. E. (1993) 'The Role of the State in Financial Markets', *Proceedings of the World Bank Annual Conference on Development Economics 1993*, World Bank, Washington, DC.

Streeten, P. (1992) 'Against Minimalism', in L. Putterman and D. Rueschemeyer (eds) *State and Market in Development: Synergy or Rivalry?*' Rienner, Boulder, CO.

Taylor, L. (1991) *Income Distribution, Inflation, and Growth: Lectures on Structuralist Macroeconomic Theory*, MIT Press, Cambridge, MA.

Toye, John (1987) *Dilemmas of Development*, Basil Blackwell, Oxford.

Vaitsos, C. (1974) *Intercountry Income Distribution and Transnational Enterprises*, Clarendon Press, Oxford.

Vandermoortele, J. (1991) 'Labour Market Informalisation in Sub-Saharan Africa', in G. Standing and V. Tokman (eds) *Towards Social Adjustment: Labour Market Issues in Structural Adjustment*, International Labour Organization, Geneva.

Vernon, R. (1966) 'International Investment and International Trade in the Product Cycle', *Quarterly Journal of Economics*, vol. LXXX, no. 2, pp. 190–207.

Wade, R. (1990) *Governing Markets*, Macmillan, London.

Weede, E. (1993) 'Rent-Seeking Dependency as Explanations of Why Poor People Stay Poor', in M. Seligson and J. T. Passé–Smith, (eds) *Development and Underdevelopment*, Rienner, Boulder, CO.

Weiss, L. W. (1966) 'Concentration and Labour Earnings', *The American Economic Review*, vol. LVI.

Widner, J. (1992) (ed.) *Economic Change and Political Liberalisation in Sub-Saharan Africa*, Johns Hopkins University Press, Baltimore, MD.

World Bank (1981) *Accelerated Economic Development: An Agenda for Action*, World Bank, Washington, DC.

——(1993) *The East Asian Miracle: Economic Growth and Public Policy*, World Bank, Washington, DC.

15

ECONOMIC RESTRUCTURING, COPING STRATEGIES AND SOCIAL CHANGE

Implications for institutional development in Africa

Yusuf Bangura

INTRODUCTION

Prospects for sustainable growth and improved levels of living appear slim in most African countries as they advance into their second decade of structural adjustment. Much of the optimism that accompanied the introduction of the reforms in the 1980s has given way to profound scepticism about the correctness of the approach that has been adopted for dealing with economies like Africa's, which have weak institutional foundations, and which face increasing marginalization in the world market. Recent estimates of weighted average GDP growth rates for forty-four African countries suggest that, at best, only a modest growth of about 2.5 per cent – less than the average rate of population growth – occurred between 1980 and 1991; and that no significant differences exist between the growth rates of 1980–1985, when the programmes were in their infancy, and 1985–1991, the period when the reforms were expected to yield greater positive results. Furthermore, countries which were believed to have applied the reform measures much more comprehensively – 'the strong adjusters' – have not performed better than those which have experienced considerable slippage, the so-called 'weak adjusters' (Mosley and Weeks, 1993).

The economic crisis is, of course, very complex, as it has affected all strata and sectors of society and has been compounded, in some cases, by civil strife and environmental pressures. Despite the influence of several interlocking factors in shaping the dynamics of the crisis, concerted attempts were made in the 1980s to tackle it from a single market-oriented policy framework. During this period, African governments lost effective control over economic policy making to the international financial institutions, after having enjoyed relative autonomy in this area for only about two decades since independence from colonial rule. Estimates indicate that a total of 241 World Bank/International Monetary Fund structural adjustment programmes were initiated by African governments between 1980 and 1989 (Jespersen, 1992). By the end of the 1980s, only eight African countries had not reached an agreement with these institutions, despite the relatively strong influence of Bank/Fund ideas in their development strategies. What is responsible for the poor economic record and how can it be remedied?

When confronted with evidence of negative economic performance in countries undergoing liberalization and restructuring, the international financial institutions often blame governments for not taking the reforms seriously enough or point to the lack of political will in regulating the activities of corrupt or inefficient bureaucrats and vested interests. Once issues of 'lack of seriousness', 'political will', 'bureaucratic corruption' and 'vested interests' are raised, it means that institutional issues are at work and need to be explained if we are to understand the problems of adjustment and economic development. This chapter seeks to focus the discussion on the social and political dimensions of the economic reforms and their implications for institutional development, drawing substantially from research work on adjustment and social change sponsored by the United Nations Research Institute for Social Development (UNRISD). The institutional issues we are concerned with relate to the capacity of state systems and interest group organizations to regulate social behaviour. Institutions are important for strategies of economic development, and knowledge of changes in social relations is a prerequisite for understanding institutional reforms. We define institutions as a bundle of rules in social relations which structure behaviour in fairly predictable ways. As systems of rules and regulations, institutions are a subset of social relations. Rules are necessary for predictable transactions, but profound changes in social relations may affect ultimately the way the rules operate.

Public institutions seek to project universal rules and regulations, establish clearly defined and predictable roles for actors to facilitate routine implementation of tasks, and develop a rational structure of incentives and sanctions to ensure institutional loyalty. The main problem is that these institutional goals have been largely ineffective in most African countries since the 1980s. A standard response by policy advisers has been to exhort leaders to get tough with bureaucrats and social actors who undermine public policies: more discipline, more probes, more policing. They recommend policies aimed at restructuring the public institutions themselves through privatization, decentralization, public expenditure cuts, retrenchment and new structures of incentives to make the state leaner and fitter.

Despite efforts at implementing these draconian measures in a number of countries, the problems of low institutional capacity remain. Two key contradictions would seem to explain why institutions have been largely

353

ineffective in crisis economies in Africa: the first is the growing contradiction between the interests of bureaucratic actors and the goals they are supposed to defend, and the second is the contradiction between the institutional set-up itself and what goes on in the wider society. To understand the way these contradictions work, there is a need to look more closely at the sets of values and relationships that anchor institutions on social systems. These are concerned with issues of social cohesion and compromise, institutional socialization and loyalties, overarching sets of values, and political authority to enforce rules and regulations. The crises in these four areas of social relations, which are, in turn, linked to the ways households and groups have coped with recession and restructuring, have altered Africa's state institutions in ways that make it difficult to carry out meaningful development programmes and public sector reforms without addressing the social relations themselves.

The first part of the chapter reviews discussions on structural adjustment and institutional perspectives, highlighting why a focus on institutions and social relations is important in the study of African economies in distress. The next two sections discuss coping strategies and issues of social change, and attempt to develop a framework that links issues relating to the crisis in social relations with those associated with problems of institutionalization. The last section returns to the analytical and policy questions of institutional reform, and outlines issues that would need to be addressed in mapping out alternative strategies of development.

STRUCTURAL ADJUSTMENT, SOCIAL RELATIONS AND INSTITUTIONS

The major assumptions of neoclassical theory have been criticized from three main perspectives: their perception of individuals as self-interested utility maximizers; their undersocialized conceptions of individual behaviour in which social relations are insignificant in making choices; and their belief in the power of the market to provide individuals with accurate information to enable them to make rational decisions (Etzioni, 1990; Granovetter, 1992). Institutions play a subordinate or invisible role in these assumptions. In the context of adjustment, it was assumed by neoclassical economic theorists that trade-based beneficiaries, such as export-oriented farmers and manufacturers, would positively respond to market signals and defend the reforms without any special institutional support from the state.

Subsequent experiences with reforms in a number of countries were to cast doubt on these underinstitutionalized assumptions, leading to a host of political science studies on ways of making the reforms politically sustainable, largely through coalition-building techniques and administratively designed resource support schemes (Nelson, 1989). These approaches took the institutional context as given in analysing the social and political strategies necessary for supporting economic change. They showed how reforms could be blocked by powerful 'rent-losing' elites, including low-income urban populations, and why spatially dispersed peasant farmers could not be expected to offer effective support to the reforms, despite their situational positions as potential winners. However, the studies did not take into account ways in which livelihood responses and changes in structures of opportunities affected the institutional contexts in which strategies of resistance and pro-reform alliance politics were being pursued.

In the field of economics itself, significant efforts were under way at the same time to correct the weak institutional foundations of the neoclassical paradigm through work that focused specifically on how institutions develop as a response to solving efficiency problems (Williamson, 1985; North, 1990). The assumption that information is perfect – and that individuals not only have equal access to it but that they can make rational decisions that are unaffected by social and cultural influences – was questioned. It was pointed out that unregulated market transactions may produce chaotic outcomes because individuals have a propensity to cheat or engage in acts of wrong-doing as they struggle to secure advantages. The market, in other words, is devoid of trust and solidarity. In this new institutional economics perspective, institutions, acting through their governance structures or regulations, are seen as specifically oriented towards solving problems of opportunism and malfeasance by reducing the potentially huge costs of quality control, reliability of employees and contract enforcement that are likely to confront economic agents if they are to be engaged in repetitive open market transactions. This approach did not challenge the neoclassical assumption of rational utility maximization and its focus on the individual in explaining economic behaviour. But the emphasis it placed upon transaction costs and imperfect information, and the low efficiency scores it accorded to collective endeavours (Williamson, 1985, p. 229), with their assumed 'free-rider' problems, kindled a new wave of research on institutional constraints in economic reform. For instance, the perspective of information constraints informs some of the theoretical work on why African peasant women have been less responsive to market incentives to relocate from relatively low-paying food crop activities to high-income export crop sectors (Lockwood, 1992). Also, the generally unimpressive record of agricultural production, despite consistent efforts in raising farm prices, has encouraged fresh research initiatives on rural institutions and possibilities of promoting an NGO sector that may overcome the institutional problems of states and markets (Brett, 1993; Uphoff, 1993).

Significantly, the insights of transaction costs are also being felt in areas concerned with the reform of African state systems (Leonard, 1993; Eggartsson, 1990). The high costs of entry into national markets associated with rent-seeking activities, and the erosion of authority relations in state bureaucracies as a result of their massive penetration by private interests, could be said to have raised the costs of economic transactions in such countries and complicated the prospects for successful adjustment. Although the new institutional approach is useful in understanding how private enterprises create new organizational arrangements to overcome costs and uncertainties, it seems doubtful whether it can be applied with the same level of rigour to state sectors that are driven by a multiplicity of interests in which key decision-making actors are not always interested in promoting efficiency (Williamson, 1985; Granovetter, 1992; Bardhan, 1989). In this regard, one could interpret recent institutional reform efforts by the World Bank as an attempt to substitute World Bank staff for the perceived lack of committed individuals or social groups in pushing for efficiency in African state systems.

We have, then, the emergence of an institutional perspective that is likely to have a strong influence on development thinking and policies. This perspective, as is the case also with many public administration approaches, sees institutional arrangements as an independent variable in shaping decisions and economic behaviour. Institutional reforms can be implemented by focusing almost exclusively on the internal structures of organizations, namely those relating to contracts; the structure of incentives and sanctions in the pursuit of organizational goals; the nature of institutional hierarchies, including role allocations and supervisory mechanisms; the elimination of waste in overhead costs; and the devolution of authority to lower levels of operations. These issues are important and need to be tackled if institutions are to function properly in any social system. The persistence of institutional inefficiency in many crisis economies that have attempted such reforms underscores, however, the limitations of this approach and the need to look more closely at the social relations that govern behaviour within institutions and in the wider society.

Recent work in economic sociology offers a useful framework for analysing the links between social relations, institutions and economic behaviour (Granovetter, 1992; Portes and Sensenbrenner, 1993; Baker, 1990). Neoinstitutionalists have been criticized for their functionalist assumptions that institutions which survive are invariably the ones that are efficient, ignoring issues of power in the defence of inefficient arrangements. They have been criticized also for ignoring questions of bureaucratic inertia, in which current actors benefit from inefficiency and continue to use institutions created by their predecessors even if they are no longer effective in solving bureaucratic tasks. Granovetter points out how organizational decisions and efficiency are often influenced not so much by formal governance structures but by personal or social relations within firms; and that social relations are important in regulating economic action irrespective of whether transactions take place within organizations or in the open market, and that these social relations play a powerful role in checking opportunism and malfeasance. The key concept in this attempt to reaffirm classical sociological and political economy approaches to the study of institutions and economic development is that of embeddedness: institutions and economic actions are rooted in a complex of social relations, which ought to be studied in order to gain a rich understanding of the character of institutions and their impact on development. This is especially relevant in the case of Africa where economic contraction has revealed personal relations, traditional values and networking as crucial to survival and accumulation strategies.

ECONOMIC VULNERABILITY AND COPING STRATEGIES

Our starting point for understanding changes in Africa's social relations is the subject of coping strategies. We understand by coping strategies the ways ordinary individuals and households organize themselves to make a living. These are largely influenced by the way individuals and groups are structured in society; their cultural values, belief systems and social networks, including their ability to mobilize family resources; the skills, assets and political connections at their disposal; the types of jobs they do; their gender; and personal motivations. This range of possible determinants makes it difficult to talk about a unified response to changing opportunities, underscoring a need always to differentiate and classify individuals in as many ways as possible. Groups dependent on fixed incomes, such as industrial workers and state employees, are likely to pay much more attention to wages, social benefits and employment contracts than peasants and informal artisans, whose primary concern may be to improve market arrangements, prices, input and labour supplies, credit facilities and land availability. And employers of labour may be concerned with wage costs, social overheads, labour contracts, market opportunities and input supplies. The range of situational contexts also demonstrates a need to examine both individual and collective responses as the two are not always the same even for individuals in the same job situation and cultural milieu. Workers in export industries, whose real wages may have firmed up as result of company gains associated with devaluation, may behave differently from those in import-substituting industries, whose incomes may have fallen drastically as companies pass on part of the costs associated with devaluation to the workforce. And within both types of industries, individual workers may have different types of social networks and motivations that may influence how they respond to incentives, or the lack of them. These different sources of livelihood responses underscore the point that price stimulants may not always be decisive in influencing economic behaviour in many contexts where agents have to weigh up other considerations. Indeed, markets are always intertwined with a complex of social and political relations, producing a multiplicity of markets, rather than the idealized, abstract market found in much of the adjustment literature (Hewitt de Alcántara, 1993).

Our treatment of the issues will be largely illustrative of the complexities of coping responses as they have affected social relations. Crisis and coping strategies obviously vary among and within countries and it is difficult to make generalizations that would apply for the whole continent. For instance, in some countries where top-level salaries have not been extensively eroded, such as Côte d'Ivoire, Senegal and Togo (before the devaluation of the CFA franc), Lesotho, Swaziland and Zimbabwe, formal sector employees have not faced the same kinds of pressures for income diversification as their counterparts in other countries, although new formal employment opportunities seem to have dried up. Strategies of groups in farming sectors and informal enterprises also vary across and within countries to render generalizations difficult. They may vary, for instance, between countries with relatively large-scale plantation or capitalist agriculture, such as Kenya, Zambia and Zimbabwe, and those with predominantly peasant producers, such as Sierra Leone, Tanzania and Uganda. There may also be differences in coping strategies among different sets of farmers in semi-arid countries of the Sahel and those in countries where the land frontier has not been exhausted, such as Angola, Cameroon, Guinea, Sierra Leone and Zaire. We make no attempt, however, to carry out a detailed desegregated country analysis as our main objective is to capture general trends, which may be present to varying degrees in most countries.

The key coping strategy we seek to highlight relates to changes in the portfolio of income-generating activities, otherwise called *multiple survival strategies*. This refers to the tendency of agents or households to diversify sources of income as single activities prove insufficient to sustain livelihoods. Diversification strategies include migration, subsistence, remunerative work on commission or wage basis, and self-employment in farming and urban informal activities. They involve participation in a range of economic activities and social networks, and the balancing of individual and collective interests in ways that challenge conventional rules and relationships. The dramatic increase in such strategies in the 1980s stems from economic vulnerability and declining levels of expectations, and affects all income groups, including business entrepreneurs. For wage sector groups, sharp declines in real wages and social benefits, growing casualization of the workforce, periodic compulsory leaves and threats of unemployment act as catalysts to diversify employment and income sources. For peasant farmers, problems of food security related to rising inflation, shortages, ecological problems and input/infrastructural costs continue to act as pressures to diversify cropping systems and to resort to or expand off-farm operations. For informal sector artisans, large migrations of formal sector workers into the informal sector have increased competition and added pressures to diversify operations. And for many industrialists, market uncertainties, high interest rates, rising import costs and shortages of raw materials have led to new accumulation strategies involving informalization of some production activities and work relations. In order to grasp the range of situational contexts among different types of groups, we examine the dynamics of these processes in three key areas: the farming, informal and urban labouring sectors.

No single pattern of adjustment has emerged in the farming sector, given the varieties of pre-reform development strategies across countries, the different ways in which market policies were implemented in the agricultural sector, and the differing cropping systems and climatic conditions (Meagher, 1991; Gibbon et al., 1993; Mosley and Smith, 1989; Demery and Addison, 1987). Farmers in export sectors where markets have been liberalized seem to have done better than those in food crop sectors, although both have been seriously hit by rising input costs associated with subsidy withdrawal, devaluation and erosion of infrastructural and technical support. An UNRISD study provides evidence of rising incomes and revived accumulation among all categories of farmers in the Nigerian cocoa economy, even though prospects for sustainability may be undermined by continued low international prices and demand, escalating input costs, ageing trees and ecological problems (Mustapha, 1992). Similar conclusions have been reached for cocoa farmers in Ghana, who were among the early beneficiaries of structural adjustment but whose real incomes have fallen in recent years as a result of setbacks in world demand and prices, and increased production costs (Sarris and Shams, 1991; Jacobeit, 1991). In countries where export crop marketing arrangements have not been fully liberalized, as in Tanzania, gains associated with the reforms have been concentrated in the less regulated food crop sector, although studies suggest strong favourable weather conditions, availability of consumer goods and possibly lower opportunities in off-farm activities as among the major reasons for the improvement (Havnevik, 1993; Gibbon et al., 1993). Farmers in countries where there has been some diversification from controlled staple food crops (such as maize in Zambia) to export crops such as wheat, soyabeans, cotton and horticultural products, seem also to have done relatively better than those in regulated food crop sectors – who are often smallholders.

As most of the gains in agriculture are associated with the export sector, it is worth stressing the point that export crop farmers constitute a minority in most farming populations in Africa. This is the case even in countries with a long history of export crop development, such as Nigeria and Ghana, where it is reckoned that about 80 per cent of the farmers are either food or non-export crop producers (Meagher, 1991; Weissman, 1990; Pearce, 1992; Sarris and Shams, 1991). Furthermore, a substantial percentage of smallholders, in some countries rising up to 50 per cent or more, are net food buyers, and their levels of living have been negatively affected by upward adjustments in food prices (Meagher, 1991; Pearce, 1992; Loxley, 1990). An empirical study in two northern Nigerian villages shows the extreme vulnerability of smallholders to price changes. Because of storage and income constraints, smallholders are forced to sell their products early when prices are low and to buy their food requirements late when prices are likely to be very high (Meagher, 1991). There are reports of land pledging and crop mortgaging by smallholders to rich farmers, because the latter have the financial resources and storage facilities to support large-scale production.

Economic pressures on smallholders have reinforced, therefore, the multiple survival strategies that were already an integral part of farming life in most food crop sectors in Africa. Concerns for food security have also acted as a constraint on high-income farmers who would have preferred to specialize exclusively on export crops (Mustapha, 1993; Berry, 1985). Data for Tanzania indicate that about 25 per cent of smallholders' income is derived from off-farm work (Sahn and Sarris, 1991; Havnevik, 1993). Nigerian smallholders earn more than half of their incomes from off-farm activities, with the figure rising to between 60 and 85 per cent in some food-deficit areas. Many such farmers use incomes earned from off-farm activities to procure basic inputs for their farming activities. Even in the export sector, where nominal incomes have been very high, about 25 per cent of all categories of farmers continue to depend on off-farm incomes for survival and accumulation (Mustapha, 1993). The choice of off-farm activities is a function of social differentiation and gender differences, with smallholders concentrating on the increasingly competitive lower ends of informal activities such as hawking, load carrying, wood collecting, weaving and barbing services; and rich peasants focusing on more remunerative activities requiring higher levels of skills, risk taking and capital: repair work, tailoring, cross-border produce trade and medium-level commerce (Meagher, 1991; Mustapha, 1992). Women of all categories are reported to be worse off in diversification strategies because of traditional household responsibilities, inequalities in land ownership and rights, differential access to labour, and gender ideologies discouraging participation in some of the high-paying off-farm jobs.

A similar pattern of diversification and differential response to economic vulnerability can be observed in the rapidly expanding informal sector. Neoliberal theory is less categorical about the positive effects of market reforms on the informal sector given the differentiated character of informal enterprises, particularly as they relate to input and output product use. However, adjustment policy itself treats the informal sector in more positive terms because of political imperatives of resettling retrenched workers in remunerated work (World Bank, 1989). Several UNRISD studies of informal sector coping strategies in Nigeria and Zambia underscore the highly differentiated character of informal enterprises and the varied forms of multiple income-generating strategies. Enterprises involving high levels of skills or capital outlays – such as transportation, metal fabrication, small-scale manufacturing, tailoring and photography – have been relatively shielded from competition, and their owners seem to be making substantial profits. A study on small-scale manufacturing enterprises in eastern Nigeria records new investments in land and equipment and rising levels of incomes among most operators (Dike, 1992). Studies on successful informal enterprises indicate that most entrepreneurs had bought their operating machines before the reforms. They have also developed networks of social support, such as the pooling of resources for electricity generation and transportation of commodities, mechanisms for extending credit facilities to members, and solidarity support in situations of harassment by local governments or the police. The rising costs of imported goods associated with devaluation and a search for local alternatives by consumers have also contributed to their success. Middle-class groups, whose living standards have been eroded, are reported in most countries to be entering the informal sector on a large scale. These groups often have the better education, technical skills and political connections which are useful in establishing flourishing enterprises. In Zambia and Nigeria they have taken advantage of special credit facilities allocated to the informal sector to launch more sophisticated services for middle-class consumers, many of whom had previously patronized traditional informal agents who now lack the resources to operate such services or to upgrade them to meet changing middle-class tastes (Meagher and Bello-Mohammed, 1993; Chiwele, 1993). Even for this category of better-off informal agents, however, there are serious supply and demand constraints relating to declines in national incomes and rising costs of raw materials and capital equipment which are likely to affect profits in the long run.

Much of the competition and stress in the informal sector is concentrated at the lower end of operations, where incomes are generally low, and activities are oriented mainly towards survival. Most informal sector agents are trapped at this basic level of survival. A Nigerian study records trends towards new forms of ownership relations emerging as a result of pressures on low-income groups. Low-income agents are being transformed into commission workers, and there is an emerging patron–client network between small-scale informals and more successful service agents, organized around the use of high-cost equipment and technical knowledge (Meagher and Bello-Mohammed, 1993). The majority of informal sector agents are under pressure, therefore, to diversify their sources of income. Estimates for the Nigerian town of Zaria indicate that 67 per cent of low-income informals are engaged in at least a second low-income activity, such as farming or petty trading (Meagher and Bello-Mohammed, 1993). The data suggest that some low-income informals who had in the past combined farming with informal sector work are being forced by competition and lack of operating capital to revert back to subsistence farming. Roughly half of high-income entrepreneurs in the Zaria study pursue at least one secondary activity. The pursuit of multiple activities is more prevalent in the more lucrative informal small-scale manufacturing sector in eastern Nigeria, where diversification of investment tends to be the norm. The data suggest that most entrepreneurs are anxious to spread their risks because of uncertainties in the economic environment. In the Nigerian towns of Aba and Nnewi, 60 per cent of the entrepreneurs sampled have diversified their investments into farming, trading, transport, real estate, restaurant services and land purchases – all high-income activities (Dike, 1992).

Household strategies have been central to the diversification of income sources among all groups. In this case, diversification involves not just the expansion of the activities of an entrepreneur, but also those of other members of his or her household, including spouses, children and dependants. Historically, female participation in remunerated work was relatively low in East and southern Africa, as compared with West Africa, where the informal sector, and women's participation in it, was central to the subsidizing of industrial wages. Zambian national household survey data indicate a rapid increase in female participation in informal sector activities, from 46 per cent in 1980 to 57 per cent in 1986, and a ninefold increase in the 12–14 year age group working in the informal sector for the same period (Chiwele, 1993). Women in Zambia tend to concentrate on a range of low-income activities, such as selling street food and collecting vegetables, which do not provide a basis for savings and enrichment. The Zaria study also indicates an increase in the proportion of women doing low-income informal jobs, including Islamic women in seclusion, who increasingly are being employed to do tedious jobs like traditional cap and gown cleaning for very low monetary returns (Meagher, 1991). However, informal women's groups in the south of Nigeria have been engaged in relatively high-income trading activities involving, in some cases, long-distance trade within and out of the country, lucrative fashion design and restaurant services. The Zaria study provides interesting evidence on correlations between household size, number of incomes per household and income strategies of different groups. Low-income informal households with an average household size of 8.5 are reported to have raised their average number of incomes by 55 per cent since the reform programme started. Commercial groups, with an average of 12.1 household members, have raised household incomes by 75 per cent. Formal wage-earning groups with an average household size of 10.3 have increased their average number of incomes by 56 per cent. By contrast, the high-income informal households with the lowest average household size (6.2) have increased their average number of incomes by only 36 per cent, indicating an intensive income maximization strategy.

It is among the industrial labouring classes that the phenomenon of multiple coping strategies has been most dramatic, given workers' attempts in the pre-crisis period to pursue a strategy of defending a 'living wage'.

Studies on Nigerian labour highlight a progressive proletarianization of the workforce in the period of the oil boom, when, as a result of increases in real wages, workers began to settle down to a life of full proletarians and disengage from strategies involving straddling factory work and farming/ petty trading activities (Mustapha, 1992; Lubeck, 1986). Zambian studies confirm a similar picture, where the copper boom of the 1960s and early 1970s strengthened the trade union movement, which was able to protect real wages and social benefits, giving rise to a high level of urban family dependence on the wage (Chiwele, 1993; Simutanyi, 1993; Bates, 1971; Jamal, 1993). The co-optation into government of the trade union movement in countries like Côte d'Ivoire, Senegal, Tanzania and Cameroon has been linked to state/private sector commitments to pay survival wages and salaries. Indeed, the gains made by industrial workers in wages and social benefits in the early period of independence were seen by reform advocates as having resulted in a 'labour aristocracy'. In the eyes of such advocates, such an aristocracy constituted a legitimate target of attack in reversing rural–urban terms of trade (Bates, 1981; World Bank, 1981; Jamal, 1993; Bangura and Beckman, 1991).

Recent ILO studies on African employment and incomes collected in the *African Employment Report* indicate that many of these assumed advantages were seriously reversed in the 1980s. In one study of twenty-eight countries for which data were available, twenty-seven showed considerable declines in real wages (30 per cent on average) in the 1980s. The real minimum wage fell by 20 per cent during the same period. Public sector wages fell faster than those in the private sector (ILO-JASPA, 1990). The share of wages and salaries in total public expenditure declined by about 14 per cent in a period of just over seven years during the 1980s (Robinson, 1990). Furthermore, there has been a sharp trend towards a compression of salaries and wages in a number of countries as wages lose their significance in the political economy. The study by ILO-JASPA of real starting salaries found that they fell in all fourteen countries surveyed, and that the lowest and highest grades narrowed considerably over a ten-year period in eleven out of seventeen seventeen countries surveyed (ILO-JASPA, 1990, pp. 35–36). Unemployment data for eleven countries, with roughly 60 per cent of the sub-Saharan population, average about 20 per cent; and the proportion of formal wage employees has drastically declined in relation to both the urban and national labour force (Jamal, 1993). Estimates for Sierra Leone, Tanzania and Zambia indicate that wage employees now constitute on average only about 16 per cent of the urban labour force (Jamal, 1993). Formal wage employees are not only a minority even in a highly urbanized country like Zambia, but the incomes and social benefits that accrue to them have dropped dramatically; annual incomes in many countries are hardly sufficient to support one or two weeks of subsistence (Chew, 1990). On top of this, workers have been made the victims of management strategies of casualization that have become prevalent among a number of private industries which seek to reduce their overhead costs, or match labour costs to the availability of raw materials and spare parts (Olukoshi, 1992; Abdullah, 1991; Simutanyi, 1993; Andrae and Beckman, 1985; Bangura and Beckman, 1991).

Wage employees have thus invaded the informal and farming sectors to a significant extent. Their response to the crisis constitutes the most significant source of competition to traditional low-income informals because of the lines of activities wage employees get drawn into: urban farming, petty trading, small-scale transportation, load carrying, food vending and repair work. Many of their farming activities are for subsistence and seem to be done mostly by workers in cities that are surrounded by farm land. Transport costs act as barriers to any meaningful form of rural farming. Skilled workers, such as those in vehicle assembly plants and those handling electrical, welding, plumbing, repair and typing activities, have been able to combine formal employment with part-time work involving the application of their skills. Successful workers in these trades have opted to forgo overtime or weekend work in order to maximize the time spent in private businesses. In some cases, this has led to conflicts with management, especially during peak periods when employers are keen to make full use of their workers' labour time. Some studies indicate an increase in the diversion of labour time and equipment to private work and a rise in industrial cases relating to dismissals (Simutanyi, 1993; Mukandala, 1994). In some cases, staying on a job is much more important than receiving the wage that goes with the job, since the job may allow a worker to use enterprise facilities, access resources or build contacts. Absenteeism and shirking are more prevalent among public sector workers than private sector ones because of more stringent monitoring in the latter. However, high rates of casualization in the private sector exert pressures on private sector workers to pursue alternative options in the informal sector. Because of their low educational backgrounds and overwhelming location on the production line, doing work that does not require any special type of skills, women have experienced higher levels of retrenchment than men in the private sector enterprises that have been studied. Their subordinate positions in industry and low levels of participation in trade unions have further increased their vulnerability in the period of crisis. Data from a Nigerian study capture these trends, and indicate that despite the growing proletarian consciousness among sections of female workers, more than 40 per cent of them still look forward to relocating fully to the informal sector where they believe they will be in control of their own lives and businesses (Abdullah, 1991).

These fundamental shifts in African coping strategies have been the subject of some theorizing in the adjustment literature in recent years, with Jamal's being among the most perceptive (Jamal, 1993; Jamal and Weeks, 1993). Jamal links Africa's failure to conform to orthodox prescriptions of adjustment with changes in the structure of its labour market: rural activities have become fused with urban ones within African extended family systems, thus immunizing both rural and urban households from the anticipated shocks of price changes. The implication of this argument is that urban workers no longer behave differently from their rural counterparts, as they both produce the same kinds of goods and services. Therefore, the terms of trade which the reform programmes have sought to correct have been internalized within extended family households who straddle rural–urban and formal–informal divisions. The two classic divisions that formed the basis for theorizing how groups and households are likely to benefit or lose from adjustment have thus become meaningless. This view is perceptive, and in some ways original. It no doubt aids our understanding of what could happen to Africa's economies if the majority of its households in urban and rural areas were exposed to the same types of employment activities and incomes. But the main question is whether this has happened to the extent suggested by Jamal's analysis. There is a tendency to assume an equalization of opportunities across households. The analysis does not take into account the profound levels of differentiation among groups engaged in multiple income activities, including the unequal ways incomes and responsibilities are distributed within – often very large – extended family households. One implication of this lack of emphasis on social differences is a tendency to underplay some of the negative effects of price changes on large sections of the urban and rural poor, and to assume implicitly that multiple survival strategies effectively cushion households from the adverse effects of adjustment. This does not capture the problems of localization, reduced consumption of goods and services, and the desperate resort to subsistence forms of livelihood that are often associated with the strategies of marginal groups. The UNRISD studies demonstrate some of these differences in group and household responses to the changes in incentives, even when employment patterns appear to be similar among groups.

COPING STRATEGIES AND CHANGES IN SOCIAL RELATIONS

What changes in social relations have been associated with the coping strategies outlined above? Here we focus mainly on the broad processes of change necessary for defining the parameters of the institutional crisis. We structure the discussion along four main themes: social polarization; multiple social identities; truncated modernization; and stalemates in the configurations of political power. Social polarization refers to key divisions that have emerged in social relations which act as constraints on efforts to promote social compromise. Polarization weakens attempts to nurture a middle ground, including 'middle-class' support groups, whose preoccupations can be identified with the pursuit of moderation and compromise.

Multiple identities refer to changes that have occurred in the values of individuals located in multiple work situations that are likely to influence institutional regulations and loyalties. Their proliferation tends to undermine efforts aimed at socializing agents in the governance structures of institutions, leading to employee indifference or sabotage of rules. Truncated modernization deals with the breakdown of the post-colonial project of development, including its underlying assumptions and values. It expresses itself in an expansion of traditional and informal practices. In institutional terms, it reflects a crisis of the overarching norms and values that are necessary for making formal rules effective in regulating employee behaviour and system-wide transactions. Furthermore, changes in the configurations of power highlight ways in which structures of power affect coalition-building strategies, institutional performance and policy implementation. These deal with the key question of political authority, whose absence in society may expose institutions to perennial conflicts and fragmented interests and loyalties.

Social polarization

The complex ways social groups and households have responded to the crisis and reforms have sharpened old social divisions and introduced new forms of polarization. These include a widening of differentials in incomes and standards of living between major reform beneficiaries and the rest of the population; divisions and conflicts within and among beneficiary groups and losers; a weakening of rural–urban relationships; and increasing inequalities among ethnic groups and regions. The first type of polarization deals with the levelling-down process that has accompanied the crisis and the pursuit of fragmented income strategies. The case studies demonstrate that this levelling-down process has affected all sectors and social groups, even if some groups have done better than others and have profited from the general decline. Among those who have done exceptionally well are small groups of individuals with secure access to foreign exchange, through either the influence they exert on state institutions or the control they wield over transactions involving the export of commodities such as precious minerals, timber products, agricultural and manufactured goods, drugs, currencies, etc. (Mustapha, 1993; Meagher, 1991; Chachaga, 1993; Mamdani, 1991). These are very diverse groups and are involved in a complex of transactions straddling the boundaries of legality and illegality. They should be distinguished from the rest of the population, including some categories of farmers, workers and informal entrepreneurs who, as we have seen, have also benefited from the reforms as a result of their association with some of these thriving sectors, but whose locations in such businesses do not allow them to capture most of the benefits. The latter groups are confronted with problems of rising costs which continue to act as pressures on profit margins and wages.

At a general level of conceptualization, one can lump these relatively better off groups with the mass of urban and rural groups which have experienced distinctly downward pressures in their standards of living. It would seem necessary also to include in this general category large sections of the middle class who currently constitute a 'new poor'. A defining characteristic of the coping strategies of all these groups is the *drastic* cutbacks they have made on their household expenditures, their resort to cheap and inferior-quality goods and services, and their pursuit of subsistence strategies for a number of commodities they previously purchased from the market. One of the best ways to capture this first level of polarization would be through data on national income distribution, but such data are unavailable for most crisis economies. In any case, even if such data were available, there still would be problems with their reliability given the informal and in some cases illicit ways high incomes are currently being earned, which national statistical systems may not be able to cover adequately. Some multilateral agencies involved in the study of long-term trends in development indicators believe that more than half of the continent's population now lives in absolute poverty, and that the incomes of two-thirds of the total labour force may have fallen below the poverty line in the 1980s (UNDP, 1990; World Bank, 1990).

This polarization is obviously the most important when considering issues of social compromise at the national level. Societies which are highly polarized in economic terms, with small or stagnating middle-income groups, find it difficult to embark on successful growth strategies, or to construct national institutions that command the loyalty of their citizens. Such groups may be too busy trying to survive the crisis and in some cases may, in fact, provide a rallying point to disaffected groups with chauvinistic political objectives. The successful growth strategies of East Asia, for instance, have partly been linked to the existence of a stable and economically secure middle-class and improvements in earnings and social services by low-income groups. Effective strategies of institution building should include, therefore, policies specifically aimed at rebuilding the middle ground and narrowing polarization. This polarization, important as it is, does not capture, however, other types of divisions that may be relevant for understanding the problems of social compromise, especially as they relate to the workplace. Our case studies and published literature suggest that patterns of divisions have emerged or deepened within each broad social category, whether it is workers, farmers, informals, business groups or the middle classes. In the case of workers, for example, those in export industries, or in firms that have been able to generate a higher percentage of their raw materials from local sources (such as textiles, breweries, plastics), or those in extractive industries earning foreign exchange, have generally done better in defending wages, employment levels and social benefits than those in import-substitution industries and the public service, which

367

increasingly face high import costs that cannot be offset by foreign exchange earnings.

This has tended to affect the dynamics of labour relations and union politics, including attempts to define common union responses or solidarity in the context of the crisis. In the case of Nigeria, for instance, changes in market opportunities have strengthened unions in export-oriented industries within the national labour movement. Unionists in weaker sectors seek affiliation to relatively more successful unions. This has led to conflicts among trade unionists within some of the not-so-successful unions in the debate over union restructuring. Furthermore, economically successful unions increasingly play mediating roles in the internal affairs of financially constrained ones. In the case of textiles in particular, which have benefited from rising export sales to neighbouring CFA currency countries, unionists have demonstrated a good record in defending workers' interests in the face of a general decline in the national real wage and employment opportunities and have come under pressure from workers in vulnerable companies for assistance in seeking employment in thriving industries. In Zambia, the Union of Mine Workers has always enjoyed a formidable presence on the Zambian labour scene because of the strategic location of the copper mines in the national economy. In recent months, it has supported management pressures for a general depreciation of the Zambian kwacha in order that salaries of workers could be paid – much to the discomfort of unions in import-substitution industries, whose workers are rapidly losing their jobs as a result of high import costs associated with the depreciation of the value of the national currency.

The deepening of intra-group divisions can also be observed in the informal sector. As many individuals get pushed into the informal economy, socioeconomic divisions there become sharp. As we have seen, a relatively small group of informal entrepreneurs, with technical skills, capital assets and, in some cases, political connections, has been successful in exploiting new market opportunities, whereas the bulk of informal agents face very stiff competition in activities that can only guarantee the most basic form of survival. A general trend is for successful enterprises to employ family as opposed to wage labour (Meagher and Bello-Mohammed, 1993; Dike, 1992; Chiwele, 1993) and for middle-class individuals to out-compete traditional informals in using state-subsidized credits that have been targeted at the informal sector. This has led to what Meagher and Bello-Mohammed refer to as a recomposition, as opposed to an equitable expansion, of the informal sector. Attempts to nurture and sustain work-based unions in the informal sector have faced serious constraints as a result of increasingly conflicting interests among agents in the same trade. Vulnerable agents have been less than enthusiastic about participating in such unions, which have attempted to maintain standard regulations in business practices. Hawkers in Zambia, for instance, defy pressures from more established traders and the government to restrict their trading activities to established trading zones (Chiwele, 1993). More than a third of informal entrepreneurs in Zaria are reported to have withdrawn from unions formed in mechanical, metal work and carpentry activities in the 1980s (Meagher and Bello-Mohammed, 1993). In some cases, such as hairdressing activities, unionists had to mobilize local governments to get members to register with the unions. Small operators, concerned basically with survival, prefer the option of autonomy to union rule fixing; whereas large operators are worried about standards and prices, which they suspect the small operators are subverting. In Zarias informal sector as a whole, only about 8 per cent of entrepreneurs continue to participate in work-based unions. Instead, there is a proliferation of ethnic-based unions, which focus on a number of welfare issues like burials, naming ceremonies and credit facilities.

Similar trends in polarization have been observed in the rural economy, where income differentials stemming from unequal access to labour, land, credits and inputs are widening between rich peasants and smallholders, particularly those in food-deficit areas, and between women and men. Such divisions take on an added dimension when we consider the plight of smallholders in food-deficit areas and rich farmers in export zones where incomes have been high (Sarris and Shams, 1991; Pearce, 1992; Weissman, 1990); or the divergence between sharecroppers and farm owners in the cocoa economy over control of the economic surplus and the distribution of farming responsibilities and input costs (Mustapha, 1992). Sharp divisions are also emerging among professionals, academics and bureaucrats as a result of the highly unequal ways individual members within each category have penetrated state institutions as well as the links they have nurtured with transnational organizations and activities involving travel, consultancy and networking. The effectiveness of professional associations has been affected by these developments (Bangura, 1994).

These two types of polarization have affected both ethnic relations and rural–urban configurations in a number of countries, further sharpening divisions in those areas. To start with, as social groups were already unevenly structured in most countries, the unequal distribution of adjustment-related costs and benefits has exacerbated ethnic and regional differences. Successful export crop zones often belong to specific ethnic groups as is the case with cocoa in Ghana and Nigeria, where northern groups hardly produce export commodities following the collapse of the groundnuts economy and the diversion of cotton products to domestic use in textile factories. Some of the ethnic conflicts in Nigeria have centred around issues of who has rights of participation and ownership in the cocoa industry, and have affected the privatization programme in that sector (Mustapha, 1992). Also, export industries may be located in specific regions and may employ a high proportion of workers from local areas as is the case with the Bemba in the copper mines of Zambia, riverine ethnic minorities in Nigeria's oil-producing states, and Ashantis in Ghana's gold mines. During periods of economic uncertainties, groups from regions where such industries are sited attempt to maintain their monopoly in the labour market or increase pressures on national policy makers to raise revenues allocated to such regions. Militant protests for a greater share of national revenue by those who live in areas where most of the national revenue is derived have been particularly sharp in the oil-producing riverine communities of Nigeria in recent years. This has led to a deployment of federal government troops to quell the protests and considerable loss of life in local populations. The most dramatic case has been that of the Ogoni people's demand in Rivers state for a greater share of the oil revenues to protect threatened livelihoods and the repressive way the government has handled their demands.

Also, some ethnic groups have had an historic advantage over others in nurturing certain types of skills and capital which are essential in taking advantage of changing structures of incentives. The dominance of Igbos in the distribution of auto-mechanic parts in all major Nigerian towns, Yorubas and Igbos in the taxi/long-distance bus service, Hausas in city bus services and in informal currency transactions, are cases in point. Many of the religious and ethnic conflicts that have taken place in northern Nigeria in recent years could be linked partly to shifts in opportunities associated with economic differentials arising from job specialization along ethnic lines. The dominance of individuals from the Middle Belt and the South in middle and lower sections of the formal sector, including middle-level enterprises, in prominent northern cities is a source of conflict between these groups and the Hausa/Fulani; as is the belief by elites from the Middle Belt that Hausa/Fulanis dominate the top echelons of most public sector establishments. The narrowing of opportunities following the collapse of oil revenues has tended to deepen hostilities. Some ethnic groups develop tightly knit networks of solidarity to dominate particular lines of economic activity and make it difficult for outsiders to gain entry and remain sustainable. This is often the source of many conflicts, as those who feel excluded or disadvantaged activate latent hatreds among their communities. This may lead to periodic violence and feelings of insecurity among their competitors, especially if the latter constitute a minority in the contested zones. The tensions that have erupted recently between ethnic groups in the mainland of Tanzania and those in Pemba and Zanzibar are linked partly to mainland fears of alleged Zanzibari domination of Tanzanian politics, following the accession of a Zanzibari to the presidency, and the belief that this group has used the institutions of the state to gain advantages in economic activities. These allegations have also been levelled against the Asian business community, which is generally seen as the main beneficiary of liberalization (Booth, 1990), given the advantages it enjoyed in commerce during the pre-adjustment period. Some African elites, who dominate the bureaucracy, complain that the previous socialist development strategy prevented Africans from using the state sector to accumulate capital, and that Africans are therefore disadvantaged in current efforts to privatize the parastatals.

Rural–urban divisions have also tended to sharpen even though reformers had expected some reverse migration to rural areas following the dramatic changes in rural–urban terms of trade. Rates of urbanization have definitely slowed down for some countries in recent years, but for many others internal strife and environmental degradation have pushed many people to urban areas and complicated the picture of urbanization. Ghana's census suggests that rural–rural migration tended to be much more pronounced in the 1980s than rural–urban migration; and in Zambia there are indications of a slowing down of the rate of growth of the urban population, already very large by African standards, vis-à-vis the rural growth rate (Chiwele, 1993). Surely, there have been small-scale remigrations to rural areas as part of long-standing traditional strategies of urban dwellers aspiring to retire to the village or cultivating rural relationships that would be useful for other social and political objectives. Researchers report such special cases, but do not find any new strategies involving a massive reorientation of economic activities by urban households towards the rural sector or of plans for relocation to that sector. Where reverse migration has occurred on a massive scale, as in the case of the Ghana returnees resettlement scheme in the 1980s, evidence suggests that most of those resettled in rural agricultural schemes have found their way back to urban areas (Dei, 1993). Urban families have responded to the food crisis and price changes not by going back to the village, but by growing their own food in the cities. Most workers may find it difficult to pursue any viable large-scale farming activity in rural areas because of low incomes and rising input costs, and the economic and social problems smallholders face in the villages are well known to urban dwellers. Private firms concerned with rising import costs of raw materials, such as textiles, breweries, and beverage and cigarette companies have been active, of course, in strategies of backward integration, which involve direct farming or investing in peasant farming activities for industrial use (Andrae and Beckman, 1985). Some companies and private individuals have also invested in agricultural trade, particularly export crops, and research indicates conflicts of interest between these external actors who are interested in quick profits in foreign exchange, and peasant producers who are concerned with protecting the gains of liberalization (Mustapha, 1992).

Studies also indicate that rural–urban ties are weakening in a number of other ways. High transport costs have drastically reduced the number and frequency of visits to rural areas and vice versa, even including those for social ceremonies like burials, marriages and festivals which were traditionally seen as important occasions to renew or consolidate ties with rural/townsfolk. A Zambian study of informal sector traders indicates that the latter have opted instead to strengthen social relations in the market place in order to be able to fulfil these social obligations in burials and marriages (Chiwele, 1993). A number of case studies also suggest that remittances from urban to rural families through the extended family system, which in the past were important in procuring inputs for agricultural production, are in serious decline (Meagher, 1991; Chiwele, 1993; Simutanyi, 1993; Mushota, 1993; Meagher and Bello-Mohammed, 1993). Urban families can no longer afford to make such payments. The circulatory patterns of rural–urban labour migration seem also to have been negatively affected by the crisis and the decline in opportunities for those trapped at the lower end of the informal sector. Many small-scale farmers used to raise part of the capital for the purchase of farm inputs by working in informal urban sectors during off-farm periods. With the economic decline and the intensification of competition in the informal sector, such opportunities are drying up. This may partly explain some of the shifts in migratory patterns along rural–rural lines that have been recorded in Ghana, where the decline in urban opportunities was very sharp in the 1980s.

Multiple social identities and loyalties

Most social groups in Africa have traditionally developed a complex of identities which encompass values based on kinship relations, ethnic affiliations and workplace socialization. Individuals often feel cross-pressured as they respond to problems at the workplace, in their ethnic environments and in national politics. Studies on group dynamics have drawn attention to problems which institutions have always faced when they try to get their members to uphold one type of identity and restrict their propensities for flexibility and ambiguity. Unions and professional associations, for instance, have been relatively more effective in mobilizing members to defend livelihoods than in getting them to follow worker/professional-based parties in national politics, where members may value other identities in structuring choice (Melson, 1971); and it is common knowledge that workplace relations have often been influenced by extra-institutional affiliations.

What has changed is not the nature of the interpenetration of workplace identity and societal values, but the character of workplace identity itself. In the past, it was fairly easy to distinguish between professionals, industrial workers, farmers, entrepreneurs and informal economic agents. However, many of the characteristics that were central in defining the identities of such groups seem dated as a result of the diversification of employment strategies. As we have seen, a worker, for instance, is likely also to be a farmer, a petty trader or an artisan; and an academic or a bureaucrat could be a business entrepreneur, a farmer, a technocrat or a transnational actor who derives a substantial part of his or her income from global relationships. And it has become much more difficult to define who an informal entrepreneur is, given the large number of qualitatively different individuals who have invaded the informal economy. At a certain level of abstraction, one can talk about an emerging fusion of identities for particular sets of groups, such as certain strata of professionals, bureaucrats and academics among the middle classes; landless rural groups and the urban poor among marginal groups; and the casual strata of the industrial labour force, large sections of traditional informal sector groups and some smallholders.

The groups classified in each of the three categories would seem to share similar types of jobs and work practices, even if they are located in different geographical and workplace settings, suggesting changes in social stratification. For example, it is becoming difficult to distinguish between certain strata of academics, bureaucrats and professionals because of the convergence of their coping strategies and work schedules. The idea of academics spending some of their time in the bureaucracy and private sector may no longer be surprising as university teachers are known to be part of an emerging technocracy for economic reform in several countries. But it is interesting to note that some bureaucrats are not only involved in the private sector and tapping overseas opportunities, but are also active in the world of academia as a result of a general shortage of full-time academic staff in some universities. Universities have been forced to hire part-time staff with an academic background from the bureaucracy and private sector to save some academic courses and departments from collapse. The labouring classes provide another example. As many industrial workers are turned into casual labourers, they come to share the characteristics of traditional informal sector groups and many smallholders, all of whom combine casual work with informal and farming activities.

As a result of these changes, the capacity of institutions to shape the workplace identities of their members has been undermined. In fact, many formal institutions have suffered a serious decline in staff time because of the fusion of work boundaries. When combined with the fusion that has also taken place in work relations among other sets of social groups at lower and upper levels of society, the implications for the functioning of regulatory regimes, codes of behaviour and the nurturing of institutional loyalties are enormous. This has implications for collective bargaining and mobilization strategies. Despite the decline in their institutional reach, most organizations continue to operate in hierarchical and non-participatory ways, further alienating the mass of their low-paid employees. However, employers increasingly find it difficult to discipline their employees since the wage/salary – although part of the overall survival strategy – may no longer be central to it. In this case, employees may be disposed to take risks that may challenge institutional regulatory mechanisms and codes of behaviour. They may not be sufficiently socialized into the **governance structures** of their organizations for the latter to be sure of their unquestioned loyalty.

Ordinarily, the power of employers is likely to increase during periods of deep recession because of high unemployment which tends to weaken union/worker militancy or individual acts of malfeasance. This has happened in private sector enterprises where employers have been able to pay existing workers wages that are higher than what such workers might receive from alternative sources. In such situations, the threat of losing a job in the face of rising unemployment acts as an effective instrument in the hands of employers to get workers to behave properly on the shop floor. In most other cases, particularly in the public sector, where wages currently constitute a small proportion of the total income or expenditure needs of workers, the power of employers over their workforce may not be so decisive in periods of high unemployment. In the public sector, even those who are supposed to supervise and discipline subordinate employees may be caught in the search for or consolidation of alternatives, making them less enthusiastic in carrying out orders. And in many private sector firms that do not pay adequate wages, despite the existence of stringent monitoring devices, employees may still find ways of evading regulation through feigning illnesses, collaborating with supervisors to be absent from work, or clandestinely converting official resources to private ends. The main point we seek to stress is that the existence of formal regulations may not be sufficient to ensure compliance under conditions of low remuneration and multiple income strategies. Even in cases where employers' hands may be strengthened by the existence of unemployment and the lack of viable alternatives for workers, the former may not always be able to dismiss workers at will because of the costs of paying retrenchment benefits and gratuity, which could be financially crippling during periods of recession. Socialization, not threats of dismissal, is a more effective way of securing employee commitment to institutional goals. This has been eroded under crisis and adjustment.

The experience of institutions with a middle-class component is illustrative of the problem of undersocialization. Professionals and academics in the public services, who were highly privileged groups in the 1960s and 1970s, have defied previously enforceable regulations of state loyalty by engaging in long periods of industrial strikes in the 1980s as the crisis and policies of restructuring eroded incomes and standards of living. Such groups have been central in mobilizing sections of the urban population against structural adjustment and authoritarian rule. Attempts by political leaders to enforce loyalty to the state and stem the rising opposition from such groups through the enforcement of existing bureaucratic regulations have been ineffective. Furthermore, civil servants in most countries have become indifferent to bureaucratic norms of discipline as they pursue livelihood and other interests that are detrimental to the proper functioning of the public bureaucracies. This incomplete or declining socialization has implications for the way disputes may be handled. Lack of commitment to institutional goals, or alienation, may encourage either apathy or violent outbursts as a form of protest. In a way, it parallels early forms of working-class incorporation into industrial life, where high levels of worker turn-over, absenteeism and seasonal work practices were observed as strategies used by workers to resist the rigours of proletarianization as they opted instead for less regulated peasant and informal sector lives. Workers' militancy relating to industrial sabotage, occasional violent assault of employers during disputes and various forms of shirking on the shop floor have been linked to workplace relations of domination, low remuneration and, significantly, **exit options** available to employees (Andrae and Beckman, 1991; Lubeck, 1986).

Problems of regulation and loyalty can also be observed in institutions that are meant to defend the interests of employees themselves, such as unions and associations. These may not always succeed in mobilizing members for group action if members are too absorbed in pursuing alternative options and the unions/associations in question do not have a good record of defending group welfare. This seems to be the case in countries like Sierra Leone, Tanzania and Uganda where union militancy is traditionally low and workers have devised low-level subsistence strategies for dealing with the crisis. Even in countries with high levels of union militancy, such as Ghana, Nigeria and Zambia, it is possible to distinguish periods when unions were much more effective in calling their members out on strike (i.e. the period of early reform when workers had not diversified their options and believed in the efficacy of union interventions) and periods when union influence in industrial relations has waned (i.e. the late reform period when workers have settled into alternatives and strikes have lost their potency as an instrument for seeking redress). Unions may still be able to organize large strikes of short duration, as demonstrated in the relatively effective Nigerian labour strike over petroleum subsidies in 1993 that contributed to a change of government, but seem highly constrained in pursuing long, drawn-out disputes which might involve continuous mobilization and use of financial resources. When disputes do drag on, as is the case with many strikes involving unpaid or badly paid teachers, satisfactory settlements are often rare and teachers seize the opportunity to consolidate their operations in the informal sector. Spectacular eruptions, not structured negotiations leading to durable and mutually respected settlements, seem to be one of the more visible outcomes of this weakening of union power.

The erosion of regulatory mechanisms at both ends of the social spectrum may largely explain why it has been difficult to work out social pacts or reach agreements that key actors in society will honour. This problem lies at the heart of Africa's institutional crisis. Existing institutions seem unable to mediate social conflicts. Social actors are increasingly faced with a 'prisoner's dilemma' of whether to abide by rules which others may not follow, especially as dominant actors seek shortcuts to the resolution of difficult conflicts by manipulating the institutions themselves.

Informalization and truncated modernization

Social relations have changed in ways that have undermined the modernization process associated with post-colonial development. The modernization project in Africa had well-defined characteristics and should not be confused with literal meanings of the term, which may identify all current activities as extensions of the march towards or away from 'modernity'. Modernization itself was associated with a particular way of organizing society, a distinct structure of accumulation, and a set of values and beliefs for regulating social behaviour and state systems. In terms of social organization and accumulation, a 'modern' society was to be created by a gradual but progressive relocation of groups into formal institutions. The informal sector was to play a subordinate and transient role in the transition to modernity, as it was assumed that the expanding formal economy would be able eventually to absorb all groups and sectors of society. In some countries in East and southern Africa, as opposed to those in West Africa, informal urban activities were severely restricted as both colonial and independence rulers attempted to maintain orderly and regulated businesses in the cities. The developed Western society was held up as a model for the emerging ideal-type African society. Peasant surpluses, rents earned from the activities of mineral-extracting companies, and foreign capital were to provide the resources for the nurturing of classes of individuals who would uphold 'modern' values in the public bureaucracy, industrial factories, university systems and corporate organizations. This was to be achieved through massive funding of formal educational and health systems, social protection schemes and a salary or wage that would guarantee a decent or adequate level of living. These groups were to be segregated partially from the rest of society through special housing arrangements provided by the state and private companies, and official regulations which insisted on the nuclear family model as the criterion for enjoying social support. Those who were better organized, or occupied strategic positions in the social structure, were much more successful in taking advantage of this relatively untargeted system of resource allocation, which meant that peasants fared worse than other groups – especially the governing/business elites and middle classes in state capitals.

The state was to play a central role in the economy, society and polity as the chief agent of modernization. It was to uphold a secularist view of development, essentially by relegating religion and tradition to the private arena, and pursuing a centralization strategy of national ethnic integration. Groups which saw themselves as the custodians of the traditions of society, such as chiefs, networks of elders, religious leaders, Koranic and traditional teachers, herbalists, hunters, secret society organizers, etc., were downgraded to the informal, 'unseen', traditional arena, even though their influence on the wider society and on many of those in the modern sector remained enormous. State actors recognized the ethnic diversities of their societies, but believed that the best way to maintain national unity was by concentrating power at the centre and promoting a national consciousness that would be devoid of ethnic cleavages. The state was to be a nation state as opposed to a multinational or multi-ethnic state. This centralization strategy delegitimized the everyday cultural and social practices of the vast majority of groups in rural and urban areas. The use of foreign languages in official discourse helped to disguise the utopian character of this strategy of integration. Agents of central power could claim linguistic/ cultural neutrality at the official level, while they remained heavily imbued in ethnic consciousness and maintained themselves in power by converting the 'nation state' into an ethnic state.

The crisis and changes in social relations associated with the coping strategies discussed above have dealt a blow to this modernization project. The formal economy not only employs less labour than the informal, but its capacity to absorb labour from informal and traditional sectors is severely blocked; it is unable to sustain a living or satisfactory wage or salary for its employees; and the romantic vision of the withering away of peasant and informal sector livelihoods has met with a rude shock. The formal economy is not only not growing, but it is no longer seen by the majority of those who work in it – and those it previously excluded – as the driving force of society. The conquest of the formal economy by forces acting informally has never been so comprehensive. The accumulation strategy on which the drive for modernization depended has been in crisis since the 1970s. Peasant surpluses and mineral rents have dried up as a result of factors ranging from low local producer prices and support services to falling international commodity prices and demand; and economic decline has been compounded by declining foreign investments, capital flight and high debt service obligations (Ghai, 1992). States' capacities to intervene effectively in the economy, in social policy and in the polity have been seriously eroded. A small and truncated formal sector rests uneasily on a vast network of informal and traditional activities.

With this loss in state capacity has come a distinct loss of legitimacy. The artificial boundaries that separated modern institutions from the rest of society have been broken. There is an unprecedented revival of religious, traditional and ethnic movements in most countries. Traditional actors have entered the social stage not so much by taking over modern institutions, but by articulating a new power of relevance at local levels where states are no longer effective in mobilizing their populations for national projects. For instance, in a village in Guinea Bissau, the failure of state agents to address the social and economic problems associated with the crisis is forcing parents to abandon modern education in favour of Koranic schooling for their children, where local religious teachers or *mallams* hold complete sway (Rudebeck, 1990). Traditional herbalists, soothsayers and syncretic religious sects are thriving in most West African cities where rising poverty, problems of youth unemployment and a lowered sense of expectations push many urban dwellers to seek solace in traditional alternatives (Ibrahim, 1991). Kingdoms which had been wiped out or undermined as centralization projects got under way, such as those in Uganda and the Lozi in western Zambia, seem to be enjoying support for their revival among their different subjects. Christian and Islamic religious leaders are making a strong showing in many countries where such forms of politics were subordinated in the past to other types of cleavages. In Nigeria, religious leaders entered the political centre stage in the mid- to late 1980s as religion became a primary medium of struggle among the country's various ethnic groups. Traditional methods of organizing political discourses, such as the village *palaver* and the *Mbongi* or lineage system, are being advocated in some places like Zaire to replace what are perceived to be failed modern forms of political representation and discourse (Wamba dia Wamba, 1992). Religious revivalist sects, secret societies and traditional hunting organizations and festivals, with a high level of middle-class participation, are enjoying renewed popularity in Sierra Leone as a cultural response to the crisis.

As these forces gain momentum, individuals in modern society, including state officials, increasingly turn to them to strengthen their hold on power and on society. The *marabous* continue to play a key role in regulating rural electoral behaviour in Senegal and both government and opposition parties compete to enlist their support. The governing party in Zimbabwe provides official support to traditional spirit mediums as a way of regulating rural behaviour and social conflicts. And various governments have rushed to set up religious affairs departments in order to regulate the activities of the new actors. Some leaders have attempted to alter the secular character of their states by declaring official support for only one type of faith (Christianity in Zambia, Islam in Sudan) or by participating in international religious organizations, such as the Organization of Islamic Conference, which compromise the religious neutrality of their states (Nigeria, Sierra Leone, Tanzania). States, political parties, unions and interest group organizations increasingly have to deal with this secular process of informalization and resurgence of religious and traditional practices, but their modes and styles of operations have not been restructured in ways that will enable them to respond constructively to the new challenges. The centralizing and modernist ideology persists and acts as an obstacle to a resolution of the crisis.

This new phenomenon of fragmentation and informality has implications for the secular and impersonal norms and values that state bureaucracies and interest group organizations have attempted to develop since colonial rule. Formal rules and regulations are likely to be ineffective in situations where the social norms and values that underpin such rules are profoundly different from the substance of the formal rules themselves. Sociological studies affirm that it is often social norms and values rather than formal rules themselves that motivate individuals to behave in desirable ways. The rules mainly act as a last line of defence against non-compliance. The erosion of the modernist project calls for a major rethink of the rules of bureaucratic behaviour. It challenges theories of development and social change that were dominant in the 1960s and 1970s. Despite the major theoretical and ideological differences that existed between Marxist and modernization scholars writing on developing countries, both had a uni-linear view of development in which social forces associated with the modern sector were expected eventually to overcome so-called atavistic values and develop into fully formed classes as they struggled to push the fledgling economies along lines of capitalist or socialist development. Both saw traditional values and forces as constraints on the projects of social transformation, but paid little or no attention to them in terms of how they should be nurtured and regulated, implying that they were unlikely to play any major positive role in the new societies that were evolving. They could only act as a setback, or an obstruction, to economic growth and develop-ment. Dependency scholars were less optimistic about growth and modern-ization, because of what they saw as an essentially externally-driven strategy of development which did not give national states sufficient auton-omy to chart their own path of development. But the recipes for the ideal-type auto-centred development paradigm which many of them advocated paid little attention to the role of traditional and informal forces in shaping the strategies of state actors expected to delink from the world market.

Stalemates in the configurations of power

Such complex changes in social development and state–society linkages are bound to alter the configurations of social forces and the balance of political power. This has happened, however, in ways that do not support the assumptions of neoliberal/development theory. Neoliberal reformers had assumed that changes in structures of incentives in favour of tradables would empower market-oriented groups, who eventually would be strong enough to enforce new rules of behaviour in state and society. Initial authoritarian and technocratic interventions to tilt the balance of opportu-nities in favour of trade-based beneficiaries were expected to give way to a new configuration of social forces in which beneficiaries would command a hegemonic status and legitimacy. The multilateral funding agencies ob-viously recognized the structural weaknesses of beneficiaries during the early phase of the reforms, which partly explains why they were unrelent-ing in their crusade to dismantle the policy-making traditions and develop-ment strategies associated with previous ways of organizing society. Apart from the well-known strategy of withholding international finance to re-calcitrant governments, the Fund and Bank attempted to swing the balance of power in favour of reformers by delegitimizing opposition to structural adjustment. A myth was propounded around the idea of 'no viable alternatives to adjustment' to silence or side-track critical and well-meaning intellectuals and labour unionists who were keen to promote national discourses that they hoped would lead to broad-based alternatives. The funding agencies also introduced a culture of secrecy in economic decision making where the informed public, including persons with professional competence, was prevented from gaining access to the details of restructuring programmes, a practice that was out of step with the post-independence traditions of open discussions of development plans. They undermined research institutions and organizations that were likely to be critical of the reform programme (witness the hasty dissolution of the Prices and Incomes Commission in Zambia following the advent to power of a government that is more committed to adjustment than its predecessor), and promoted new national research institutions and regional research and training networks to provide intellectual and technical support to the new policy.

This strategy of changing the balance of forces in favour of the reforms met with a lot of resistance from many African governments and societies. In countries with fairly well-defined traditions of development strategies, such as Tanzania and Zambia, in which post-independence regime change had been low or non-existent, resistance to the reforms came from both interest groups in the state bureaucracy or ruling party and groups located in the wider society. Societal interest group resistance was strong in countries such as Zambia where urban groups were much better organized and the state's developmentalist philosophy less penetrating. Rapid postcolonial regime change in other countries, such as in Nigeria and Ghana, made it easier for new governments to accept the reforms even though there were varying degrees of implementation. Resistance in this set of countries emanated primarily from organized interest groups. However, whichever set of countries one deals with, the evidence indicates that in no country were the configurations of social forces restructured in ways that ensured the establishment of a solid support base for the reforms. Even in the case of Ghana where the reforms were much more rigorously implemented than in any other country, the critical change in the structure of power was achieved before the reforms were put in place. The key political change occurred during the 'revolutionary' phase of the regime in 1982–1983 when powerful groups in business, politics, the professions and the army were treated to a shock therapy of repression as the new government attempted to rid the society of what it saw as corrupt practices. That earlier militant and violent intervention profoundly changed the political culture and discourse by introducing deep divisions and suspicions between state officials and critical sections of society, which the reform efforts subsequently consolidated and deepened. It may partly explain the failure to build a solid pro-reform coalition in the country after more than ten years of adjustment, and why the business class remains staunchly opposed to the chief architects of the reforms, Rawlings and the PNDC/NDC (Provisional National Defence Council/National Democratic Congress), despite the gains many of them made during the reform years.

The changes in social relations highlighted in previous sections make it unlikely that any *simple* coalition of forces can be built either to support or to resist the reforms or offer alternatives that can be defended over any extended period. Given the various levels of polarization and complex ways social relations are being restructured, no theory of group dynamics that is based on an assumed profile of fully formed winners and losers is likely to provide sufficient insights into the options that may be available to construct social coalitions for group or state action. There are no simple winners and losers, and a variety of social contradictions mediate economic behaviour and connect winners and losers in complex and non-deterministic ways. The only clear winners, as we have seen, are the disparate groups of individuals linked to transactions involving the movement of currencies. Many of their activities are so non-transparent that they are unlikely to provide any credible leadership to the increasingly distressed majority population in rebuilding the battered institutions. Much of society is structured in ways that require a series of trade-offs if large groups of individuals are to be fully attracted to national projects or coalitions for effective development. Such trade-offs will have to take into account not only the disparities that have emerged in levels of living and social relations among and between groups, but also the differentiation that has occurred along ethnic and regional lines and between rural and urban communities. These are tasks that are likely to demand much more time, effort and resources than the situation obtaining during the pre-crisis period when the divisions were not so complex. The new social realities call into question attempts of governments and financial institutions to impose narrowly defined reform programmes on these societies. The stalemates in the power configurations exacerbate already evident weaknesses in national structures of authority whose resolution is crucial if state institutions are to be provided with the foundations for purposeful developmental action.

SOCIAL CHANGE AND INSTITUTIONAL DEVELOPMENT

What general conclusions can be drawn from this discussion that will contribute to an understanding of the problems of institution building in crisis economies? As we stated in the introduction, we understand by institutions a bundle of rules in social relations which structure behaviour in predictable ways. These need not take organizational forms, although the institutions we are concerned with, namely states and interest group formations, are organizational in character. Institutions are necessary for the proper functioning of markets and political systems. They ensure that outcomes in economic and political transactions are converted into the conventions, norms and ultimately traditions which are necessary in regulating conflicts and allocating benefits and punishments. Institutions can act as constraints on individuals who may wish to impose their will on society, while at the same time they can facilitate orderly programmes of transition to new social arrangements. While creating spaces in civil society through rising state incapacity to control dissent, Africa's institutional crisis simultaneously makes it difficult for recent gains in civil liberties to be extended to other critical sectors of the political system, and to push through viable economic development programmes.

The previous section attempted to establish a connection between changes in social relations and problems of institutionalization. It posited a link between, on the one hand, issues of polarization, multiple identities, truncated modernization and stalemates in the power balance, and on the other hand, problems of social compromise, socialization in governance structures, overarching norms and political authority. The linkages at these four levels would need to be kept in mind in any discussion of institutional development, particularly as it relates to state systems. The first part of the linkage provides the social context in which current institutions function and the second highlights the structural constraints which influence the pursuit of institutional goals, i.e. the third part of the linkage. A successful strategy of institutional reform must focus on all three dimensions of the problem: changes in social relations, the crisis of institutionalization, and institutional goals. A focus on just the institutional goals is unlikely to grasp the significance of the qualitatively different pressures that are being brought to bear upon formal institutional actors who are expected to defend the goals. An exclusive focus on the goals or the internal arrangements of organizations would be justified only in situations where external social processes and values are in fundamental agreement with the values and objectives of the institutions. Where these diverge, policy would need to pay great attention to social relations and institutionalization constraints. These linkages are highlighted in Figure 15.1.

Indeed, the institutional goals themselves will need rethinking and profound reform if they are to be relevant in the context of current changes in social relations. There are three basic elements of the institutional goals that are worth considering. The first concerns the establishment of *rules and regulations* which have the same meaning and relevance for social groups and individuals acting within different organizational settings in a given territorial space. In the context of the changes we are dealing with, such rules and regulations must attempt to break the hollow dichotomy between formal and informal transactions by making informal and traditional interests and values central to national standards. They must aim to legitimize

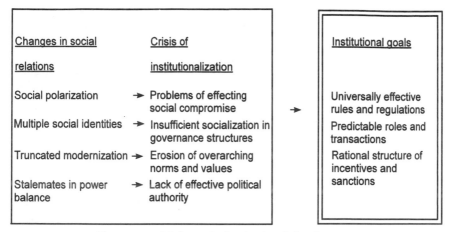

Figure 15.1 Linkages in institutional development

the traditional and open up issues in those areas for public discourse so that national laws will be both just and non-discriminatory in the way they allocate advantages and disadvantages among groups and communities. Part of this effort would require a new approach to national programmes of education which, in most countries, have largely ignored traditional rights and legal/belief systems. While upholding the principles of human rights and civil liberties, national institutional rules and regulations must make sense to all segments of society in order that individuals and office holders can be held accountable in different social contexts for their actions. This is all the more relevant under conditions of multiple coping strategies where individuals move in and out of a complex of socioeconomic settings. It will help regulate current practices in which dominant elites and office-holders commit crimes or acts of malfeasance in the public arena and seek refuge and support in traditional settings.

Institutional goals also concern the development of *predictable roles and transactions* as embodied in organizations with a high level of bureaucratization, or in village/tightly knit community settings where trust and personal interactions help to check opportunism. How such predictable transactions can be established in largely informalized societies undergoing rapid change is one of the contemporary challenges of development theory and practice. Using the impersonal market instruments of legal contracts and the institutions of private property rights seems insufficient for the complex transactions and levels of market penetration that exist in such societies. Finally, institutional goals deal with the pursuit of *rational structures of incentives and sanctions* necessary for influencing the behaviour of actors who are expected to enforce institutional rules and objectives. This includes issues of salaries, social benefits, training, career advancement, accountability and participation. Issues of incentives cannot be handled effectively outside of the context of social pressures affecting institutional actors as they try to cope with changing economic opportunities and respond to the coping strategies of other groups.

As we can see, some of the tasks of institution building are internal to the institutions themselves, while others have a much more societal dimension and may require more long-term strategies of regulating social behaviour. The nature of the crisis and social change suggests that a focus on just the internal institutional goals is likely to produce inadequate results and evade the need for fundamental reform. Many of the World Bank's efforts in the area of institutional reforms have concentrated on the internal governance structures of bureaucracies. The excessive focus on the internal has been informed by earlier assumptions of the need for a passive state in promoting a market economy that reformers believed was ready to be liberated. In this view, African states were seen as inefficient and overextended, unable to serve society equitably and effectively, and blocking the emergence of private entrepreneurs whose profit-maximizing strategies would minimize inefficient transactions and raise national income levels. Institutional reforms were concerned, therefore, with rolling back the state and have focused on retrenchment, privatization, decentralization, organizational restructuring and the promotion of non-governmental organizations (NGOs). Of these five areas, the only policy that deals with wider societal issues is that on NGOs. Furthermore, none focuses directly on questions of democracy except the policy on decentralization, which has tended to be formalistic as it hardly challenges existing power structures in national and local government bureaucracies.

The major work in institutional reform has been in the areas of retrenchment and privatization. Retrenchment is seen as necessary to reduce budget deficits and inflationary trends, and to introduce higher remuneration to motivate existing staff. Despite the strong focus on this area of reform, the empirical evidence indicates that most countries failed to reduce their budget deficits and inflation rates in the 1980s (Jespersen, 1992). Expenditures on salaries and wages declined relative to total public expenditures in the 1980s (ILO-JASPA, 1990), and they constituted much smaller proportions of national expenditures than those incurred on debt servicing and military obligations. Furthermore, payments of retrenchment benefits compounded the problems of attaining budgetary balance and had to be rescheduled or scaled down in a number of countries. Much more importantly, there is no country where the policy of retrenchment has been offset by a pay and benefits policy that is adequate for maintaining staff livelihoods. Retrenchment and salary realignments have not weakened multiple survival strategies, nor have they won back the institutional loyalties of staff in any significant way.

The policy of privatization has proceeded rather unevenly across Africa. Quite apart from the weak or non-existent financial institutions in most countries, which make it difficult for markets to discipline private entre-preneurs, many of the companies that have been put up for sale have not been bought, partly because of their loss-making records and low levels of optimism in investment decisions pertaining to manufacturing. In some cases, uncertainties over the future of the companies and the status of their personnel have aggravated the institutional crisis and affected the supply of critical goods and services. The attempt to sponsor NGOs to take over the delivery of some key services, particularly in rural areas, has been fraught with problems. NGOs, like the states they wish to supplant, are faced with problems of efficiency and accountability (Brett, 1993; Vivian and Maseko, 1994) and it is doubtful whether they can substitute for local organizations and states in rebuilding national institutions. Recipients tend to see NGOs as donors who ultimately may disappear from the scene, as their activities are not embedded in the social traditions of the communities they serve. A Zimbabwean study found that rural people were much more prepared to make claims on government institutions – even when they did not always get what they demanded – than they were with regard to NGOs, suggesting a very low level of NGO institutionalization (Vivian and Maseko, 1994).

Strategies aimed at supporting a process of institutionalization that would lead to effective rules, predictable transactions and viable incentives for institutional actors would need to address three main issues. These have a bearing on the four dimensions of social change highlighted in previous sections. The first concerns questions of livelihood, social polarization and multiple identities. A crisis in livelihoods affects the internal functioning of institutions in two fundamental ways: employees' use of office time to pursue non-institutional goals, and the channelling of institutional resources to private ends. Given the massive erosion of living standards among most social groups, and the shifts that have occurred in strategies of income maximization, it would seem unlikely that any one institution, let alone the state, would be able to guarantee secure livelihoods to its employees in the foreseeable future. Even if incomes were raised to 'satisfactory levels', the widening gulf between international and national incomes would sug-gest that most individuals in bureaucracies, some of whom have developed transnational linkages, would resist attempts to restrict their income sources to one institution. At one level, this trend is not unique. Flexible work specialization has also been observed in industrial economies undergoing profound changes in accumulation. The rise of post-modernism has been associated, in fact, with shifts in work practices (Harvey, 1989). However, a major difference in the changing structures of work between developing and industrial countries is the presence in the latter of social regulations and remuneration which ensure that staff time and resources are allocated more or less according to institutional requirements. A key issue that would need to be confronted in highly informal developing economies is how to create standard societal rules and regulations that individuals would be accountable to as they move from one set of institutions to another. In order that such rules may be effective, organizations may need to be restructured in ways that would encourage transparency in transactions and internal democracy in decision making. This will enable concerned bureaucrats and their allies in society to expose institutional malpractice.

A related problem is the issue of remuneration and how this is linked to the deepening processes of polarization. Poverty in most countries is so extensive, and the divisions among groups, sectors and regions so deep and pervasive, that it simply would not make sense to recreate a privileged minority in the formal economy and institutions. What may be required is a massive intervention in the social sector to guarantee fulfilment of basic needs in education, health, transportation and nutrition. Much of the traumatic experience of hitherto privileged groups relates to the very large expenditures they have had to incur by way of private provisioning to maintain satisfactory standards in basic social services. The response that is required in promoting and protecting social standards should not be bogged down by the kind of debate over universalism and targeting in which the World Bank and other agencies have been involved recently, but should take a hard look at the crisis of social provisioning in specific countries as it affects families, social groups, regions, ethnic groups and urban and rural areas. Such national systems of provisioning should have solid in-built arrangements for community and social group participation in order to prevent more powerful groups from diverting funds and services to their own ends. The social crisis is so deep and extensive in some sectors of provisioning that to focus social policy only on 'vulnerable groups' undermines the vision that is required to come to terms with the crisis. In some cases, vulnerable groups are not a minority group, but encompass the majority of the population itself. Furthermore, institutional actors are connected to a wide range of families and social networks, whose crises may affect the way such actors are likely to perform their bureaucratic roles. Some basic level of social protection for all categories of individuals in key areas of basic health, education and transportation would seem necessary to ease some of the social pressures on institutional actors. The recent shift in Fund/Bank thinking to incorporate social provisioning issues in policies of economic reform represents a positive move, but work in this area is still very limited and seems to be driven by a single ideology. Not enough funds and analytical resources have been allocated by states to their national social programmes, and the key ministry responsible for planning the interventions, social affairs, continues to occupy a very peripheral place in the bureaucratic structures of most governments. The kinds of interventions necessary in this field would require properly functioning statistical systems to monitor progress, and well-trained and committed individuals with an excellent knowledge of the social stratification and traditions of their societies.

The second issue that would need to be addressed in order to support a viable process of institutionalization concerns the role of culture in social development and institution building. This has both theoretical and policy relevance. At the theoretical level, it would seem obvious that a narrow focus on a single utility paradigm is unlikely to capture complex patterns of socioeconomic behaviour in economies undergoing rapid change. Furthermore, state practices are not determined or shaped by only one type of rational behaviour. As we have seen, economic transactions are embedded in complex webs of social relations and state actors respond to various, often conflicting, demands. When societies experience prolonged periods of crisis, traditional/cultural practices become key elements in the economic decisions of social actors. These traditions are not static, however, but are constructed by different actors as they respond to new problems and needs. Relations of domination and subordination are reproduced and restructured in complex ways as actors attempt to interpret, utilize and mobilize traditional values to support their economic goals. This produces outcomes that may not correspond to a priori assumptions, underlying a need always to ground theoretical insights on strong empirical foundations when dealing with such societies.

At the policy level, a focus on culture has implications for the way the public/private dichotomy that has afflicted African state systems can be managed in ways that will promote institutionalization. One of the ways neoliberals have tried to handle rent-seeking problems is through liberalization and marketization. This strategy is often combined with conventional approaches that emphasize public probes on corruption and the imposition of penalties on wrongdoers. The fact that problems of rent seeking have persisted in economies undergoing reform indicates a need to consider alternatives. Rent-seeking agents have always relied on informal traditional networks to frustrate efforts at regulating their activities in the public sphere. The point, of course, is that these traditional networks are not private, but have been made to look that way by government policies which provide legitimacy only to formal networks (Eke, 1975).

All social systems have mechanisms for ensuring accountability and for disciplining wrongdoing. Traditional mechanisms of accountability will need to become an integral part of national systems of accountability if anti-institutional practices of dominant groups are to be regulated. Legitimizing the traditional public sphere as an integral part of national accountability systems will not, of course, on its own, produce positive results. Many local societies are deeply divided and patron–client networks may ensure that small privileged groups continue to pilfer public resources by playing off one set of communities against another. Effective processes of accountability also need some level of awareness by community members of public issues and readiness to criticize public policies and actions of officials. Such traditions of critical scrutiny of local authorities may be absent in some societies, but they already exist in a number of others, where traditional rulers have to ensure that public functions and services are carried out to maintain their legitimacy among their subjects, even when they allocate to themselves a larger share of the resources. Given the low levels of literacy in such societies, budgets will have to be translated into tangibles (such as number of bore holes, drugs, educational materials, fertilizers, farm implements, etc.) for members to be able to monitor their disbursement and be interested in defending their entitlements. This means that low-income groups in traditional/informal sectors, which constitute the majority population, will have to be given large concessions in resource allocation and political leverage for them to feel part of national development efforts and be concerned with disciplining rent-seeking individuals who claim to represent their communities. The fact that rent-seeking activities make most people worse off suggests that efforts aimed at tilting the system of resource allocation and decision making in favour of underprivileged groups are likely to generate considerable support. Anti-corruption probes have always been popular among most sections of society when new governments come to power. Such probes have been ineffective, however, because of the missing elements of resource distribution and political control in favour of groups in traditional and informal settings. This analysis also has implications for activist individuals concerned with probity and positive social change. They would need to focus a good part of their struggles in informal and traditional sectors to prevent rent-seeking and neotraditionalist groups from monopolizing the discourse on culture and tradition.

The third issue concerns the role of social forces in disciplining institutions. Social struggles are central to the process of institutionalization, and organized interest groups play a key role in this process. Pressures from groups disadvantaged by policies of exclusion and institutional inefficiencies are essential for the setting of boundaries to state and private corporate power, ensuring public probity, and promoting individual rights and good governance. This relates to the issue of establishing effective authority relations. Institutions are likely to be ineffective in situations where political authority is absent or largely inoperative. Throughout the 1980s, the Fund and Bank were sceptical about the positive roles of social groups in promoting development and good governance, since the activities of such groups tended to put many of the reform policies into question. All organized groups were seen as having vested interests which needed to be repressed if the reforms were to have any chance of being implemented (World Bank, 1989; Beckman, 1992). Given the fragmentation dynamic and the presence of diverse groups and interests in society, it seems highly unlikely that centralized dictatorship would provide the political authority necessary for rebuilding the weakened institutions. Political liberalization and real devolution of power to lower levels of authority are the logical policy frameworks for responding to fragmentation and informalization.

In this regard, there have been shifts in World Bank policy towards some support for democratization in recent years as struggles for political liberalization intensified in most African countries in the 1990s, and as major bilateral donors tried to tie international assistance to issues of democratization and human rights. However, the pattern of democratization has been highly uneven and prospects for the creation of stable and effective political authority seem ambiguous because of a failure to rethink the question of power and its distribution among social groups and ethnic/regional formations under new circumstances. As in the policy of structural adjustment, there has been an attempt to impose on these societies a single political formula with strong 'winner takes all' electoral arrangements, which might make sense only in relatively more homogeneous, stable and economically prosperous societies. Relatively free and fair elections have been held in ten countries (Benin, Burundi, Cape Verde, Lesotho, Madagascar, Malawi, Mali, Niger, South Africa and Zambia) even though the military has attempted a come-back in two of these, with considerable loss of life to local populations in Burundi. Civil strife or wars rage on in eight others (Angola, Chad, Liberia, Mozambique, Rwanda, Sierra Leone, Somalia and Sudan). And incumbents have refused to let go of power in a majority of the remaining cases as either elections are rigged or opposition groups are frustrated in long, drawn-out national conferences. Even in countries that have conducted free elections, winning parties continue to flout basic procedures of democratic practices, and it is doubtful whether future elections will be as free as the first ones. Existing institutional arrangements seem unable to mediate interest group and state strategies which will break the deadlock that informs most political processes in the continent. Political authority, the backbone of institutional development, cannot be nurtured under conditions of stalemate.

The key problem is how to ensure that key institutions are sufficiently insulated from the control of any single group, or coalitions of narrowly defined groups, while they continue to serve the public interest. Based on the evidence of social fragmentation and anxieties over exclusion and vulnerability, it would seem counterproductive to impose a single formula of democratization on these societies. Electoral systems and political frameworks would need to be devised that would have in-built provisions for power sharing among ethnic groups under competitive party arrangements, so that potential losers in electoral contests would not always feel threatened by the possible negative consequences of defeat. These would need to be backed up by programmes of devolution of real power and resources to the lowest strata of society where groups are much more likely to have effective control over their representatives. Such transparently administered political pacts at various levels of society, reviewed periodically, would allow political parties, interest groups and non-governmental organizations to protect some of the gains they have made in civil liberty in recent years, and deepen their work of mobilization and organization without the ever-present threat of state or opposition violence/arbitrariness, much of which is associated with feelings of insecurity by office-holders/seekers and their allies in society. Such arrangements might also allow institutional actors to develop some degree of autonomy from the governments they serve. They might help to demystify the electoral process which currently blocks discussions of other pressing issues of social accountability in the allocation and administration of public resources, and facilitate the nurturing of an independent media and judiciary.

Finally, two conditions are necessary to promote the kinds of institutional reforms discussed in this chapter. The first concerns the retrieval of national sovereignty in policy making from the international financial institutions. Successful national institutions can only be built by those who run, or benefit or suffer from, their operations. External agencies and interests should facilitate, not lead, processes of national development and institution building. Where national actors have failed to grasp the need for and direction of change, no external force, however powerful and well meaning, can substitute for the missing national capacity and vision. It will only postpone the necessity of building that capacity. What happened in the 1980s with respect to structural adjustment should not be allowed to repeat itself in the search for effective institutional arrangements to promote economic development and democracy. The second condition concerns the need to approach development issues from a multi-faceted perspective and avoid the temptation to indulge in single-formula ideological prejudices. The problems are so complex and the changes under way so profound that a standard prescription cannot work in one country, let alone for all countries. To paraphrase Barraclough's imagery of markets and states: markets can be good servants when properly supervised, but they have been historically bad masters when they have been allowed to dictate the course of development in social life. The key issue in social development is not whether there should be state or market interventions, but 'what kind of interventions and how much' (Barraclough, 1991, p. 258).

REFERENCES

Abdullah, H. J. (1991) 'Women in Development: A Study of Female Wage Labour in Kano's Manufacturing Sector, 1945–1990', unpublished PhD thesis, University of Hull, Hull.

Andrae, G. and Beckman, B. (1985) *Industry Goes Farming: The Nigerian Raw Material Crisis and the Case of Textiles and Cotton*, Research Report no. 80, Scandinavian Institute of African Studies, Uppsala.

——(1991) 'Textile Unions and Industrial Crisis in Nigeria: Labour structure, organisation and strategies', in I. Brandell (ed.) *Workers in Third World Industrialisation*, Macmillan, London.

Baker, W. (1990) 'Market Networks and Corporate Behaviour', *American Journal of Sociology*, vol. 96, no. 3.

Bangura, Y. (1994) 'Intellectuals, Economic Reform and Social Change: Constraints and opportunities in the formation of a Nigerian technocracy', *Development and Change*, vol. 25, no. 2.

Bangura, Y. and Beckman, B. (1991) 'African Workers and Structural Adjustment: A Nigerian case study', in D. Ghai (ed.) *The IMF and the South: The Social Impact of Crisis and Adjustment*, ZED Books/UNRISD/UWI, London.

Bardhan, P. K. (1989) 'The New Institutional Economics and Development Theory: A brief critical assessment', *World Development*, vol. 17, no. 9.

Barraclough, S. (1991) *An End to Hunger? The Social Origins of Food Strategies*, ZED Books/UNRISD/South Centre, London.

Bates, R. H. (1971) *Unions, Parties and Political Development*, Yale University Press, London.

—— (1981) *Markets and States in Tropical Africa: The Political Basis of Agricultural Policies*, University of California Press, Berkeley, CA.

Beckman, B. (1992) 'Empowerment or Repression: The World Bank and structural adjustment in Africa', in P. Gibbon *et al.* (eds) *Authoritarianism, Democracy and Adjustment: The Politics of Economic Reform in Africa*, Seminar Proceedings No. 26, Scandinavian Institute of African Studies/UNRISD/CMI, Uppsala.

Berry, S. (1985) *Fathers Work for Their Sons: Accumulation, Mobility and Class Formation in an Extended Yoruba Community*, University of California Press, Berkeley, CA.

Booth, D. (1990) *Structural Adjustment in Socio-Political Context: Some Findings from a Local Study in Tanzania*, Hull Papers in Developing Areas no. 4, Centre of Developing Area Studies, University of Hull, Hull.

Brett, E. A. (1993) 'Voluntary Agencies as Development Organisations: Theorising the problem of efficiency and accountability', *Development and Change*, vol. 24, no. 2.

Chachaga, C. S. L. (1993) 'Forms of Accumulation, Agriculture and Structural Adjustment in Tanzania', in P. Gibbon (ed.) *Social Change and Economic Reform in Africa*, Scandinavian Institute of African Studies, Uppsala.

Chew, D. (1990) 'Internal Adjustments to Falling Civil Service Salaries: Insights from Uganda', *World Development*, vol. 14, no. 6.

Chiwele, D. (1993) *Crisis, Adjustment and Social Change in Zambia's Urban Informal Sector* (Mimeo), UNRISD, Geneva.

Dei, G. J. S. (1993) *Hardships and Survival in Rural West Africa: A Case Study of a Ghanaian Community*, CODESRIA, Dakar.

Demery, L. and Addison, T. (1987) 'Food Insecurity and Adjustment Policies in Sub-Saharan Africa: A review of the evidence', *Development Policy Review*, no. 5.

Dike, E. (1992) *Economic Crisis, Structural Adjustment and Micro-Level Coping Strategies: Urban Informal Sector Small-Scale Industrial Entrepreneurs in Nigeria* (Mimeo), UNRISD, Geneva.

Eggertsson, T. (1990) *Economic Behaviour and Institutions*, Cambridge University Press, Cambridge.

Eke, P. (1975) 'Colonialism and the Two Publics in Africa: A theoretical statement', *Comparative Studies in Society and History*, vol. 17, no. 1.

Etzioni, A. (1990) *The Moral Dimension: Towards a New Economics*, The Free Press, New York.

Ghai, D. (1992) *Structural Adjustment, Global Integration and Social Democracy*, UNRISD Discussion Paper no. 37, UNRISD, Geneva.

Gibbon, P., Havnevik, K. and Hermele, K. (1993) *A Blighted Harvest? The World Bank and African Agriculture in the 1980s*, James Currey, London.

Granovetter, M. (1992) 'Economic Action and Social Structure: The problem of embeddedness', in M. Granovetter and R. Swedberg (eds) *The Sociology of Economic Life*, Westview Press, Oxford.

Harvey, D. (1989) 'From Fordism to Flexible Specialisation', in D. Harvey (ed.) *The Condition of Post-Modernity: An Enquiry into the Origins of Cultural Change*, Blackwell, London.

Havnevik, K. (1993) *Tanzania: The Limits to Development from Above*, Scandinavian Institute of African Studies, Uppsala.

Hewitt de Alcántara, C. (ed.) (1993) *Real Markets: Social and Political Issues of Food Policy Reform*, Frank Cass, London.

Ibrahim, J. (1991) 'Religion and political turbulence in Nigeria', *Journal of Modern African Studies*, vol. 29, no. 1.

ILO-JASPA (International Labour Organisation – Jobs and Skills Programme for Africa) (1990) *African Employment Report*, ILO-JASPA, Addis Ababa.

Jacobeit, C. (1991) 'Reviving Cocoa: Policies and perspectives on structural adjustment in Ghana's key agricultural sector', in D. Rothchild (ed.) *Ghana: The Political Economy of Recovery*, Rienner, London.

Jamal, V. (1993) *Adjustment Programmes and Adjustment: Confronting the Parameters of African Economies*, Paper presented at the Rural Development Studies Research Seminar, Institute of Social Studies, The Hague, November.

Jamal, V. and Weeks, J. (1993) *Africa Misunderstood or Whatever Happened to the Rural-Urban Gap?*, Macmillan, London.

Jespersen, E. (1992) 'External Shocks, Adjustment Policies and Economic and Social Performance', in G. Andrea Cornia *et al.* (eds) *Africa's Recovery in the 1990s, a UNICEF study*, Macmillan, London.

Leonard, D. (1993) 'Structural Reform of the Veterinary Profession in Africa and the New Institutional Economics', *Development and Change*, vol. 24, no. 2.

Lockwood, M. (1992) *Engendering Adjustment or Adjusting Gender? Some New Approaches to Women and Development in Africa*, Discussion Paper no. 315, Institute of Development Studies, Brighton.

Loxley, J. (1990) 'Structural Adjustment Programmes in Africa: Ghana and Zambia', *Review of African Political Economy*, no. 24.

Lubeck, P. (1986) *Islam and Urban Labour in Northern Nigeria: The Making of a Muslim Working Class*, Cambridge University Press, Cambridge.

Mamdani, M. (1991) 'Uganda: Contradictions in the IMF programme and perspective', in D. Ghai (ed.) *The IMF and the South: The Social Impact of Crisis and Adjustment*, ZED Books/UNRISD/UWI, London.

Meagher, K. (1991) *Priced out of the Market: The Effects of Parallel Trade and Market Liberalisation on Smallholder Incomes in Northern Nigeria*, Research report prepared under a Robert McNamara Fellowship, Zaria, Nigeria.

Meagher, K. and Bello-Mohammed, Y. (1993) *Informalisation and its Discontents: Coping with Crisis and Adjustment in Nigeria's Informal Sector* (Mimeo), UNRISD, Geneva.

Melson, R. (1971) 'Ideology and Inconsistency: The "cross-pressured" Nigerian worker', *The American Political Science Review*, vol. 65, no. 1, March.

Mosley, P. and Smith, L. (1989) 'Structural Adjustment and Agricultural Performance in Sub-Saharan Africa', *Journal of International Development*, vol. 1, no. 3.

Mosley, P. and Weeks, J. (1993) 'Has Recovery Begun? "Africa's adjustment in the 1980s" revisited', *World Development*, vol. 21, no. 10.

Mukandala, R. S. (1994) *Alternative Livelihood Strategies Among Current and Former Parastatal Employees in Tanzania* (Mimeo), UNRISD, Geneva.

Mushota, R. (1993) *Crisis, Adjustment and Social Change among the Urban Poor in Zambia* (Mimeo), UNRISD, Geneva.

Mustapha, A. R. (1992) 'Structural Adjustment and Multiple Modes of Livelihood in Nigeria', in P. Gibbon *et al.* (eds) *Authoritarianism, Democracy and Adjustment:*

The Politics of Economic Reform in Africa, Seminar Proceedings no. 26, Scandinavian Institute of African Studies/UNRISD/CMI, Uppsala.

——(1993) *Cocoa, Farming Households and Structural Adjustment in Nigeria* (Mimeo), UNRISD, Geneva.

Nelson, J. (1989) *Fragile Coalitions: The Politics of Economic Adjustment*, Transaction Books, New Brunswick, NJ.

North, D. (1990) *Institutions, Institutional Change and Economic Performance*, Cambridge University Press, Cambridge.

Olukoshi, A. (1992) *Crisis, Adjustment and Social Change: The Experience of the Kano Manufacturing Class* (Mimeo), UNRISD, Geneva.

Pearce, P. (1992) 'Ghana', in A. Duncan and J. Howell (eds) *Structural Adjustment and the African Farmer*, ODI/James Currey/Heinemann, London.

Portes, A. and Sensenbrenner, J. (1993) 'Embeddedness and Immigration: Notes on the social determinants of economic action', *American Journal of Sociology*, vol. 98, no. 6.

Robinson, D. (1990) *Civil Service Pay in Africa*, International Labour Office, Geneva.

Rudebeck, L. (1990) 'The Effects of Structural Adjustment in Kandjadja, Guinea-Bissau', *Review of African Political Economy*, no. 49.

Sahn, D. E. and Sarris, A. (1991) 'Structural Adjustment and the Welfare of Rural Smallholders: A comparative analysis from sub-Saharan Africa', *World Bank Economic Review*, vol. 5, no. 2.

Sarris, A. and Shams, H. (1991) *Ghana Under Structural Adjustment: The Impact on Agriculture and the Rural Poor*, New York University Press, New York.

Simutanyi, N. (1993) *Crisis, Adjustment and Survival Strategies of Workers in Zambia: A Case Study of Railway Workers, Kabwe* (Mimeo), UNRISD, Geneva.

UNDP (United Nations Development Programme) (1990) *Human Development Report*, Oxford University Press, New York.

Uphoff, N. (1993) 'Grassroots Organisations and NGOs in Rural Development: Opportunities with diminishing states and expanding markets', *World Development*, vol. 21, no. 4.

Vivian, J. and Maseko, G. (1994) *NGOs, Participation and Rural Development: Testing the Assumptions with Evidence from Zimbabwe*, Discussion Paper no. 49, UNRISD, Geneva.

Wamba dia Wamba, E. (1992) 'Beyond Élite Politics of Democracy in Africa', *Quest Philosophical Discussions*, vol. VI, no. 1.

Weissman, S. R. (1990) 'Structural Adjustment in Africa: Insights from the experiences of Ghana and Senegal', *World Development*, vol. 18, no. 2.

Williamson, O. E. (1985) *The Economic Institutions of Capitalism*, The Free Press, New York.

World Bank (1981) *Accelerated Development in Sub-Saharan Africa: An Agenda for Action*, The World Bank, Washington, DC.

——(1989) *Sub-Saharan Africa: From Crisis to Sustainable Growth*, The World Bank, Washington, DC.

——(1990) *World Development Report*, Oxford University Press, Oxford.

16

FROM GATT TO WTO

A potential for or a threat to LDC development?

Göte Hansson

INTRODUCTION

In December 1993, after more than seven years of negotiation, the Uruguay Round was completed and in April 1994 the new agreement on international trade was signed by around 122 countries. If successful, the process of ratification should make the agreement come into force from 1995. The completion of the Uruguay Round means that a new era begins in the field of international trade and trade-related policies. The new agreement includes areas that previously have not been covered by the General Agreement on Tariffs and Trade (GATT). Furthermore, and in the long run this may be of even greater importance, it has been decided that the existing GATT secretariat shall be replaced with a new multilateral trade organization, the World Trade Organization (WTO).

The new organization and the revised trade agreement it will administer and control have both met with great appreciation from the rich developed world and the business community, whereas questions have been raised about the pros and cons of the new international trade system for the less and least developed countries as well as for the global environment.

The objective of this chapter is to analyse the new trade agreement and its potential short-term and long-term effects on less developed countries.

In the next section we give a brief background to the whole issue of trade, growth and development. This section also presents a brief analysis of the increasingly important issue of the relationship between trade and national sovereignty in politically sensitive policy areas like working conditions and environmental standards. Is there a need for complementing international trade agreements with agreements on, or conditions related to, labour standards and environmental policy? Then we analyse the treatment of LDCs in the international trade system. After a brief discussion of the recent pre-WTO development we focus on the relevant changes for LDCs in the new trade agreement, and the consequences of these changes for the

LDCs are analysed. Finally, some concluding remarks and aid implications of the new intended international trade system are presented.

TRADE, DEVELOPMENT AND NATIONAL SOVEREIGNTY – AN ISSUE OF CONTROVERSY AND DEBATE

Trade and development

As early as 1776, in *An Inquiry into the Nature and Causes of the Wealth of Nations*, Adam Smith observed and emphasized the role of foreign trade in solving the economic problems in a country with a rapidly growing population and limited agricultural resources. The free trade doctrine has since then become one of the most central doctrines in international economics and international politics. To quote Paul Krugman (1987, p. 131): 'If there were an Economist's Creed, it would surely contain the affirmation "I understand the Principle of Comparative Advantage" and "I advocate Free Trade".' However, trade has not always been seen as something solely positive. Economists such as Myrdal, Prebisch, Singer and Emmanuell have all pointed to factors that recommend a more moderate or even reserved attitude towards free international trade. Gunnar Myrdal, in the mid-1950s, stated:

> it is not self-evident but, indeed, very much up to doubt whether today a freer trade would necessarily lead to less international inequality.
>
> (Quoted from Meier, 1976, p. 688)

> If left unregulated, international trade and capital movements would thus often be the media through which the economic progress in the advanced countries would have backsetting effects in the under-developed world.
>
> (Quoted from Meier, 1976, p. 691)

Another line of argument against trade as an engine of growth is known as the Singer–Prebisch argument. According to this argument, productivity growth (through technical progress) in less developed countries gives rise to a negative development of terms of trade (UNDEA, 1949; Prebisch, 1950). On the other hand, in 1959 one prominent economist, Gottfried Haberler, wrote that:

> Marginal interferences with the free flow of trade, if properly selected, may speed up development. But I do not want to leave any doubt that my conclusion is that substantially free trade with marginal insubstantial corrections and deviations, is the best policy from the point of view of economic development.
>
> (Quoted from Meier, 1976, p. 702)

Haberler continues:

> If we were to estimate the contribution of international trade to economic development, especially of the underdeveloped countries, solely by the static gains from trade in any given year on the usual assumption of given production capabilities...we would indeed grossly underrate the importance of trade...trade bestows very important indirect benefits, which also can be described as dynamic benefits, upon the participating countries.
>
> (Quoted from Meier, 1976, p. 704)

Among these effects Harberler mentions the possibility to import various material means for economic development, the transmission of ideas and technological knowledge, and the role of trade as a vehicle for the international movement of capital. He also points out that free trade works as an important anti-monopoly policy.

Dynamic effects are, however, difficult to assess and quantify. Therefore, when discussing the role of trade in the process of development it is important to recognize the complexity of the development and growth process. As underlined by Södersten:

> The growth process is obviously a complex result of economic, sociological, psychological, religious, etc. forces. It is hardly possible that economics alone could, even in principle, explain economic growth.
>
> (Södersten, 1964, p. 14)

Looking at recent development in various parts of the world and also at recent economic theory on growth and economic development, the issue of the causes of economic growth is still puzzling and to some extent even more so today than in the early 1960s. Growth performance and standards of living differ largely between continents but also between countries within the same continent.

The question of the role of trade in this process has, however, still not been solved. Things have become even more complex with the recent development of the theory of international trade where the traditional and basic assumptions of constant returns to scale and perfect competition have been relaxed. Instead, important characteristics of the real world, such as imperfect markets and the existence of economies of scale, have been introduced into the models. The new models, according to one of the orginators of the 'new' trade theory, Paul Krugman,

> call into doubt the extent to which actual trade can be explained by comparative advantage [in the sense of Ricardo and Heckscher Ohlin]; they also open the possibility that government intervention in trade via import restrictions, export subsidies, and so on may under some circumstances be in the national interest after all.
>
> (Krugman, 1987, p. 131f)

From the point of view of economic theory the free trade argument is sometimes questioned since the real world is a world with frequent imperfections. According to the theory of second best, therefore, we cannot be sure whether the elimination of some, but not all, imperfections, such as trade barriers, will improve the situation or make it even worse.

However, there are still strong arguments in favour of trade liberalization, such as the static effects that lower costs of production and increase the consumption possibilities, and particularly the dynamic effects that are set in motion through international trade. Thus, departures from free trade should be analysed carefully before being introduced. Therefore, notwithstanding the developments in trade theory and the implications of the second-best theory, both of which have produced arguments for protectionism, it is not difficult to agree with Krugman who has concluded that:

> free trade is not passé, but it is an idea that has irretrievably lost its innocence. Its status has shifted from optimum to reasonable rule of thumb. There is still a case for free trade as a good policy, and as a useful target in the practical world of politics, but it can never again be asserted as the policy that economic theory tells us is always right.
>
> (Krugman, 1987, p. 132)

This conclusion is in conformity with that reached by Greenaway and Chong Hyun Nam who concluded in 1988 that 'We may not be entirely clear of the precise determinants of growth; the potential for trade strategy in discouraging growth is, however, rather more apparent' (Greenaway and Chong Hyun Nam, 1988, p. 433). What these authors refer to are the negative effects of an inward-oriented trade strategy. This should, however, not exclude possibilities to perform a successful import-substitution strategy based on the infant-industry argument, even if success stories are rare and the failures are quite frequent (see e.g. the experiences reported in the various contributions in Hansson (1993)).

Trade, 'unfair' competition and national sovereignty

One important aspect of increased internationalization that is crucial from the point of view of political economy is its effects on national sovereignty. This issue, along with the liberalization of capital movements, has been the subject of intense debate. As noted by Mhone (1994, p. 34), 'increasingly, national sovereignty, and protective barriers to trade have become a fetter on globalisation and the free reign of international capital'.

Capital, organized in transnational companies, is assumed to make extensive use of the differences that exist between countries. Trade based on the utilization of these differences produces arguments for trade restrictions or against the idea of international trade at large (see e.g. Daly 1993). Furthermore, a related problem is 'the rapidity with which shifting competitive advantages in international transactions are transmitted to national economies' (Mhone, 1994, p. 34). This has frequently resulted in increased use of protective barriers in developed countries in order to protect domestic production and employment. As a rule, the trade barriers have been introduced outside GATT. Furthermore, they have mostly taken the form of quotas and other non-tariff measures that, compared with tariffs, are inferior from the point of view of global welfare and in most cases are inferior from the point of view of national welfare in the protective countries also (see e.g. Hansson (1990, Chapter 3) for an analysis).

To make the arguments for protectionist measures politically acceptable, the differences behind the revealed comparative advantages are often classified as 'unfair'. It is, however, seldom a straightforward matter to make a definition of what should be seen as 'unfair'.

It is important to remember that all division of labour, on a domestic as well as on a global level, is based on differences in resources and abilities among individuals, firms and nations. These differences produce differences in costs of production and thus a pattern of comparative advantages.

When discussing the basis of comparative advantage it is important to make a difference between what can be called *natural* comparative advantages, i.e. differences in factor abundance, natural resources and existence of technology gaps and economies of scale, and comparative advantages that are *created* by the politicians through legislation and economic policy.

Confidence in the free operation of markets was an important basis for the creation of the present international economic system, especially for GATT. However, as noted above, real economies do not satisfy the conditions of a perfect market economy. Therefore, it is necessary to adjust for market imperfections in order to make the global allocation of resources optimal. However, even without market imperfections we should not expect politicians in various countries to be passive with regard to resource allocation issues. The reason is to be found in international differences in the valuation of different aspects of life. Income distribution objectives may well lead to differences in tax rates, social insurance systems and in labour market legislation also. Furthermore, different valuations of intergeneration aspects may well lead to differences in environmental legislation. The important question to ask is who should decide upon issues of this kind?

It is obvious that along with the internationalization and liberalization of trade and capital movements, this type of differences is becoming increasingly important and thus also a growing source of dispute and conflict.

As early as the beginning of the nineteenth century, the potential conflict between unilateral national legislation and the possibility to maintain competitive strength in international markets was observed in connection with labour market legislation. The trade argument for international labour legislation from this period can be exemplified by the following quotation from the French liberal economist Jérome Blanqui who in 1838–1839 wrote:

> There is only one way of accomplishing it [labour legislation] while avoiding its disastrous consequences; this would be to get it adopted simultaneously by all industrial nations which compete in the foreign market. Will people be willing to do this? Can it be done? Why not? Treaties have been concluded between one country and another by which they have bound themselves to kill men; why should they not be concluded today for the purpose of preserving men's lives and making them happier?
>
> (Quoted from Hansson, 1983, p. 12)

Blanqui and others were quite unsuccessful in getting labour standards incorporated into trade treaties. Even though the creation of the International Labour Organization in 1919 can be seen as one result of the demands for international labour standards during the nineteenth century, this organization has no explicit links to trade policy. Thus, the demands have continued, and will continue to do so, along with the process of internationalization, in particular when developing countries begin to take advantage of their abundance of low-wage labour. However, the issue of harmonization of social policy and labour standards finds little if any support in economic theory as long as such a harmonization is not assumed to be a measure to reduce the use of non-tariff trade barriers that have been introduced on the basis of the cheap-labour argument (see e.g. Hansson, 1983, Chapters 1 and 5 and references therein).

It is reasonable to assume that we will have to continue to live with the debate about whether the rapid development of competitive strength as reflected in international markets is based on 'fair' or 'unfair' competition. During periods when unemployment figures are high in developed countries, increased competition from low-wage countries in labour-intensive lines of production can be expected to be met with protectionist arguments based on the concept of 'unfair labour standards'.

If efficiently implemented, the Uruguay Round Agreement will pave the way for increased international division of labour. As large parts of the developing world still have an abundance of labour, and thus have a potential competitive strength in labour-intensive and slow-growing lines of production, tensions between developed and less developed countries can be expected to increase. People with little education and in low-skilled work in the developed countries will tend to lose against this competition and will try to make their politicians introduce various types of trade barriers (see Daly (1993) who argues against free trade on this basis). In fact during the last week of March 1994, the USA and France wanted to complement the new international trade agreement and make child labour an illegal factor of international competition.

As noted in Hansson (1983) history shows that there are reasons to expect that the demands for incorporating labour standards in trade agreements will seldom be presented as purely protectionist arguments. Frequently, partly because of poor understanding of the situation in the exporting countries and partly for political reasons, such demands have been and will most likely continue to be presented as arguments about solidarity with workers in less developed countries. However, this line of argumentation should be subject to critical analysis. In Hansson (1983, p. 182f.) it is concluded that only the incorporation of basic trade union rights into trade treaties can be characterized as an action of solidarity with foreign workers that do not have such rights. Other types of more specific working conditions, e.g. wages, hours of work, working environment, and even the existence of child labour, are of much more dubious value from the point of view of international solidarity. Although some workers in the developing countries may become better off, these gains must be weighed against the losses of other workers in those countries who may well end up receiving lower wages or become unemployed, *ceteris paribus*. In the case of trade restrictions that are based on the existence of child labour, the income redistribution may be detrimental to large-size families but should be weighed against the potential gains for child welfare that can arise from a reduction in this type of labour.

Recently 109 Nobel prizewinners have taken an initiative to stop child exploitation under the motto 'Child Right Worldwide'. This initiative is interesting, not only because of the eminent individuals who have taken it, but also because they approach important international organizations such as the World Bank and the International Monetary Fund. Like the advocates of social clauses, the initiative by the Nobel prizewinners seems to emphasize sanctions rather than positive assistance. Thus, in their brief message they mention boycotts of companies that exploit children (child labour being one example) (Nobel Prizewinners Worldwide Initiative to Stop Child Exploitation, 1994).

It is important, however, not only to introduce measures that stop child labour by various types of threat but also to complement such measures with social and educational policy actions. Without substantial social and educational policy measures, a social clause on child labour, or boycotts of products produced by means of child labour, will most likely lead to a worsening of the situation for the children, making them work in the informal sector, e.g. as prostitutes and young criminals, under conditions even worse than those existing in the export industries and, moreover, much more difficult to combat through international economic actions (for a theoretical analysis of a social clause on child labour, see Hansson (1983, pp. 94–103)).

One problem closely related to the issue of 'fair' and 'unfair' competition concerns environmental aspects of international trade. In a highly critical article against the free trade doctrine and the new international trade agreement, Daly (1993, p. 26) writes:

> Economists rightly urge nations to follow a domestic program of internalizing costs into prices. They also wrongly urge nations to trade freely with other countries that do not internalize their costs... free competition between different cost-internalizing regimes is utterly unfair.

There is no reason to argue against the idea of cost internalizing *per se*. However, it is far from easy to determine what full costs really are. First, not all the effects of various activities are known. Second, in cases where the effects are known it is not always easy to make a correct or fair evaluation of the effects. This is largely an issue where history, culture, political ideology, etc., play important roles.

Notwithstanding the problems of evaluation, it is important to state that compared with the advocates of labour standards in trade policy, the environmentalists have more well-founded arguments. However, they have frequently shown a tendency to press their arguments too far. In contrast to the conclusion of international harmonization of labour standards, there is a clear case for international harmonization of environmental policy, for instance by incorporating an environmental clause in multilateral trade agreements, provided that the harmonization is limited to transfrontier environmental problems. For purely domestic environmental problems, like the case of labour standards, there is no economic reason for international harmonization. Instead those problems should be dealt with on a national basis with due respect to national sovereignty.

From the point of view of political economy, it seems very difficult to reach efficient international agreements on pollution control, since politically important groups in low-standard countries can be expected to work against the harmonization efforts. External pressure through international taxation by means of trade barriers can be one way to obtain changes in the production processes, so that the transfrontier pollution from resistant foreign producers is reduced. In this way, from the point of view of economic theory, the efficiency in the global allocation of resources may well be improved. However, it is important to stress that this is only true for transfrontier pollution problems and that trade policy is never the optimal policy. Instead the solution should be solved through international harmonization agreements. Here it is interesting to note that in the Uruguay Round Agreement it was decided to include the issue of trade and environment in the work programme of the WTO (IBRD, 1994a, p. 1).

A specific trade-related problem is transport. It is important not to forget that also within a country transportation plays an important role and thus uses a lot of energy and produces pollution. This is a direct consequence of the division of labour within national borders. Therefore, the issue of

401

environmental problems related to transport should not be restricted to the issue of international trade. Furthermore, the costs of energy and environmental damage related to transportation must be weighed against the cost differences related to energy and environmental damage in the production of the traded goods. Agreeing with the principle of full cost internalization, it is easy to see that international trade and transportation may well reduce the total costs of energy and pollution that follow from the production and consumption of a specific commodity in energy-efficient and low-polluting industries, but of course they do not always do so. Thus, like many other potential trade-related problems, the issue of trade, transport and the environment must be dealt with in a general equilibrium rather than a partial equilibrium context.

Before we close this section, it is important to stress the importance of being careful in using the argument of 'unfair' competition. Such an argument can easily be used to underpin the right of sovereign nations to design their society. As a rule, from the point of view of economic welfare, there is no need for harmonization of economic policy. This does not mean that there will be no such harmonization, however. In fact, the liberalization of international capital movements will mean an increase in the cost of introducing ambitious (i.e. cost-increasing) policies, in the field of environmental standards or working conditions, for example. Therefore, one can expect that governments in countries with higher ambitions in such fields will have strong incentives to take on the role of leadership in the process of international harmonization. However, trade restrictions are never the optimal policy and differences in these fields of economic policy should not be used as arguments against free trade. To argue, like Daly (1993), that the free trade argument is no longer valid, because of the free international mobility of capital, is false. What motivates trade are the differences among countries in the opportunity costs for various products. A country that prices itself out of the market, losing market shares and losing footloose capital, has to adjust its economic policy (relaxing some of its cost-increasing political ambitions), adjust real factor prices (e.g. reduce wages), and/or devalue its currency in order to restore competitiveness. Daly overlooks these fundamental forces. The following conclusion by Paul Krugman is better founded in economic theory:

> Free trade can serve as a focal point on which countries can agree to avoid trade wars. It can also serve as a focal point on which countries can agree to avoid trade wars. It can also serve as a simple principle with which to resist pressures of special-interest politics. To abandon the free trade principle in pursuit of the gains from sophisticated intervention could therefore open the door to adverse political consequences that would outweigh the potential gains.
>
> (Krugman, 1987, p. 143)

LDCs AND THE INTERNATIONAL TRADE SYSTEM

The recent pre-WTO development

During the past decade there have been some interesting features character-izing developments in the field of international trade. In the rich parts of the world, regional integration has developed quite rapidly and bilateralism has thus come to play an increasingly important role. In large parts of the rest of the world, the World Bank and the IMF have demanded quite far-reaching trade liberalization as part of various types of structural adjust-ment or economic recovery programmes that have been introduced in indebted countries as a prerequisite for debt reductions and favourable loans. By that means these less developed and generally poor countries have become more open to international competition. At the same time, there seems to have been a general agreement that a revision of the existing GATT was urgently needed so that bilateralism and non-transparency, where the unequal economic power among nation states tends to harm the poor countries, can be replaced with a multilateral transparent system of international trade policy.

The recession that followed upon the oil crisis in the early 1970s pro-duced a break in the trade liberalization that was initiated by the formation of GATT in 1947. It is worth noting that the introduction of various types of trade barriers since 1973 was directed mainly against exports from Japan and less developed countries that had begun to take advantage of their abundance of cheap labour. The export of labour-intensive manufactures from the *Newly industrialized countries* (NICs) placed many domestic firms in the old industrial world in a weak competitive position. As a consequence, demands for protectionism were advanced, frequently based on the argument of 'unfair' working conditions. In many cases these de-mands led to the introduction of various types of non-tariff barriers also.

To give an exact measure of the magnitude of the rise in protectionism since the 1970s is very difficult since much of the trade policy has been designed in a way that conceals it from detection. GATT estimated that some 3–5 per cent of total world trade was affected by the protective measures that were introduced by the developed market economies be-tween 1974 and 1977 (UNCTAD, 1978, p. 16). It should be noted that this figure does not include trade policy measures that had been introduced and implemented before 1974 and that were still restricting trade during the period in question. Thus, trade in textiles and clothing, approximately some 5 per cent of world trade, was not included in the estimate. As these measures also were directed mainly against imports from LDCs, we note that those LDCs that had tried to diversify their economic structure away from a more or less complete reliance on agricultural goods and other primary commodities were the big losers in the trend away from compliance with GATT, towards bilateralism outside GATT (for an interesting and highly informative analysis of the issue of protectionism since the mid-1970s, see Bhagwati (1988, Chapter 3)).

The above trade policy development took place notwithstanding the fact that in 1965 a special section on trade and development had been introduced in GATT. In this section it was stated that:

> There is need for a rapid and sustained expansion of the export earnings of the less-developed contracting parties.
>
> There is need for positive efforts designed to ensure that less-developed contracting parties secure a share in the growth in international trade commensurate with the needs of their economic development.
>
> (GATT, 1986, p. 53f.)

As a consequence, the developed countries made a number of commitments, among which we note that these countries

> shall to the fullest extent possible – that is, except when compelling reasons, which may include legal reasons, make it impossible – give effect to the following provision[s]:...refrain from introducing, or increasing the incidence of, customs duties or non-tariff import barriers on products currently or potentially of particular export interest to less-developed contracting parties.
>
> (GATT, 1986, p. 55)

Thus, the developed contracting parties of GATT in 1965 made quite far-reaching commitments in relation to trade policy towards less developed countries. In real policy, however, the commitments proved to be less far reaching.

An organization that has come to be seen as the trade organization for less developed countries in particular is the United Nations Conference on Trade and Development, UNCTAD, which was established in 1964. However, unlike GATT, UNCTAD does not deal only with trade issues but also includes issues concerning investments, foreign aid, transnational companies and the issue of technology transfers between developed and less developed countries. Among the relatively few concrete results of the work in UNCTAD it is interesting to note the generalized system of tariff preferences (GSP) that was introduced in 1971. However, these preferences have mainly accrued to a small number of less developed countries. In a study from 1977 it was concluded that 75 per cent of the GSP trade comes from twelve less developed countries, mainly NICs (Baldwin and Murray, 1977).

In conclusion, the developed countries have made important commitments through both GATT and UNCTAD. However, as noted above, parallel to the tariff reductions that have taken place during the last thirty years since the formation of UNCTAD and the inclusion of a section about trade and development in GATT, the developed countries have introduced a number of non-tariff barriers outside the frame of these two organizations. These measures have frequently been directed towards the less developed countries. At the same time the developed countries have tried to convince, and through the World Bank and the IMF also pressured, less developed countries to turn away from inward-oriented policies and to open up their economies to increased international trade and competition.

Finally, it is interesting to note that the trade expansion of the LDCs during the 1980s was just around one-third of the growth of total world merchandise trade or around 1.6 per cent annually. Thus, the LDCs' share of global trade decreased from 28 to 21 per cent (Goldin and van der Mensbrugghe, 1992, p. 8). This reduced share fell mainly on non-manufacturing LDCs, i.e. mainly the poorest countries. This is clearly indicated by the fact that between 1970 and 1990, LDCs' share of total manufacturing trade increased from around 10 to around 20 per cent (IBRD, 1994a, p. 2). However, as can be seen in Figures 16.1 and 16.2 the participation in and contribution to world trade differ largely among the different developing regions. Sub-Saharan Africa (excluding the South African Customs Union) contributed just around 5 per cent of the 19 per cent of total world merchandise exports coming from low- and middle-income countries in 1990, i.e. just 1 per cent of total world merchandise exports, while low- and middle-income countries in East Asia and the Pacific as a group contributed 7 per cent to world merchandise exports.[1]

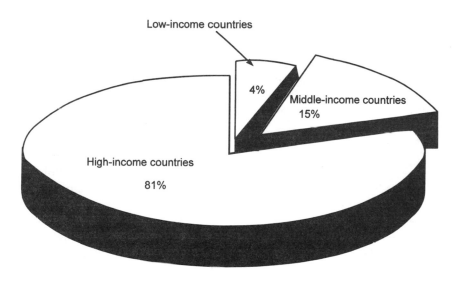

Figure 16.1 Origin of world merchandise exports, 1990
Source: *World Development Report* (1992, Table 14)

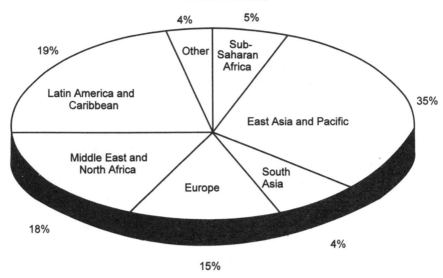

Figure 16.2 Merchandise exports from low- and middle-income countries, 1990
Source: *World Development Report* (1992, Table 14)

The results of the Uruguay Round – the LDC perspective

Considering the development of the international trade system during the last few decades, it is easy to agree with Hufbauer and Schott who in 1985, i.e. the year before the start of the Uruguay Round, stated:

> Few countries are content with the way the world trading system now operates. Rules are vague and weakly enforced.... While trade negotiations are not a panacea for ills of the world economy, neither are they a placebo. In conjunction with appropriate monetary and fiscal policies, trade reforms can contribute to economic growth and employment.
>
> (Hufbauer and Schott, 1985, p. 97)

Then, what were the changes of the international trade rules that eventually resulted from the Uruguay Round? This section presents a brief survey of the most important changes that can be expected to have a direct impact on the trade and thus on the growth and development potential of the LDCs. It should be noted that in this section we do not make any assessment of these latter effects. Such an analysis will be presented in the next section.

One of the most important results of the Uruguay Round is that the resulting World Trade Organization, the WTO, is not intended to be a free trade organization even if it has the objective of promoting trade liberalization. Instead, the WTO will be an organization that should promote and supervise the adherence to transparent and predictable rules. It will not by itself introduce sanctions against those who deflect from them but its rules make it possible to authorize members to withdraw most favoured nation (MFN) treatment from the transgressors.

Furthermore, decision making within the WTO will be based on qualified unweighted majority voting. This will clearly favour LDCs. Around 80 per cent of the members of GATT, and the intended WTO also, are LDCs. However, because of lack of capacity in terms of qualified civil servants and negotiation specialists, it is obviously a problem for the LDCs to utilize this potential.

In terms of trade liberalization and policy areas covered by the Uruguay Round Agreement, the following points should be noted (for more details see e.g. IBRD (1994a, Annex 1), which is the main source of our summary if not otherwise stated):

(a) *Tariffs*: The objective is to produce an overall cut of 33 per cent.

Tariffs on *manufactures* will be reduced in five equal annual reductions from the date when the WTO is put into operation. It has been agreed (provisional results from November 1993) that the industrial countries should produce a 38 per cent cut in their tariffs on manufactures. Lower than average tariff cuts have been agreed in 'sensitive sectors, such as textiles, clothing, footwear and transport equipment' (IBRD 1994a, Annex 1, p. 1). LDCs have agreed to increase tariff bindings, i.e. legal maximum rates, from 12 to 56 per cent of manufacturing imports.

In the case of *tropical products*, the provisional information from November 1993 'indicates a 42% reduction in tariffs on agricultural tropical products (simple average), and 57% on industrial tropical products in industrial countries (import-weighted average)' (ibid.). This means a reduction in the import-weighted average industrial country tariff on industrial tropical products from 4.2 to 2.3 per cent (ibid.).

For tariffs on *natural-resource-based products* the preliminary information from November 1993 shows a 34 per cent cut in tariffs, from a weighted average of 3.2 per cent to 2.1 per cent (ibid.).

(b) *Agriculture*: The objective is to establish a market-oriented trading system with stronger multilateral rules.

In this new field of the GATT system the Uruguay Round produced a number of important results:

- The start of a gradual liberalisation process in the sector – initially over 6 years for industrial countries and 10 years for developing countries.
- Restrictions against imports are subject to a 'tariffication' commitment, with average tariff cuts by industrial countries of 36% over 6 years from 1986–88 base, and a minimum cut of 15% on all tariff lines.

- Tariff bindings increased from 81% to 95% of imports in industrial countries, and from 23% to 90% in developing countries.
- Domestic supports...must be reduced by 20% from a 1986–88 base over the implementation period....The so-called 'green box' subsidies – certain government service programs, decoupled income support, social safety-net programs, structural adjustment assistance, environmental programs, and regional assistance programs – are exempted from reduction commitments.
- Export subsidies must be reduced by 36% in value and 21% in volume over the implementation period from a 1986–90 base.
- Special safeguard provisions, triggered by volume increases or price reductions, permit the imposition of additional duties up to specified limits.
- Several provisions introduce greater flexibility for developing countries.

(IBRD, 1994a, Annex 1, p. 2f.)

Among these provisions we note the following:

- Reductions in tariffs, domestic supports and export subsidies are set at two-thirds the levels specified above, and spread over ten years.
- Least-developed countries are exempted from all reduction commitments.
- Exemption from the tariffication commitment on any agricultural product that is a primary staple in a traditional diet...
- Exemptions from domestic subsidy commitments when subsidies relate to investment...diversification away from production of illicit narcotic crops, and input subsidies for low-income producers.
- Exemptions from export subsidy reduction commitments when the subsidies relate to export marketing and internal transport.
- Food aid exempted from export subsidy commitments...

(IBRD, 1994a, Annex 1, p. 3)

(c) *Textiles and clothing*: The objective is to phase out the Multifiber Arrangement and make trade in these products follow the mainstream multilateral trade rules.

For this sector, which is often labour intensive, and thus important for low-income countries, the Uruguay Round produced an agreement that included:

- Gradual integration of the sector into the WTO (GATT 1994)...over 10 years.
- Outstanding quota restrictions shall be expanded by the prevailing quota growth rate plus 16% annually in the first three years,

by 25% in the subsequent four years, and by 27% in the final three years.

- A commitment is made to take the necessary anticircumvention measures to deal with transshipment, rerouting, false declaration of origin, and forgery.
- Provisions to redistribute quotas in favor of quota-constrained and efficient exporters.

(IBRD, 1994a, Annex 1, p. 4f.)

(d) *Changes in the rules of international trade*: In addition to the above changes regarding *market access*, the Uruguay Round also changed the rules of international trade. For example, the *safeguards* clauses were improved and put under tighter discipline. In particular we note that:

- Developing country exporters accounting for less than 3% of a country's imports of a product shall be exempt from safeguard action, provided that all developing Members with less than a 3% share account for less than a 9% share overall.
- Voluntary export restraints (VERs) and similar measures on exports or imports are to be eliminated within four years, although each Member has the right to maintain one VER until the end of 1999. Governments are not to encourage or support the adoption of VER-like measures by public or private enterprises.

(IBRD, 1994a, Annex 1, p. 5f.)

In relation to *anti-dumping* measures the new agreement means a strengthening of the rules on such measures. For developing countries it is stated that 'developing countries are to be given special consideration, and the possibility of constructive remedies explored, before antidumping action is taken against their exports' (IBRD, 1994a, Annex 1, p. 6).

Also the rules on *subsidies* are reformed by the new agreement. Here we note that:

- Least-developed countries are allowed to maintain export subsidies, as are other developing countries whose per capita income is less than US$ 1,000 per annum. Developing countries that are not, or cease to be, in these categories are required to phase out export subsidies within eight years (with the possibility of extension). Economies in transition are granted a seven-year period within which to eliminate prohibited subsidies.
- The prohibition of subsidies linked to the use of domestic over imported products shall not apply to developing countries for five years, and to least-developed countries for eight years.
- ...The *de minimis* provisions establish exemptions for developing countries from countervailing duties when subsidy levels do

not exceed 2% ... or import shares are less than 4%, and cumu-
latively among countries benefitting from this provision, less
than 9% of total imports.

(IBRD, 1994a, Annex 1, p. 7)

(e) *New areas and a new institutional framework*: In addition to the
above areas, it should be noted that the new international trade
agreement contains articles on trade issues that previously have not
been included in GATT, i.e. *rules of origin, technical barriers to trade,
and sanitary and phytosanitary measures*. The objective of these
articles is to harmonize and provide disciplines for rules of origin,
to improve transparency and coverage disciplines to prevent the use
of technical norms and testing procedures as barriers to trade, and to
establish rules to clarify and harmonize sanitary and phytosanitary
measures to prevent their use as unnecessary obstacles to trade.

Finally, some new trade-related areas have been included in the
Uruguay Round Agreement. One such very important area is *trade-
related intellectual property rights* (TRIPS). Here the objective is to
develop rules that should protect such rights. Here we note that in
relation to LDCs:

A one-year delay period is envisaged for the implementation of
the TRIPS agreement following the establishment of the WTO.
Developing countries and transition economies are permitted to
delay implementation for a further four years, except for the
national treatment and most-favored-nation commitments.
Where patent protection is called for in areas of technology not
actually so protected in developing countries, a grace period of an
additional five years is provided in respect of the technologies in
question. The least-developed countries are permitted ten years
on the same basis, with the possibility of further extensions....
Notwithstanding the above transition provision, all patentable
inventions on pharmaceuticals and agricultural chemical products
made after entry into force of the WTO must be protected. Least
developed countries may have the transition period extended
upon request.

(IBRD, 1994a, Annex 1, p. 11f.)

Other new areas include trade-related investment measures (TRIMS) and
trade in services. In the latter area the objective is to liberalize trade and
to establish multilateral rules and disciplines. For the developing
countries, the liberalization of trade in services 'is anticipated as a gradual
process' (IBRD, 1994a, Annex 1, p. 13).

Finally, the institutional framework of the international trade system is
strengthened, mainly through the creation of the World Trade Organization. This new organization aims to:

Enhance GATT surveillance, improve overall effectiveness of GATT, increase its contribution to coherence in policy making.

(IBRD, 1994a, Annex 1, p. 14)

Here it is important to note that the membership in the WTO:

implies acceptance of the revised GATT (GATT 1994) as well as all Uruguay Round agreements. The single undertaking concept underlying the WTO means that developing countries are assuming more extensive and higher levels of obligations than ever before.

(IBRD, 1994a, Annex 1, p. 14)

Trade liberalization and trade expansion

When analysing the percentage figures for tariff reductions it is important to note that these reductions must be looked upon from the current tariff levels. A small percentage reduction in a high tariff level may well give rise to a greater trade expansion than a greater reduction in a low tariff level. Therefore, in order to assess the Uruguay tariff reductions it is interesting to know the pre-Uruguay tariffs and the offer.

The message in Figure 16.3 is summarized by GATT (1993, p. 23) as follows:

(i) the proposed cuts in the developed economies' tariffs on "textiles and clothing", "fish and fish products", "transportation equipment" and "leather, rubber, footwear" are below the average for all industrial products;

(ii) the reductions for "metals", "mineral products and precious stones", "wood, pulp, paper and furniture", and "non-electric machinery" are well above average;

and

(iii) the reductions for "wood, pulp, paper and furniture", "metals", "non-electric machinery" and "mineral products and precious stones" are larger when weighted by imports from developing countries than when weighted by imports from all sources, which means that, within each of these product categories, specific products of greater interest to developing economies are receiving relatively greater tariff reductions;...For each of the developing economies' three top value product categories...the percentage tariff reduction is greater for the mix of products imported from developing economies than for the mix imported from all sources.

It is important to remember that Figure 16.3 is limited to tariff reductions. In the field of textiles and clothing large parts of LDC exports are restricted by the Multifiber Arrangement. This means that the liberalization for this

411

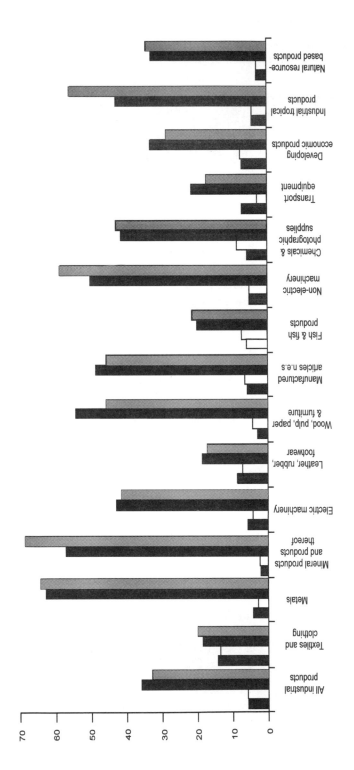

Figure 16.3 Developed economies' pre-Uruguay Round rates and offered reductions

Source: GATT (1993, Table 11)

group of products will be much more far reaching when the Uruguay Round Agreement is fully implemented, than what is indicated in the figure.

AN ASSESSMENT OF THE URUGUAY ROUND AGREEMENT FROM THE POINT OF VIEW OF LDCs

When, in December 1993, the Uruguay Round came to a successful completion, it is interesting to ask whether the prospects for growth and development in the poorest countries have been positively affected or not. In the previous section, we summarized the content of the Uruguay Round Agreement with special reference to less developed countries. It is important to note that these countries have been much more active in the Uruguay Round than in previous GATT rounds. One explanation for this is of course that with the economic reform process in most LDCs, and thus the liberalization and opening up of their respective economies, it becomes increasingly important for these countries, which are small from the point of view of the international economy, to work actively for a reformation of the international trade system away from bilateralism and towards a well-functioning multilateral system with transparent and predictable rules. Since 1986 over sixty LDCs have reported unilateral trade liberalization measures to GATT, twenty-four have become members of GATT, and more than twenty less developed countries and former centrally planned countries are in the process of acceding (IBRD, 1994a, p. 2).

There seems to be a general agreement that on a global level the results from this GATT round will contribute to increased trade, incomes and investment (IBRD, 1994a, p. 9; Friis Bach, 1994, p. 2). Guay Mhone, who has produced a critical article about the implications of the Uruguay Round for developing countries, writes 'There is no doubt in anybody's mind that the world is better off with, than without, GATT' (Mhone, 1994, p. 34). However, when it comes to the issue of the distribution and character of the gains and losses opinions vary, mainly because of the time perspective.

The LDC commitments can be summarized by quoting IBRD (1994a, Box 1):

i) Increase in the number of duties bound and some tariff reduction on both industrial goods and agriculture. Tighter disciplines of agricultural policies.

ii) Over 70 developing countries made commitments in services including many least-developed countries.

iii) Developing countries have agreed to remove prohibited export subsidies and submit their policies to international rules.

iv) Trade distorting investment measures are to be eliminated in 5–7 years (local content requirements, trade balancing).

v) Protection of intellectual property will gradually be extended in several areas.

vi) Developing countries will adopt the framework agreement on services.

It is obvious that these commitments are quite far reaching considering the present situation in large parts of the developing countries. However, as noted in the previous section, the special needs of LDCs have in many cases led to longer periods of implementation for these countries (in the case of least developed countries some commitments are completely exempted). Notwithstanding these special treatments, it is obvious that the commitments made by the LDCs are far reaching and in comparison with the developed countries this means a heavier demand for domestic policy actions.

According to Mhone the LDC commitments have been more or less forced upon the LDCs:

> in the Uruguay Round its [GATT's] guiding principles of non-discrimination, reciprocity and transparency have been used by some Northern countries to intimidate the South into submitting to the dictates of the globalised international division of labour, driven by Northern capital and technology primarily.
>
> (Mhone, 1994, p. 34f.)

Friis Bach argues that the new agreement can give rise to a negative effect on the problem of poverty (Friis Bach, 1994, p. 2). By referring to estimates from the World Bank and the OECD, Friis Bach concludes that in the industrial countries the daily per capita gain from the agreement will be 2.75 DKK while the same gain for the average LDC inhabitant will be 0.25 DKK, and for the very poorest countries the effects of the Uruguay Round will be a loss. In the case of Africa, according to Friis Bach (1994, p. 2) every inhabitant will lose 0.07 DKK every day as a result of the agreement. As noted by Friis Bach the calculations are very uncertain and incomplete. Nevertheless, the estimates should give rise to critical rethinking about the distribution aspects of the free trade system and of how to complement the Uruguay Round with various forms of foreign assistance from the great gainers to those countries that are not yet in a position to reap the great benefits of the reformed free trade system. As noted by Goldin and van der Mensbrugghe:

> The overall gains from liberalisation greatly exceed the losses. However, the potential losses facing low-income countries require an enhanced commitment to compensation and development assistance.... The overall gains in terms of increasing world income range from $195 billion per annum in the case of a partial reform [Uruguay Round Agreement], to $477 billion per annum in the case of complete liberalisation [assuming that all trade restrictions and subsidies have been removed]. While there are regions which lose from

reform, the overall gains are significantly larger than the losses, so that compensation mechanisms can be implemented which could ensure that all regions gain from trade reform.

(Goldin and van der Mensbrugghe, 1992, p. 14)

Of the estimated annual gain of $195 billion 1992 dollars from the partial liberalization by the year 2002, $104 billion are estimated to accrue to OECD countries and $91 billion to the developing countries. Among the developing countries some countries, net food importers, will lose. However, as noted by Goldin and van der Mensbrugghe, a fact that also has been reflected in the Uruguay Round Agreement, 'the total $7 billion in losses is small compared to the gains, and could be compensated for by a transfer of 3.5 per cent of the gains, equivalent to less than 20 per cent of official development assistance' (Goldin and van der Mensbrugghe, 1992, p. 11)

It is important to note that the figures concerning the magnitude and distribution of the gains and losses of the agreement are just estimates and should be interpreted with great caution even if the estimates are based on a quite ambitious study with a world economy computable-equilibrium model (see e.g. Goldin and van der Mensbrugghe, 1992, pp. 27ff.). However, the model only captures the effects of trade liberalization and the elimination of subsidies. For the less developed countries, in particular those least developed countries that can be classified as net food importers and that at present are implementing far-reaching economic reform programmes, the effects estimated in the above model are probably a clear underestimate of the gains. The reason is that changes in important systemic reform components, for instance privatization and increased reliance on decentralized decision making where markets and incentives will play a central role, are not included in the model.

In addition to the above remark about the underestimation of the gains for countries that are now implementing economic systemic reforms, GATT (1993, p. 44) states that its estimates are based on product-by-product analysis of the Uruguay Round Agreement which is clearly a limitation that also points to an underestimation of the total effects.

The new areas covered by the Uruguay Round Agreement, services (GATS), trade-related intellectual property rights (TRIPS) and trade-related investment measures (TRIMS), seem not to have been included in the estimates that were quoted above. The quantitative effects of incorporating these policy areas in the agreement are difficult to estimate. According to GATT (1993, p. 39f.), however, GATS should be positive for the LDCs. The reason is that services are relatively labour intensive and in many cases, like tourism, they demand relatively high inputs of low-skilled labour. Thus, foreign investments in LDCs' services sectors should be expected to follow upon the implementation of GATS.

The inclusion of TRIMS and TRIPS in the new multilateral trade agreement can also be expected to be positive from the point of view of attracting foreign investments to LDCs. However, in the case of TRIMS the sovereignty of the respective country will be restricted and the power of owners of international capital will increase. However, for many of the poorest countries, the problem is probably not that foreign investments are queuing up for making investments and therefore should be controlled, but rather that there is little or no interest from foreign capital in making investments in these countries. The limited interest for investments in most countries in Sub-Saharan Africa is not due to trade-related aspects of investments but is rather due to political risks of nationalization, and economic policy at large. When structural adjustment programmes have been completed, however, it is to be hoped that the picture can change. Here it is important to note that most of these programmes are consistent with the new trade agreement.

In the case of TRIPS, finally, the possibility for LDCs to imitate products and production methods without permission will gradually be reduced. On the other hand, the inclusion of TRIPS in the agreement can be expected to lead to an increased inflow of foreign investments in LDCs. Furthermore, as noted by IBRD (1994a, p. 8), 'A number of developing countries will derive benefits from the agreement, especially those that have started to develop and export knowledge-intensive products and services' (e.g. computer software). Thus, the implications of TRIPS can be expected to differ largely between countries, depending on their level of industrialization and development. In order to get a better understanding of how the agreements on TRIMS and TRIPS, respectively, affect the location of internationally mobile capital and the respective host countries, it is an important task for future research to make a closer investigation of the characteristics of foreign investments in LDCs.

Notwithstanding the above remarks about the limitations of the estimates of the effects of the new multilateral trade agreement, it is clear that the estimates presented by OECD, GATT and the World Bank also indicate quite high magnitudes of the gains from an efficient implementation of the Uruguay Round Agreement.

Looking at various groups of developing countries, Mhone (1994, p. 40) concludes that least developed countries are among the potential winners of the agreement, since they are exempted from more or less all commitments and thus are free to use various types of measures to promote trade and economic development. However, in reality and at least in the short to medium term, these countries will face considerable problems in utilizing the advantages of the new trade agreement, owing to lack of capacity, both institutional and in terms of human capital. In the short run the net food importers within this group will be worse off because of the liberalization of agricultural trade and the dismantling of agricultural subsidies in the developed countries. However, here it is important to remember that the low prices that have existed as a consequence of subsidization have made it difficult for agriculture in less developed countries to compete both in their respective domestic market and in the international market. In the long term the changes introduced in the Uruguay Round Agreement mean an important potential for many developing countries, not the least in Sub-Saharan Africa, to make profitable agricultural investments and to become competitive and efficient producers of agricultural goods. Such a development will be particularly positive for the peasants.

The group of developing countries that a priori seems to lose from the new agreement is the NICs who now have to compete on equal terms with the developed countries. On the other hand these countries can be expected to gain from the dismantling of the Multifiber Arrangement and similar trade restrictions in the field of electronics, etc.

One important starting point for an assessment of the effects of the Uruguay Round on LDCs is the current characteristics of the trade of these countries.

From Figure 16.4 it can be concluded that the commodity composition of LDC exports varies largely between various groups of LDCs. Manufactures dominate exports from Asian and European LDCs while agricultural and mining products dominate exports from LDCs in other parts of the world. Statistics on LDC exports of industrial products show that:

(i)   one-half of developing economies have a substantial export interest in natural resource-based products (the share in export earnings exceeds 20 per cent), and for one-half of the members of this group, natural resource-based products account for the majority of export earnings;

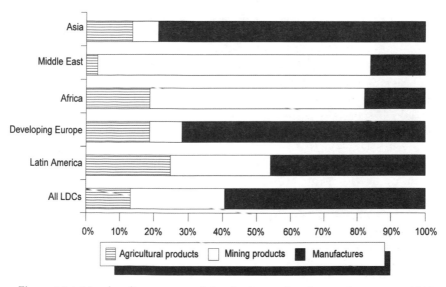

Figure 16.4 Merchandise exports of developing regions by product group, 1992
Source: GATT (1993, Table 2)

(ii)   one-third of developing economies have a substantial export interest in textiles and clothing, and just under one-third of developing economies have a substantial export interest in metals and in mineral products and precious metals and stones;

(iii) electric and non-electrical machinery are important in the aggregate exports of developing economies (a combined share of 23 per cent) due to the importance of these two product categories in the exports of the leading exporters of manufactures among developing economies; and

(iv)   almost all of the least-developed economies are at present dependent on a single product category for the majority of export earnings from industrial products, and products of particular interest include natural resource-based products, textiles and clothing, and mineral products and precious metals and stones.

(GATT, 1993, p. 13)

The same source concludes that in relation to LDC exports of agricultural products:

(i)   two-thirds of developing economies have a substantial export interest (exceeding 20 per cent of earnings from exports of agricultural products) in agricultural tropical products, and for two-thirds of the members of this group agricultural tropical products account for the majority of export earnings;

(ii)   over one-half of developing economies have a substantial export interest in coffee, tea, cocoa, etc. (tropical beverages and other tropical products such as sugar), and for half the members of this group, this product category accounts for the majority of earnings from exports of agricultural products;

(iii) just over one-third of developing economies have a substantial export interest in fruits and vegetables; and,

(iv)   almost one-half of the least-developed economies at present depend for the majority of earnings on exports of agricultural products, with products of particular interest including tropical beverages, as well as fruits and vegetables, oilseeds, fats and oils, and other agricultural products.

(GATT, 1993, p. 16)

Finally, on one of the new fields included in the Uruguay Round Agreement, trade in services, from GATT (1993, p. 17f. and Tables 6 and 7) it can be concluded that for those LDCs where there are available statistics on trade in commercial services:

(i)   almost one-half receive a substantial share of their total foreign-exchange earnings (more than 20 per cent) from exports of commercial services;

(ii) within the group of developing economies with a high or very high export interest (more than 21 per cent of total foreign exchange earnings), travel is of particular interest.

It should be noted also that the export composition is changing rapidly for all developing regions and that between 1979 and 1988:

new products were relatively more important in the trade structures of developing regions at the end of the 1980s than for developed countries, although their average number of principal exports remained lower. The proportion of new products in the structure of their exports to developed countries ranged from twice (Asia) to three times (Africa) the 15 per cent figure for developed countries.

(GATT, 1993, p. 18)

Furthermore, for the following analysis it is interesting to quote GATT (1993):

Although textiles and clothing remain the dominant export in terms of their share in total merchandise exports (excluding fuels) of developing East Asia, South Asia and Sub-Saharan Africa, while non-ferrous metals dominate for Latin America, the product composition of their exports is changing rapidly.

For Sub-Saharan Africa, rapidly growing product groups include textiles and clothing, chemical elements and compounds, fruits and vegetables, manufactured fertilizers, machinery, wood and wood products, non-ferrous metals, iron and steel, non-metallic metals, animal feeds, leather goods and footwear, transport equipment, metal manufactures, plastic material, dyes, coffee/tea/cocoa, tobacco and meat.

(GATT, 1993, p. 19)

Thus, it seems to be of the utmost importance for LDCs to diversify their economic structure and exports. However, such a diversification demands a transparent and predictable international trade system so that the protectionist experiences from the mid-1970s become unlikely to be repeated. One important field where the new trade agreement will mean a clear improvement for the less developed countries is trade in textiles and clothing. This sector, with its intensive use of relatively low-skilled labour, has been important in many of the Asian countries' process of transformation to industrial economies. By removing the Multifiber Arrangement this sector opens up significant export potentials for the African continent also.

Textiles and clothing is the sector that is expected to grow most up to the year 2005, with a growth of 60 per cent for clothing and 34 per cent for textiles (GATT, 1993, p. 45). For trade in agricultural goods also, in particular trade in agricultural tropical products, high growth rates are expected. The growth figures for agricultural and fishery products are estimated at 20

419

per cent. Roughly the same expected growth, 19 per cent, has been calculated for processed food and beverages.

Without a successful completion and implementation of the Uruguay Round, not only would the world be worse off but the poorest countries should be expected to be the big losers. Even if Myrdal was right in stating that there is an inherent tendency that inequalities between rich and poor countries will increase through trade, both groups may well be absolutely better off. This is also indicated by the estimates from the IBRD and the OECD. The exceptions mentioned by Friis Bach (1994) are mainly countries that can be characterized as net food importers. According to these calculations, Africa is the continent where the losers dominate. However, it should be remembered that most countries in Sub-Saharan Africa today are implementing far-reaching economic reform programmes where market forces are given a central role in determining the structural changes of the economy and where international openness is one of the main characteristics of the intended economic system. This means that we should expect these countries to become gradually more able to adjust to changing international conditions and also to become more export oriented. Therefore, the calculations should be interpreted with great caution. The outcome depends critically on the outcome of the respective national reform programmes and the respective countries' possibilities to attract internationally mobile capital. This, in turn, depends critically on the predictability of the international trade system, something that will increase by the results from the Uruguay Round, and on the political development in the respective countries. Along with the process of not only economic reforms but of democratization in the African countries as well, the risks of nationalization of capital will most likely fall and thus international capital will find it more attractive to make investments in these countries. Therefore, the new trade agreement and the WTO, according to our view, incorporates a much higher growth potential than what is shown in the IBRD and OECD calculations.

CONCLUDING REMARKS AND AID IMPLICATIONS

If ratified and successfully implemented, the multilateral trade agreement that resulted from the Uruguay Round will mean a clear improvement of the institutional framework for international trade. Through the agreement the rules of international trade will increase in transparency and predictability. This is very important, in particular for poor countries with a weak bargaining position. There seems to be a close to general agreement that the world economy will be better off with the new trade agreement than without it. This is a view that is not only shared but also emphasized by LDCs. In fact, these countries have been very active in the negotiations and have made a number of quite far-reaching commitments.

This does not mean that the effects of the new trade system will be entirely positive for all LDCs. For the least developed countries that are often net food importers, there will be important transition problems when the production and export subsidies in OECD agriculture are eliminated. On the other hand, the gradual elimination of the Multifiber Arrangement will produce an important potential for diversification of production and exports from these countries, provided that the Multifiber Arrangement is not replaced with a new set of non-tariff barriers.

In the Uruguay Round Agreement the developed countries have committed themselves to assist the less developed countries. It is not clear whether this will result in real policy actions in favour of the LDCs or whether domestic structural adjustment problems will lead to various forms of restrictions, motivated by arguments based on, for instance, environmental problems or the use of cheap labour in export production abroad. Considering the historical evidence from the 1970s, this risk should not be underestimated.

Even if the overall impression is that the LDCs will gain from the new international trade agreement, we should not overlook the fact that the OECD countries are the great winners. Furthermore, the LDCs need various types of assistance to be able to reap the potential benefits of the agreement. Such assistance should not only be limited to helping the net food importers to overcome their transition problems but also, and this is as important in a long-term perspective, aim at increasing the administrative and bargaining capacity of these countries. In the fields of trade-related labour standards and environmental standards assistance of various types is needed also. For the currently very sensitive issue of child labour, quite ambitious social and educational programmes have to be introduced rather than just prohibiting trade in products that have been produced by children. Pure trade restrictions will most likely lead to an even worse situation for children and low-income, large-size families.

Mhone (1994) presents an interesting discussion about the various parts of the Uruguay Agreement from the point of view of LDCs. Even if he is positive and states that 'the world is better off with, than without, GATT' (Mhone, 1994: pp. 34 and 40), he points to a number of important problems that the new agreement can give rise to and where the developing countries may need assistance from the richer contracting partners. His notes refer to issues that will become critical in implementing the new agreement, e.g. the rules of origin where harmonization is needed and where monitoring institutions must be created or improved in developing countries, and the anti-dumping code, where developing countries lack monitoring capacity also. In another field, where the prospects of the new agreement look bleak from the point of view of efficient implementation, there are technical barriers to trade. Here safety and health aspects may well be used as an argument against free trade. If so, the losers will be found among the less developed countries with little capacity and competence to satisfy the standards set by the developed countries. Here it may be of some interest to note that the European Community has been trying for a long time to harmonize technical standards. However, the process has been slow and beset by a host of problems (see e.g. Hansson, 1990, p. 180 and Chapter 4). Therefore, it is reasonable to agree with Mhone when he concludes that even if limitations of the use of technical standards were to benefit developing countries

> it is most likely that the Agreement on Technical Barriers to Trade will work to the disadvantage of the lesser developed countries in the South by limiting their exports, to the North, of manufactured goods, especially processed foods, textiles, durable consumer goods and indigenous products.
>
> (Mhone, 1994, p. 37).

Also in this field it is important to note that most developing countries lack the capacity to interpret and apply technical standards in their export production. Therefore, extensive foreign assistance in creating capacity and building institutions is needed.

However, one should not exaggerate the problems related to the new multilateral trade agreement. Instead one should ask what would have happened without a new agreement. It is reasonable to assume that countries which, from a global economic point of view, are very poor and less developed, and which have a weak bargaining position, would have been even worse off in such a situation, because of increased bilateralism, less transparency and thus increased uncertainty.

In a draft resolution on the evaluation of the results of the Uruguay Round the Council of Ministers of the Organization of African Unity (OAU) in February 1994 invited international organizations 'to jointly provide technical assistance...on all technicalities of the Final Act and related agreements of the Uruguay Round' and called upon the Secretary-General of the OAU 'to elaborate a programme of technical assistance for the benefit of African countries, to respond to and cope with the results of the Uruguay Round in the short, medium and long-term perspectives' (IBRD, 1994b).

The ongoing economic systemic changes in many LDCs are necessary for improving the situation of these countries. However, these reforms are not sufficient; they must be complemented with reforms of the international trade and payment systems. The Uruguay Round Agreement is one important step in this process but the LDCs must be given assistance to face the emerging new international institutional framework. Therefore, it is of the utmost importance that the developed countries take the invitation from the Council of Ministers of the OAU seriously if the current unfavourable situation of LDCs in world markets is not to become permanent.

NOTES

1 **Classification of countries:** The classification is based on 1990 GNP per capita, calculated with the World Bank Atlas method. *Low-income countries* includes all countries with up to $610 per capita income. *Middle-income countries* includes all countries with a per capita income of $611–7619. *High-income countries* includes all countries with a per capita income of $7620 or more.

In the figures Sub-Saharan Africa does not include countries in the South African Customs Union (South Africa, Namibia, Lesotho, Botswana and Swaziland).

REFERENCES

Baldwin, R. E. and Murray, T. (1977) 'MFN Tariff Reductions and Developing Country Trade Benefits under the GSP', *Economic Journal*, vol. 87.

Bhagwati, J. N. (1988) *Protectionism*, MIT Press, Cambridge, MA and London.

——(1993) 'The Case for Free Trade', *Scientific American*, November, pp. 18–23.

Daly, H. E. (1993) 'The Perils of Free Trade', *Scientific American*, November, pp. 24–29.

Friis Bach, C. (1994) *Skuespillet – Hvordan u-landene kan komme i klemme i GATT-aftalen*, Nord/Syd Koalitionens Handelsgruppe, Copenhagen.

GATT (1986) *The General Agreement on Tariffs and Trade*, The GATT Secretariat, Geneva.

——(1993) *An Analysis of the Proposed Uruguay Round Agreement, with Particular Emphasis on Aspects of Interest to Developing Economies*, The GATT Secretariat, Geneva.

Goldin, I. and van der Mensbrugghe, D. (1992) *Trade Liberalisation: What's at Stake?*, OECD Development Centre, Policy Brief No. 5, OECD, Paris.

Greenaway, D. and Chong Hyun Nam (1988) 'Industrialisation and Macroeconomic Performance in Developing Countries under Alternative Trade Strategies', *Kyklos*, vol. 41.

Haberler, G. (1959) *International Trade and Economic Development*, National Bank of Egypt Fiftieth Anniversary Commemoration Lectures, Cairo; partly reprinted in G. M. Meier (ed.) (1976) *Leading Issues in Economic Development*, Third Edition, Oxford University Press, Oxford, pp. 702–707.

Hansson, G. (1983) *Social Clauses and International Trade*, Routledge, London and Canberra; St Martins Press, New York.

——(1990) *Harmonisation and International Trade*, Routledge, London and New York.

——(ed.) (1993) *Trade, Growth and Development: The role of politics and institutions*, Routledge, London and New York.

Hufbauer, G. C. and Schott, J. J. (1985) *Trading for Growth: The next Round of Trade Negotiations*, Institute for International Economics, Washington, DC.

IBRD (1994a) *The Uruguay Round: A Preliminary Assessment*, 2 February, International Bank for Reconstruction and Development, Washington, D.C.

——(1994b) *The Uruguay Round: Resolution Adopted by the Council of Ministers of the Organization of African Unity on the Evaluation of the Results of the Uruguay Round of Multilateral Trade Negotiations*, 15 February, International Bank for Reconstruction and Development, Washington, DC.

Krugman, P. R. (1987) 'Is Free Trade Passé?', *The Journal of Economic Perspectives*, vol. 1, no. 2, pp. 131–144.

Mhone, G. C. Z. (1994) 'GATT – Implications of the Uruguay Round for Developing Countries', *Southern African Political and Economic Monthly*, February, pp. 34–40.

Myrdal, G. (1956) *Development and Underdevelopment*, National Bank of Egypt Fiftieth Anniversary Commemoration Lectures, Cairo; partly reprinted in G. M. Meier (ed.) (1976) *Leading Issues in Economic Development*, Third Edition, Oxford University Press, Oxford, pp. 688–692.

Nobel Prizewinners Worldwide Initiative to Stop Child Exploitation (1994) *A Message from the Nobel Prizewinners to the Makers of the Future*, Amsterdam/ The Hague/Washington, DC, 12 April.

Prebisch, R. (1950) *The Economic Development of Latin America and Its Principal Countries*, United Nations Economic Commission for Latin America, New York.

Södersten, B. (1964) *A Study on Economic Growth and International Trade*, Almqvist & Wiksell, Stockholm.

UNCTAD (1978) *Growing Protectionism and the Standstill on Trade Barriers against Imports from Developing Countries* (TD/B/C.2/194), UNCTAD, Geneva.

UNDEA (1949) *Relative Prices of Exports and Imports of Under-Developed Countries*, United Nations, Department of Economic Affairs, New York.

World Development Report (1992) Oxford University Press, New York.

17

GOVERNMENT, TRADE AND INTERNATIONAL CAPITAL MOBILITY

Ronald Findlay

The role of international factor mobility in shaping the evolution of the modern world economy has not followed any simple linear trend. While its heyday was undoubtedly in the *belle epoque* of the 1870–1913 period, when not only did Europeans colonize the world but tens of millions of Indians and Chinese moved about the less developed regions in their wake under the aegis of their empires, it has revived markedly again after experiencing a severe decline in the 1930s and 1940s as a result of depression and world war. The revival of capital mobility, however, has been much more evident than that of labour, despite the phenomena of the 'brain drains' and the flow of refugees generated by ethnic and other tensions in the newly independent states of the Third World.

The economies of the advanced industrial world have witnessed a withdrawal of government from intervention in the markets for tradable goods, within the frameworks of the European integration movement and the successive GATT agreements. The phenomenal advances in communications technology and the freeing of capital and exchange controls have meant that capital has become so much more mobile, with labour more or less fixed within national frontiers, and the perception has grown that each nation's prosperity is a function, to a large extent, of its ability to compete as a destination for this massive, footloose global pool of investible resources. What are the sources of the ability to act as a relatively more effective magnet for internationally mobile capital? Increasingly, it seems that the main factor is the provision of 'infrastructure' in the very broad sense that includes not only the 'physical overhead capital' of roads, bridges and electronic communications systems but also the 'social infrastructure provided through public education' that raises the quality of the labour force. The role of government, lessened in the arena of specific market interventions through tariffs, quotas and subsidies, has become increasingly enhanced in terms of the provision of infrastructure, consistently with Adam Smith's enumeration of the 'duties of the sovereign'.

Thus the relevant action in the field of government policy in relation to trade and investment issues has shifted away from the traditional emphasis on the effects of direct trade interventions that the vast literature of the subject has concentrated on, as surveyed for example in the well-known book by Corden (1974). Even the so-called 'new' trade theory, emphasizing increasing returns and monopolistic competition, and the associated literature on 'strategic' trade policy, has continued to concentrate on the traditional instruments, even though in a different market setting of oligopoly instead of perfect competition.

Discussion of these interesting new aspects of the role of government seems to require a model, however simple, that will *explicitly* incorporate the difference that the existence of governmental institutions makes to an economic system. The key point, stressed by writers from Hobbes to David Hume and Adam Smith, is that the existence of a sovereign authority that exercises Max Weber's 'monopoly of the legitimate use of force' to preserve law and order and enforce contracts enhances the productivity of resources in the private sector, and therefore constitutes what can be classified as a public intermediate input. It is 'intermediate' in the sense that it is not a 'final' use by consumers or investors but an essential component of the means by which final goods themselves can be provided in enhanced amounts by comparison with a state of anarchy. It is 'public' in the sense that it is 'non-rival' and 'non-excludable' as emphasized in the famous contributions by Lindahl and Samuelson.

Provision of the public input withdraws resources from the private sector and thus has a counterbalancing negative impact on final output. With the usual assumptions about diminishing returns it is easy to show that final output will be a *concave* function of the level of resources devoted to the public input, which therefore have a well-defined optimum at the point where the marginal value of public input is equal to the marginal costs of the resources withdrawn from the private sector to provide it. Whether or not this optimal level of public input is provided depends upon whatever *positive* theory of the political economy of government behaviour one finds most applicable to a given situation. In Findlay and Wilson (1987) where this model was first expounded we considered two alternative hypotheses. One, called 'surplus maximization', assumed that the objective of the government entity was to extract the maximum potential surplus, the difference between total revenue and expenditure on the public input. This surplus could then be used to maintain the ruling group and its clients or to dispense to the masses in favours if so desired. It is shown that on this hypothesis the level of the public input is *below* the optimum level for society as a whole. Traditional monarchies and some modern dictatorships could fit this mould.

An alternative hypothesis is that the level of the public input is determined by a process in which the objective is to maximize the size and power of the bureaucracy, subject to a balanced budget constraint. If the level of revenue attainable is sufficiently high this would result in a level of the public input *above* the optimum. If we assume that the public sector is more labour intensive than the private sector, this could result in wages being higher than at the socially optimal level. Thus a worker-oriented political party could have a common interest with the state bureaucracy in overexpanding the government, since it raises labour's share at the expense of capital, even though it reduces final output for the society as a whole. Perhaps the Swedish experience corresponds to such a model of an overexpanded government sector.

The simple Findlay–Wilson model that I have been describing up to now can be extended in any number of ways to provide a richer structural specification. One important modification is to introduce final public services, such as garbage disposal and concerts in the parks, along with public inputs as already described. Revenue would thus be used to provide a mix of public activities, final services as well as 'infrastructure' that enhances the productivity of the resources engaged in the private sector. Suppose that all agents have identical preferences and derive satisfaction from consuming both private goods and public services. Taking government initially as a faithful agent of its principal, the representative consumer, it is easy to specify an optimal level of public activity, and the optimal division of the activity between the public input and the final public services. This will simply be the allocation that maximizes the utility function of the representative consumer, subject to the technology and the factor endowment of the economy.

Suppose, however, that the policy maker has an agenda of his or her own, one that puts greater emphasis on the provision of infrastructure to production in the private sector than to public services. This could be because the policy maker regards 'high-tech' manufacturing, say, as giving greater prestige to the nation than the humdrum provision of public services such as sewers and parks. If so, the economy will have a larger and more productive private sector, because of the additional infrastructure, even though the utility of the representative consumers is lower. In a fully open democratic pluralist system one would expect such a policy maker to be voted out of office unless there is, as in Japan for example, a powerful entrenched bureaucracy that manages the economy more or less independently of whichever politicians are in office.

In a number of recent papers (Clarida and Findlay, 1991, 1992, 1994) Richard Clarida and myself have introduced international trade and capital mobility into this extended model. We enrich the production structure of the private sector to differentiate between a subsector that is more responsive to infrastructure spending by government, say high-tech manufacturing, and another one that is less so, say low-tech labour-intensive goods. We show that given technology and factor endowments the economy in which the representative consumer has a greater relative preference for private goods, as opposed to the final public services, will require a greater optimal provision of the public input and a smaller provision of public services. Because of the assumption of differential responsiveness to public input provision this economy will enjoy a comparative advantage in high-tech manufacturing, holding technology and factor endowments constant across countries.

If trade is opened up between these economies, identical except for this difference in tastes between private goods and public services, the economy that prefers private goods will export high-tech manufactured goods and import the labour-intensive goods, with trade inducing *further* provision of the public input and *further* contraction of final public services, while the opposite would happen in the other country. Trade thus *widens* the difference in comparative advantage that induced it in the first place, with the difference in preferences being the fundamental underlying determinant. Each economy will enjoy its gains from trade in terms that stress the component of its utility that matters more at the margin: private goods in one case and public services in the other.

In terms of the 'competitiveness' of high-tech manufacturing trade enhances it in the former country and reduces it in the latter since the public input is raised in the exporter of high-tech manufactures and reduced in the exporter of low-tech goods. Thus advocates of an industrial policy associated with trade intervention may arise in the latter country, hoping to increase the provision of the public input by subsidizing high-tech production through tariffs or other measures. Needless to say consumers would lose.

The implication of differences in tastes for private goods and public services drawn here will of course all be amplified if these differences are enhanced by 'political economy' considerations of the sort that we discussed earlier, in which more public inputs were provided by 'high-tech' production advocates in one case as labour-intensive public services were overprovided in a social democratic welfare state model of Scandinavian type. Trade will result in further expansion of high tech through provision of more infrastructure in the first case, while less infrastructure and more public services would be provided in the second, with low-tech labour-intensive exports expanding to pay for more high-tech imports.

It is interesting to note that in the ongoing discussions of USA–Japan trade problems the American side has been urging the Japanese to alleviate the 'structural impediment' of too little provision of public services in that economy. The new Hosokawa government itself appears to agree that the bureaucracy in the Finance Ministry and MITI has too much control over the Japanese economy. Thus the perception of the Japanese economy as a highly efficient and dynamic creation of an East Asian Development State, as described by Chalmers Johnson (1982) and other so-called 'revisionists', is but the other side of the coin of the price that the Japanese consumers have to pay in the form of cramped living space and limited public amenities.

To summarize our discussion to this point, we can contrast our two stylized extremes of the 'developmental state' and the 'welfare state'. In the former there is a higher level of public inputs in the form of infrastructure, resulting in an 'absolute' as well as a comparative advantage in high-tech manufacturing. The return to capital will be higher and the real wage lower than in the worker-oriented social-democratic 'welfare state', where the provision of final public services will be higher. These differences come about, assuming similar technological knowledge and factor endowments, either from differences in tastes alone, as between private goods and public services, or from these amplified by the deviation of the policy makers' own tastes as to the appropriate configuration of the economies under their control, which are not subject to discipline by well-informed voters in a fully competitive democratic process. Long periods of one-party rule, despite periodic fair elections, as in post-war Japan and Sweden, could give rise to this 'autonomy of the state' in either case.

Up to now we have been assuming that both capital and labour remain within their national borders in the two types of economies. Let us now suppose that capital is perfectly mobile internationally. What will be the effects? Clearly it will tend to flow from the 'welfare state' to the 'developmental state' since the rate of return on capital is higher, and the real wage lower, in the latter, due to the greater provision of public infrastructure and the relative neglect of labour-intensive final public services. The inflow of capital into the 'developmental state' will expand the high-tech manufacturing sector even further, contract the low-tech production sector and pull more labour out of public services. The impact on factor prices will be to raise the real wage and lower the return to capital. In the welfare state the opposite effects will happen. The reallocation of capital between the two economies will cease when the rates of return to private capital are equalized. Since there is more infrastructure in the developmental state the real wage will be higher there than in the welfare state, with the same technological knowledge and labour force in the two countries.

But this is not the end of the story. The expansion of the private sector in the developmental state, with the public input at its initial level, means that the rate of return on that variable has been increased, while the rise in the real wage has raised the cost of final public services. The government budget must therefore respond by providing even more public input to the private sector, and less labour to public services, expanding high-tech exports even further and raising the return on capital once again and thereby inducing a further capital inflow. In the welfare state the opposite effects will again happen. The private sector will get less infrastructure, lowering the return on capital and inducing even more export of capital. The fall in the real wage would put more labour into public services.

The full long-run equilibrium will therefore only be established when the levels of public inputs and public services have been adjusted *endogenously* to equate the rates of return on private capital. The disparity in real wages will be even greater than before the endogenous adjustments of public inputs and services. Trade will also be enhanced, with even more high-tech exports from the developmental state and low-tech exports from the welfare state. The development state will have to run an export surplus to pay the return on its capital imports from the welfare state. GDP will rise in the developmental state but fall in the welfare state, with GNP going up in both owing to the receipt of returns on its capital exports by the latter.

The ideas about the importance of public inputs and the role of government in relation to trade in a world of high international capital mobility that we have been discussing here resemble somewhat the approach taken by Robert Reich, now the Secretary of Labor in the Clinton administration, in his book on *The Work of Nations*. In this work he seems to repudiate his earlier advocacy of selective intervention, i.e. attempting to 'pick winners', in favour of general productivity-boosting measures such as providing physical infrastructure and improving the skill level of the labour force. Such measures would act to make the USA a 'magnet' for the attraction of mobile global capital, raising the real wages and standard of living of American workers as a result.

The budget deficit problem and the unpopularity of raising taxes has prevented the current administration from implementing anything substantive along the lines of Reich's vision, though it might be a longer-term objective should Clinton be re-elected.

Looking at the USA in terms of the highly stylized model spelled out here it seems that the system of checks and balances built into the political system by James Madison and the founding fathers has prevented the country from following either the 'developmental state' model of the East Asian economies, led by Japan, or the 'welfare state' model of the Scandinavian countries and Western Europe generally. While critics accuse the USA of 'muddling along' and lacking a long-term vision of the two alternative sorts, it may not be entirely an accident that the US economy is actually outperforming both Europe and Japan at the present time. It could be that the overconfident bureaucracy in Japan has expanded capital facilities too far in the manufacturing sector while the welfare state in Europe has overexpanded the public high-tech sector. Not only the relative *laissez-faire* of the economic arena, but also the balance of forces countervailing each other in the political arena, may be providing the pragmatism and flexibility that make the economic system of this country continue to be the leader in the world, contrary to many confident predictions of its demise at the hands of either of its interventionist rivals.

In the light of the analysis outlined in this chapter, it is possible to stretch two alternative scenarios for the future of European integration, which now appears to be stalled after all the hype about 1992. One possibility is of course 'Fortress Europe', an attempt to stimulate high-tech manufacturing and services behind a wall of protection while continuing with the generous public services of the traditional welfare state. It seems clear that this can only lead to stagnation and postponement of the inevitable structural adjustment. The other possibility is to re-emphasize the hopes of 1992, with a focus on substitution of coordinated infrastructure projects at the expense of cutting some of the more generous welfare state provision. This would divert more of the global pool of investible capital towards Europe and revitalize European exports.

Japan, on the other hand, would have to move closer to the American middle from the other direction, cutting back its excessive past investments in manufacturing capital and providing more amenities to its long-suffering consumers and trimming the powers of its bureaucracy.

There is no need for governments to override the wishes of consumers in either direction when it comes to the choice between private goods and public services. The 'duties of the sovereign', at the turn of the century, can keep them sufficiently occupied.

REFERENCES

Clarida, R. and Findlay, R. (1991) 'Endogenous Comparative Advantage, Government and the Pattern of Trade', NBER Working Paper No. 3813, August.
—— (1992) 'Government, Trade and Comparative Advantage', *American Economic Review*, vol. 82, no. 2.
—— (1994) 'After Maastricht: Public Investment, Economic Integration and International Capital Mobility', *Economica*, vol. 61, no. 243.
Corden, W. M. (1974) *Trade Policy and Economic Welfare*, Oxford University Press, Oxford.
Findlay, R. and Wilson, J. D. (1987) 'The Political Economy of Leviathan', in A. Razin and E. Sadka (eds) *Economic Policy in Theory and Practice*, Macmillan, London.
Johnson, C. (1982) *MITI and the Japanese Miracle*, Stanford University Press, Stanford, CA.
Reich, R. (1991) *The Work of Nations*, Alfred Knopf, New York.

INDEX

Adam, C. 330
Adesina, Jimi 332, 342
Adiseshiah, M. 173
Africa: agencies of restraint 282–98, *see also* agencies of restraint; agricultural exports 359–60; agricultural sector 359–60, 364, 369; apartheid 167; average GDP growth rates 352; casualization of labour 364, coping strategies 357–65, *see also* coping strategies; corruption 283–95; democratization of 168, 342; deterrents to private investment 282–98; developmental regionalism and 166; donor conditionality and 285–8; economic policy 60–1; economic vulnerability 357–65; entrepreneurs 62–3; environmental deterioration 167; ethnic conflict 76, 167, 369–70; farming sector 359–60, 364, 369; financial markets 333–5; government corruption 283–8; growth and 55–64; harmonization of political cultures 168; incentive structures 60; income levels 363–4; industrial policies 344; industrial workers 362–3; informal sector 360–2, 364, 368–9, 372–3; informalization 376–9; institutions 61–2, 352–90; Intergovernmental Authority on Drought and Development 167; labour markets 331–3, 342–3, 365; Lagos Plan of Action 166; learning from other economies 339–41; loyalty to employers 373–5; marginalization of 166; market size of economies 330–1; market structures 328–9; modernization project 376–9;

multiple social identities 366, 372–5; multiple survival strategies 358–65; Organization for African Unity (OAU) 166; politics 62–4; post-apartheid regime 167, predatory states 263–4, *see also* predatory states; private investment 60–1, 282–98, 333–5; privatization 384–5; public sector corruption 288–94; regional cooperation 166–8; resource accumulation 58–60; resource allocation 60–1; retrenchment 384; role of the state 335–9; rural–urban divisions 369–72; SADC 166–7; SADCC 166–7; 'second liberation' 168; smallholders 359–60; social change and institutional development 381–90; social polarization 365, 366–72, social relations 356–7, 358, 365–81, *see also* social relations; 'strong adjusters" 352; stylization of economies of *see* stylization of economies; Sub-Saharan *see* Sub-Saharan Africa; technology and 59–60, 329, 344; trade unionism 363, 368, 375; wage bargaining 331–3, 362–3; 'weak adjusters' 352; women workers 362, 364; workplace identities 372–5
African Economic Community (AEC) 166
agencies of restraint: in Africa 282–98; audit professions 294–5; budget rules 284; democracy and 285; donor conditionality 285–8; external agencies 285–6; financial liberalization and 284–5; on government 283–8; judiciary 295; limitations of 283–95; limits on

borrowing from central bank 284; on private agents 294–5; on public sector corruption 288–94
agricultural land: deforestation and 180; irrigation of 178–9; salinization of 178–9, *see also* environmental issues; environmental resources; grazing land; soil
agriculture: Uruguay Round Agreement and 407–8, 418, 419–20
aid *see* development aid; emergency relief
Alam, G. 139–40
Alesina, A. 63
Amadeo, E. 342, 343
Amsden, Alice H. 44, 61, 105, 106, 271, 276, 334
Anand, S. 188
Andvig, Jens Christopher 265, 289
appropriate technology xxv, *see also* technology and technology transfers
aquifers: excessive extraction and 179; pollution of 179; as renewable resource 179; saltwater intrusion in 179; soil cover and 179, *see also* water
Arnold, J. E. M. 176
Arrow, Kenneth 159, 191, 210
Asia: developmental regionalism 170–1; growth in 57; market interventions in 61; resource accumulation 57; 'shared growth' 63–4, *see also* East Asia; India; South Asia; South Korea; Southeast Asia
Asia Pacific Economic Cooperation (APEC) 171
Asia–Pacific region 162, 171
Association of Southeast Asian Nations (ASEAN) 170
atmosphere: as environmental resource 177, 185, 225–6; global warming 185–7; Montreal Protocol on the protection of the earth's ozone layer 203; ownership of 225–6; pollution of 177, *see also* environmental resources; pollution
Axline, A. 168

Bach, Friis 414
Bahl, R. 239, 245
balance of payments: India 143; Latin America 33–4, 39; support xviii–xix

Balassa, B. 85
Baldwin, R. 91
Banuri, T. 342, 343
Baran, Paul A. 256
Bardhan, P. 333, 344
Barrett, S. 216
Barro, R. J. 56, 68, 73, 74, 78, 83, 85
Barros, A. 344
Basu, P. 84
Bates, Robert 255, 331, 337
Bauer, P. T. 314
Baumol, W. J. 56
Becker, Gary 308–10
Bell, M. 343
Ben-David, D. 60
Bentley, A. F. 307
Bevan, D. 84–5
Bhagwati, Jagdish N. 256, 264, 266
Bienen, Henry S. 262, 267
biodiversity: Convention on Biological Diversity 203, 210, 214, 215, 219, deforestation and 206, *see also* deforestation; exotic capital 219–20, loss of 206–15, *see also* environmental loss; niche competition 206–8; protection of 1; species extinction 207–8, *see also* environmental issues; environmental resources; global agreements on the environment; global environmental markets; global environmental value
biomass-based subsistence economies 176, *see also* environmental resources; rural poor
Blanqui, Jérome 399
Bleaney, M. 86
Bliss, C. 91
Bogetíc, Z. 239, 243
Bovenberg, A. L. 231
Brennan, Geoffrey 310
Bretton Woods system 159, 163
Bromley, D. W. 203
Brown, K. 207
Brundtland Commission: definition of sustainable development xix
Buchanan, James M. 310
Buzan, Barry 171

capital accumulation 324–5
capital markets: environmental degradation and 179; rural poor and 179

capital mobility *see* international capital mobility

carbon emissions: private sector carbon offset deals 216–18; tradeable emission permits (TEPs) 227

carbon storage *see* forests

Cardoso, E. 86

Caribbean Basin: developmental regionalism and 168–70; NAFTA and 169; political homogeneity 169; regional cooperation 169; risk of marginalization 169; sufficient size argument 168–70

Caribbean Free Trade Association (CARIFTA) 168

Chakravarty, S. 182

Chambers, Valerie 173

Chiang Kai-shek 271

Chibber, A. 60

child labour 400

Chong Hyun Nam 397

Clapham, Christopher 259

Clarida, Richard 427–8

Clark, Colin 125

Clark, J. 317

climate: forests and 180; Framework Convention on Climate Change 203, 210, 215, *see also* environmental issues; rainwater

coastal waters: niche competition and 207; regional problems 165; saltwater intrusion into coastal aquifers 179, *see also* water

Collier, Paul 91, 92

Collins, S. 335

commodity price fluctuations 85

commodity taxation 225, 235

Convention on Biological Diversity 203, 210, 214, 215, 219

convergence hypothesis 2, 57–8; 'conditional' convergence effect 70, 73–5

coping strategies 357–65; in Africa 358, 365–81; changes in social relations and 358, 365–81; multiple survival strategies 358–65

Corden, W. Max 268, 426

cost–benefit analysis: of development aid 204, *see also* social cost–benefit analysis

credit markets: rural poor and 179

Cukierman, A. 283

current account disequilibria 30, 36

Daly, H. E. 401, 402

Das, T. K. 143

Dasgupta, P. 184, 185, 191, 194

De Long, J. B. 59

de Lucia, R. 216, 220

de Melo, J. 60–1, 239

De Tocqueville, A. 304–6

Deacon, R. 220

Deaton, A. 85

debt crisis: in India 143; in Latin America 29–30, 32, 36–9

debt overhang: Sub-Saharan Africa 80–1, 87

debt relief xix

debt-for-nature swaps 220

Decalo, Samuel 264

deforestation xxiv, 1, 180; carbon storage and 211–13; loss of biodiversity and 206; population change and 207; tropical 207, *see also* environmental issues; environmental resources

Demas, W. G. 168

democracy: agencies of restraint and 285; democratization of Africa 168, 342; economic growth and 63, 299–322; elections xviii, 312–14; encouragement of xviii; mass participation 312–14; median voter models 312–13; NGOs and 304–19; participatory 304–19; pressure groups 306–12; role of parties 312–13; sustainable development and xviii; voter apathy 312–14; World Bank policy and 314–19, *see also* human rights; legal institutions/systems; political reforms

Denison, E. D. 104

development aid: cost–benefit analysis 204; criticism of xvii; cuts in 225; donor conditionality 285–8; Dutch-disease impacts of 84; environmental issues 204, 205–6; Uruguay Round Agreement and 420–2

development cooperation *see* Swedish development cooperation

developmental regionalism 160, 164–75; Africa 166–8; APEC 171; ASEAN 170; Asia–Pacific 162; Caribbean Basin and 168–70; closed regionalism 161, 171; coastal waters 165;

collective self-reliance 165; development integration and 166; double movement and 163; EAEC 171; EAEG 171; ecological issues 160, 164–5; economic blocs and 165; effective articulation argument 165, 170–1; European Community 161–2; GATT 160, 161, 162; globalism and 163, 165; ground water 165; hegemonic stability 159–60; market regionalism 165; meaning of 160; Middle East and 171–2; NAFTA 162; new regionalism 160, 161, 163, 164–5, 166, 167; 'North Americanization' 162, 169, 170; old and new regionalism distinguished 161, 164–5; open regionalism 161, 163, 170; peace dividend argument 165, 171–2; Polanyi and 163; regional cooperation and 163; regional integration and 160, 166; regionness 161–2, 165, 173; rivers 165; SAARC 172, 173; SADC 166–7; SADCC 166–7; security dimension 160, 161, 165, 172; social order 159–60; South Asia and 172–3; Southeast Asia and 170–1; strategy of development regionalism 164–6; Sub-Saharan Africa 166–8; sufficient size argument 165, 168–70; sustainability argument 166, 172–3; viable economy argument 165, 166–8

disaster relief xix
Dixon, R. 217, 218
Dornbusch, R. 313
Downs, A. 312
Dreifus, A. 170
drylands: management of 178

Earth Summit in Rio de Janeiro 1992 see Rio Earth Summit 1992
East Asia: capital accumulation 57; development states in 272, 274; human capital formation 57, 89; industrial policy 88–90; research and development 138–9; state intervention 89, see also Asia
East Asia Economic Caucus (EAEC) 171
East Asian Economic Grouping (EAEG) 171

Easterly, W. 56, 57, 58, 60, 74, 75, 78, 83, 239, see also endogenous growth model
Eatwell, J. 323
ecological issues see environmental issues
economic growth: convergence hypothesis see convergence hypothesis; coordination failures 32, 33, 35; democracy and 63, 299–322; economic integration and 91; endogenous model of 56–7, 58–9, 69–70, 78; entrepreneurs and 62–3; environment and xxiii–xxiv, 2–16; exogenous shocks and 75–6; external shocks see external shocks; government consumption and 77–8; income convergence see convergence hypothesis; income levels and 57; innovation and 2–16; institutions and 61–2; intercountry differences 56–8; investment ratio 76; long-wave theories see long-wave theories; macroeconomic stabilization and see macroeconomic stabilization; neoclassical model of 58–9; New Growth Theory 1, 2; openness of economy 76–7; policy variables 76–8; political instability and 75–6; population growth and 2; post-War 56–8; rent-seekers and 62–3; resource accumulation and 57, 58–60; sociopolitical instability and 75–6; technological progress and 2, 58–60; trade barriers and 76; transaction costs and 61–2
economic reforms xviii–xix; balance of payments support xviii–xix; debt relief xix; economic analysis and management xix; encouragement of market economics xviii, xix, 16–17; macroeconomic stabilization xviii–xix, xxiii, 3; Ministries of Finance xix; policies xviii; political reforms and xxiii; restoration of growth xviii; structural reforms xviii
economies of scale scenario 329
education xxv; brain-drain 137; higher education 136–7, 154; India 134–5, 136–7, 153–5; inverted educational pyramid 136; Latin America 41; primary education 136–7; science and

education (*contd.*)
technology 134–5; secondary education 134–5, 136; social status and 137; South Korea 135, 136, 154; vocational training 135
Edwards, S. 76, 313
effective articulation argument 165, 170–1, *see also* developmental regionalism
Eggertsson, Thráinn 268–9
Ehrlich, P. 177, 178
Elbadawi, I. 83
elections *see* democracy
emergency relief xix
endogenous growth model 56–7, 58–9, 69–70, 78
entrepreneurs: growth and 62–3
environmental issues xvii, 1; biodiversity *see* biodiversity; carbon emissions 216–18; deforestation *see* deforestation; development aid 204, 205–6; developmental regionalism and 160; economic failure as cause of environmental loss 208–15; economic growth and xxiii–xxiv, 2–16; environmentally sensitive resource transfers 205–6; fossil fuels 180, 238; global issues *see* global agreements on the environment; global environmental markets; global environmental value; global warming; international trade and 400–2; irrigation 178–9; pollution *see* pollution; population growth *see* population growth; poverty and xxiv; soil *see* soil; species extinction 207–8; sustainable development *see* sustainable development; trade and 400–2, *see also* environmental loss; environmental taxation
environmental loss: biodiversity loss 206–15; decline in stock 180; degradation of renewable natural resources 177; economic failure as cause of 208–15; global appropriation failure 210–15; intervention failure 208–9
environmental management: clean-up costs 227; drylands 178; of global commons 226; of national resources 226, policy instruments 226–8, *see also* environmental taxation; problems of

180, 226; tradeable emission permits (TEPs) 227
environmental resources: agricultural land 178–9; aquifers *see* aquifers; atmosphere *see* atmosphere; biomass-based subsistence economies 176; Brundtland Report 177; carbon storage 211–13, 216–19; climate *see* climate; competing uses of 180; debt-for-nature swaps 220; defining 177–80; development economics and 177; environment as capital asset 179; environmentally sensitive resource transfers 205–6; exotic capital 219–20; fertility rate and 179; forests *see* forests; fossil fuels 180, 238; global agreements on *see* global agreements on the environment, global public goods 203, *see also* global environmental value; grazing land 179; loss of xxiv; management of *see* environmental management; niche competition 206–8; non-linear dose-response relationship 177; optimal development 180, 182–7; overexploitation of 203–23; ownership of 225–6; parasitic relationships 177–8; rainwater *see* rainwater; rationing demand for 226; regeneration 177; renewable natural resources 177–9; resource basis of rural production 176–7; rural poor and 176–7, 179; soil *see* soil; sustainable development *see* sustainable development; symbiotic relationships 177–8, 179; transfers of 204, 205–6; tropical forests *see* tropical forests; water *see* water; welfare economics and 180, *see also* environmental taxation; global environmental markets; global environmental value
environmental taxation: choice of policy instruments 226–8; choice of tax base 236–7; commodity taxes 225, 235; corporate income tax 241; domestic taxes on goods and services 243; 'double dividend' argument 230–4; effects of 236, 237–9; excise taxes 235; on factors of production 236; fuel taxes 243; implementation in one

country 235–6; income tax 225, 235, 239–41; in the LDCs 243–5; on luxury goods 245; ownership of natural resources and 225–6; Pigouvian taxes 227–8, 236; in real world economies 234–5; reform of 224–48; taxes on international trade 241; transport taxes 245; value-added taxes 235, 236, *see also* environmental issues; environmental management; environmental resources; taxation

Epstein, G. 335

Eskeland, G. S. 239, 243

Estache, A. 239, 246

Euh, Y. 334

European Community 161–2; 'Fortress Europe' 162, 171, 431; Single Market 169

Evans, Peter B. 255

exchange rate: Latin America policies 48–51; macroeconomic stabilization and 29; real exchange rate misalignment (RERMIS) 72, 77, 78, 95–7

exotic capital 219–20

external shocks: foreign real interest changes shock 81–3; growth and 83–6; investment and 86; net capital flows shock 81–3; Sub-Saharan Africa 79–87; terms of trade trade shocks 81–3, 84, 87

factor-price equalization theorem 59–60

Fairi, R. 60–1

Falconer, J. 176

Fanelli, J. 41, 80

Fankhauser, S. 212

Felix, David 325, 328, 329, 345

fertility rate xxv; environmental resources and 179, *see also* population growth

Findlay, Ronald 255, 269; Findlay–Wilson model 426, 427

Fischer, S. 60

Fishlow, Albert 34

Fon, V. 236

foreign aid *see* development aid

foreign investment: in India 145, 146, 148; in Latin America 38

forests: carbon storage 211–13, 216–19; climate and 180; deforestation *see* deforestation; Forests Absorbing Carbon Dioxide Emissions (FACE) 216; protection of soil in 180; reforestation 216; social value of 180; tropical *see* tropical forests, *see also* environmental resources

Foroutan, F. 288

fossil fuels 180, 238

Framework Convention on Climate Change 203, 210

free trade *see* global free trade system

Freeman, C. 115, 131

Freeman, R. 325

Friis Bach, C. 414, 420

fuel taxes 243

General Agreement on Tariffs and Trade (GATT): developmental regionalism and 160, 161, 162; India and 162; LDCs and 403–5; opposition to 162; trading blocs and 162, 163; Uruguay Round *see* Uruguay Round, *see also* World Trade Organization

Gerschenkron, Alexander 56, 74, 253, 276

Ghose, A. K. 134, 151

Gilbert, M. 125

Gintis, H. 335

Giovanni, A. 334

global agreements on the environment 203–4; Convention on Biological Diversity 203, 210, 214, 215, 219; Framework Convention on Climate Change 203, 210; Montreal Protocol 203

Global Environmental Facility 204, 210

global environmental markets: buying down private risk 220; creating 215–20; exotic capital 219–20; global good citizenship 217–18; government–government trades 215–16; private sector carbon offset deals 216–18; regulation-induced markets 215–17

global environmental value: actions for global benefit 204; carbon storage 211–13, 216–18; economic failure as cause of environmental loss 208–15; environmentally sensitive resource transfers 205–6; fundamental causes of global environmental change 206–15;

global environmental value (*contd.*)
generally 203–5; global agreements
see global agreements on the
environment; global appropriation
failure 210, 215; global markets *see*
global environmental markets;
transfers for global benefit 204, *see
also* environmental resources
global warming: social cost–benefit
analysis 185–7
globalism: developmental regionalism
and 163, 165
Goldin, I. 405, 414–15
Goodland, R. 124
Göransson, Bo 122
Granovetter, M. 356
grazing land 179, *see also* agricultural
land; environmental issues;
environmental resources
'green revolution' 104
Greenaway, D. 86, 397
Greene, J. 86
Grilli, E. R. 93
groundwater: excessive extraction 179;
regional problems 165, *see also* water
growth *see* economic growth
Gunning, J. 91, 92

Haberler, Gottfried 395–6
Hammond, P. J. 59
Harris, J. R. 343
Harris, Nigel 262
Harrison, Paul xxiv
Hassan, F. 239, 243
Heal, G. M. 184, 185
Heckscher, Eli 301
hegemonic stability 159–60
Heggie, I. G. 236, 239
Helleiner, G. 59, 85, 88, 90, 124, 329
Heller, Peter S. 331
Helpman, E. 329
Heston, Alan 125
Hikino, Takashi 105, 106
Hill, P. 84
Hirschman, Albert 312, 335
Hodgson, G. M. 163
Holt, S. L. 315–16
Hotelling, H. 225, 313
House, W. 332, 342
Hufbauer, 406
human capital 104; development of 1;
in East Asia 57, 89; New Growth

Theory 1, 2; technological progress
and 2
Human Development Index xxiii
Human Development Reports xxiii
human rights: promotion of xviii;
sustainable development and xviii, *see
also* democracy; political reforms
Hume, David 301, 303
Hussain, I. 89
Hussein, Sadam 172

import protection: as export promotion
88
import-substitution strategy 88, 94;
Latin America 34, 36
income convergence *see* convergence
hypothesis
income tax 225, 235, 239–41, *see also*
taxation
India: abolition of licensing system 144;
acquiring capacity for using and
replicating imported standard-modern
technology 132–3; balance of
payments support 143; brain-
drain 137; capital goods 131, 132,
133, 147; commitment to capitalism
129–30; communist bloc and 130;
consumer goods 132, 146–7; Council
of Scientific and Industrial Research
(CSIR) 138; education 134–5, 136–7,
153–5; export of capital goods 133;
export liberalization 145; five-year
plans 130; 'foreign collaborated
firms' 130; foreign investment 145,
146, 148; foreign personnel 145;
GATT and 162; government research
laboratories 138–40, 154; graduate
unemployment 137; high-tech 131;
higher education 136–7, 154; highly-
modern technology 131, 132; import
of capital goods 132–3, 144, 145–6;
import liberalization 129, 142–3, 145–
6; imports of consumer goods 132,
133; in-house R&D 140–2, 152–3;
Indian Institutes of Technology
(IIT) 138–40; industrial infrastructure
151; industrial policies 129, 130,
144–9; industrial productivity 137,
150–2; industrial restructuring after
SAP 146–9; innovation 131, 132;
knowledge and skills 131, 133–7,
149–50; large-scale industry 148;

machinery imports 132, 133; meaning
of 'modern technology' 130–1;
mergers 145; national laboratories
138–40, 154; oligopoly 146–7; 'open
door' policy for foreign investment
145; primary education 136–7; private
sector 129–30, 145; production for
domestic market vs. foreign market
147–8; productivity 137, 150–2;
protection of domestic markets 130;
public investment 151; public
sector 129–30, 145, 148–9;
redundancy 150–1; research and
development 131, 132, 137–42, 153–5;
restructuring of industry 146–9;
retraining 149–50; retrenching of
public sector 148–9; reverse
engineering 142; scale encroachment
147; scientific workers 134–5;
secondary education 134–5, 136, 154;
small-scale industry 151; smallness of
firms 142; stabilization and structural
adjustment programme (SSAP) 142–3;
standard-modern technology 131;
standard-tech 131; state intervention
129–30, 132, 138–40; structural
adjustment in 129–58; structural
adjustment programme (SAP) 129,
142–6; takeovers 145; technological
implications of SAP 149–55;
technological policies in 129–30,
144–6; technological workers 134–5,
150–2; technology absorption 141–2,
152–3; technology agreements with
foreign suppliers 130, 145;
technology estates for small industry
152; technology imports 129–58;
trade liberalization 129, 142–3, 145–6;
Trans-European Network (TENS)
Programme 151–2; vocational training
135; workforce skills 131, 133–7
industrialization see late-comer
industrializers; technology and
technology transfers
inflation: in Latin America 30, 37, 38;
macroeconomic stabilization and 30,
37
information and communication
technology (ICT): late-comers and
104, 120–2; state intervention
and 121–2
Ingham, B. 84

innovation: capacity to innovate 131;
economic growth and 2–16;
India 131, 132; Latin America 41;
macroeconomic stabilization 30, 41;
national innovation systems 155;
Schumpeter innovation cycle 114–15,
see also research; technology and
technology transfers
institutions: in Africa 61–2, 352–90;
development of 61–2; economic
growth and 61–2; legal see legal
institutions/systems; social change
and 381–90
international capital mobility: Findlay–
Wilson model 426, 427; government
action and 425–31; infrastructure
and 425, 427–31
international trade 1, 16; child labour
and 400; and development 395–7;
environmental aspects of 400–2;
import protection as export
promotion 88; labour standards
and 398–401; LDCs and 403–20;
national sovereignty and 397–402;
protectionism 76, 88, 398, 403–4;
Singer–Prebisch argument 395;
technical barriers to 410; UNCTAD
404–5; 'unfair' competition
and 397–402; Uruguay Round
Agreement see Uruguay Round
Agreement, see also General
Agreement on Tariffs and Trade
investment see foreign investment;
private investment; public investment
irrigation 178–9; salinization and 178–9,
see also environmental issues;
environmental resources; soil
degradation; water

Jacobsson, Staffan 121–2
Jamal, V. 364–5
Japan 17, 431; EAEG 171;
education 154; research and
development 138
Jayawardena, L. 89
job creation: technology and xxv
Johnson, Chalmers 428
Johnson, S. 203
Jones, R. 88

Kemp, Tom 336
Keynes, John Maynard xxiii

Khan, M. 80
Khartala, 334
Killick, Tony 338
Kim, E. M. 334
King, K. 203
King, R. 76
Klitgaard, 288
Knight, M. 80
Kondratiev cycles/long waves 114, 115, 116, 120, see also long-wave theories
Koo, H. 334
Koopmans, Tjalling 182, 183, 185
Korea see South Korea
Krasner, S. D. 159
Kravis, I. B. 125
Krueger, Anne O. 34, 90, 255, 256, 258
Krugman, Paul 35, 88, 94, 327, 329, 395, 396, 397, 402
Kurz, M. 191

Lal, Deepak 255, 257, 258, 268, 270, 310, 313, 337, 344
Lall, S. 133, 135, 328
Larsen, B. 239, 246
late-comer industrializers 104–6, 325; catching up 118–22; ICT revolution and 104, 120–2; 'late' late-comers 105; levels of development 104–5, long waves 113–22, see also long-wave theories; patterns of growth 105, 106–16; purchasing power parity 105; softnomization and 123–4; Soviet model of growth 116–18; techno-economic paradigms (TEP) 115, 120–1; technology transfer basis xxv
Latham, E. 306
Latin America: allocative efficiency 41; balance of payments 33–4, 39; capital flight 36–9; capital inflows 38–9; capital markets 40, 46–8; coordination failures 32, 33, 35; current account disequilibria 30, 36; debt crisis 29–30, 32, 36–9; domestic savings 37, 40, 41–6; economic crisis of 1980s 36–8; education 41; evolution of external sector 38–9; exchange rate 29, 33–4, 37; exchange-rate policy 48–51; external financing 33–4, 39; external gaps 35, 36–9; financial systems 40; fiscal gaps 35, 36–9, 40; fiscal policy 41–6; foreign direct investment 38; gaps

35–9; import-substitution strategy 34, 36; inflation 30, 37, 38; innovation 41; international interest rate and 37, 38, 39, macroeconomic stabilization 29–53, see also macroeconomic stabilization; MERCOSUR 162, 170; monetary and financial policy 46–8; monetization 40; 1990s in 38–9, predatory states in 263, see also predatory states; predatory states in 262, 263; private savings 37, 40, 41–6; public investment rate 29, 30, 37, 38, 40, 41–6; relative prices 34; reversal of capital flows 38–9; state intervention 34; tax policies 42–4; term maturity of financial instruments 40; trade surplus generation 36–7, 39
Lee, J. 68, 74, 83, 85
Lee Kwan Yew 304
legal institutions/systems: supporting xviii, see also democracy; political reform
Lenin 118
Lensik, R. 335
Letwin, S. 312
Levi, Margaret 264, 267, 268, 271
Levine, R. 57, 60, 62, 76
Lewis, Arthur 254, 333
Lewis, W. A. 332
Liang, N. 344
Lindauer, David 332
Lipset, S. M. 313, 314
Little, I. M. D. 191
Lockwood, M. 355
long-wave theories 114–16; catching up and 118–22; Kondratiev cycles 114, 115, 116, 120; Soviet growth model and 116–18; techno-economic paradigms (TEP) 115, 120–1, see also late-comer industrializers
Lundahl, Mats 263, 266

McKinnon, R. 326, 334
McLeod, D. 84
macroeconomic stabilization xviii–xix, xxiii, 3, 29; capital markets and 33, 34; development policies and 29–53; effects of policies 29; employment and 30; exchange-rate policy 48–51; fiscal policy 41–6; growth and 29, 30, 31–5; income distribution and 29, 34; inflation and 30, 37; innovation

and 30, 41; investment and 29, 30, 37, 38, in Latin America 29–53, *see also* Latin America; learning and 30; market equilibrium and 32–3, 35; monetary and financial policy 46–8; objective of policies 30, 40; policies 4–5, 29–53; real value of government deficits and 34; structural reform policies and 31–5, 38; tax policies 42–4; thin capital markets and 33

Maddison, Angus 105, 125

Madison, James 430

market economy xxii, xxiii; encouragement of xviii, xix, 16–17; social order and 159

market equilibrium: disequilibrium and gaps 35–6; macroeconomic stabilization and 32–3, 35

market regionalism 165, *see also* developmental regionalism

Martin, William 167

Mauro, P. 282

Meltzer, A. 313

mercantilism 301–2; neomercantilism 160, 303; predatory states 272–4

MERCOSUR 162, 170

Merhav, M. 328, 330

Mhone, Guay 397, 398, 413, 414, 416, 421, 422

Middle East: Arab nationalism 171; Arab–Israeli conflict 172; developmental regionalism and 171–2; peace dividend 171–2; regional hegemony 172; security issues 172

Milgate, M. 323

Mirrlees, J. A. 182, 184, 191

Mkandawire, Thandika 334, 336

Moene, Karl Ove 265, 289

Molvaer, R. K. 167

Montreal Protocol on the protection of the earth's ozone layer 203

Moran, C. 85

Moran, D. 207, 219, 220

Mosley, S. 332

Munasinghe, M. 203

Muni, S. D. 172

Murphy, K. M. 62, 63

Murphy, P. 220

Musgrave, R. 188

Mwega, F. M. 334

Myint, Hla 255, 257, 258, 268, 270, 310, 313

Myrdal, Gunnar 395, 420

Mytelka, Lynn 164

natural resources: renewable 177–9, *see also* environmental resources

Nelson, Joan 332, 354

Nelson, P. 123

Nelson, Richard 41

Nelson, R. R. 155

neoclassical economics: model of economic growth 58–9; stylization of economies 325–7

neomercantilism 160, 303, *see also* mercantilism

net national product: in a deterministic environment 191–5; in a dynamic economy 190–7; economics of optimal control 190–1; project evaluation and 187–90; well-being and 187–90

New Growth Theory 1, 2; capital formation 1; human capital formation 1, 2; technology and 1, 2

'new international economic order' 159

'new world order' 159, 163

Newcombe, K. 216, 220

niche competition 206–8, *see also* environmental resources

Nie, N. H. 312, 313

Nissanke, M. 334

Nkrumah, Kwame 271

non-governmental organizations (NGOs): World Bank and 314–19, *see also* democracy

North, Douglass C. 62, 252, 355; North's law 259–60; predatory states 261, 264, 267, 271, 272, 274; property rights 261

North American Free Trade Area (NAFTA) 162; Caribbean and 169; 'North Americanization' and 162, 169, 170

Norton-Griffiths, M. 214

Noss, A. 153

Nurske, R. 335

Oakeshott, Michael 301

Olson, Mancur 260, 261, 262, 266, 307–8

optimal development 180, 182–5;
second-best optima 185–7
optimal taxation theory 228–30, 239
option values theory 187
Organization for African Unity
(OAU) 166
Ostergaard, Tom 166
Ostrom, E. 226

Palmer, N. D. 172
Pavitt, K. 343
peace dividend: in Middle East 165,
171–2
Pearce, D. 181
Peltzman, S. 313
Perez, Carlota 120, 121, 123
Perotti, R. 63
Pigou, A. C. 227
Pitelis, C. 337
Polanyi, Karl 163, 307
political instability: growth and 75–6
political reforms xviii; economic
reforms and xxiii; elections xviii;
legal institutions xviii; legal system
xviii, see also democracy; human
rights
pollution: of aquifers 179; of
atmosphere 177; global international
agreements see global agreements on
the environment; trade policy and
401, see also environmental issues;
environmental management;
environmental resources
population growth xxv–xxvi;
deforestation and 207; economic
growth and 2; environmental
degradation and xxiv, 178; niche
competition 206–8, see also
environmental issues; environmental
resources; fertility rate
predatory states 257–8, 260–75; in
Africa 263–4; availability of
alternative rulers 268; bribery 265;
bureaucracy 265; competition for
power 262; corruption 265–6;
creation of leaders 261; definition
of 263; establishment of 260–4;
exercise of power 260–2; in Latin
America 262, 263; limitations on
predation 267–9; mercantilist states
272–4; need for third party
enforcement 262; paradox of 266–7;

productive predatory states 269–70;
property rights 261; rivals for
power 262, 263, 274; role of external
pressure 272–5; self-seeking
behaviour 258; size of ruling
clique 263; the three levels of rent
seeking 264–6; transaction costs
268–9, 274, see also state intervention
pressure groups 306–12, see also
democracy
Pritchett, L. 83, 288
private investment: in Africa 60–1,
282–98, 333–5; deterrents to 282–98;
external shocks and 86; stylization of
economies and 333–5; in Sub-Saharan
Africa 86; terms of trade
improvement and 86
project evaluation: cost–benefit
analysis 183–5; measurement of net
national product and 187–90
property rights 259–60, 261
public investment: external shocks
and 86; India 151; Latin America 29,
30, 37, 38, 40, 41–6; macroeconomic
stabilization 29, 30, 37, 38;
Sub-Saharan Africa 86; tax incentives
for 42–4

Quah, D. 57

Rahman, Ziaur 172
Rain Forest Alliance 216–17
rainwater: deforestation and 180;
renewal of aquifers 179, see also
climate; water
Ranis, G. 331
Ravallion, M. 188
real exchange rate misalignment
(RERMIS) 72, 77, 78, 95–7
reforestation 216, see also forests
regional cooperation 163, 166, 169, 172
regional integration 160, 166; in
Africa 166
regionalism see developmental
regionalism
regionness 161–2, 165, 173
Reich, Robert 430
Rempel, H. 332
rent seeking: economic growth and
62–3; predator states and 264–6
Repetto, R. 178
research 1, 131; East Asia 138–9;

government research
laboratories 138–40; in-house 140–2,
152–3; India 131, 132, 137–42, 152–5;
Japan 138; South Korea 138; state
intervention 137–40; Taiwan 138, see
also industrialization; innovation;
technology and technology transfers
resource accumulation: growth and 57,
58–60
resource allocation: Africa 60–1; theory
of 188
resource growth xvii
reverse engineering 142, see also
technology and technology transfers
Richards, S. 313
Riddell, Roger 330
Riley, Stephen 168
Rio Earth Summit 1992 203, see also
global agreements on the environment
rivers: developmental regionalism
and 165
Robinson, Joan 324, 328, 333
Robson, Peter 166
Rodriguez-Clare, A. 59
Rosenstein-Rodan, P. 335
rural poor: biomass-based subsistence
economies 176; capital markets
and 179; credit markets and 179,
environmental resources and 176–7,
179, see also environmental resources;
importance of domestic animals 179;
nomads 179; resource basis of
production 176; Sub-Saharan
Africa 179
rural–urban divisions: in Africa 369–72

SADC see Southern Africa
Development Community
SADCC see Southern Africa
Development Cooperation
Conference
Sala-i-Martin, X. 73
salinization of soil 178–9, see also
environmental issues; environmental
resources; irrigation
Sandesara, J. C. 129
Sandmo, A. 230
savings: in Latin America 37, 40, 41–6;
tax incentives for 42–4
scale scenario 329
Schattschneider, E. E. 311
Schleifer, A. 282, 288, 291

Schmoller, Gustav 272
Schneider, R. 213
Schott, 406
Schumpeter, J. A. 114–15, 312, see also
long-cycle theories
Scitovsky, 335
Seers, Dudley 161
Seidman, A. 330
Sen, A. 188
Shah, A. 239, 246
Shorne, Parthasarathi 44
Sigurdson, J. 139
Smith, Adam 301, 306, 395, 425
social cost–benefit analysis: and global
warming 185–7; measurement of net
national product 190–7; social
discount rates 183–5, see also cost-
benefit analysis
social order: developmental regionalism
and 159–60; market system and 159
social relations: in Africa 356–7, 358,
365–81; and coping strategies 358,
365–81; ethnic conflicts 369–70;
informalization 376–9;
modernization and 376–9; multiple
social identities 366, 372–5; social
polarization 365, 366–72
socialism 168, 169
sociopolitical instability: growth
and 75–6
Södersten, B. 396
softnomization 123–4, see also late-
comer industrializers
soil: aquifers and 179; deforestation
and 180; degradation of 1, 178–9; in
drylands 179; forests and 180;
irrigation and 178–9; land degradation
xxiv; loss of topsoil 178; salinization
of 178–9; soil value of forests 180;
symbiotic role of microbes 179, see
also environmental issues;
environmental resources
Solorzano, R. 190
Solow, R. M. 58, 59, 181, 185, 191
South Asia: developmental regionalism
and 172–3; political tensions 173, see
also Asia
South Asian Association for Regional
Cooperation (SAARC) 172, 173
South Korea: education 135, 136, 154;
research and development 138;
secondary education 136, 154;

South Korea (*contd.*)
technological workers 135;
workforce skills 133–4, *see also* Asia
Southeast Asia xxiii, 17; ASEAN 170;
developmental regionalism 170–1;
'Indochinese' area 170; state
intervention xxiii, 17, 34; technology
transfer xxv, *see also* Asia
Southern Africa Development
Community (SADC) 166–7
Southern Africa Development
Cooperation Conference (SADCC)
166–7
species extinction 207–8, *see also*
biodiversity; environmental issues;
environmental resources
Staniland, M. 341
state intervention: administration
costs 256; administrative
obstacles 256; benevolent
states 256–7, 270–1; developmental
states 258, 270–7; economic failure as
cause of environmental loss 208–10;
economic policies xxiii; economists'
views of the state 251–5; education
see education; ICT revolution
and 121–2; information-related
obstacles 256; international capital
mobility and 425–31; in Latin
America 34; mercantilist
states 272–4; North's law 259–60,
272; patrimonial societies 259;
predatory states *see* predatory states;
property rights 259–60, 261; role of
external pressure 272–5; Southeast
Asia xxiii, 17, 34, technology and
technology transfers xxv, *see also*
technology and technology
transferstransaction costs 256, 268–9,
274; varieties of inefficient states 255–9
Stevens, Christopher 169
Stevens, J. 203
Stigler, G. 313
Stiglitz, Joseph 333, 334, 343
Stokes, William 260
Streeten, Paul 252, 328, 338
stylization of economies:
alternative 327–35; capital
accumulation 324–5; financial
market 326, 333–5; generally 323–4;
investment policy 333–5; labour
markets 325–6, 331–3, 342–3; market

size argument 330–1; market
structure 328–9; neoclassical 325–7;
role of the state and 335–9; scale
scenario 329; technical conditions
329; technological change 325–6;
wage bargaining 331–3
Sub-Saharan Africa 59, 67–99;
apartheid 167; commodity price
fluctuations 85; 'conditional'
convergence effect 70, 73–5; debt
overhang 80–1, 87; debt
democratization 168; dependence on
imports for production 80;
developmental regionalism and 166–8;
Dutch-disease impacts of aid 84;
economic integration and growth
91–3; economic stagnation in 68–79;
endogenous growth model and 69–70;
environmental deterioration 167, 178;
ethnic conflict 76; exogenous
shocks 75–6; export instability 85–6,
87; exports and investment 80;
external gaps 80–1; external shocks
see external shocks; fiscal gaps 80–1;
foreign exchange constraint on
growth 79; foreign real interest
changes shock 81–3; government
consumption 77–8, 84; import
instability 85–6; imports and
production 80; industrial policy
88–90; Intergovernmental Authority
on Drought and Development 167;
investment 76, 80, 86, 87; loss of
topsoil 178; net capital flows
shock 81–3; nomads 179; policy
variables 76–8; post-apartheid
regime 167; private investment 86;
public investment 86, 87; regional
cooperation 166–8; regional
integration and growth 91–3; rural
poor 179; SADC 166–7;
SADCC 166–7; sociopolitical
instability 76; soil degradation 178;
terms of trade trade shocks 81–3, 84,
93; trade integration 91–3; transport
policy 91, *see also* Africa
subsidies: Uruguay Round Agreement
and 409–10
subsistence economies: biomass-
based 176, *see also* rural poor
sufficient size argument 165, 168–70,
see also developmental regionalism

Summers, Larry xxiii, 59
Summers, Robert 125
sustainable development xvii, xviii, xix, 1, 180–2; Brundtland Commission definition xix; defining xix, 181; democracy and xviii; determination/ distribution of intergenerational well-being 181, 182–90; developmental regionalism and 166, 172–3; discount rates and 183–5; human rights and xviii; net national product and *see* net national product; optimal development and 180, 182–5; resource substitution 181, *see also* environmental taxation; welfare economics
Sutton, A. C. 118
Swanson, T. 208
Swedish development cooperation xvii–xx; aim of xvii–xviii; analysing results of xx; choice of development partners xviii; Country Strategies xx; improvements in governance xviii; increasing effectiveness of xx; orientation of xviii; subobjectives of xvii–xviii

Tait, Alan 331
Taiwan: research and development 138
Tanzi, Vito 44, 243
taxation 224–5; commodity taxes 225, 235; corporate income tax 241; developing countries 239–43; domestic taxes on goods and services 243; excise taxes 235; on factors of production 236; of foreign capital 225; fuel taxes 243; income tax 225, 235, 239–41; on international trade 241; Latin America 42–4; of luxuries 225, 245; macroeconomic stabilization 42–4; optimal taxation theory 228–30, 239; Pigouvian taxes 227–8, 236; Ramsey tax rule 229, 310; tax incentives 42–4; Third World 224–5; of trade 225; transport taxes 245; unemployment and 235; value-added 235, 236, *see also* environmental tax
Taylor, L. 327, 328, 329
technology estates 152
technology gaps 104–5
technology and technology transfers

xxv, 2; acquiring capacity for using and replicating imported standard-modern technology 132–3; Africa 59–60, 329, 344; agreements with foreign suppliers 130, 145; appropriate technology xxv; economic growth and 2, 59–60; factor-price equalization theorem 59–60; failures of xxv; human capital formation and 2; impact of technological change on labour market 325–6; importing 129–58; India 129–58; job creation xxv, late-industrializers and xxv, *see also* late-industrializers; New Growth Theory 1, 2; reverse engineering 142; scale economies and 2; scale scenario 329; Schumpeter innovation cycle 114–15; softnomization 123–4; Soviet model of growth 116–18; state intervention and xxv; techno-economic paradigms (TEP) 115, 120–1; technology absorption 141–2, 152–3; transition from standard-tech to high-tech 131–2; unemployment and xxv, *see also* industrialization; innovation; research
Tendler, J. 317
terms of trade trade shocks 81–3, 84, 87
Thomas, Clive 168
Thomas, V. xxiii
Tilly, George 273
Tirole, J. 289, 293, 294, 295
Todaro, M. P. 343
Tostensen, Arne 167
Toye, John 341
trade *see* international trade
trade surplus generation 36–7
trade-related intellectual property rights (TRIPS): Uruguay Round Agreement and 410, 415–16
trade-related investment measures (TRIMS): Uruguay Round Agreement and 410, 415–16
tradeable emission permits (TEPs) 227
trading blocs: GATT and 162, 163
Trans-European Network (TENS) Programme 151–2
transaction costs 61–2, 256, 268–9, 274
transport taxes 245, *see also* taxation
tropical forests 180; carbon storage 211–13, 216–18; deforestation *see* deforestation; genetic pool 180;

tropical forests (*contd.*)
  Rain Forest Alliance 216–17, *see also* environmental resources
Truman, D. B. 306, 307
Tullock, Gordon 261, 273

unemployment: graduate unemployment 137; in India 137, 150–1; taxation and 235; technology and xxv
United Nations Conference on Trade and Development (UNCTAD) 404–5
Upendranath, C. 136, 137
Uruguay Round xviii, 394; LDCs and 406–11, results of 406–11, *see also* Uruguay Round Agreement; tariff reductions 411; trade expansion 411; trade liberalization 411; World Trade Organization *see* World Trade Organization, *see also* General Agreement on Tariffs and Trade
Uruguay Round Agreement: agriculture 407–8, 418, 419–20; aid and 420–2; anti-dumping measures 409; changes in rules of international trade 409; LDCs and 413–20; market access 409; Multifiber Arrangement and 408, 411, 419, 421; natural-resource-based products 407, 417; new areas 410; new institutional framework 410; rules of origin 410; sanitary and phytosanitary measures 410; subsidies 409–10; tariffs 407, 411; technical barriers to trade 410; textiles and clothing 408–9, 418, 419; trade in services 418–19; trade-related intellectual property rights (TRIPS) 410, 415–16; trade-related investment measures (TRIMS) 410, 415–16; tropical products 407, *see also* World Trade Organization

Vaitsos, C. 328
value-added tax 235, 236, *see also* taxation
van Bergeijk, P. 335
van de Walle, Nicolas 262, 267
van der Mensbrugghe, D. 405, 414–15

Vandermoortele, J. 332
Vedovato, Claudio 266
Verba, S. 312, 313
Vernon, R. 328
viable economy argument 165, 166–8, *see also* developmental regionalism
Villanueva, D. 86
Viner, Jacob 258, 275
Vishny, R. W. 282, 288, 291
von Amsberg, J. 181
von Braun, J. 178
von Weizsäcker, Ernst xxiv
Vyasulu, V. 130

wage bargaining: Africa 331–3, 362–3
Warford, J. 208
water: irrigation *see* irrigation; pollution 179; rivers 165; underground basins 179, *see also* aquifers; coastal waters; groundwater; rainwater
Weber, Max 426
Weeks, John 327, 352
Weiner, M. 312
Weiss, L. W. 332
welfare economics: determination/distribution of intergenerational well-being 181, 182–90; environmental resources and 180; global warming 185–7; net national product and *see* net national product; sustainability constraint 181, *see also* social cost–benefit analysis; sustainable development
Wheeler, D. 84, 85
Williamson, J. 88
Williamson, Jeffrey 332
Wilson, John 269; Findlay–Wilson model 426, 427
World Bank policy: participatory democracy and 314–19
World Trade Organization (WTO) 394, 406–7; aims of 410–11; decision making in 407; membership of 411; objective of 406, *see also* General Agreement on Tariffs and Trade

Yamakage, S. 170

Zheng, K. 239, 246